PARENTS AS PARTNERS IN EDUCATION
Families and Schools Working Together

SIXTH EDITION

EUGENIA HEPWORTH BERGER

Professor Emerita, Metropolitan State College of Denver

PEARSON

Merrill
Prentice Hall

Upper Saddle River, New Jersey
Columbus, Ohio

Library of Congress Cataloging-in-Publication Data

Berger, Eugenia Hepworth.
    Parents as partners in education : families and schools working together / Eugenia
Hepworth Berger.—6th ed.
        p. cm.
    Includes bibliographical references and index.
    ISBN 0-13-048110-6 (pbk.)
    1. Home and school—United States. 2. Education—Parent participation—United States. I. Title.
LC225.3.B47 2004
371.19'2—dc21   2003041265

Vice President and Executive Publisher:
Jeffery W. Johnston
Publisher: Kevin M. Davis
Editorial Assistant: Autumn Crisp
Production Editor: Sheryl Glicker Langner
Production Coordination: Emily Hatteberg,
Carlisle Publishers Services
Design Coordinator: Diane C. Lorenzo
Photo Coordinator: Cynthia Cassidy
Cover Designer: Linda Sorrells-Smith
Cover Image: Corbis
Production Manager: Laura Messerly
Director of Marketing: Ann Castel Davis
Marketing Manager: Amy June
Marketing Coordinator: Tyra Poole

This book was set in Zapf Humanist by Carlisle
Communications, Ltd. It was printed and bound
by R. R. Donnelley & Sons Company. The cover
was printed by Phoenix Color Corp.

Photo Credits: Todd Yarrington/Merrill, pp. 2, 383, 399;
Silver Burdett Ginn, p. 2; Shirley Zeiberg/PH College,
p. 2; Eugenia Hepworth Berger, pp. 3, 6, 10, 16, 17, 19,
28, 53, 60, 66, 69, 71, 72, 73, 74, 92, 99, 105, 106,
108, 113, 119, 149, 153, 180, 187, 192, 194, 215, 223,
235, 262, 271, 287, 290, 319, 320, 321, 328, 330, 335,
349, 464, 465, 472, 474; Catherine Smith, pp. 9, 134;
Debra McClave, pp. 12, 84, 95, 136, 205, 463, 480;
Courtesy of the Metropolitan Museum of Art, pp. 34, 36,
37, 39, 40, 42, 43, 45, 46, 51, 52, 55, 58, 62, 64;
Courtesy of the Saint Louis Museum of Art, p. 56;
Ethelynn Fortescue, p. 65; John and Ellen Machina
Berger, p. 75; Glenn Morris, p. 131; Peggy Lore, p. 139;
Audrey Gilden, pp. 163, 283, 309; Richard & Carol Ann
Myers, p. 173; Bob and Marian Jensen, p. 337; Andrea
Berger, p. 346; Barbara Schwartz/Merrill, p. 368, Dan
Floss/Merrill, p. 371; Tom Watson/Merrill, p. 375; Anne
Vega/Merrill, p. 396; Barton D. Schmitt, pp. 416, 420,
427, 439; Elena Machina Berger, p. 460; Margy Dudley,
p. 478.

Pearson Education Ltd.
Pearson Education Singapore Pte. Ltd.
Pearson Education Canada, Ltd.
Pearson Education—Japan

Pearson Education Australia Pty. Limited
Pearson Education North Asia Ltd.
Pearson Educación de Mexico, S.A. de C.V.
Pearson Education Malaysia Pte. Ltd.

10 9 8 7 6 5 4 3 2
ISBN: 0-13-048110-6

DEDICATION

To the memory of my husband, Glen Berger
  To the rest of my extended family,
  my parents, Gladys and Richard Hepworth
  and Anna and Henry Berger
  my children, Dick, Debra, and John
  my grandchildren, Jevon, Jeni, Caroline, and Andrea, and
  my sisters, Cora, Marian, and Jo.

It was through my participation in an extended family that I became aware of the importance of support, nurturance, and love.

2 About the Author

 Eugenia Hepworth Berger became interested in parent involvement when she and her husband, Glen, became the parents of three children who attended public schools. A professional in early childhood education, sociology, family-life education, and parent education for 30 years, she has two master's degrees and a Ph.D. in sociological foundations of education. Eugenia is active in many professional organizations, including the Association for Childhood Education International, the National Council on Family Relations, the National Association for the Education of Young Children (life member), the National Council for Social Studies, and the American Sociological Association. In 1994–1995 she served on the board of the National Association of Early Childhood Teacher Educators. She has been a board member of the Colorado Association for Childhood Education, served as president of the Rocky Mountain Council on Family Relations for three years, and served on the board of the Colorado Association for the Education of Young Children, 1998–2001. She has coordinated many conferences, ranging from the Colorado Year of the Child in 1979 to ACEI and RMCF state conferences in the 1980s and 1990s. Prior to becoming a college professor, she was a public school teacher and director of a parent education program. A faculty member at Metropolitan State College of Denver since 1968, she wrote the early childhood education certification program and the minor in early childhood, and coordinated the early childhood education program for eight years. She retired in December 1997 and is now professor emerita of education.

Eugenia has been elected to a variety of honorary associations, including Pi Kappa Lambda, Mortar Board, Mu Phi Epsilon, Pi Lambda Theta, and Kappa Delta Pi. She received the Distinguished Service Award from Metropolitan State College of Denver. She is included in *Who's Who in the West* and *Who's Who of American Women*.

Preface

The beginning of a new century makes one reflect on the accomplishments and disappointments of the past as well as the opportunities that lie ahead. During the past decades there was change from distancing families from their children's education toward engaging families and communities more completely as partners in education. A look at today's families, schools, and communities shows that, although they remain the same in their roles of nurturing, educating, and providing services, they differ in their delivery systems. But diversity in meeting the needs of children increases the chances that those needs will be met.

No longer do we question whether parents should collaborate with schools. Now we try to design an appropriate and successful partnership that meets the needs of individual schools and school districts.

When I wrote the first edition of *Parents as Partners* in the late 1970s, I did so because of my great interest in parent-school collaboration. This developed from my roles as a parent, a public school teacher, and a college professor, as well as my experience as director of a Parent Education and Preschool Program in the early 1960s. It was my aim to project this enthusiasm for parent-school partnerships to preservice students, school personnel, and parents.

Now, writing this sixth edition, I am overwhelmed by the proliferation of reports, books, and journals filled with suggestions for collaboration and successful partnerships. The U.S. Department of Education has focused on the home and parents as necessary components in education. I visited with school principals and teachers and found exciting programs that include parents. Parents as first teachers and continuing partners in education are becoming accepted by the education community.

This edition, like its predecessors, includes a comprehensive look at parent-school partnerships, and it also updates the national emphasis on home-school participation. Professional and commercial organizations have responded with articles, materials, and programs that offer suggestions for enhancing parent involvement. With its comprehensive coverage, this book offers practical information that enhances school-parent collaboration, and it includes an annotated bibliography in the Appendix to serve as a reference to the new national emphasis.

ORIENTATION TO THE TEXT

Interdisciplinary. The text studies parent involvement from an interdisciplinary approach and looks at home-school collaboration using historical, educational, psychological, ethnic-social diversity, and sociological perspectives. In this edition there was a strong effort to include immigration patterns and the history of diversity in the United States, as well as recognition of the original inhabitants, the Native Americans. It is hoped that this will make all diverse groups feel recognized as contributing members of society.

Theory and Research. Theory and research underpin each chapter of the text. New research emphasizes the need for collaboration between families and schools.

Practical Application. A teacher, administrator, parent, or student can pick up this book and find suggestions and descriptions of specific programs that will enable collaboration between families and schools.

Readability. Reviewers and students have commented on the readability of the text. It is written in an easy-to-read style.

Illustrations. More than a hundred photographs enrich the narrative. Classical paintings from leading art museums illustrate Chapter 2, "Historical Overview of Family Life and Parent Involvement."

Drawings and Graphs. Many drawings and graphs are included in the text. Enlargements of these figures are included in the instructor's manual so that transparencies can be made easily.

Comprehensive Coverage. The text moves beyond the typical discussion of parent involvement to include history and current research on parent involvement and a look at diverse families. There are activities and programs to enrich parent-school collaboration, communication necessary for partnerships, leadership for parent programs, school-based and home-based programs, child abuse detection, the exceptional child's education, and elucidating the rights and responsibilities of schools and parents. Previous reviewers and users of the text consistently comment on its comprehensive coverage.

SPECIAL FEATURES

Instructor's Manual. The instructor's manual includes multiple-choice, short-answer, and essay questions help instructors compose tests.

Activities. Each chapter suggests activities that enhance the opportunities for learning about parents and schools.

Situational Vignettes. Vignettes bring alive situations that typically occur in parent-school relationships.

Advocacy. Preparation and suggestions for advocacy, plus facts about children in the United States, give parents and educators the knowledge they need to help them encourage active involvement in issues.

Annotated Bibliography. A comprehensive annotated bibliography describes resources, books, and associations for parent information, family diversity, and parent-school collaboration.

Historical Outline. An outline in Chapter 2 of historical dates of parent education and education highlights succinctly illustrates parent involvement.

✍ ACKNOWLEDGMENTS

Many people are involved in producing a book. I thank everyone who allowed me to use their work. They were cooperative and gracious, and their encouragement helped me to continue.

First, I thank my sister, Jo Spidel. Jo wrote the original chapter on children with disabilities and continued to revise it with each edition. Jo was a great asset in writing about children with disabilities because she was knowledgeable and actively involved in teaching.

Professionals—Phyllis Levenstein, Joyce Epstein, Don Davies, Julia Herwig, Marion M. Wilson, Bettye Caldwell, Miriam Westheimer, Cynthia Franklin, Loretta Fuddy, Virginia Plunkett, Romie Tobin, Virginia Castro, Kevin Swick, Colorado Department of Education, Parent Education and Assistance for Kids (PEAK) Parent Center, and the Utah Parent Center—all have shared materials with me in the past or present. A husband and wife, Kelly and Bruce Stahlman, generously wrote about their experiences with twins who have cerebral palsy. I appreciate their contributions. Pat Welch and David Denson of the C. Henry Kempe Center for the Prevention and Treatment of Child Abuse and Neglect gave me information and the Barton Schmitt photographs that appear in Chapter 10. In addition to those who shared information with me personally, I must acknowledge James Comer, the National Information Center for Children and Youth with Disabilities, the American Humane Association, the C. Henry Kempe National Center for Prevention and Treatment of Child Abuse and Neglect, the Population Reference Bureau, and the U.S. Department of Education for their continued efforts to benefit children and share their information with others. I am also indebted to my MSCD students, who were helpful with suggestions, discussions, and responses to my class presentations. Bretta Martinec and Rosina Kovar gave me suggestions for two case studies.

The Metropolitan Museum of Art and the Saint Louis Art Museum allowed me to use prints from their collections. Audrey Gilden, Debra McClave, John and Elena Machina Berger, and Andrea Berger graciously shared and were responsible for the photographs.

My family was an essential ingredient in the entire project each time around: first, my husband, Glen, who was my great support throughout my life and whose confidence in my ability to write and revise helped me throughout the first five editions; second, my three children, Dick, Debra, and John, who were responsible for my entrance into the field of parent education; third, my parents, who were my first educators, and who set an unexcelled example of supportive childrearing; and last, but not least, my four grandchildren, who arrived after the first edition, but who have kept me in touch with schools, teachers, and the parent component.

I want to thank everyone on the staff of Merrill/Prentice Hall for their continued support. Most supportive were my editor, Kevin Davis, who guided the revisions and suggested changes, and the editorial assistant, Autumn Crisp, who answered questions. I would also like to extend special thanks to production editor, Sheryl Langner, who was instrumental in guiding this edition, and to Carlisle Communications for the production services provided.

Finally, I want to thank the following individuals for their comments and suggestions during the development of this text: Mary Ellen Dallman, Valdosta State University; Diane E. Karther, University of Akron; and William O'Bruba, Indiana University of Pennsylvania.

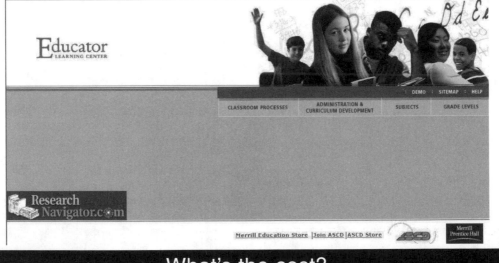

Discover the Companion Website Accompanying This Book

THE PRENTICE HALL COMPANION WEBSITE: A VIRTUAL LEARNING ENVIRONMENT

Technology is a constantly growing and changing aspect of our field that is creating a need for content and resources. To address this emerging need, Prentice Hall has developed an online learning environment for students and professors alike—Companion Websites—to support our textbooks.

In creating a Companion Website, our goal is to build on and enhance what the textbook already offers. For this reason, the content for each user-friendly website is organized by topic and provides the professor and student with a variety of meaningful resources. Common features of a Companion Website include:

FOR THE PROFESSOR—

Every Companion Website integrates **Syllabus Manager™**, an online syllabus creation and management utility.

- **Syllabus Manager™** provides you, the instructor, with an easy, step-by-step process to create and revise syllabi, with direct links into Companion Website and other online content without having to learn HTML.

- Students may logon to your syllabus during any study session. All they need to know is the web address for the Companion Website and the password you've assigned to your syllabus.

- After you have created a syllabus using **Syllabus Manager™**, students may enter the syllabus for their course section from any point in the Companion Website.

- Clicking on a date, the student is shown the list of activities for the assignment. The activities for each assignment are linked directly to actual content, saving time for students.

- Adding assignments consists of clicking on the desired due date, then filling in the details of the assignment—name of the assignment, instructions, and whether or not it is a one-time or repeating assignment.

- In addition, links to other activities can be created easily. If the activity is online, a URL can be entered in the space provided, and it will be linked automatically in the final syllabus.

- Your completed syllabus is hosted on our servers, allowing convenient updates from any computer on the Internet. Changes you make to your syllabus are immediately available to your students at their next logon.

FOR THE STUDENT—

- **Introduction**—General information about the topic and how it will be covered in the website.

- **Web Links**—A variety of websites related to topic areas.

- **Timely Articles**—Links to online articles that enable you to become more aware of important issues in early childhood.

- **Learn by Doing**—Put concepts into action, participate in activities, examine strategies, and more.

- **Visit a School**—Visit a school's website to see concepts, theories, and strategies in action.

- **For Teachers/Practitioners**—Access information you will need to know as an educator, including information on materials, activities, and lessons.

- **Current Policies and Standards**—Find out the latest early childhood policies from the government and various organizations, and view state, federal, and curriculum standards.

- **Resources and Organizations**—Discover tools to help you plan your classroom or center and organizations to provide current information and standards for each topic.

- **Electronic Bluebook**—Paperless method of completing homework or essays assigned by a professor. Finished work can be sent to the professor via email.

- **Message Board**—Virtual bulletin board to post and respond to questions and comments from a national audience.

To take advantage of these and other resources, please visit the *Parents as Partners in Education: Families and Schools Working Together,* Sixth Edition, Companion Website at

www.prenhall.com/ berger

⚇ Brief Contents

CHAPTER 1   **Family Involvement—Essential for a Child's Development**   1

CHAPTER 2   **Historical Overview of Family Life and Parent Involvement**   33

CHAPTER 3   **The Family and Community**   91

CHAPTER 4   **Effective Home-School-Community Relationships**   147

CHAPTER 5   **Communication and Parent Programs**   191

CHAPTER 6   **Collaborative Leadership—Working with Parents**   233

CHAPTER 7   **School-Based Programs**   281

CHAPTER 8   **Home-Based Programs**   327

CHAPTER 9   **Working with Parents of a Child with Disabilities**   367

CHAPTER 10   **The Abused Child**   415

CHAPTER 11   **Rights, Responsibilities, and Advocacy**   459

Resources for Home and School Programs   493

Bibliography   519

Index   545

Contents

CHAPTER 1

Family Involvement—Essential for a Child's Development   1

Introduction   2
Challenges   3
Family Systems   7
Parents: First Educators   8
Brain Development   15
Early Theories Concerning Intellectual
   Development   19
Implications for Parents and Other
   Caregivers   22
Developmental Continuity and
   Discontinuity   23
Programs Across the Nation   26
Reconsidering Children's Early Development
   and Learning   29
A Look Ahead   30
Summary   31

CHAPTER 2

Historical Overview of Family Life and Parent Involvement   33

Introduction   34

Part 1—Early History   35

Prehistoric Parent Education   35
Formal Education in Early Societies   35
Parent Involvement in Education and Family
   Life in Greece   36
Parent Involvement and Family Life
   in Rome   37
European Children During
   the Middle Ages   38
People in Other Parts of the World   39
Influence of the Reformation and Invention
   of the Printing Press   41

The Beginnings of Modern Parent Educators
   and Child Development Theorists   41
European Children in the 17th and 18th
   Centuries   44
The Family in Colonial North America   47
Early Education in the Spanish
   Southwest   48
Development of the Family Concept   48
Native Americans in the 1700s
   and 1800s   49
Childrearing in the 1800s in the
   United States   50
Immigration and Annexations   52
Civil War   53
Change in Education   55

Part 2—More Recent History of Parent Education and Child Development   58

1880 to 1890   59
1890 to 1900   61
1900 to 1910   62
1910 to 1920   63
1920 to 1930   66
1930 to 1940   68
1940 to 1950   70
1950 to 1960   71
1960 to 1970   74
1970 to 1980   78
1980 to 1990   80
1990 to 2000   82
2000 to 2004   84
Summary   87

CHAPTER 3

The Family and Community   91

Families   92
Population Count   93
Definitions of Race   93

Family Structure and Roles   96
Family Forms   101
Growth of a Nation   103
Greater Amount of Education
    for Parents   103
Child Count and Child Welfare   104
Working Mothers   106
Greater Involvement of Fathers
    with Their Children   107
Divorce   111
Single-Parent Families   113
Blended Families   116
Poverty   119
Families and Individuals
    Without Homes   123
Working with Culturally Diverse Groups   127
Cultural Diversity   129
The First Inhabitants of North America   130
Arrival of Other Ethnic Groups   133
Spanish Americans   133
African American Families   136
Asians   139
Diversification of Present-Day
    United States   143
Summary   144

CHAPTER 4

**Effective Home-School-Community
Relationships   147**

Parent-School Cooperation   149
School Climate and Parental Attitudes   149
The Case for Improved Relationships   151
Roles of Parents, Teachers,
    and Administrators   156
School Activities and Resources   163
Parents as Resources   169
Parents as Partners in Education
    at Home   170
Contacts Early in the School Year   170
What Works   173
Meeting the Needs of Your School Area   176
Building Family Strengths   178
Volunteers   179
Summary   189

CHAPTER 5

**Communication and Parent
Programs   191**

Communication   192
One-Way Communication   194
Two-Way Communication   201
Roadblocks to Communication   204
Effective Communication with Parents   207
Parent Education Programs—P.E.T., Active
    Parenting, STEP   212
Parent-Teacher Conferences   215
Dealing with Concerns Throughout
    the Year   231
Summary   231

CHAPTER 6

**Collaborative Leadership—Working
with Parents   233**

Family Involvement   234
Develop Collaborative Leadership Skills   234
Parent Education   235
Needs Assessment   237
How Parents Learn Best   242
Group Discussions   242
Leadership Training   243
Using Technology   246
Establishing a Positive Atmosphere   246
Group Roles   249
Dynamics of Roles within Groups   250
Role Descriptions   251
Productive Groups   252
Types of Meetings   255
Arrangements for Meetings   255
Summary   271
Appendix A: Parent Needs Assessment   273
Appendix B: Promoting Children's
    Self-Esteem   279

CHAPTER 7

School-Based Programs   281

Seven Levels of Parent Involvement   282
Six Types of Involvement   285

Comer Process   286
Early Childhood Longitudinal Study   290
Middle and Secondary Schools   292
Characteristics of Effective
    Collaboration   293
A Walk Through an Elementary School   293
School and Center Programs   294
School-Based Parent Involvement   301
Math and Science Associations that Support
    Parent Involvement   303
Reaching All Families   303
Title Programs   304
Helping Parents Work
    with Their Children   305
Workshops at School for Parents
    to Use at Home   306
Reaching Reticent Parents   310
Parent Education for Teenagers   315
Parenting Skills   316
Comprehensive Service Delivery—Family
    Resource Centers   318
Making Programs Happen   323
Summary   325

CHAPTER 8

Home-Based Programs   327

Home Visiting   327
Home-Based Education   328
Programs That Work   329
Five-Step Guide to Learning Activities   344
Development of a Home Activities File   346
Deciding on a Home-Based Program   349
Deciding on a Program   350
Screening for Better Understanding   355
Homeschooling   357
Homework   360
Summary   366

CHAPTER 9

**Working with Parents of a Child with
Disabilities   367**

Development of Special Education   368
Legislation for People with Disabilities   372

Individuals with Disabilities Education Act
    Amendments of 1997 (P.L. 105-17)   376
Positive Collaboration of Parents
    and School   385
Students Who Are Gifted and Talented   385
Definitions of Disabilities
    or Exceptionalities   388
Child Find Project   393
Part C of IDEA 97   395
The Individualized Family Service Plan
    and Family Survey   397
Children with Disabilities in Head Start
    and Child Care   398
Parent-School Partnerships   399
How Parents Can Help the School-Age
    Child at Home   401
Communication Between Professionals and
    Parents of Children with Disabilities   403
Parental Reactions to Disabilities   406
Parents Share Their Feelings   408
Concern for Those Who Work with Children
    with Disabilities   411
Rights and Services Available
    to Parents   412
Maslow's Hierarchy of Needs   412
Summary   413

CHAPTER 10

The Abused Child   415

Responsibility to Report   416
Background   418
Extent of Child Abuse and Neglect   421
Categories of Maltreatment   425
Neglect   425
Physical Abuse and Neglect   426
Emotional Abuse   426
Sexual Abuse   429
Bullying and Violence in Schools   432
Corporal Punishment in Schools   434
Who Reports Maltreatment Cases?   435
Behaviors and Attitudes of Parents and Children
    That May Indicate Child Abuse   437
Behavioral and Psychological Characteristics
    of the Child in School   440

Why Do Abuse and Neglect Continue
   to Happen?   443
Characteristics and Risk Factors of Abusive
   Parents   443
Roots of Violence   445
Why Is There Abuse?   447
Development of Policies   448
How to Talk with Children and Parents   450
Programs to Prevent Abuse   451
Intervening in Sexual Abuse   453
Summary   456

CHAPTER 11

Rights, Responsibilities, and Advocacy   459

Origin of Parents' and Children's Rights   460
Parents' Right to Select Their Child's
   Education   462
Student Records—Open Record Policy   465
Rights and Responsibilities of Students
   and Parents   467
Developing Criteria Together   475

Child Advocacy   476
The Child Advocate   479
Preparing for Advocacy   481
Facts on Children and Families   485
Advocacy for Children Around
   the World   488
Summary   491

APPENDIX

**Resources for Home and School
Programs   493**

Bibliography   519

Index   545

NOTE: Every effort has been made to provide accurate and current Internet information in this book. However, the Internet and information posted on it are constantly changing and it is inevitable that some of the Internet addresses listed in this textbook will change.

1 Family Involvement— Essential for a Child's Development

Research on the brain makes it clear that children must have a loving, warm, interactive environment. Communities and schools can enable families to flourish by providing support and caring.

Author

It seems clear that we cannot have islands of academic excellence in a sea of community indifference.

Boyer, 1991, p. xvii

Simply put, family involvement in education is too important to ignore if we really want to create a stronger, safer, and more enriching future for our children.

U.S. Department of Education, 1994, p. 2

In this chapter on the importance of parents, you will read about needs and successes when parents, schools, and communities collaborate and advocate together. After completing the chapter, you should be able to do the following:

- Discuss the increase in collaboration among families, communities, and schools.
- Cite research that supports the significance of education and family, school, and community involvement.
- Identify and explain research on attachment that illustrates the need for early attachment of children with a parent or significant caregiver.
- Discuss breakthroughs in neuroscience research on brain development and what it means for families and education.
- Discuss the developmental theories of Piaget and Vygotsky and Hunt's book *Intelligence and Experience* as they describe development and challenge the assumption of fixed intelligence and predetermined development.
- Define *developmental continuity* and *discontinuity* and explain why it is important for families, schools, and social agencies to work together.
- Recognize and identify the five dimensions of readiness.

✇ INTRODUCTION

The information age of the 21st century will require an educated populace. Like the change from an agricultural society with both parents at home and the family working as a unit, to an industrial world with the father no longer staying home, the change to an information age, often with both parents working, causes a corresponding change in the needs and roles of family, school, and community.

The attack on the World Trade Towers in New York City and the Pentagon in Washington, DC, on September 11, 200l, increased the need for the populace to work together and support one another. The response of those in New York and Washington, DC, and across the country, helped strengthen the resolve of both the nation and the individuals and families living here. Schools, the one institution that touches families at all income levels and from all ethnic groups, now more than ever are charged with the responsibility of not only educating students but also supporting families. Although this is not entirely a new role for educators, the need is critical for schools and families to develop a partnership that will strengthen and help both the school and the family.

Throughout the world, parents, educators, political leaders, professionals, and concerned citizens of all ages, socioeconomic groups, and ethnic backgrounds recognize that strong families are essential for society. Although there is no consensus on specific needs of families, there is agreement that families are important and that society must give families the time and resources necessary to provide the support and attention their children need.

As society becomes increasingly dependent on technology and members of extended families are separated from one another, it becomes apparent that schools and communities must help families provide a caring environment for children. The need to promote human interactions becomes even stronger than in previous generations, when extended families had more time and

Parents are their children's first and most important nurturers, socializers, and educators.

incentive to provide for the caring of children. A rallying cry for collaboration among schools, families, and communities has spread across the nation. Ingredients for successful collaboration include adequate and supportive child care, small class sizes in the early years to ensure individual attention for children, and the active involvement of parents in their children's development and education. To create a literate society, we must care for children and give them the opportunity to develop skills and become educated citizens. The U.S. Department of Education (1994) shared these views on education: "Within this rapidly changing society, few areas are as essential to a successful future as education, both as a means of learning basic and advanced skills and as a process for helping to develop responsible, compassionate citizens who are ready to make valuable contributions to their family, community, state, and nation" (p. 1).

CHALLENGES

The challenges that our society faces include (1) promoting caring schools and communities, (2) encouraging caring family environments, (3) providing adequate and enriching child care, (4) providing positive before- and after-school care, and (5) creating and supporting collaboration among parents, teachers, and the community.

Teachers, reaching out to children in a caring, supportive way, let children know that they matter and that they belong.

Caring Schools and Communities

When teachers, parents, and members of the community reach out to children in a caring, supportive way, children know that they belong. They are able to form attachments and respond in a positive, caring way. Parents, child care providers, and teachers must recognize the need for children to have a caring environment. Schools, families, and communities are called on to increase their involvement and collaboration to support the children.

Coleman (1994) discusses the issue by describing social capital, financial capital, and human capital as components of society. He defines *social capital* as the social relationships of "adults in the family and community in the lives of children" (p. 23). *Financial capital* includes the economic support of institutions, primarily schools, to provide the skills children need to participate as members of society. Social and financial capital are needed to provide the human capital: "the investment of the social and financial capital of one generation in the creation of human capital in the next generation" (p. 28). Coleman sees financial capital as available and able to support schools, but says that social capital, the caring commitment, is lacking.

> New investments in social capital are both in demand and socially desirable. These new institutions are analogous to the school in that the demand for them arises as the mother leaves the household, just as the demand for mass schooling arose as the father left the household. Yet, they cannot be exactly like the school traditionally has been in kinds of qualities that engender in children. For the social capital that is now eroding leaves a more fundamental vacuum. They must be institutions that induce the kinds of motivations, the kinds of attitude, and the conception of self which children and youth will need to succeed in school and as adults. (pp. 36–37)

According to Comer (1997), "exclusion and overblown individualism" are detrimental to the development of a healthy society. He continues, "A huge body of social and behavioral science research shows that good development and a sense

of belonging in a supportive environment produce better individual and group behaviors than the opposite" (p. 209).

How can schools and families develop a caring environment? Swick (1997) suggests, "The strength of great societies is in their ability to reach out to each other through mutually enriching services" (p. 151). Guiding principles of human responses include:

- Value each person's integrity.
- Reach out to each other in truly humane and understanding ways.
- Respect and value human differences.
- Serve others in meaningful and nurturing ways.
- Build charitable and responsible "habits" into our daily lives.
- Build in children and in ourselves a belief in the goodness of people. (pp. 151–152)

What temperaments do caregivers need to enable them to provide a caring environment? They must see themselves as caring, capable individuals who have a positive sense of identity. Swick (2001) stated that there are four sets of dispositions needed by individuals to provide caring environments for their students: (1) healthy sense of self, (2) caring skills and behavior, (3) prosocial relationships with others, and (4) helping and serving skills and relationships (p. 131). The first, a healthy sense of self, develops from relationships with significant others—parents, teachers, role models, and those who had an impact on the child.

The development of caring skills and behavior is strengthened further by interactions, modeling, and guidance with other caring individuals. Children model what they experience; prosocial behaviors are learned through prosocial relationships with others.

The acquisition of caring and serving skills is a constructionist process where the child's involvement with parents and other significant adults is critical to the child's continued growth in becoming a caring individual (Swick, 2001, p. 132). The process includes modeling when children are involved in caring and service; educators are role models and need to build mutual trust and respect with the students. Suggestions for becoming a caring, competent teacher include (1) building mutual trust—be honest; (2) cultivating communication skills—be a role model; (3) adjusting the schedule—be flexible, (4) altering perspectives—be empathetic; (5) promoting humor—be human; and (6) promoting a positive self-image—be kind (Krall & Jalengo, 1998–1999).

Comer (1997) describes the "common threads" that result in successful schools: "positive school relationships; caring, responsible, predictable adults in the lives of students; a sense of belonging in constructive groups engaged in challenging learning and activities; and opportunity for students to sense direction and purpose" (p. 72).

There is a need for a more caring community for children and youth from early childhood to young adulthood. The use of illicit drugs, alcohol, and tobacco by young people illustrates this need. Involved, caring adults in the community who offer alternatives, such as social activities, programs devoted to music and the arts, physical fitness and recreational opportunities, as well as educational enrichment, can help children grow into physically and emotionally healthy young adults. These alternatives can help reduce the temptation to use these harmful substances, despite their widespread availability.

How can schools and families develop a caring environment? Teachers and parents can reach out to one another with genuine interest and support. They can take time to get to know one another and to recognize and respect one another's beliefs, values, and concerns. Most important, if parents and teachers show respect for one another, they can develop a caring partnership (Berger, 1996a, 1996b; Swick, 1997).

Children Speak Out

Children are responding to the increasing violence in schools. In 2002, Galinsky and Salmond

of the Families and Work Institute of New York published a booklet containing the results of a study they conducted with the support of the Colorado Trust. From October through December of 2001, 1,012 students in the 5th through 12th grades in Colorado were interviewed. Interviewers also questioned 1,001 young people of a nationally representative group. Thirty-five percent of those interviewed suggested that students in the schools need to "stop or change the smaller things that lead to more extreme violence" (p. 5). They suggested stopping the acts of emotional violence such as bullying, meanness, insults, gossiping, teasing, and making fun of each other. In addition, they responded that students need to be nice and friendly and get along with each other, and that the physical violence must stop—no more fighting, hitting, pushing, or shoving. Instead, there should be tolerance, respect, and an end to hatred and racial discrimination. The children suggested getting young people to "talk it out" with one another and having adults talk with them about alternatives and consequences (Galinsky & Salmond, 2002).

Caring Families

The importance of parents giving attention, support, love, and encouragement to children is well established. Findings show that the primary causal factor in a child's success or lack of success in school is not socioeconomic status (Epstein, 1996; Zill, 1996), but the caring support and encouragement given by their parents. Although concern about finances makes it more difficult to concentrate on emotional and educational needs of the family, low-income families who provide caring for their children supply the base for their educational and social needs. At every level of income, in all cultures, and in different family forms, it is essential that children have enriching and loving families that guide and help them as they grow.

Boyer (1991) states, "There is no evidence that today's parents are less committed or less caring" (p. 4). Parents have not changed, but the "loss of

For children to achieve their potential, it is essential for families and educators to show support and caring.

community, the increased fragmentation of family life, the competing, often conflicting, pressures" affect their ability to provide the family life that children so desperately need (p. 4). It is recognized that having children who are "ready to learn" does not mean they come to school with specific academic skills in place. It means that children have the care, conditions, environment, health provisions, and nutrition that allow them to be ready to learn.

Adequate and Enriching Child Care

The family is the most important child care provider. A national survey of employed mothers found that nearly half of children younger than 5 were cared for by the respondent's parents or other relatives when the mother worked outside the home. Twenty-two percent preferred having a relative care for their children, especially for very young children (Larner, 1996). Other options included family child care providers and child care centers. Those who used child care centers and home-based child care were most concerned about safety, the attention children receive, cleanliness, communication with the parent, and the provider's warmth (p. 30).

The increased use of child care centers requires that care providers work with parents to provide a loving, supportive environment for the children. Parents must also provide loving care when they are with their children, recognizing that the child is their most important responsibility and asset.

Child Care Providers

The urgent need for child care when parents work outside the home is evident. Parents worry most about the quality of care, the expertise and caring ability of providers, and the turnover rate of staff members. Children need continuity in caregivers to develop caring relationships, and parents want providers who show caring and warmth to their charges. Because child care providers generally are poorly paid, the turnover rate of workers is high. It is necessary to recognize the importance of high-quality child care and acknowledge that child care providers require a sufficient income to stay in the profession.

Kagan and Cohen (1996) point out that care and education have never been entitlements for the preschool infant and child as they have been for school-age children:

Beyond concerns that many early care and education programs provide custodial care at best and place children at the risk of harm at worst, little attention has been directed to the quality of the early care and education system as a whole. (p. x)

This is a challenge that needs to be met.

Positive Before- and After-School Care

Over the past decade, there has been growing concern about the increasing amount of time that school-age children spend unsupervised and often alone, before and after school. It is recognized that unsupervised after-school time not only fails to support children's development, intellectually and emotionally, but also creates an opportunity for children to become involved with drugs, smoking, and other illegal activities. Collaboration among schools, recreation services, human services, and/or arts in residence needs to occur so that children have a safe environment before and after school. "It is a demand for care, first, all day from birth to school age; second, after school every day until parents return from work; and, third, all summer" (Coleman, 1994, p. 36).

Collaboration Among Parents, Teachers, and the Community

The demand for schools to work with families and communities to become involved has exploded on the education scene. Epstein (1996) points out that the question is no longer whether there is a need for collaboration between schools and parents, but what is the most effective way to work together and how should it be accomplished.

Schools that have reached out to parents are guideposts for those schools that have not begun to do so. Parents, schools, and communities may access information from the U.S. Department of Education by telephone, fax, correspondence, and the Internet. In the late 1990s, the department offered videos, articles, booklets, and newsletters concerning family and school partnerships. These offerings must continue in the 21st century. Schools need to be innovative in their effort to reach families. If they need help, information is available (see the Appendix). Schools have an obligation to take the lead in developing partnerships.

✑ FAMILY SYSTEMS

Just as schools are systems with teachers, principals, superintendents, students, and ancillary personnel interacting with the goal to educate, so the families they serve are entities or systems. Each child and parent is affected by the family system in which they participate. Broderick (1993) describes the family as "an example of an open, ongoing, goal-seeking, self-regulating, social system . . . shaped by its own particular structural features (size, complexity, composition, life stage, the psychobiological characteristics of its individual members) . . . and its sociocultural and historic position in its larger environment" (p. 37). Family systems are guided and influenced by their cultural and historical backgrounds as well as by the composition of the members of the family with their own psychobiological characteristics and structure.

Systems Vary

Family system theories are derived from diverse sources and are varied (Rosenblatt, 1994). A family that lives in a rural area will have a different structure from a family in the city. On a farm, the family needs to work as a team to accomplish the tasks of caring for animals and producing crops. Children participate within the system as necessary cogs in the operation. In the city, many children are unable to contribute to the family's well-being. There is no role that helps them feel productive, thus the systems that result are different.

Families native to the area where they live will have a different frame of reference from new arrivals. Immigrant families may have systems derived from their place of origin. They may adapt to the new society or they may prefer to keep their original system intact. If children live with a prescribed frame of behavior in their own family system that is at odds with the families of their classmates, they may have great difficulty adjusting to the opposing systems.

Changes in a System

When a family undergoes a transitional event such as the birth of a child, a move to a new location, or an illness of a family member, the system will need to adapt to accommodate the change. Change occurs in a variety of ways. It may be sudden or gradual, positive or negative. The change may be minimal or shattering. Divorce causes children to lose the family system as they knew it and adapt to an entirely new one. Teachers need to know what is happening in a student's family so that they can respond in an appropriate manner and be helpful to the child.

Three Levels of Systems

The child's development is related to experiences in the entire environment. Bronfenbrenner (1979, 1986) recognized three levels of systems:

1. The *microsystem* includes face-to-face relations with family and peers, with parents as the major influence on a child's interactive ecological system (O'Callaghan, 1993).

2. The *mesosystem* involves face-to-face relationships with more formal organizations such as schools, scouting groups, recreation facilities, and religious groups.

3. The *exosystem,* which is further removed from personal interaction, still influences children through their parents and their parents' employment and government actions. Focus now on the microsystem, parents, families, and caregivers essential for a child's development.

✆ PARENTS: FIRST EDUCATORS

Home is the first classroom. Parents are the first and most essential teachers. (Boyer, 1991, p. 33)

Parents are the first nurturers, socializers, and educators of their children. It is almost impossible to overemphasize the significance of the role of parents. The parents' role in their children's early years is significant in many ways, but it has three essential aspects: (1) Society would not survive if a culture stopped procreating or rearing its young. (2) Children who do not have the opportunity to form attachment to a significant other during the first two years of life find it difficult or impossible to overcome the lack of that emotional bond. (3) Brain research shows that experiences, both good and bad, during the first three years of life affect the connections and the "wiring" of the child's brain.

Survival of Society

Infants cannot survive without being nurtured by someone who feeds and cares for them. The manner of nurturing infants varies within each subculture as well as across cultures. A child's well-being is affected by both the quality of care and the child's resiliency. One child may thrive whereas another may deteriorate in environments that seem identical. The child, the caregiver, and the environment intertwine in the childrearing process, making each child's experiences unique.

The essential commitment between caregiver and child emphasizes the significance of the parent's role. Other roles such as breadwinner, food gatherer, or food producer are necessary but can be fulfilled in a variety of ways, depending on the culture. In childrearing, however, certain obligations and responsibilities transcend all groups of people. Every child must be fed, touched, and involved in communication—verbal and nonverbal—to grow and develop. Childrearing, whether by parents or alternative caregivers, requires a nurturing environment. Perhaps the ease with which most men and women become parents diminishes the realization that parenthood is an essential responsibility. Many have assumed that parenthood is a natural condition and that simply becoming a parent or caregiver transforms the new mother or father into a nurturing parent. As a result, society has not demanded that parents have the prerequisite knowledge that would ensure competence in one of the most important occupations—childrearing. Some basic understanding of child development on which to base parenting skills, allowing for individualization and cultural diversity, should be expected.

Attachment

The ability to nurture does not blossom automatically when one gives birth to a child. It involves many diverse variables, ranging from parent-child attachment to previous modeling experiences to environmental conditions that allow and encourage a positive parent-child relationship. Many parents have not had the good fortune to learn from a positive role model. They need advice and a support system of family, friends, and professionals.

Issues related to readiness to learn are the child's feelings of attachment, security, and well-being. An area of research of paramount importance to parents is that of human attachment. Since the 1930s there has been increasing research on bonding and attachment. Experts recognize attachment as an essential ingredient for a healthy personality. *Attachment* is defined as a form of behavior that has its "own internal motivation distinct from feeding and sex, and of no less importance for survival"

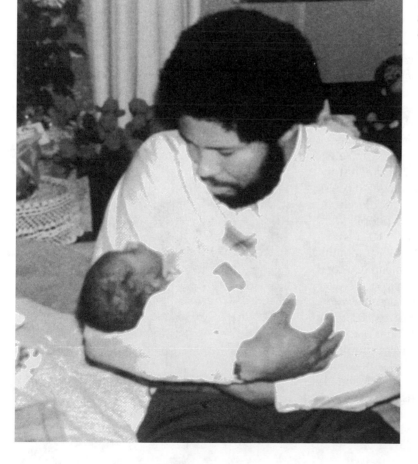

Father and infant begin the attachment process through caring and eye to eye contact.

(Bowlby, 1988, p. 27). Attachment behavior is the behavior that a person exhibits to obtain and maintain proximity to the attachment figure, generally the mother but also the father and, in their absence, someone the child knows. It is strongest when the child is sick, tired, or frightened. Human attachment is crucial throughout the life cycle.

The recognition of the importance of the first few years in the development of attachment came through studies of children who did not thrive. Skeels, Spitz, and Bowlby did *not* do controlled studies that gave some children love and withheld it from others. Instead, they looked at what had happened to children who had failed to thrive. Why had this happened? What did these children lack that the other children had?

Skeels

It was during the 1930s that questions about the importance of human attachment in the young child were raised. Harold Skeels, a member of the Iowa group of child researchers, studied the effect of environment on the development of children during a period when most researchers were studying maturation or behaviorism (e.g., Gesell and Watson). One study, a *natural* history investigation, had startling findings (Skeels, 1966). Skeels placed 13 infants and toddlers from an orphanage in an institution for people with mental retardation. The 13 children—10 girls and 3 boys—ranged in age from 7.1 to 35.9 months and had IQs from 36 to 89, with a mean IQ score of 64.3. Children in the control group of 12, also chosen from children in the orphanage, between 12 and 22 months old, had IQs of 50 to 103, with a mean IQ of 86.7 points. The children placed in the wards for mental retardation were showered with attention by the attendants and supervisors. They were cared for, played with, loved, and allowed to go along on excursions. Almost every child developed an attachment to one person who was particularly interested in the child and

his or her achievements. The control group of children in the orphanage, however, received traditional care with no special treatment. When retested, after varying periods from 6 to 52 months, the children in the institution for mental retardation had gained 27.5 IQ points, but those left in the orphanage had lost an average of 26.2 IQ points.

Although the research could be criticized because variables were not controlled—there were more girls than boys placed in the wards—and changes in IQ can be partially explained by statistical regression, the results were so dramatic and unexpected that the effect of early environment had to be considered. Skeels (1966) followed up on the subjects of this research almost 20 years later and found evidence to reinforce his initial findings. Of the 13 children in the experimental group who had been transferred to the mental institution, 11 had been adopted and reared as "normal" children. Twelve of the 13 had become self-supporting adults, achieving a median educational level of 12 years of schooling. Of the 12 control group children who had been left in the orphanage, four were still in institu-

Eye contact fosters human attachment, a necessary component for healthy development.

tions; one was a gardener's assistant; three were employed as dishwashers; one was a floater; one was a part-time worker in a cafeteria; and one had died. Only one individual had achieved an educational level similar to that of the experimental group—a man who as a child had received different treatment from the others. He had been transferred from the orphanage to a school for the deaf, where he received special attention from his teacher. The children who had been placed in a mental institution and later adopted, received love and developed human attachments; they had achieved a lifestyle more typical of children outside the orphanage, whereas those left in the orphanage had only a marginal existence. Evidence strongly supports the importance of a nurturing early environment and also indicates that a poor initial environment can be reversed by enriched personal interaction (Skeels, 1966).

Spitz

René Spitz, a physician, also became involved in the observation of infants during the 1930s. In *The First Year of Life* (1965) he described his research and observations of the psychology of infants. He studied babies in seven situations: private families, foster homes, an obstetrics ward, an Indian village, a well-baby clinic, a nursery, and a foundling home.

Both the nursery and foundling home were long-term institutions that guaranteed constancy of environment and dramatically illustrated the necessity of human attachment and interaction. Both institutions provided similar physical care of children, but they differed in their nurturing and interpersonal relationships. Both provided hygienic conditions, well-prepared food, and medical care. The foundling home had daily visits by a medical staff, whereas the nursery called a doctor only when needed. The nursery was connected to a penal institution where delinquent girls, pregnant on admission, were sent to serve their sentences. Babies born to them were cared

for in the nursery until the end of their first year. The mothers were primarily delinquent, psychopathic, or socially maladjusted minors. In contrast, some of the children in the foundling home had well-adjusted mothers who were unable to support their children. Others were children of unwed mothers who were asked to come to the home and nurse their own and one other child during the first three months.

Spitz (1965) filmed a representative group of the children he studied in both institutions. He studied 203 children in the nursery and 91 in the foundling home. The major difference in the care of the two sets of children was the amount of nurturing and social interaction. The nursery, which housed 40 to 60 children at a time, allowed the mothers or mother-substitutes to feed, nurse, and care for their babies. The infants had at least one toy; they were able to see outside their cribs and to watch the activities of other children and the caregiving mothers. The babies thrived.

In the foundling home, however, the babies were screened from outside activity by blankets hung over the sides and ends of their cribs, isolating them from any visual stimulation. They had no toys to play with, and the caretakers were busy tending to other duties rather than mothering the children. During the first three months while they were breast-fed, the babies appeared normal. Soon after separation, however, they progressively deteriorated. Of the 91 foundling home children, 34 died by the end of the second year.

Spitz (1965) continued to follow up on 21 children who remained in the foundling home until they were 4 years old. He found that 20 could not dress themselves; 6 were not toilet trained; 6 could not talk; 5 had a vocabulary of two words; 8 had vocabularies of three to five words; and only 1 was able to speak in sentences. Spitz attributed the deterioration of the infants to lack of mothering. Although the children in the nursery had mothering, those in the foundling home did not.

Absence of mothering equals emotional starvation. . . . This leads to progressive deterioration engulfing the child's whole person. Such deterioration is manifested first in an arrest of the child's psychological development; then psychological dysfunctions set in, paralleled by somatic changes. In the next stage this leads to increased infection liability and eventually, when the emotional deprivation continues into the second year of life, to a spectacularly increased rate of mortality. (p. 281)

Bowlby

In 1951, John Bowlby reviewed studies of deprivation and its effects on personality development. In a systematic review for the World Health Organization, he described those works that supported theories on the negative aspects of maternal deprivation. In a monograph, Bowlby (1966) stated: "It is submitted that the evidence is now such that it leaves no room for doubt regarding the general proposition that the prolonged deprivation of the young child of maternal care may have grave and far-reaching effects on his character and so on the whole of his future life" (p. 46).

Development of Attachment.   Bowlby (1982) described attachment in a family setting. Most babies about 3 months old show more attention and are more responsive to their primary caregiver than to others by smiling at, vocalizing to, and visually following their parent or other primary caregiver. At about 6 to 8 months of age, infants develop stranger anxiety. They become con-

The brain is affected by the nourishment, care, and stimulation that it receives. Early nurturing is essential to a child's development.

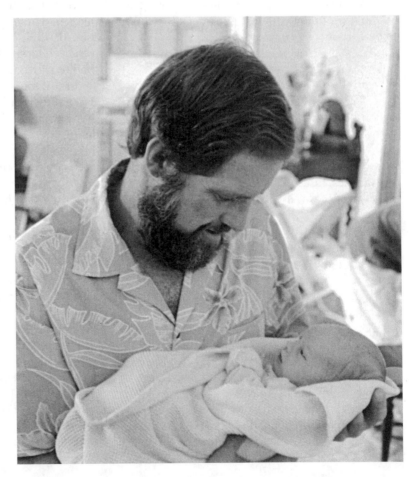

cerned about being near their caregiver and fearful of those they do not know. This attachment to primary caregivers continues and strengthens in intensity from 6 to 9 months, although when the child is ill, fatigued, hungry, or alarmed, the intensity increases. During the same period the infant demonstrates attachment to others as well, primarily the father, siblings, and caregivers. Attachment to others does not reduce the attachment to the mother or primary caregiver. At 9 months, most children try to follow primary caregivers when they leave the room, greet them on return, and crawl to be near them. This behavior continues throughout the second year of a child's life and on into the third. When children reach about 2 years 9 months to 3 years of age, they are better able to accept a parent's temporary absence.

Bowlby (1966) emphasized that the greatest effect on personality development is during the child's early years. The earliest critical period was believed to be during the first 5 or 6 months, while mother-figure and infant are forming an attachment. The second vital phase was seen as lasting until near the child's third birthday, during which time the mother-figure needs to be virtually an ever-present companion. During a third phase, the child is able to maintain the attachment even though the nurturing parent is absent. During the 4th to 5th year, this tolerable absence might extend from a few days to a few weeks; during the 7th to 8th years, the separation could be lengthened to a year or more. Deprivation in the third phase does not have the same destructive effect on the child as it does in the period from infancy through the 3rd year.

Orphanages in Romania

Research in the 1990s on infants raised in Romanian orphanages reaffirmed the findings of Spitz, Skeels, and Bowlby and furthered the study of causal factors. "Evidence began accumulating that sensory stimulation plays a crucial role not only in the early development of the brain's sensory- and motor- and memory-processing circuitry, but also

in the development of the neural and hormonal systems that regulate our response to stress" (Carlson, 2002). The researchers looked specifically at the dismal patterns of cortisol secretion. "Touch is critical to the establishment of this mechanism for maintaining the body's homeostatic balance" (Carlson). Thirty of the children were in the control group of standard orphanage care, where 1 caregiver would look after 20 children. Many of these children were withdrawn and exhibited repetitive movements. Although they received adequate care and medical attention, they were not called by name and were moved frequently from caregiver to caregiver. "Clearly, the social networks in which children grow up bear on the development of the neural networks that mediate memory, emotion, and self" (Carlson).

Maternal or Human Attachment?

Rutter (1981) and Bower (1982) questioned whether the term *maternal deprivation* was too restrictive to cover a wide range of abuses and variables. They suggested that maternal deprivation was too limited a concept—that human attachment and multiple attachment should be considered, and that warmth as well as love be regarded as vital elements in relationships. Rutter suggested that the bond with the mother was not different in quality or kind from other bonds. In addition, individual differences among children resulted in some children being more vulnerable to "mother deprivation."

Tizard and Hodges

Questions regarding the irreversibility of deprivation were raised. Would sound childrearing reverse early deprivation? It appeared that good childrearing practices and a good environment would help the child, but early deprivation continued to be a problem and deprived infants often remained detached. Tizard and Hodges (1978) studied children raised in an institution to see if the lack of personal attachment had lasting effects. Children who were adopted did form bonds as late as 4 or 6 years of age, but they exhibited the same attention and social problems in school as those who remained in the institution. "Being one in a class of many other children may for the child have repeated some of the elements of the nursery 'family group,' leading to a similar pattern of competitive attempts to gain the attention of the teacher and poor relationships with other children" (Hodges, 1996, p. 71).

Rutter

In reviewing the research, Rutter (1981) said, "It appears that although attachments can still develop for the first time after infancy, nevertheless fully normal social development may be dependent on early bonding" (p. 190). Rutter broadened his work to include many aspects of the environment that affect the child. He found that lack of parent attachment did not harm intellectual development in the same way that it harmed psychosocial development if the child was reared with opportunities for learning experiences and stimulation. Did multiple risks hinder the ability of a child to survive, not only intellectually but also socially and emotionally? Rutter's evidence established that disturbed family relationships were key variables in resulting conduct disorders and delinquency in children. Adequate parent relationships in infancy, though seemingly essential, cannot necessarily protect the child from multiple risk factors that may arise later in life. One of these factors is which school the child attends. A good school makes a difference in the mental and intellectual health of a child. Rutter concluded that risks, loss, and discordant families all affect children, but "it may be that the first few years do have a special importance for bond formation and social development" (p. 217).

Ainsworth

Ainsworth (1973) wrote that parent-child attachment is necessary for the development of a healthy personality, but that attachment may occur beyond the early "sensitive period." Ainsworth identified three classifications of attachment: avoidant/ insecure, ambivalent/insecurely, and securely attached (Shore, 1997).

Brazelton and Yogman

In their extensive studies of infants, Brazelton and Yogman (1986) analyzed the process of early attachment and wrote specifically about the interaction between infant and parent, covering even the effects of experiences in utero. The child appears to be born with predictable responses, including the ability to develop a reciprocal relationship with the caregiver.

The authors described four stages vital to the parent-infant attachment process, which lasts from birth to 4 or 5 months. In the first stage the infant achieves homeostatic control and is able to control stimuli by shutting out or reaching for stimuli. During the second stage the infant is able to use and attend to social cues. In the third stage, usually at 3 and 4 months, the reciprocal process between parent and child shows the infant's ability to "take in and respond to information" as well as to withdraw. During the fourth stage the infant develops a sense of autonomy and initiates and responds to cues. If the parent recognizes and encourages the infant's desire to have control over the environment, the infant develops a sense that leads to a feeling of competence. This model is based on feedback and reciprocal interaction and allows for individual differences.

Concerns

Three groups of parents may pose particular concern when developing parent-child attachments. The first is made up of parents who have never had models of good parenting or have been reared in abusive homes. They need help in learning how to care for children. The second group contains parents who tend to be isolated and insecure and do not have a support system. These groups could be helped by supportive home visitors (Jacobson & Frye, 1991). The third group includes parents who are busy and away from home for extended periods. The importance of early bonding and attachment development is such that these parents should be aware of the consequences of not devoting time to their young children.

Maltreatment of children, from infancy on, may have enormous effects on their social interaction. These children are often aggressive in their relationships with other children in a school setting. Youngblade and Belsky (1989) describe the effects that maltreatment might have on toddlers and older children, extending into adulthood. It sometimes results in dysfunctional relations not only between parent and child with insecure attachments, but also with peers. The authors state that "maltreated toddlers are, on average, more aggressive, less prosocial, and more disturbed in interaction with age-mates than are comparison children" (p. 11). Therapy can ameliorate the effects on children of dysfunctional parenting and maltreatment. Intervention with parents who may be prone to abusing their children is also essential.

Parents who are at risk for abusing children can be helped. Bowlby (1988) described a Home Start program in Leicester, England, in which volunteers visited parents in their homes and helped them with their roles as parents. The C. Henry Kempe Center in Denver and Hawaii's Healthy Start Program have also worked with parents who were likely to become child abusers and with parents who had already abused their children. Having good child care models and support during periods of stress helps parents develop more appropriate childrearing skills.

The attachment process and the early life of a child are the first steps to the child's total growth. They provide the necessary emotional trust that allow the child to continue to develop relationships.

Hospitalism

Bowlby (1982) also cited research that illustrates the need for concern for young children who must go to a hospital for an extended length of time or who must have institutional care. His research revealed that when children ages 15 to 30 months are placed in residential nurseries or hospitals in a strange environment away from the mother-figure and other familiar people, they commonly go through three stages: (1) protest, (2) despair, and (3) detachment. The phases do not start and stop abruptly, but may involve days or weeks of transition or shifts back and forth.

The first phase, protest, may last from a few hours to a week or more. The child reacts to the environment and may cry, display distress and anger, and seem to be looking for the missing parent. The second phase is a period of despair when the child withdraws, makes no demands, and appears to be in a state of mourning. The final stage is the detachment period, which may appear to be adjustment and recovery but is actually a withdrawal from the parent and an absence of the attachment behavior that is normal for the child's age. The child becomes more sociable, accepting food and toys from nurses, but withdraws from the former attachment figures. If separation continues, the child may not attach to anyone and may appear to care for no one. The child will become detached. Most hospital staff members are concerned about children's attachment to their parents and thus will encourage a parent to stay with the child or visit often.

BRAIN DEVELOPMENT

Theories on attachment and brain development emphasizing the importance of the first years of life have gained support from recent research (Brazelton & Greenspan, 2000; Carnegie Corporation of New York, 1994; Education Commission of the States, 1996; Greenspan, 2002; Newman, F. 1996; Shore, 1997). Scientists use ultrasound to study fetus brain development and neural functioning and scanning techniques such as magnetic resonance imaging (MRI) and positron emission tomography (PET) to learn how the brain works postnatally.

"Functional MRI provides information about changes in the volume, flow, or oxygenation of blood that occur as a person undertakes various tasks, including not only motor activities, such as squeezing a hand, but also cognitive tasks, such as speaking or solving a problem" (Shore, 1997,

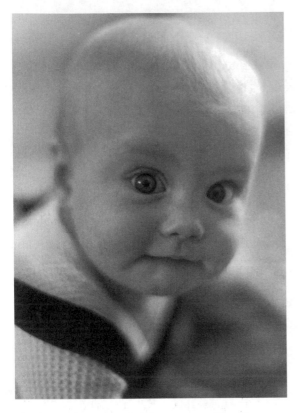

The brain of an infant develops at an exhilarating rate.

p. 8). A PET scan, employed when a child is thought to have neurological problems, requires an injection of a tracer chemical, making it an invasive procedure, which researchers generally avoid. Since PET scans cannot be considered non-invasive, the research comes from situations in which the child has needed the scan for medical reasons. By analyzing the results of PET scans researchers have furthered scientific knowledge: "Scientists can visualize not only the fine structures of the brain, but also the level of activity that is taking place in its various parts" (p. 9). Prior to these technological advances, brain research was accomplished only when operations were performed or people had strokes, and neither situation revealed what was happening in the brain at specific times.

Wiring of the Brain

Experience is critical in the "wiring" of a child's brain. When a stimulus activates a neural path, the synapses receive and store a chemical signal. If synapses are used repeatedly, they are strengthened, reach a threshold level, and become permanent. If not used repeatedly, they are pruned and eliminated (Shore, 1997).

> In the first decade of life, a child's brain forms trillions of connections synapses. Axons hook up with dendrites, and chemicals called neurotransmitters facilitate the passage of impulses across the resulting synapses. Each individual neuron may be connected to as many as 15,000 other neurons, forming a network of neural pathways that is immensely complex. This elaborate network is sometimes referred to as the brain's "wiring" or "circuitry." (p. 17)

Early interactions directly affect the way the brain is wired.

Nonlinear Development of the Brain

The brain does not develop one area and then the next in a straight, linear pattern. It develops in an integrated fashion. Structures that control cognition (thinking), perception (sensing), and action (moving) develop at the same time, though not in lock-step fashion. They are linked by a network of interconnections, separate but functioning parallel to one another (Goldman-Rakic, 1996).

Learning is part of memory. "Learning is what happens when information is presented; memory is the gradual process of manipulating that information into a form it will maintain over time, so that it can be consciously retrieved and applied" (LeDoux, 1996, pp. 16–17).

Active Brains of Children 0–3

The development of the brain proceeds at an exhilarating rate. The number of synapses reaches adult level by age two. By age three, a child's brain is two-and-one-half times more active than the brain of an adult, and the synapses do not begin

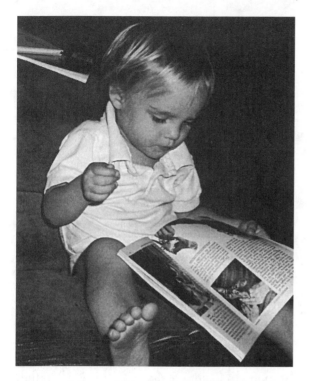

Infants and young children are primed for learning

they are very young. Children benefit most from reading aloud when they discuss stories, learn to identify letters and words, and talk about the meaning of words. (p. 9)

There are many ways parents can encourage reading, but the most significant are reading to children and relating stories to everyday events. Thus development, learning, and caring come together.

Coupled with a discussion of brain development and reading is the continuing need for emotional attachment. When the environment is nurturing and stimulating, it results in both neurological brain development and human attachment.

Inherent Capacities: Language Development

Inherent capacities of children are speech, language, movement, and emotional development. Children are primed to acquire language and basic skills, but not to learn to read or solve complex arithmetic problems. Watching children as they learn to crawl and walk without being taught to do so shows that certain developments are inherent. The ability to acquire language illustrates the inherent nature of language development.

to decline until puberty. For the first three years, production of synapses is greater than elimination. "This suggests that young children—particularly infants and toddlers—are biologically pried for learning" (Shore, 1997, p. 210). By age three, the child's brain has 1,000 trillion synapses. The number holds steady for the first decade. After approximately 10 years of age the synapses decline in density, and by late adolescence half of the synapses have been discarded and 500 trillion remain (Shore).

These findings make the research on reading and suggestions for development of reading concepts ever more valuable. The U.S. Department of Education (1986) pointed out that one of the most promising directions of parent partnerships with schools involves the ability to read. It reported:

The best way for parents to help their children become better readers is to read to them—even when

Within the first 6 months, as infants listen to a caregiver's speech, their perceptual systems are configured to their native tongue. Kuhl (1996) described the process as "language magnets" that attract infants to their native language. "Babies are born with an ability to distinguish among all vowel sounds, but if a sound doesn't occur in the baby's language the ability to discern it will decline" (p. 13). For example, the Swedish language has 16 vowel sounds; English, eight or nine; and Japanese, five. Swedish children retain the ability to distinguish the vowels that are not in the language they hear. "Babies learn to categorize their languages' specific vowel sounds simply by listening the their parents' speech. At six months, even before they can produce and understand words, infants' perceptual systems are configured to acquire their native languages" (pp. 13–14).

This ability to hear and learn language at a young age illustrates why the prime time to teach children multiple languages is when they are infants and toddlers with caregivers who speak different languages.

Effect of the Environment

The brain is affected by the environment. This finding resolves forever the question of whether it is nature or nurture that is most important for the child's development. Children's brain development is not fixed at birth—as Hunt, Piaget, and Vygotsky have already told us. The brain's development is a dynamic interplay between both nature and nurture. The brain is affected by the nourishment, care, and stimulation that it receives.

- How a brain develops hinges on a complex *interplay* between the *genes* you're born with and the *experiences* you have.
- *Early experiences* have *decisive impact* on the architecture of the brain, and on the nature and extent of adult capacities.
- *Early interactions* don't just create a context; they *directly affect* the way the *brain is "wired."*
- Brain development is *non-linear:* there are prime times for acquiring different kinds of knowledge and skills.
- By the time children reach age three, their brains are twice *as active* as those of adults. Activity levels drop during adolescence. (Shore, 1997, p. 18)

See Chapter 10 for a discussion of the negative effects of maltreatment on infants and children.

Interplay Between Genes and Experiences

Genes play an important role in a child's development, but they are only "part of the equation; it is the dynamic relationship between nature and nurture that shapes human development" (Shore, 1997, p. 15). The brain is affected by care, nourishment, stimulation, and environmental conditions.

Even before birth the environment has an impact. Trauma and abuse can harm the brain and interfere with its development. Exposure to nicotine, alcohol, or other drugs affects the child before and after birth. It not only influences the child's general development but also affects the wiring of the brain.

The implication inherent in recognizing the important role of experiences in children's development is the need to promote nourishing, caring, responsive environments for children.

Early Experiences

Children are primed for learning during the early years. Their experiences in the first three years affect their growth and abilities for the rest of their childhood and as adults. "Early stimulation is essential to normal development" (Newman, L. 1996, p. 15). Early care and nurturing have an impact on how children develop and learn as well as the state of their emotional development. Parents must be able to read their babies' cues and respond to infants' feelings, knowing when they need stimulation, when they need to be left alone, and when they need comforting. Nurturing is essential to a child's development and helps protect the child against stress (Education Commission of the States, 1996; Shore, 1997).

Emotion and Intellect

Steps to developing emotional and intellectual health in children are described by Greenspan (2002). At the first level, infants respond "with attention, interest, and pleasure to sensations such as touch and sound provided by a familiar caregiver. These emotions help babies organize their senses and motor responses and develop a sense of security" (Greenspan). When children do not receive interaction from their caregiver, they become apathetic and despondent.

"By four months," the second level of development, "the baby is exhibiting organized, joyful engaging and by nine months, we can see two-way, affect-based communication . . . mother talks;

baby vocalizes back . . . thus initiating early forms of communication and thinking" (Greenspan). Emotional responses can be observed by watching a four- or five-month-old baby smile in response to another's smile. Emotional responses precede the child's motor ability.

The emotional abilities developed earlier become the building blocks in the third level at 12 to 18 months. The child has greater ability to problem solve. The fourth level focuses on the toddler who needs to increasingly develop the use of emotional cueing, more often referred to as affect cueing.

The fifth level includes symbols that have purpose and meaning such as seen in preteen play. At the sixth level, the "child learns symbolic causes-and-effect thinking through bridging his own emotions and intent with the ideas of someone else. This is the basis for reality testing,

impulse control, concentration, and judgment" (Greenspan, 2002).

In the book *The Irreducible Needs of Children,* Greenspan lists questions that parents, caregivers, and others can use to appraise the child's emotional and intellectual developmental level from 3 months to 12 years (Brazelton & Greenspan, 2000).

EARLY THEORIES CONCERNING INTELLECTUAL DEVELOPMENT

Theories developed by Hunt, Piaget, and Vygotsky were not based on neuroscientific evidence, yet much of their work supports the findings now available through brain scans.

Piaget and Vygotsky

Piaget (1896–1980) and Vygotsky (1896–1934) were both born in 1896, but Piaget's work began influencing American education in the late 1950s; Vygotsky's influence occurred later. Both believed that children construct their own understanding. Piaget emphasized that knowledge is constructed as a result of the child's interaction with physical objects, whereas Vygotsky focused on language and the child's interaction with adults. Piaget believed that children progressed through their intellectual developmental level independent of a cultural context; Vygotsky wrote that the culture in which a child lives influences the child's development. For Vygotsky, "competence is developed through language and through interaction with adults and other children in everyday problem-solving activities. Adults and capable peers provide a child with guidance and 'scaffolding,' as well as support calibrated to the child's abilities" (Kagan, Moore, & Bredekamp, 1995, p. 37). The major difference would be obvious while watching teachers interact with students. The Vygotsky theorist would aim at skills the child is developing, not those already developed. Scaffolding a child to an emerging concept would be appropriate in a Vygotsky classroom (Bodrova & Leong, 1996),

The interplay between a child's genetic makeup and positive experiences enables the brain to develop.

whereas a Piagetian would be working with the child's current development.

Hunt

Hunt was one of the first theorists in the United States to raise questions concerning the development of intelligence in children. He recognized that children are not born with fixed intelligence. In *Intelligence and Experience* (1961), Hunt challenged the assumptions of fixed intelligence and predetermined development. The belief in fixed intelligence had far-reaching implications for education and childrearing. If IQ were fixed, intellectual growth could not be affected. The role of parents, therefore, had been to allow intellectual growth to unfold naturally toward its predetermined capacity. Hunt cited that, between 1915 and 1935, parents were even warned against playing with their infant, lest overstimulation interfere with the child's growth. Hunt's belief that IQ is *not* fixed led to a change in perception of the parental role from one of passive observation to one of facilitation.

Piaget

Hunt (1961) focused on the effects of experience on the development of intelligence. He thoroughly reviewed research on the development of intelligence in children. He devoted a large portion of his book to the works of Jean Piaget, a genetic epistemologist who wrote a prodigious number of books and articles on knowledge and cognitive development.

Piaget emphasized that development involves the interaction of the child with the environment. Piaget's book *To Understand Is to Invent* (1976) succinctly illustrates his basic concept of the importance of activity on the part of the learner—the need to act or operate on the environment in the process of developing knowledge. It is through this interaction with the environment that the child develops intelligence. Piaget saw this as an adaptive process that includes *assimilation* of experiences and data into the child's understanding of the world; *accommodation,* by which the child's

thought processes are adjusted to fit the new information into the schemes or models already constructed; and finally *equilibrium* that results from the adaptive process. This model of acquiring new knowledge was important to the cognitive theorists and affected the educator's curriculum because it emphasized the importance of experience to the developing child. A child without a rich environment was at a disadvantage.

Another aspect of Piagetian theory that reinforces his description of the developmental process of learning is his analysis of the developmental stages of the child's thought. In the process of acquiring intellect, children differ from adults in the way they form concepts. Children relate to experience at their own levels of understanding. Hunt (1961) described these three major stages—sensorimotor, preconceptual, and formal:[1]

SENSORIMOTOR

The first period of intellectual development, the sensorimotor, lasts from birth till the child is roughly between 18 months and 2 years old. The reflexive sensorimotor schemata are generalized, coordinated with each other, and differentiated to become the elementary operations of intelligence which begin to be internalized and which correspond to the problem-solving abilities of sub-human animals. During this period, the child creates through his continual adaptive accommodations and assimilations, in six stages, such operations as "intentions," "means-end" differentiations, and the interest in novelty (Piaget, 1936). On the side of constructing reality, the child also develops the beginnings of interiorized schemata, if not actual concepts, for such elements as the permanence of the object, space, causality, and time (Piaget, 1937).

CONCRETE

The second period of concrete operations in intellectual development, beginning when the child is about 18 months or 2 years old, lasts till he is 11 or 12 years old. It contains, first, a preconceptual phase

---

[1] From *Intelligence and Experience* (pp. 113–115), by J. M. Hunt, 1961, New York: John Wiley & Sons. Copyright 1961, John Wiley & Sons. Reprinted by permission of John Wiley & Sons, Inc.

during which symbols are constructed. This lasts to about 4 years of age, and during it the child's activity is dominated by symbolic play, which imitates and represents what he has seen others do, and by the learning of language. The accommodations forced by the variation in the models imitated along with the assimilations resulting from repetitions of the play-activities gradually create a store of central processes which symbolize the actions imitated (Piaget, 1945). As the images are established, the child acquires verbal signs for those which correspond to the collective system of signs comprising language. At this point the child comes under dual interaction with the environment, i.e., with the world of things and the world of people. The child's action-images greatly extend the scope of his mental operation beyond the range of immediate action and momentary perception, and they also speed up his mental activity, for the sensorimotor action is limited by the concrete sequence of perceptions and actions. This period contains, second, an intuitive phase. This is a phase of transition that lasts till the child is 7 or 8 years old. In the course of his manipulations and social communications, he is extending, differentiating, and combining his action-images and simultaneously correcting his intuitive impressions of reality (space, causality, and time). It contains, third, the phase of concrete operations. As the child interacts repeatedly with things and people, his central processes become more and more autonomous. Piaget (1945, 1947) speaks of his thought becoming "decentred" from perception and action. With greater autonomy of central processes come both differentiations and coordinations, or groups, of the action-images into systems which permit classifying, ordering in series, numbering. . . . The acquisition of these "concrete operations," . . . bring a distinctive change in the child's concrete conceptions of quantity, space, causality, and time.

FORMAL OPERATIONS

The third period of formal operations starts at about 11 and 12 years when the child begins to group or systematize his concrete operations (classifications, serial ordering, correspondences, etc.) and thereby also to consider all possible combinations in each case.

Piaget's theories clearly indicate that intellectual development is a process that commences in in-

fancy and continues throughout childhood. The early years are important even though the development of intelligence in young children differs from that in older children.

Hunt's book kindled interest in Piaget as well as in the importance of experience for young children during the time when their parents are the prime caregivers and teachers.

The time was ripe for consideration of intervention and parent involvement. Equal educational opportunity was a high priority. The nation had been aroused by the Soviet Union's launching of *Sputnik* in 1957. Many people wondered if children were learning as well as they should, and there was concern that the United States was falling behind the Soviets in scientific discovery. It was hoped that an emphasis on early childhood education would help overcome learning and reading deficiencies. These considerations supported arguments for early intervention in education.

Appropriate Practices in Early Development

Elkind (1987a) warned against pressured learning in early childhood. He described the scores of intelligence tests at age 4 as predicting with an accuracy of 50 percent what a child's scores will be at age 17. This does not mean, however, that children at age 4 must have half of all the skills they will gain by age 17. Nor does it mean that "this calls for formal, teacher-directed learning. . . . We serve [children] best by providing an environment rich in materials to observe, explore, manipulate, talk, write, and think about" (p. 10). Neurological researchers and educators echo this warning (Brazelton & Greenspan, 2000; Carnegie Corporation of New York, 1994; Education Commission of the States, 1996; Greenspan, 2002; Newman, F., 1996; Shore, 1997).

Although research guides and describes the brain, there is both promise and peril in its use. "The peril rests in believing that these 'windows of opportunities' are so absolute that failing to take advantage of one will lead to unfavorable outcomes for children" (Puckett, Marshall, & Davis, 1999, p. 8). These authors see the promises, but warn that the focus should continue to be on the whole child with continuing best practices and that the research on the working of the brain not be misused. Yet, the brain research supports the understanding developed in earlier studies, and can, if used wisely and appropriately, strengthen childhood programs. "Much of what scholars and practitioners in child development and early childhood education have been proposing for years finally can enjoy the confirmation of scientific 'hard' data" (Puckett et al., p. 12).

℘ IMPLICATIONS FOR PARENTS AND OTHER CAREGIVERS

1. *First, do no harm* (Shore, 1997). Parents must not subject their children, born or unborn, to tobacco, alcohol, or other drugs.

    Parents and other caregivers must not abuse their children emotionally, sexually, or physically.

    Parents and caregivers should follow a child's cues. Do not overstimulate, cause stress by expecting too much, or encourage overkill of the child's potential. Respond to the child's signals of interest and physical condition.

2. *Give your child quality time.* Tune in to your child's interests and needs. Echo the sounds of an infant; listen and respond to the toddler; ensure language development by listening and talking with children at all ages.

    Encourage inquisitive, discovery behavior. Provide objects that the child can manipulate safely. Provide language, music, movement, and enriching experiences. Continue to have an appropriate environment for older children. Use positive reinforcement and love to guide the child. Have behavior parameters for older children that allow them freedom within the boundaries.

3. *Share the knowledge.* Implications for childrearing challenge all parent educators. New

parents should be encouraged to become actively involved with and responsive to their infants. To achieve these goals, all high schools should offer child development and family life courses that include information on attachment and intellectual development. Continuing or adult education programs should offer childrearing classes for parents who are no longer in school. Innumerable channels exist for disseminating information to a wide audience through health services, schools, television, and social agencies.

A more comprehensive discussion of these issues with suggestions for improving school-home collaboration is found in the following 10 chapters.

Policy and Practice

The reforms to change schools emphasized parental participation with community, university, and school involvement. Changes included site-based education, standards for the curriculum, and accountability. Families gained more power in the selection of public education for their children with the creation of charter schools and the continuation of magnet schools in the 1990s. Magnet schools, originally endorsed in 1975 and 1976, each specialized in a specific area such as math-science-engineering, multicultural studies, computer science, humanities, and the arts. These schools had been used earlier to reduce segregation and improve the quality of education. The number of magnet schools more than doubled, going from 1,019 in 1981–1982 to 2,433 in 1991–1992, with a threefold increase in enrollment (American Institute for Research, 1994). Children not living within the traditional attendance area of a magnet school were allowed to enroll if space was available.

> Magnet schools represent a significant effort on the part of the federal government as well as state and local educational agencies to attain two goals: first, to promote the desegregation of American schools, and second, to provide quality education for all students. (American Institute for Research, 1994, p. 1)

Charter schools, authorized with the passage of a 1994 law as part of the Improving America's Schools Act, enable parents to control their children's education. Parents elect their own board, which plans the school. The charter school allows privatization with associations, firms, and groups of parents able to develop their type of private school using public funds (Michel, 1996). Funding comes from the district where the school is located.

> Charter schools are public schools under contract— or charter—from a public agency to a group of parents, teachers, school administrators, or others who want to create alternatives and choices within the public school system. The schools are free, open to all, and designed to be publicly accountable as well as creative, flexible, and responsive to students' and parents' needs. (U.S. Department of Education, 1996, p. 1)

The use of charter schools has continued to increase in the first decade of the 21st century.

Evidence in Support of Home-School Collaboration

The public outcry in the 1990s to improve students' academic success and reduce the dropout rate has elicited a strong response from many professionals and governmental organizations. The links among home, school, and parental involvement are recognized as very important (American Association of School Administrators, 1991; Anastasiow, 1988; Anderson, Hiebert, Scott, & Wilkinson, 1985; Bloom, 1986; Boyer, 1991, 1995; California Task Force on School Readiness, 1988; Center for the Future of Children, 1995; Clark, 1983; Coleman, 1987, 1997; Coleman & Schneider, 1993; Comer, 1988; Comer & Haynes, 1991; Davies, 1987, 1990; Epstein, 1986, 1987a, 1987b, 1994, 1995, 1996; Epstein & Dauber, 1991; Fagnano & Hughes, 1993; Fagnano & Werber, 1994; Families and Work Institute, 1994; Gotts, 1989; Henderson, 1987; Henderson & Berla, 1994; Hess & Holloway, 1984; Kagan & Zigler, 1987; Levenstein, 1988; Lipsky & Gartner, 1989; Macchiarola & Gartner, 1989; Michel, 1996; Moles, 1996a, 1996b; NASBE, 1988,

1991; National Commission on Children, 1991; National Commission on Excellence in Education, 1983; O'Callaghan, 1993; Rigsby, Reynolds, & Wang, 1995; Rioux & Berla, 1993; Schweinhart, Barnes, & Weikart, 1993; Silvern, 1988; Umansky, 1983; U.S. Department of Education, 1986, 1991a, 1991b, 1994, 1997, 1998a, 1998b; Walberg, 1984; Wasik, 1983; Watson, Brown, & Swick, 1983; Wilson, 1991).

No longer is the push for parental involvement directed primarily toward children with a high risk of educational concerns, health problems, disabilities, neglect, or possible abuse. All children need the support of family involvement in their education. The strong emphasis began in 1983 with a report from the National Commission on Excellence in Education that still rings true in the 21st century. In *A Nation at Risk: The Imperative for Educational Reform,* the commission told parents:

> You bear a responsibility to participate actively in your child's education. You should encourage more diligent study and discourage satisfaction with mediocrity and the attitude that says "let it slide"; monitor your child's study habits; encourage your child to take more demanding rather than less demanding courses; nurture your child's curiosity, creativity, and confidence; and be an active participant in the work of the schools. (p. 35)

DEVELOPMENTAL CONTINUITY AND DISCONTINUITY

Throughout childhood, many caregivers—teachers, child care workers, doctors, and administrators— are involved with the child and family. Ideally, they can provide a stable environment where each of society's institutions contributes to the child's growth in an integrated and continuous approach. *Developmental continuity* is defined as a coherent whole or an uninterrupted succession of development. *Discontinuity* means a lack of continuity or logical sequence and refers to changes or disruptions in a child's development.

From a population that finds strength in its diversity, it is impossible to produce a curriculum that ensures perfect developmental continuity for all, but it is possible to work toward support systems that foster the child's continuous development. To provide continuity today, the professional must look beyond the individual to the social system in which the child lives. Children whose parents come from a different country experience great differences between their home experience and school. It is particularly difficult for children from non-Western cultures who attend a Western school (Kellaghan, Sloane, Alvarez, & Bloom, 1993).

> Other groups of children who are likely to experience cultural discontinuities at school are minority and subordinate group children. Examples of such groups in the United States are blacks, American Indians, Chicanos, and Puerto Ricans. . . . The result is that, even though they may know a good deal about the culture of the dominant group, they do not accept it for themselves because of its negative associations in their history and experience." (pp. 22–23)

Change pervades all parents' lives. High mobility, a decrease in extended families living nearby, an increase in poverty, and the devastating effect of drugs are some concerns of today's parents. Parents, schools, child care programs, recreation centers, and public agencies must work together to ensure continuity of provisions, discipline, and nurturing.

Parents can more easily adapt to new conditions, and children can handle change better, if they can depend on some stability in their environment. Families, child care programs, and schools are the first line of defense in the provision of this stability. Those who work with children need to know what provisions, discipline, and nurturing the child is receiving from each of the other providers—family, schools, recreation facilities, churches, child care providers, and public agencies. Only then can they offer the continuity that children need.

The tension and the differences that exist between different preschool programs and elementary education are noted by Caldwell (1991). Not only are programs quite varied, but there is also an "absence of sincere networking. . . . The transition is bound to be difficult for the children and minimally efficient for those who will be their mentors at the next level" (pp. 73–74).

Lombardi (1992) proposes three elements to ensure continuity. The first is a developmentally appropriate curriculum that will fit the needs of the child. The second is parent involvement with the school at all levels of collaboration, such as support groups, parent education, volunteers, decision makers, and staff. The third requires community support and services offered by social agencies in collaboration with the school.

Concerns

Two concerns—responsive school environment and developmentally appropriate curriculum—need to be addressed. First, it is the school's responsibility to create an environment that enables children to succeed while providing enough continuity so that the children feel as though they belong. This is important for both young children and adults. The school should be culture-sensitive and respond positively to the language and culture of the home.

The second concern calls for a developmentally appropriate program. Barbour and Seefeldt (1993) refer to developmental continuity, which is a "term used to describe a way of designing early childhood instruction. Curriculum is designed to provide learning experiences that are linked to children's prior knowledge, that flow in a natural progression across the preschool and primary grades toward more sophisticated and complex content, and that permit progress according to each child's rate and style of learning" (p. 11). In the effort to advance our children educationally, some educators have tried to push the first-grade curriculum into kindergarten and early childhood programs. Many school districts, in an effort to improve test scores and reading ability, have added more and more rote academics to the young child's educational experience.

This has to be done with great care to ensure the growth of the child, and not the failure. Continuity is more difficult to achieve and failure may be forced on children who otherwise would succeed. If schools provide a positive environment with a developmentally appropriate curriculum, they will enable the child to be successful.

Programs for young children should not be seen as either play-oriented or academic. Whether in preschool or in a primary classroom, developmentally appropriate practice should respond to the natural curiosity of young children, reaffirm a sense of self, promote a positive disposition toward learning, and help build increasingly complex skills in the use of language, problem solving, and cooperation (Lombardi, 1992, p. 1). A curriculum that provides developmental continuity is based on the "whole" child, including social, emotional, physical, and intellectual development, and is adjusted so that children experience success. Artificial barriers are eliminated, and curriculum provides a smooth transition from preschool through the grades (Barbour & Seefeldt, 1993).

If the curriculum is not developmentally appropriate, the environment changes into a hostile arena where children cannot accomplish their tasks. Responding to concerns over incorporating inappropriate curricula into kindergarten and early childhood programs, several professional organizations have endorsed positions on what is appropriate (see Bredekamp, 1987; Bredekamp & Rosegrant, 1992; National Association of Elementary School Principals, 1990).

Is all continuity beneficial? Silvern (1988) and Kontos (1992) point out that continuity in and of itself is not always positive. If children come from an ideal home environment, they will benefit from an educational climate that incorporates the positive aspects of a nurturing home environment. If children come from culturally diverse homes, they will feel more comfortable if the school acknowledges cultural diversity and enriches the curriculum by incorporating aspects of home cultures into the school setting. This will help children make the transition from home to school.

However, discontinuity is clearly appropriate for children from sterile or abusive homes. Rather than continue an oppressive situation, the school must provide a nurturing environment, including lunches and/or breakfasts when necessary.

Early childhood settings can be homelike in their approaches to space, time, and language, allowing children, within guidelines, to feel secure. The home provides space that is "characterized by dimensions of warmth, closeness, sharing, security, and support" (Silvern, 1988, p. 150). School space is often individual and insecure. The home is flexible in time, but school schedules are usually rigid. The home encourages a shared understanding of language meanings, whereas language at school is formalized. Therefore, early childhood programs and schools can furnish "continuities that allow children to make sense of the world and discontinuities that afford children important experiences that they do not obtain at home" (p. 149).

Elementary, middle, and secondary schools provide additional challenges. For primary school children the change from one teacher to another may cause a change in continuity. Students in middle and secondary schools routinely have a variety of teachers, each with their own methods and personalities. Children at all ages have to make these transitions. Are they able to do it successfully? The Center on Families, Communities, Schools, and Children's Learning is studying the transition from grade to grade and how it affects the child's continuity. Researchers (Bright, 1994; Hildago, 1994; Sui, 1994; Swap, 1993) studied changes in family involvement from kindergarten to second grade with families of varying cultural backgrounds. Epstein (1996) states, "Many studies still are needed, however, to learn how partnerships change or remain the same across the grades from birth through high school; the challenges that families meet at each stage of their children's development; and the results for students, parents, and the schools of partnerships across the grades" (p. 220).

Children whose first language is not English come to school as experienced users of another language.

Children do not acquire language skills out of context or despite a cultural milieu; rather, language is embedded in that context. When the tasks, demands, and interactions of a young child's everyday experiences are similar to and continuous with those of the school, then the child's prior experiences facilitate success in school. But when the child's experiences differ from those encountered in school—when they are discontinuous—it is more difficult for children to apply previously acquired abilities in school and to acquire new ones. (Kagan et al., 1995, p. 34)

Ensuring continuity for children is an enormous challenge to families, schools, and communities and is an issue that will require continued efforts.

Although children progress through similar stages of development as they move across the preschool and primary grades, this development is not equal or identical. It is time to recognize that children learn best as they are allowed to construct knowledge and that schools—whether child care centers, preschools, or public schools—must provide environments that ensure that children's educational experiences will support their growth, development and different modes of learning. It is time to mobilize all those who are concerned about children's education and to include teachers, parents and community support groups in the process of reorganizing schools for developmental continuity. (Barbour & Seefeldt, 1993, p. 86)

✍ PROGRAMS ACROSS THE NATION

Many programs show what can be done to improve the lot of children. Some of these programs have been replicated, encouraging the adaptation of successful efforts.

Two early and highly successful programs based on parental involvement are the Saturday School and Parents As Teachers (PAT) programs developed in Missouri. Another is the Home-Oriented Preschool Education (HOPE), created in 1966 by the Appalachia Educational Laboratory, with a detailed five-phase follow-up study completed in 1989.

Cities like New York, Indianapolis, St. Louis, New Haven, Baltimore, Chicago, and Los Angeles developed programs that involve parents (Chapman, 1991; Hyde, 1992; Jackson & Cooper, 1992; Reed, 1991; U.S. Department of Education, 1994). (Refer to Chapter 7 for a discussion of programs in these cities and Missouri's PAT and the Appalachian HOPE programs.)

In many cases, parents need to be empowered before they can participate fully with the schools. Both Comer (1997), who developed a program in New Haven, Connecticut, and Epstein (Epstein, 1996; Epstein & Dauber, 1991), who did research in Baltimore schools, found that meaningful activities in the schools helped parents become involved with schools in a productive way. "When teachers help them, parents of all backgrounds can be involved productively" (Epstein & Dauber, 1991, p. 290).

Comer's Program in New Haven

One school system that reached out to parents succeeded in such a turnaround of parent participation that the program has been extended to more than 50 schools. Comer (1988, 1997; Comer, Haynes, Joyner, & Ben-Avie, 1999) and the Yale University Child Study Center started working with two schools in the New Haven school system in 1968. Initially, Comer found a misalignment between home and school. This was overcome by involving parents in restructuring the school. Parents were involved on three levels: as aides in the classroom, as members of governance and management teams, and as general participants in school activities. Parents' distrust of the school needed to be overcome, and this could happen only when they and the school cooperated with each other.

Students were viewed as having unmet needs rather than as being uninterested, having behavior problems, or being bad children. These children were served by a mental health team that attempted to understand their anxiety and conduct. A Discovery Room encouraged children to regain an interest in learning, and a Crisis Room provided positive alternatives to children who had behavior problems. The greatest turnaround in intellectual development occurred when social skills were incorporated into the program. Parents were able to join in as partners, and the school became a force for increased self-esteem and desire for learning. Comer's program has been replicated in schools across the nation.

Touchpoints

Parents need friends and professionals who can support them as they raise their children. To respond to this need, especially illustrated by parents of a child with special requirements, Brazelton developed a program called Touchpoints (see Table 1.1). "Touchpoints are like a map of child development that can be identified and anticipated by parents and providers" (Brazelton & Greenspan, 2000, p. 184). The Touchpoints cover the first 3 years.

Brazelton and Greenspan (2002) also developed a three-level training program—individual level, community level, and faculty level—to implement the Touchpoints program. For more information, contact *touchpoints@tch.harvard.edu*.

Each of the Touchpoints is based on child development, and the training is essential to perform the guidance and leadership that is seen as necessary to accomplish the aim of Touchpoints.

Ready to Learn

The first proclamation in the national goals for 2000—all children in America will start school *ready to learn*—promotes readiness and calls for enormous interest in early childhood and the family. If the statement means children of all ages must be ready to learn when they start school, then societal and environmental conditions must change for this goal to be accomplished. Are children who live in poverty-stricken or violent communities able to come to school ready to learn? Often, they are not. Schools must change, communities must change, and families must become cohesive units to accomplish the first national goal. Children of

TABLE 1.1   Each Touchpoint corresponds to a specific age and focus.

Touchpoint	Age	Focus
1	Prenatal	Imagining the baby, the parent, considering the realignment of relationships, and preparation
2	Newborn	Health, parental emotions, the baby's characteristics, and attachment
3	3 weeks	Parental exhaustion, feeding, individuality, and relationships
4	6–8 weeks	Sociability, parental self-confidence, and relationships
5	4 months	Attachment, interest in the world patterns of care, baby's demands, and father engagement
6	7 months	Motor abilities, feeding, sleeping, and object permanence
7	9 months	Mobility, social referencing, person permanence, and control
8	12 months	Independence, motor skills, learning, and irritability
9	15 months	Autonomy, play, motor skills, dependence, and language are the areas of discussion
10	18 months	The parents and staff are concerned with cognition, language, sense of self, and battles for control
11	24 months	Pretend play, language, autonomy, and motor skills
12	36 months	Imagination, fears and phobias, language, peer relations, and social understanding

Brazelton and Greenspan, 2000.

all ages need to be able to come to school ready to learn. The proclamation, however, addresses the young child in particular and focuses on the early years of the child and the child's family. The young child entering kindergarten or first grade must be ready to learn. The child must come to school healthy, well-nourished, alert, and ready to respond to the challenges of school.

Boyer

In *Ready to Learn: A Mandate for Our Nation,* Boyer (1991) lists seven basic questions that need to be answered for each child to be ready to learn.

How can we ensure that all children have a healthy start?

How can every child live in a supportive, language-rich environment, guided by empowered parents?

How can we make available to all children quality child care that provides both love and learning?

How can work and family life be brought together through workplace policies that support parents and give security to children?

How can television become a creative partner in a school-readiness campaign, offering to preschoolers programming that is mind-enriching?

How can we give to every child a neighborhood for learning, with spaces and places that invite play and spark the imagination?

How can we bring the old and young together with new intergenerational arrangements that provide a community of caring for every child? (p. 11)

These seven questions are necessary for support of all children, from birth until graduation from secondary school. Add to them the necessity for schools to be ready for the children.

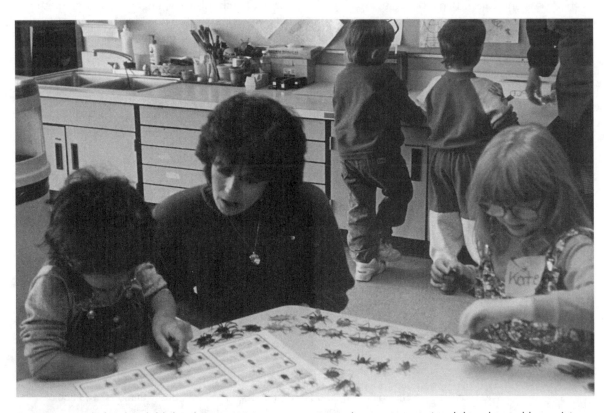

Caring support helps the child develop cognitive competencies such as representational thought, problem solving, mathematical knowledge, social knowledge, and imagination.

Listening to Parents

A national survey of 2,017 parents found that 88 percent of the children had access to pediatric health care. Stated a different way, it showed that over 1 out of 10 children did not have health care. Ninety-seven percent of those who had had health care felt that overall pediatric care was either excellent or good, but many parents were less satisfied with the extent of help concerning the child's growth and development. Fifty-four percent wanted more specific information on how to encourage learning, 42 percent wanted help with discipline, and 23 percent had discussed either of these concerns with a health professional. Only 35 percent had ever attended a class or a discussion on children (McLearn, Davis, Schoen, & Parker, 1998). The study underscores the recognition that multiple professionals are involved with children and each can reinforce the necessary understanding of childrearing. Working together, families can help their children develop well and be ready to learn.

✍ RECONSIDERING CHILDREN'S EARLY DEVELOPMENT AND LEARNING

To clarify the issues involved in being ready to learn, the National Goal Panel established the Technical Planning Group for Goal I. The planning group examined children's early development and, in doing so, shifted from a strictly cognitive approach of readiness to a discussion of five dimensions: (1) physical well-being and motor development; (2) social and emotional development; (3) approaches toward learning; (4) language development; and (5) cognitive and general knowledge. (See Kagan et al., 1995, for a complete narrative of *Reconsidering Children's Early Development and Learning*.) After reading the discussion, this author believes that most of the issues apply to all children, from early ages to secondary school.

The following sections summarize the five dimensions discussed by Kagan and colleagues.

Dimension 1. Physical Well-Being and Motor Development

Physical development considers rates of growth, physical fitness, and body physiology, including health and well-being, diseases, and disabilities.

Physical abilities are measured by four motor skills: (1) gross—walking, running, jumping; (2) fine—manual dexterity; (3) sensimotor—hearing, touch, kinesthesis, and vision; and (4) oral—sucking and the uses of vocal cords, tongue, lips, jaw, and palate that allow one to speak.

> Children who deviate significantly from normative patterns of physical development may possess strengths in other areas and demand close attention from schools and other social institutions to maximize their learning potential. (p. 16)

Dimension 2. Social and Emotional Development

Emotional development includes self-concept, self-esteem, and self-efficacy.

> Early parent-child interactions are an important influence on children's emotional development. Children initially learn to express and interpret emotions through interactions with primary caregivers. . . . Children's ability to express their feelings appropriately is considered crucial to their overall health, behavior, and well-being. Such expression may manifest itself as the ability to communicate one's attitudes and feelings effectively, which involves possession of the knowledge and skills to communicate verbally and non-verbally (pp. 18–19).

Social development involves the "ability to form and sustain social relationships with adults and friends," which is "central to children's preparedness for school" (p. 19).

> Social and emotional development must be understood as cumulative, contextually driven, and based on the interaction of multiple characteristics or variables. (p. 21)

Dimension 3. Approaches Toward Learning

"Gender, temperament, and cultural patterns and values all predispose children to different approaches to learning" (p. 24). Learning styles include cognitive approaches to a challenge, motivation, persistence, creativity and inventiveness, and ability to reflect. Styles can develop and change.

Dimension 4. Language Development

> By definition, language development is the acquisition of linguistic forms and procedures, and social rules and customs for acts of expression and interpretation. Such knowledge has three essential components: content (meaning), form (structure), and use (function). (p. 29)

Verbal language includes not only meaning and vocabulary but also speaking, listening, questioning, and social and creative use of language. By age 5, children have not achieved adult level in language. Although they need a language to be able to communicate, express thoughts, and as a symbol for developing concepts, these skills are developing but are not a prerequisite to school. Rather, the refinement of language is a "shared task of schools, families, and communities" (p. 31).

Dimension 5. Cognition and General Knowledge

The report identified three types of knowledge: physical (physical properties of objects); logico-mathematical (relationships, similarities, differences, and associations); and social-conventional (school-learned knowledge). Children develop the following cognitive competencies: representational thought; problem solving; mathematical knowledge, social knowledge, and imagination. A lack of social-conventional knowledge does not make a child unable to learn (pp. 36–39).

Conclusions

The Technical Planning Group recommends that

> energy be devoted to examining the readiness and capacity of the nation's schools to receive young children. . . . Specifically, the report has encouraged a shift from a primarily cognitive orientation to one that embraces multiple dimensions . . . early development and learning must no longer be regarded solely, or even primarily, as a cognitive issue. . . . There must be a match between the nature of the child's learning environment and the child. . . . In order for children to thrive, they must be in environments that foster rich developmental experiences (pp. 41–44).

✍ A LOOK AHEAD

The following synopses provide an overview of the remaining chapters.

Chapter 2, Historical Overview of Family Life and Parent Involvement, contains a summary of education history and trends as they relate to parents. Parental involvement is not new; parents have always been prime educators of their children, but, through the years, the emphasis of parents as partners in education has changed. Since the 1960s, increased concern for school and home cooperation has resulted in parents' participation in schools and home visitation programs. Chapter 2 describes the growth of education programs for parents and notes the historical changes in childrearing practices. In closing, it outlines the issues that face the nation today.

Chapter 3, The Family and Community, describes families in the United States today. Demographic changes in the nation since the 1950s place many families at high risk. These changes include high rates of mobility, women working outside the home, out-of-wedlock births to teenage mothers, divorce, and poverty. The chapter discusses how schools can respond to rapid changes and high levels of stress in society.

It also addresses cultural diversity, including a discussion of blacks, Hispanics, Native Americans, and recent immigrants from Vietnam, Cambodia, and Thailand.

Chapter 4, Effective Home-School-Community Relationships, includes the special activities that schools need to offer parents. Techniques are suggested for using parents and other community members as volunteers.

Chapter 5, Communication and Parent Programs, focuses on communication among parent, child, and school. One-way communication, in the form of newsletters and notes, is illustrated. Suggestions are given for two-way interactions between parents and schools to help parents feel welcome. Open responses, listening skills, and ways to encourage good communication help parent, teacher, and child communicate more effectively. Techniques of good parenting (as illustrated by such programs as Systematic Teaching of Effective Parenting, Parent Effectiveness Training, and Active Parenting) are included. Tips for parent-teacher conferences, acknowledged as one of the most effective means of communication between parent and teacher, are discussed in detail.

Chapter 6, Collaborative Leadership—Working With Parents, deals with leadership training and types of meetings. The chapter gives tips on leading meetings and suggestions on the types of meetings to use for parent education.

Chapter 7, School-Based Programs, describes some schools' special characteristics that make them effective in collaborating with parents.

Chapter 8, Home-Based Programs, details programs for working with the family as well as the individual child in the home. These programs are seen as ways to educate and support all members of the family. The chapter describes new approaches to home-based education, reviews research done by Home Start, and addresses increased interest in homeschooling and homework.

Chapter 9, Working With Parents of a Child With Disabilities, originally written by Jo Spidel, an educator who held an advanced degree in learning disabilities, has been revised to include new policies on special education. The chapter discusses inclusion, the development of the Individualized Education Program, and the unique needs of children with disabilities and their families.

Chapter 10, The Abused Child, includes data on child abuse and recommends procedures for dealing with this problem. Teachers and child care workers must be able to recognize abuse and respond appropriately.

Chapter 11, Rights, Responsibilities, and Advocacy, concerns student rights and responsibilities. The example of advocating for good child care is used to illustrate the responsibility of advocating for change that will help children and families.

The book closes with an Appendix listing books, pamphlets, organizations, and references that can be used to develop a parent education program. Descriptions of parent programs can also be helpful to individuals working with parents. From infancy to young adulthood, varying needs require different types of programs. Brief descriptions of programs related to age levels are discussed to provide the reader with an overview of current parental involvement.

SUMMARY

Parenthood is an essential role in society. The support given by parents, interrelated with other agencies—particularly the school—should be integrated and continuous. Programs that respond to parents' needs range from infancy, preschool, and primary and intermediate grades to secondary and young adult programs.

Five areas are considered: (1) caring schools and communities, (2) caring families, (3) adequate and enriching child care, (4) positive before- and after-school care, and (5) collaboration among parents, teachers, and the community.

Families are social systems that impact and impart their history and culture. Systems vary, and they change related to the circumstances in the family.

Parents are their child's first educators and, as such, are responsible for the child's survival and for providing an environment that facilitates attachment and brain development in their child. All three responsibilities are extremely important for the child's subsequent development. The chapter discusses brain development from infancy through 3 years of age.

The renewed interest in parental involvement, which manifested itself in concern over the child's intellectual development, was reinforced by the writings of Piaget, Vygotsky, and Hunt.

Studies on human attachment, including those by Skeels, Spitz, Bowlby, Ainsworth, and Tizard, emphasized the significance of a nurturing and warm parent-figure.

Developmental continuity with a caring environment, an appropriate curriculum, and smooth transitions is important. Discontinuity is needed when the child comes from an abusive or sterile environment.

Child care providers and educators must be advocates for children. Research on the quality of child care centers shows a need for improvements. In response to the question, "What does it mean to be ready to learn?" five areas were considered: (1) physical well-being and motor development, (2) social and emotional development, (3) approaches toward learning, (4) language development, and (5) cognitive and general knowledge.

✎ SUGGESTED CLASS ACTIVITIES AND DISCUSSIONS

1. Survey a preschool, elementary school, or middle or high school in your area to find out how the school involves parents.
2. Visit a child care center or primary-grade classroom and survey the variety of families in a class. How many are two-parent families, single parents, or foster parents? What ways would you suggest that the school could work with families to provide caring environments for the children? How can families help the teacher enrich the caring classroom?
3. Using the three levels of family systems—microsystem, mesosystem, and exosystem—analyze how your own family system is influenced by each.
4. Review the information on brain development. How would you relay this information to parents?
5. Look into the research on attachment. How are both parents important to the infant?
6. Give Piagetian-type tests to children at ages 3 months to 9 years. Focus on the way the children think and the differences in ability. Add a scaffolding activity (Vygotsky) with a child. Did the child respond positively to the help or did the child show discouragement?
7. Visit an infant center or nursery. Observe the extent to which children are actively involved in their environment. Are some more actively involved than others?
8. Discuss the importance of Hunt's book *Intelligence and Experience.* How has it helped change the belief in fixed IQ?
9. Invite a social worker to discuss the problems involved in foster home and institutional placements.
10. Visit a Head Start center. How are parents involved in the program?
11. Visit a preschool cooperative organized and run by parents—a parent cooperative. Talk with some parents about their responsibilities in the preschool program. Interview the director and discuss the roles parents play in the total program.
12. Investigate and analyze the goals of *Call for Action for American Education in the 21st Century.*
13. Describe how you can defend the importance of parents as teachers of their own children and parents as partners with the school.

2 Historical Overview of Family Life and Parent Involvement

As each decade passes, society goes through changes in feelings, beliefs, and goals. Each time reflects its own color, shape, and sound. With the passing of the 20th century, it is time to reflect on the goals, standards, and beliefs that are needed for the 21st century. What will the future reflect?

Author

In this chapter you will learn the history of parent education and involvement through the years. After completing the chapter you should be able to do the following:

- Recognize that theories on parent education and child development change as the political climate and beliefs of the culture evolve.
- Enumerate societies in ancient times that were concerned with child-rearing and identify their characteristics.
- Identify Plato, Aristotle, and Cicero, their lands of origin, and their beliefs about families and childrearing.
- Describe how children were educated during the Middle Ages.
- Identify and discuss major advancements or changes in society during the 15th and 16th centuries that affected children's education.
- Describe childrearing in Europe during the 17th and 18th centuries.
- Describe the religious zeal of the New England Puritans and the child-rearing practices in the early colonies.
- Identify the contributions of Comenius, Locke, Rousseau, Pestalozzi, and Froebel.
- Identify Elizabeth Peabody and Henry Barnard and their contributions to early childhood education and the kindergarten movement.
- Describe the early civilizations in the Americas and the Europeans' treatment of the native population.
- Describe the growth of parent education and the development of women's associations.
- Describe childrearing in the United States from the 1890s to the present.
- Discuss patterns of immigration and migration in the United States.
- Discuss current issues and concerns in family life and education.
- Recognize that movement in political thought results in changes in education and family life.

✍ INTRODUCTION

A new emphasis on the best way to involve families in their children's education brings an increased dimension to family involvement. Although the explosion of parent education and parent involvement programs in recent decades has tended to obscure the roots of the parent education movement, it is recognized that families have always been involved in the education of their children.

A traditional concept was being reemphasized. The many new programs that resulted were rich in design and control and produced additional knowledge about the whys and hows of programs involving parents. There have been periods, however, when parents *were* the natural advocates for their children and partners in the educational process.

It is meaningful to compare the emergence of educational programs with the economic conditions and social thought of corresponding historical periods, for there is a relationship between a time's societal developments and its childrearing practices and educational theories. Note the effect the Russian *Sputnik* success had on the U.S. emphasis on cognitive development during the 1960s. Or go back further into history and relate the needs of poverty-stricken children in Switzerland in the 1700s to the educational beliefs and practices of Pestalozzi. The history of parent education and involvement can be pictured as the ebb and flow of the ocean's tide. Some eras portray a calm; others are characterized by tumult. As rapid changes, social problems, poverty, and political unrest produce turbulence for families, their need for stabilizing forces increases. So in the 1960s with the calls for a War on Poverty and the Great Society, there emerged a focus on the family as one institution that could affect the lives of millions of disadvantaged children. The powerful call resulted in renewed interest in programs in child care centers, home-based education, and combined home-school intervention projects. Meeting the challenges of the 21st century requires that children be educated, and that can be accomplished only if families and schools work together.

The picture of mother and child depicts loving care of parents to children throughout the centuries. *Jean-Baptiste-Corot (French, 1796–1875). Mother and Child, probably 1860s. Oil on wood. (The Metropolitan Museum of Art, H.O Haremeyer Collection, The Gift of Mrs. P. H. Frelinghuysen, 1930. ([30.13])*

PART 1
Early History

❧ PREHISTORIC PARENT EDUCATION

Since the beginning of civilization, family groups and parents have been involved with the rearing of their young. Before the development of written records, which is believed to have occurred between 6000 and 5000 B.C., early human beings had developed a primitive culture. To ensure survival they had to develop means to obtain food and water for sustenance and provide protection from harsh weather and predators. Picture a primitive family group with children modeling their parents' actions. Children accompanied their parents on forays, learning to obtain food through hunting, fishing, and gathering wild foods, or, in later periods, by growing crops. Parents also taught their children rules for participating as members of both the family group and the larger society. A study of contemporary primitive groups in Brazil and Indonesia substantiates the fact that nonliterate people use the oral tradition to pass on time-tested wisdom and practices.

Primitive societies did not develop schools; the prime educators were the family and community. Children were valued for their contribution to survival and for their implied continuance of society. They were the future—they would carry on the traditions of the culture as well as provide for the basic needs of the group.

For thousands of years, children have learned and internalized the important customs, rules, values, and laws of their society so they could function within their cultural groups. This process of socialization is prevalent in all groups, primitive or highly developed. Without it, children do not develop into functioning human beings as defined by the culture in which they live. During prehistoric times, just as today, the first teachers—the socializers—were parents and families.

❧ FORMAL EDUCATION IN EARLY SOCIETIES

Our knowledge of education in ancient civilizations with written records is more extensive. In the valleys of the Tigris-Euphrates and the Nile rivers, where the ancient civilizations of Sumeria, Babylon, Assyria, and Egypt flourished, formal learning joined forces with informal learning. During the Old Kingdom in Egypt, 5510–3787 B.C., children were educated at home. During the Middle Kingdom, 3787–1580 B.C., there are indications that school outside the home developed (Frost, 1966; Osborn, 1991). Artwork depicts Egyptians as holding their children in high esteem. Adults showed affection for their children by holding them on their laps and embracing them. Children were also portrayed in art as carefree—running, playing with balls, dolls, board games, and jumping at leapfrog and hopscotch (Bell & Harper, 1980; Osborn, 1991). In Sumeria, both boys and girls were important to the family and were given opportunities to learn (Chambliss, 1982). Formal systems of education also existed in ancient India, China, and Persia, as well as in the pre-Columbian Americas, especially in the cultures of the Mayas, Aztecs, and Incas.

✸ PARENT INVOLVEMENT IN EDUCATION AND FAMILY LIFE IN GREECE

The Athenian state produced philosophy and social thought that is still studied in schools. As far back as the 6th century B.C., regulations governed schools. Parents were responsible for teaching their sons to read, write, and swim; schools were to be in session for a certain number of hours; a public supervisor was appointed; and free tuition was provided for sons of men killed in battle. Schools were nonetheless private, and parents had the right to choose the pedagogue or school they desired for their children.

Greeks viewed children as children but also as a link to the future, the conveyors of culture and civilization, as well as valued members of the family. They focused on close supervision rather than physical punishment as the way to guide children (Bell & Harper, 1980).

Plato

Real concern over education blossomed during the golden age of Greece. Plato (427–347 B.C.) questioned theories of childrearing in his dialogues in the *Republic.*

> And shall we just carelessly allow children to hear any casual tales which may be devised by casual persons, and to receive into their minds ideas for the most part the very opposite of those which we wish them to have when they are grown up? We cannot. (Plato, 1953, p. 221)

Plato even believed the games children played should be controlled. He believed so strongly that a child could be molded to fit the needs of society that he wrote in his *Laws:*

> To form the character of the child over three and up to six years old there will be need of games. . . . For when the programme of games is prescribed and secures that the same children always play the same games and delight in the same toys in the same way and under the same conditions, it allows the real and serious laws also to remain undisturbed. (Bell & Harper, 1980, p. 15)

Egyptian boys were educated at home during the Old Kingdom. During the Middle Kingdom, schools developed outside the home.
Portrait panel from a mummy. Encaustic on wood panel, 2nd century A.D. (The Metropolitan Museum of Art Gift of Edward S. Harkness, 1918. [1917–])

Plato designed an ideal city-state in which genetics and procreation would be controlled by the state to produce children who, when grown, would be capable of administering affairs of state (Chambliss, 1982). Parent education was not for the benefit of the family or its individual members; it was designed to strengthen the communal state.

Aristotle

Although Aristotle (384–323 B.C.) disagreed with Plato about the desirability of a communal ideal state, he agreed that education was too important to be determined by the financial ability of the parents. Like Plato, he believed that education did not exist for the benefit of the family or its individual members but was designed to strengthen the state.

🌿 PARENT INVOLVEMENT AND FAMILY LIFE IN ROME

During about the same period, family life in Rome was flourishing, and parents were actively involved in their children's education. The high priority placed on children resulted in concern for their development, with the parents being their children's first educators.

Polybius and Cicero

Polybius (204–122 B.C.) and Cicero (106–43 B.C.) both wrote of the importance of the family in the development of good citizens. Cicero declared:

> For since the reproductive instinct is by Nature's gift the common possession of all living creatures, the first bond of union is that between husband and wife; the next, that between parents and children, then we find one home, with everything in common. And this is the foundation of civil government, the nursery, as it were, of the state. (Chambliss, 1982, p. 226)

Cicero believed, as Aristotle had, that man is a social and political creature and that human virtues are developed through social participation.

Mother as First Teacher

In Rome and Sparta, the mother was the first teacher of her children, but the Roman mother had a greater role in academic education than the Spartan mother, and taught the children to read. The mother taught her daughters the obligations,

Families were important to Romans, and fathers placed high priorities on their sons' educations. *Ghirlandaio, Domenic (Domenico di Tommaso Curradi di Doffo Bigordi) (born c. 1448, died 1494). Francesco Sassetti (1429–1490) and his son Teodoro. Fifteenth Century Portrait. Tempera on wood. (The Metropolitan Museum of Art. The Jules Bache Collection, 1949 [49.7.7])*

responsibilities, and skills necessary to be a homemaker. The father encouraged his sons to learn to read and write, develop physical skills as well as business acumen, and practice citizenship. This changed in the middle of the second century B.C. when schools were established and fathers began to use tutors or schoolteachers (Bell & Harper, 1980; Frost, 1966; Osborn, 1991).

Infanticide

It should be noted that from primitive times through Greco-Roman days to modern times, laws and customs illustrate that infanticide, abandonment to exposure, and sale of children have been common practices (see deMause, 1974, pp. 25–33). Roman children had few rights. Roman fathers held the power of determination over their children, even to the extent of deciding upon life or death. The need for survival became a guide for practices of infanticide. "Sometimes it was under the direction of the state, as in ancient Sparta, or among the Romans, whose Twelve Tables forbade the rearing of deformed children, or at the discretion of the parents, as among the Athenians" (Bossard & Boll, 1966, p. 491). In most societies where infanticide or similar practices occurred, once the decision was made to keep children, they were raised in the same way as the other children within the culture.

Concern for eradication of child desertion, infanticide, and the selling of children began to grow about the first century A.D. By 318 in Rome, Emperor Constantine decreed that killing infants was a crime (Osborn, 1991). Rewards were offered to those who reared an orphan. Refuge and asylum for abandoned children were offered by the church, which further testified to the emergence of concern for children (Bossard & Boll, 1966). Finally, in 374, an imperial edict prohibited the exposing and consequent death of infants (Bell & Harper, 1980).

Education and family life had become important during the golden civilizations of Greece and Rome and in early Christian times. A subsequent decline in the importance of the family occurred during the Middle Ages, and the concern for parent involvement did not emerge again until many centuries later.

✍ EUROPEAN CHILDREN DURING THE MIDDLE AGES

As the Roman Empire declined, turmoil, famines, and warfare made family life difficult, if not impossible. The major concern was for survival. Adults and children were not given different treatment (Bell & Harper, 1980).

Feudal System

A feudal system emerged, which provided a protective though restrictive social order for the people. During the Middle Ages, about 400–1400, children were very low among society's priorities. "The prevailing image of the child was that of chattel, or piece of property consistent with the ideology of serfdom" (Elkind, 1987a, p. 6). Children of serfs and peasants learned what they could from their parents and peers. There was no system of education and, due to the lack of privacy, very little family life. Living conditions did not provide the poor with an opportunity for privacy or time with their families. Thus, learning came through working with parents to fulfill the menial tasks required to subsist on feudal estates (Aries, 1962; Frost, 1966). As children worked and participated in everyday life, they were socialized into the way of life—the values, customs, and means of existence—for the poor.

Children of Nobility

By contrast, children of nobility were reared and taught in their homes until the age of 7. Life in a medieval castle, built for defense rather than for family life, was difficult for children.

The children of nobles were precursors of the emerging middle- and upper-class families of the 17th and 18th centuries. They inherited property and were educated for their future duties. They, too, were socialized into the values and social graces of their families, but beyond that they were also taught reading, ciphering, and penmanship. Because the men were often away on missions and women were left to run the estates, both genders were taught the practical skills needed to care for the household and land. Children were expected to be miniature adults, "mingling with older adults in an undifferentiated common stream of association and activity" (Handel, 1988, p. 22). After the age of 7, boys were sent to work as apprentices with another family. Boys from the upper classes learned skills and duties befitting a noble and the art of chivalry, while commoners

Noble children, dressed as young adults, were treated very much like adults.
Hyacinthe Rigaud (1659–1743). Louis XV (1770–1774) as a Child. (The Metropolitan Museum of Art, Purchase, Bequest of Mary Wetmore Shively in memory of her husband, Henry L. Shively, M.D. 1960. [60.6])

were apprenticed to learn a craft, a trade, or agriculture. The custom of education by apprenticeship existed for many centuries.

✑ PEOPLE IN OTHER PARTS OF THE WORLD

Great civilizations were in progress in Asia, Africa, and the Americas during Europe's Middle Ages, A.D. 400 until A.D. 1400. The following in-complete descriptions of the ancient civilizations are included to illustrate that the multicultural makeup of the United States includes many people whose ancestors had great learning and civilizations. Children were raised by their families within the traditional cultural expectations of the time period. Children in classrooms come from a variety of cultural backgrounds. Recognition of their heritage helps make the classroom family-friendly.

Africa

The Egyptian calendar has a recorded date of 4241 B.C. People began to settle along the Nile around 4000 B.C. The Kush kingdom of Nubia (Sudan) was established in 1600 B.C. Between A.D. 400 and 900 several kingdoms developed on the African continent, including Jenne, Gao, Yoruba, Hausa, and IgboUkwu (Kullen, 1994, p. 17). The civilizations that flourished before and during the period of world explorations were Ghana (A.D. 1000); Mali (A.D. 1300); Kongo, Swahili, and Monomotapa (A.D. 1400); and Songhai, Kanem-Bornu, Bunyoro, and Luanda (A.D. 1500). The Songhai Empire reached it zenith under Askia Muhammad I in the mid-1500s (p. 34).

Asia

The Xia dynasty ruled China from 2205 to 1766 B.C., a period of improvement in farming, irrigation, and writing. The Shang dynasty ruled China from 1766 to 1122 B.C. The Zhou dynasty, 1066–221 B.C., was the period in which the teachings of Confucius became important. The Great Wall of China was begun in 256 B.C. The Han dynasty ruled China from 206 B.C. until A.D. 220. "The writing brush, paper and ink come into wide usage, and the first dictionary is compiled" (Kullen, 1994, p. 13).

There was cultural contact among the Asian countries. Trade from India went as far as Malaya, the Philippines, Formosa, and the Celebes by 100 B.C. As early as A.D. 109 China and Persia were trading goods over land routes.

The Chinese were early sailors, engaging in maritime activity from the middle of the 7th century. They traveled back and forth between countries in the southeast. Both China and Japan remained relatively isolated from outside interference, however, until the 19th century.

Americas

As early as 10,000 to 5,000 B.C., villages were built in the Americas. Although the first year of the Mayan calendar was 3111 B.C., the golden age of the Mayans was 600–500 B.C. The civilization continued until the abandonment of their cities in A.D. 1400–1450.

Adults had ambivalent feelings about children in the 17th and 18th centuries. Change was taking place in society as well as in the family.
Don Manuel Osorio Manrique de Zuniga (1784–1792). Goya y Lucients, (1746–1828).
(The Metropolitan Museum of Art, the Jules Bache Collection, 1949. [49.7.41])

The Olmec civilization developed near Veracruz, Mexico, in 2000 B.C. and flourished from 1250 to 1200 B.C. Through much of Central America they established "trade routes, highly developed art and architecture, and a form of writing" (Kullen, 1994, p. 4).

Other civilizations in the Americas included the Toltecs in central Mexico (A.D. 850–900), the Hohokam and Anasazi in present-day Arizona and New Mexico (A.D. 100–900), the Mochica and Nazca civilizations in Peru (A.D. 100–900), and the Aztec and Incan empires (A.D. 1200–1500). The Incan Empire ruled over an estimated 16 million people and stretched through the Andes from present-day Ecuador to Santiago, Chile. It continued until 1553, almost 60 years after Columbus came to the Americas (Kullen, 1994).

INFLUENCE OF THE REFORMATION AND INVENTION OF THE PRINTING PRESS

The Reformation, coupled with the invention of the printing press, brought about great change in Europe. An awareness of childhood began to evolve in the 12th century, gaining ground through the 17th century. The invention of movable type for printing in 1439 by Johannes Gutenberg made books available to a much larger segment of the population, even though only the wealthy were able to purchase them for personal use. By 1500 "there were nearly 2,000 printing establishments in Europe and more than three million books had been produced" (Osborn, 1991, p. 21). The increased number of books brought about great change in society and also revealed the changing times. Children's lives between the 14th century, when children were still tied to apprenticeship systems, and the 17th century, when the family was organized around children, were illustrated by the change in etiquette books. Those published in the 1500s were restricted to etiquette for adults, while *La Civilitie Nouvelle,* written in 1671, included children as part of the family system. One of the very early parent education books contained directives for parents to use as they taught children their letters. It even included the proper way to discipline and control children (Aries, 1962). For the first time in history, authors were speaking directly to parents.

Luther

European societies, emerging from a time of suffering and hardship and influenced by the Protestant Reformation and the Catholic Counter-Reformation, viewed the child as one in whom evil must be suppressed and the soul nourished (Bell & Harper, 1980). Throughout the Middle Ages, the Catholic church had been a primary influence on people's behavior. When Martin Luther (1483–1540) introduced his Ninety-five Theses in 1517, he opened the floodgates for religious change. The most important aspect of the Protestant Reformation was the concept of a priesthood of believers, in which people were expected to learn to read and study the Bible for themselves and thereby find their own salvation. Luther believed people should be able to read the Bible in their own language. He brought his beliefs to the people and wrote the Sermon on the Duty of Sending Children to School, in which he pointed out to parents that they should educate their children. He recommended that children learn their catechisms, and he encouraged the use of Aesop's fables for the teaching of morals.

Church in Medieval Times

As the church grew in medieval times, children began to be viewed as pure and innocent, representative of the Virgin Mary and infant Jesus on the one hand, and depraved and evil because of original sin on the other (Bell & Harper, 1980).

The Catholic Counter-Reformation saw the founding of the Jesuit Order, which made much progress in religious education. These advancements in education permeated educational practices both in Europe and the United States. The religious tenor of the times also influenced social thought and, consequently, childrearing practices for centuries.

THE BEGINNINGS OF MODERN PARENT EDUCATORS AND CHILD DEVELOPMENT THEORISTS

The modern parent educator began to emerge during the 17th and 18th centuries, but the general population was not affected until the 19th century. New ideas about education and the importance of the home in the education of children were developed by social thinkers such as Comenius, Locke, Rousseau, Pestalozzi, and Froebel, all of whom rejected the concepts of original sin and depraved children.

Poverty and deprivation caused the underclass to resort to begging.
Style of Louis Nain. Beggars at a Doorway. *Oil on canvas. (The Metropolitan Museum of Art, Purchase, 1871. [71.80])*

John Amos Comenius (1592–1670)

Born in Moravia in 1592, Comenius was a member and bishop of the Moravian Brethren who believed in the basic goodness of each child as opposed to the concept of original sin. This idea is reflected in his writing about education methodology; his thinking was more advanced than that of many others who lived during the same period. In *Didactica Magna,* a large treatise on education, he discussed the importance of the infant's education: "It is the nature of everything that comes into being, that while tender it is easily bent and formed, but that, when it has grown hard, it is not easy to alter. Wax, when soft, can be easily fashioned and shaped; when hard it cracks readily" (Comenius,

1967, p. 58). In the *School of Infancy,* written in 1628, he emphasized that education begins at home and described in detail the manner in which young children should be educated. Comenius also wrote textbooks for children. *Orbis Pictus* (The World in Pictures) is considered the first picture book for children (Morrison, 1991). Although a prolific writer, Comenius was unable to change the direction of education during his lifetime.

John Locke (1632–1704)

Locke, an Englishman who was educated at Christchurch College, Oxford, had far-reaching and innovative ideas concerning government and education. He probably is best known for the concept that the newborn's mind is a *tabula rasa,* or blank slate, at birth. All ideas develop from experience; none are innate. It is incumbent upon family and teacher to provide the optimum environment and valuable experiences for the child's mind to thrive.

Locke, who lived during the period when hardening of the child was in vogue, was a staunch supporter of the concept. If children were exposed to cold baths and other methods of hardening, according to the belief, they would become more resistant to diseases and ailments. "A sound Mind in a sound Body is a short, but full Description of a Happy State in this World" (Locke, 1989, p. 83).

Jean Jacques Rousseau (1712–1778)

Rousseau was another giant in the development of changing European social thought. As thoughts of greater freedom for human beings evolved, stirrings of freedom for children also emerged. As a political analyst, Rousseau wrote *Social Con-* *tract* in 1762, in which he described government through consent and contract with its subjects. This desire for freedom extended into his writings concerning children. Although Rousseau allowed his five children to be placed in foundling homes soon after birth, he wrote charming books about child development. In *Emile,* written in 1762, he urged mothers to "cultivate, water the young plant before it dies. Its fruits will one day be your delights. . . . Plants are shaped by cultivation and men by education" (Rousseau, 1979, p. 38).

Johann Heinrick Pestalozzi (1747–1827)

Pestalozzi was a Swiss educator and a sensitive social activist influenced by the writings of Rousseau. He was 5 when his father died, and he was reared by his mother and nurse in a sheltered, restrictive environment. His greatest joy came during visits to his grandfather, Andrew Pestalozzi, pastor at Hoenigg near Zurich. He accompanied

Life was not all work and no play. Cards, blindman's buff, and blowing bubbles were some of the recreational diversions.
Cardin, Jean Batiste-Simeon (French, 1699–1779). Boy Blowing Bubbles. *Oil on canvas. (The Metropolitan Museum of Art, Wentwork Fund 1949. [49.24])*

his grandfather on pastoral calls and saw the mean and hungry depths of abject poverty starkly contrasted with the accumulated luxuries of wealth. These impressions and his later work at the university fermented into a zeal for righting the wrongs inflicted on the poor.

He read Rousseau's *Emile* and was so impressed that he used it as a guide for the education of his own child. Pestalozzi believed in the natural goodness of children and struggled for many years teaching and caring for poor children in his home.

Pestalozzi based his teaching on use of concrete objects, group instruction, cooperation among students, and self-activity of the child. To teach mathematics, he used beans and pebbles as counters and divided cakes and apples to demonstrate fractions. The child's day also included recreation, games, and nutritious snacks and meals (Gutek, 1968). Pestalozzi is remembered primarily for his writings; in his first successful book, *How Gertrude Teaches Her Children*, he emphasized the importance of the mother and included teaching methods for parents. It was the first comprehensive education book for parents. Pestalozzi can be hailed as the father of parent education. He stridently emphasized the importance of the home. "As the mother is the first to nourish her child's body, so should she, by God's order be the first to nourish his mind" (Pestalozzi, 1951, p. 26). He saw the effects of the environment on the young charges he taught and noted the significance of parents in this way: "For children, the teachings of their parents will always be the core, and as for the schoolmaster, we can give thanks to God if he is able to put a decent shell around the core" (p. 26).

Friedrich Wilhelm Froebel (1782–1852)

Froebel, known as the father of kindergarten, was born in 1782, 35 years after Pestalozzi. Froebel is most noted for his development of a curriculum for the kindergarten, but he also recognized the importance of the mother in the development of the child. He saw the mother as the first educator of the child and wrote a book for mothers to use with their children at home. The book, *Mother Play and Nursery Songs with Finger Plays*, included verses, pictures, songs, and finger plays still used today, such as "pat-a-cake, pat-a-cake." Froebel's plan for education grew around a concept of unity. He organized his curriculum to follow the natural unfolding of the child with the mother assisting in the development. The child and mother enjoyed the language and interaction. Visualize the small child and mother playing the following game:

Count your baby's rosy fingers.
Name them for him, one by one.
Teach him how to use them deftly.
Ere the dimples all are gone;
So, still gaining skill with service,
All he does will be well done.

(Blow & Eliot, 1910, p. 147)

The mother was involved in teaching her child, guided by Froebel's curriculum.

Froebel's development of kindergarten curriculum had a significant effect on the current philosophy of education. Instead of a prescribed curriculum designed by the adult to teach the child to read, write, and be moral, the curriculum was developed from the needs of the child. The concept of child development and teaching to the individual levels of each child was a radical departure from lock-step education.

EUROPEAN CHILDREN IN THE 17TH AND 18TH CENTURIES

Ambivalent feelings about children and their place in the social system were reflected during the 17th and 18th centuries in Europe. The well-to-do commonly employed wet nurses to breastfeed their children. Although sometimes necessary, the practice separated the mother from her infant. Another characteristic of the period was the swaddling of young infants, which seems to have been done primarily to provide warmth, because buildings were damp and drafty. The infants were bound from head to toe in a cloth band (a maillot) about two inches wide with their

Outdoor activities were also enjoyed by children. *Raeburn, Sir Henry (1756–1823)*. The Drummond Children. *(The Metropolitan Museum of Art, Bequest of Mary Stillman Harkness 1950. [50.145.31])*

arms at the sides and legs extended. Later, between the first and fourth month, the arms were released, and the child could use them. Usually at 8 or 9 months, the infant was unswaddled. Babies also were unwrapped when it was necessary to clean them. Although it may seem that swaddling would have retarded growth and development, this does not appear to be the case. After they were unswaddled, babies were soon encouraged to walk. Louis XIII, who had been swaddled, was running by 19 months of age and playing the violin and drum at about 18 months (Hunt, 1970).

Social Change

The 18th century was one of tremendous upheaval, filled with social change and restlessness. In France this political and social unrest resulted in the French Revolution. In England, growth in industry created a demand for labor. Toward the latter half of the 18th century and during much of the 19th century, the Industrial Revolution created an atmosphere of poverty and misuse of children as laborers.

Families tended to fit into one of three categories: the wealthy, who allowed others to rear their offspring and who exhibited indifference to children; the emerging middle class, who wanted to guide, direct, and mold their children in specific patterns (Lorence, 1974); or the poor and poverty stricken, who lacked the means to have much semblance of family life.

Wet Nurses

The lack of interest of the wealthy in their children encouraged the continued use of wet nurses. In France and England mothers placed their children with countrywomen to be cared for until they were 2 or 3 years of age. Or, if very wealthy, they hired nurses to come into their homes.

The use of wet nurses was not condoned by authorities in England and France. The French physician Guillemeau, in *De La Norriture et Government des Enfans* stated, "There is no difference between a woman who refuses to nurse her own children and one that kills her child as soon as she has conceived" (Lorence, 1974, p. 3). William Cadogan criticized the practice when he wrote in 1748, "I am quite at a loss to account for the general practice of sending infants out of Doors to be suckled or dry-nursed by another woman. . . . The ancient Custom of exposing them to wild Beasts or drowning them would certainly be much quicker and humane ways of despatching them" (pp. 3–4).

During the nineteenth century, three theories of childrearing prevailed: strict childrearing as reflected in the Puritan ethic, hardening of the child as suggested by Locke, and looking at children as flowers that needed to be nurtured.
John Hopponer (British, 1758–1810). The Sackville Children. Oil on canvas. (The Metropolitan Museum of Art, Bequest of Thomas W. Lamont, 1948. [53.59.3])

Parental Guidance

These writings and those of Comenius, Rousseau, Pestalozzi, and Froebel illustrate a new spirit of humanism and a recognition of children as human beings with some rights. Sometimes these rights were subjugated to the belief that children must be totally obedient to their parents to grow properly. These parents represent the second category of families, the emerging middle class who wanted to guide, direct, and mold their children in very specific patterns.

Susanna Wesley, mother of John Wesley, the founder of the Methodist religious movement in England, could never be criticized for overindul-

gence. Regarding her childrearing beliefs, she wrote:

> I insist upon conquering the will of children betimes, because this is the only strong and rational foundation of a religious education, without which both precept and example will be ineffectual. But when this is thoroughly done, then a child is capable of being governed by the reason and piety of its parents, till its own understanding comes to maturity, and the principles of religion have taken root in the mind. (Moore, 1974, p. 33)

Children of poor families were often sent to workhouses or foundling homes, and these were hardly nurturing environments for the young. As soon as the child was old enough to work, apprenticeships were found and, most often, the child was misused as a source of cheap labor.

Children's Recreation

Despite the strict discipline imposed on the young of all classes, there were some light and free times for some children in England. The theater was immensely popular, and upper-class children occasionally accompanied their parents. More often, however, children attended puppet shows. They also played organized games, including many that are still popular today, such as blindman's bluff, hide-and-seek, teeter-totter, cricket, hockey, and football (Bossard & Boll, 1966). Rhymes and fairy tales prevailed. Mother Goose tales, published in 1697, gave parents a collection of rhymes and stories to read to their children. Many of the favorite nursery rhymes read to children today originated during this period, including, among others, "To Market, To Market"; "Little Boy Blue"; "Baa, Baa, Black Sheep"; "Jack and Jill"; "Who Killed Cock Robin?"; "Tom, Tom, the Piper's Son"; and "The House That Jack Built." Many of the rhymes were political statements of the times but were used then, as today, as poems to read to children.

Such were the diverse methods of childrearing in Europe at the time of the settling and colonization of the future United States. Depending on their station in life in the old country, settlers had varied childrearing practices, but there was some homogeneity within the colonies. More consistency developed as colonists faced common conditions in a new frontier.

✌ THE FAMILY IN COLONIAL NORTH AMERICA

Colonists settled three major areas: New England, the middle colonies, and the southern colonies. In the new country, the concept of the family had unique importance. Children were valued in the frontier because cutting home sites from raw land, constructing houses and outbuildings, tilling the soil, and harvesting the crops required great physical efforts. Eager hands were needed to survive.

Puritans

The religious zeal of the New England Puritans permeated family life and influenced childrearing practices as it defined the duties of parents and children, husbands and wives, and masters and servants. Benjamin Wadsworth, in a 1712 essay titled *The Well Ordered Family: Or Relative Duties,* gave directives on proper marital relationships. Husbands and wives were to be supportive of and loving toward one another. "Though they owe duty to one another, yet to God's Law that declares and prescribes what that duty is; when therefore they fail in duty, they not only wrong each other, but they provoke God by breaking his Law" (Wadsworth, 1712/1972, p. 41).

Wadsworth further advised parents on their relationships with their children. He outlined the duties of the children to their parents. Both mothers and fathers should love their children as Abraham had loved Isaac, he said. Mothers were expected to nurse their children. Parents were required to provide religious instruction, pray for their children, and see that they were well "settled in the World" (p. 58). Although parents were to care for their children, they were not to be overindulgent. Children were to be brought up with diligence and have respect for the law.

Children were not "to laugh or jear at natural defects in any, as deafness, blindness, lameness, or any deformity in any person but teach them rather to admire God's mercy; that they themselves don't labour under such inconveniences" (p. 87). Children were to love, fear, revere, and honor their parents. They were to be obedient and faithful, for "when children are stubborn and disobedient to Parents, they're under awful symptoms of terrible ruine [sic]" (p. 97).

Wadsworth's essay was followed by Eleazar Moody (1775/1972) in *The School of Good Manners.* In the preface a quote from Proverbs 22:6 supported his theme: "Train up a Child in the Way he should go, and when he is Old he will not depart from it." The complete title explains the purpose of the essay: *The School of Good Manners: Composed for the Help of Parents in Teaching Children How to Behave During Their Minority.* Indeed, this was a parent education book for the colonies. The second chapter contained 163 rules for children, including rules governing behavior at the meeting house, at home, at school, and in the company of others. Following are a few of the rules:

> Be not hasty to run out of the Meeting-house when the Worship is ended, as if thou wer't weary of being there. (p. 7)
>
> Never sit in the presence of thy Parents without bidding, tho' no stranger be present. (p. 8)
>
> Approach near thy Parents at no time without a Bow. (p. 8)
>
> Dispute not, nor delay to Obey thy parents Commands. (p. 8)

Schools

New England schools reinforced stern discipline and instruction in good manners, as well as providing religious teachings. Breaking the will of obstinate young pupils was handled through corporal punishment. The birch rod, the flapper (a six-inch-wide leather strap with a hole in the center), ferules (flat pieces of wood used to smart the palms), and the cat-o'-nine-tails were used in schools to enforce discipline (Bossard & Boll, 1966).

Three Regions: North, Middle, and South

The essays of Cotton Mather, Benjamin Wadsworth, and Eleazar Moody, all published in Boston, reflected the lifestyle in New England. Childhood in the northern colonies implied adherence to a strict and complicated code. The families in the middle colonies were a more heterogeneous group, ranging from the Dutch in New York to the Quakers in Pennsylvania and the Catholics in Maryland. Those who settled in the south did not come because of religious persecution and, though as concerned about their children, were more gentle and solicitous in their guidance.

The families in all three regions were patriarchal: the father's word was law for children. Colonial laws supported parental authority. An early New York law exemplified the extreme to which demands for respect of parental authority could be carried:

> If any Child or Children, above sixteen years of age, and of Sufficient understanding, shall smite their Natural Father or Mother, unless provoked and forct for their selfe preservation from Death or Mayming, at the complaint of said Father or Mother, and not otherwise, they being sufficient witness thereof, that Child or those Children so offending shall be put to Death. (Bossard & Boll, 1966, p. 504)

The early settlers had brought a diversified and rich cultural heritage from Europe. They were still influenced by European social thought, but they were developing their own individual lifestyles and educational systems. Through the colonial years, the "family carried the greatest burden. . . . The family continued to be an important center of training even after colonial society developed" (Middlekauff, 1969, p. 281).

❧ EARLY EDUCATION IN THE SPANISH SOUTHWEST

While family life on the eastern seaboard of North America was developing, Spain was extending its settlement of Mexico and the American Southwest. Spain's initial reason for exploring north of the Rio Grande was to seek wealth. Later, settlements were established to claim the land for Spain and spread the Catholic faith.

Life in these settlements developed quite differently from the structures of the eastern colonies of the northern Europeans. Some of the Spaniards had been given land for their military service; others obtained their land by "squatters' rights." Spanish colonists included continentals (those born in Spain), Spaniards born in the New World, mestizos (offspring of Spanish and Indian marriages), Indians, and slaves. Each of the first three classes looked down on the other classes. Wealthy Spaniards, who received land grants from the viceroys, seldom mixed with the mestizos or Indians, except to employ them as overseers for their haciendas. The major educational force was the family, with religious guidance coming from Catholic missionaries. Families resulting from intermarriage, however, tended to mix religious customs. The parents of the Indian child, as well as the parents of the mestizo and the Spanish child, were the major educators of their children. Parents and the extended family were responsible for what was largely the informal education of their children into the customs and work ethic of the area.

The Jesuit and Franciscan priests, who wanted to convert all people to Catholicism and teach Spanish to the Indians, were not encouraged by the viceroys from Spain to establish schools, so no formal system of education was developed during the early days in the Southwest. Uneducated settlers were easier to control than those who had an education. Children did not need to learn to read the scriptures because priests cared for their religious needs.

❧ DEVELOPMENT OF THE FAMILY CONCEPT

Concurrent with a view of the child as a unique individual was the development of the family into a more cohesive and private unit. In 18th-century Europe, however, this evolution was limited to families of means. In the early 19th century, the greatest proportion of families, those who were poor, lived as they had in medieval days, with children often separated from their parents.

Living conditions were crowded, and there was little privacy. Children were either apprenticed at a young age or remained with their parents and labored from dawn to dusk to earn their keep. Between the 18th and 20th centuries, the European concept of family did not change, but the ability to have a family life extended to those who were not wealthy (Aries, 1962).

Families in the New World

In this respect, the pattern in the colonies and in the Southwest differed from that in Europe. Families were able to become cohesive social entities in early colonial life. They were able to establish homes and work together to provide food for the table.

African Americans

The land of opportunity did not exist, however, for people brought to the New World as slaves. Family life was not allowed to develop; mothers and children were separated from fathers at the whim of their owners. It was not until after the Civil War that former slaves were free to redefine their family roles and structures. This early loss of human rights had a complex and continuing effect on the economic and social history of the Black family in the United States.

❧ NATIVE AMERICANS IN THE 1700S AND 1800S

The Native American nations had similarity in their reverence for nature, but each nation developed its own culture. From the time of the arrival of the Europeans, their lives were disrupted by clashes among the British, French, and Spanish, with some Indian nations collaborating with the French and others the English in the wars. Their expectations, after fighting with the European nations, were to benefit from the success in

battle. This did not occur. As time progressed the European settlers moved the Native Americans to the Indian Territory west of the Mississippi.

Settlements

The Native Americans in the east and south tended to live in permanent residences where they farmed and hunted. Those to the west were migratory, foraging for food and using movable homes such as the teepee.

The Iroquois and the Cherokee are two fine examples of Indian culture. The Iroquois confederation was found in what is now upstate New York. The Cherokee settled in areas in and around present-day Georgia and the mountains of North and South Carolina and Tennessee.

Resistance

There are many examples of resistance by the Native people. In 1680 the Pueblo Indians, led by Pope, a medicine man, destroyed 21 missions and drove 2,300 Spanish colonists out of New Mexico and Arizona. These settlers fled to El Paso, but the Spanish returned and reconquered New Mexico and its capital, Santa Fe, in the 1690s.

The tales of cowboys and Indians reflect the Native people protecting their land.

American Indian Removal

Although the Supreme Court recognized the rights of American Indians to use their property at their own discretion, they could not sell their land to anyone other than the U.S. government. This was followed in 1829 by a policy established for removal of Native Americans to lands west of the Mississippi. In 1830 Congress passed the Removal Act, and five southeastern tribes were forcibly marched to west of the Mississippi.

The Cherokee, fearing they would follow, took their case, *Cherokee Nation v. Georgia*, to the Supreme Court. The court found that the Cherokee had a right to their land. The land was settled by the Cherokee who had homes, schools, government, and a published newspaper. However, gold had also been found in the area, and White settlers wanted the land. In 1838 the entire nation (except for those who fled to the hills) was forcibly marched to Indian Territory in present-day Oklahoma. Many died along the route known as the Trail of Tears.

The removal of Native people continued. The Winnebago ceded lands to the government and moved west to Iowa in 1840. In 1848 and 1849 they were moved again, this time to Minnesota. The Potawatomie were moved to a 30-square-mile reservation in Indian Territory in present-day Kansas. The Shawnee, who had dominated trade with the European Americans in South Carolina, met the same fate and were relocated in Indian Territory near the Potawatomie.

It is difficult to move from this inhuman practice of uprooting families and relocating them to reservations to discussing the theories of childrearing of the families settling in former American Indian country. Were the now-dominant Whites unable to see that strong families and the opportunity to rear their young were just as important to those earliest Americans as it was for the newest settlers in the New World?

〰 CHILDREARING IN THE 1800S IN THE UNITED STATES

The colonies declared independence from England in 1776. Soon, the first hard years of recovering from a war for independence, of building a new nation, and fighting the War of 1812 would be past. Instead of looking to Europe, considering the Native peoples, or relying on the religious guides of the clergy, families began to develop their own beliefs in childrearing. There were steadily increasing publications on the topic in the United States.

Early Literature

Robert Sunley analyzed this period by drawing from original works concerning childrearing in 19th-century magazines, journals, reports, children's books, medical books, and religious texts. Some of the earliest included *Advice to Mothers on*

the Management of Infants and Young Children, written by W. M. Ireland in 1820, and *Hints for Improvement of Early Education and Nursery Discipline* by Louise Hoare, published in 1829. *Mother's Magazine* published "To Mothers of Young Families" and "Hints for Maternal Education" in 1834 and "Domestic Education" in 1838 (Sunley, 1955). *Parents' Magazine* (not related to the current publication) was published from 1840 until 1850. Childrearing advice consistently emphasized the significance of the mother's role in the care and upbringing of the child. Fathers were, for the most part, ignored in the childrearing literature.

Mothers were encouraged to breast-feed their children. Babies were to be weaned between 8 and 12 months of age, and mothers were not to extend the period by many months. Loose, light clothing was recommended, but heavy layers seemed to be prevalent, and swaddling was customary in some areas. Cradles were used, although mothers were not to rush to the side of the cradle if the baby cried. Immediate response to a baby's crying was thought to encourage more crying.

Early toilet training was recommended as a means of "establishing habits of cleanliness and delicacy" (Sunley, 1955, p. 157). Standards for personal neatness and cleanliness were high, and children were expected to wash often.

Articles advised strict moral training, reflecting the Calvinist doctrine of infant depravity, which required strict guidance reminiscent of earlier days. Children were not to be spoiled, and parents were to expect total and immediate obedience. "It was considered fatal to let the child win out" (Sunley, 1955, p. 160). Breaking children's wills freed them of what was believed by many to be children's basically evil natures. European influence was thereby evident and reflected a strong cultural carryover.

Three Theories of Childrearing

Mothers were intent on their responsibilities of childrearing. Brim (1965) cited parent group meetings as early as 1815 in Portland, Maine. Mother study groups were formed before 1820 in other parts of the country as well. Called Maternal Associations, these parent groups generally consisted of middle-class members of Protestant-Calvinist religious groups. They were interested in proper moral training and discussed methods of childrearing that included discipline and breaking the child's will.

Sunley pointed out that there were two other theories of childrearing besides the religious moral emphasis discussed earlier. One was the idea of "hardening" the child, which probably stemmed from Locke and Rousseau. "Children should become strong, vigorous, unspoiled men like those in early days of the country" (Sunley, 1955, p. 161).

A third theory had the more modern ring of nurturing. Sunley cited the theory as being rooted in Europe. Children were treated in a gentle and persuasive manner with "understanding and justice" and with "consistency and firmness" underlying the nurturing. This guidance was thought to enable children to reach their potential.

It seems that the third theory reflected the thought of Pestalozzi and Froebel. Their influence was felt in the United States through the interest of professional educators and new prominent German immigrants. In 1856, Margaretha Schurz founded the first kindergarten in the United States in Watertown, Wisconsin (Weber, 1969). This school, based on Froebelian theory, was in marked contrast to the authoritarian and rigid traditional schools of the period.

The third theory of childrearing viewed children as beautiful youths who should be treated with understanding and justice. The Calmady children illustrate this well.
Lawrence, Sir Thomas (1769–1830). The Calmady Children (Emily; 1818–1906, and Laura Anne, 1820–1894). *(The Metropolitan Museum of Art. Bequest of Collis P. Huntington, 1900. [25.110.1])*

Music continued to be important to families and their children. Lutes, violins and the piano in this painting were some of the musical instruments that were enjoyed.
Renoir, Pierre-Auguste (1841–1919). The Daughters of Catulle Mendes (Claudine; Huguette, 1871–1964; and Helyonne), 1888. Oil on canvas. (The Metropolitan Museum of Art, The Walter H. and Leonore Annenberg Collection, Partial Gift of Walter H. and Leonore Annenberg, 1998 [1998.325.3])

✒ IMMIGRATION AND ANNEXATIONS

Between 1820 and 1930 about 38 million people immigrated to the United States. In addition, there were approximately 2.9 million African Americans, including 386,000 who were free, as reported in the 1840 U.S. Census.

Journey to the New World

Whether it was made on sailing ships like those that Columbus sailed or, later, on crowded steamers, the journey across the Atlantic was ex-

tremely hard on the immigrants. For those who were forced by religious intolerance, social upheaval, or lack of opportunities in their homelands, the decision to come to the United States to find their freedom or fortune was difficult.

First, they were leaving the society and home they knew. Many never saw their loved ones again. Second, they had to save up money and gather food in order to afford the trip. Many were forced to travel by foot to a port city where they might wait months before a ship was ready to sail.

As they waited they used resources and food planned for the voyage. Ship owners wanted to make as much money as possible so ships were crowded. Many of the immigrants became ill on the voyage. Some suffered from hunger. When they arrived in the Americas, they might already be ill and destitute. Many of those who had few resources stayed in the cities where they landed, trying to accrue enough so they could move on. Those with more money were able to journey on and obtain land.

Each group of immigrants had its trials. Those who arrived after the country obtained independence also found discrimination. When new arrivals differed from those settlers already established, they were considered less desirable. There was great discrimination against the Irish who arrived after the potato famine (1845–1849) in Ireland. Chinese immigrants felt great discrimination when they arrived on the West Coast in the 1850s. In 1882 the Chinese Exclusion Act that barred Chinese laborers was passed. Subsequently, it was extended for years. Later, Italians and other people from southern and eastern Europe (1890–1924) faced prejudice. As time passed, those who looked like the original settlers faced less discrimination; those who were physically identifiable have had a continuing battle for equality.

German Immigrants

In the 1840s, there was a large amount of political unrest in Germany. When reform they desired did not take place, thousands of Germans with liberal political beliefs fled to the United States.

They had enough capital to be able to settle beyond the coastal cities. (The first kindergarten, established in Wisconsin by Margaetha Schurz, was a result of her family leaving Germany for political freedom.) When they came to the United States, they were able to establish German-speaking schools and tried to retain their culture. They and the Irish, who also came in huge numbers in the 1840s but for a different reason, are the two largest ethnic groups, besides the British, to immigrate to the United States.

Irish Immigrants

The Irish had been coming to the United States over the years, but the potato famine of the 1840s sent huge numbers of starving, poverty-stricken Irish streaming to the United States. An estimated 800,000 Irish refugees came during the 1840s; more than 105,000 came in 1847 alone.

Unlike the Germans, most of whom who had financial backing, most of the Irish were poor. Many spoke Gaelic, wore homemade clothes, and had to settle in coastal cities because they could not afford to move inland.

People of Irish descent were persecuted in the United States for their differences, one of which was their Roman Catholic faith. Since the Puritans (Protestants) had fled because of religious persecution, they did not want the Roman Catholic Church to have any influence in the United States. This persecution continued with killings and church burnings until the Civil War took the focus off the Irish Catholics. The concern about a Roman Catholic becoming president of the United States and putting the nation under the influence of the Roman Catholic Church continued into the 1920s and was even a factor in the 1960 presidential campaign of John F. Kennedy.

Texas and the Mexican-American War

Texas revolted against Mexico in 1835 and won its independence. Ten years later it was annexed to the United States. This was one of the contributing factors to the subsequent Mexican-American War, which began in 1845. In the 1848 Treaty of Guadalupe Hildalgo, Mexico ceded California, Nevada, Utah, and parts of New Mexico, Arizona, Wyoming, and Colorado to the United States. The region's inhabitants were allowed to move to Mexico or stay in the United States. Residents were supposed to retain all rights and property; however, many lost their land due to taxes they were unfamiliar with as well as through illegal land dealings.

Thus, shortly before the Civil War, many people in the Southwest, new to the laws and rules of the country, became U.S. citizens.

✑ CIVIL WAR

In the 1860s, the country was torn apart by the Civil War. Although the slave trade had been outlawed in 1808, slavery continued in the United States. States' rights, including the related issue of slavery, resulted in the Southern states seceding from the union.

The Civil War tore the country apart and changed it forever.

Slavery

Slavery—the practice of owning another person, providing their keep but using their labor—has existed for thousands of years. The earliest slaves were either captured in war or were in debt and forced to pay off their debts as slaves. Rules controlled the practice of slavery. According to the laws of Moses, slaves of their own people were to be freed after 6 years and foreign slaves, twice every century. Greeks obtained slaves through war and bought them from pirates. The Romans had slavery throughout the period when they conquered other countries. But the practice of slavery did not sanction lifetime slavery or ownership of a slave's offspring.

In 1418, Portuguese Prince Henry the Navigator began the exploration of Africa. As Portugal continued exploring Africa and building forts, it began trading with the kingdom of Benin and became involved in the slave trade. In 1442 the Portuguese explorer Antam Goncalvez kidnapped some African nobility. As ransom he received 10 Africans whom he sold into slavery. Thus began the slave trade that would later impact the Americas (Kullen, 1994, p. 2). In 1497, Vasco da Gama sailed around southern Africa's Cape of Good Hope. The following year he reached India, the country that Columbus had tried to find by sailing west. The Portuguese exploration of Africa and the wealth resulting from obtaining slaves and selling them, mixed with the discovery of North and South America, led to the horrendous practice of slavery in the Americas.

In 1501 the Spanish king, Ferdinand II, sanctioned the introduction of African slaves into the colonies (Kullen, 1994). In 1516, Catholic cardinal Cisneros, regent of Spain, banned the use of slaves in Spanish colonies. In 1517 the bishop Bartoleme de Las Casa petitioned that each household emigrating to the colonies be allowed 12 slaves. He later regretted this and opposed slavery. By 1518, however, there was extensive slave trade in San Juan Bautista (Puerto Rico). By the late 1800s, almost four centuries later, as many as 30 million people had been brought from Africa and forced into slavery in North and South America.

When the Spanish first came to the New World, they had expected to use the indigenous people as slaves. The practice of providing a grant of land with accompanying unpaid, forced labor—called *encomienda*—did not work out because the slaves knew the territory and were able to run away. In addition, many died from diseases of European origin. They were extremely susceptible to these diseases because they had not developed resistance to them.

Africans were able to handle the climate, the environment, and the heavy work—positive attributes that contributed to a devastating and sad period in American history. Slavery was used because it was profitable. Laws continued to be made that restricted African Americans. In 1663, in Maryland, all imported Africans were considered to be slaves and, if a free European American woman married a slave, she also lost her freedom. In 1664, enslavement was for life and transferred to the children through the mother (Kullen, 1994).

Changes for African Americans

During the Civil War and Reconstruction, change came about for African Americans. In 1865 the 13th Amendment to the Constitution abolished slavery. A year later, in 1866, the 14th Amendment made African Americans U.S. citizens. In 1870 the 15th Amendment gave them the vote. These changes held great promise of freedom for African Americans, but reality delivered continued prejudice and restrictions. In 1896 the U.S. Supreme Court ruled in *Plessy v. Ferguson* that separate but equal facilities were constitutional.

Changes for Women

During the Civil War, women began to take over farm work and carry out the obligations generally reserved for their husbands. Women also filled

Even after emancipation, African Americans had a difficult life and worked long hours while they attempted to keep their families together and cared for. *Thomas P. Anshutz, (1851–1912). Cabbages. (The Metropolitan Museum of Art, Morris K. Jesup Fund, 1940. [40.40])*

the void left by men who resigned from teaching to fight in the war (Calhoun, 1960), and their experience with children brought forth a more nurturing environment in the educational system.

After the Civil War, women did not return to the same subservient positions they had held previously. Calhoun described the change:

> The whole movement signifies an extension of woman's economic independence of man, and the breaking down of that barrier of inequality that had so long served to keep woman in a subordinate place in the household. While the Civil War did not start the movement, it did greatly stimulate, and . . .

helped to unsettle the foundation of "mediaeval" family which was now passing out and through a transition of storm and stress yielding to the new family of equality and comradeship. (Vol. 2, pp. 361–362)

The change in the woman's role in the family and the new feeling of equality encouraged the formation of women's clubs and the resultant emphasis on parent education within those organizations.

✐ CHANGE IN EDUCATION

Change was coming to education as well as to family life. During this same period, the mid-1800s, the kindergarten movement was gaining strength. Henry Barnard, Secretary of the Connecticut Board of Education and later U.S. Commissioner of Education, became enthused by Froebelian materials at the International Exhibit of Education Systems in London in 1854. Barnard disseminated information in the *American Journal of Education* and a volume that he edited, *Kindergarten and Child Culture Papers*. He became recognized as the father of the kindergarten movement in the United States.

Elizabeth Peabody

Elizabeth Peabody, a sister-in-law of Horace Mann, was also a staunch supporter of the kindergarten movement and helped to spread the "good word" about the kindergarten methods of Froebel. Most important, Peabody crusaded to introduce kindergarten throughout the land and spread her beliefs about the natural goodness of children. Throughout her life, she was an apostle of Froebelian kindergarten. She believed that the system had come to him through revelation (Weber, 1969). Since she and Barnard had great stature in educational circles, they were able to have a substantial effect on educational thought.

Froebel's *Mother Play and Nursery Songs* was translated into English, giving parents an opportunity to use Froebelian activities in their homes. In

Change was coming to education. Women were called upon to teach in the schools and take the place of male teachers who left to fight the war.
Winslow Homer (1836–1910). The Country School, 1871. (The Saint Louis Art Museum. Purchase)

1870 there were only four books on kindergarten, but by the end of the decade five more had been translated, four more had been written, many articles had been printed and distributed, and two journals, *The Kindergarten Messenger* and *The New Education,* were flourishing (Vandewalker, 1971).

Peabody and Barnard firmly established Froebelian kindergarten in the United States. Pestalozzi and Froebel influenced the educational roles of parents with the belief that parents are integral components of education. A climate for change, the possibility of the perfectibility of humans, and reverence for motherhood prevailed. Thus, the time was ripe for the parent education movement to begin.

Table 2.1 highlights the events and people who influenced ideas about children and child-rearing from early times until the 1880s.

TABLE 2.1   Events and people who influenced ideas about children and childrearing, 6000 B.C.–A.D. 1800.

6000–5000 B.C.	Primitive cultures developed. Parents modeled behavior for children to learn.
5510–3787 B.C.	Egyptian children were educated in their homes in the Old Kingdom of Egypt.
3787–1580 B.C.	Schools outside the home developed in Egypt.
427–347 B.C.	Plato questioned theories of childrearing, suggesting that a controlled environment would promote good habits. Infanticide was practiced by Greeks, Romans, and others.
384–323 B.C.	Aristotle, father of the scientific method, promoted childrearing and education by the state.
204–122 B.C.	Polybius noted the importance of the family in developing good Roman citizens.
106–43 B.C.	Cicero emphasized the family's role in the development of the Roman citizen.
A.D. 318	Emperor Constantine declared infanticide a crime.
A.D. 400–1400	The Roman Empire declined and the feudal system emerged. Wealthy children were apprenticed to nobles; commoners were apprenticed to tradesmen. Peasants worked in the fields.
A.D. 1450	The printing press was invented, but books were available only to the wealthy.
1483–1540	Martin Luther introduced the Ninety-five Theses and began the drive for all to learn to read the Bible.
1500–1671	Etiquette books began to include etiquette for children.
1592–1670	Comenius, a Moravian educator, wrote books on progressive educational theories.
1632–1704	John Locke believed the newborn's mind was like a blank slate—everything is learned.
1697	Mother Goose tales were published.
17th & 18th centuries	Wealthy European children were cared for by wet nurses. Colonial American children were taught to follow Puritanical religious beliefs and were trained to be obedient and faithful. Spanish-Indian Catholic children in the Southwest United States were reared in extended, close-knit families.
1703–1791	John Wesley, founder of Methodism, was raised by his mother, who believed in breaking the will.
1712–1778	Rousseau, author of *Emile,* wrote that children should grow up untainted by society.
1747–1827	Pestalozzi, father of parent education, developed a curriculum based on concrete objects and group instruction, cooperation among students, and self-activity.
1782–1852	Friedrich Froebel developed a curriculum for the young child based on the concept of unity. He is regarded as the father of kindergarten.
19th century	American parents began to rely on American publications in addition to European ideas and the tenets of the church.
1815	Parent group meetings were held in Portland, Maine.
1854	Henry Barnard, U.S. Commissioner of Education, supported Froebelian concepts.
1856	A German-speaking kindergarten was established in Wisconsin by Margaretha Shurz.
1860	Elizabeth Peabody established the first English-speaking kindergarten in the U.S.
1860–1864	During the Civil War women were encouraged to replace men as teachers.
1870	The National Education Association was founded.
1870–1880	A great extension of the kindergarten movement and parent education occurred.
1871	The first public kindergarten in North America was established in Ontario, Canada:
1873	Susan Blow directed the first public kindergarten in the U.S., opened by Dr. William Harris in St. Louis.

PART 2

More Recent History of Parent Education and Child Development

Parent education and childrearing practices reflect the times in which they occur. The first parent education programs in Maine in 1815 reflected the concern of the time—breaking the will of the child. In the United States, children were still viewed as willful and depraved, in need of having their sinfulness banished.

The free kindergarten programs of the 1890s reflected the perceived need for immigrant and poor children to learn the ways of the establishment, particularly in regard to health habits and cleanliness. Many of the parent education programs established in the 1920s were the consequence of the tuberculosis epidemic and the need to spread information about health.

As you read the rest of this chapter, reflect on the changes in childrearing practices. Note the effects of G. Stanley Hall, Freud, Watson, Skinner, Erikson,

The Hatch family illustrates the extended family which emphasizes the importance of mothers to nurture and care for the children while the fathers were the providers.
Johnson, Eastman (American, 1824–1906). The Hatch Family, 1871. (The Metropolitan Museum of Art. Gift of Frederick H. Hatch, 1926. [26.97])

Spock, and Piaget. As their theories became known, childrearing practices changed. Relate that to today as the process of sharing information continues to change. The remainder of this chapter is divided into decades that reflect the changing parenting skills and childrearing practices.

🕮 1880 TO 1890

Toward the close of the 19th century there was a growing belief in the perfectibility of humans and society. Education was viewed as an avenue to that end. Kindergarten was believed to be an excellent instrument to reach children while they were still young enough to be guided in their moral development.

Settlement Houses

Settlement houses were established in the 1880s and 1890s for the urban immigrant groups who arrived in the new land destitute and without a livelihood. The kindergarten was used by the settlement houses to alleviate the suffering of children. Educators were also able to reach parents with information about childrearing and the Froebelian curriculum. "Industry, neatness, reverence, self-respect, and cooperation were seen as results of the properly directed Froebelian kindergarten, and these moral beliefs were linked to both individual and societal advancement" (Weber, 1969, p. 39).

The Women's Christian Temperance Union (WCTU) also supported the kindergarten movement and education of parents by establishing WCTU kindergartens in at least 20 cities (Weber, 1969). Free Kindergarten Associations were formed throughout the United States. By 1897 there were more than 400 of these associations actively involved in the education of young children and parents. The WCTU developed a course using Froebel's belief in unity with a sequential curriculum for use with mothers of young children. Settlement houses and Free Kindergarten Associations worked with the lower socioeconomic groups and new immigrants. The concern and interest shown

the poor and the philanthropic commitment to alleviate suffering reflected the awakening of renewed social conscience. The kindergarten movement and parent education were strengthened by the development of humanism and the belief in the child's innate goodness (Weber).

Women's Associations

By the 1880s this growing emphasis on childrearing and education emerged from two additional sources, women's associations and the child study movement. Associations organized by women in the late 1800s were the first source and included the Child Study Association of America (CSAA), formed in 1888 by a group of New York City mothers; the American Association of University Women (AAUW), founded in 1882 by college graduates; the National Congress of Mothers, later changed to the National Congress of Parents and Teachers, the PTA, organized by women who gathered from across the nation at a meeting in 1897; and the National Association of Colored Women, established in 1897.

The associations founded in the 1880s and 1890s had a lasting effect on parent education in the United States. Throughout its history, the CSAA has emphasized child study and parent education; it was the oldest and largest organization solely committed to the study of children. Its earliest programs were studies by authorities of the time: Spencer, Rousseau, Froebel, and Montessori (Brim, 1965). The organization engaged in a variety of activities and services—all related to children and parents. (Brim, 1965; Fisher, 1933; National Society for the Study of Education, 1929; Schlossman, 1976).

The American Association of University Women has implemented a diverse educational program, including the study of children and parent education. The PTA has been concerned with parent-school relationships since its inception. The National Association of Colored Women has focused on civic service, social service, and education with committees on home and the child, mothers, and legislation. Another group, the General Federation of Women's Clubs, formed in 1889, ushered in an even greater interest in women's roles as leaders. These organizations, with the exception of the CSAA, are still actively involved in the field of education.

Child Study Movement

When G. Stanley Hall, a charismatic psychologist at Clark University, was elected president of the university in 1889, he founded a child study center. Children had not been the center of scientific research before then. Hall wanted to determine what was in children's minds. Using a questionnaire method of research, he first used associates and assistants at the university to gather data. As his research progressed, he extended the use of questionnaires to teachers throughout the country and then to thousands of parents. To answer the ques-

tions, parents needed to observe their child's speech and behavior. This natural observation was a learning experience for the observer as well as a device for collecting data. Although many of the completed questionnaires contained questionable answers, Hall and his associates—Patty Smith Hill and Anna Bryan—compiled some provocative recommendations. "Above all, he counseled parents, be indulgent with young children; treat them as young animals, who simply have to behave as they do. Childhood was an easygoing, cavorting stage which youngsters must pass through peaceably if they were eventually to become mature, self-controlled adults" (Schlossman, 1976, p. 443).

Even though Hall's child study movement was short-lived, replaced by the research of Thorndike, Cattell, and Watson in the 1900s, he remains important to parent education for his institutionaliza-

Many immigrants settled in the cities. The country, however, was primarily rural with, families living in small towns or on farms like the one pictured here.

tion of child study and his influence on the founding of the PTA. Since then, the development of effective childrearing practices and parent education is no longer the effort of just a few interested individuals. Hall made child study a part of a college program, and strong organizations, founded and sustained by dedicated men and women, are actively involved in parent education today.

1890 TO 1900

The 1890s centered on the family, with well-defined roles for mother, father, and children. The father's duty was to financially support the family while the mother controlled the home. Women's clubs flourished. Well-to-do mothers were able to join one of the many clubs available to them. Those who were on a lower socioeconomic level were served by settlement houses and the Free Kindergarten Association.

Stendler (1950) analyzed the first year of every decade from 1890 until 1950 in articles in three popular magazines, *Good Housekeeping, Ladies' Home Journal,* and *Woman's Home Companion.* He found an immense amount of interest in childrearing in the 1890s and early 1900s. The home environment was recognized as important in the formation of character. Mothers were idolized as the epitome of purity and goodness, and children were thought to model the mother in their character development. It was important then that the mother be the right kind of person. The father was earning the family fortune, and the mother was looked up to as knowledgeable and capable of rearing children. The articles reflect those who were financially secure, not the many who were poverty stricken.

Native Americans

At the same time that the home environment was recognized as important for formation of character, American Indian children were being removed from their homes and placed in boarding schools. In 1894, Hopi children were forcibly gathered and placed in European American–type schools. In 1911, the United States Army entered the Navajo and Hopi reservations and captured more than 60 Hopi children to take them to boarding schools (Kullen, 1994, p. 258). This separation of families was damaging to both child and parent.

In 1901 citizenship was conferred on people in more than 30 tribes in Indian Territory: Navajo, Creek, Apache, Caddo, Cheyenne, Arapaho, Comanche, Delaware, Iowa, Kaw (Kansa), Kickapoo, Kiowa, Modoc, Miami, Osage, Otoe and Missouria, Ottawa, Pawnee, Peopria, Ponca, Potawatomi, Quapaw, Sac (Sauk) and Fox (Mesquakie), Seneca and Cayuga, Shawnee, Tonkawa, Wichita, and Wyandotte (Kullen, 1994, p. 246).

Immigration

In the late 1890s and the early 1900s, immigrants continued arriving. In 1892 Ellis Island was opened, replacing Castle Gardens (New York City) as the port of entry for immigrants. Open until 1954, over 20 million immigrants were processed through its gates. Cursory examinations were given during which officials determined who could enter the United States and who would be deported.

As each wave of immigrants arrived in the United States, it was believed that they needed to discard their old cultures and adapt to the culture in America.

Spanish-American War

At the conclusion of the Spanish-American War in 1898, Spain ceded the Philippines, Guam, and Puerto Rico to the United States under the Treaty of Paris; Spain received $20 million in consideration of its losses.

Puerto Rico

By 1900 Congress had established a relationship between the United States and Puerto Rico. The newly acquired territory would have a governor and executive council appointed by the president of the United States and a house of delegates and resident commissioner elected by popular vote (Banks, 1991). This continued

Country schools educated many of the youth in the primarily rural United States during the 19th and early 20th centuries. This famous 1872 painting depicts young men playing "crack the whip" during recess.
Homer, Winslow (1836–1910). Snap the Whip. *(The Metropolitan Museum of Art, Gift of Christian A. Zabriskie, 1950. [50.41])*

until 1916, when the Jones Act gave Puerto Ricans U.S. citizenship. Many Puerto Ricans began migrating to the United States, especially to New York City.

The Philippines

The Filipinos wanted independence instead of being part of the United States and fought for it but were defeated. In 1898 the United States established a five-person commission to govern the islands. This continued until the Jones Act of 1916, which allowed the Philippines to have its own legislature. The Tydings McDuffie Act provided for the Commonwealth of the Philippines and promised freedom in 1946. Following World War II, in 1946, the Filipinos were given their freedom.

1900 TO 1910

The first decade of the 19th century continued focusing on the family. In 1908 the American Home Economics Association was formed. Primarily an organization of teachers of home economics in colleges, public schools, and after 1914, extension programs, the association emphasized home management skills related to homemaking and parenthood, such as food preparation and nutrition. Emphasis gradually included child development and family enrichment (Brim, 1965; National Society for the Study of Education, 1929). In 1909 the National Committee on Mental Hygiene was formed. Because there was concern with improving mental hygiene, the emphasis on mental health increased during succeeding decades. In 1950 this group merged with others to form the National Association of Mental Health.

Changes in Education

This period saw change emerging in education as well as in childrearing. John Dewey, along with Hall, emphasized the need for change in childhood education. Dewey, William Kilpatrick, Francis Parker, and Patty Smith Hill drew away from traditional structured educational practices toward a curriculum that included problem solving, learning by doing, purposeful activity, and social aspects of education.

Montessori

While educators in the United States were moving toward a child-oriented, problem-solving curriculum, Maria Montessori was establishing another educational form in Italy. Concern for poverty-stricken children prompted Montessori, an Italian physician, to establish Casa dei Bambini, a children's home in a tenement section of Rome. In 1907, she designed a specific program, structured so that children learn by doing. By teaching children precisely how to use equipment, she was able to help children overcome their impoverished environment. Her methodology—more structured than that of American theorists—did not find wide acceptance in the United States until the 1960s.

First White House Conference

Poverty-stricken children in the United States were often forced to work under horrendous conditions at a very young age. These children, who were undernourished, neglected, or abused, prompted a rising social concern. As a result, the first White House Conference on Care of Dependent Children was called in 1909. The Children's Bureau was created in 1912 as a consequence of the conference, a first step in government concern for children.

Immigration

In the late 19th century and the beginning of the 20th century, immigration continued at a high rate. Ellis Island, which opened in 1892, processed thousands of immigrants as they made their way to a new life in the United States. Between 1890 and 1914, 15 million Europeans, mostly from southern and eastern Europe, arrived. Their customs and physical appearance differed from those already in the United States, and were, therefore, considered inferior. "Each group experienced discrimination, lived in ghettos, and . . . many of them eventually became culturally assimilated, attained social mobility, and moved to the suburbs of cities such as New York, Boston, and Chicago" (Banks, 1991, p. 90).

✥ 1910 TO 1920

Soon after the 1909 White House conference, the government began disseminating information on child care. The first *Infant Care,* which would become a popular parent education book on child care for infants, was published in 1914 by the federal government agency that is now the U.S. Department of Health and Human Services. Government entered the field of parent education through creation of the Children's Bureau, provision for county demonstration agents, and concern for children's health.

College Research Centers

Colleges and universities also became involved by establishing research and teaching centers devoted to the study of children. The State University of Iowa instituted a child study center in 1911. Its purpose was the "investigation of the best scientific methods of conserving and developing the normal child, the dissemination of the information acquired by such investigation, and the training of students for work in such fields" (National Society for the Study of Education, 1929, p. 286).

Thus, preschool laboratories for psychological studies and an infant laboratory for study of nutrition were established. The first concerted effort to distribute findings to parents did not occur until the 1920s, when programs in parent education were offered throughout Iowa. The Yale

The title of this painting "First Steps," describes the wonderful interaction between parents and child. The little child, taking her first steps, reaches for her father.
Vincent Van Gogh. First Steps, after Millet. *(The Metropolitan Museum of Art. Gift of George N. and Helen M. Richards [64.165.2])*

Psycho-Clinic and the Merrill-Palmer School of Homemaking were also pioneers in the study of children and made valuable contributions to the understanding of children and the development of parent education (National Society for the Study of Education, 1929).

First Parent Cooperative

Twelve faculty wives at the University of Chicago—with guidance from the university—established the first parent cooperative in the United States in 1916. The women wanted high-quality child care for their children, parent education, and time to work for the Red Cross during the war (Taylor, 1981). This cooperative, the only one established in that decade, followed the tradition of English nursery schools established in 1911 by Margaret McMillan.

Nursery School

McMillan originally designed an open-air school for the poor in England. She emphasized health, education, play, and parent education, rather than mere child watching. The concept of the nursery school was welcomed by middle-class American families, as illustrated by the first parent cooperative in Chicago. Thus, parent cooperatives and the growth of nursery schools in the United States strengthened and promoted parent education.

Change in Discipline

Although authorities during the 1890s and early 1900s had emphasized love and affection in the formation of character, a new trend suggested that discipline through punishment was necessary to ensure character development. Parents were advised to use more discipline in the establishment of character in their children. Stendler (1950) found that discipline (reward or punishment) was discussed in 14 percent of the surveyed magazine articles in 1900 and jumped to 34 percent in both 1910 and 1920. Providing a good home influence had commanded the attention of 53 percent of magazine articles in 1900, but was the focus of only 30 percent in 1910 and dropped to 12 percent in 1920 (Stendler). The increased attention to strict child-rearing was illustrated by the first issue of *Infant Care*. Autoerotic activities, such as thumb-sucking and masturbation, were thought to be extremely dangerous. It was felt that if such activities were not brought under control, they could permanently damage the child. "While he was in bed, he was to be bound down hand and foot so that he could not suck his thumb, touch his genitals, or rub his thighs together" (Wolfenstein, 1953, p. 121). During the day, thumb-sucking was handled by covering the hand with cotton mittens or making the hand inaccessible to the child (Wolfenstein).

A drastic change in attitude was reflected by scheduling the infant's activities rather than responding to the baby's needs. In 1890 the infant's life was loosely scheduled. By 1900, 22 percent of the articles recommended tight scheduling for infants; by 1910, 77 percent of the articles called for rigid scheduling (Stendler, 1950). Although breast-feeding was still highly recommended, a supplemental bottle could be given at 5 months, and the child was supposed to be completely weaned by the end of the first year (Wolfenstein, 1953). Mothers were told to expect obedience, ignore temper tantrums, and restrict physical handling of their children. These severe attitudes continued into the 1920s when all magazine articles on the

The period between 1890 and 1910 witnessed an explosion of population interest in children, as evidenced by the great number of magazine articles on child development. G. Stanley Hall, who felt children should be kept out of school until they were 7 or 8, represented the growing academic interest in children.

topic recommended strict scheduling of infants (Stendler, 1950).

Throughout these periods there were exceptions to every trend (Brim, 1965). Although strict scheduling began around 1910 and continued through the 1920s and early 1930s, a book published in 1894, Holt's *The Care and Feeding of Children,* recommended "strict, routinized care of the child" (Brim, 1965, p. 169). Watson's *Psychological Care of Infant and Child* stated, "There is a sensible way of treating children. . . . Let your behavior always be objective and kindly firm. Never hug and kiss them, never let them sit in your lap. If you must, kiss them once on the forehead when they say goodnight. Shake hands with them in the morning" (Vincent, 1951, p. 206). Published in 1928, Watson's book appeared "when Freudian theory was well in its ascendancy" (Brim, 1965, p. 169).

Between 1910 and 1920 the Child Study Association of America was emphasizing "love, support, and intelligent permissiveness in child care, based on the work of Freud, G. Stanley Hall, and other leaders in the clinical movement" (Brim, 1965, pp. 169–170). Vincent (1951) also noted that overlaps in theories occurred with reference to "tight scheduling" as late as 1948, and a preference for self-regulation appeared as early as 1930. Even though the period of 1890 to 1910 stressed love and freedom, the period of 1910 to 1930 emphasized strict scheduling and discipline, and self-regulation appeared in the late 1930s and 1940s, other theories were interwoven with these during the same periods.

Family reunions showed the interest in families. Before the increase in transportation through airlines and high speed highways, families tended to live near one another.

✒ 1920 TO 1930

Early childhood as an important period for character formation was stressed in the 1920s. This belief was at the other end of the spectrum from Hall's belief in allowing the child to grow free and unrestricted. Behaviorists warned that parents should "do it right early or else" (Schlossman, 1976, p. 462).

Child Care Beliefs

During the 1920s many teenagers and young adults were viewed as reckless, overindulged, and spoiled (Schlossman, 1976). To reverse this scandalous situation, children were to be trained early to be responsible, well-behaved individuals. Watsonian behaviorism was beginning to be felt. This child-drearing theory was mixed in the 1920s with the learning-by-doing theories of Dewey, a small portion of Freudian psychology, and Gesell's belief in natural maturation and growth. Although each theorist had a different approach, all recognized the importance of early experiences and the influence of the environment on the child's development.

The 1923 edition of *Infant Care,* issued by the Children's Bureau, admonished parents that "toilet training may begin as early as the end of the first month. . . . The first essential in bowel training is absolute regularity" (Vincent, 1951, p. 205). Although breast-feeding was recommended for six to nine months, once weaning was commenced it was to be accomplished in two weeks. If the parents insist on substitution to "artificial food . . . the child will finally yield" (Wolfenstein, 1953, p. 125).

An explosion of parent programs accompanied the prosperity of the 1920s. The era reflected a swing from parent education offered by settlement houses for immigrants and free kindergartens for the underprivileged to the involvement of many middle-class parents in study groups for their own enlightenment and enjoyment.

Parent Cooperatives

Parent cooperatives emerged in five locations in the 1920s: (a) Cambridge, Massachusetts, (b) the

University of California at Los Angeles, (c) Schenectady, New York, (d) Smith College in Northampton, Mass., and (e) the American Association of University Women in Berkeley, California. The last, called Children's Community, has continued to flourish over the years and is the oldest continuous parent cooperative program in the United States (Taylor, 1981).

The parent cooperative movement, which developed rapidly in California but grew more slowly elsewhere until after World War II, was a way for parents to obtain high-quality education for their children (Osborn, 1991). To participate, parents must share responsibilities—an excellent example of parent involvement.

Parent Education

Organizational membership growth also illustrated increased interest in parent education. PTA membership expansion depicted, in terms of sheer numbers, the growth in interest in parent programs. The organization grew from 60,000 in 1915 to 190,000 in 1920, to 875,000 in 1925, to nearly 1.5 million in 1930 (Schlossman, 1976). AAUW membership rose to 35,000 in the 1920s, and each issue of its journal contained a column on parent education. Concurrently, the Child Study Association of America, recognized as the educational leader in parent education during the 1920s, grew from 56 parent groups in 1926 to 135 in 1927 (National Society for the Study of Education, 1929).

Child Study Manual

In the 1920s Benjamin Gruenberg published *Outlines of Child Study: A Manual for Parents and Teachers,* a text on childrearing that many parent groups used as a study guide. Succinct discussions on issues of child development were included in each chapter (Gruenberg, 1927). Parents, along with a professional or lay leader, could read and discuss the issues. A need for trained leaders resulted in CSAA sponsorship of the first university course in parent education at Columbia University in 1920.

Across the country many school systems implemented parent education and preschool programs. The Emily Griffith Opportunity School (Denver public school system) initially funded a parent education and preschool program in 1926. Its early emphasis on health education for families expanded to childrearing theories and other parent skills as interests and needs changed.

Special Concerns

Concern for children with mental retardation emerged during the 1920s, with separation and custodial care seeming to be the answer. "In regard to all mentally deficient children, it may be said that while we cannot improve their mentality we have reached the point where, by recognition of their capabilities and limitations, we can so place them in our social scheme that they may lead happy and useful lives" (Gruenberg, 1927, p. 230). This thinking has gradually changed over the years to the positions supporting mainstreaming for children with disabilities in the 1970s and inclusion in the 1990s and 2000s along with increased parent involvement and advocacy by parents of children with exceptionalities.

The effect of early childhood concerns and parent education was so great during the 1920s that the National Society for the Study of Education (1929) devoted its *Twenty-Eighth Year Book* to preschool and parent education. This issue described programs and listed conferences and agencies engaged in parent education during the 1920s. Refer to the *Twenty-Eighth Year Book* for a comprehensive report on the 1920s.

Restrictive Legislation on Immigration

Fear of the rapid increase of immigrants during the late 19th century and the first two decades of the 20th century resulted in restrictive legislation. The Johnson Reed Act in 1924 established a quota system for immigration from each country that was based on a percentage of those who lived in the United States in 1890. The Chinese Exclusion Act of 1882 had closed down Chinese immigration. The 1924 Act extended this ban and made all Asians ineligible for citizenship. Paradoxically, in the same year, the Citizenship Act granted Native

Americans full citizenship, along with the right to vote, a right that should have been theirs since the independence of the nation.

Immigration policies were reformed in 1965, effective in 1968, when original national quotas were removed. Since that time there has been a great increase in immigration from Asia, South America, and Latin America.

The Coming of the Depression

As the 1920s drew to a close, middle-class parents were active in parent groups, optimistic about the future, and concerned about health, nutrition, and shaping their children's actions. The financial crash of 1929 brought a tremendous change in the lifestyle of many families and set the stage for the Great Depression of the 1930s.

✑ 1930 TO 1940

The 1930s ushered in the depression era with a necessary response to the needy and a broadening of concern for the family and family relationships as well as for the individual child (Fisher, 1933; Gruenberg, 1940).

White House Conference

The decade began with a White House Conference on Child Health and Protection in November 1930. Attended by more than 4,000 specialists, the conference produced the following statement on parent education:

> This Committee strongly recommends that various educational associations and organizations and the educational departments of the different states be requested to study the possibilities for organizing parent education as part of the system of public instruction and that the professional groups and organizations concerned with children be asked to study their opportunities and obligations for parent education. (Pennsylvania Department of Public Instruction, 1935, pp. 9–10)

Childrearing Practices

The 1930s reflected varying viewpoints on childrearing, ranging from strict scheduling to self-regulation. Fewer articles were written in the early 1930s than in the early 1920s, and when published, they emphasized physical development, nutrition, and character formation. Character formation began to take on broader meanings. Whereas it had meant moral development earlier in the 1900s, articles in magazines now included personality development (Stendler, 1950). Thumbsucking was still considered dangerous, but parents were admonished to divert the child's attention, rather than use restraints. "It is a natural habit . . . it should not excite parents unduly" (Wolfenstein, 1953, p. 123).

Parent education continued at a high level of participation during the first half of the decade. For example, the Pennsylvania Department of Public Instruction's (1935) Bulletin 86, *Parent Education*, reported that parents were being reached through study groups, with more than 700,000 parents involved in group participation. Parents in the United States also were receiving information through the mass media: radio series, lectures, magazines, and distribution of more than 8 million copies of *Infant Care*. The following statement from Bulletin 86 emphasized the importance of parent education:

> More and more it is being recognized that educators have a responsibility for providing professional leadership and for furthering the coordination of parent education activities in their communities. The job of the school is only half done when it has educated the children of the nation. Since it has been demonstrated beyond doubt that the home environment and the role played by understanding parents are paramount in the determination of what the child is to become, it follows that helping the parent to feel more adequate for his task is fully as important from the point of view of public education and the welfare of society as is the education of the children themselves. Moreover, an educated parenthood facilitates the task of the schools and insures the success of its educational program with the child. (p. 12)

This mother reading to her children illustrates the emphasis on parent education which expanded in the 1920s and continued into the 1930s.

Social and economic conditions were having an effect on family life and, consequently, on children within the family. The depression and a need to support families by offering information on budget, clothing, health, physical care, and diet precipitated parent education for the poor. Rehabilitation projects of the 1930s, such as the Works Progress Administration (WPA), offered a forum for mothers who were not active in women's clubs or parent-teacher associations to learn about home management practices. Established in October 1933, the Federal Emergency Relief Administration (FERA) authorized work-relief wages for unemployed teachers and others to organize and direct nursery schools; about 75,000 children were enrolled during 1934 and 1935 (Goodykoontz, Davis, & Gabbard, 1947). It was the intention of FERA that the nursery programs be taken over by the schools when funds from the federal government were terminated. "It is my desire that . . . schools shall be so administered in the states as to build toward a permanent and integral part of the regularly established public school program" (pp. 60–61). Few, however, were taken over by the schools.

Poverty

Poverty made it very difficult for families to provide for their children during the depression years. In rural communities families had gardens to help with the necessary nutrition for the children. Being poor was not unusual so that a family in poverty was no disgrace. All or most of the child's friends were also poor.

Treatment of Minorities

Minority children had a double handicap to overcome: prejudice against children of color prevailed. In many areas, children of Spanish heritage were not allowed to speak in their family's native language, a problem that continued for many decades. This told them that their background was not proper, not up to standard. Much of the United States followed the separate-but-equal doctrine, operating separate, usually substandard programs for African Americans. It was not until 1954 that the U.S. Supreme Court declared the practice a violation of the Constitution.

Child Development

In the early 1930s the scientific method of discovering truth gave immense credibility to Watsonian psychology and behaviorism as opposed to the sentimentality of earlier childrearing practices. However, during this same period, the Freudian view of infantile fixation and the need for expression of repressed emotion by the child began to influence beliefs about children. This set the stage for the concern about emotional development prevalent in the 1940s.

✍ 1940 TO 1950

The tendency of parents in the 1920s and early 1930s to follow the specific rules of behaviorists changed in the 1940s when parents began to recognize that no one answer could work for all situations (Brim, 1965). The emotionally healthy child was the goal for professionals and parents. Stendler (1950) pointed out that in 1940, only 33 percent of the surveyed magazine articles on infant discipline favored behaviorism, whereas 66 percent endorsed self-regulation. "The swing from the 'be-tough-with-them, feed-on-schedule, let them cry-it-out' doctrines of the twenties and thirties was almost complete" (Brim, 1965, pp. 130–131). Self-regulation allowed the development of trust and automony in the young child.

Baby Decade

Vincent (1951) suggested that the decade between 1935 and 1945 could be called "baby's decade" with the mother "secondary to the infant care 'experts' and the baby's demands" (p. 205). By the early 1940s, mothers were told

that children should be fed when hungry, and bowel and bladder training should not begin too early. Babies were to be trained in a gentle manner after they developed physical control. The latest version of *Infant Care* depicted children as interested in the world around them and viewed exploring as natural. "Babies want to handle and investigate everything they see and reach. When a baby discovers his genital organs he will play with them. . . . A wise mother will not be concerned about this" (Wolfenstein, 1953, p. 122).

Wolfenstein described the change in attitude toward the basic nature of human beings:

> On of the most striking changes in American thinking about children from the nineteenth and early twentieth centuries to the more recent past and the present is the radical change in the conception of the child's nature. From the 19th-century belief in "infant depravity" and the early 20th-century fear of the baby's "fierce" impulses, which, if not vigilantly curbed, could easily grow beyond control and lead to ruin, we have come to consider the child's nature as totally harmless and beneficent. (Mead & Wolfenstein, 1963, p. 146).

Spock

Shifts in beliefs about children were reflected in the childrearing practices of the period. In 1946 Benjamin Spock, a national best-selling author and parent educator, published *The Common Sense Book of Baby and Child Care.* He believed the rules and regulations imposed on parents during the 1920s and 1930s caused undue pressure, and he advised parents to enjoy their children and the role of parent. In the 1957 edition of his book, Spock described predominant attitudes at the time of the 1946 edition:

> When I was writing the first edition, between 1943 and 1946, the attitude of a majority of people toward infant feeding, toilet training, and general child management was still fairly strict and inflexible. However, the need for greater understanding of children and for flexibility in their care had been made clear by educators, psychoanalysts, and pediatricians, and I was trying to encourage this. Since then a great

change in attitude has occurred, and nowadays there seems to be more chance of a conscientious parent's getting into trouble with permissiveness than with strictness. So I have tried to give a more balanced view [in the 1957 edition]. (pp. 1–2)

Spock's book answered questions on feeding, sleeping, clothing, toilet training, management, and illnesses; he had answers for almost all the questions a new parent might have. It continued to have great influence on childrearing through the 1950s and beyond as children raised by Spock's methods became parents.

Parent Groups

The 1940s, although consumed by the outbreak of World War II, saw no reduction in offerings in parent education. Parent groups continued in public schools, and county extension programs prospered. Although services continued and emergency-relief nursery schools for workers involved in the war effort expanded, research and training in child development declined (Brim, 1965).

Both the Great Depression and World War II brought federal support for children's services at younger ages. FERA regulated the child care funds originally, followed by WPA, and, during World War II, the Federal Works Agency (Goodykoontz et al., 1947). The need to provide child care for families during the depression emanated from the necessity for parents to work to get back on their feet and support their families. During World War II, women needed child care services so they could join the war effort.

Parent education found added direction in the 1940s through the mental health movement. In 1946 the National Mental Health Act was passed, authorizing states to establish mental health programs and related parent education (Goodykoontz et al., 1947). The need to understand oneself and one's children was recognized as necessary for healthy parent-child interaction.

The decade ended quietly. The war was over, and the establishment of families, delayed by the war, was in full swing.

Two World Wars were fought in the twentieth century: World War I (1914–1918) and World War II (1941–1945). After World War II, soldiers returned home, and many returned to school on the G.I. bill.

1950 TO 1960

The 1950s were years of relative calm, with emphasis on children and family life. Schools were feeling the increase in numbers of children and were rapidly expanding to meet their needs. Many young adults had postponed marriage and family during the war. But now, the "baby boom" began gathering ever more steam. The PTA had more than 9 million members and thousands of study groups among its 30,000 local chapters. Study groups used material on childrearing and special concerns of parents published by the PTA. Parents were involved with the schools as room parents and fund-raisers for special projects. The view, "Send your child to school, we will do the teaching; your responsibility as a parent is to be supportive of the teachers and schools" prevailed as the basic philosophy between school and parents. The formal learning of reading, writing, and arithmetic started when the child entered first grade, just as it had for many decades.

Emphasis on Family Life

A survey by the National Education Association revealed that family life was the topic of 32 percent of adult education classes (Brim, 1965). Parent education and preschool programs, part of adult education in many school districts, continued as a vital source of childrearing information. Pamphlets from the Child Study Association, the Public Affairs Committee, Science Research Associates, and the Parent Education Project of Chicago, plus books by authorities such as Arnold Gesell, Erik Erikson, B. F. Skinner, Benjamin Spock, Lawrence Frank, and Sidonie Gruenberg, were used as curriculum guides. During the 1950s James L. Hymes wrote his first book on home-school relations.

Orville Brim, sponsored by the Russell Sage Foundation and the Child Study Association, examined the issues involved in parent education in his book *Education for Child Rearing* (1965). His analysis of the effects of parent education continues to be relevant to the study of parent education today.

Your Child from 6 to 12, published by the U.S. Department of Health, Education and Welfare (1949), illustrated the attitude that prevailed in the 1950s and beyond. The preface of the booklet reflected the change from the absolutism of the 1920s and 1930s: "There are many more things that we don't know than we know about children. . . . Every child is unique in temperament, intelligence, and physical make-up" (p. 39).

In the early 1950s, thumb-sucking was viewed as a natural occurrence rather than a negative one. A baby "may try to get pleasure out of his thumb or fingers. Sucking is a poor substitute for

Following World War II, families rejoiced over the return to family life and the baby-boom began.

being held, or talked to, or fed; but it is better than nothing" (Wolfenstein, 1953, p. 124).

Mental Health

Concern for mental health gave parents double messages; it was difficult to combine firm guidance and advice on emotional health. One such view on emotional health stated, "Any action that causes children to feel guilty . . . should be avoided. It is often better to say nothing whatever to the children, for fear of saying too much, or the wrong thing. Instead, divert their minds, give them new interests" (U.S. Department of Health, Education and Welfare, 1949, p. 38).

Erikson

Erikson (1986) popularized the eight stages of personality development in *Childhood and Society*, first published in 1950. His neo-Freudian theories emphasized social and emotional development based on interdisciplinary theories from biology, psychology, and sociology. His theory outlines eight stages of growth from infancy to old age. The stages begin with development of trust versus mistrust for infants; autonomy versus shame and doubt for toddlers; initiative versus guilt for preschoolers, and industry versus inferiority for school-age children. The later stages involve adolescents forming identity versus identity diffusion; for young adults, intimacy versus isolation; for adults, generativity versus self-absorption; and for mature adults, integrity versus despair. Erikson and the childrearing practices of the 1950s reflected the belief that social and emotional health were of utmost importance to the child.

Analysis of Parent-Child Relations

In a content analysis of *Ladies' Home Journal, Good Housekeeping,* and *Redbook* from 1950 to 1970, Bigner (1985) found articles primarily concerned with parent-child relations, socialization, and developmental stages. Spanking was condoned by some in the early 1950s, but by the end of the decade it was consistently discouraged and described as an inefficient and barbaric

method that does no more than show the youngster that parents can hit. Most articles encouraged self-regulation by the child. Parents were told it was important that children feel loved and wanted. Parents were advised to hold, love, and enjoy their children and to rely on their own good judgment in making childrearing decisions.

Parents were encouraged to provide a home life that was supportive of individual differences and allowed each child to grow into a well-adjusted adult. Development was a natural process, and maturation could not be pushed. Gesell's work on development in psychomotor and physical areas supported the theory that children proceed through innate developmental stages. As a consequence, parents were encouraged to provide a well-balanced, nutritional diet and an environment that allowed children to grow and learn at their own rate.

The 1950s were characterized by fathers working and mothers staying home to care for the children.

The Department of Health, Education and Welfare, established in 1953 with the Social Security Administration, Office of Education, and Public Health Service under its jurisdiction, continued a diversified approach to parent education.

Toward the end of the 1950s, the nation's calm was disturbed. Russia's success in launching *Sputnik* into space caused a ripple effect across the United States. Why had the Soviets achieved a feat not yet accomplished by the United States? Americans looked for an answer.

ᘑᘒ 1960 TO 1970

The 1960s was a decade of sweeping changes in parent involvement, social and civil rights, and family characteristics. The family had been gradually changing since the early part of the century when the family was viewed with great sentimentality, mothers were revered, and the family was a sacred institution that few dared to question. By the 1960s it was common for all institutions—family, education, religion, economics, and government—to be criticized and questioned. Great changes in the American family took place between 1890 and 1960 as the country changed from a basically rural nation to an urban nation. The majority of families had been self-sufficient rural families with authoritarian parents; now most became dependent on others for income. As a mobile society evolved, one person in five moved each year for a better job or a better education. Children were no longer economic assets who helped their parents with the family farm or business; instead, they became financial liabilities, costing $20,000 to raise from infancy to 18 years of age (Hill, 1960). The many

The need for parent education was recognized. Programs were offered by schools, hospitals, and social agencies.

women who had continued working after World War II were joined in the 1960s by many more who entered the labor force to supplement their husband's income or increase their own economic freedom. For many other women, who were single parents or were a supporting member of a two-parent family, working was an economic necessity.

Focus on Development

The 1960s began a period of concern for intellectual and cognitive development in the young, but little change was evident between the 1950s and 1960s concerning social and emotional child-rearing practices.

Father Involvement

The importance of the father's relationship with his children was stressed and, although his obligations to his children were not the same as the mother's, early interaction with his newborn baby was recognized as very beneficial. "Fathers who feel comfortable giving physical attention to their babies at the start are lucky" (U.S. Department of Health, Education and Welfare, 1962, p. 29).

Publications

Parents had many child care books and booklets from which to choose. Publications from the Child Study Association and Science Research Associates and public affairs pamphlets covered many of the problems parents faced. Benjamin Spock continued to publish books on child care, and in them he advised firm, consistent guidance of the child. "A child needs to feel that his mother and father, however agreeable, have their own rights, know how to be firm, won't let him be unreasonable or rude.

The importance of fathers in the child's development began to be emphasized in the 1960s and 1970s.

He likes them better that way. It trains him from the beginning to get along reasonably with other people" (Spock, 1957, p. 326).

Ginott

Spock's efforts were aided by psychologist Haim Ginott (1965), who offered parents a method for talking about feelings and guiding the child in a manner that avoided placing guilt and helped the child understand the parents' feelings, thus disciplining the child in a positive manner.

Piaget

Professionals working with children and parents were greatly influenced by Piaget's theories of cognitive development. His ideas, clearly discussed by Hunt in his book *Intelligence and Experience* (see Chapter 1 of this book), emphasized active involvement of the child with the environment. Parents became much more concerned about their child's intellectual development and were no longer satisfied that development would unfold naturally.

White House Conferences

When the Golden Anniversary White House Conference on Children and Youth convened in 1959, it delved into concerns about the family and social change, development and education, and problems and prospects for remediation (Ginsberg, 1960). This conference was followed by a White House Conference on Mental Retardation in 1963.

The time was ripe to meet the needs of all people—not just the dominant social class. The Great Depression of the 1930s and World War II of the 1940s had kept the country occupied with emergencies. The affluent 1950s, impaired by the Korean War and the Cold War with the Soviet Union, gave cause for reflection. The 1960s brought forth many questions. Was the United States able to provide advantages for all its people? Were democracy and the free enterprise system capable of providing the best life for the most people? Could the United States surpass the Soviets in the space challenge? These were some of the difficult questions, concerning millions of people, that faced the nation.

Equal Educational Opportunity

The social climate of the nation during the 1960s mandated a concerted effort to provide equality of opportunity, as reflected in the Civil Rights Act of 1964. One result was a comprehensive national survey of 645,000 students in 4,000 schools. These findings were revealed in *Equality of Educational Opportunity* by Coleman et al. (1966). Although the main thrust of the report was to investigate the effects of de facto and de jure segregation on educational achievement, the report had implications for educators who might institute early intervention. The researchers found that school curricula and expenditures on facilities and materials did not affect school achievement, but the quality of teachers did. The students who achieved believed they had some control over their own destiny. "Minority pupils, except for Orientals, have far less conviction than whites that they can affect their own environment and futures" (Coleman et al., p. 23). The most important factor shown to affect achievement was family background. Notable variables included the home's effective support of education, number of children in the family, and parents' educational levels.

War on Poverty

Although prosperity was within reach for most U.S. citizens and the standard of living had steadily improved to the highest in the world, minorities, people with disabilities, and the economically disadvantaged were still underemployed, often poverty stricken, and largely ignored. The government had high hopes for a Great Society where poverty would be eliminated for all citizens. In the War on Poverty programs, children of the poor—who were undernourished, in ill health, without proper housing, and lacking educational opportunities—were chosen as a major target to realize hope for the future.

The works of behavioral scientists and educators presented overpowering evidence that early environment has a profound effect on a child's development (Bloom, 1964; Hunt, 1961; Skeels, 1966; Spitz, 1965.). (See Chapter 1.) These reports, along with the national mood of the mid-1960s supporting equal rights and opportunity, propelled the country to respond to the needs of the poor and disadvantaged. One of the most effective responses was to provide educational intervention for the children of the poor.

If children could be given equal environmental opportunities, the cycle of poverty could be broken. The stage was set for the birth of Head Start. As research indicated that parent involvement and family background were positively correlated with academic success, the inclusion of parents in their child's education program was entrenched from the beginning of the Head Start program. There is a recognition that the powerless must be instruments of their own change; as a result, parents were included on advisory councils, in career development programs, and in education of children. Parents had become involved in the educational process again.

Head Start

In 1965 the Office of Economic Opportunity began an 8-week summer program for disadvantaged preschool children. The proposed projects had a two-pronged approach. The child would benefit from an enriched early education program, and the parents would be an integral part of the programs as aides, advisory council members, or paraprofessional members of the team. As a result of these beliefs the first Head Start centers were opened in the summer of 1965 as part of the War on Poverty. Head Start was a comprehensive program of health, nutrition, and education as well as a career ladder for economically disadvantaged families. Rather than wait for results of the long-range effects of early intervention, the trial program was enlarged in the fall to encompass many Head Start programs, funded by federal money but administered by local agen-

cies. Its name described its aims. Children who were disadvantaged would be given a head start on school.

Research on Head Start

Researchers in the 1960s demonstrated startling gains in IQ in children enrolled in Head Start and other programs (Caldwell, 1968; Deutsch & Deutsch, 1968; Gray & Klaus, 1965; Weikart & Lambie, 1968). Those looking for sustained intellectual gains, however, were disappointed with the results of one of the first studies, the so-called Westinghouse Report/Ohio State University Study (Westinghouse Learning Corporation & The Ohio State University, 1969), which indicated no sustained intellectual development (see Consortium for Longitudinal Studies, 1983; Lazar, Darlington, Murray, Royce, & Snipper, 1982).

ESEA

Shortly after the formation of Head Start, the Office of Education, Department of Health, Education and Welfare, undertook direction for the Elementary and Secondary Education Act (ESEA) of 1965. Suddenly, twice the amount of federal money poured into schools that applied for and received grants. Public schooling, although still controlled by local boards of education, began to be influenced by federal spending. The federal money, funded through state agencies, was used to help eliminate the educational disadvantages of children in the public schools. Some of the Title projects under ESEA included:

1. Title I, which assists local school districts in improving the education of educationally deprived children. From its inception, parents were involved in the program.

2. Title IV-C (formerly Title III), which promoted the innovative programs that enrich educational opportunities. Many of these projects included home visitation programs for preschool children, identification of handicapped children before school entry, and working with the parents for the benefit of their children.

Concern about continuity of educational success after Head Start resulted in the implementation of the Follow Through program as part of the 1967 Economic Opportunity Act. Designed to carry the benefits of Head Start and similar preschool programs into the public school system, parent participation was a major component of the program, and, as with the Head Start program, parent advisory councils were mandated.

Civil Rights Act of 1965

Although not directly connected with parent education, the Civil Rights Act of 1965 had great influence on the role of minorities and women during subsequent decades and, through this, affected the family. Affirmative action, requiring minorities and women to be treated equally in housing, education, and employment, resulted in psychological as well as empirical changes in conditions for these populations. Although the increase in equality was not accomplished as the Civil Rights Act demanded, heightened awareness on the part of minorities and women had profound effects on their understanding of themselves, their relationships within the family unit, and their concern for equal opportunities.

Vietnam War

Throughout most of this decade the Vietnam War affected family relationships, values, and social change. The war diminished the opportunity for success of the Great Society by funneling money and energy away from domestic programs. It also had an immense effect on family unity because many families were torn apart over diverse values concerning drug use, participation in the war, and moral responsibilities. Parents of adolescents cried for direction and guidance when confronted with overwhelming value changes in their children. Television, peer group influence, lack of consistent social and moral guidance, and involvement in the Vietnam War thrust parents into an arena for which they were not prepared by the modeling of their parents or by education.

Emphasis on Services for Low-Economic Groups

The decade closed with greater emphasis on parent involvement and education for families of low socioeconomic levels than in any previous era. Backed by federal money, the War on Poverty attacked many areas. Whereas early programs were structured to inculcate immigrants and the poor with the values and customs of the dominant culture, the 1960s attempted to recognize the importance and viability of diverse cultural backgrounds and draw from the strengths of diversity with parents as active advocates for their children and themselves. Blacks, Chicanos, Puerto Ricans, underprivileged Whites, and others of low socioeconomic background had the opportunity to express their needs and desires, and the Head Start program reflected each community.

1970 TO 1980

The enormous number of programs implemented in the 1960s came of age in the 1970s. Development occurred in both private and public sectors with churches, local agencies, public schools, and clubs, as well as state and federal agencies, showing concern for families caught in the stream of social change. The country was still confronted with the Vietnam War at the beginning of the decade. With the end of U.S. involvement in 1973, one of the major disruptive forces on family unity was resolved.

Advocacy

The decade could be described as the era of advocacy. Groups were no longer willing to sit and wait for someone to do something for them; they had learned in the 1960s that the way to help is through self-help and self-determination. Parents of children with disabilities, individually and through organizations such as the Association for Retarded Children, the Council for Exceptional Children, and the Association for Children with Learning Disabilities, advocated equal rights for the special child and won (see Chapter 9). Advocate groups for children sprang up across the land with training sessions on political power and the means to implement change and protection for children.

The public schools were not immune. Parents began to question programs and their participation with schools and teachers. Forced integration and required busing were issues confronting schools and parents.

Changes in Parent Involvement

Over the years, parent involvement in school decision making had diminished. Families in earlier centuries had the prime responsibility for education of their children. When formal education joined with informal education, parents still had decision-making rights in regard to their child's schooling. In colonial days the church and family were the major institutions for the socialization of children. During the 18th and 19th centuries the community school increased in importance, but parents were still involved in decision making. Schools were small. Many country schools were dispersed across the nation, and schoolteachers were hired by the local school board, lived in the community, and were responsible to the local school district. Between 1890 and 1920 there was a shift from community to urban schools (Butts & Cremin, 1953; Goodson & Hess, 1975). The dramatic shift from a rural society to an urban society resulted in a change in the control of schools. The process transferred control of schools from the community to professionals. Consolidation of rural schools into larger, centrally located schools improved equipment, facilities, and diversity of staff, but it took away parent influence. From the 1920s until the 1970s the steady flow from rural to urban areas increased the separation of school and families. Minorities and the poor were most alienated from the educational process.

Research

Studies conducted in the 1970s consistently demonstrated the importance of an enriched early home environment to the child's school success (Hanson, 1975; Shipman, Boroson, Bidgeman, Gart, & Mikovsky, 1976; White, Kaban, Attanucci, & Shapiro, 1973). Shipman et al. (1976) studied African American children of low socioeconomic status. The mother's educational aspirations and expectations were higher for children who scored high in reading than for those who scored low in reading. A higher level of parental education was also associated with children's overall academic success.

In 1975 the Consortium for Longitudinal Studies (1983) set out to determine the effect of the experimental early intervention programs of the 1960s on children. The consortium selected 11 research groups for analysis. Although the programs differed, they were all well designed and well monitored, so there was an excellent database.

The consortium's findings emphasized the importance of early intervention (Consortium for Longitudinal Studies, 1983; Gray, Ramsey, & Klaus, 1982; Lazar et al., 1982; Levenstein, 1988; Spodek, 1982). In a summary of the consortium's findings, Lazar (1983) discussed two important points. First, a good preschool program pays off in two ways: benefits for children's development and financial savings as a result of less special education placement. Second, "closer contact between home and school and greater involvement of parents in the education of their children are probably more important" than generally realized by administrators (p. 464).

A follow-up study of Weikart's Perry Preschool Program vividly illustrated the effect that early educational intervention can have on children's lives (Berrueta-Clement, Schweinhart, Barnett, Epstein, & Weikart, 1984). The Perry Preschool Program followed children to age 19, 4 years beyond the report published by the consortium. Berrueta-Clement et al. compared children who had attended the Perry Preschool with children who had not. The researchers found that former Perry Preschool students grew up with more school success, placed a higher value on school, had higher aspirations for college, had fewer absences, and spent fewer of their school years in special education than children in a control group. Although Weikart's program had a strong parent-involvement component, the contributions of parents to the program's success were not analyzed because the researchers were unable to separate parent involvement from the preschool effect. In fact, however, the influence of caregivers, whether teachers or parents, cannot be separated from the well-being of the child and the success of a program.

In 1972, 16 Home Start programs serving 1,200 families were launched. Eleven Child and Family Resource programs serving 900 families were started in July 1973. "These programs, all built around a Head Start program, promote continuity of service by including all children in the participating family from prenatal stage through age 8, and broaden the program focus from the age-eligible child, to the entire family" (U.S. Department of Health, Education and Welfare, 1974, p. iii).

Developmental Continuity

Concern about the link between Head Start and the public school resulted in funding for developmental continuity. Two program designs were investigated. One was based on a cooperative model with both Head Start and the schools working out a continuous educational program for the child. The other caused change within the existing school system and included programs for children 3 years and up as part of the school system as well as a curriculum structured for preschool ages through age 8. Both programs involved parents throughout preschool and school years.

Children in the 1970s, according to the experts, continued to need love, consistent guidance, and an enriched and responsive environment. Concern over parent-child separation, particularly in a required hospital stay, was evident in advice given to parents. They were told to stay with the child if hospitalization was necessary. Bonding and the importance of early child-parent interaction was reflected in the research of Ainsworth (1973), Bowlby (1966, 1982, 1988), Brazelton (1987), Klaus and Kennell (1982), and Spitz (1965).

Child abuse and neglect were recognized as debilitating and destructive forces against children, and the concerns of the 1960s became a mandate to report all suspected cases of child abuse and neglect (see Chapter 10).

Sexist references in texts, which implied innate differences between boys and girls or referred to children in masculine terms only, became noticeable by their absence. Feminists joined civil rights activists and advocates of rights for disabled persons in elimination of stereotypes and inequality of opportunity. The 1970s moved forward, slipped backward, and consolidated gains for many who were not a part of the mainstream of life in the United States.

Government publications ranged from the traditional *Infant Care* and *Your Child from One to Six* to curriculum materials for Head Start, Home Start, Follow Through, and two new series, *Family Day Care* and *Caring for Children*. Attention continued to focus on the total family rather than on the individual child. The Office of Child Development became the Administration for Children, Youth and Families.

The decade closed with school, government, social agencies, and families concerned with educational programs and support systems for children and parents. Plans for the White House Conference for Families were under way. The diversity of underlying philosophies was exemplified in the concern for a definition of family composition. Differing opinions ranged from those who believed families were composed of two parents and children to those who believed any unit living together was a family. The times were difficult; inflation was causing great hardships. From among the many issues, one concern raised hope for the future—parents were vitally concerned about the future of the family.

1980 TO 1990

White House Conference

The 1980s commenced with the White House Conference on Families, which took place in July

1980 at three locations: Baltimore, Minneapolis, and Los Angeles. Interest was high. Families were important to the citizens, but divisive interests complicated the work. Despite this, the conference approved 20 recommendations to support families, including flexible work schedules, leave policies, job sharing, more part-time jobs, and more child care services.

The decade ended with little movement toward achievement of these recommendations. Few companies offered flexible work schedules and job sharing. Congress defeated the Family and Parental Leave Act in 1988. Child care was viewed by two presidents as a private or state concern, not a federal issue, although the child care tax credit was implemented. The ambivalence and reaction of the federal administration toward the well-being of families and children was exemplified by the cancellation of the White House Conference on Children and Youth, which had been scheduled for December 1981, and had taken place every decade since President Theodore Roosevelt convened the first conference in 1909. The 1960s and the 1970s were times for expansion of civil rights and family programs; the 1980s were a time for retrenchment.

Head Start

Of all the programs that were started in the late 1960s and 1970s, the most politically enduring was Head Start. It continued to receive funds throughout the 1980s, but was able to reach only 18 percent of eligible children and families.

Family Concerns

Families in this decade were under stress caused by financial pressure, lack of available time, high mobility, lack of an extended family in close proximity, drugs, abuse, violence on the streets and on television, health concerns, inadequate nutrition, and difficulty in obtaining or providing adequate child care. On the positive side, inflation steadied in the 1980s. Those who did not have housing, however, were caught in a crunch. Home buyers were faced with high down payments or ex-tremely high monthly payments. Many could not afford any housing, and the number of homeless increased to become a national disgrace.

Poverty existed in all parts of the United States—32.5 million people were poor, 12.5 million of whom were children. One child out of five lived in poverty. The ratios were even higher for two minority groups: Nearly one in two Black children and one in three Hispanic children lived in poverty (Children's Defense Fund, 1989b). Poverty was most evident in the core cities. Shelters and churches offered warmth to the homeless on cold nights, and food lines were set up by many private and church groups. In rural areas where poverty was not so evident, little hope was available. Many children attended school without their basic nutritional needs being met. School lunches were a necessity for them.

In sharp contrast, the 1980s were also characterized by greater affluence. High salaries were available for those in business, technology, and communication. Education was recognized as one way out of poverty. Dealing drugs was another. Children and families living in central cities with high crime rates and widespread drug abuse needed comprehensive support to enable them to realize a more promising destiny (Schorr & Schorr, 1988). Poverty, social programs, and education were intertwined in an effort to lower the high risk of poverty.

Two concerns that contributed to high risk for children were the increased numbers of teenage pregnancies and unmarried mothers. Very young mothers are not prepared physically, educationally, or mentally to rear children, yet one in five infants was born to an unmarried teenager in the 1980s (Hymes, 1987). In addition, the increased numbers of single mothers due to divorce, death of a spouse, or preference also heightened the risk of poverty.

In more than half of two-parent families in the United States, both parents worked (O'Connell & Bloom, 1987). This gave families a higher standard of living. However, time became a precious commodity, and some families found it difficult to save time for themselves and their children. Articles on handling stress and programs for stress reduction continued to grow in popularity. Parent education programs such as STEP, PET, and Active Parenting were offered by schools, hospitals, and social agencies (see Chapter 5).

Many baby boomers began families of their own, and some chose to use birthing rooms in hospitals so that parents and infants could have time together when the infant was first born. Lamaze classes helped prepare parents for the birth, and the La Leche League helped mothers with nursing. Many baby boomers had waited to start having children and were eager recipients of the parent education offered by these and other groups.

Acquired immuno deficiency syndrome (AIDS) frightened the entire society. The deadly disease was recognized in the early 1980s.

Parent Education

The need for more parent education for teenagers and all parents was recognized. The country was divided throughout the 1980s, just as it had been during the White House Conference on Families. The far right decried public interference in rearing of children, but polls showed that most people favored family life education. Abortion clinics were bombed as the "right to life" faction demonstrated against the "right to choice" faction. "Pro-family" had different meanings for different people.

Developmentally Appropriate

The National Association for the Education of Young Children (NAEYC) prepared a position statement that outlined the components of developmentally appropriate curricula for young children.

Interest in programs for 4-year-olds increased in individual states, and states began to fund programs that would meet the needs of 4-year-olds who were at risk. The federal government, in the form of P.L. 99–457, offered incentive grants to support programs for children with physical and learning disabilities from birth until age 2.

Child Development Associate

An issue was the lack of qualified child care staff. The Child Development Associate (CDA) pro-

gram continued, moving from Bank Street College of Education to the Council on Early Childhood Professional Recognition, under the auspices of the NAEYC. More than 31,000 people were credentialed by the end of the 1980s. Colleges across the nation continued to offer two-year associate and four- or five-year teacher certification programs. After obtaining credentials or a certificate, however, those who worked in child care were paid such low salaries that many could not afford to work in the field if they were sole support for a family.

International Change

Citizens and governments of many countries exhibited concern about nuclear waste and the environment. Political and economic changes occurred in China and the Soviet Union: China began to accept tourists and exchanged students and goods with the rest of the world, and the Soviet Union, under Mikhail Gorbachev, began a restructuring and concurrent openness to dissent. There was hope these changes could bring the dawning of a new period of peace and prosperity to the world.

Although some positive signs of change were evident, the social concerns of poverty, at-risk children, AIDS, undereducated youth, drug and alcohol abuse, stress on families, environmental pollution, and homelessness plagued the country into the 1990s.

⅋ 1990 TO 2000

Focus on Family

The 1990s could be called the Decade of Focus on the Family. Parent involvement changed to family involvement. From focusing on mothers in the 1950s and both fathers and mothers in the 1960s and 1970s, a shift occurred toward viewing family environment as the most important factor in a child's education. The Department of Education emphasized the strengthening of families and issued a paper, *Strong Families, Strong Schools: Building Community Partnerships for Learning* (1994). Family partnerships with school were encouraged. In 1990, the Center on Children, Schools, Families, and Children's Learning was established.

Federal influence on schools continued with federal programs such as Title I, Even Start, and the Elementary and Secondary School Act. The introduction of Goals 2000: Educate America and the development of national standards were criticized by some as taking away the constitutional rights of states to control education. At the same time, parents were given more power to influence the education of their children. Many schools began restructuring and turned to site-based management, an educational design that had parents working with school personnel in the establishment of goals and direction. There was also a movement for choice in school selection. Charter schools became available in many states commencing in 1996 and 1997. Parents could elect their own board and choose their own curriculum for their charter schools, funded by the school district in which they were located.

Family Resource Centers

Family resource centers were funded. Their goals were to strengthen and empower families. The centers designed their programs according to the needs of their populations with offerings that might include parent education, programs for children, and literacy programs.

Family Literacy

Family literacy programs were established to help those who could not read. The classes helped newcomers who did not speak or read English well as well as those who had not learned to read in school. Family literacy programs recognized that parents could help their children more if the parents were able to read and support their children.

Homeschooling

Homeschooling became more popular during this decade, and support groups helped parents who wanted to teach their children at home.

States enacted certain requirements for parents to continue homeschooling. For example, children must take tests every 3 years and place no lower than the 19th percentile. It was recommended that schools work with homeschooling parents so that children could participate in activities that the home is unable to offer, such as band, chorus, and athletics.

Concerns

The 1990s started with continued dissatisfaction with what the government was doing about unemployment, AIDS, homelessness, drug and alcohol abuse, and the budget deficit.

The Cold War had ended. The Soviet Union split into several countries, and throughout eastern Europe, ethnic factions began fighting for independence and control. Particularly tragic were the civil wars in the former Yugoslavia. The 1990s have been times of change and reassessment in many countries.

Family and Medical Leave Act

Congress finally passed the Family and Medical Leave Act in early 1993, providing 12 weeks of unpaid leave for employees with such family concerns as childbirth, adoption, or a serious illness of a child, spouse, or parent. The bill required all companies with 50 or more employees to guarantee jobs and provide health benefits to workers when they returned after the leave.

Temporary Assistance for Needy Families

Welfare was revamped in 1996 with the Personal Responsibility and Work Opportunity Reconciliation Act. AFDC (Aid to Families with Dependent Children) had provided assistance for poor, single-parent families since 1935. It was replaced with Temporary Assistance for Needy Families (TANF), which provides block grants to states who run their own programs within federal guidelines. The law requires mothers to join the workforce if they receive assistance for more than 2 years. It places a 5-year lifetime limit on eligibility for assistance. In carrying out the law some concerns have emerged, including child care, health care, poor job skills of some former AFDC recipients, and child care workers who earn low wages.

Pro-life and Pro-choice

Advocates for stronger families and better conditions for children were strong in their positions. The two largest camps were those in favor of no abortions and those who favored abortion under certain circumstances. Although both groups were strong advocates, the pro-life advocates differed from the pro-choice advocates in their approach to strengthening families.

The new century arrived with the country strong in spirit. Will it support its schools and families?

IDEA 97

The Individuals with Disabilities Education Act, IDEA 97 (P.L. 105-17) was reauthorized in 1997. It addressed the participation of parents in the development of their child with disability's program.

✨ 2000 TO 2004

Emphasis on Education

The 21st century opened with continued emphasis on education. Programs that had originated in the 1960s from the War on Poverty, such as the Elementary and Secondary Education Act and Head Start, continued into the new century. The importance of families in the education of children was emphasized, and programs for the very young child were increased.

Response to Terrorism

On September 11, 2001, the Twin Tower Center in New York City and a section of the Pentagon in Washington, DC, were destroyed by terrorists.

The focus on education continued in schools, home, and community, but the national focus changed to a war on terrorism. Special forces were sent to Afghanistan to conduct a war against the Al Qaeda and Osama bin Laden, their leader. The war on terrorism, however, would continue to be a concern throughout the decade because it was recognized that there were terrorist cells in various countries around the world.

The people in the United States and their allies responded strongly to the terrorism with determination that they would not submit to fear. There was, however, much stronger control and inspections at events such as the winter Olympics in Salt Lake City, in airports, and at government buildings.

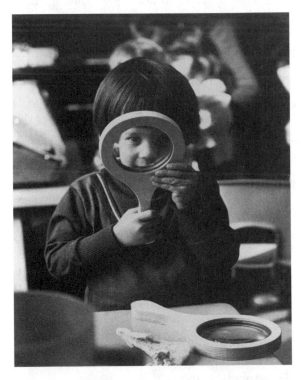

The focus on learning, educational programs, and systems of delivery continued to be tried, researched, and delivered.

Schools remained open and teachers and families continued in their pursuit of good education for their children.

White House Summit on Early Childhood

The government focused on improving education. The previous White House Conference on Early Childhood Development and Learning on April 17, 1997, made many educators aware of the importance of the early years on brain development. (See Chapter 1.)

A White House Summit on Early Childhood was held on July 26 and 27, 2001. Its focus was to raise public awareness of the importance of early childhood. The topics covered were varied, with speakers who discussed brain development, poverty and how it affects children, and intervention skills.

Prior to the summit, the National Education Association (NEA), a professional organization with 2.6 million members, challenged the focus on literacy, recommending that health, nutrition, and brain and social development of infants and young children must also be included.

A seminar was held in Washington, DC, on February 6, 2002, to consider research. The question, "What is scientifically based research and how is it achieved?" was addressed.

Programs that were specially developed to help families with young children included the Child Care Development Fund and Early Head Start. In addition, individual school districts continued a trend toward funding all-day kindergartens. The National Education Goals Panel continued the emphasis on Goal 1, All Children Ready to Learn and Goal 8, Parental Involvement.

Partnerships for Family Involvement in Education

The U.S. Department of Education offered information and support through the establishment of Partnerships for Family Involvement in Education.

In addition, the Center on Families, Communities, Schools, and Children's Learning, which was established at Johns Hopkins University, continued to provide research, policy, and a National Network of Partnerships.

National Education Goals Panel

The National Education Goals Panel was created in 1990 as a bipartisan group of two members appointed by the president, four state legislators, four members of Congress, and eight governors. The panel was dissolved in 2002 by a congressional mandate.

A number of Promising Practices Policies resulted in various improvements in the schools during the panel's existence. Reports on accomplishments by individual states and the Department of Defense (DOD) were recognized by the panel. According to reports, schools improved due to downsizing to smaller schools and classrooms, more strategic planning, and better accountability. Each of the eight goals were considered. Goal 3, Student Achievement, reported that the study of mathematics has shown statistically significant positive change in average scores. However, it had not reduced gaps between the top and bottom quartiles, majority and minority students, or students eligible and not eligible for reduced cost or free lunches. "During the 1990s fourth grade students made more improvement in mathematics achievement than in reading in most states" (Barton, 2002). Other findings include: "Good readers are getting better at the same time weak readers are losing ground" (Barton, 2002) The achievement gap between White and minority students and between top and bottom quartiles had not been reduced in nearly all of the states.

The eight National Education Goals Panel called for greater levels of student achievement and citizenship; high school completion; teacher education and professional development; parental participation in the schools; literacy and lifelong learning; and safe, disciplined, and alcohol- and drug-free schools. The goals also called for all children to be ready to learn by the time they start school and for U.S. students to be first in the world in mathematics and science achievement (Barton, 2002).

No Child Left Behind Act of 2001

A new law, No Child Left Behind Act of 2001, was signed into law on January 8, 2002. "The new law is considered to be the most sweeping reform of the Elementary and Secondary Education Act since it was enacted in 1965" (U.S. Department of Education, 2002).

The law requires that states test third through eight graders annually in reading and mathematics. The object of testing is to require that states and school districts develop systems of accountability. States will be required to provide annual report cards on school performance and statewide results. At the same time, states and school districts are to have more local control and flexibility in decision making on how increased learning and testing will be obtained.

It is proposed that parents of children in schools that are designated as failing may transfer their child to another school, traditional or charter, that is performing better. When schools continue to fail, supplemental service such as after-school programs, tutoring, and summer school may use Title I funds. More federal funding in reading instructional materials and in improving teacher quality was also approved (U.S. Department of Education, 2002).

Charter Schools

By 2001, 36 states, the District of Columbia, and Puerto Rico had enacted laws for charter schools. In 1992 only two states had charter schools which, although public schools, are organized differently and offer an alternative type of education for parents and students. Charter schools find and develop their own facilities, hire their own teachers, and design their own curriculum. They are usually smaller than the traditional public schools, are popular with parents, and have a more di-verse population than the traditional school. In traditional public schools the school population typically is 59 percent White; 18 percent Hispanic; 17 percent Black; 4 percent Asian; and 1 percent American Indian. In charter schools, White students generally account for only 49 percent of the school population; Hispanic students for 10 to 21 percent; Blacks from 17 to 24 percent; and American Indian students from 1 to 3 percent. The number of Asian students is reduced from 4 to 3 percent (Dervarics, 2001).

Whether the charter schools are accomplishing better education for their students is still unclear. Current research has not found that charter schools have higher academic achievement than traditional schools. More research comparisons will be available in the future (Dervarics, 2001).

Family and Medical Leave Act

The Family and Medical Leave Act, which offers 12 weeks of unpaid leave from work, was favored by most citizens. From 1993 when it was signed into law, it has been estimated that 356 million men and women have used the leave to care for newborn or newly adopted children, care for children, spouses, or parents with health problems, or recover from a condition or illness themselves. It was found, however, that 78 percent of those who needed leave were unable to take it because one salary was not enough to support their families. Some states are looking at options that would supplement the one salary by allowing the parent staying home with the infant to take out unemployment benefits or temporary disability insurance. In 2000, the U.S. Department of Labor adopted regulations encouraging states to provide unemployment benefits to working parents who take leave to care for newborns or newly adopted children (Asher & Lenhoff, 2001).

Technology

"Computer technology has transformed society in profound ways. For better or worse, the increasing persuasiveness of computer technology is a reality no one can ignore" (Shields & Behrman, 2000). The number of computers in the schools has increased from 250,000 in 1983 to 8.6 million in 1997. Access to computers at home range from 22 percent of families with less than $20,000 income to 91 percent of families with incomes of $91,000, according to a 1989 survey (Becker, 2000).

Making computers a useful tool in the early childhood classroom requires that the teacher be knowledgeable and supportive. Children should be 3 or 4 years of age before they explore and use appropriate computer software. Kindergarten and primary-grade children continue with exploration, using developmentally appropriate software, but as they become more familiar with computers, their explorations may lead to composing short stories.

In the early 1980s most computers were found in institutions of higher education. The use of computers, started for general use in the 1980s, exploded in the 1990s, and continues into the 21st century. With the explosion of computer use, and the information available through the Internet, it is essential in the 21st century that older children become competent computer users.

Population Diversity

Schools' student populations show increased diversity in the 21st century. During the 1990s and early 21st century, immigration rose to its highest level since the beginning of the 20th century. Early in the 20th century, one million immigrants arrived each year. Since 1992, almost one million immigrants have arrived each year as well, accounting for 9 percent of the total population. The greatest number of immigrants come from Asia and Latin America. Those migrating from Asia are often from China and the Philippines, whereas the majority of Latin Americans come from Mexico (Martin & Midgley, 1999; Martin & Widgren, 2002). This influx of immigrants and refugees (through both legal and unauthorized entry) impacts the schools, with enrollment of many non-English-speaking students. In 2000, the foreign-born population in the United States totaled almost 30.5 million: 15.5 million Latin Americans;

8.3 million Asians; 4.7 million Europeans, 836,000 Africans; 835,000 Northern Americans, and 181,000 Oceanians (U.S. Census Bureau, 2001). These students enhance the diversity of the schools, but they also require special programs such as English as a Second Language (ESL), to help the children adjust to education in the United States.

Living with Change

The nation looks forward to a new century with many changes happening around the world. To understand the future, it is also necessary to understand the past. As the new century begins, the nation faces the need for a continued response to terrorist threats, conflict with Iraq, nuclear concerns, and continued unrest in the Israeli-Palestine area. Around the world, many live in dire conditions that need to be ameliorated. Challenges abound. How will the nation respond to make the world a better place for all children?

Table 2.2 highlights the events and poeple who influenced ideas about children and child-rearing from the 1880s to modern times.

✆ SUMMARY

Parental involvement in the education of children has been present since prehistoric times (see Tables 2.1 and 2.2 for a brief overview of important ideas about children over the centuries). The family provided the first informal education for the child through modeling, teaching, and praise or discipline. From the times of early Egyptian, Sumerian, Hebrew, Greek, and Roman days, parents were actively involved in the selection of teachers and the education of their children.

During the Middle Ages (A.D. 400–1400), at 7 years of age, children of nobility were sent to live in another noble's home, and others became apprentices in trades. Children were treated as miniature adults rather than children. It was not until the 15th to 17th centuries that the concept of family began to develop.

Strict discipline was imposed on all classes of children. This philosophy prevailed until the writings of Rousseau, Pestalozzi, and Froebel in the 18th and early 19th centuries brought a touch of humanism to the rearing of children.

TABLE 2.2   Highlights of events and people who influenced ideas about children and childrearing, 1880–2004.

1882	The American Association of University Women was established.
1884	The Department of Kindergarten Instruction of the National Education Association was formed (later the Department of Elementary-Kindergarten-Nursery Education; dissolved in the mid-1970s).
1888	The Child Study Association of America was founded.
1889	The General Federation of Women's Clubs was founded. G. Stanley Hall began the first child study center.
1890–1900	Settlement houses were established to aid the poor and new immigrants.
1892	The International Kindergarten Union was established (now the Association for Childhood Education International).
1895	Patty Smith Hill and Anna Bryan studied with G. Stanley Hall.
1896	The Laboratory School at the University of Chicago was started by John Dewey. The National Association of Colored Women was established.
1897	The Parent Teachers Association (PTA) was founded.
1898	*Kindergarten Magazine* was first published.
1905	Maria Montessori established Casa del Bambini in Rome. Sigmund Freud wrote *Three Essays of the Theory of Sexuality*.
1909	The First White House Conference on Care of Dependent Children was held.
1911	Margaret McMillan designed an open-air nursery for children of the poor in England. Gesell started the Child Development Clinic at Yale University.
1912	The Children's Bureau was established. It published the first edition of *Infant Care* in 1914.
1916	The first parent cooperative was established in Chicago.
1917	The Smith-Hughes Act was passed. The Iowa Child Welfare Research Station was established.
1920s	Twenty-six parent education programs were established.
1920	The Child Welfare League of America was founded. Watson, a behaviorist, believed that children should be strictly scheduled and should not be coddled.
1922	A nursery school was established in Boston by Abigail Elliot. Benjamin Gruenberg wrote the *Child Study Manual*.
1925	The National Council of Parent Education was established. Patty Smith Hill began the National Committee on Nursery Schools (now the National Association for the Education of Young Children).
1927	The first Black nursery school in the U.S. was founded by Dorothy Howard in Washington, D.C.
1928	The nursery school movement expanded from 3 schools in 1920 to 89 in 1928.
1930	The White House Conference on Child Health and Protection recommended parent education as part of the public school system.
1932	Parent education courses were offered in 25 states.
1933	The Federal Emergency Relief Administration authorized work-relief wages for nursery school teachers.
1934–1938	*Parent Education*, the journal of the National Council of Parent Education, was published.
1940s	A new emphasis on mental health for children emerged.
1940	The Lanham Act provided money for child care so that mothers could join the war effort.
1946	Benjamin Spock published *The Common Sense Book of Baby and Child Care*.
1949	*Your Children from 6 to 12* was published by the Children's Bureau.
1950	Erik Erikson wrote *Childhood and Society*, which included the eight stages of personality growth. James Hymes wrote *Effective Home-School Relations*.
1952	Jean Piaget's work *The Origins of Intelligence in Children* was translated into English.

1957	After the launching of *Sputnik*, new emphasis was placed on children's intellectual development. *Parenthood in a Free Nation* was published by the Parent Education Project of the University of Chicago.
1960	The Golden Anniversary White House Conference on Children and Youth was held. The Parent Cooperative Preschools International was founded.
1960	The Day Care and Child Development Council of America was founded.
1962	J. McVicker Hunt wrote *Intelligence and Experience*, which questioned the concept of fixed IQ.
1963	The White House Conference on Mental Retardation was held.
1964	The Economic Opportunity Act of 1964 began the War on Poverty.
1965	The Civil Rights Act was passed. Head Start was established. The Elementary and Secondary School Act was passed; Title I provided money for educationally deprived children.
1967	The Follow Through program was begun to provide continuity for former Head Start students.
1970	The White House Conference on Children and Youth was held.
1972	The National Home Start program, which involved parents in teaching, was initiated.
1975	The Education for All Handicapped Children Act, P.L. 94-192, was passed.
1980	The White House Conference on Families was held.
1987	PL 99-457; designed to serve handicapped children with disabilities up to age two, was passed.
1990	National Education Goals 2000 was established.
1993	The Family and Medical Leave Act of 1993 was passed.
1996	Temporary Assistance for Needy Families (TANF) replaced Aid to Families with Dependent Children (AFDC).
1997	The White House Summit on Early Childhood was held July 26 and 27.
1997	The Individuals with Disabilities Education Act of 1997 was reauthorized.
2001	The No Child Left Behind Act of 2001 was passed.
2001	On September 11, the Twin Towers Center in New York City was destroyed by terrorists.

Family life in the United States was able to flourish from the early days. Childrearing practices varied according to country of origin, but were basically tied to the religious background of the family. The nation is culturally diverse with immigrants from many countries arriving from the 1600s to the present time. The major exceptions were the indigenous population and Black families brought from Africa to serve as slaves, who were not allowed to have a normal family life. The indigenous people (American Indians) were also mistreated and moved to reservations by the late 1800s, a destructive process for their family lifestyles.

Childrearing practices of the former Europeans were reflected by the Puritan belief in breaking the will of the child and the need for perfect behavior. The parent education groups in the early 1800s were based on the need to rear children according to these religious principles.

The modern parent education movement began in the 1880s and 1890s. Prominent women founded the National Congress of Mothers, later known as the National Congress of Parents and Teachers (PTA), the Child Study Association, and the American Association of University Women. Each included childrearing as a part of its program. G. Stanley Hall created the first child study center in the United States at Clark University. In addition, philanthropic organizations included parent education in their settlement schools and Free Kindergarten Association programs.

The federal government became involved in family life with the first White House Conference on Care of Dependent Children in 1909. As a result, the Children's Bureau was established in 1912, and the first issue of *Infant Care* was published in 1914. Colleges and universities showed their concern for research in child development by the establishment of research and child study centers.

The years during the 1920s were the most productive in terms of the establishment of parent education programs. Twenty-six parent education organizations were founded during the decade, and many parent education groups emerged across the nation. Change had also come in terms of childrearing practices. Although authorities in the 1890s and the early 1900s emphasized love and affection in the formation of character, the 1920s focused on strict scheduling and discipline.

During the 1940s parent education programs continued, bolstered by child care money for mothers working in the war effort.

The 1950s showed more concern for the mental health of the child. The writings of Freud and Erikson on social-emotional growth, plus Benjamin Spock's famous child care book, helped shift attitudes from the strict scheduling of the 1920s to the "on demand" feedings and concern for mental health of the 1950s.

In the late 1950s the Soviet Union launched *Sputnik.* Suddenly, there was concern for the intellectual development of American youth. This forecast the emphasis toward cognitive development in the 1960s and 1970s. The total child—emotional, social, intellectual, and physical—was the focus of many professionals, and although cognitive development was emphasized and Piaget's theories on cognitive development had a great effect on education, this developmental theory complemented the belief in the need for physical, social, and emotional health. Head Start, Follow Through, and Title I programs looked toward the child's total needs. The family was brought into the development and ongoing commitments of federal programs.

In the 1960s and 1970s Americans were confronted with great social change. The 1980s began with the first White House Conference on Families, attended by men and women representing diverse philosophic beliefs about families.

Parent involvement was recognized as an important element in a child's success at school. Monetary support for family support programs, however, decreased in the 1980s. Head Start continued but served only one fifth of eligible children. Societal problems include increased drug and alcohol abuse by school-age children and poverty for one in five children. Families are faced with a shortage of time and increased stress in a turbulent world.

In 1987, P.L. 99–457—legislation to serve exceptional young children—was passed. The 1990s saw the Family Medical Leave Act pass in 1993. Family resource centers, family literacy, and Even Start supported parents in their search for literacy and family strengths.

In 1996, welfare revamped as Temporary Assistance for Needy Families (TANF) was enacted to replace the Aid to Families with Dependent Children (AFDC).

In 2002, the No Child Left Behind Act of 2001 was passed. All children are required to be tested annually in mathematics and reading, grades third to eighth. The 21st century arrived facing many challenges.

≈ SUGGESTED CLASS ACTIVITIES AND DISCUSSIONS

1. Ask a librarian to help you find books from art museums throughout the world. Examine these for trends in childrearing practices and beliefs.
2. Find a library that has federal publications. Look through books published by the Children's Bureau. Examine the changes in beliefs about child development.
3. Get a copy of the *Twenty-Eighth Year Book, Parts I and II, Preschool and Parent Education* by the National Society for the Study of Education. Compare the programs on parent education in the 1920s with the programs in 2000.
4. Concern about the poor was strongest during the 1890s, the early 20th century, the 1930s, and the 1960s. What were the differing causes of poverty? Why did the concern seem to lessen in intervening decades?
5. Why did nursery schools serve the poor in England? Why do they tend to serve middle-class parents in the United States? How did their origins differ?
6. Identify some of the Native Americans' nations. How has their way of life changed over the past 150 years?
7. Discuss federal intervention. Trace its history from the "hands off" approach of Spencer to the start of the Children's Bureau. How has federal involvement grown since 1910?
8. Examine your community. How many new types of programs for children have begun since Head Start was initiated in 1965?
9. Describe the changes in immigration. How have various immigrant groups differed in their treatment after arriving in the United States?
10. Contact school officials and see how they have implemented the Individuals with Disabilities Education Act requirements.
11. Contact school officials and discuss the changes in education that have occurred since they became involved.
12. Use your computer and e-mail or call with requests for information on education and family involvement. (Obtain telephone numbers and e-mail addresses in the Appendix.)

3 The Family and Community

The People strengthen themselves as they become a mosaic of diverse shapes and colors bound together in a supportive, cooperative whole, more complete combined than segregated.

Berger, 1998

All of our children ought to be allowed a stake in the enormous richness of America.

Kozol, 1991, p. 233

In this chapter on the diversity of families you will find information that will help you examine the strengths and needs of families and enable you to do the following:

- Define the term *family*.
- Cite population changes in the United States.
- List and discuss social needs of families in the United States.
- Describe changes occurring in society that affect families.
- Discuss the greater involvement of fathers in rearing their children.
- Discuss poverty in the United States and the effect it has on families.
- Identify considerations that should be given to diverse families—for example, single-parent, recently divorced, blended, and culturally or ethnically different families.
- Identify strengths that allow families to have positive, constructive, and enabling lives.

✏ FAMILIES

Families in the United States and around the world are living with change, but the essence of the family remains stable, with family members needing a permanent relationship on which they can count for consistency, understanding, and support.

The importance of the family unit in the socialization of children cannot be overstated. It is essential that children have a supportive interactive environment that provides a loving, caring relationship. Families can provide the necessary caring that enables children to develop emotionally, intellectually, and physically.

The family is the most stable component of society. Countries emerge and disintegrate, but the family remains—changed in form, but not in essential functions. If there is a bond among its members, with young children receiving necessary nurturing as well as shelter and food, then the family unit will survive. If the family is connected, reducing isolation and alienation, then the family and those within it will flourish. As it bends with the winds of time, its basic structure and functions are amazingly secure. As the provider for and socializer of children, the family has no match. It might be a nuclear two-parent family, a single-parent family, or an extended family, but as long as it gives the nurture and support needed by its members, it is a viable, working unit.

If you walked down a street in the United States today and knocked on a door, would you find a mother, father, and child or children in the house with the mother working as a homemaker? Probably not. In 2000, only one in five families fit that description. What was once considered a typical family—two parents and children—is not the average family in the United States.

As a provider for and socializer of children the family has no match, but only one in five families fit the description of mother, father, and one or two children as shown in this illustration. There are a variety of family configurations.

❧ POPULATION COUNT

The 2000 census surprised the demographers with the increase in population. Although the projection for 2000 had been for 275 million people, the census identified 281,421,906 people in the United States. On July 1, 2001, there were 284,796,887 people, an increase of over 3 million persons or 1.2 percent. This was due to a 61 percent natural increase of births over deaths; however, immigration (international migration) was responsible for 30 percent (U.S. Census Bureau, 2001b).

The population is varied. Some are young; some are senior citizens; some are middle-aged; and any of these may be single, divorced, widowed, or married.

Table 3.1 is divided into two sections. The top section shows the total population, with the White category including Hispanics or Latinos. The lower section separates the Hispanic/Latino population from the White category and adds the category "Some other race." As the note states, in 1990 individuals could choose only one race. The inclusion of more than one race changes the numbers and percentages. By using the lower section of Table 3.1, which includes race alone or in combination, the following percentages were computed: eighty-three percent are White, including 12.5 percent Hispanic White; 12.5 percent are Black; 4 percent, Asian; and 1 percent, American Indian, Alaskan Native; 0.25 percent are Native Hawaiian and Other Pacific Islander; and 0.6 percent are Some other race (U.S. Census Bureau, 2001a).

❧ DEFINITIONS OF RACE

The categories of race and Hispanic origin changed in the 2000 census to include persons who view themselves as more than one race. In addition, Pacific Islanders were removed from the Asian category and joined with Native Hawaiians.

In order to count the census, six categories of persons from one race alone and a new category for those from two or more races were included. The addition of a category for those with multiracial identification was an important addition to the 2000 census. There are 15 separate response categories and three areas that allow the respondents to write in their choice of race. These categories follow five questions that classify persons of Spanish/Hispanic/Latino race. Figure 3.1 (p. 96) illustrates how the 2000 census offered the respondents opportunities to describe how they defined their racial background.

The categories of race and Hispanic/Latino status in Table 3.1 are defined as follows:

American Indian and Alaska Native. A person having origins in any of the original peoples of North America, who maintains cultural identification through tribal affiliation or community recognition.

Asian. A person having origins in any of the original peoples of the Far East, Southeast Asia, and the Indian subcontinent. This area includes, for example, China, India, Japan, Korea, and the Philippine Islands.

Black or African American. A person having origins in any of the Black racial groups of Africa.

Hispanic or Latino. A person of Mexican, Puerto Rican, Cuban, Central or South American, or other Spanish culture or origin, regardless of race.

White. A person having origins in any of the original peoples of Europe, North Africa, or the Middle East.

Some other race. A person who identifies with a race not listed. (Day, 1996a, p. 31; Census 2000).

Those who chose more than one race (2.4 percent) were referred to as two or more races or more than one race (see Figure 3.1). Five and one-half percent chose a race different from those listed. "The concept of race the Census Bureau uses reflects self-identification by respondents; that is the individual's perception of his/her racial identity. The concept is not intended to reflect any biological or anthropological definition" (U.S. Department of Commerce, 2000).

TABLE 3.1 Population by race and Hispanic/Latino status.

	1990 Census		Census 2000 (mil.)	
	Number (mil.)	Percent of total population	Race alone[1]	Race alone or in combination[2]
Total population[3]	**248.7**	**100.0**	**281.4**	**281.4**
White	199.7	80.3	211.5	216.9
Black or African American	30.0	12.1	34.7	36.4
American Indian and Alaska Native	2.0	0.8	2.5	4.1
Asian	6.9	2.8	10.2	11.9
Native Hawaiian and Other Pacific Islander	0.4	0.1	0.4	0.9
Some other race	9.8	3.9	15.4	18.5
Hispanic or Latino (of any race)[3]	22.4	9.0	35.3	35.3
Not Hispanic or Latino[3]	226.4	91.0	246.1	246.1
White	188.1	75.6	194.6	198.2
Black or African American	29.2	11.7	33.9	35.4
American Indian and Alaska Native	1.8	0.7	2.1	3.4
Asian	6.6	2.7	10.1	11.6
Native Hawaiian and Other Pacific Islander	0.3	0.	0.4	0.7
Some other race	0.2	0.1	0.5	1.8

Note: Because individuals could report only one race in 1990 and could report more than one race in 2000, and because of other changes in the census questionnaire, the race data for 1990 and 2000 are not directly comparable.

Thus the difference in population by race between 1990 and 2000 is due both to these changes in the census questionnaire and to real change in the population.

[1] One of the following six races: (1) White, (2) Black or African American, (3) American Indian and Alaska Native, (4) Asian. (5) Native Hawaiian and Other Pacific Islander. (6) Some other race.

[2] Alone or in combination with one of more of the other five races listed. Numbers for the six race groups may add to more than the total population and the six percentages may add to more than 100 percent because individuals may indicate more than one race.

[3] Hispanic or Latino population may be of any race.

Source: From the U.S. Census Bureau, Administrative and Customer Services Division. Statistical Compendia Branch (2001).

Immigration was responsible for 30 percent of the country's population increase from approximately 250 million in 1990 to approximately 285 million in 2001.

Households

Census reports include two groups of household types: family household and nonfamily household. The *family household* is one in which the householder and at least one other person are related, categorized as married couple, female with no spouse present, or male with no spouse present. The *nonfamily household* may have only one person or may have others, but none are related. It is categorized as either female nonfamily or male nonfamily.

The number of both types, family and nonfamily, of households cited in 2000 was 104.7 million, with family household accounting for 72 million (69 percent). Married couples live in 55 million houses; male householders, 4 million, and female householders over 12 million (see Table 3.2) Of these householders, 34.6 million were families who lived with their own children. Twenty-five million were married couples, 4 million male householders, and 7.5 million female householders. The average size of a family in 2000 was 3.17 persons, slightly lower than the 3.29 persons recorded in 1980.

Families with no children account for 37.4 million householders. Of these, there were 30.1 million married couples, 2.2 million male householders, and 5.1 million female householders.

Nonfamily householders account for 32.6 million persons (31 percent). Of these, 14.5 million were male and 18 million were female. Over 26 million (25.5 percent) of the nonfamily householders lived alone (U.S. Census Bureau, 2000a).

Bryson (1996) compared the changes in households between 1970 and 1995. As illustrated in

→ Note: Please answer BOTH Questions 5 and 6

5. Is this person Spanish/Hispanic/Latino? *Mark* ☒ *the "No" box if not Spanish/Hispanic/Latino*
   - ☐ No, not Spanish/Hispanic/Latino
   - ☐ Yes, Mexican, Mexican Am., Chicano
   - ☐ Yes, other Spanish/Hispanic/Latino—*Print group* ↘
   - ☐ Yes, Puerto Rican
   - ☐ Yes, Cuban

   | | | | | | | | | | | | | | |

6. What is this person's race? *Mark* ☒ *one or more races to indicate what this person considers himself/herself to be.*
   - ☐ White
   - ☐ Black, African Am., or Negro
   - ☐ American Indian or Alaska Native—*Print name of enrolled or principal tribe.* ↘

   | | | | | | | | | | | | | | |

   - ☐ Asian Indian
   - ☐ Chinese
   - ☐ Filipino
   - ☐ Other Asian—*Print race* ↘
   - ☐ Japanese
   - ☐ Korean
   - ☐ Vietnamese
   - ☐ Other Pacific Islander—*Print race* ↘
   - ☐ Native Hawaiian
   - ☐ Guamanian or Chamorro
   - ☐ Samoan

   | | | | | | | | | | | | | | |

   - ☐ Some other Race

   | | | | | | | | | | | | | |

FIGURE 3.1   2000 Census questions on race and Hispanic origin

Source: From Census 2000, by the U.S. Census Bureau, retrieved August 21, 2002, from *http://www.census.gov/dnd/www/pdf/do2p*

Table 3.3, major changes occurred in family composition. These changes include the number of families maintained by women with no husband present. The number rose from 5.6 million in 1970 to 12.1 million in 1995. There is also an increase in the number of families maintained by men with no wife present, from 1.2 million in 1970 to 3.2 million in 1995.

✎ FAMILY STRUCTURE AND ROLES

Parents who collaborate with teachers and child care workers are a varied group. Some belong to two-parent families, others are never-married single parents. Some may be same-gender couples, divorced single parents, or single parents whose spouses have died. Most parents who divorce soon remarry, so blended or reconstituted families may involve joint custody, stepparents, stepbrothers and stepsisters, half-brothers and half-sisters, and brothers and sisters. Thirty-one percent were nonfamily householders, with 14.6 million male householders and 18 million female householders (see Figure 3.2). In 2000, 26.7 million (25.5 percent) nonfamily householders lived alone. Seven percent were other families without children. Almost one-fourth, 24.1 percent, were married couples with children, and 8 percent were other families with children. The largest group, however (28.7 percent), were married couples without children.

TABLE 3.2 Households, families, subfamilies, and married couples: 1980 to 2000.

Type of unit	1980	1985	1990	1995	1997	1998	1999	2000	Percent change 1980-90	Percent change 1990-2000
Households.............	80,776	86,789	93,347	96,990	101,018	102,528	103,874	104,705	16	12
Average size	2.76	2.69	2.63	2.65	2.64	2.62	2.61	2.62	(X)	(X)
Family households.......	59,550	62,706	66,090	69,305	70,241	70,880	71,535	72,025	11	9
Married couple	49,112	50,350	52,317	53,858	53,604	54,317	54,770	55,311	7	6
Male householder[1]	1,733	2,228	2,884	3,226	3,847	3,911	3,976	4,028	66	40
Female householder[1] ...	8,705	10,129	10,890	12,220	12,790	12,652	12,789	12,687	25	17
Nonfamily households	21,226	24,082	27,257	29,686	30,777	31,648	32,339	32,680	28	20
Male householder......	8,807	10,114	11,606	13,190	13,707	14,133	14,368	14,641	32	26
Female householder....	12,419	13,968	15,651	16,496	17,070	17,516	17,971	18,039	26	15
One person	18,296	20,602	22,999	24,732	25,402	26,327	26,606	26,724	26	16
Families...............	59,550	62,706	66,090	69,305	70,241	70,880	71,535	72,025	11	9
Average size	3.29	3.23	3.17	3.19	3.19	3.18	3.18	3.17	(X)	(X)
With own children[2].......	31,022	31,112	32,289	34,296	34,665	34,760	34,613	34,605	4	7
Without own children under[2]	28,528	31,594	33,801	35,009	35,575	36,120	36,922	37,420	18	11
Married couple	49,112	50,350	52,317	53,858	53,604	54,317	54,770	55,311	7	6
With own children[2]	24,961	24,210	24,537	25,241	25,083	25,269	25,066	25,248	2 2	3
Without own children[2] ...	24,151	26,140	27,780	28,617	28,521	29,048	29,703	30,062	15	8
Male householder[1].......	1,733	2,228	2,884	3,226	3,847	3,911	3,976	4,028	66	40
With own children[2]	616	896	1,153	1,440	1,709	1,798	1,706	1,786	87	55
Without own children[2] ...	1,117	1,332	1,731	1,786	2,138	2,113	2,270	2,242	55	30
Female householder[1].....	8,705	10,129	10,890	12,220	12,790	12,652	12,789	12,687	25	17
With own children[2]	5,445	6,006	6,599	7,615	7,874	7,693	7,841	7,571	21	15
Without own children[2] ...	3,261	4,123	4,290	4,606	4,916	4,960	4,948	5,116	32	19
Unrelated subfamilies	360	526	534	674	615	575	522	571	48	7
Married couple..........	20	46	68	64	50	41	50	37	(B)	(B)
Male reference persons[1] ..	36	85	45	59	77	72	64	57	(B)	(B)
Female reference persons[1]	304	395	421	550	487	463	408	477	39	13
Related subfamilies	1,150	2,228	2,403	2,878	2,907	2,870	2,901	2,984	109	24
Married couple..........	582	719	871	1,015	1,012	947	1,029	1,149	50	32
Father-child[1].............	54	116	153	195	244	250	281	201	(B)	31
Mother-child[1].............	512	1,392	1,378	1,668	1,651	1,673	1,591	1,634	169	19
Married couples	49,714	51,114	53,256	54,937	54,666	55,305	55,849	56,497	7	6
With own household	49,112	50,350	52,317	53,858	53,604	54,317	54,770	55,311	7	6
Without own household ...	602	764	939	1,079	1,062	988	1,079	1,186	56	26
Percent without	1.2	1.5	1.8	2.0	1.9	1.8	1.9	2.1	(X)	(X)

*In thousands, except as Indicated (80,776 represents 80,776,000). As of March. Based on Current Population Survey; includes members of Armed Forces living off post or with their families on post, but excludes all other members of Armed Forces: see text, this section, and Appendix III. For definition of terms, see text, this section. Minus sign (2) indicates decrease.]
B Not shown: base less than 75,000.   X Not applicable.   [1]No spouse present.   [2]Under 18 years old.

Source: From, *Current Population Reports,* P20–515, and unpublished data, by the U.S. Census Bureau. Retrieved, March 5, 2002 from *http://www.census.gov/prod/2001pubs/statab/sec01.pdf*

TABLE 3.3   Changes in family composition between 1970 and 1995.

1970	1995
1. Married couples with children made up 40 percent of households.	1. Married couples with children made up 25 percent of households.
2. The average was 3.14 people household.	2. The average was 2.65 people per household.
3. One out of every five had five or more people.	3. Only one out of every 10 households had 5 or more people.
4. People living alone made up one-sixth of households.	4. People living alone made up one-fourth of households.
5. 5.6 million families were maintained by women with no husband present.	5. 12.1 million families were maintained by women with no husband present.
6. 1.2 million families were maintained by men with no wife present.	6. 3.2 million families were maintained by men with no wife present.
7. Two out of three households were in metropolitan areas.	7. Four out of five households were in metropolitan areas.
8. 44 percent of families had no children under 18 at home.	8. 51 percent of families had no children under 18 at home.

Source: From "Household and Family Characteristics, March 1995," by the U.S. Bureau of the Census, *Current Population Reports,* pp. 20–488, October, 1996.

FIGURE 3.2   Household composition: 1970 to 2000.

Source: From "Household and Family Characteristics: March 1995," by the U.S. Bureau of the Census, in *Current Population Reports,* P20–488 and P20–515 and unpublished data.

Percent of total households

Traditional two parent families, unmarried couples, skip generation households, widowed parents, single parents, gay and lesbian, and singles make up the vast array of family forms.

Roles of Parents

Although their forms vary, families provide similar functions. It is expected that the roles within families provide for the needs of the children and that parents have rights and responsibilities. Swick (1986) described these roles as "(1) nurturing, (2) guiding, (3) problem solving, and (4) modeling" (p. 72). Cataldo (1987) described similar roles providing "care, nurturance, and protection"; socialization; "monitoring the child's development as a learner"; and supporting "each youngster's growth into a well-rounded, emotionally healthy person" (p. 28).

The first function of a family is to nurture and supply nutrition, protection, and shelter. Families provide interaction, love, and support. The family has a right to rear the child as it sees fit and a responsibility to see that the child receives adequate care.

Parents socialize their children to follow the norms of society in accordance with the parents' cultural beliefs. Socialization varies, depending on the culture. Families in some cultures demand respect toward their elders; others socialize their children in a democratic style that depends on mutual respect. There are also variations within cultures that often result from how the parents were raised. In the rearing process, most children learn and internalize their parents' value system.

Parents also have the obligation to see that the child is educated both at home and at school. In some families, education is not recognized as a function of the family, but learning or lack of learning is very much a part of any family system. Parents are the first educators of their children, so the child's ability to function well in school rests to a great extent on the home's nurturance and environment.

Therapists have come to recognize that it is a mistake to send an emotionally disturbed child back into the same ecosystem in which the disturbance developed. Therapists must work with the family as well as the child. Therapists also need to understand the larger community in which the family lives. How does the larger community affect the family? Are there cultural norms that influence their communication skills? Is the family under stress? Is under- or unemployment a factor? Only when therapists arrive at an understanding of the concerns and culture are they able to guide the family and child toward healthier relationships. Working with children at school is similar. Teachers need to know their school neighborhood and the issues and problems that parents face to understand the children under their charge.

Stages in Family Life

In addition to recognizing the many family forms, professionals find it helpful to view parenthood as divided into different stages. Sometimes families are in several stages simultaneously, such as families with a large number of children whose births are spread over 20 or more years. The stages developed by Galinsky (1987) divide parenthood into six levels of development much like the child's stages of development. The first stage, the *image making* stage, takes place before the birth of a child. Images are formed and preparation is made for the birth. The second stage is the *nurturing* period during infancy, when attachment develops. In the third period, the *authority* stage, families help their child understand the norms of the society. During the fourth stage, from preschool to adolescence, parents offer *guidance* and children learn to interpret their social reality. The *interdependent* years, the teens, make up the fifth stage of family development. When the children are ready to go out into the world for themselves, parents enter their last stage: *departure*. During each of these stages, parents provide the guidance necessary for that stage of development.

Parenting Styles

Ideally, families provide a support system that allows the child to grow into a healthy, responsible person. Parenting styles (some of which are more effective than others) are often identified as *authoritative, authoritarian,* or *laissez-faire* (see Table 3.4).

Each of these types has different ways of handling issues and concerns within the family. In addition, depending on the circumstance, responses in families may vary. The style recommended by parent educators is the authoritative, democratic style, because it is thought that children raised under that style will achieve, be dependable and responsible, and feel good about themselves.

Children raised with authoritative parents will be allowed to analyze and recognize the issues confronting them. Guidance will be available but will not be dictated. Children will learn to make decisions. Working and talking together, they will be able to learn why angry, quick decisions do not work.

TABLE 3.4 The manner in which families socialize their children varies. Three major theories, authoritative, authoritarian, and laissez-faire, include a multitude of styles.

Family Type	Characteristics
Authoritative	Democratic decision making Guidelines and parameters Effective communication Problem solving Self-discipline and responsibility
Authoritarian (might be overprotective)	Demanding parent Absolute rules Restrictive environment Punitive control Strong guidelines
Laissez-faire (might be very indulgent)	Anything goes Neglectful parent No one cares Withdrawal from parental responsibilities
Dysfunctional (includes authoritative, authoritarian, and laissez-faire families)	Alcohol- or drug-addicted Neurotic or mentally ill Abusive

Children with authoritarian parents are expected to mind their parents without any question about what precipitated the issue. The children do not get an opportunity to resolve an issue or learn from actions except to learn that punishment will follow no matter what the situation. They receive little training in decision making. Children may learn to mind, but they also learn to avoid being caught and, perhaps, to lie when they are.

Children of laissez-faire rearing often think that their parents are not interested in them. The children may be depressed, act out, or take risks because they do not feel their parents care. In addition, they get no guidance to help them make decisions. Too much freedom makes it possible for children to think that they do not matter.

Eating meals together, at dinner or breakfast, with open discussion is important. It helps families to know each other and to bond. In addition, a weekly family meeting with shared leadership (each person taking a turn) helps families understand one another and make satisfactory and fair decisions. It can be a time when children and parents can share their feelings, help make decisions, and receive encouragement. See "Building Family Strengths" in Chapter 4 for more discussion of strong families.

Two subtypes do not fit into the three major types. The overprotective parent can often become authoritarian; the indulgent parent may not guide the child. Dysfunctional families—including those that are abusive, addicted to drugs or alcohol, mentally ill, or neurotic—may fluctuate between authoritarian to the point of abuse, and laissez-faire, with abdication of parental roles. One of the most difficult issues that children face is the inconsistency in dysfunctional families. Dependable families in which children understand the guidelines and can communicate with and rely on their parents are extremely important to children's mental health.

If the types of families are multiplied by the number of configurations of families (single, two-parent, and blended) and the individual personality differences of each child and parent, it becomes apparent that to work effectively with parents, teachers and child care workers must individualize their suggestions and responses.

Children who arrive at the school's door represent these many varieties of families. Nearly 15 percent are born to unmarried mothers, half of whom are teenagers. It is estimated that 90 percent of unwed women keep their children and raise them alone or with help from their families. This results in many children being raised by grandparents or aunts and uncles. This so-called "skip-generation parenting" results in children growing up in an extended family with cousins and a variety of interrelationships. The National Center for Lesbian Rights estimates that 2 million children are being raised by lesbian or gay mothers or fathers. "Most gay couples . . . describe themselves and their families as conventional in most ways, even boring" (Johnston, 1990, p. 5).

FAMILY FORMS

Traditional two-parent families, unmarried couples, skip-generation households, widowed parents, single-parent families, gay and lesbian couples, and singles make up a vast array of family forms (Johnston, 1990). "To judge one kind of family structure as 'right' and another as 'wrong' creates a distance" (p. 7) between the parents and the school and makes it difficult if not impossible to create the kind of working relationship essential for parent-school collaboration.

Some commonalty stands out. Both men and women questioned in polls placed importance on the family and were willing to adapt and make sacrifices to keep the family together. Keep in mind that parents often view their child as an extension of themselves. If parents are approached in a way that lets them know the teacher wants the child to succeed as much as the parents do, a true collaboration can take place.

The structure, stage of family development, family size, and ages and gender of the children all figure in to the makeup of each unique family.

The families described here are representative of the many types of families. Add to the list with your own descriptions.

Single-Parent Family

Tina is a young divorced mother with one son, Tommy, age 3. They live with Tina's parents. In addition to working part time at a department store, Tina takes 6 hours of classes at the community college. Each morning she gets up, prepares breakfast for Tommy and herself, bundles him into his coat during cold weather, hopes that her aging automobile will start, and heads into her long day. First, she deposits Tommy with her sister who runs a family child care home. She feels fortunate to have a relative who enjoys children to care for Tommy. He has been anxious ever since his father left, and the security of spending his days at Aunt Georgia's helps compensate for his loss.

Tina figures that with family help and her part-time college work she will be able to graduate in a little more than 2 years, just about the time Tommy will start school. Her ex-husband Ted does not send support money consistently, and Tina knows her parents can help only so much. As she works as a clerk in the department store, she dreams of the time when she will make enough to give Tommy the home and opportunities he needs.

Unwed Single Teenage Mother

As Sherrill thinks back, she can't remember when she didn't want a baby. "When I have a baby," she thought, "I'll be treated like an adult by my mother, and I'll also have a baby all my own who will love me." Already, though, Gerald, age 3 months, has become a real handful.

Sherrill turned 15 yesterday, and instead of being able to bum around with her friends, she had to take care of Gerald. "If only my mother hadn't had to work," Sherrill complained, "I would have had a couple of hours between feedings just to get out. I never dreamed a baby would be so demanding. What makes him cry so much?"

The school down the street offers a program for teen mothers and their infants. Sherrill is on the waiting list and plans to enroll at the end of summer. "I never thought I'd want to go back to school," she says, "but they help out by caring for my baby while I'm in class and my mother says that I need to be able to make a living for Gerald. Temporary Assistance to Needy Families (TANF) will help me for only 24 months. I really don't like school, but I guess I'd better go. If only Gerald would start being more fun."

Two-Parent Homeless Family

When Barbara married Jed, the future looked good. Young, handsome, and willing to work, Jed thought his job at the plant would last forever. But who would have expected the layoffs? Jed's father worked at the plant for 25 years before he retired. Now Jed and Barbara, along with Jessie, age 2, and Bob, age 6, are moving west in hopes of finding work.

It's hard to live out of a car. Barbara worries about Bob because he is missing first grade. She and Jed put him in school whenever they are in a city for any length of time, but schools want his permanent address. It embarrasses Barbara to say their family is homeless, so she finds out the name of a street near the school and pretends they live there. Bob doesn't like school anyway. He says the children make fun of him and the teacher gives him seatwork that he doesn't understand.

Jed feels as if he has failed as a father and provider for his family. If he could just find a good job. Minimum wage doesn't give him enough to pay for rent, let alone buy clothing and food. Last month they spent time at a church-run mission for the homeless. Jed was glad that they were in a town far from home so that none of his old school friends recognized him and Barbara. Maybe a good factory job will turn up.

Two-Income Family

"Joe, the alarm. It's your turn to get up and start breakfast." Maria turns over to get 10 more minutes of sleep before the drive to school. Each day

Maria teaches 28 second graders in the adjoining school district. Joe teaches mathematics at the local middle school. It works exceedingly well for them. The children, Karen and Jaime, stay with a neighbor until it is time for them to walk to school. Joe and Maria take turns dashing home early enough in the afternoon to supervise the children after school.

At times, the stress of work and the demanding days get to Joe and Maria. Some days their schedules do not blend, and they scurry to find someone to care for the children after school. Karen and Jaime occasionally have been "latchkey" children. Neither Joe nor Maria want their children to be left on their own. They see too many children in their classrooms in similar situations who feel as if no one cares. Joe tries to be a nurturing father who also helps with the home, but he relies on Maria to clean, shop, and cook.

Summers are the best time for the family. Joe works for a summer camp, but Maria is able to spend more time at home, enjoying the children and organizing for the coming year. Periodically she thinks about how much easier it would be for her to quit teaching and be a full-time homemaker, but then reality sets in. They could not make the house payments if they were not a two-income family—and a family needs a home.

✌ GROWTH OF A NATION

The first United States census in 1790 reported a population of 3,939,326. By the 1940s, the country had grown to a bustling, heterogeneous land of 131,409,119 (Kaplan, Van Valey, & Associates, 1980, p. 25). During this period, the nation changed from small and rural to large, industrial, and urban. From 1940 to 1990, about 118 million more inhabitants were added to the United States. The official report of the Bureau of the Census gave a total of 249,632,692 people in 1990, an increase of 10.21 percent over the 1980 census of 226,504,425 (U.S. Bureau of the Census, 1991a).

The resident population, as illustrated in Figure 3.3, increased dramatically during the twentieth century. The population grew from approximately 76 million in 1900 to over 281 million in 2000. The resident population numbers differ slightly from the population numbers above, but both figures dramatically illustrate the change. The nation grew from almost 4 million in 1790 and will reach 300 million in the 21st century.

In just 50 years, from 1940 to 1990, the population nearly doubled. Most of the increase was from the net increase of births over deaths rather than from immigration. Infant mortality was reduced, and people were living longer. During the 1970s the birth rate declined to about 13 million, but with the arrival of refugees and immigrants and the increased number of senior citizens, the population steadily grew. In the 1990s, as indicated previously on the information on population count, natural increase of birth over death accounted for 61 percent, but immigration was also high at 39 percent.

In the 1980s, children of the baby boom era—those born from 1947 to 1964—began having children. Many had delayed marriage and childrearing, and their children were becoming ready for school in the 1990s. Most of these mothers would continue working.

✌ GREATER AMOUNT OF EDUCATION FOR PARENTS

Today, many workers need more education because of the large number of technical jobs. These better educated parents are generally comfortable in their dealings with the school. In 1940, only 36 percent of men and 40 percent of women (24 to 29 years old) had completed high school, and only 7 percent of men and 5 percent of women had completed college (Howe, 1988). By 1999, 83 percent of both men and women had completed high school. Whites had the highest percentage with 84.3 percent; Blacks, 77 percent; Asian and Pacific Islanders, 64.7 percent, and Hispanics, 56 percent. Those 25 years and older who had completed 4 years of college included 27.5 percent men and 23.1 percent women. Of these 25.9 percent were White; 15.49 percent

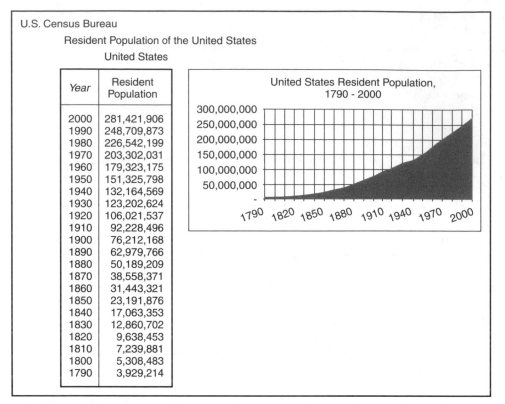

U.S. Census Bureau

Resident Population of the United States

United States

Year	Resident Population
2000	281,421,906
1990	248,709,873
1980	226,542,199
1970	203,302,031
1960	179,323,175
1950	151,325,798
1940	132,164,569
1930	123,202,624
1920	106,021,537
1910	92,228,496
1900	76,212,168
1890	62,979,766
1880	50,189,209
1870	38,558,371
1860	31,443,321
1850	23,191,876
1840	17,063,353
1830	12,860,702
1820	9,638,453
1810	7,239,881
1800	5,308,483
1790	3,929,214

FIGURE 3.3 The 20th century has seen a dramatic increase in resident population.

Source: From the U.S. Census Bureau, 2000. Retrieved February 14, 2003, from http://www.census.gov/dmd/www/resapport/states/unitedstates.pdf

were Black; 42.4 percent, Asian and Pacific Islander; and 10.9 percent Hispanic (U.S. Department of Commerce, 2000).

Parents who have not had educational opportunities are often very supportive of the schools and want an education for their children, but some feel uncomfortable with teachers and principals. Parents who have had to quit school or who had an unpleasant experience in their own schooling may fear the schools and find it difficult to become a partner with the professional. The school must reach out to these reticent parents.

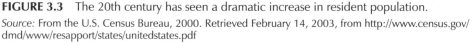 CHILD COUNT AND CHILD WELFARE

The number of children in the United States in 2000 was 72,293,812, a 14 percent increase

since 1990 (Annie E. Casey Foundation, 2001). Table 3.5 illustrates the number of children according to race. Sixty-one percent or over 44 million are White; 15 percent or 10.5 million are Black; 17 percent or over 12.3 million are Hispanic; 3 percent or more than 2.5 million are Asian/Pacific Islander; and 1 percent or 686,000 are American Indian/Alaskan Native. Three percent or almost 2 million chose more than one race, and 192,326 chose some other race (Annie E. Casey Foundation, 2001).

These figures illustrate the "largest increase in the number of children living in the United States since the 1950s, foreshadowing major new challenges to the nation's schools and social services (Annie E. Casey Foundation, 2001). Improvements in the last decade include decreases in infant mortality, teenage and children's death rates, and the

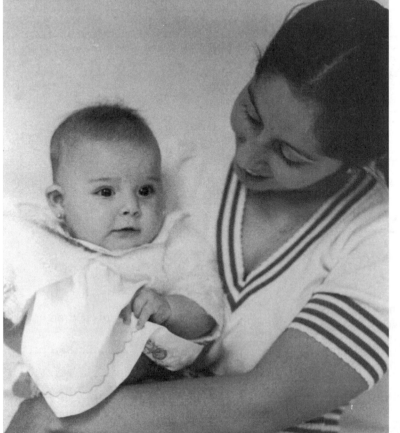

Workers need more education in societies with high technological opportunities. The percentage of both men and women completing high school has increased from 40 percent of women and 36 percent of men in 1940, to 83 percent of both genders in 1999.

high school dropout rate. Poverty rates declined to 16.9 percent in 2000 from a high of 22.7 percent in 1992. Births to teenagers declined from 37 percent in 1990 to 30 percent in 1998 (Annie E. Casey, 2001). However, *KIDS COUNT* found that 10 million children have employed parents who struggle to make ends meet. Infant mortality (deaths per 1,000 live births) rates were reduced from 16.1 percent in 1975 to 7.1 percent in 1999. Child death rates were also reduced. For children aged 1–14 the rate was 44 per 100,000 in 1975, and was reduced to 24 in 1999 (Annie E. Casey Foundation, 2002).

Other encouraging data on children's welfare include the rate of teen deaths due to accident, homicide, or suicide. For teenagers aged 15–19,

the rate fell from 73 per 100,000 in 1975 to 53 in 1999. The high school dropout rate was also reduced for teenagers aged 16–19 from 12 percent in 1975 to 9 percent in 2000. The number of children who live in families that have no parent with full-time year employment fell from 33 in 1975 to 23 in 2000. However, the increase of single-parent families rose from 17 percent in 1975 to 29 percent, nearly one third in 2001 (Annie E. Casey Foundation, 2002).

At the time this chapter was revised, the outcome of the possible 2001–2002 recession and the September 11, 2001, Twin Towers attack, was not resolved. Although the prognosis for a recovery is evident, the future remains uncertain. Will high employment rates be achieved?

TABLE 3.5 Number of children by race and Hispanic origin: 2000 Census.

	Number	**Percent**
Total population under age 18	72,293,812	100%
One race only*	58,045,361	80.3%
White*	44,027,087	60.9%
Black or African American*	10,610,264	14.7%
American Indian or Alaskan Native*	685,911	0.9%
Asian*	2,420,274	3.3%
Native Hawaiian or other Pacific Islander*	109,499	0.2%
Some other race*	192,326	0.3%
More than one race*	1,906,192	2.6%
Hispanic	12,342,259	17.1%

*Non-Hispanic

Source: From Census 2000 data, in the *KIDS COUNT Data Book* (p. 24), by the Annie E. Casey Foundation, 2001.

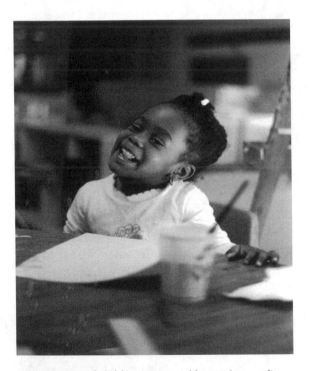

The number of children increased by 14% according to the 2000 census. Of the 72 million children counted, 61 percent were white; 15 percent, Black; 17 percent, Hispanic; 3 percent, Asian American, and 1 percent, Native American.

Working parents of preschool children provide child care in a variety of ways. The Families and Work Institute survey of 1997 found 55 percent of the parents of preschoolers relying on parents or other relatives to care for their preschoolers (Bond, Galinsky, & Swanberg, 1998). In 1997 the Census Bureau reported that 41 percent of parents of preschoolers in families with employed mothers counted on relatives to help out; 35 percent used family child care homes or child care centers; 12 percent used both relatives and child care; 30 percent used a relative (grandparents or other relatives); and 12 percent used fathers. A few mothers (4 percent) were able to use siblings to care for their children while they worked. Generally these parents either worked from their home or administered their own business (U.S. Census Bureau, 1997).

In 2004, similar child care arrangements for preschoolers are necessary. Information (Ehrle & Tout, 2001) on infants and toddlers under the age of 3 shows that parent care (27 percent) and relative care (27 percent) provide the greatest percent of child care arrangements. This is followed by center-based care (22 percent), family child care which is similar to family child care homes cited above (17 percent), and nanny care (7 percent). The percentages, although they differ, show that parents continue to rely heavily on relatives and on adjusting their own time schedules so that they can help care for their young children.

⟨⟩ WORKING MOTHERS

Today, mothers who work outside the home outnumber mothers who work solely in the home. In 1996 more than half (68 percent) of married women living with a spouse and children younger than 6 were in the labor force, with 28 percent employed full time, year-round. For married mothers living with a spouse and school-age children (6–17), 80 percent worked, with 44 percent working full time, year-round (Bianchi & Spain, 1996, p. 21). The school-age children will need before- and after-school care or they will be latchkey children.

Since 1940 there has been dramatic changes in workforce patterns. In 1940 almost 70 percent were breadwinner/homemaker families, and both parents worked in less than 10 percent of families (Ahlburg &.De Vita, 1992). In 2000, 60 percent of families with children under six years of age had both parents in the labor force (U.S. Bureau of Labor Statistics, 2001). The changes are continuing.

Insights for Teachers and Administrators

1. Parents of school-age children rely heavily on schools to provide care for the children with school hours and after-school programs or after-school child care programs. Some children become latchkey children and provide for themselves after school. Other children are cared for in their own homes or in other homes with relatives and neighbors providing before- and after-school care for them.

2. If a mother works full time she does not have the opportunity to volunteer in the classroom during the week, so offer her other ways in which she can contribute. A form with options and with room for suggestions that can be answered by a parent and returned to school, can help parents connect with their child's school.

3. Adopt before- and after-school programs that offer enriching activities for the child and safe child care for the family.

4. Keep the parents informed on the progress of their child. Set aside some time each week during which the parents can telephone you.

5. Initiate telephone calls at a convenient time for both you and the parents share something positive about the child.

6. Hold a get-acquainted evening program for parents. Ask them to fill out a chart so they may share needs with others. Allow parents to decide on the extent of their participation.

7. Videotape class activities or programs that are important to the children so that the parents who were unable to attend may view them later.

8. Make home visits at a time convenient for the family.

Today, women are not as likely as they once were to leave the labor force when they have children. Mothers with one or two children are most likely to work outside the home; as family size increases, outside employment decreases.

⟨⟩ GREATER INVOLVEMENT OF FATHERS WITH THEIR CHILDREN

Roles of fathers have changed and increased in the past two centuries. From the early Puritan times until industrialization, a "good" father was breadwinner and provider of moral guidance. Fathers have long held these two roles, but in the 20th century the importance of fathers' roles in their children's development has undergone change based on social conditions and beliefs as well as research in child development. At the turn of the 21st century fathers exhibit willingness to provide expanded roles as companions, standard-setters, guidance counselors, play partners, teachers, providers, caregivers, and role models.

Children do better cognitively and intellectually if both parents are involved in caregiving.

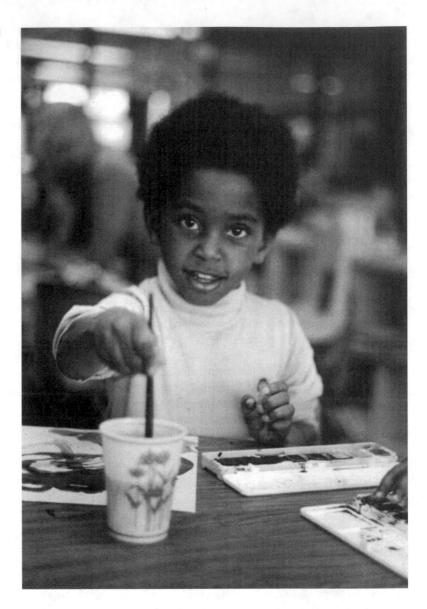

The Children's Bureau, established in 1912, provided information to families in caring for their infants in the publication *Infant Care*. Although fathers were mentioned in the publication, the advice was directed to mothers. Fathers were not considered as important to the child's development until the 1940s. Awareness of the father as a gender-role model came about toward the end of World War II, but it was not until the 1970s that the role of nurturant father was emphasized (Lamb, 1997).

Some advocates for fathers argue that in the 1990s fathers were viewed as superfluous. "The retreat from fatherhood began in the 1960s, gained momentum in the 1970s, and hit full stride in the 1980s" (Horn, 1997, p. 24). In the 1990s, organizations that focused on fathers included the National Institute for Responsible Fatherhood and

Family Development, Promise Keepers, National Centers for Fathering, and the National Fatherhood Initiative. These groups responded to data about the negative aspects of being raised without a father, including the fact that such children are "three times more likely to fail at school, two to three times more likely to experience emotional or behavioral problems requiring psychiatric treatment . . . three times more likely to commit suicide as adolescents . . . five times more likely to be poor" (p. 27). When income was controlled, children without a father present continued to fare worse than those who had both parents (Horn, 1997). In two-parent families it is important that family members are supportive of one another and that conflict and abuse are absent.

Research

In the 1980s, 1990s, and continuing in 2000s, research shows that, although fathers have a more physical style of interacting with their children, this supports and adds to the nurturing and verbal style of the mother (Horn, 1997; Lamb, 1997). If the parents have supportive relationships with one another and their children, the children thrive. "Children who have secure, supportive, reciprocal, and sensitive relationships with their parents are much more likely to be well-adjusted psychologically than individuals whose relationships with their parents—mothers or fathers—are less satisfying" (Lamb, 1997, p. 13). It is the parent's feelings and attitudes when projected onto the child that impact the child's feelings of well-being. It is the characteristics of the man as a father, not as a man, that influence the child's development (Pruett, 1996). A study in 1997 by the U.S. Department of Education showed that children do better cognitively and emotionally if they have both parents involved rather than just one.

The National Center on Fathers and Families has developed a Fathering Indicator Framework with six fathering indicator categories. The categories include: (1) father presence, (2) caregiving, (3) children's social competence, (4) cooperative parenting, (5) father's healthy living, and (6) ma-

terial and financial contribution. The operational categories accompany the fathering indicator categories to be used by programs to guide research (National Center on Fathers and Families, 2002).

Although many boys without fathers develop normally, if the combination of mother and father support one another, provide a better economic base for the family, and provide a nurturing environment for their children, then that combination is preferred over a single-parent family.

Father Involvement

Heightened interest in fatherhood goes hand in hand with the increasing number of women who work outside the home. More than ever, mothers need a cooperating husband to help with all the duties of homemaking. More important, many young fathers see the expression of love toward their children as a way of fulfilling their own lives with meaningful relationships. Some fathers are full-time homemakers and care for the children while their wives work outside the home.

Single parents, both men and women, often substitute a network of friends and kin to handle emergencies and everyday obligations. This extended network helps parents meet the demands of nurturance and role model.

Fathers in two-parent families tend to be playmates with the children, rather than being responsible for children's care and rearing or obtaining child care for the children. Although fathers and mothers are similar rather than dissimilar in their connection with their children, fathers tend to be more physically stimulating with unpredictable play whereas mothers tend toward containment and soft, repetitive verbal expression. Both types of interaction are beneficial for the child (Lamb, 1997).

In the National Association for the Education of Young Children (NAEYC) accredited child care programs, fathers preferred involvement in (1) family activities, (2) Daddy and Me programs, (3) activities for both parents to learn about their child's future, (4) activities for both parents to learn about child development, and (5) sporting events (Turbiville, Umbarger III & Guthrie, 2000, p. 77).

A survey conducted by the Families and Work Institute in 1997 found that fathers had increased their interaction with their children. Fathers spent an average of 2.3 workday hours doing things with or caring for their children, an increase of 30 minutes per workday since a 1977 survey was conducted. Working mothers spent another hour each day, but the total time spent caring for children had not increased. On days off, fathers spent six hours with their children, and women, eight. Even with the new emphasis on father nurturance, 56 percent of employed mothers wished that fathers would spend more time with the children, and 43 percent wished that fathers would help more with household chores. Both parents would like more time with their children: 70 percent felt that they do not have enough time with children. The amount of personal time dropped to 1.6 hours a day for men—a decrease of 36 minutes from the 1977 survey—and 1.3 hours for women—a decrease of 24 minutes. In caring for sick children or other needs, 22 percent of fathers said they take time off from work, compared to 83 percent of employed mothers. On average, however, men work longer hours than women, with men working 50.9 hours a week and women, including part-time workers, averaging 41.4 (Bond et al., 1998). The amount of paternal involvement depends on (a) motivation; (b) skills and self-confidence; (c) support, especially from the mother; and (d) institutional practices.

Swick and Manning (1983) and Levine and Pittinsky (1997) recommended ways in which fathers can participate in the family. Their suggestions included the father reinforcing the mother's efforts in child care; communicating with her about the children; playing, listening, and exploring with the children at all ages; and being involved in their education from the first preschool through the upper grades.

Other positive suggestions include:

1. Be there. Engage in activities with your child from the early caregiving, bathing and bedroom routine, to later when you can read to your child, share your own stories, and play together.

2. Accept your child. Accept your child for who she or he is. Each child has an individual personality. Trying to change a quiet child into a boisterous one or an uncoordinated child into an outstanding athlete, makes the child feel unaccepted.

3. Use positive parenting. Praise is better than punishment in guiding children. Help the child express anger constructively.

4. Share parenting. Work as a team with your spouse.

5. See fathering as worthwhile and satisfying. "Children need their fathers to help them with skills and decision making, and to feel competent and good about themselves (Ballantine, Winter, 1999/2000, p. 105).

Involving Fathers in Schools and Centers

Research shows that children whose fathers are positively involved in their school activities complete more school and have stronger emotional and cognitive development (Byrne, 1997; Engle & Breaux, 1998; Lamb, 1997; Levine, Murphy, & Wilson, 1993). The reverse is true for children without father involvement. They are three times more apt to fail, have more emotional problems that need psychiatric treatment, have more behavioral problems, have lower reading scores, and are three times as apt to commit suicide (Byrne, 1993; Horn, 1997; Levine et al., 1993).

Many schools and centers have developed ways to involve men. Fourteen of these programs are described in *Getting Men Involved* (Levine et al., 1993). The first step in getting fathers, brothers, uncles, and interested high school seniors and juniors involved is to create a father-friendly environment. The term, *father*, extends to all father-substitutes. Because many children do not have a father in the home, encouragement and inclusion of father-substitutes are extremely important. Encourage family friends, uncles, grandfathers, stepfathers, and other father-substitutes to become lowing insights, the term *father* includes any father or father-substitute.

Insights for Teachers and Administrators

1. When fathers drop off or pick up their children at school, make an effort to talk with the father as well as the mother.

2. Encourage fathers to participate in the classroom.

3. Send newsletters to fathers and other male relatives. Send a newsletter to noncustodial fathers, unless the courts object to contact with the noncustodial parent. Include a picture and an article about a father participating in the classroom.

4. Schedule conferences at times that are convenient for both parents. Encourage the father to come and participate.

5. Have a special conference with the noncustodial parent, if the courts permit, if it appears to be counterproductive for both custodial and noncustodial parents to be present at the same time.

6. Make telephone calls letting both parents know about something the child has done that was interesting and positive.

7. Ask a father who participates to recruit another. Or pair up two fathers so that the new father can model the father who is familiar with the classroom.

8. Make home visits at a time when both parents will be there.

9. Videotape children in the classroom to share with parents. Include fathers working in the classroom in the video so that fathers see they are welcome to participate.

10. Include activities that appeal to fathers. Let them help with all types of classroom involvement, but also have activities such as games, exercise, or physical activities that some fathers would feel comfortable overseeing.

11. Present a workshop that allows parents to participate in the class so they become familiar with the expectations and activities. Encourage them to attend workshops on helping in the classroom, parenting skills, and conflict resolution.

12. Plan field trips such as visits to a zoo, farm, or museum. Ask parents to accompany and participate.

13. Plan a family evening where parents come and read with their children.

14. Learn from and listen to the fathers. Appreciate their contributions.

DIVORCE

Divorce involves change for both parents and children. The effects of divorce on children are related more to the previous situation and the subsequent events that affect the child than on the divorce itself. Children are usually ashamed of the divorce and feel rejected because of a parent's departure. Wallerstein (1985) found that younger children seem to suffer the most at the time of the divorce, but in a 10-year follow-up, older girls still harbored feelings of betrayal and rejection by men, making commitment to their own relationships difficult. If the quality of life after the divorce was good, children did well. If parents continued to fight over the children or burdened their children with too much responsibility, "in short, if stress and deprivation continue after the divorce—then children are likely to suffer depression and interrupted development" (p. 8).

On the other hand, divorce may improve the situation for a child in cases where a successful reestablished single family or a remarriage provides the child with a good quality of life. The initial effect of divorce is reduced over time. Children adjust to it and their risk at school is much lower a year after the divorce than immediately following it. Shaw (1992) listed conditions that affect the adjustment of children to divorce:

- Relationships of parents following divorce. Are the parents amicable, or do they use the children as ammunition against one another?
- Separation from a parent who is significant to the child.
- The parenting skills and relationship of the children with the custodial parent.
- The relationship of children to the nonresidential parent.
- Economics and financial ability to keep a standard of living. (p. 182)

Insights for Teachers and Administrators

1. Children do better following a divorce if they are able to have positive relationships with both parents unless the parents are extremely hostile toward one another (Lamb, 1997).

2. Parent hostility versus parent cooperation causes major problems for children who may be buffeted between the two parents. Research that compared intact homes with marital conflict to single homes without conflict have shown that children in the conflict-free homes have fewer emotional problems (Lamb, 1997; Shaw, 1992).

3. Teachers and administrators must also recognize that during the period of divorce, the family may be in turmoil. Children will bring their distress with them to the classroom.

4. The school can offer the child a stable and sensitive environment—one the child can count on—during that period. The school may be the only environment during this period that remains the same, so it may be the only place where children can count on structure and guidance to offer security. This is especially important for children going through a recent divorce. When they come to school, they do not want to be singled out as if there were something different about them because a divorce has occurred in their family, but they do need support and understanding.

5. Especially during the first year of divorce, children experience not only change and feelings of loss, but also the disorganization and reorganization of their parents' lives. Parents are sometimes distant; other times they may be more possessive of their children. Children are affected if they perceive abandonment by one parent (Lamb, 1997). If parents use their children as part of their conflict, the children suffer.

6. Children often yearn for their parents to reconcile and may blame themselves for the divorce. Children may respond to divorce by externalizing or internalizing problems or experiencing cognitive deficits. Boys, more than girls, show early negative reactions by being more quarrelsome and acting out. They externalize their change and loss. Children who are unhappy in their life situations, whether a divorce or not, tend to internalize their concerns and/or become less successful in school.

7. Keep positive expectations for the children. Be kind, but encourage them to keep up with their classwork.

8. Find ways that the child can contribute to the class. Use special projects or activities that may interest the child.

9. Make phone calls to both parents to share a school activity or a positive contribution the child has made to the class.

Decline of Economic Well-Being

A concrete change, and one of the most significant, is the decline in economic well-being of women who have custody of their children after divorce. "Most women and children will experience a decline in their economic well-being following marital disruption which will precipitate stress and affect other aspects of their lives" (Mauldin, 1990, p. 145).

After divorce, about half of eligible women receive some child support. There are a variety of reasons that child support is not available. In a survey by the U.S. Census Bureau, only 26 percent of women received the full amount to which they were entitled. Twelve percent who were supposed to receive payment received none, whereas another 12 percent received a partial amount. Forty-four percent were not awarded any support. Twenty-seven percent of these women wanted support but were not awarded any (U.S. Bureau of the Census, 1991d, 1995). Men did not fare any better when they were the sole support of a family. Fifty-nine percent were not awarded any support money; 28 percent were to receive support, but only 18 percent received any (U.S. Bureau of the Census, 1995).

If the woman is dependent on her own salary, she has the disadvantage of earning less income based on her gender. Women earn less than men no matter what their educational level. The wage gap continues. In 1996 women's median annual earnings for year-round, full-time jobs were 73.8 percent of men's salaries (U.S. Bureau of Census, 1998).

✑ SINGLE-PARENT FAMILIES

The 1970 census showed that 9 percent of children lived with a single parent. In 2001, 29 percent did. Two factors have increased single parenthood. One is the increase in birth to unmarried women, and the other is the increase in the divorce rate. In the early 1990s the trend toward an increase in single parents continued, and in 2001, the percentage was at 29 percent (Annie E. Casey Foundation, 2002a). See Figure 3.4.

Single-parent families are not a new phenomenon. From the 1860s until the mid-1960s there was no increase in the proportion of single parents because the growing divorce rate was offset by the declining death rate. Young children in the last half of the 1800s and first half of the 1900s were raised in single-parent families most often because the mother was widowed. Twenty-five percent lost a parent to death (Amato, 1994). Single-parent mothers worked hard to raise their children by taking in boarders, doing laundry, and somehow managing—with help from their children—to rear the family.

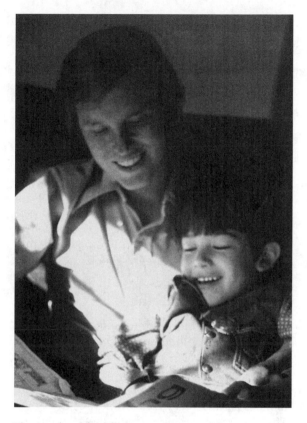

The number of single parents increased from 9 percent in 1970 to 29 percent in 2001.

FIGURE 3.4 Percent of families with children headed by a single parent, 1975–2001.

Source: From Census 2000 data, in the *KIDS COUNT Data Book* (p. 7), by the Annie E. Casey Foundation, 2001.

By the 1960s, however, the divorce rate had risen to such a degree that the number of single-parent families increased because of divorce rather than death (Furstenberg, 1994; Thornton & Freedman, 1983). The divorce rate doubled from 1963 until 1979, but appeared to have stabilized by the 1990s. Nearly half of all recent first marriages will end in divorce, with most children (88 percent) having their mothers as the custodial parent (Bogolub, 1995; Norton & Glick, 1986; Shiono & Quinn, 1994). During the period that a mother is raising her children alone, she has a much higher risk of poverty. Most divorced parents remarry, however, making it possible for 80 percent of children to live in two-parent homes most of the time they are in school.

Out-of-Wedlock Births

One third of all births are to unmarried women. Many of these mothers are very young and so will continue to live with someone in their extended family ("related subfamilies"), as opposed to divorced single parents who live in "unrelated subfamilies" (Carlson, 1992; Norton & Glick, 1986). There is great concern about the alarming increase in out-of-wedlock births, especially among teenagers. Eighteen percent of all children are born to unmarried mothers. The birth rate for unmarried women ages 15 to 19 increased steadily from 1940 through 1980 and then leveled off because of a decrease in the number of teenagers. These increasing birth rates outside of marriage do not mean there are more teenage mothers, but that there are more unwed teenage mothers. Girls now do not marry as young as their counterparts in the 1950s, and teenagers are having babies without marrying the fathers. For many young mothers, marrying the father is not a viable option; many of these young men are unable to obtain employment that would bring the family out of poverty.

Two factors—an increase in births out of wedlock and decreases or delays in births to married women—increased the percentage of births to unmarried mothers from 5 percent in 1970 to 14.2 percent in 1975, 18 percent in 1980, and 32.6 percent in 1994 (Children's Defense Fund, 1997; Thornton & Freedman, 1983). This startling figure points to the need for more family life education in the schools, especially for young mothers, and it also calls for an educational system that meets the needs of low-income families.

One in every five young females with below-average educational skills who lives in a below-poverty-level home becomes a mother while still a teenager. No matter whether young people are White, Black, or Hispanic, they are more apt to become pregnant if they are below average in academic skills. Higher infant mortality rates and greater risks to the child are just two of the problems associated with teenage pregnancies. Very young women are not prepared emotionally, economically, or physically to take on the challenge of childrearing.

Insights for Teachers and Administrators

What does this mean for a teacher? First, schools must accept the fact that single-parent families can supply the components necessary for a flourishing, functioning family. However, single parents have special needs. Unless they have established a strong network of friends or family, they may have difficulty meeting all the requests and obligations in their involvement with the school.

1. If children become part of a single-parent family through the death of one of their parents, they also need the teacher to recognize the change that is happening to them.

2. Opportunities for talking with teachers and counselors or attending group sessions with other children who have lost a parent through death or divorce can be helpful (Lewis, 1992).

3. Parents and teachers need to communicate throughout a child's education, but it is essential during periods of change to know what is happening both at home and at school and to help children overcome the isolation and distress they feel. Although only

one in every five children will probably be from a one-parent family at any given time, half of all children will spend part of their childhood in a one-parent family.

4. Offer convenient times for parent-teacher conferences. Single parents (and many two-parent families) need early-morning, evening, or weekend times for their conferences. A form such as the one suggested in Figure 4.8 will help teachers find out when parents are available. Single parents may also need child care while they attend a conference. This service is helpful for two-parent families as well, to allow both parents to attend.

5. Acknowledge and communicate with non-custodial parents. If noncustodial parents receive report cards and other information, they likely will be more interested in the child's work and better able to be involved with the child. Most noncustodial parents are men, and the percentage of men who pay child support is low. Schools can help sustain or even increase the father's interest by keeping him informed. Most fathers already have a keen interest in their child's schooling. They want to know what is happening without questioning the child. Honor their position; send them frequent reports unless the courts have specified that the noncustodial parent should not have contact or information about the child.

6. Learn parents' names. Always check the records to determine the names of the children and the parents, because they may not be the same. This applies equally to two-parent families, because half of them will have had a divorce. Calling the parents by their correct names is a simple gesture of courtesy.

7. Help parents become involved easily. Find ways that single parents can be involved without putting great stress on the family. Parents who work outside the home might be able to attend early-morning breakfasts, especially if child care is provided and the children get breakfast, too. Keep the number of parents at each breakfast small so you can talk with each parent individually. Find out how they would like to be involved, what their needs are, and if they have any ideas for their partnership with the school. Acknowledge their suggestions for improved home-school collaboration.

8. Encourage communication among parents. Establish a newsletter that allows parents to communicate with other parents. Let the parents include what they want to say in the newsletter. Better yet, make it a parent-to-parent newsletter, so they can establish their own networks.

9. Use care in communication. In all partnerships with parents, one of the most important elements of cooperation and understanding is the ability to communicate. The first objective is to have effective communication. The second objective is to prepare written materials that project positive and knowledgeable feelings toward the parent. Take care when preparing invitations to programs. Perhaps you may wish to emphasize one group, but make sure the child and parent know that they do not need to have a father, mother, or grandparent to attend. For example, saying "Bring your grandparent or a grand friend to class next week" implies that the visitors, not their titles, are important. At the program make sure you have some get-acquainted activities so that no one feels left out or alone. Activities also encourage networking among parents, and may be the best opportunity for new single parents in the neighborhood to become acquainted with others. (See Chapter 4 for more school activities, and Chapter 6 for ways to make group meetings work.)

10. Reach out. To involve both single and working parents, Moles (1996a) suggests: "Develop a single unobtrusive system to keep track of family changes, such as these examples: At the beginning of the year ask for the names and addresses of individuals to

be informed about each child and involved in school activities. At mid-year send a form to each child's parents or guardians to verify that the information is still accurate. Invite the parents or guardians to indicate any changes. . . . Work with local businesses to arrange released time from work so that parents can attend conferences, volunteer or in other ways spend time at their child's school when it is in session" (p. 49).

Based on a study of seventh- and eighth-grade children and their parents, Wanat (1992) recommended that the school, in addition to providing stability, acceptance, and parent involvement, provide students with special attention from teachers, counselors, and administrators. The single parents wanted to be the parent and did not want the school to assume that they had abdicated that role, but they could be helped by offering (a) extra educational help, (b) tutoring for the children, and (c) before- and after-school study time.

If the parent remarries, the child is affected again, and concerns arise regarding the following:

- The loss of the parent as the sole caregiver and the strong relationship that may have developed between parent and child.

- The relationships between the stepparent and the children. These are discussed in the following section.

✖ BLENDED FAMILIES

School personnel tend to view families as they have in the past. They look to the residential family—the family and children located within their school district—as the one family involved with the school and children. School policies must recognize the unique concerns of the blended family and avoid detrimental effects on the growing number of stepchildren.

There is a complex social organization in blended families. In the remarried families, some children may be offspring of the mother, some of

the father, and the remaining may be born to the remarried couple. A child may be living in a home with a brother or sister, a stepbrother or stepsister whose biological parent is the mother or father in the home, and a half-sister or half-brother who is the child of the remarried couple. In addition, they may have visitation with their other biological parent and have the same types of configurations when they are living or visiting there. Families may have as many as 30 configurations (Manning & Wootten, 1987).

Blended Family Cycle

When two people marry and one or both have children from a previous relationship, the road to a secure, happy family is difficult. It can be accomplished, but the original thoughts of delight on the part of the children and acceptance of the new arrangement by ex-spouses are complicated by the realities of the situation. One of the complicating circumstances occurs because both parent and child have come from single-parent family status. During the single-parent stage, parent and child tend to become extremely close. The parent may have turned to the children for emotional support and decision-making help in the absence of the former spouse. Children of the newly married couple often see the remarriage as a double loss. First they lost a parent through divorce. Now they are losing their special relationship with the other parent by having to share their custodial parent with a new stepparent.

Thus begins the blended family. Sixteen percent of all families include a stepchild or stepchildren (Dainton, 1993). Initially, the newly married couple fantasize that all the children will enjoy one another and both adults. The children, however, come into the remarriage generally hoping their biological parents will get back together. Therefore, fantasy is the first stage of the blended family cycle (see below for a description of the stages).

The cycle of the blended family as developed by Papernow (1993) starts with an early stage, where family members move from fantasy to recognizing their problems and needs. The cycle moves to a middle or restructuring stage, and then enters a final stage of solidifying the new family. In the first three stages, the family is generally divided according to biological line. The early stage includes three components: fantasy, immersion, and awareness.

During the fantasy stage, parents visualize that the new marriage will provide a supportive, loving family, although the children probably want their biological parents back together. "Both partners may imagine that because the adults in the new family adore each other, stepparents and stepchildren will also" (p. 13). In the second stage, immersion, the nonbiological parent becomes the outsider parent, not able to relate in the same way a biological parent does to the biological children. It is a period of sinking versus swimming. During immersion, the parents may be concerned about the family with negative feelings occurring. During the awareness stage, parents become more able to understand the dynamics of the new relationship. The bond between biological parent and child is acknowledged by the outsider parent, and they are ready to go to the next stage. If parents can recognize the areas of concerns of the first three stages and deal with them in the next, the family will probably thrive, but, if they get stuck in the first three stages, the family will probably dissolve.

The middle or restructuring stage includes mobilization, during which the airing of differences occurs; and action—power struggles are resolved and new agreements are made, with changes in family structure and new boundaries. "Every family activity is no longer a potential power struggle between insiders and outsiders" (p. 16).

The final stage includes contact, during which intimacy and authenticity in real relationships are forged. "The marital relationship becomes more of a sanctuary and source of nourishment and support, even on step issues" (p. 16). Finally, resolution occurs. Although issues may recur and the family may reexperience the stepparenting cycle, the family is able to go forward. Differences no longer threaten the family.

The entire cycle affects the children. During the first stage, while the children are still feeling a loss, their participation in school often suffers. They may go through stages of grief similar to those experienced after divorce, death, or moving away from loved ones. Children may act out in class; they may be despondent, and they may have no interest in schoolwork. For school-age children the school is a stable environment and can be a support for them. Staying in the same school with their friends can ease the transition.

During the early stage, stepparents become aware that they are not able to nurture children in the same way that biological parents do. Biological parents already have a strong bond with their children. Parents develop an awareness of these family pressures. Both partners recognize what they can handle and which attitudes need to be changed. In some cases the family is never able to restructure their lives, and many of these marriages do not succeed.

The restructuring period of stepfamily development allows for more openness in discussion of change. Parents and children continue to have strong biological ties, but the differences lead to action. In this action phase, family boundaries are clarified and the couple attempts to work together to find solutions.

In the final stages, the roles of each stepparent have been more clearly defined. The stepparent has a specific role relationship with the stepchildren. Acceptance of the new family structure is evident.

Blended family stages cannot be rushed. Papernow (1993) found that from four to seven years were needed to complete the entire cycle, and some families were never able to develop their blended family into a strong family.

Insights for Teachers and Administrators

Crosbie-Burnett and Skyles (1989) suggest that schools must improve in four areas to meet the needs of stepfamilies: (1) focus on cooperative co-parenting by the biological parents; (2) change the idea that there is a dichotomy between involved and uninvolved parents, but instead view the involvement as falling along a continuum; (3) view the stepparent as an additional parent, not a replacement; and (4) recognize that the extended family (nonresidential biological parents, residential or nonresidential stepparents, grandparents, or other relatives) has potential to support the child and the school. The exception to the authors' suggestions is the noncustodial parent who does not have visitation or other legal rights.

Support for blended families may be provided by implementing the following practices (adapted from Crosbie-Burnett & Skyles, 1989; Kelly, 1995; Manning & Wootten, 1987; and Visher & Visher, 1979).

1. Provide workshops for teachers to explain the varying configurations and the developmental stages of blended families. Review the possible effects on children according to age, gender, and needs.

2. Provide workshops on developing family traditions that strengthen families.

3. Eliminate the use of terms like *broken home* that may offend remarried or single families. Survey the parents to determine whether *reconstituted, step,* or *blended* are preferred terms. Children can devalue themselves if they hear terms that appear to be derogatory. Other children might conclude that some students are different and inferior.

4. Mail report cards, newsletters, and other informational items to both custodial and noncustodial parents.

5. Include noncustodial parents on field trips, in special programs, and in school activities.

6. Be aware of days when the student is likely to go on a visitation. Time messages accordingly.

7. Encourage children to make more than one Mother's Day or Father's Day card if they have more than one parent of the same gender.

8. Appoint parents from blended and single-parent families to serve on advisory councils, Parent Teacher Associations, or other organizations.

9. Be sensitive to a child whose parent has just remarried. This is a period of stress for both the child and the family. Children may act out and need special handling during the transition.

10. Include family information and positive stories about children in blended families or single-parent families within the curriculum.

11. Provide peer support groups for stepchildren or single-parent children where they can meet, talk, and realize that they are not the only ones in a blended family.

12. Offer books, articles, and lists of resources about stepfamilies and single-parent families for parents and school personnel. Subscribe to the *Stepfamily Bulletin* from the Stepfamily Association of America (see Appendix).

13. Adolescent stepchildren have greater well-being if the stepparent (usually the stepfather) is able to be nurturing, warm, and accepting. These skills may be taught to the stepparent (Crosbie-Burnett & Giles-Sim, 1994).

"Schools are in a position to help support children during this life transition by giving them a safe place to express and explore their feelings, questions, and concerns about parental marriage" (Crosbie-Burnett & Skyles, 1989, p. 59).

Grandparent Maintenance Families

The number of grandparents maintaining families increased from 2.2 million in 1970 to 3.9 million in 1997, a 76 percent increase (Casper & Bryson, 1998, p. 1). Six and seven-tenths percent of children under 18 were maintained by grandparents. These are families in which parents may live with the family, but where the grandparents provide the financial support, different from the families who have a grandparent move in with them. These families have a variety of composition including 34 percent of the families who had both grandparents present along with some parents and their children. Twenty-nine percent were

Grandparent maintaining families have increased from 2.2 million in 1970 to 3.9 million in 1997.

grandmothers only who had grandchildren and some parents present. Fourteen percent were children with no parents present living with the grandmother alone. Seventeen percent live with both grandparents with no parents present, and 6 percent live with the grandfather alone (p. 5).

Although some grandparent maintenance families do not have low income or insufficient education, the research indicates that the majority of grandparent-maintained families differ from households maintained by parents.

These differences include the educational level of the grandparent who may not have graduated from high school, and who is unable to obtain a high-income job. Even when grandparents work and have health insurance, the insurance programs do not cover grandchildren living with them. Children cared for in grandparent homes are younger, the grandparent is older, they are apt

to be living in the central city, to be poor, and to be uninsured. "Grandparents and their grandchildren would benefit greatly if policies and programs intended to help traditional parent-child families in times of need could be uniformly extended to grandchildren" (p. 12.) The concerns and insights that schools have for single parents should be also used with grandparent maintenance families.

✺ POVERTY

The poverty rate for children in 2000 was 16.2 percent, down from 22.7 percent in 1993. Children under 18 have a higher poverty rate than any other age group. Children make up 39 percent of the poor, but they are only 26 percent of the population (U.S. Census Bureau, 2000c).

Prevalence of Poverty

The number of poor in 2000 was 31.1 million—1.1 million less than in 1990, even though there was a population increase. The overall poverty rate was 11.3 percent, down from 11.8 percent in 1999 (U.S. Census, 2002c). However, in 2002, the Census Bureau reported that poverty of families with children increased from 12.7 percent in 2000, to 13.4 percent in 2001 (U.S. Census Bureau 2002a). Black families with children had the highest rate with 26.6 percent in poverty. Hispanics followed, with 23.7 percent. In 2000, the median household income of the following groups were: Blacks, $30,439; Hispanics, $33,447; Non-Hispanic Whites, 45,904; Asian and Pacific Islanders, $55,521; and a three year average for American Indian and Alaska Natives, $31,799. The income for Blacks and Hispanics was at an all-time high. Women with no husband present had median incomes of $28,116 (U.S. Census Bureau, September 25, 2001). Median income points to the middle of incomes rather than the average; half of each group was below the median income, and half were above.

Definition of Poverty

Poverty is defined in the United States according to the income of the person or family. In 2000, the poverty threshold for a family of four was $17,603 annual income; for a family of three, the poverty threshold was $13,738 (U.S. Census Bureau 2002). In 1990 a family of four who earned less than $13,359 was classified as in poverty (U.S. Bureau of the Census, 1991c). In 1996 the poverty threshold was $16,036 for a family of four. With inflation, the poverty threshold continues to increase by the same annual average as the Consumer Price Index. In 1996, the total income of almost 40 percent (14.4 million persons) of those in poverty had less than half the poverty index. Many in poverty do not have money to provide for the basic needs of housing, food, and clothing (Lamison-White, 1997).

Destructive Nature of Poverty

To exist in the culture of poverty means to feel depressed, powerless to effect change, and unable to control one's destiny. Alienation, anomie, isolation, and depression are common partners of poverty. Parents who are depressed and unable to control their own world pass that feeling on to their children.

Children in poverty are apt to have poor health, inadequate maternal care, and negative educational experiences. They score poorly on standardized tests, drop out of school, and experience violence, and many are prone to die in childhood.

Length of Time Families Are in Poverty

Contrary to popular belief, only a portion of the impoverished are poor for eight years or longer. Most people who become poverty stricken move back out of poverty in one to two years. In the 1990s one in three children spent at least one year in poverty. For poorly educated, young, minority, or disabled persons, poverty may remain for long periods of time.

Long-term poverty is rare among White children, however: less than one percent are in poverty for more than ten years, and six percent, for five or more years. But long-term poverty affects 29 percent of African American children for more than ten years, and almost half for more than five years. Children who live in extreme poverty or are in poverty for long periods of time suffer the most. If poverty occurs during early childhood years, the consequences are more severe than if it occurs in a child's later years (Brook-Gunn & Duncan, 1997). Education influences whether a family is in poverty and whether it remains in poverty. As education increases, poverty decreases. There is an urgent need for schools to prepare all children for successful educational accomplishments.

Whom Does Poverty Affect?

Poverty is not as prevalent now as when the War on Poverty began in 1966. At that time, one in every five families—39.5 million people—earned so little they fell below the poverty level. This was reduced to 24.1 million in 1969. It remained fairly constant throughout the 1970s, until the 1980s, when 4.8 million more became impoverished. In 1986, 32.4 million people lived below the poverty level (Shapiro & Greenstein, 1988). In 2000, 33.1 million people lived below the poverty level. See Figure 3.5A, which shows the total number of poor and the poverty rate for 1959–2000, and Figure 3.5B, which reflects the poverty rate by race and Hispanic origin.

In 2000, poverty rates were 21.2 percent for Hispanic children and 22.1 percent for African American children. The three year average poverty rate for American Indians and Alaska Natives was 25.9 percent. Poverty rates for all groups except Whites were at their historic low (U.S. Census Bureau, 2000c).

"Children living in mother-only families were more than five times more likely to be poor than those living in two-parent families: 38 percent compared with 7 percent" (Corcoran & Chaudry, 1997, p. 41). Although African Americans and Hispanics have a greater chance of being in poverty, more Whites are below the poverty level because there is a greater number of Whites in the United States. Numerically, 60 percent of all poor people are White children, but proportionately, 90 percent of the children in long-term poverty are African American (pp. 45, 47).

African Americans, with a 22.1 percent poverty rate, have over 8 million in poverty; Hispanics have a 21.2 percent poverty rate with 7.5 million people living in poverty. Non-Hispanic Whites with a 7.5 percent poverty rate have 14.5 million in poverty. The two

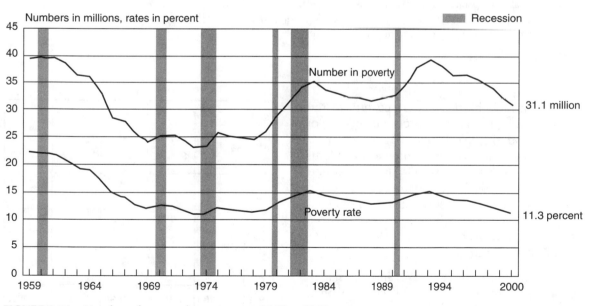

FIGURE 3.5A   Number of poor and poverty rate: 1959 to 2000.

Note: The data points represent the midpoints of the respective years. The latest recession began July 1990 and ended in March 1991; data does not include the 2002 recession.

Source: From the *Current Population Survey,* by the U.S. Census Bureau, March 1960–2001, retrieved August 22, 2002, from *http://www.census.gov/hhes/poverty/poverty00/pov00.html*

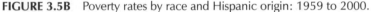

FIGURE 3.5B Poverty rates by race and Hispanic origin: 1959 to 2000.

Note: The data points represent the midpoints of the respective years. The latest recession began July 1990 and ended in March 1991. Data for Blacks are not available from 1960 to 1965. Data for the other race and Hispanic origin groups are shown from the first year available. Hispanics may be of any race.

Source: From the *Current Population Survey,* by the U.S. Census Bureau, March 1960–2001, retrieved August 22, 2002, from *http://www.census.gov/hhes/poverty/poverty00/povrac00.html*

groups that are hardest hit by poverty in the United States are Black children and children of female-headed single families. There has been a significant reduction of children living in families where no parent has full-time, year-round employment. It was reduced from 33 percent in 1975 to 23 percent in 2000. (See Figure 3.6).

Insights for Teachers and Administrators

1.   One of the greatest problems that half of all single mothers face is insufficient income. When working with these mothers, teachers should recognize not only their time constraints but also their financial bind and avoid pressure in either area.

2.   Find ways to involve parents, for they need to know that they are important and wanted.

FIGURE 3.6 Percent of children living in families where no parent has full-time, year-round employment, 1975–2000.

Source: From Census 2000 data, in the *KIDS COUNT Pocket Guide* (p. 6), by the Annie E. Casey Foundation, 2002.

3. Parents who are depressed and unable to control their own world pass that feeling on to their children.

4. Children in poverty are apt to have poor health and inadequate care. Before viewing a child as being neglected, however, find out the source of the problem.

5. Teachers in a central city are likely to have many children who are in low socioeconomic levels in your classes. A higher percent of children who live in the central city are in poverty, but no matter where they work teachers will find children from families having financial problems.

6. Families who have always been self-sufficient and suddenly find themselves without employment face tremendous psychological adjustments as well as difficulty in providing shelter and food.

7. For some, using social welfare is an acknowledgment of defeat and they would rather do without some necessities than accept such help. If they are open to suggestions, help by providing information on social services. The school can also provide exchange options where out-grown clothes may be substituted for ones that fit.

8. To exist in the culture of poverty means to feel depressed, powerless to effect change, and unable to control one's destiny. Alienation, anomie, isolation, and depression are common partners of poverty.

Ways to Counteract Poverty

To counteract the stress of poverty on families, parents and children need at least the following:

- A decent standard of living (jobs that pay enough to adequately rear children).
- More flexible working conditions so children can be cared for.
- An integrated network of family services.
- Legal protection for children outside and inside families.

Family Support Programs

Programs to support families are being offered across the United States. They range from family resource centers to family literacy programs. "By strengthening families' ability to nurture their children physically, emotionally, and intellectually, family support programs increase the likelihood that children will grow up healthy, safe, and successful" (Allen, Brown, & Finlay, 1992, p. 1). These programs will be discussed in more detail in Chapter 8 and are listed in the Appendix.

FAMILIES AND INDIVIDUALS WITHOUT HOMES

Over 3 million persons (women, children, and men) were homeless in 2001. Demand for shelter rose 13 percent according to the U.S. Conference of Mayors' December 2001 report on homelessness. The Department of Housing and Urban Development (HUD) found that 4.9 million low-income households paid more than 50 percent of their income on rent, an amount much too high to allow them adequate income for other necessities (National Law Center on Homelessness and Poverty, 2002a).

The U.S. Conference of Mayors revealed the following data on the homeless:

40% are families with children

57% are single-parent families

22% are mentally disabled

20% work

4% are unaccompanied children

Of these

50% are African American

35% are White

12% are Hispanic

2% are Native American

1% are Asian (National Law Center on Homelessness and Poverty, 2002a, Overview, p. 1)

Only 38 percent of the single young women who are mothers have ever held a job longer than six months. They are generally undereducated, have few job skills, probably have abused alcohol and other drugs, and are the recipients of domestic violence. The homeless lack more than just housing (Nunez, 1996).

Other people without homes, in addition to young single mothers with children, include unemployed two-parent families; single men and women; jobless people with mental illness; people with mental and physical disabilities; homeless independent children and young adults; alcoholics; and transients. It is estimated that families with children make up 40 percent of the homeless. Schools are directly concerned with single- or two-parent families with children who should be in school and runaway children who have dropped out of school.

The Stewart B. McKinney Homeless Assistance Act

The Stewart B. McKinney Homeless Assistance Act of 1987 (P.L. 100–77) was reauthorized in January 2002 as the McKinney-Vento Amendment. The act was designed to ensure that homeless children have access to education. Although it offers incentives and nominal grants to encourage states to provide for homeless children, the responsibility is left to each state (National Law Center on Homelessness and Poverty, 2002b; Stronge & Helm, 1991). The authorized federal funding is $70 million. The minimum amount of funding any state receives is $150,000 (National Law Center on Homelessness and Poverty, 2002b).

Authorized Rights for Students in a Homeless Situation

Children and youth who are eligible for special consideration include those who are living with someone who cannot afford or has lost their home, be they a friend, relative, or someone else. It also includes those staying in a motel, hotel, or emergency shelter because they do not have adequate accommodations (National Law Center on Homelessness and Poverty, 2002b).

The reauthorization has the following requirements with guidelines for academic achievement, school selection enrollment, dispute resolution, transportation, liaison, and segregation.

Students in homeless situations have the following protections in school selection:

- Local educational agencies (LEA) must keep students in the school they attended when they had a permanent home or the school they last attended if at all feasible and if it is not against the parent's or guardian's desire.

- Students may stay at their original school until the end of the school year in which they move into permanent housing.

- If the LEA does not enroll the students in their school of origin, a written explanation to the parent/guardian is required and may be appealed. Dispute resolution is available.

- Students in homeless situations without a guardian or parent must be helped to choose and enroll in a school.

- States must have a McKinney-Vento plan that describes how students in homeless situations will be given the same opportunity to reach academic standards as other students.

- Students in homeless situations should have access to education and services they might need to ensure that they meet the academic standards.

- Students in homeless situations must be enrolled even if they do not have all the required documents needed.

- At the parent's or guardian's request, transportation must be provided to transport the child to and from their school of origin. To ensure that the children and youth in homeless situations are able to access the availability of education, the LEA must have a designated appropriate staff person to help them with information and assistance in obtaining services and education (National Law

Center on Homelessness and Poverty, 2002b, pp. 1–6).

A more complete copy of the reauthorization can be obtained on the Internet at *http://www.nationalhomeless.org/reauthoriztion.html*, or use the Internet address in the Bibliography at the back of this book.

The National Law Center for Homelessness and Poverty recognized some issues that need to be addressed to help persons who are homeless. Less than 30 percent eligible for low-income housing receive low-income housing. Only 11 percent of the 40 percent eligible for disability receive disability. Only 37 percent have food stamps even though most are eligible for them. Similarly, most are eligible for welfare benefits, but only 52 percent receive them. Regretfully, in spite of the law, some 12 percent are still denied their education (National Law Center for Homelessness and Poverty, 2002a, pp. 1–2).

Concern for Children in Homeless Situations

When families are dislocated because of losing their home, they may move to various locations, such as shelters or relatives' homes in other school districts. Not only do the children lack the security of living in a stable environment, but they also face uncertainty, moving time and again. It is a problem for these children to continue their schooling if the school will not accept them because of residency requirements. Concern of administrators and teachers for the welfare of homeless children should include (a) the opportunity for education, (b) acceptance by staff and peers, and (c) referrals as needed for special services. Swick (1999) suggests that centers or schools assign a teacher, staff member, or liaison to help the child and family during times of crisis. To do this the liaison may need to advocate for the family to get the needed services.

Teachers found learning difficulties, speech delays, behavioral problems, depression and anxiety, short attention span, aggression, and withdrawal in homeless children (Bassuk & Rubin, 1987; Klein, Bittel, & Molnar, 1993; McCormick & Holden, 1992).

Homeless children have a higher risk of nutritional deficiency and other health problems including delayed immunization, poor iron levels, and developmental difficulties. In a study of homeless children compared with low-income children who had homes, it was found that the homeless children were delayed in their growth (Fierman et al., 1991). It may be a combination of factors—malnourishment, diarrhea, asthma, elevated lead levels, or social factors including family violence, drug-exposed babies, alcohol abuse, mental disorders, and child abuse and neglect—that affect the child's growth (Bassuk, 1991; Fierman et al., 1991).

Homeless children who come to school are usually ashamed of not having a home, of living out of a car, tent, or shelter. They need support, not blame; they need acceptance, not rejection or shame; and they need a curriculum that allows them to succeed. They may need special tutoring, and a buddy assigned to help them learn the routine. If they are continuing in the same school that they attended before becoming homeless, they need to be assured that they are still valued.

Because the family and children are under a lot of stress, it is better to let them offer information than to inquire into personal concerns. Homeless children revealed their feelings in interviews by Berck (1992): "If being a poor child living in a rich city is a crime, I'm guilty. . . . People have no right to punish me for something I have no control over" (p. 32).

Parents' Desires

In a research survey (McCormick & Holden, 1992), homeless parents indicated they would like assistance with transportation; developmentally appropriate child care; opportunities to share with others; flexible opportunities to be involved; respite opportunities; mental health self-esteem groups; information on services; an easy intake process for preschool participation; and classes.

Children's Feelings

Walsh (1992) pictured homeless children through their conversations. Sam writes about how he feels about losing his pet dog, Ralphy, when he had to move to a shelter:

> I had a dog for a long time before I came here. We had to give him to a friend because we couldn't bring him down ere wit us. The shelter say "No animals." And, even if we move out of here, we can't get him back because e likes the people he's with right now. And me and him were best friends. His name was Ralphy. I always still remember him. I just hope he remembers me. (p. 77)

Juan expresses his feelings of sadness, not just for himself, but also for his parents:

> Being here makes me sad but I don't cry. I feel sad about it by myself. Sometimes I talk to my mother about it. I tell her how sad I am. She says she knows I'm sad. She knows because she feels the same way. I don't know if she cries about it. If she does I never see her. I think she does though. I don't like to talk about this stuff too much. (p. 82)

Insights for Teachers and Administrators

Teachers cannot solve the problems of homeless families, but they are in a position to greatly ameliorate the damage done to children.

1. Establish a buddy system in the classroom. Assign a buddy to all children new to the room (not just the homeless). Make it a classmate-friendly room.

2. Have clear, simple outlines that allow children to fit into the class schedule. (For children enrolling for the first time, let a buddy discuss the routine with the new child, mentor and guide the child through the procedures.)

3. Have a procedure for transitions from one activity to another. Music, rhythm, and movement give children extra creative activities as well as providing organized transitions.

4. Provide a place where children can keep their school materials and a supervised area where homework or enrichment activities can be completed at school.

5. Help the new child catch up, and individualize the assignments for the new child.

6. Provide health provisions (toothbrushes, soap, etc.) and clothes.

7. Encourage parents to become involved. Let the parents of homeless children participate in the classroom. As with all parents, they will need to know how you want them to participate. Plan a workshop for parents, or mentor them individually. Their involvement will not only provide extra help in the classroom, but it can also become an educational program for parents. They may learn more about how they can help their children.

All these suggestions can help the family, but families need time to develop skills and stability. The way homeless shelters are usually set up, the family can stay only limited amounts of time. Some programs have begun to recognize that this does not provide homeless families enough time to gain skills for employment or enough stability to provide for the family. Nunez (1996) described the American Family Inns, where parents and children can live for a year establishing stability in the family and allowing the parents to become self-sufficient. The American Family Inn meets the educational needs of each parent, children have supplemental help to compensate for skills they need to develop, and infants and preschoolers go to child development centers, giving the children a jump-start. Recreation and cultural programs are also provided. Similar programs have been established across the country. They provide single mothers and two-parent families time to develop skills and establish stable lifestyles.

The extra effort works. After a family moves from the American Family Inn to their own permanent housing, they are provided with aftercare services for an additional year. Studies show that approximately 94 percent who lived in an American Family Inn were still self-sufficient and living independently 2 years later (Nunez, 1996, p. 76).

The continuing concerns for homeless families and the children affected by homelessness requires giving top priority to schools and programs that help these families survive and flourish. The United States has a challenge from other nations: the United States ranks 16th among industrialized countries in living standards for our poorest one fifth of children, 17th in efforts to lift children out of the lowest poverty level, 18th in the narrowest gap between rich and poor, and 18th in infant mortality (Children's Defense Fund, 1997, p. xv).

❧ WORKING WITH CULTURALLY DIVERSE GROUPS

Children are like snowflakes.
At first they appear to be alike,
But on close examination
they are all different.
Focus on their similarities,
But understand their differences.

What is the best way teachers can meet the needs of children? How can they help children accept themselves and others in an environment that is fair regardless of ability, gender, or race? How can they encourage all children to achieve their potential in a supportive environment? Four approaches to one's work with children are included here. Those who help children develop—teachers and other personnel—should:

1. *Focus on Self.* Know their own biases, beliefs, and culture. Why do they feel the way they do? What do they value? What would they change? Teachers must examine their own lifestyles and beliefs.

2. *Focus on Children's Understanding and Appreciating Themselves.* Encourage children to know themselves through an environment of acceptance, encouragement, and inquiry. Interactions with children should be based on knowledge of child development in order for the interaction among children and adults to be appropriate and enabling.

3. *Focus on Collaboration With Parents and Community, Acceptance of Others, and Understanding of Cultural History as Well as Individual Family History.* Recognize history and culture and its influence on the lives of children and families.

4. *Focus on Caring and Teaching.* Strive for practices that acknowledge the child's development and needs. Recognize that there are a variety of learning styles that can be enhanced through teaching strategies that individualize for the strengths and needs of the students.

Focus on Self

Examine family history. What values are internalized that really came from childhood and the manner in which children are socialized? How much do you model after your parents, other relatives, or friends? Examine the lives of those who have been significant to you—family, teachers, friends, or someone famous. What was their cultural background? What did they believe? What values did they live by? Have they influenced you?

When did your family or ancestors move to the United States? How easy or hard was the transition from their native country? What are the beliefs that carried down to your generation? What changes were made? How did they influence you, or did they influence you? Or, if you are American Indian, where did your ancestors live? How did they fare when settlers from other countries arrived? What was their value system?

The questions you can ask yourself are endless. If you find some prejudicial feelings, you may be able to examine them, recognize they are not based on fact, and work them out so that you can be prejudice-free.

Activities

One activity that may help you on your journey to understanding yourself is the answer to the question, "Who am I?"

Make a list of who you are. List the points of how you see yourself, as the thoughts come to mind. Do not dwell on what the answers mean. Make a list five to ten items long. Now you can look at the list and see what you placed first. Was it teacher, mother, father, husband, or wife? When you think of yourself, what roles are paramount? Your view of who you are may change depending on what stage of life you are in. You may not even agree with the list you just made. Are there other roles more important to you? The list is unimportant. What is important is your review of the roles and thinking about what they mean to you.

Another activity is something both you and your students can work on. Make a family history. Talk with relatives and find out what you can about the family. Record stories they may want to share.

If you have a computer, you can use a computer program of Family History, or you can write a narrative about the family. Use a scanner to include pictures of your ancestors and living relatives. You will learn a lot about your family and yourself.

Focus on Children and Culture

Many books have been written since the late 1960s that examine multicultural education. Each has its own positions and strengths. Each focuses on its beliefs on how teachers can approach diversity within the classrooms. The focus on children and culture is defined by De Gaetano, Williams, and Volk (1998):

> *Kaleidoscope* is deeply rooted in an understanding that children are intimately connected to their family, their ethnicity, religion, race, gender, abilities, and disabilities, sexual orientation, and life experiences—in short, their culture. This approach requires that teachers observe children carefully, seeking the essence of who and what students are, their strengths, and their world. (p. 5)

A book written for preschool teachers and their charges is the *Anti-Bias Curriculum: Tools for Empowering Young Children* by Derman-Sparks and A.B.C. Task Force (1989). It focuses on ways to help children see themselves and others in a positive light.

The authors point out that children notice gender and racial differences as early as the second year of life. By age 3 they may have been exposed to biases that are "pre-prejudice." By ages 3 and 5 they are sorting out aspects of their own self, their gender, and race. For these reasons an antibias curriculum program for young children is important (Derman-Sparks and A.B.C. Task Force, 1989):

> Bicultural, bicognitive education means children (1) learn the beliefs, values, rules, and language of their own culture in the learning/teaching style appropriate to their culture, and also (2) learn the beliefs, values, rules, language, and learning style of the dominant culture.

> The ideal early childhood program would incorporate both an anti-bias approach . . . and, where appropriate, bicultural, bicognitive curriculum. (p. 6)

Basic principles that undergird the teaching of children include:

- Affirming the cultures of all children, not simply those of the dominant culture.

- Integrating the experiences and culture of all children into the content and process of schooling to motivate and promote learning.

- Weaving cultural diversity into the transmission of values, knowledge, and skills that occurs in schools.

- Enabling students to become socially and politically responsible people. (De Gaetano, Williams, & Volk, 1998, p. 12)

The *Anti-Bias Curriculum* book helps early childhood educators provide the opportunity for preschool children to examine their gender and cultural identities. When children ask questions, their questions are not ignored. They are answered directly and given opportunities so that they are able to develop their understanding of self and others. Color and cultural blindness and ignoring the questions would be fine if these realities did not exist, but they do. Rather than rejecting the examination of our gender and culture, it is best to recognize it and learn to appreciate differences.

The antibias curriculum seeks to avoid the trap of tourist examination of cultures where holidays and customs are the only adventures into cultural identity. A preschool curriculum includes:

1. Many books that reflect differences in gender, race, disabilities, geographic location, and socioeconomic class.
2. Opportunities for dramatic play with costumes, clothing, and equipment that allow for diversity.
3. Identity books such as *I Am Special* or *All About Me.*
4. Music of all countries.
5. Art from all countries.
6. Diversity in the types of dolls.
7. Visuals so that all groups are represented on posters, in pictures, videos, and computers. (Derman-Sparks and A.B.C. Task Force, 1989)

Enable Children

Enable children to handle their anger and frustrations. Children with troubled lives need support in order to work out their problems in a positive manner. When a child acts out, find out what is causing the problem, rather than reacting with punishment (Comer, 1997).

Get Acquainted with the Community

Because of the influx of new minority groups into the United States, teachers are realizing they need to increase their understanding of different cultures. This is not an easy task, and it requires an essential commitment. The first and most important thing to remember when working with culturally diverse groups is to avoid stereotyping. Although it is essential to understand a group's culture, it is also necessary to allow them to be individuals. Every group is composed of individuals, and those individuals may or may not fit the norm.

The only way to get to know the families in the community, in addition to inviting them to the school, is to go out into the community to meet them on their territory.

School personnel should get acquainted with the school neighborhood before school starts. Take "block walks" with small groups in nice weather. A complete, integrated study unit may also be developed on the neighborhood early in the school year.

CULTURAL DIVERSITY

Our nation is culturally diverse. It includes diverse family configurations, many ethnic groups, varying socioeconomic levels, and religious differences, as well as rural and urban influences. For over 300 years, men and women in the United States have been marrying others who have different countries of origin. Our society is made up of Irish Americans, Italian Americans, Asian Americans, Polish Americans, Albanian Americans, Native Americans, German Americans, African Americans, English Americans, French Americans, Spanish Americans, and many others. Most of these have a multi-American cultural background such as French American, Native American, African American, and Irish American combined, or Irish American, German American, and Italian American combined.

Most of the new arrivals (85 percent of foreign-born) who are living in the United States are legal residents. Of this group, most (78 percent) of the children attend school in five states (California, 45 percent; Illinois; Texas; New York; and Florida). Schools will find an increase in the number of students as well as children from many different countries. It is projected that the number of children in school will grow from 34 million in 1990 to 42 million in 2010. Of these, 9 million will be children of immigrants, 22 percent of the school-age population (Board on Children and Families, 1995, p. 75). School personnel should be aware of and ready to respond to the cultural diversity.

Culture: A Way of Life

School personnel and parents may not understand the cultures that make up the school population. The term *culture* is most easily understood when viewed as a way of life. Other descriptions are "blueprints for living" and "guidelines for life." Culture includes the way in which life is perceived. It is the knowing, perceiving, and understanding one brings to a situation. Culture may include artifacts such as housing, clothing, and utensils. It is easier to recognize that different artifacts stem from different lifestyles than it is to discern that individuals are perceiving information differently—viewing a situation or communication with varying interpretations.

Culture is both *learned* and *internalized* by the child. Children of any ethnic background learn the cultural patterns in which they are raised. They come to school with those perceptions. For example, the concept that a child should be seen and not heard is common in various cultures. Such a child is usually well behaved, but does not offer to answer questions or is not comfortable talking in class. This cultural trait does not work to the child's advantage in a school when the student is called upon. Teachers should be aware of this cultural pattern and make sure that the child has many opportunities for expression in an encouraging, safe environment. They must be aware that the child has internalized the quiet behavior. It will be difficult for the student to change, but acceptance of the child's positive behavior plus encouragement and reinforcement of the desired behavior will help the child participate in the school's culture. High expectations based on knowledge and understanding of each child sets the stage for growth.

Exploring Your Culture

When people first arrive in the United States, intermarriage with those from other countries of origin may or may not have occurred. But the mixture in the United States increases as people interact with one another. Children in a classroom may not even be aware of their ethnic background. Encouraging them to explore their ancestors results in greater understanding of culture with its historical and geographical background.

Challenges

Two challenges face the schools as they work with culturally diverse students. One is accepting, understanding, and working with each child. The other is helping the children to accept themselves. The more the school and home become involved with each other in a positive relationship, the greater the opportunities for understanding the family and reducing discrimination.

Since the end of the Vietnam War, refugees from most of Indochina—Laotians, Hmongs, Cambodians, Chinese, and Vietnamese—have entered our schools. In addition, many new arrivals have come from Mexico, Latin America, and South America. Immigration has continued from other countries as well, so you may find children in the schools speaking languages from Europe, Asia, Africa, and the Americas.

Caring Strategies

Some teaching and caring strategies may be more effective than others in working with children. Consider (a) group problem solving; (b) peer reading and tutoring; (c) cooperative learning; (d) group pride, sharing, and replacing competition against others with self-competition; (e) culturally relevant materials; (f) parent volunteers; (g) flexibility in timed events, and (h) dramatizations, sharing of folk tales, and journal writing (Berger, 1997; Gilliland, 1988; Little Soldier, 1985). Observe the children and analyze their learning strengths and interests. As you learn about your students, adapt your class to the best ways of learning for individual children and the class as a group.

ᘑ THE FIRST INHABITANTS OF NORTH AMERICA

American Indians, the Native Americans, are indigenous to what is now the United States. The most prominent theory of their origin asserts that their ancestors crossed a land bridge through the Bering Strait from Siberia into North America as early as 40,000–10,000 B.C. (Kullen, 1994). Although often portrayed as a homogeneous people, they are diverse both culturally and physically. Their facial features, height, and hair textures vary; skin colors range from dark brown to very light (Banks, 1997).

When the Europeans first came to the Americas, as many as 18 million Native Americans were living in North America (John, 1988). Estimates of the number of spoken languages range from 300 (John, 1988) to 2,200 (Banks, 1991). Anthropologists have attempted to group the Indian nations who resided in what is now the United States. These groupings include the following areas: Eastern Woodland, Great Lakes Woodland, Southeastern, North Central Plains, South Central Plains, Southwest, California, Northwestern Plateau, and Northwest Pacific Coast.

When studying the American Indian (Native American), it becomes clear that there is diversity as well as commonality among the nations.

Contributions to Civilization

Native Americans have made important contributions to the U.S. and world cultures. Their contributions to agriculture, architecture, irrigation, and government are outstanding. As early as 10,000 B.C. the Native Americans had domesticated corn. They were accomplished horticulturists. In addition to corn, some of the more common foods developed by the Indians of North and South America are potatoes, peppers, tomatoes, peanuts, squash, maple sugar, and beans. (The Irish potato originated with Native Americans.) These foods are used extensively in the world today. Indians in the Southwest developed an elaborate irrigation system. Pyramids of Teotihuacan in Mexico, Tikal pyramids in Guatemala, and Cahokia pyramids in the Mississippian culture as well as the Taos pueblos illustrate their architectural achievements (Kullen, 1994; Weatherford, 1991, 1988).

Their concept of representative government, which was practiced by the Iroquois confederacy of Five Nations (Mohawks, Oneidas, Onondagas,

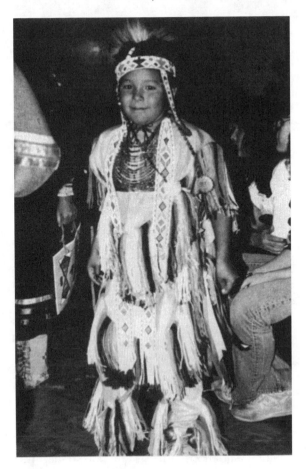

Visit with families, attend a powwow. Get to know the parents and/or grandparents of the child.

Cayugas, Senecas, and later the Tuscaroras) had great influence on the establishment of the U.S. government. Benjamin Franklin studied this confederacy and learned about their representative government before the U.S. Constitution was written (Weatherford, 1988). These and other contributions help show a more accurate picture of the Native American.

By the time Cristoforo Colombo (Christopher Columbus) arrived, there were more than 300 nations established in all parts of North America. The population ranged from 2 or 3 million to 18 million.

Movement West

Within each area, numerous Indian tribes flourished. As Europeans settled the eastern portion of the United States, those people indigenous to the East were pushed westward.

Indian tribes were placed on reservations with most of the reservations in the midwestern and western parts of the United States. The treatment of the Native American is characterized by broken treaties, genocide, and persecution—an oppressive chapter of American history.

Most descriptions of the European expansion into North America misrepresent the resistance of the Native American. This distortion of history influences the view other Americans hold about Native Americans, as well as erodes the Native American's self-esteem. A study of different Indian nations, including the people indigenous to the area in which you live, will provide a more accurate picture of the history of the Native American.

Education for Native Americans

In the 1990s two landmark efforts were made to describe Indian education and to make specific recommendations for its improvement. Two groups working toward these aims were the Indian Nation a Risk Task Force and the White House Conference on Indian Education (WHCIE). Suggested basic research included the study of bilingualism, the inclusion of Native American languages, as well as the health issue of fetal alcohol effects. It was also recommended that Native American should do more research—that an insider view is essential.

Suggestions include:

- Alternative assessment or unbiased standardized tests to assess student achievement and abilities.
- Effective parent support programs (WHCIE).
- Instruction, curriculum, and program administration for exceptional American Indians and Alaska Natives of all ages (WHCIE).

Insights for Teachers and Administrators

1. Because Native Americans come from diverse cultures, it is important that teachers who have these children in their classes learn as much as possible about their specific cultures and backgrounds. "The acculturation of Native Americans should be looked upon as a continuum ranging from 'traditional orientation' to 'assimilated'" (Little Soldier, 1985, p. 186).

2. Visit in the neighborhood, talk with parents in informal settings, attend a powwow (unless it is a closed ceremony), and visit the parents in their homes after they feel comfortable having you there. "Visit with the people in the community at every opportunity" (Gilliland, 1988, p. 24).

3. As is the case in all ethnic groups, individual preferences and values exist. Use the background on culture as a guide to help you understand the individual child, not as a stereotypical absolute.

4. In working with the parents of Native American children, teachers need to show interest and acceptance. Teachers must expect to reach out to the parents and the extended family. Help them feel comfortable with you and the classroom. When they are at ease, invite them to share their specialties, perhaps crafts and folklore, with the class.

5. Curriculum in the schools needs to include an accurate history of Native Americans to overcome the stereotypical misrepresentation of them as savage hunters of the plains. The study of Indian nations that represent a variety of lifestyles and governmental forms can show the diversity and accomplishments of American Indians prior to the coming of the Europeans.

6. Some cultural traits that may cause misunderstanding unless the teacher is aware of them include (Gilliland (1988):

a. *Eye contact.* To many Indians, looking down is a sign of respect. In some Indian groups, a person looks another in the eye only to show defiance.

b. *Time.* Time has a different meaning for many Indians, far different from the way many European Americans view the concept. For example, European Americans "say 'time flies.' To the Mexican 'time walks.' However, the Indian tells, 'time is with us' " (p. 26). Patience is a highly valued characteristic.

c. *Family.* The extended family is important to the Native American child, so grandparents may be the ones to attend parent-teacher conferences. If the child is separated from the extended family by a move to the city or some other circumstance, the child may experience a loss of the sense of security.

d. *Nature and spirituality.* Native Americans respect nature, and spirituality is an important part of the Indian culture. "Harmony with nature, and spirituality, are also necessary to good health" (p. 31).

e. *Age and wisdom.* The focus in the dominant U.S. society is on youth; in the Native American tradition, there is respect for age and the wisdom associated with elderly people.

ARRIVAL OF OTHER ETHNIC GROUPS

Some believe that artifacts in Mexico indicate that Africans were the first to discover America, but no settlement or lasting impact occurred. It is known that around A.D. 1000, Norse explorers Leif Ericsson and Thorwald Ericsson made voyages to Newfoundland. Since Norse settlements did not survive, their impact on the continent did not continue. The next group of people to explore the Americas were the Spanish. The Portuguese, French, and British followed.

SPANISH AMERICANS

When the Europeans came to the Americas there were two continents that already had 300 nations, each designated by individual nation names and each with its own culture developed in response to the environment and to answer its people's questions about life and death. The continents were named after Amerigo Vespucci, a navigator and explorer, because German cartographer Martin Waldessmuller published a map with the name America on it.

Christopher Columbus, sailing for Spain and searching for Asia, reached the Caribbean in 1492. He landed on the island of San Salvador in the Bahamas, explored Cuba and Hispaniola, made three more voyages, and claimed all the land for Spain. In 1496 Santo Domingo was established by Christopher Columbus on the southwestern shores of Hispaniola, the earliest continuously inhabited settlement of Europeans in America. Spanish explorations included present-day Puerto Rico, Florida, Mexico, and the southwestern United States. In 1559, Arellano became governor of La Florida. One thousand colonists and 500 soldiers brought 240 horses and settled near present-day Pensacola. In 1560, Durango in north central Mexico was founded. Others were becoming interested in the new land. In 1564 French Huguenots built Fort Caroline on the St. Johns River in Florida. The Spanish drove out the Huguenots, destroyed Fort Caroline, and in 1565 established a colony at St. Augustine.

The Spanish explorations were far flung. Missions were established as far north as present-day San Francisco and beyond.

Throughout the 1500s the Spanish explorers continued to develop a Spanish empire in the Americas. Coronado marched north into Arizona and New Mexico. De Soto reached the Mississippi River in 1542. Spanish explorers including Ponce de Leon, Cortes, Coronado, and Balboa explored what is now Florida, Mississippi, New Mexico, and other parts of the western and southern United States as well as Mexico and South America.

Children are very important to Spanish-surnamed or Hispanic families.

One area in the United States that was settled as early as 1581 and still retains the beauty of some of its early culture is southern Colorado and New Mexico. In 1581, Juan de Onate helped found a settlement and Franciscan missions in the Rio Grand Valley of New Mexico. In 1600 the colonists moved to San Gabrielle on the Rio Grande. Onate served as governor until 1607. The city of Santa Fe, the first capital in the United States, was established in 1609. Many of the descendants of the early conquistadors and families who were given Spanish land grants still live in Colorado and New Mexico.

This first group of Spanish-surnamed citizens in the United States were in North America before the Pilgrims arrived. Hardly immigrants, they had settled and lived with the Pueblo Indians long before the United States was interested in the territory. These Spanish colonialists, given land grants by the Spanish viceroys, continued their Spanish lifestyle in areas including Santa Fe, San Antonio, and San Diego. Missions, Spanish-style architecture, their methods of ranching, and irrigation systems show their contributions to the lifestyle of the Southwest. Many of these people do not want to be called Mexican American or Chicano; their heritage is Spanish and the terms *Spanish American, Hispanic,* or *Latino* better fit their culture and their heritage.

Diversity in Present-Day Hispanics

Although the Spanish-surnamed residents of the United States share some linguistic and cultural traits, each wave of immigrants from Spain, Cuba, Latin America, and Mexico, as well as U.S. citizens from Puerto Rico, has brought its own unique attributes. Varied social status and educational levels in their countries of origin, the isolation or hardships encountered on arrival, their desire to acculturate, and the length of their family's residence in the United States all contribute to a heterogeneous Hispanic American population. Teachers must work to dispel any stereotypical ideas they may have about their Spanish-surnamed students.

The southwestern United States was Spanish territory until 1821 when Mexico gained independence from Spain. The Southwest was part of Mexico until Texas gained freedom in 1836 and was annexed by the United States in 1845. Arizona, New Mexico, Nevada, and parts of California and Colorado were acquired by the United States as the result of the Mexican-American War. Thus, by 1848 many people whose ancestors had lived in traditionally Spanish-speaking areas since the 1600s suddenly became citizens of the United States.

The great influx of Mexican Americans did not begin in the United States until about the time of the Mexican Revolution in 1910. Many of the first immigrants were upper-class Mexicans, refugees escaping for political reasons. Their assimilation into U.S. society was relatively easy. A second influx of immigrants occurred in 1916 when Mexicans were hired to help maintain the railroad system across the United States. They were expected to work and return home, but many remained. They suffered bitter discrimination, especially from those who felt that they were taking jobs from U.S. citizens. Nonetheless, the descendants of this group of Mexican Americans are now assimilated into the society.

During World War II the United States needed help with its farm crops, so the bracero program was instituted. Mexicans were invited to work temporarily in the gardens of California and other states. In 1951, the Migratory Labor Agreement (P.L. 78) established a new bracero program (Banks, 1997).

After World War II many Spanish-surnamed people migrated to cities and northern states to work. Some came from Mexico, but many were U.S. citizens who moved up from New Mexico, Texas, and southern Colorado to work in cities and on ranches. These were the natives of the Southwest who were forced off their land when the mines closed and farms were automated. They were a rural people, trying to assimilate into an urban culture.

The use of braceros and migrant workers set a pattern for Mexican workers to come to the United States. Many began crossing the border illegally. In 1954 U.S. immigration authorities began deporting illegal Mexicans, but thousands of Mexican Americans continued to pour across the borders (Banks, 1997). An amnesty bill passed by Congress and implemented in 1988 allowed illegal residents who could prove they had lived in the United States for five years to become citizens.

Illegal immigration continues today. The economies in Mexico and other Latin American countries are poor. Many of these immigrants are grasping at an opportunity to provide for their families. The children come to school knowing little or no English. These children need special care and help to succeed in our educational system. This new group of Spanish-speaking Americans, coupled with the rural-to-urban movement of longtime citizens of Hispanic background, present a challenge to the schools to provide both bilingual education and a strong program in language enrichment.

Insights for Teachers and Administrators

It should be remembered that Spanish Americans were the first to settle in America—in New Mexico, Texas, Colorado, Arizona, Florida, and California—so there are many levels of assimilation and diversity. Sharing the knowledge of the contributions of all Hispanic groups helps children respect and honor that heritage.

1.   Spanish-surnamed children work best in a cooperative, rather than competitive, atmosphere.

2.   For the newly arrived Hispanic, opportunities for language expression need to be encouraged at all levels of education. Small group discussions, cooperative games that increase language skills, use of language on the computer, role-playing, creative dramatics, puppetry, and general encouragement of language use are all essential for language development. Classrooms in which children are encouraged to talk with each other also promote language development. If children are not allowed to talk in the lunchroom, the importance of language development is being ignored.

3.   As is the case with all children, teachers working with Spanish-surnamed children must get to know the parents and work with them and their children to meet their needs.

4.   Recently arrived immigrants may be reluctant to get involved in the school—many fear being identified as illegal immigrants, even though schools are required to educate all children and are not responsible for determining who is legal and who is not. Many of these parents have not had a good experience in school themselves and feel threatened by the school. See Chapters 4, 7, and 8 for ideas on how to involve this challenging group of parents.

✌ AFRICAN AMERICAN FAMILIES

African Americans have been a part of the Americas since Diego el Negro sailed with Columbus in 1502. Blacks helped Coronado explore present-day Kansas in 1541 and helped establish St. Augustine, Florida, in 1565 (Banks, 1991). As indentured servants, Blacks landed on the eastern shores of the United States in 1619. When they were brought over as slaves, their culture was eradicated as much as possible. (Refer to Chapter 2 for a discussion of slavery.) Family life was discouraged, and families were broken up if the master wanted to sell one member of the family and not the other. Children were most often left

African-American families often have strong kinship bonds and a distinct work and achievement orientation.

with their mother until they were old enough to be on their own. Most were not allowed to learn to read; schooling was usually forbidden.

Achievements of African Americans

Throughout the history of the United States there have been African Americans who were free, and many who were slaves educated themselves. Those who were free worked for the emancipation of other African Americans who were under the bondage of slavery. African Americans contributed to the growth and development of the United States. They were leaders, teachers, and scientists. In 1766 Crispus Attucks, the first to die for independence, was killed during the Boston Tea Party, a protest against taxes levied by England. Banneker

(1731–1806) was an inventor and mathematical genius. Harriet Tubman (1826–1913) conducted the Underground Railroad, a system of helping slaves escape bondage. Frederick A. Douglass (1817–1895), a great orator, denounced the evils of slavery. James P. Beckwourth (1798–1867) was a pioneer in the West. Early members of Congress included Jefferson Long (1836–1900), who served from 1870 to 1871; Hiram Revels (1822–1901), who served from 1870 to 1871; Robert B. Elliott (1842–1884), who served from 1871 to 1874; James T. Rapier (1839–1884), who served from 1873 to 1875; Robert Smalls (1839–1915), who served from 1875 to 1887; John Mercer Langston (1829–1897), who served from 1889 to 1891; Richard H. Cain (1825–1887), who served from 1873 to 1875 and 1877 to 1879; and John R. Lynch (1847–1939), who served from 1879 to 1883 (Adams, 1991).

African Americans continued to contribute as scientists, artists, business leaders, agronomists, musicians, educators, and authors. Elijah McCoy (1843–1929) was a Black inventor who had 57 patents; Dr. Daniel Hale Williams (1856–1931) was the first person to perform heart surgery; Dr. Ernest E. Just (1883–1941) was a noted biologist; and Charles Drew (1904–1950) was a pioneer in blood plasma preservation. Children know about Martin Luther King Jr., but many do not know the heritage of other African Americans. The African American heritage includes a high development of music, art, literature, and an emphasis on religion. In many families there is a strong commitment to church, so children grow up in families where faith and religion are important. Many Black leaders have been ministers (for example, Martin Luther King Jr. and Jesse Jackson). Music is an essential expression in their religion. Black musicians developed jazz. Although many Blacks have a remarkable creative ability in music, this does not mean that all Blacks are great musicians, nor do all Blacks use the church as a focal point in their lives.

The strengths found in African American families include strong kinship bonds, an achievement orientation, a strong work orientation with a desire for upward mobility, adaptability of family roles, and an emphasis on religion (Billingsley, 1992; Hale-Benson, 1986; Hill, 1992). These strengths encourage parent-teacher cooperation, and school personnel should approach the collaboration with a winning attitude. The extended family, along with flexible family roles, allowed families to survive the hardships and trials that have been a part of their lives in the United States.

Comer (1997) recommends that for African Americans to become part of the "Good Society," the first step is that scapegoating of Blacks and others must decrease. This is necessary so that all can focus on and handle the problems and opportunities that exist. Second, schools must help solve the cultural and societal problems of the nation rather than reflect them. Last, it is possible to have a "win-win culture," still competitive but also enabling and caring (pp. 14–15).

In order for families to survive and thrive in a democracy, Comer (1997) states that the society must (1) develop a sound and growing economy that permits the participation of all its citizens, and (2) maintain sound community and family functioning so that critical tasks, particularly child-rearing, can be performed well. The culture must value families, allowing them to participate in a strong economy and facilitating a sound family and community. (p. 11)

African American students need to have a caring school community and a supportive family. They also need the opportunities for their families to participate fully in the society.

Insights for Teachers and Administrators

Sharing the knowledge of the contributions of African Americans helps children respect and honor their heritage. Focus on discovering the many contributions made by African Americans and other ethnic groups. Help children know the dream.

1. Each child, of any cultural group, is unique. Culture depends in great part on the location and socioeconomic status of the family. The culture—Black or White—in a lower income neighborhood is much different from that in a middle-class and upper-class area. Middle- and upper-class African Americans tend to have culture similar to that of others in middle- and upper-class society in the United States.

2. Impoverished Black families have different strengths and different problems. Black parents in ghettos face problems of poverty, powerlessness, alienation, and a negative environment. Their children rarely see models of financial success as a result of education and hard work. A good standard of living is impossible if the parent is unemployed or earning only minimum wage. These children are raised in a culture of dropouts and school failure, as well as with the love of their extended family.

3. Encourage parents and compliment their effort to encourage their children to achieve. Clark (1983) and Comer (1997) suggest that family lifestyle is a stronger indicator of a child's success in school than socioeconomic level. Clark found that children who were high achievers came from homes that supported and helped their children achieve, regardless of their income. The interpersonal communications within these families showed encouragement in their academics, nurturing interaction with frequent dialogue, established rules and clear guidelines, and monitoring of their learning activities.

4. Collaboration with parents can encourage success for both the child and the parent. When parents participate in decision making and learning activities, it allows them to be involved with the schools in positive ways. "When engaged in task-oriented activities with stipulated objectives and expected outcomes, the individual experiences his or her effort as being valued and accumulates strength that is generated by the realization that he or she is able to make things happen. In a society in which one is defined by what one does, a mother's identity and self-worth begins to be reaffirmed by virtue of her work in schools" (Winters, 1993, p. 99)

5. Children who speak a Black dialect of English at home will come to school knowing different language patterns than those who are surrounded by standard English. They will have to practice standard English—which is not always an easy task. "Speaking, listening, labeling, storytelling, chanting, imitating and reciting" (Hale-Benson, 1986, p. 161) are activities that should be encouraged in an early childhood classroom. There should be ample opportunity for all children to enjoy them.

6. Black families often have a strong network among family members and friends. Aunts, uncles, and grandparents help and support one another (Stevens, 1982).

7. Hale-Benson (1986) connects the roots of West Africa with the childrearing culture of African Americans. "Black children may have distinctive learning and expressive styles that can be observed in their play behavior" (p. 5).

8. A model early childhood classroom for all children includes (a) a supportive environment with frequent touching and lap sitting; (b) an emphasis on the development of self-concept through success experiences, compliments, and display of work; (c) opportunities for creative expression in music, dramatics, and visual arts; (d) involvement in arts and crafts with African American and African art as part of the curriculum; (e) activities that involve physical movement, play, and dance with as much self-direction as feasible; (f) exposure to artifacts, stories, and other aspects of African culture; (g) extracurricular activities that include bringing the community into the school and taking field trips; and (h) celebration of holidays that include the holidays of many cultural groups (Hale-Benson, 1986). A child care center, Visions for Children, founded by Hale in a Cleveland suburb, is based on the program described here. "Visions for Children's focus is on language skills. This includes expressive as well as receptive language; too often children receive language through listening but do not have enough opportunity to engage in expressive language. Expressive language includes holding con-

versations with adults, telling stories for pictures, engaging in sociodramatic play, and responding to questions in complete sentences" (Hale, 1994, p. 175). The teacher must be aware of body language and be sensitive to its cues, model standard English, encourage the children to talk, emphasize group learning, incorporate music into the curriculum, and have a variety of learning activities that reach children with a variety of learning styles.

Until prejudice and discrimination are eliminated in the United States, most Black children will receive mixed messages. Schools that include their parents as active partners, recognizing their contributions, will enable children to feel acknowledged and accepted. At school, children need to receive one message: All children will succeed because they are first-class citizens.

ASIANS

Since 1965 and the passage of the Immigration and Nationality Act Amendments of 1965 and the end of the Vietnam War in 1975, many immigrants have arrived from Asia. In 1997 Asian Americans were 24 percent Chinese; 21 percent Filipino; 13 percent Asian Indian; 11 percent Vietnamese; 10 percent Korean; 10 percent Japanese; 5 percent Cambodian, Hmong, and Laotian; and 7 percent other Asian—for an estimated 9.6 million Asian Americans, who make up less than 4 percent of the total U.S. population. Most (70 percent) came to the United States after 1970 (Lee, 1998). Those coming from Southeast Asia were primarily refugees from the Vietnam War. This section focuses on that group, because their dislocation or relocation was not their choice.

Southeast Asians

One of the easiest mistakes for teachers to make is to presume all Southeast Asians—from Vietnam, Laos (including the Hmong), Cambodia, and Thailand—share a common background. The first major group of refugees arrived from Vietnam in 1975 after the fall of the country to the North Vietnamese. This group included wealthy

and poor people and highly educated scholars and professionals as well as unskilled workers. Most were literate, but 18 percent had no education (Banks, 1991). The second wave of Indochinese refugees was more diverse and included Hmong, Laotians, and Kampucheans (Cambodians). They were more homogeneous in their lack of education and their inability to speak English.

French Indochina, first proclaimed the Indochinese Union by the French in 1893, was made up of Vietnam, Cambodia, and Laos. Until that time, the countries were separate political entities; after the union they continued to differ from one another in language, history, and culture. The term *Indochinese* was given by the French and may be used to describe an area but should not be used to designate individual countries. The countries of Laos, Cambodia, and Thailand were influenced by India; Vietnam and the Hmong regions (the mountains of Laos) were influenced by

Asian parents are very supportive and interested in the educational success of their children.

China. However, these countries do not view themselves as one area; they are separate countries. Throughout their long history, these countries were often enemies, controlled by one or the other as one empire thrived and was then destroyed. When working with children from this area of Asia, find out which country was the parent's homeland.

Language differences in these countries are illustrated in Figure 3.7 and Table 3.6. These children will have to use English as a second language to communicate with each other. Indochinese families also have different placement of names.

The Vietnamese, Cambodians, and Laotians are addressed by their first name, although many of the refugees have adapted their names to fit traditional name placement found in the United States. Schools may not find as much confusion in 2000 as they did in the 1970s.

During the 2,000-year history of Indochina, its inhabitants were influenced by Chinese, Indian, Oceanic, and European cultures. The variety of religious traditions are indicative of the many cultures in the region. Buddhism spread from India; Taoism and Confucianism originated in China; and Christianity was introduced much later. An Indochinese person may believe in more than one religion because Eastern religions are based on philosophies of behavior more than deification of their leaders. In addition to the major religions, animism and ancestor worship are practiced in many rural areas. Polytheism is accepted. Most Eastern religions share an emphasis on the individual's search for peace and harmony, a reverence for ancestors, and a respect for elderly persons.

Insights for Teachers and Administrators

It will be necessary for the teacher to determine whether the families of students who are from Asia have lived in the United States 20 to 30 years or if they are new arrivals.

1. If children come from a culture where there is no formal education, they may have problems adjusting to school. Teachers need to recognize these children's experiences and backgrounds and plan a curriculum to address their strengths and needs.

2. Southeast Asian children who were in school before coming to the United States were taught largely through lecture and memorization; active participation in the learning process may be new to them. Others may not have attended school at all.

3. Most Indochinese families form close-knit extended families. They often try to reunite when they arrive in the United States. They also work hard to save money, often sacrificing, to bring other members of their families to their new home. Use journals for older children and creative art for younger and older children to help them express feelings.

4. Teachers should be sensitive to gestures and mannerisms that may have unintended meanings. For example, Southeast Asian students may not look steadily in the eyes of the teacher because such behavior is a sign of disrespect. A pat on the child's head may be meant as a kindly gesture, but it is likely to offend. Be sure not to criticize children in front of others; they need to be able to "save face." Indochinese pupils may come to school with small round bruises on the arm, but coining (pressure by coins) is used as a method to reduce illness or pain and is not a sign of abuse.

5. Most Asian American families value education, and generally Vietnamese, Cambodian, Chinese, and Laotian students work hard to obtain an education. Often parents or siblings will tutor young children or others before school. Their respect for education extends to teachers, so most Indochinese parents will not question the teacher's decisions or expertise.

Lus tshaj tawm: kom teb cov teebmeem hauv qab no ua lus hoob. tom qab, yog koj teb tau kom teb cov teebmeem uas pom hauv no ua lwm yam lus.

1. koj lub npe hu li cas? _____

2. koj nyob qhov twg tuaj? _____

Hmong
(Hmong)

ຄຳຊີ້ແຈງ

1. _____?

2. _____?

(Lao)

Lời Chỉ Dẫn: Trả lời hai câu hỏi dưới đây bằng tiếng việt. Sau đó, trả lời những câu hỏi trên thẻ này bằng các ngoại ngữ khác.

1. Em tên họ là gì? _____

2. Em từ đâu tới? _____

Tiếng Việt
(Vietnamese)

指示：請用中文回答下列兩個問題。如可能答其他語言問題，請用千此丄個回答問題。

1. 你尊姓名﹖ _____

2. 你從那裏來﹖ _____

中文
(Chinese)

FIGURE 3.7 These examples illustrate the variety of written languages of the Indochinese people.

Source: From *Indochinese Students in U.S. Schools: A Guide for Administrators* (pp. 49–50), by the Language and Orientation Resource Center, 1981, Washington, DC: Center for Applied Linguistics.

TABLE 3.6 Name placement varies among the Indochinese ethnic groups.

	Last name	Middle name	First name	Addressed as*
Vietnamese				
Nguyen Hy Vinh (M)	Nguyen	Hy	Vinh	Vinh
				Mr. Vinh
Hoang Thi Thanh (F)	Hoang	Thi	Thanh	Thanh
1. Married (to Mr. Vinh)				Mrs. Thanh
				Mrs. Vinh
				Thanh
2. Unmarried				Miss Thanh
Cambodian				
Sok Sam Bo (M)	Sok	(none)	Sam Bo	Sam Bo
				Mr. Sam Bo
Rith Bopha (F)	Rith	(none)	Bopha	
1. Married (to Mr. Sam Bo)				Bopha
				Mrs. Sam Bo
2. Unmarried				Bopha
				Miss Bopha
Lao				
Vixay Siharath (M)	Siharath	(none)	Vixay	Vixay
				Mr. Vixay
Douangkeo Malaythong (F)	Malaythong	(none)	Douangkeo	Douangkeo
1. Married (to Mr. Vixay)	Siharath	(none)	Douangkeo	Mrs. Douangkeo
2. Unmarried				Douangkeo
				Miss Douangkeo
Hmong				
Chu Sao Thao (M)	Thao	Chu	Sao	Chu
	(clan name)			Mr. Chu Sao
May Xee Vang (F)	Vang	May	Xee	
	(clan name)			
1. Married (to Mr. Chu Thao)				May Xee
				Mrs. Chu Sao
2. Unmarried				May Xee
				Miss May Xee

*Adding *Mr., Mrs., Miss* makes the form of address more formal.

Source: From Indochinese Students in U.S. Schools: A Guide from Administrators (pp. 49–50), by the Language and Orientation Resource Center 1981, Washington, DC: Center for Applied Linguistics.

🙰 DIVERSIFICATION OF PRESENT-DAY UNITED STATES

To understand the immigration of today, it helps to view the history of immigration and diversification of the United States.

British Explorations

Other European countries followed the exploration of the Americas started by the Spanish and Portuguese. In 1578 and 1579 Sir Francis Drake, sailing for Britain, explored the California coast and claimed upper California for Queen Elizabeth I. In 1584, Sir Walter Raleigh explored Virginia. A colony was established on Roanoke Island, Virginia, in 1585. There were no survivors found. A second attempt was made in 1587, but it also failed.

The first successful colony in present-day United States was established by the London Company at Jamestown, Virginia, in 1607. Three German colonists were with the first group and the following year, 1608, skilled Polish and German glassmakers as well as Italian and French emigrated to Jamestown. In 1613 Pocahontas, daughter of the Algonquin chief, Powhatan, married James Rolfe in Jamestown. The inclusion of English, Italian, French, Polish, and German settlers and the marriage of Pocahontas could have been an omen for the future diversification in the Americas.

The *Mayflower* brought the Pilgrims to an area near Jamestown in 1620. These separatists from the Church of England had moved to the Netherlands in 1608 to escape religious persecution. They returned to England in 1618 and set sail for the Americas.

Irish colonists arrived in 1621 at Newport News, Virginia. In 1634, a Roman Catholic colony at St. Mary's, Maryland, became home to Irish immigrants who came as indentured servants. Two thirds of European immigrants came to America as indentured servants (Kullen, 1994,

p. 74). They were able to work off their debts. The first African Americans came in 1620 as indentured servants. The first African American baby was born free in 1624. Later laws made the conditions for African Americans and their freedom extremely harsh.

English colonists continued to come to North America and settled as far north as present-day New Hampshire and Maine.

French Explorations

The French were also exploring. They explored the northeastern coast off Newfoundland as early as 1540. Jacques Cartier sailed to an area near present-day Quebec. In 1634 Jean Nuolet explored Wisconsin for the French. By 1682 La Salle had explored the Mississippi to the Gulf of Mexico. The French empire extended from Quebec to the mouth of the Mississippi.

The French Huguenots established a town in New York in 1677. In 1685 thousands of Huguenots fled France and settled in New York and South Carolina.

Pennsylvania

King Charles II granted land to William Penn primarily as a haven against religious persecution of the Quakers in 1681. Penn welcomed others who had been persecuted for religious beliefs. Among those who found refuge were many German Mennonites who migrated in 1683. In 1687, Philadelphia, Pennsylvania was founded.

Santa Fe

In the Southwest, Santa Fe was established in 1609. It is the oldest state capital in the United States. A regular supply route between Mexico City and Santa Fe was established in 1610. By 1630 Santa Fe had a population of 1,000 people: 200 Spaniards and 800 mestizos (children of a marriage between a Native American and a Spaniard).

Immigration

In 1765 there were approximately 1,850,000 settlers in the eastern part of the United States. Of these, most were from Britain (approximately 85 percent). In addition, there were 175,000 Germans, 55,000 Dutch, 40,000 French Huguenots, 20,000 Swiss, 15,000 Swedes, and 1,500 Jews.

Immigration has continued since the first settlements. In the 1840s there was an influx of Germans escaping from social unrest in their country and Irish escaping from a potato famine. In the late 1800s and early 1900s there were many immigrants arriving from southern and eastern Europe.

Each time large groups of immigrants arrived in the United States there was discrimination against them, especially if they looked different and were poverty stricken. The discrimination against the Irish is an example of the difficulty of acceptance. From 1820 until 1865, 1,900,000 Irish arrived in the United States. The Roman Catholic Church grew from 650,000 to 1,600,000. Since many of the other, earlier immigrants had come to the Americas for religious reasons, they had a distrust of the Catholic Church. In 1831, the St. Mary's Catholic Church in New York City was burned. A convent in Charlestown near Boston was burned in 1834. Three days of rioting took place in Philadelphia in 1844. Churches were burned, and 13 people were killed. Anti-Catholic agitation continued in the 1850s. The St. Louis riot of 1854 ended with 10 people killed. Bloody Monday, in 1855 in Louisville, Kentucky, resulted in 100 Catholics slain. The Civil War caused the nation to focus on different issues, and the persecution of Irish dissipated.

Teachers can ameliorate prejudice and discrimination by treating all children with care and understanding. If they model nonprejudicial behavior and recognize the strengths of each child, they will help children become bias-free.

This chapter points out many of the diverse challenges that face teachers, parents, and schools. The changing world—accompanied by the birth and growth of a new generation and the arrival of newcomers from other lands—requires dedication to the task.

> Families are like blossoms
> in a wild flower garden
> Mixed in color, size, and configuration
> All the flowers lend to the beauty
> of the garden
> So it is with families
> Each adds to the beauty of the community

✺ SUMMARY

Families around the world are living with change, but the family, the most stable component of society, flourishes. Marriage and family life are important.

The population of the United States has increased dramatically in the last 50 years. Along with growth in numbers, several trends are evident. More mothers are working outside the home. More people are completing high school and college. Out-of-wedlock births, especially to teenagers, have increased alarmingly. Twenty-nine percent of children live with single-parents. Fathers are getting more involved with their children; thus, in the 1990s and 2000s, the emphasis was on families and father involvement.

Poverty in the United States increased in the last decade and leveled off by 2000. Almost one in every five children lives in poverty. The greatest proportions are among children of single-parent mothers and children in Black families.

Black families still face covert prejudice, although strides have been made to reduce overt discrimination. Immigration of Southeast Asians—Vietnamese, Hmong, Laotians, and Cambodians—has challenged our schools. These immigrants have adjusted to the environment extremely well considering the great cultural shock and language differences.

Although it is important to understand cultural differences, teachers will encourage success in their students when they focus on the strengths of each child.

✺ SUGGESTED CLASS ACTIVITIES AND DISCUSSIONS

1. Count the number of moves the members of your class have made. Why have they moved?

Where have they moved? How many times have they moved?

2. Survey your class members. How many different cultural lifestyles are represented in your class? Discuss.

3. How can teachers support fathers' involvement and support of their children?

4. Interview a single parent. Find out the advantages and disadvantages of rearing children alone. Which support systems do they need?

5. How is family life changing in the United States? How does this affect parent education programs? Discuss the changes that have occurred during your lifetime.

6. What is an ideal family? Discuss. List the values and strengths you look for in an ideal family. Why did you choose them?

7. Investigate methods school districts are using to help Vietnamese, Cambodians, Cubans, Laotians, Chicanos, and other immigrants acculturate into the school system. Ask for materials from your school district that are being used by teachers.

8. Monitor the food stamp program, changed by the 1996 welfare law, Personal Responsibility and Work Opportunity Reconciliation Act (PRWORA). Is it working, is it causing hardship for children, or has it been changed?

9. Research the effect of Temporary Assistance for Needy Families (TANF) on child care and families. Has it been helpful? Are there any concerns?

10. Discover your heritage by researching your family's past. If adopted and your heritage is not revealed to you, make up a heritage that you would like to have.

4 Effective Home-School-Community Relationships

Education should consist of a series of enchantments, each raising the individual to a higher level of awareness, understanding, and kinship with all living things.

Anonymous (Frank, 2001, p. 232)

Where can anyone find an opportunity to impact a child's world as easily and as well as in a school or home, leading children to discover their own distinct way to grow and develop?

Know you what it is to be a child? . . . It is to believe in love, to believe in loveliness, to believe in belief; it is to be so little that the elves can reach to whisper in your ear; it is to turn pumpkins into coaches, and mice into horses, lowness into loftiness, and nothing into everything, for each child has its fairy godmother in its own soul.

Thompson, 1988, p. 300

In this chapter on parent involvement in schools, you will learn about ideas and programs that will enable you to collaborate successfully with parents and also do the following:

- Set up a program that encourages parents to participate.
- Develop a school that welcomes parents.
- Inform parents of their importance and role in the school-home partnership.
- List and explain services that schools can offer to help families accomplish the task of parenting.
- List and explain services that help parents become partners with their schools.
- Provide parents with access to information about school and homework.
- Provide a family resource center.
- Develop a parent advisory council.

Box 4.1

OVERHEARD IN THE TEACHER'S LOUNGE: WHICH SCHOOL WOULD YOU CHOOSE?

"It happened again today," Gloria complained in ever-increasing disgust. "Sara came to school late, obviously tired, without a coat, and when I asked her where her coat was, she burst into tears. Her parents just don't care. What am I supposed to do? I wrote her mother a note last week, but she hasn't responded."

"Did you really expect an answer?" Melody asked. "I thought when I moved to suburbia my problems would be over, but the parents of the children in my room don't volunteer, and only half of them show up for conferences. I've thought about calling them, but I'm just too busy."

"Don't complain," Susan responded. "I'd rather have parents who stay away from my classroom than those who are so involved that they pester you and even try to tell you how to work with their child. A good parent is a quiet parent. Just teach to the exams and make sure the students' scores are above average. I was at one school where parents were so involved that they had a fit when we scored below the 50th percentile. Have you heard about. . . ?"

Or

The programs at school and outside resources really helped me this fall. One child came from a family who seemed disinterested in the welfare of their child. "Sara came to school obviously tired, without a coat, and when I asked her where her coat was, she burst into tears."

The social worker shared with me what she knew about Sara's circumstances. It seems that her father was in a terrible automobile wreck, and has been hospitalized and out of work for the last 6 months. The mother is overwhelmed with the lack of finances, caring for her children, and fear for her husband's condition.

I called Sara's mother and let her know that we would be supportive of Sara and help her be successful in her schoolwork. We also discussed the resources available at the school as well as social services and nonprofit organizations. She had not known about most of the resources available to her. Then we used the exchange room to find some new clothes for Sara.

Guess what? She came to back-to-school night. Other parents offered to baby-sit her children so she can get out, visit her husband, and take a part-time job. She was so appreciative. It will be a long struggle, but this family will make it. It really makes me feel good to know that we were able to help.

And

"Ann, do you think you could help me with the workshop on family math? Eighteen families showed up last night for the first session. They got so involved and were so appreciative that we're planning another the week after next. We're going to make manipulatives that they can use at home with their children."

"Sounds great," Ann said. "I've been thinking of developing a workshop on inventive spelling and writing. I also want to involve the parents in developing an authors' library. My students are so excited about writing their own books. Let's brainstorm together and plan both of the workshops. It will be more exciting if we work together, and don't forget that I have four parents who are fantastic volunteers. I'm sure they will want to help. We need to check on child care, too. I know some parents have difficulty finding someone to take care of their children. If we get Nadine to plan for the children, we can let the parents observe her interaction with them. She's wonderful, sensitive, and has so many enriching ideas."

✒ PARENT-SCHOOL COOPERATION

Parent-school cooperation brings the strengths of the home and the expertise of the school into a working partnership. Every issue, concern, and educational goal involves the family of the child. Separation of the child from the family is impossible, because every child is socialized into a family culture. Even those reared in an institution are affected by the culture of the institution—their substitute family. Children bring the ideas, feelings, strengths, and weaknesses of the home into their life at school. If homes and schools are connected through the children, clearly a working partnership will strengthen the effectiveness of the school. Home-school partnerships are an essential step forward. Working together, schools and homes will succeed in educating the next generation.

Recent research emphasizes increased opportunities for children's success when the home and school work together (U.S. Department of Education, 1986, 1987, 1991a, 1991b, 1993, 1994). More parent-school involvement is needed from birth through high school (Bloom, 1981; Daresh, 1986; Davies, 1990; Epstein, 1986, 1987a, 1987b, 1994, 1995, 1996; Epstein & Dauber, 1991; Fehrmann, Keith, & Reimers, 1987; Loucks, 1992; Meyerhoff & White, 1986; Moles, 1987, 1996a, 1996b; NASBE, 1988, 1991; Warner, 1991). This chapter focuses on the goal of good school-home-community relationships with suggestions for procedures and methods to start the process.

✒ SCHOOL CLIMATE AND PARENTAL ATTITUDES

When you walk into a school, are you able to sense its spirit? Does it seem to invite you to visit? Or does it make you feel unwelcome? Can you pinpoint the reasons for your feelings? Each school differs in its character (usually set by the administrators) and reflects the morale and attitudes of the personnel. Some say, "Come, enjoy with us this exciting business of education." Others say, "You are infringing on my territory. Schools are the professional's business. Send us your children. We will return them to you each evening, but in the meantime, let's each keep to

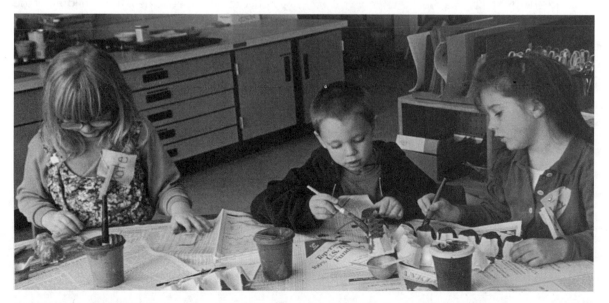

Centers and individualized instruction can happen when parents are involved with the classroom.

our own responsibilities." In the first instance, there is joy in the educational spirit. In the second, fear and avoidance are dominant.

Parents bring different attitudes into the home-school relationship. One parent may feel excitement and anticipation about a forthcoming visit to the school, whereas another may be struck with dread over a required conference. Parents come from diverse backgrounds. If their past school experiences were pleasant and successful, they are likely to enjoy visiting schools again. If their experiences were filled with failures and disappointments, whether real or imagined, the thought of school is depressing; if they do approach the school, it is with trepidation. When you recognize, understand, and respect parents' cultural and social backgrounds, you are more likely to succeed at bringing those parents into a partnership with the school.

Coupled with the parents' past experiences are current pressures. In some districts the burden of poverty will consume the parents. Parents concerned with mere subsistence have little energy left for self-fulfillment or for meeting their children's emotional and educational needs. Maslow's (1968) hierarchy of needs stresses that basic needs must be met before a person can climb to higher rungs of the ladder toward self-actualization. Parents contending with unemployment, inflation, and social change will need special understanding. "Humans of all ages get caught in a powerful web spun of two strong threads; the way they were treated in the past, and the way the present bears down on them" (Hymes, 1974, p. 16). The school must be a support system working cooperatively with the home rather than another agency viewing the parents as failures.

Add the parents' concerns for their children's welfare and you will recognize why school-home relationships can be either negative encounters or effective partnerships. Hymes (1974) eloquently described the parent-child-teacher relationship when he said that parents love their children, and if the teacher "feels this same love, then parents are your friends. Show your interest in a child and parents are on your side. Be casual, be off-handed, be cold toward the child and parents can never work closely with you. . . . To touch the child is to touch the parent. To praise the child is to praise the parent. To criticize the child is to hit at the parent. The two are two, but the two are one" (pp. 8–9).

Debilitating experiences with schools, feelings of inadequacy, poor achievement by children, and current pressures can cause some parents to stay away from the school. On the other hand, some parents tend to dominate and are compulsively involved with the schools. Between these two extremes are (a) parents who need encouragement to come to school, (b) parents who readily respond when invited, and (c) parents who are comfortable about coming to school and enjoy some involvement in the educational process (see Figure 4.1).

Each group requires a different response from the professional staff. The parents who tend to stay away will need time to overcome past negative experiences and learn to appreciate that the school can be trusted to help their children. If the school has an inviting and responsive climate, the three groups of parents in the middle ground will feel welcome. These groups, which encompass the largest portion of parents, will soon begin contributing to the school's activities. They can also form a supportive advocacy for future school plans.

Parents in the domineering group can also become positive assets. Let them lead by taking on a responsibility, such as fund-raising or organizing a social get-together. Offering a variety of tasks and different degrees of involvement assures parents that they may contribute according to their talents and available time and allows all of them to be comfortable about coming to school and enjoying involvement in the educational process.

| Parents who avoid schools like the plague | Parents who need encouragement to come to school | Parents who readily respond when invited to school | Parents who are comfortable and enjoy involvement in school | Parents who enjoy power and are overly active |

FIGURE 4.1 Parents respond to schools based on their past experiences and their current situations.

✇ THE CASE FOR IMPROVED RELATIONSHIPS

Schools have more contact with families than any other public agency. Almost every child from the age of 5 spends nine months a year, five days a week, five or six hours a day in school. When child care centers and preschools are included, the school-home-community relationship begins even earlier. Locally controlled schools can respond to the needs of the community. If schools and community join forces in a coordinated effort to support families and children, they can have an enormous effect. The school and home also have a natural opportunity to work together. With the community, they can achieve their goals for children.

Research

The 2001 Phi Delta Kappan/Gallup poll found that 51 percent of the respondents graded their own schools with either A's or B's. Those closest to the schools, the parents, graded the public schools even higher with 19 percent A's and 43 percent B's for a total of 62 percent A and B responses.

It seems that those who are most knowledgeable about their particular school district grade their schools higher than they grade schools in the nation as a whole. Only 23 percent gave grades of A and B in the national total.

The respondents also showed support of their schools by choosing to reform the system rather than changing to an alternative (Rose & Gallup, 2001).

In an extensive research project, Williams (1992) found both school personnel and parents concerned about the necessity of parent involvement in schools. He found that 86.8 percent of teachers and 92.1 percent of 2,300 principals believed teachers needed parent-involvement training.

In another survey (Harris & Associates, 1987), 75 percent of teachers wanted to have parents involved inside the school and 74 percent of parents wanted to be involved. The group who thought it did not have enough contact included teachers working in inner-city schools, parents of secondary students, and single parents who work full time. Strong home-school links strengthen teacher satisfaction and thus increase the likelihood of the teacher continuing in the profession (Harris & Associates). The results of the survey bring up the question of *who* is responsible for initiating and fostering parent-teacher interaction. It supports the findings of Williams (1992), who believed teachers need parent-involvement training.

Seefeldt (1985) called for parent involvement in which there is concern for the welfare of parents as well as children. She recommended that schools be sensitive to the needs of families, offer real support for families, and provide true collaboration between home and school. Parents' decision-making powers might include "decisions about the school's budget, selection of staff, and general operating procedures" (p. 102).

Epstein found that teachers who were leaders in parent-involvement practices enabled all parents, regardless of the parent's educational level, to be involved. These teachers asked parents to conduct learning activities at home, such as reading aloud, asking their children about the school day, playing games, visiting the classroom, going to the library, and helping children with their homework. Teachers who did not involve parents had attitudes that stereotyped less-educated single parents and low-socioeconomic parents (Epstein, 1986; Epstein & Dauber, 1991).

Family Involvement

Five types of involvement were suggested by Epstein and Dauber as a result of research in the Baltimore schools (Epstein & Dauber, 1991). They concluded that the schools have a basic responsibility to do the following:

1. Enable families to provide the skills and knowledge needed to help their children at each age level.

2. Communicate with families through notes, telephone calls, conferences, and other types of communication. Communication was also studied by Loucks (1992), and parents responded that parent-school communication could be strengthened by more opportunities in (a) one-on-one contact with school personnel, (b) participation in the curricula that their children experience, (c) joint problem solving between the school and home rather than by the school alone, (d) precise suggestions on how parents can help their children, and (e) more observations of children as they are involved in school activities. Students indicated that their parents were discouraged from being involved positively with the schools. Instead, they were contacted when there were discipline concerns or problems in the academic area. The students said they would feel better if their parents attended school functions, were used as volunteers, served on committees, and participated with the ongoing activities of the school.

3. Include parents as volunteers and assistants in the classrooms and other areas of school. Make it possible for parents to attend school functions (Epstein & Dauber, 1991). In 1997, 69 percent (73 percent of women, and 64 percent of men) of respondents to a Gallup poll said they would be willing to work as a volunteer without pay. The highest percentages were those with college degrees (73 percent) and those who were public school parents (78 percent) (Rose, Gallup, & Elam, 1997).

4. Guide parents so they can help their own children through monitoring, discussing, and helping with homework.

5. Involve parents in decision making. Provide training for them to communicate with other parents. Include parents in governance and advocacy. Encourage participation in PTO/PTA and advisory councils.

A sixth type of family involvement, which was not part of Epstein's original research, extends the involvement of the school to include the larger community. Draw on community resources, social agencies, health services, and businesses, and provide programs that give children and families the support that they need.

Parent involvement, parent education, and more community involvement in the support of families as they raise their children are three areas of challenge.

Strategies for Supporting and Involving Families

Kaufman (2001) describes a process to involve and support families. Start out by establishing "strong relationships between the center and the home," using empathy and patience to forge relationships. Families need to know that they and their ideas are respected (p. 83). Second, the family's concerns need to be validated without being judged. The following discussion between the family and center professional helps evaluate the options and possible appropriateness of action and assistance. Third, know the resources available and be able to recommend them and offer addresses and telephone numbers. If the parents have limited English skills, try to locate volunteers who can translate for them. Fourth, adapt communication to the parents. Recognize that some parents may have limited reading ability; others may not speak English well. Discuss in language that is easily understood. Kaufman also recommends methods of communication with parents including newsletters, open-door policy, greeting and seeing parents at drop-off and pick-up times. The final recommendation is the collaboration with other agencies such as Head Start ESL classes, GED programs, advocacy programs, and public schools (Kaufman, 2001).

Teachers who are leaders in parent-involvement practices enabled parents to be involved.

Public Response

In the 1992 Gallup Phi Delta Kappa poll, respondents showed recognition of society's needs and evidence of restructuring community responsibilities. It showed that most people (77 percent) favor using public school buildings for extended services in the community. Eighty-seven percent favored keeping the buildings open after hours on school days, 67 percent were in favor of keeping them open during weekends, and 72 percent wanted use of the buildings during vacations (Elam, Rose, & Gallup, 1992). This would make it possible for health and social services to use public school buildings as support centers for youth services.

In the same survey, respondents also believed that preschool programs would help low-socioeconomic children do better in schools. Seventy-four percent said that providing preschool programs would help either quite a lot or a great deal. Only 21 percent thought these programs would not help much or not help at all. Forty-nine percent were willing to pay more taxes to make this possible, and 64 percent were in favor of federally subsidized child care (Elam et al., 1992).

Private schools, and virtually all colleges and universities, plan many occasions to bring their alumni back to their campuses to keep them interested in the school. The public schools could adopt the same policy to their advantage, inviting not only alumni to attend such events but also members of the community who have attended schools in other areas.

Home-School Continuity

Continuity between home and school is a necessary and important support system for families today. One in five families has a single-parent mother; one in two children has both parents working outside the home. This was not the case 30 years ago. More than half of school-age children go home to empty homes or alternative child care. Families cannot afford to be caught in an adversarial position with the school. They need cooperation, support, and facilities that make it possible to supply their children with a stable environment. If you do not know their needs, you will not be able to respond to them.

A good way to improve relationships between school and home is to do a needs assessment or survey to determine what the families in the school area desire. The questionnaire in Figure 4.2 is just an example. If you know several of the parents or have access to the parents' addresses, asking them what topics they want or need included on the questionnaire would make the assessment more meaningful.

School schedules that involve split sessions or classes finishing at 2:30 p.m. and a lack of after-school programs are indicators that our society has little concern for the family. Tradition controls the time school is in session, as well as how school buildings are used.

The public is apparently in favor of having after-school programs. In a 1997 National Opinion Research Center poll, 77 percent of parents of primary-age children and 82 percent of parents of middle school students favored after-school programs (U.S. Department of Education, 1998b). This finding is similar to a 1988 Gallup poll that showed 70 percent of parents favoring before- and after-school programs. Forty-nine percent of those who favored such programs, however, believed they should be paid for by school taxes; 34 percent did not. Nearly half the respondents believed summer programs should also be offered. Community outreach to help families is a positive step toward achieving continuity.

Continuity needs to be a cooperative effort. Groups such as recreation program leaders, library services personnel, special after-school teachers, and artists in residence should be enlisted to help extend the school day to accommodate parents' schedules. Parents who are not employed outside the home could volunteer or be paid to help with before- and after-school programs. Enrichment activities, physical development, and social opportunities should be provided for children who have working parents and for others who wish to partake of the opportunities. The coordination of school programs with

PARENT QUESTIONNAIRE

1. What I want to know about the school:

	Very important	Somewhat	Not at all
1. What curriculum will my child have?			
2. How is the school organized?			
3. What is the procedure for seeing school personnel?			
4. If I have a problem with the school, not the class, whom do I see?			
5. How is reading taught?			
6. What books are used in the school?			
7. What books should I use with my child?			
8. How is mathematics taught?			
9. How should I help my child with math?			
10. Other			

2. How I would like to be involved with the school:

	Very interested	Somewhat	Not at all
1. Be a classroom volunteer			
2. Serve on policy committees			
3. Make games for the classroom			
4. Help with money-raising events			
5. Collect resources for the classroom			
6. Be a room parent			
7. Organize a volunteer program			
8. Share expertise or experiences			
9. Work in family resource room			
10. Other			

Comments: _____

FIGURE 4.2   This questionnaire is a simplified needs assessment of what parents want to know about the school and how they would like to be involved. Asking these questions at the beginning the year shows interest in the parents and can help the school plan meetings and activities.

social agencies, recreation departments, and other community resources will greatly enhance the chance of successful continuity.

Parent-School Collaboration

Not everyone in the school will be comfortable with increased parent-school collaboration. Epstein (1986) pointed out two conflicting theories. One encourages homes and schools to work together because they share the same goals for the students. The other theory argues that schools can achieve their goals to educate most efficiently when school and home remain separate, that "professional status is in jeopardy if parents are involved in activities that are typically the teacher's responsibilities" (p. 277).

Of course, most teachers are also parents. Their role confusion was dramatically illustrated at a workshop involving parents, teachers, and administrators. The participants were asked to raise their hands if they were parents. Almost every person in the room raised a hand. Suddenly the teachers and administrators were in their parental rather than professional roles. Teachers described how different their feelings were when their roles switched.

The emotional change between being a parent receiving services or being a professional responsible for the education of someone else's child was felt immediately. Before coming to the workshop, participants held varying views on parent involvement. Some believed in working with parents, some were already highly successful at parent involvement, and some wanted to keep parents at a respectable distance. As they experienced the change of roles, they recognized how trying to understand parents' feelings and concerns is a giant step toward creating effective home-school relationships.

Picturing parents as a group separated from the school sets up an artificial barrier. Parents are no special breed. We are the parents of the current generation of young people. To understand ourselves as parents is to begin to understand others. What makes us effective participants in home-school-community relationships are those same qualities that make others productive members of the home-school-community team.

≈ ROLES OF PARENTS, TEACHERS, AND ADMINISTRATORS

Roles of Parents

Within each school, parents may assume a variety of roles (see Figure 4.3). Most commonly, parents observe what the school does with their children in the educational process. But parents may also assume other roles simultaneously.

The room-parent, for example, who provides treats and creates parties, is an accessory or temporary volunteer. Volunteers can provide needed services, but their involvement is geared only to a specific time and task.

Increasingly, parents are serving as more regularly scheduled resources to the schools. Some parents spend a morning or a full day each week working in the resource center, developing materials and sharing with other parents. You may find others making books with children's stories or listening to children read and discussing ideas with them. Still others work as unpaid aides in the classroom.

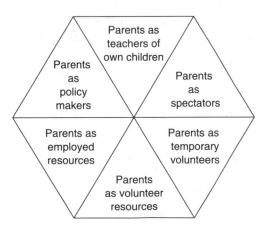

FIGURE 4.3   Possible roles for parents in schools.

Note: These roles for parents in schools are typical of those that emerge in the interaction of parents and schools. It is important to have parents involved as more than spectators.

Parents may also help make policies. Local school boards have been composed of community leaders charged with educational policy making for many years. Early control of schools was accomplished by local community leaders who were generally the elite of the area. At least 50 percent of the Parent Advisory Councils in Head Start must be composed of parents served by the program. Chapter 1 recommends parent involvement, including input into the program. With this representative membership, policy control has reached down to the grass roots of the constituency being served. The decisions of policy-making parents directly affect the schools their own children attend.

Collaborative decision making brings parents of children in the schools into the decision-making process. Also called site-based management, the process involves teachers and parents as well as the traditional mix of administrators, principals, and superintendent. Together they determine the needs of individual schools and make decisions and plans that they believe will make their school more effective. (Chapter 7 discusses site-based managed schools in more detail.)

Clearly, parents are teachers of their own children. There is now emerging an increasing awareness of the link between informal and formal instruction. Parents can enhance the informal education of their children by understanding the formal education process, although they are encouraged to teach in an informal manner. Daily incidental teaching of language and problem solving, for example, encourages development of intelligence in the young child. Infants learn as they listen, look, touch, and are touched. As the parent lets the child select socks that match the color of the child's shirt, the preschooler is learning color discrimination and matching. Setting the table and putting away the dishes involve classification of articles. Programs to help parents in their role as the child's early educator have been successful. Parents who are aware of their roles in the educational development of their adolescent children promote the successful completion of their formal education. Parents are the one continuous force in the education of their children from birth to adulthood.

The Teacher's Role in Parent Involvement

The teacher is central to parent involvement in the educational process. Teacher roles include facilitator, teacher, counselor, communicator, program director, interpreter, resource developer, and friend. These roles are illustrated through the activities described later in this chapter and in Chapter 5—for example, parent-teacher conferences, volunteer programs, and program development.

Teacher Attitudes and Feeling

The school needs personnel who accept parents, but sometimes teachers and administrators are unaware of how they feel toward parents. The questions in Figure 4.4 were developed to help teachers assess their attitudes toward parents.

It is also helpful for teachers to discuss their work with another person, ask a close colleague to evaluate apparent values, and compare their real with their ideal values. This will help teachers focus on their attitudes about working with parents. There are no right or wrong answers; the purpose is to recognize values and attitudes.

Classroom Management

One of the issues involved in education today is the concern about classroom management. If a room is chaotic, the children cannot learn, and the teacher cannot teach. If parents and teachers work together and communication is ongoing, parents can help teachers in their role of classroom manager. If the expectations of the teacher are for children to be responsible and learn and if the expectations of the parent are for the same, consistency between the two can be very helpful. Regular contact with parents whose children have trouble staying on task may actually save time. Sometimes teachers spend an exorbitant amount of time correcting a child when plans could be made to help the child use time effectively. New programs on conflict control, resolution, alternatives, and mediation can be used to help children recognize how they can control emotions that result in outbursts and disobedience.

"Defend our practices, or work together toward a common goal?" (National Association for the Education of Young Children [NAEYC], 2000 p. 86). An interesting study resulted from an ethical dilemma in the November 1999 issue of *Young Children,* NAEYC's journal. It described Aaron, a child who was successful in all areas of his schoolwork. His parents, however, did not think that he was challenged enough and wanted him to spend part of each day in the first grade. The article asked for readers to respond to which principles and ideals of NAEYC's *Code of Ethical Conduct* applied to this situation. Two principles relate to the situation: P-2.2—"We shall inform families of program philosophy, policies, and personnel qualifications, and explain why we teach as we do—which should be in accordance with our ethical responsibilities to children"; and P-2.4—"We shall involve families in significant decisions affecting their child." In the responses to the ethical dilemma, P-2.2 was referred to a number of times, but P-2.4 was never mentioned. Thus the title of the NAEYC article. Parents and teachers need to work together toward a common goal.

	How You See Yourself		How You Wish You Were	
As a Teacher I . . .	Yes	No	Yes	No
1. Feel that parents are more work than help.	❑	❑	❑	❑
2. Feel tense when parents enter my room.	❑	❑	❑	❑
3. Prefer to work alone.	❑	❑	❑	❑
4. Compare brothers and sisters from the same family.	❑	❑	❑	❑
5. Feel threatened by parents.	❑	❑	❑	❑
6. View parents as a great resource.	❑	❑	❑	❑
7. Believe that low-income children have parents who do not care.	❑	❑	❑	❑
8. Enjoy working with several outside persons in the classroom.	❑	❑	❑	❑
9. Have prejudiced feelings about certain groups.	❑	❑	❑	❑
10. Feel that parents let children watch too much television.	❑	❑	❑	❑
11. Feel that parents are not interested in their children.	❑	❑	❑	❑
12. Work better with social distance between the parent and myself.	❑	❑	❑	❑
13. Believe parents who let their children come to school in inappropriate clothing are irresponsible.	❑	❑	❑	❑
14. Feel that a close working relationship with parents is necessary for optimal student growth.	❑	❑	❑	❑
15. Am pleased when all the parents are gone.	❑	❑	❑	❑
16. Anticipate parent conferences with pleasure.	❑	❑	❑	❑
17. Feel that parents have abdicated the parental role.	❑	❑	❑	❑
18. Enjoy working with parents.	❑	❑	❑	❑

FIGURE 4.4 Teachers can assess how they feel about collaboration with parents by answering these questions.

	As a Teacher I . . .			As a Teacher I Believe That I Should . . .	
	Always	Sometimes	Never	Essential	Not Important
1. Listen to what parents are saying.	❑	❑	❑	❑	❑
2. Encourage parents to drop in.	❑	❑	❑	❑	❑
3. Give parents an opportunity to contribute to my class.	❑	❑	❑	❑	❑
4. Have written handouts that enable parents to participate in the classroom.	❑	❑	❑	❑	❑
5. Send newsletters home to parents.	❑	❑	❑	❑	❑
6. Contact parents before school begins in the fall.	❑	❑	❑	❑	❑
7. Listen to parents 50% of the time during conferences.	❑	❑	❑	❑	❑
8. Contact parents when a child does well.	❑	❑	❑	❑	❑
9. Allow for differences among parents.	❑	❑	❑	❑	❑
10. Learn what objectives parents have for their children.	❑	❑	❑	❑	❑
11. Learn about interests and special abilities of students.	❑	❑	❑	❑	❑
12. Visit students in their home.	❑	❑	❑	❑	❑
13. Show parents examples of the student's work.	❑	❑	❑	❑	❑
14. Enlist parent volunteers for my classroom.	❑	❑	❑	❑	❑
15. Ensure a caring environment.	❑	❑	❑	❑	❑
16. Encourage both mother and father to attend conferences.	❑	❑	❑	❑	❑
17. Make parents feel comfortable coming to school.	❑	❑	❑	❑	❑
18. Include parents in educational plans for their children.	❑	❑	❑	❑	❑
19. Try to be open and honest with parents.	❑	❑	❑	❑	❑
20. Send notes home with children.	❑	❑	❑	❑	❑
21. Include students along with parents during conferences.	❑	❑	❑	❑	❑
22. Let parents sit at their child's desk during back-to-school night.	❑	❑	❑	❑	❑
23. Keep both parents informed if parents are separated.	❑	❑	❑	❑	❑
24. Consider parents as partners in the educational process.	❑	❑	❑	❑	❑

FIGURE 4.4 *continued*

The Administrator's Role in Parent Involvement

School climate—the atmosphere in school—reflects the principal's leadership style. Five aspects of school-parent interaction are affected by this leadership. First, the *spirit* of the school and the enthusiasm of its staff reflect the administrator's role as morale builder. Supportive guidance, with freedom to develop plans based on individual school needs, allows the principal to function with productive autonomy. The principal builds staff morale by enabling staff members to feel positive, enthusiastic, and secure in their work with children and parents.

With the increase in violence in the schools and the recognition of bullying in its many forms (see Chapter 10), it is imperative for administrators to recognize the signs of bullying and the lack of a caring environment in their schools. It is necessary to provide an environment for children in which they feel safe and an accepted member of the school.

A second leadership role, *program designer,* involves implementing the educational program. The principal needs to recognize the importance of home-school-community relationships in the success of the educational program and strive toward implementation of such a working relationship. If the principal allows teachers the autonomy to work with parents, using volunteers and aides in the development of individualized curricula, the school is on its way to an effective program of parent involvement.

The administrator's third role requires the development of an effective *principal-parent relationship.* The principal determines whether the school atmosphere makes parents feel welcome. Besides influencing the general spirit and morale of the school, the principal is responsible for maintaining an open-door policy, scheduling open houses, providing and equipping resource areas for parents, arranging parent education meetings, developing parent workshops and in-service meetings, and supporting the PTA or PTO.

Fourth, the principal serves as a *program coordinator.* Individual teachers may develop unique programs using the talents of parents, but the achievement of continuity requires the principal's coordination of parent-involvement programs.

Finally, the principal has a *leadership* role in developing site-based management and leading advisory councils and decision-making committees. This new role needs strong leadership ability to encourage and enable teachers, staff, and parents to work together and develop an educational program specific to their community's needs.

In order to achieve the roles, an administrator who uses collaborative or shared decision making with other members of the staff and with the community, including parents, has others who have come to the same decisions and who will be comfortable with and supportive of the decisions.

Administrators need to be able to diffuse anger by listening, treating others with respect, paraphrasing the issues, and responding with plans for what will be done (Meadows & Saltzman, 2000).

Ways to Enhance School-Home-Community Relations

Why does one school have superb relationships with parents and community whereas a nearby school does not? Most often the leadership of the administration and individual teachers makes the difference. Their leadership has made the school responsive to the parents and the parents supportive of the school. Schools usually do not change overnight, but gradually the school, home, and community can become united in a joint effort.

Many of the techniques geared to improve home-school-community relationships are already in place. This chapter is a reminder to keep doing the positive activities that have helped in the past, increase attention to making a partnership, and change negative attitudes. It focuses on five areas: (a) school atmosphere and involvement of parents, (b) school activities and resources for parents, (c) contact early in the school year, (d) meeting the needs of the school area, and (e) volunteers.

Chapter 5 focuses on communication and the need for positive communication with parents. One-way and two-way communications can increase contact between family and school. Communication ranges from the simplest note sent home by the teacher to a complicated news report in the media. Parents want to know what is happening at school and are interested in program development and curriculum decisions. This chapter, along with effective communication discussed in Chapter 5, can turn a school around.

School Atmosphere and Acceptance of Parents

Schools let parents know how welcome they are. The attitude of the school personnel is reflected in the way parents are met in the principal's office, the friendly or unfriendly greetings in the hall, and the offerings in the school. If visitors walk into the school and the secretaries ignore them for a period of time, the body language and the attitudes reflect that the school would prefer that they not visit. If schools want to collaborate with parents, they must make sure the office is staffed by people who can make a visitor feel welcome. This, along with positive school policies and services, indicates whether the school recognizes families as important.

Restructuring of schools is only one aspect of restructuring needs. Employment, elimination of discrimination, and the opportunity for all to participate meaningfully in a democratic society will be necessary before schools can meet their challenge. Davies (1990) points out that "profound educational reform requires a dramatic social, political, and economic transformation reaching far beyond education institutions alone" (p. 68). He suggests that the educational change will probably occur in "small stages, gradually and painfully, with many starts and stops" (p. 68). But these changes in schools will be only one aspect of change in the nation.

Situation

"I thought when we moved to this school district that Josi would receive an excellent education, but she is so upset over the way the children in her room are treating her that she cries when she comes home from school. I have to force her to go to school in the mornings. I wish we hadn't moved. Having a larger house just isn't worth the pain," Susan mournfully told her friend, Elizabeth.

"What's going on?" Elizabeth asked.

"The school just doesn't care about my child," Susan said. "I've talked with the principal several times, and I go visit every week and talk with the teacher, but she doesn't respond to my concerns at all. Miss Block, her homeroom teacher, thinks it is just natural for children to have a hard time in a new school. I think the children pick on Josi because she is small and defenseless, but Miss Block insists that Josi stands up for herself and just complains because she wants attention. She thinks Josi enjoys this attention. Oh, she also says that her self-esteem in the new school is not strong yet and that she doesn't have any friends, but that will come if we just let the children work it out for themselves."

"That attitude must really be hard on you and Josi," Elizabeth replied.

"It makes me angry! I think that the principal and teacher hate me and my child," Susan said, her voice trembling.

1. Could this situation have been avoided? How?

2. What can the teacher and parent do to turn Susan's concerns into a collaborative effort rather than a confrontation?

3. What could Susan do to help Josi?

4. What could be done in the classroom to eliminate the concern?

Open-Door Policy

An open-door policy is more an attitude of the school than a series of activities, although periodic open houses, forums, coffee hours, and interactive seminars can add to the receptive climate of the school. Parents are welcome at any time in schools with an open-door policy. Schools that have unpleasant announcements rather than welcome signs on their doors or that require appointments to visit the principal, teachers, or classrooms are saying, "Come only by request or when you want to discuss a problem." Schools and parents need to avoid the problem-conference syndrome. Dialogue between parents and schools should occur before a problem develops. This can be done through coffee klatches and seminars. Parents can give suggestions and get answers; school personnel can ask questions and clarify school procedures and curriculum long before an issue develops into a problem. By establishing two-way communication early, the climate is set for parents and school to work together on behalf of, rather than suffer a confrontation over, a child.

Parent Advisory Councils and Site-Based Management

All schools can establish parent advisory councils. Title I components establish two parent advisory councils, a districtwide council, and a local council for each involved school. The councils give input on the planning, implementation, and evaluation of the Title I program. Head Start and Home Start have had participatory advisory councils since the 1960s, but public schools were not required to have such parent participation until 1974. Fifty percent of council members should be selected from among parents of students receiving Title I services.

The success of parent advisory councils in Head Start, Home Start, and Title I programs has demonstrated that parents can be involved in policy and decision making in a meaningful and constructive way. Although schools can implement a parent advisory council related to their own situation, they can also learn from the Title I experience, in which schools actively solicit parents' participation and give them the information and training needed to become effective policy and decision makers.

Site-based management has been established in schools across the nation. Still in its infancy, the site-based management theory lies in the belief that those closest to an issue are the ones who can make decisions and find the most appropriate answer. Parents are on the team, which includes teachers, school personnel, and community representatives. Usually led by the principal, the team determines the best way to administer the school, develop curriculum, and respond to the needs of the students and community.

Family Center

Parents need a place within the school where they can meet, share information, work, and relax. Ideally, parents will have a room similar to that traditional haven, the teachers' lounge, as well as a space within each classroom.

The family room can be equipped and stocked by the parents. Typical items include a sofa, comfortable chairs, table, coffeepot, microwave, telephone, typewriter, computer, bulletin board, storage area, supplies, and reading materials. If a room is not available, a small area shared in a workroom, an area in an unused hall, or a large closet would give minimal space. In each, both storage space and a bulletin board for notices should be available.

Teachers can help parents develop a base in each classroom. An extra desk, a corner, or a bulletin board lets parents claim a spot within their child's classroom. If the area contains information on current assignments, new curriculum ideas, activities to be used at home, taped messages from the teacher, or a display of children's work, parents will make a point to stop by. Parents of preschool, kindergarten, and elementary children can use the corner to find activities that will continue the educational experience in the home or to talk or work with individual children or small groups. Teachers can use the corner for short conferences with parents.

The parents' room implies that parents are expected to be in the building. There is a place for them to stop and a base from which they can reach out in their involvement.

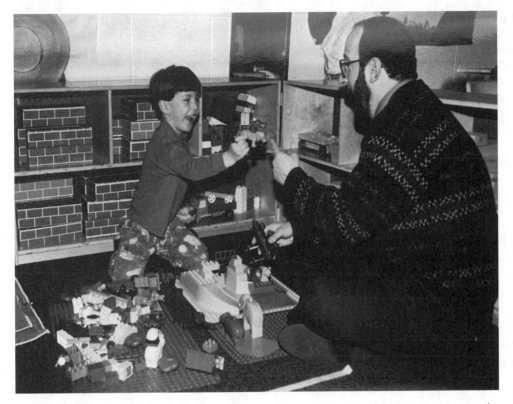

Schools should let parents know they are welcome. The participation of parents can give teachers the opportunity to expand their activities and offerings.

� SCHOOL ACTIVITIES AND RESOURCES

The following school activities and resources encourage parent participation.

Back-to-School Nights

A time-tested school event, the back-to-school night has proved very successful. Teachers often complain that the parents who need to learn about the educational program are the very ones who do not show up, but this type of evening program nevertheless has improved home-school relationships from preschool through secondary schools. Parents enjoy sitting in the desk normally occupied by their child, viewing the curriculum materials, observing the displays in the room, and listening to the teacher. Parents expect the teacher to tell them about school programs. Following a presentation of the course objectives, there is usually a period for questions and answers. Back-to-school night is not a time for talking extensively about individual children, although the teacher should identify which parents belong to which students. It is a good time to set up a special conference if you have concern about the progress of a student.

A variation on the back-to-school night is the Saturday morning session. Some working parents have difficulty attending evening programs, and offering an alternative time can increase parental participation. The Saturday morning activity can be a workshop with parents participating in their children's normal activities, or it can be a presentation-discussion similar to the evening session. Saturday morning programs can become a meaningful educational experience for both children and families by involving a series of parent-child programs.

Alumni Events

Private schools have long used alumni activities and events to keep their graduates as members of a cohesive group. Public schools that encourage alumni to come back for special events also develop alumni support for the school. Alumni can help with school morale, as well as with developing programs that tie the school with business, industry, or social services. Strong alumni can rise to the occasion and support the school in many areas.

Sharing Reading

A practice that has had promising results is inviting parents, community celebrities, and school personnel to share a book they enjoy with the children in the class. The book, of course, needs to be one that interests the developmental level of the children and short enough to be read in one session. Parents enjoy the opportunity of coming to the class to read a story to the children during sharing time. Principals can use this as an opportunity to get to know children better. Afterward children will be able to relate to the principal as someone who spent time reading with them. Children are excited to meet a celebrity who comes to share with them. Following the visits, letters may be written to thank the contributor.

Parent Education Groups

Parent education groups are discussed in detail in Chapter 6. Meetings can range from a one-day workshop to an organized series of workshops throughout the year. Individual teachers use the parent group meetings for in-service training of volunteers in their rooms, dissemination of information to parents, or presentation of programs that answer parents' needs. Parents become real resources for the school through parent educa-

tion meetings, which teach them to become effective tutors and school volunteers.

Parent education may be offered whenever the need arises. The school can have a list of workshops available or determine the needs of the community. If a telephone answering machine is available, parents could call any time for school-related information. Besides workshops, articles or individual conferences can be arranged to help the parents.

Parent education meetings offered by schools are viable for those with children at any age level. The parent of a young child may be interested in child development, enrichment activities, and promotion of creativity. Parents of children of all ages are concerned about drugs and alcohol. Parent education groups, allowing parents to meet and discuss common concerns, are an essential part of the educational program. Interestingly, middle and high schools have very few parent education groups, but the parents of these students are vitally concerned about their children's futures. Manning (1992) suggests that education for parents of adolescents must focus on three factors. First, they need to understand the developmental level of their youth. Early adolescence is a "unique time between childhood and adolescence; 10- to 14-year-olds represent a highly diverse group who demonstrate characteristics of both children and adults" (p. 25). Second, parents need to treat their young adolescent appropriately, recognizing the relationship between the child's development and behavior. The third issue in parent education involves the transition to middle school. An appropriate parent-education curriculum would include adolescent development, adolescent behavior, and the transition to a new school. There are training materials written especially for the young adolescent, but Manning suggests an individualized program related to the community and parents might be even more beneficial.

Parents of adolescents need information but, just as important, they need the support system that a parent education group offers. If parents of adolescents can discuss problems and understand that other parents have the same concerns, they can cope with pressures better. An advocacy group for children and parents can be formed. Responsibilities and guidelines for students, determined by parents and students in a specific community, can support parents in the rearing of their children. Schools need to offer parent education. In doing so, they strengthen parent-school-community relationships.

Parent Networks

Parent networks may form naturally out of parent education groups, but many parents with no interest in parent education might want to join a network group of parents. Now, more than ever, parents need to cooperate with one another to handle the pressures of the social world. Drugs, alcohol, and teenage pregnancies hurt many school children. Parents in a network can cooperate to approach a problem from two vantage points. First, they can advocate for better facilities for students. Young people need places to gather, socialize, and have fun. They need programs after school that enrich their lives and give them an opportunity to belong to a group. Second, parents can develop a code that all families can support as a guide for their children. In this way, the students may not feel as if they are the only ones who have to follow rules. The community will be united in its support of children.

School-Home Activity Packets

Parents appreciate knowing activities and enrichment ideas that support the school curricula. Many teachers make calendars that describe what the child will be learning at school. Sending home packets with activities that support the curriculum enhances parents' involvement in their children's education. The activities need to be relevant to the curriculum within each class and each school. These packets may be supported by workshops in which parents learn about the activities, or they may be ongoing informational packets related to what the child is learning at school.

One workshop could be developed in which parents make tote bags their children can use to bring ideas and materials for the activities to be done at home. At this workshop the ideas behind the take-home activity kits could be explained and discussed. Research that supports family involvement can be shared (Binkley, 1988; Boyer, 1991; Epstein & Dauber, 1991). Some families have difficulty completing home-school activities. Communicate with them; develop quick activities for parents who do not have a lot of time, and try to encourage interactions between parent and child that are positive and fun. Some early childhood classrooms send home a stuffed teddy bear, asking the family to include the bear in their weekend and then write a story about the bear's adventures. Other schools send home fish, gerbils, or other live animals to be cared for during break. These activities are similar to those in school-home activity packets, but the kits usually include many educational activities, with some, but not all, related to the family. For example, children might measure their parents' height, design the week's menu, plan a garden, calculate the number of times each person can jump while playing jump rope, or write a story about their family. Think about the children and families with whom you work. Recognize their interests and their needs, and plan how to organize the school-home activities.

1. School-home activity packets should relate to the curricula.

2. Activities should be interesting and enjoyable for the parent and child.

3. The packets should include any special materials needed to complete the activity, unless the materials are common to the homes in your area.

4. Send home clear instructions; be available to answer questions by telephone.

5. Stress that the activities are to be enjoyed; if they cause stress rather than a positive interaction, do not insist that they be completed.

6. Ask parents to complete an evaluation form that is included with the instructions.

7. If the activity kit has permanent equipment, make sure that it is returned the following day.

School Programs and Workshops

Remember when the introduction of "modern math" made it impossible for some parents to help their children with homework? Parents in that predicament appreciated workshops that explained the new terminology and processes. Schools can offer programs and workshops to the community with the same success. Parents from the community can plan and implement some of the workshops; speakers can be obtained; projects can be started.

A project in which parents make books of their children's work can be a great success and also create remembrances to be kept for years. Simple construction-paper books, as well as hardback books, can be developed. Books containing stories and poems composed by parents or children can be placed in the library and classroom for all students to use.

Try to arrange alternate times to offer workshops. If you offer meetings during the day, in the evening, and on Saturdays, parents will be able to come to the ones that fit their schedules.

District or School Conferences

Professionals go to conferences to gain information and be stimulated to try something new. Why not have the same kind of conference for parents? Instead of a workshop, plan a half-day or full-day conference where teachers and other professionals hold sessions for parents and community personnel to attend. These sessions could include such subjects as phonics, family math, whole language, music and movement, art, language arts, social studies, science, and computers.

School Projects

Enlist parent help if you plan to add to the playground or build a reading loft in your classroom.

Most parents enjoy contributing their time for something permanent. Children will be proud that their parents helped build the jungle gym or plant the elm tree in the school yard. Saturday sessions give ample time to develop, plan, and build. Many fathers find this the most comfortable way to contribute to the school. Working on a project can start a relationship that brings them into a partnership with the school.

PTO or PTA

The tradition of parent-teacher associations (PTAs) extends back to the 1890s. Their influence on parent-school relationships has been demonstrated over the years. The PTA publishes material for parents and strives for parent-school cooperation. Many parent-teacher groups, generally called parent-teacher organizations (PTOs), do not join the national PTA but have similar structure and interaction with the schools. Both PTAs and PTOs can serve as avenues toward greater parent-school interaction.

Fairs, Carnivals, and Suppers

Traditionally the PTO or PTA sponsors spaghetti suppers, potluck dinners, dinner theaters, or similar activities that promote a community spirit, give families a night of fun together, and usually increase the treasury. Parents and children flock to school to attend a carnival produced by parents and school staff. Money earned is generally spent on materials or equipment for the school program.

Exchanges

Children grow; toys get tiresome; books are read. Why not have an exchange? A popular exchange is to have children bring boots, heavy jackets, and raincoats to school to be traded or sold. Boots seldom wear out before they're outgrown, so a boot exchange works very well. Toys can also be exchanged. How often have you seen toys sit for months without being used? Some schools have children bring two toys, one for exchange and one to give to another child. Children swap the toy they brought for a different one.

Children also tire of some books and can exchange their old ones for books they have not read. A parent volunteer checks in the books and issues tickets to be used to "buy" another one. Children look through the books until they find a book they want and then use the tickets to buy it.

Learning Centers

Parents or volunteers from the community can be put in charge of learning centers. Use the resource room to furnish ideas and supplies for parents, or have a workshop to demonstrate how to plan and prepare a learning center. Learning centers can include, for example:

- A place for games
- A reading center
- A center for writing and making books
- A puzzle center
- A center for problem-solving activities
- A science area
- A talk-and-listen center
- A place for music and tapes
- A weaving center
- An art project center

Rules and regulations for using the center should be posted.

Telephone Tutor

With call-forwarding, which is available in most communities, the school can set up a tutor aid program through telephone calls in the evening. Volunteers or teachers can answer the telephone in the afternoon at the school. Later calls can be forwarded to the homes of a volunteer or paid aide working with the children that night. In a well-coordinated program the volunteer could know what curriculum is being covered in the class. If the entire district uses the telephone tutor, special numbers could be assigned for mathematics and language arts.

If call-forwarding is not available, a telephone answering machine could direct students to help by listing the names and phone numbers of tutors on call for that night. An excellent way to draw attention to the needs of the school district is to enlist important people in the community to serve as volunteer tutors. Their leadership will provide publicity and credibility to the volunteer program.

Resource Room

When parents see they can contribute to a project that has obvious benefits for their children, some will become actively involved. A resource room can be beneficial to both school and parents. Resource materials located in an empty room, a storage closet, the corner of a room, or a metal cabinet can be a great help to teachers. Involve parents in developing a resource center by holding a workshop to describe and discuss the idea. Brainstorm with parents and other teachers on ideas that might be significant for your school. Parents can take over after the workshop to design, stock, and run the center. Later, as assistants in the classroom, they will make use of it. They can help supply the center with articles on teaching, ideas and materials for games, and recycled materials to use in activities.

Articles on Teaching

Parents and community volunteers check old magazines related to teaching and classify useful articles according to subject and student age level. These are filed for use by teachers and aides. In searching for and classifying the articles, parents learn a great deal about teaching activities for home and school so the exercise is beneficial for the parent and the school.

Games

Parents check books, magazines, and commercial catalogs for ideas for games and adapt them to the school's needs. Volunteers make universal game boards for reading, spelling, and math from poster board or tag board. Felt markers are used to make lines and note directions; games are decorated with artwork, magazine cutouts, or stickers. Game materials should be laminated or covered with clear plastic.

Recycled Materials

Volunteers collect, sort, and store materials for classroom teachers. Items such as egg cartons, wood scraps, wallpaper books, cardboard tubes, felt, fabric remnants, and plastic food holders are used for many activities. Egg cartons, for example, can be used to cover a dragon, make a caterpillar, hold buttons for classification activities, and hold tempera paint for dry mixing. Milk cartons are used for making items from simple computers to building blocks. Science activities are enriched by a collection of machines, for example, motors, radios, computers, clocks, and typewriters. The articles can be used as they are or taken apart and rebuilt. Recycling is limited only by lack of imagination.

Libraries

A collection of magazines and books can be useful to parents or teachers in the development of teaching aids—such as games and learning activities—or for information on how children learn. From ideas therein, a toy lending library, an activity lending library, a book and magazine library, or a video lending library can be developed. Items can be checked out for a week or two. Checkout and return are supervised by parent volunteers.

Toy Lending Library

The toy lending library is developed with educational toys for young children (Nimnicht & Brown, 1972) or with a collection of toys for older children. The toys for young children can be built and collected by parents. Toys for older children can be collected from discarded toys left over after the toy exchange, or they can be built by parents and children.

Activity Lending Library

Games and activities developed by parents and children can be checked out for a week or two.

Book and Magazine Library

Discarded magazines and books can be collected and used to build a comprehensive lending library. Professional magazines have many articles on child development, education, and learning activities. Booklets distributed by numerous organizations can also be loaned. Refer to the Appendix for lists of organizations that handle pertinent books. Pamphlets and articles cut from magazines can be stapled to file folders and loaned to parents. To keep track of the publications, glue a library card pocket in each book or on each folder. Make a card that states the author and title of the publication, with lines for borrowers to sign their names. As each is taken, have the borrower sign the card and leave it in the card file. When the publication is returned, the name is crossed out, and the card is returned to the pocket.

Video Lending Library

Videotapes made by teachers to illustrate their lessons on math, social studies, language arts, art, physical education, music, and other subjects or activities can be very helpful to parents. Homework or "homefun" assignments can be explained on the videos. Teachers can also share creative activities that families would enjoy together. This would be especially beneficial during breaks or weekends.

Actual classes can also be the subject of videos so that parents can see their child at work or play during the school hours. This type of video is often used to accompany parent-teacher conferences, but could also be available in the family resource room. Selected videos and videos of student activities would offer a look at students at school; homefun or homework assignments; educational movies; videos on educational programs such as language, a writer's workshop, mathematics, geography, or science; and age-appropriate movies for entertainment.

Summer Vacation Activities

Parents can keep students, particularly elementary-age children, from losing academic gains during the summer. Teachers should "let parents know their help is not just incidental but vital to their child's success" (Casanova, 1987, p. 21).

Research shows that the parents who are involved by teachers become more positive about the teachers and rate the teachers higher in interpersonal skills and teaching ability. The most significant feature of parent-school involvement is providing activities for the parent to use with the child (Epstein, 1986; Epstein & Dauber, 1991).

Casanova (1987) suggested that teachers identify children who will be in their class the next fall and offer the parents simple suggestions, such as going to the library and reading stories. This is a step toward becoming acquainted with the parents in a positive manner before the child comes into your group.

Teachers should also offer suggestions to their departing class as a farewell gift to the parents and children. Choose the activities carefully. Casanova (1987) cautioned, "Remember that summer vacation provides children with a break from school routines. Try to structure activities that strengthen children's thinking skills in a natural setting" (p. 21). Children might plan the meals for a week, using math to estimate costs and quantities and knowledge about nutrition to balance the meals.

Based on Epstein's study of parent involvement, Berliner (1987) suggested that parents of all children be involved in summer tutoring, reading to children, listening to children, playing learning games, and discussing stories. "Teachers should consider a program of parental involvement in at-home learning activities as a way to arrest summer drop-off of students' skill levels" (p. 21).

� PARENTS AS RESOURCES

Parents should be asked early in the year if they have any talents or experiences they would like to share with classes. Parents might share information about their careers, or they might have a hobby that would spark student interest or supplement learning programs. Storytelling is an art that is often overlooked. Invite some senior citizens to tell about their childhoods. The resources in the community are unlimited.

Book Publishing

One of the most beneficial activities that has developed from the emphasis on reading, writing, and writing workshops is the opportunity for parents to be involved in helping children publish their own books. The activity may be done at home or at school. Some schools have the equipment that allows the parent to volunteer to be a book publisher. The child may develop a story during a writing workshop period, a session on whole language, or traditional reading and writing sessions. After the story is completed, it can be published with or without editing, although editing helps the child learn conventional spelling and grammar in a positive situation. If parents are available, they can help with the process. The following steps are usually taken:

1. The story is written during a writing workshop or (for the younger child) the story is dictated to the parent.

2. The story is edited by the student, by the student and the parent, or by the parent alone. In some classes an editing panel is established and students edit together.

3. The story is typed on a computer or typewriter by the student or parent. If the story is to be published in handwritten form, this step is eliminated. Copies of the stories may be made on a copy machine.

4. If the book is going to be handled and read by many students, the pages should be laminated. A laminating machine or clear contact paper can help make the book permanent.

5. The book is bound. Many schools have spiral binding equipment available for the parent to use. In other schools, binding may be done by simply stapling the pages together and covering the book with heavy paper. Traditional bookbinding can also be accomplished by parents. A

bookbinding workshop would show parents how to sew the pages together and make the outside cover. The outside sheet between the cover and the inside pages is a plain sheet of construction paper. The construction paper is glued to the outside cover. Depending on the material used, the outside cover can also be laminated.

6. The completed works should then be recognized and shared. Some schools have complete libraries of children's books displayed in the front halls or rooms. Others have classes that keep their published books in their own rooms. One school has the books circulate from room to room with an insert that allows children to write that they have read the book and to add a complimentary comment. The young writer receives recognition for the work!

Career Day

Plan a day or a series of days when parents and community volunteers come in and explain their careers. Rather than have parents talk to the whole class, let them work at a center. Have them explain their careers, the pros and cons, the necessary skills, and the satisfaction obtained from their work. If feasible, the parents can provide some activities the children could do related to the career. For example, a carpenter could bring in tools, demonstrate their use, and let the children make a small project, supervised by the carpenter and an aide or another parent.

Talent Sharing

Let parents tell stories, sing folk songs, lead a creative dramatics project, or share another talent. You might persuade some to perform before the class; some may wish to work with a few children at a time and let the children be involved. Some parents may have a collection or a hobby to share. Quilting is popular and could be followed by a lesson in stitchery. Basket making, growing orchids, stamp collecting—all provide opportuni-

ties for enriching the classroom learning experiences. Bring those educational and fun lessons out to enjoy.

▧ PARENTS AS PARTNERS IN EDUCATION AT HOME

Reading at home throughout the year should be encouraged. Figures 4.5 and 4.6 illustrate a way to get parents involved in a home reading program. First, a letter is sent to parents describing the program (Figure 4.5). An explanation could also be given at back-to-school night or during a workshop. After the children read a book, they color in a book on the sheet sent home with the letter. When all the books on the sheet are colored in, a certificate is awarded (Figure 4.6). Each teacher sends home a list of books that are appropriate for the child to read. Bookmarks with the titles of books related to the age of the child are a good idea. In addition, books from the school library can be checked out and taken home.

▧ CONTACTS EARLY IN THE SCHOOL YEAR

Many teachers have found that early communication is well worth the time it takes, even during summer vacation. It is quite common for kindergarten teachers to invite the new kindergarten class and their parents to a spring orientation meeting. Generally, these functions are scheduled in the hope that the strangeness of school will diminish and that, as a result, subsequent entry into kindergarten will be more pleasant. Just as important is the message to the parents that the school cares. This idea can be carried over into other levels of education with results that are just as gratifying.

Letters in August

Some teachers send letters, with pictures of themselves enclosed, to each new student coming to their classes. The student and parents learn the

[School Letterhead]

Dear Parents,

I would like to invite you and your child to participate in
Read-Aloud Month during October. This statewide project is
sponsored by the Colorado Council of the International
Reading Association. The purpose is to encourage parents and children to read aloud
together. Children who are read to become better readers—it's a fact!

Each student who participates in Read-Aloud Month will be given a time sheet to take
home. This will be used to record time you or other adults spend reading aloud to your
child. For every 15 minutes of read-aloud time, your child may color one book
on the time sheet.

To successfully complete this project, all the characters on the time sheet must be
colored in by the end of October. Each child who completes the time sheet will receive a
certificate rewarding participation in the project.

Setting aside time to read with your child helps your child learn and develop an
interest in reading. Take a few minutes each day to share the joy of reading with
your child!

Sincerely,

*P.S. I'm also sending home a bookmark, an annotated bibliography with suggestions for good
books to read aloud, and a Join the Read-Aloud Crowd poster for your refrigerator door or family
bulletin board. Be sure to read the suggestions on the back of the poster.*

FIGURE 4.5   Encouraging parents to be involved in their child's reading is a positive way to accomplish good read-ing habits and communicate with parents.

Source: Printed with permission. Colorado Council International Reading Association.

FIGURE 4.6 Attractive certificates, suggested books, and posters highlight the importance of reading.

Source: Art by Richard Florence.

teacher's identity and know that the teacher cares enough to write. A good rapport between teacher and home is established before school begins.

Neighborhood Visits

Rather than waiting until the regular conference period arrives or a problem arises, teachers should contact each parent early in the year. Visits to the neighborhood are excellent ways to meet parents.

Block Walks

Try a block walk while the weather is warm and sunny. Map the location of all your students' homes (this may be a class project) and divide the area into blocks. Schedule a series of block walks, and escort the children living in each block area to their homes on a selected day. Have the students write letters or notes in advance indicating that you will visit a particular block. Choose an alternate day in case of rain. On the appointed day, walk or ride the bus to the chosen block. Meet the parents outside and chat with them about school. You may also accumulate some curriculum materials such as leaves, sidewalk rubbings, or bits of neighborhood history to be used later by the children in the classroom. This initial contact with parents will be positive, and possibly make a second meeting even more productive. You can reinforce the positive aspect of an early meeting by making an interim telephone call to inform the parents of an activity or an interesting comment made by their child.

Bus Trips and Coffees

An all-school project, with teachers riding a bus to tour the school's enrollment area, allows parents and teachers to meet before the opening of school. If prior arrangements are made for coffees at parents' homes, other parents may be invited (Rich & Mattox, 1977).

Picnics

A picnic during the lunch hour or while on a field trip during the early part of the year will afford teachers the opportunity to meet some parents. Plan a field trip to a park or zoo and invite the parents to a bring-your-own-lunch gathering. Have another picnic after school for those who could not come at lunchtime. After the lunch or picnic, call to thank those who came. Because some parents work and will be unable to attend either picnic, you might wish to phone them for a pleasant conversation about their child.

✑✑ WHAT WORKS

Research has revealed that parents who provide active support of their children contribute more to their child's success in school than those who provide passive support. The least effective parents—in terms of the child's ability to succeed—are those who are nonsupportive. Parents must actively help their children as well as encourage them to achieve (Epstein, 1996; Liontos, 1992; Rich, 1988; Watson et al., 1983). Parent behaviors that support the child's cognitive development include:

1. Talk with children and listen to their concerns.
2. Read to children and listen to them read.
3. Establish daily routines that include study time for homework in an area conducive to study (if the child is old enough to have homework).
4. Provide opportunities for exploring and play.
5. Eat meals together.
6. Have appropriate bedtime schedules.
7. Guide and monitor out-of-school time.
8. Model good values and positive behavior.
9. Have high expectations of achievement.
10. Gain knowledge of child development and parenting skills.
11. Use authoritative rather than authoritarian control.
12. Take a strong interest in the schools.
13. Communicate with the teacher.
14. Collaborate with and support the school (Berger, 1996a, 1996b; Epstein, 1996; Hess &

Reading begins early. Children enjoy sharing their reading skills.

Holloway, 1984; Liontos, 1992; Rutter, 1985; U.S. Department of Education, 1994).

Research from the U.S. Department of Education on Follow Through, Title I, Title VII Bilingual, and the Emergency School Aid Act and from Epstein's work at the Center for Families, Schools, Community, and Children's Learning, found that:

- Children do better in school if their parents help them. The children also behave better and are more diligent than children whose parents do not involve themselves.

- Teachers and principals show greater respect to parents who participate in school activities and also have better attitudes toward the children of these parents.

- School personnel find out about how parents feel and what they need and are better able to respond to them when there is caring and parent involvement (Lyons, Robbins, & Smith, 1983; Swick et al., 2001).

- When teachers involve families, they rate the parents more positively and do not stereotype single parents and those with less education. The teachers recognize that parents are equally willing to help and follow through at home. When they do not work with single parents or parents with less education, they rate these parents as less willing to help and follow through at home.

- Work at home with one subject—for example, reading—resulted in increased scores in that subject, but did not transfer to other subjects—for example, math.

- Parents are able to influence and make a contribution to the education of their children.

- Students, parents, and school personnel all agree that parent involvement is important.

- The way teachers work with parents is more important than the family background, including class, race, marital status, and whether both parents work (Epstein, 1996). Socioeconomic status is not the primary causal factor in school success or lack of success; it is parental interest and support of the child.

Watson et al., (1983) examined environmental influences of neighborhood support, home support, income, and educational level of the parents in an attempt to determine their individual and collective effects on children as they entered school. They found a significant relationship between the support that a parent is given by the environment and the support the parent gives the child. Couple this relationship with one that shows that the support given to the child at home makes a difference to the child's achievement in first grade. "Regardless of the income and/or educational level of the home, the [supported and supportive] home was effective in helping the child achieve" (p. 178).

Research on What Works

A report from the U.S. Department of Education (1986) emphasized the "curriculum of the home." It states:

> Parents can do many things at home to help their children succeed in school. . . . They do this through their daily conversations, household routines, attention to school matters, and affectionate concern for their children's progress. Conversation is important. Children learn to read, reason, and understand things better when their parents:
>
> - Read, talk, and listen to them.
> - Tell them stories, play games, share hobbies.
> - Discuss the news, TV programs, and special events.
>
> To enrich the "curriculum of the home," some parents:
>
> - Provide books, supplies, and a special place for studying.
> - Observe routine for meals, bedtime, and homework.
> - Monitor the amount of time spent watching TV and doing after-school jobs.
>
> Parents stay aware of their children's lives at school when they:
>
> - Discuss school events.
> - Help children meet deadlines.
> - Talk with their children about school problems and successes.
>
> Research on both gifted and disadvantaged children shows that home efforts can greatly improve student achievement. For example, when parents of disadvantaged children take the steps listed above, their children can do as well at school as the children of more affluent families. (p. 7)

America Goes Back to School, Partner's Activity Kit, 1996–97 emphasized parent involvement and literacy as two of the important challenges for the nation (U.S. Department of Education,

1997). The Department also published a booklet to help parents tutor their children. In *Read Write Now: The Partners Tutoring Program* (Venezky, 1995), an effective tutoring program included:

1. Create a supportive, safe situation for tutoring. Safe means "not judgmental."

2. Be honest in responding, but do not correct speech. Model correct speech instead.

3. Don't overexplain.

4. Help learners to think independently. Try a response such as, "How do you think we could find an answer to this?"

5. Be relaxed, and don't worry about making mistakes.

In *Becoming a Nation of Readers: What Parents Can Do,* Binkley (1988) emphasized the importance of parents in the reading process. "Learning to read begins at home. Just as your children naturally learned to talk by following your example, they may naturally learn a great deal about reading before they ever set foot inside a school building" (p. 1).

Booklets covering educational issues are available to help the No Child Left Behind concept succeed. One booklet, "Helping Your Child Become a Reader" cited simple strategies from "Reading Tips for Parents" (U. S. Department of Education, 2002). The suggestions include:

• Invite your child to read with you every day.

• When reading a book where the print is large, point word by word as you read. This will help your child learn that reading goes from left to right and understand that the word said is the word seen.

• Read your child's favorite book over and over.

• Read many stories with rhyming words and repeated lines. Invite your child to join in on these parts. Point, word by word, as your child reads along with you.

• Discuss new words. For example, "This big house is called a palace. Who do you think lives in a palace?"

• Stop and ask about the pictures and about what is happening in the story.

• Read from a variety of children's books, including fairy tales, song books, poems, and information books.

Information on these government publications may be obtained by calling 1-800-USA-LEARN.

School-Home Support

The National Association of Elementary School Principals (1994) give suggestions that have worked in Blue Ribbon Schools. PALs, parent-assisted learning, in Graysville, Georgia, included PAL packets, which were sent home with students on a rotating basis several times a week. The packet includes a book to read as well as games and activities designed for parents and children to complete together.

The Canfield Avenue School in Mine Hill, New Jersey, has Friday Folders, which are sent home each Friday with a weekly calendar and a "tip sheet" on home learning as well as all graded papers and assignments completed for the week. The folder is returned on Monday with a signature showing that the parent received the folder.

In Elm Grove Elementary in Wheeling, West Virginia, SOS, Students on Saturday, offers two 45-minute classes for students on Saturdays throughout the year. Parents and the principal work together to plan and offer the program, and they utilize parents and community resources to conduct the classes, which include anything from baseball, astronomy, and photography to kung fu.

For more descriptions of these programs, refer to the *Best Ideas from America's Blue Ribbon Schools* by the National Association of Elementary School Principals (1994).

✌ MEETING THE NEEDS OF YOUR SCHOOL AREA

Schools can make a special effort to help families function more effectively. Some parents travel constantly; the stay-at-home partners in those families have many of the same problems that a single parent has (see Chapter 3). A parent with a disability may need help with transportation or child care. An early survey of families will disclose what parents need and suggest ways the school can encourage participation.

Work-Site Seminars

Meet the needs of parents by offering seminars and parent education at companies and businesses during the lunch hour. Some corporations hire a parent educator to set up a program for their employees. School personnel could coordinate with them and be a resource for the parent educator. Topics for seminars range from school activities and parent-child communication to child development. If the company does not have an employee to set up the program, the school could offer seminars on an ongoing basis.

Telephone Tree

A "telephone tree" set up by the PTO or PTA can alert parents quickly to needs in the community. One caller begins by calling four or five people, who each call four or five more. Soon the entire community is alerted.

Transportation

If a parent group is active, it can offer transportation to those who need help getting to the school or to the doctor's office. Those in need might include people with disabilities and families with small children or a child who is ill.

Parent-to-Parent Support

Parents without an extended family living nearby can team up with other parents. The parent organization can set up a file on parents that includes their needs, interests, children's ages, and location, with cross-references for parents to use. Parent education group meetings tend to promote friendships within the group. Isolated parents are often the ones who need the help of another parent the most. One parent may be able to manage the home efficiently, whereas another needs tips and help. Some parents were not exposed to a stable home environment and need a capable parent as a model. Although educators may not want to interfere in the lives of parents, they must remember that they meet and work with all parents and thus have the greatest access to the most parents of any community agency.

Child Care

Child care during conferences can be offered to families with young children. Older children can participate in activities in the gymnasium, while young children can be cared for in a separate room. It is difficult for some parents to arrange for child care, and a cooperative child care arrangement with parent volunteers would allow greater participation at conferences.

Crisis Nursery

A worthwhile project for a parent organization is the development of a crisis nursery. Schools would have to meet state regulations for child care to have a nursery within the school, but it provides a great service and a chance to meet parents and children before school starts. An assessment program, similar to Child Find, might alert parents and schools to developmental problems, such as hearing loss or poor sight.

A neighborhood home can also be used as a crisis base. If a parent with several children must take one child to the doctor, the crisis center can care for the other children during the parent's absence. Abusive parents can use the crisis center as a refuge for their children until they regain control of their emotions.

After-School Activities

Schools can become centers for the community. One step toward greater community involvement is an after-school program. With so many working parents, many children become latchkey kids, going home to an empty house. If schools, perhaps working with other agencies, provide an after-school program for children of all ages, a great service is accomplished. Teachers should not be expected to be involved in after-school programs. However, recreation workers, trained child care workers, and volunteers can implement a program that supplements the school program. Children can be taught how to spend leisure time through participation in crafts, sports, and cultural programs.

Although it is generally recognized that young children need supervision, the needs of secondary students are often ignored. Older students may have three to four unsupervised hours between the time they are out of school and the time their parents arrive home. School dropouts are rarely involved in school activities. If you look at community structure, it becomes clear that schools are the major link between the family and the community.

Family Literacy Programs

Parents who can read with their children are better able to help and encourage the children in their reading and learning. Family literacy programs are needed by families new to the United States for whom English is a second language, as well as the many parents who went through school without learning to read. (See Chapter 8.) Join with a family literacy program and offer space and help in providing literacy development, or develop the school's literacy program. This program could be enhanced by including programs for those who are able to read. Expand by offering family literacy, workshops on great books for children, Great Books, and Great Decision programs. Solicit volunteers from the community, including retired teachers who might enjoy the challenge.

Skill Training

Offer workshops that provide skill training for the amateur as well as for the person who needs a skill to get a job. Courses in computer training, carpentry, typing, financial management, and organizational skills would all be appropriate workshops to help the parents in the community.

Underemployed parents may need to develop more skills to become self-sufficient. Offer life-skills training. Teach classes on parenting, relationships, anger management, and leadership.

Help identify the abilities and needs of fathers. Provide literacy, job training, and employment opportunities, information, and referrals (Governor Romer's Responsible Fatherhood Initiative, 1997).

Emotional and Educational Support for Homeless Parents

In order to meet the needs of your school area, you should respond to and advocate for those who could use your help. Children from homeless families will benefit from a family-friendly school environment.

1. Attitude counts. Be sure the classroom accepts and values all children—all ethnic groups, diversity, and conditions including homelessness.
2. Make it easy for a homeless family to enroll in the school with friendly, immediate, and trouble-free registration procedures.
3. Provide breakfasts, snacks, and lunch, without stereotyping people who receive these meals, at reduced prices or free.
4. Provide child development centers for infants and toddlers.
5. Offer early childhood classes for preschoolers.
6. Provide parent education and parent participation programs.
7. Provide English as a Second Language (ESL) courses as well as family literacy programs.

8. Offer classes or find classes that can help the parent become ready for employment.

9. Provide support meetings that help parents deal with depression and anxiety.

Advocacy

1. Assign a teacher, staff member, or liaison to help the child and family during crisis.

2. Advocate for the family, if necessary, to get needed services.

3. Help with job search and placement.

4. Mentor the family. (Adapted from Eddowes, 1992; Klein et al., 1993; McCormick & Holden, 1992; Nunez, 1996; Swick, Da Ros, & Kovach, 2001; Stronge, 1992)

✒ BUILDING FAMILY STRENGTHS

All families have strengths. They are expressed in a variety of ways, but the approach that schools and agencies must take when working with families is to focus on their strengths and, through this focus, eliminate their problems. Research shows that parents respond positively to schools that set out to collaborate with them. During 2001–2004 many families have had breadwinners who are out of work and having difficulty finding work that allows them to provide for their families. Other families have both parents working, so time becomes a scarce commodity. If projections hold true, three fourths of parents with school-age children and two thirds of parents with preschoolers will be working outside the home as well as providing caregiver roles in the home after work hours. Schools can help make this dual role easier for parents by providing or allowing other agencies to use the school building to provide before- and after-school care.

We tend to look at the half-full glass as half empty. Even if a majority of both parents will be working outside the home, there are still many families who have one parent as caregiver at home with the children. Many of these parents sacrifice to have one parent remain home, and they are willing to be partners with the school.

Others can provide the needed security and support their children need to make the school's responsibility of educating easier. Programs such as the Building Family Strengths program, designed at the University of Nebraska, focus on areas that parents need to address to keep their families strong. These include the following:

- *Communication.* Effective communication in strong families involves clear, direct channels between the speaker and listener. Families develop complicated ways of communicating. Strong families have learned to communicate directly and use consistent verbal and nonverbal behaviors (see Chapter 5).

- *Appreciation.* Appreciation involves being able to recognize the beautiful, positive aspects of others and letting them know you value these qualities. It also means being able to receive compliments yourself.

South African diamond miners spend their working lives sifting through thousands of tons of rock and dirt looking for a few tiny diamonds. . . . We sift through diamonds, eagerly searching for dirt. (Stinnett & DeFrain, 1985, p. 49)

Appreciative family members look for the diamonds.

- *Commitment.* Commitment in strong families means that the family as a whole is committed to seeing that all members reach their potential.

- *Wellness.* Family wellness is the belief in positive human interaction. This belief helps family members trust others and learn to give and receive love. Family wellness is not the absence of problems. Strong families have their share of troubles, but their trust and love enable them to deal with their problems effectively.

- *Time together.* Spending time together as a family can be the most rewarding experience for humans. Two important aspects of time together are quality and quantity. Members of a strong family spend a lot of meaningful time with each other. This gives a family an identity that can be had in no other way.

- *The ability to deal with stress, conflict, and crisis.* All the previous strengths combine to make an inner core of power for families. This core serves as a resource for those times when conflict and crisis come. Strong families are able to survive and even grow in the face of hard times (Achord et al., 1986).

Developing these strengths takes time and energy, but realizing their significance can help a family focus on the important interactions within the family. Many families do not realize the importance of spending time together, communicating clearly with one another, and showing appreciation. These last two strengths take no extra time; they may take practice, but clear communication and showing appreciation can become a natural part of family life.

Families benefit from programs offered at the school or from home visits by school personnel who are able to share ideas about developing family strengths, discipline, school activities, and "homefun." Chapter 5 has more discussion on communication and parent programs.

✑ VOLUNTEERS

Have you ever wondered why some teachers have extra help? One answer lies in the recruitment of volunteers and the subsequent interaction with them.

Parents want the best for their children; most will respond to an opportunity to volunteer if the options for working are varied and their contributions are meaningful. When both parents work, short-term commitments geared to their working hours will allow and encourage participation from this group. Although the world is a busy place, time spent at school can bring satisfaction and variety to a parent's life.

Volunteers: Used or Users?

Volunteerism has been criticized by some as inequitable and an exploitation of "woman power."

To avoid such accusations, try to choose volunteers who can afford the time, or allow busy parents to contribute in such a way that they enjoy the time away from their other obligations. If education and training are included in your volunteer program, the participants can gain personally from the experience. For many, volunteering in school may be the first step toward a career.

If you are alert to the needs of parents, using them as volunteers can become a means of helping their families. If you work with them over a period of time, listen and use your knowledge of community resources to support the families in solving their problems. Volunteerism should serve the volunteer as well as contribute to the school.

Who Should Ask for Volunteers?

All teachers can benefit from the services of volunteers, but they should first determine the extent to which they are ready to use the assistance. Volunteer programs vary in their scope and design. Individual teachers may solicit volunteers from among parents; individual schools can support a volunteer program; or school districts can implement a volunteer program for the total system.

A teacher who has not used aides, assistants, or volunteers should probably start with help in one area before expanding and recruiting volunteers for each hour in the week. In preschools, the free-choice period is a natural time to have added assistance. In elementary schools, assistance during art projects is often a necessity. Add to this initial use of volunteer help by securing extra tutors for reading class. In secondary schools, recruitment for a special project provides an excellent initial contact.

Easing into use of volunteers may not be necessary in your school. Because most preschools and primary grades have used assistance for many years, their teachers are ready for more continuous support from volunteers. Yet involving other people in the classroom program is an art, based on good planning and the ability to work with and supervise others. Successful involvement of a few may lay the groundwork for greater involvement of others at a later time.

Enlist volunteers to work in the schools. Their help makes possible programs that would be difficult to offer otherwise.

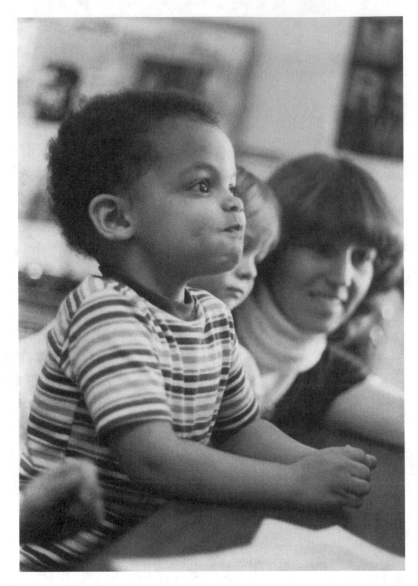

Recruitment of Volunteers by Individual Teachers

Many teachers have been successful in implementing their own volunteer programs from among the parents of their students. If you have used volunteers previously and parents in the community have heard about your program from other parents, recruitment may be easy. Early in the year, an evening program, where

the curriculum is explained and parents get acquainted, is an effective time to recruit parents into the program. If parents have not been exposed to volunteerism, encourage them to visit the room and give them opportunities to participate in an easy activity, such as reading a story to a child or playing a game with a group. Ask them back for an enjoyable program so they begin to feel comfortable in the room. Sharing their hobbies with the children introduces many parents to the joys of teaching. Gradually the fear of classroom involvement will disappear, and parents may be willing to spend several hours each week in the classroom.

Invitations That Work

Suppose you write notes inviting parents to visit the school or publish an invitation in the newsletter, but nobody comes. If you have had this experience, you need a "parent-getter." Judge your activity and invitation by the following questions:

- Does the event sound enjoyable?
- Is there something in it for the parents?
- Are the parents' children involved in the program?
- Does the program have alternate times for attendance?

The first criterion, making the event sound enjoyable, can be met by the wording of the invitation. The second and third vary in importance; one or the other should be addressed in each bid for parent attendance. Scheduling alternate times depends on your parents' needs.

One teacher complained that the parents at her school were just not interested in helping. Only three had volunteered when they were asked to clean up the playground. When asked if there were any other enticements for the parents to volunteer to help, the teacher said no. "Would you have wanted to spend your Saturday morning cleaning up the playground?" she was asked. The teacher realized she would not have participated, either, if she had been one of the parents. An excellent means of determining the drawing power of a program or activity is your own reaction to the project. Would you want to come? Had the Saturday cleanup project included the children, furnished refreshments, and allowed time for a get-together after the work was completed, the turnout would have been much better. Make it worth the parents' time to volunteer.

Performances

Many schools have children perform to get parents to turn out. The ploy works; parents attend! Some professionals discourage this method because they believe that children are being exploited to attract parents. However, it is probably the manner in which the production is conceived and readied rather than the child's involvement that is unworthy. What are your memories of your childhood performances? If the experiences were devastating, was it the programs themselves or the way they were handled that led to disappointment? If the performance is a creative, worthwhile experience for the child and does not cause embarrassment, heartache, or a sense of rejection for the child who does not perform well and if all children are included, this method of enticing parents can be valuable for both child and parents. Experience in front of an audience can develop poise and heightened self-concept—and be fun for the child. Parents invited to unpolished programs enjoy the visit just as much as if they had attended refined productions. Small, simple classroom functions, scheduled often enough that every child has a moment in the limelight, are sure to have high parent turnout. The more parents come to school and get involved with the activities, the better chance you have of recruiting assistance.

Field Trips

Use a field trip to talk with parents about volunteering in the classroom. Parents will often volunteer for field trips, during which teacher and parent can find time to chat. See if the parents' interests include hobbies that can be shared with the class. Be receptive to any ideas or needs that parents reveal. The informal atmosphere of a field trip encourages parents to volunteer.

Want Ads to Encourage Sharing Experiences and Expertise

Parents have many experiences and talents that they can share. Who lived on a farm? Who just traveled to Japan? Who knows how to cook spaghetti? Who can knit? Who has a collection of baseball cards? Who can speak a different language? Who has some stories to tell? Who is a geologist? Who is a food server? Ask parents to share their talents, hobbies, and experiences with your class. Send home a want ad to parents (see Figure 4.7) and ask them to return a tear-off portion, or call them and ask them personally to come to the school. Schedule each parent at a time that is convenient for parent and teacher. If possible, a follow-up in class of the ideas presented will make the visit even more meaningful. After the presentations, write thank-you notes with suggestions that parents might come to class again, providing another means of recruiting potential volunteers.

Invitations to Share

Sending home invitations with the children asking parents if they are interested in volunteering is a direct way to recruit. Each teacher should design the invitation to fit the needs of the class. A letter that accompanies the form should stress to parents how important they are to the program. Let them know the following:

- Teachers and children need their help.
- Each parent is already experienced in working with children.
- Their child will be proud of the parents' involvement and will gain through their contributions.

Friendly requests along with suggestions enable parents to respond easily. Be sure to ask parents for their ideas and contributions. You have no way of knowing what useful treasures you may find! Let parents complete a questionnaire, such as the one in Figure 4.8, to indicate their interests and time schedules. Perhaps a parent cannot visit school but is willing to make calls and coordinate the volunteer program. This parent can find substitutes when regular parent volunteers call in to say they must be absent. Others who are homebound can aid the class by sharing child care, making games and activities at home, designing and making costumes, writing newsletters, and making phone calls.

Parents who are able to work at school can perform both teaching and nonteaching tasks. Relate the task to the parents' interests. Nothing discourages some volunteers as much as being forced to do housekeeping tasks continually, with no opportunity for interaction with the children. The choice of tasks should not be difficult, however, because the opportunities are numerous and diversified, as the following lists indicate:

Teaching Tasks

Tutor.

Supervise learning centers.

Listen to children.

Play games with students.

Tell stories.

Play instructional games.

Work with underachievers or students with learning disabilities.

Help select library books for children.

Teach children to type.

Help children prepare and practice speeches.

Help children write.

Take children to the resource center.

Read to children.

Help children create a play.

Supervise the making of books.

Show filmstrips.

Supervise the production of a newsletter or newspaper.

Assist in learning centers.

Share a hobby.

Speak on travel and customs around the world.

Demonstrate sewing or weaving.

Demonstrate food preparation.

Nonteaching Tasks

Make games.

Prepare a parent bulletin board.

Help Wanted
Positions Available

Tutor for Reading
Do you have an interest in children learning to read? Come tutor! We will train you in techniques to use.

Good Listener
Are you willing to listen to children share their experiences and stories? Come to the listening area and let a child share with you.

Costume Designer
There will be a class presentation next month. Is anyone willing to help with simple costumes?

Tour Guide
Do you have memories, slides, or tales about other states or countries? Come share.

Talent Scout
Some talented people never volunteer. We need a talent scout to help us find these people in our community.

Good-will Ambassador
Help us make everyone feel an important part of this school. Be in charge of sending get-well cards or congratulatory messages.

Reader of Books
Read to the children.
Choose a favorite book or read one chosen by the teacher.

Photographer
Anyone want to help chronicle our year? Photographer needed.

Collector
Do you hate to throw good things away? Help us in our scrounge department. Collect and organize.

Game Player
We need someone who enjoys games to spend several hours a week at the game table.

News Editor
Be a news hound. Help us develop and publish a newsletter. The children will help furnish news.

Book Designer
The class needs books written by children for our reading center. Turn children's work into books.

Volunteer Coordinator
The class needs volunteers, but we also need to know who, when, and how. Coordinate the volunteer time sheet.

Construction Worker
Are you good at building and putting things together? Volunteer!

SIGN UP IN YOUR CHILD'S CLASSROOM OR RETURN THIS FORM WITH YOUR INTERESTS CHECKED.

Tutor_____ Listener_____ Costume Designer_____ Tour Guide_____ Talent Scout_____ Ambassador_____
Photographer_____ Collector_____ Game Player_____ News Editor_____ Book Designer_____
Volunteer Coordinator_____ Construction Worker_____ Other_____

_____   _____   _____
Name   Address   Telephone

FIGURE 4.7   One way to solicit school volunteers is through a want ad.

Please Share With the School

Dear Parents:

We need volunteers to help us with our school program. You can share your time by helping while you are at home or at school. If you want to share in any way, please let us know.

Are you interested in volunteering this year? _____ Yes _____ No

Check the ways you want to help.

_____ In the classroom

_____ In the resource center

_____ At home

WHAT WOULD YOU LIKE TO DO?

_____ Share your hobby or travel experience

_____ Help children in learning centers

_____ Be a room parent

_____ Work in a resource room

_____ Supervise a puppet show

_____ Go on field trips

_____ Care for another volunteer's children

_____ Substitute for others

_____ Develop a learning center

_____ Tutor reading

_____ Tell stories

_____ Check papers

_____ Check spelling

_____ Help with math

_____ Read to children

_____ Make games

_____ Listen to children read

_____ Play games with children

_____ Make books

_____ Share your recipes

Any other suggestions? _____

_____

Comments _____

When can you come?

	Monday	Tuesday	Wednesday	Thursday	Friday
	AM | PM	AM | PM	AM | PM	AM | PM	AM | PM

Can you come each week? _____ Other _____

What time can you come? _____

How long can you stay? _____

_____   _____
Name   Telephone

FIGURE 4.8   Questionnaires are another way to obtain parents' interests and time schedules.

Repair equipment.

Select and reproduce articles for the resource room.

Record grades.

Take attendance.

Collect lunch money.

Plan a workshop for parents.

Grade and correct papers.

Organize cupboards.

Help with book publishing.

Contributions From Home

Serve as telephone chairperson.

Collect recycling materials.

Furnish refreshments.

Furnish dress-up clothes and costumes.

Wash aprons.

Make art aprons.

Design and/or make costumes.

Repair equipment.

Make games.

Care for another volunteer's children.

Write newsletters.

Coordinate volunteers.

Teaching embraces creative ideas and methods; volunteers, responding to the challenge, can provide a vast reservoir of talent and support. Book publishing is an excellent example of an effective volunteer activity that is both a teaching and a nonteaching role.

Management Techniques

Use management skills in organizing and implementing your volunteer program. A parent coordinator can be very helpful in developing effective communication between teacher and parent. Two types of charts—time schedules and volunteer action sheets—can clarify the program and help it run more smoothly.

Time Schedules

Time schedules can be adjusted if weekly charts are posted at school and sent home to parents. When parents can visualize the coverage, the class will not be inundated by help in one session and suffer from lack of help in another.

Volunteer Sheet

Because volunteers are used in many ways, developing an action sheet that describes each person's contribution is helpful. Figure 4.9 illustrates the scope of involvement within one classroom. With this list the parent coordinator can secure an effective substitute for someone who must be absent. If the teacher needs games constructed, the parent coordinator can call on parents who have volunteered for that activity. Special help in the resource center or with a student project may be found quickly by calling a parent who has already indicated an interest in helping this way. The responsibility for the volunteer program does not need to rest solely on the teacher's shoulders. Parents and teachers become partners in developing a smoothly working system.

Increasing Volunteer Usage

Although permanent volunteers are more effective in establishing continuity in a program than periodic contributions by occasional volunteers, both are needed. As the year progresses, some parents may find they enjoy teaching immensely. These parents may extend their time obligation and in doing so, bring more continuity to the program. Ideally, an assistant should tutor a reading group or a child for several sessions each week rather than just one. When initiating a program, it is best to start out with easily handled time slots and then expand the responsibilities of parents after they become secure and familiar with the class, the objectives, and the material.

Volunteer Training

Suppose that several parents have indicated interest in being permanent volunteers in your

Name	Telephone	Classroom Regularly	Classroom Substitute	Special Presentation	Child Care	Make Games at Home	Work in Resource Center: Help Students	Work in Resource Center: Develop Resources — Type	Work in Resource Center: Develop Resources — Make games
Names of volunteers	555-5555							X	
"		X	X						
"		X	X						
"	X	X	X		X				
"	X		X	X	X				
"			X		X				
"	X			X	X	X	X	X	
"	X	X							
"	X	X	X						
"						X	X	X	
"	X				X				
"		X	X	X	X		X	X	
"		X		X					
"		X			X				
"		X							
"		X		X			X		
"				X					
"		X	X	X	X		X		
"					X		X		
"		X				X	X	X	
"		X	X	X					
"		X	X	X					

FIGURE 4.9 Volunteer action sheets help organize an orderly volunteer program.

classroom. What is your next step? The time spent explaining your routine, expectations, and preferences for teaching will be well worth the effort in the parents' abilities to coordinate with you in your classroom. Most teachers have specific preferences for teaching that they will want to share with the volunteers helping them. These, in addition to some general guidelines, will help prepare the volunteer. The following humanistic guidelines for working with children are appropriate for all volunteers:

- A healthy, positive self-concept is a prerequisite to learning.

- The act of listening to a child implies that you accept the child as a worthwhile person.

- The child will develop a better sense of self-worth if you praise specific efforts rather than deride failures.

- Provide tasks at which the children can succeed. As they master these, move on to the next level.

- Take time to know the student as a person. Your interest bolsters confidence in your relationship. (Adapted from DaSilva & Lucas, 1974)

Many children who need extra help with their work also need their self-concepts strengthened. Volunteers can provide an extra touch through kindness, interest, and support.

The Teacher's Responsibilities to the Volunteer

As teachers enlist the help of volunteers, certain responsibilities emerge. The teacher's responsibilities follow:

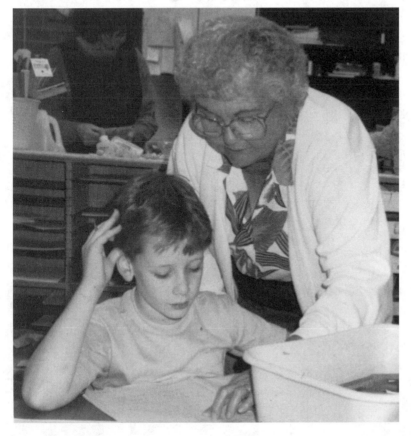

Senior citizens are participating as excellent volunteers in the schools.

- Make volunteers feel welcome. Smile and reassure them.
- Explain class rules and regulations.
- Introduce volunteers to the resources within the school.
- Explain the routine of the class.
- Describe your expectations for their participation.
- Remember that volunteers are contributing and sharing time because of satisfaction they receive and to help the child.
- Give volunteers reinforcement and recognition.
- Meet with volunteers when class is not in session to clarify, answer questions, and, if needed, give instruction and training.
- Appreciate, respect, and encourage volunteers.

Awareness of these points will make the cooperative effort of teacher and volunteer more fulfilling for both.

The Volunteer's Responsibilities to the Teacher

If parents or others in the community volunteer to help in the school, they accept certain responsibilities, which include the following:

- Be dependable and punctual. If an emergency requires that you miss a session, obtain a substitute or contact the volunteer coordinator.
- Keep privileged information concerning children or events confidential. Do not discuss children with people other than school personnel.
- Plan responsibilities in the classroom with the teacher.
- Cooperate with the staff. Welcome supervision.
- Be ready to learn and grow in your work.
- Enjoy yourself, but do not let your charges get out of control.
- Be fair, consistent, and organized.

Volunteer aides are not helpful if they continually cancel at the last moment, disrupt the room rather than help it run smoothly, or upset the students. They are immensely helpful if they work with the teacher to strengthen and individualize the school program.

Recruitment by Schools and School Systems

Many schools and school districts assist teachers by recruiting volunteers for their classes. The first step in initiating a volunteer program for a school or school system is the development of a questionnaire to ascertain the teachers' needs. The teachers complete a form, based on the curriculum for each age level of students. After the forms are completed, the coordinators can determine the requirements of each room.

After teachers have indicated their needs, the coordinator begins recruitment. Many avenues are open for the recruiter. A flyer geared to the appropriate age or level of children, asking people to share their time with the schools, can bring about the desired results. Organizations can also be contacted. The PTA or PTO, senior citizen groups, and other clubs have members who may want to get involved as volunteers in the school.

The points discussed earlier for obtaining volunteers for the individual classroom are also appropriate for volunteers who are solicited on a larger scale. The major differences are organizational and include the following:

- Teachers should contact the volunteer coordinator or reply to the coordinator's questionnaire if they want a volunteer.
- Districts usually require volunteers to fill out an application stating their background, giving references, and listing the hours they are available.
- Many school districts have an extensive compilation of resource people who have agreed to volunteer in the schools. An alliance with

businesses encourages companies to allow their employees to visit schools and tell students about their careers. These resource people and experts can share their knowledge with classes throughout the school district. Lists of topics with resource people available to share expertise can be distributed throughout the district. Teachers can request the subject and time they want a presentation.

- Outreach such as a community study hall can be initiated and staffed by the volunteer program. Volunteers can tutor and work with children after school hours in libraries, schools, or other public facilities (Denver Public Schools, n.d.).

- Certificates or awards distributed by the district offer a way to thank the volunteers for effort and time shared with the schools.

Individual teachers tend to use parents as aides and resource people in the room. The district most often furnishes resource people, drawn from the total population, in schools throughout the district. The school's volunteer coordinator uses both approaches, enlisting volunteers to tutor and aid in the classroom and recruiting resource people from residents of the school's population area to enrich the curriculum.

✐ SUMMARY

Understanding parents' feelings and concerns provides the basis for creating effective home-school relationships. Schools have character; some invite parents to participate; others suggest they stay away. Parents have feelings about schools that range from a desire to avoid the school to such a high interest that they are overly active. Parents participate in schools as spectators, accessory volunteers, volunteer resources, paid resources, policy makers, and teachers of their children.

Schools can develop attitudes that welcome parents and conduct activities that invite them into the school. Personnel in the school need to understand and examine their own attitudes toward parents. The use of questionnaires helps in the recognition of these attitudes.

An open-door policy with open forums, coffees, and seminars invites comments from parents. Initial contact should be made early in the year or even during the summer before the school year begins. Suggestions for early contact include neighborhood visits, telephone calls, home visits, and breakfasts.

A resource room, established and staffed by parent volunteers, makes parents significant educational resources. The resource room includes articles on teaching, games, recycled materials, and a lending library for toys, books, and games. A family center gives parents a place to stop and a base from which they can reach out to help children.

Parents today are more involved as policy makers than in the past. Parent advisory councils are part of Title I, and parents confer with school administrators on program planning, implementation, and evaluation.

Schools can become community centers and meet the needs of families in the area by organizing parent volunteers for parent-to-parent groups, child care centers, crisis centers, and after-school programs. If schools focus on family strengths they will help families develop and keep these strengths, which are effective communication, commitment, wellness, time together, and the ability to deal with stress, conflict, and crises.

Parents and others from the community can also be included in the schools as volunteers. Teachers need to develop skills to recruit, train, and work with volunteers as part of an educational team.

✐ SUGGESTED CLASS ACTIVITIES AND DISCUSSIONS

1. Make a list of suggestions from this chapter. Use it as a checklist to test your school's response to parents.
2. Contact the president of the PTA or PTO in a neighborhood school. What are his or her goals for parent involvement in the school? Which programs have been planned for the year? Which direction would he or she like the PTO or PTA to take?
3. Discuss why some parents may feel intimidated by schools and why some teachers may be reluctant

to have parents involved. Role-play the teacher and parent roles and share your feelings.

4. Describe an ideal parent-teacher relationship. List five things a teacher can do to encourage such a relationship. List five ways a parent can work with the school.

5. List what makes you feel comfortable or uncomfortable when you visit a center or school.

6. Visit a school and look at bulletin boards, notices, and family centers that might welcome parents. Make a list of things that might invite parents as well as things that might intimidate parents.

7. Examine the offerings of a school system or an individual school. What programs or activities does the school offer? List and describe the offerings such as Head Start, family literacy, telephone tutoring, resource rooms, exchanges, prekindergarten programs, and parent advisory council.

8. Describe the different families you might find in the school in your neighborhood and in a different neighborhood. What are their living arrangements, their values, their ambitions, their hopes for the future?

9. Write guidelines for parents to use when they visit or work in the classroom. Describe the guidelines on a poster or handout.

10. Examine your community and develop a list of field trips and home-learning activities. Plan a packet for parents to use with their children during spring break.

11. Design a want ad or letter that invites parents to become volunteers in the classroom.

12. Search the community for resources that can be used in the school. Include specialists, materials, and places to visit.

13. List the strengths that help families. What other strengths might you add? How would you help families build their strengths?

5 Communication and Parent Programs

To really communicate one must listen, one must share true meaning, and one must reflect upon the message being shared.

Author

"The time has come," the walrus said,
"To talk of many things:
Of shoes—and ships—and sealing wax—
Of cabbages and kings
And why the sea is boiling hot—
And whether pigs have wings."

Carroll, 1968, p. 78

In this chapter on communication you will find methods for effective communication that will enable you to do the following:

- Discuss effective communication.
- Identify and use one-way communication.
- Identify and use two-way communication.
- Describe roadblocks to communication.
- List elements of effective communication with parents.
- List steps to improving listening skills.
- Define *rephrasing, reframing, open responses, problem ownership,* and *reflective listening.*
- List and describe parent education programs.
- Work on concerns that emerge in relationships with students and parents.
- Develop a plan for an effective parent-teacher conference.

❧ COMMUNICATION

What do you have in mind when you think of effective communication? Is it the transmission of feelings, information, and signals? Is it the sending and receiving of messages? Is it a verbal exchange between people—for example, parents and teachers?

Definition of Communication

Most definitions of *communication* encompass more than mere interchange of information. They range from the definition given in *Webster's Encyclopedic Unabridged Dictionary of the English Language* (1989)—"the imparting or interchange of thoughts, opinions, or information by speech, writing, or signs"—to definitions that focus on the effect a message has on the receiver. Is the message received with the meaning that the sender intended to convey? In working with parents, it is essential that messages are sent and received as intended.

Messages

Each message has at least three components: (1) the words or verbal stimuli—what a person says; (2) the body language or physical stimuli—

the gestures; and (3) the vocal characteristics or vocal stimuli—the pitch, loudness or softness, and speed (Gamble & Gamble, 1982).

The sender gives a message; it is received and interpreted by the receiver. If the intent of the message is accurately received, effective communication has occurred. For this to happen, the listener must be an active participant. The listener must be able to hear the message, the feeling, and the meaning of the message.

Communication includes (a) speaking, (b) listening, (c) reflection of feeling, and (d) interpretation of the message. It is a complicated process because so many variables come into play. The sender's voice and body language, the message itself, the receiver's reaction to the sender, and the receiver's expectations all affect the message. To be effective in communication, speakers need to understand their own reactions and the reaction of others to them, and they must listen to the meaning of the message.

The receiver must correctly interpret the meaning of the message and the sender's intent. If the message—or the receiver's response—is misinterpreted, miscommunication occurs. Miscommunication can be overcome. The receiver may check out understanding by rephrasing and recycling the

If the intent of the message sent is accurately received by the listener, good communication has occurred.

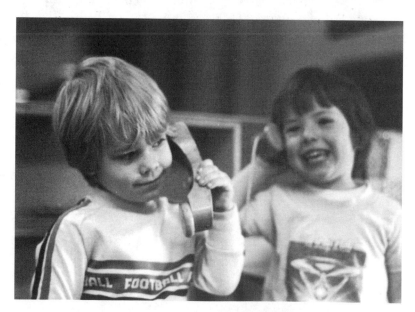

conversation or by further questioning within the context of the subsequent discussion.

Miscommunication

Interpersonal communication may be visualized as messages within an ongoing circle or oval configuration. As pictured in Figure 5.1, the message (filtered through values and past experiences) goes to the receiver (where it also is filtered through values and past experiences), is decoded, responded to, and sent back to begin the cycle again. Communication is a dynamic, continuous process that changes and evolves.

Visual Messages

When talking with one another it is easy to assume that what one says is the most important element in the conversation. However, research shows that oral, verbal messages (the spoken words) account for only 7 percent of the input; vocal and tonal messages (the way in which the words are spoken) account for 38 percent; visual messages (body language) account for 55 percent (Miller, Wackman, Nunnally, & Miller, 1988). If this is the case, teachers, principals, and child care professionals need to focus on their total communication system and be aware of their body language and tone of voice, as well as their verbal messages.

One- and Two-Way Communication

One-way communication from the school merely informs parents about the school's plans and happenings. Two-way communication, which requires interaction among participants, allows parents to

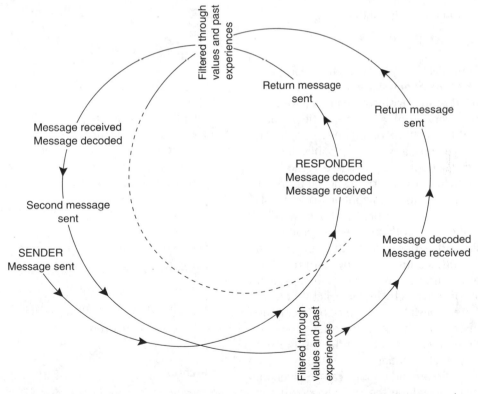

FIGURE 5.1 Messages are filtered through the receiver's value system and experiences before they are decoded and responded to. Communication is a dynamic, continuous process.

give feedback to the school on their knowledge, concerns, and desires. Both the school and parents gain. The steps to achieve effective communication among school, home, and community are easy to implement once the importance of effective communication is acknowledged. A number of strategies for establishing improved communication are described on the following pages. Choose the ones that fit your individual needs, and add others that work for you.

ℬ ONE-WAY COMMUNICATION

A newsletter may be used by the school as a message from the principal, or it may be sent home by each teacher. It is a simple form of one-way communication, and the format varies with the goals and objectives of each newsletter. Design ranges from a very simple notice to an elaborate and professionally written letter.

Simple Newsletters

The more newsletters you write, the easier they become. Not every newsletter contains all information, for it is an ongoing communication. The design may vary from a simple notice that is hand-printed and photocopied (see Figure 5.2) to a letter created through a desktop publishing program on the school computer (see Figure 5.3). Items may include the children's activities in curriculum areas such as math contracts or contests, reading projects, group presentations in social studies, hands-on work in science, practice in music skills, art experiences, field trips, care of classroom pets, contributions by resource people, creative drama experiences, and accomplishments or remarks by individual children.

Newsletters may also be used at the secondary level with sections blocked for each course of study. Communication between home and secondary schools is essential.

Students who are old enough can be given the responsibility of writing the periodic newsletter. This way, the newsletter serves two purposes: curriculum and communication. The students are

Let the children help with the newsletter.

challenged to write neatly, spell correctly, and construct a readable newsletter. Younger children can make individual contributions by painting a picture or making a comment that can be shared.

Consider using the following in your newsletter:

- Clear headlines that identify the topic
- Colorful paper
- Calendar of the week or month
- Book suggestions
- Recognition of birthdays
- Children's or students' work
- Quotes of children
- Artwork

Preschool

Publication of newsletters at this stage is the teacher's responsibility, although children can contribute drawings and stories.

FIGURE 5.2 Newsletters may take many forms, ranging from this informal design to very sophisticated publications.

❋❋❋❋❋❋❋❋❋❋❋❋❋❋❋❋❋❋❋❋❋❋❋❋❋❋❋❋

PARENT NEWSLETTER

▪▪▪▪▪▪▪▪▪▪▪▪▪▪▪▪▪▪▪▪▪▪▪▪▪▪▪▪▪▪▪▪▪▪

YOUR SCHOOL   *SEPTEMBER*

2000 CENTURY STREET
SOMEWHERE, UNITED STATES

●●●●●●●●●●●●●●●●●●●●●●●●●●●●●●●●●●

ANNOUNCEMENTS   *Dates to Remember*

BACK TO SCHOOL NIGHT   *Thursday, September 12*
Go to your child's classroom at 7:00 P.M.
Refreshments at 8:30 p.m.

+++

Workshop on Conferences   *Tuesday, September 17*
Auditorium at 7:00 P.M.

Conferences   *Thursday, September 19*

Sign your forms and return them

To your child's teacher

+++

The Adventurer Room   Space Adventurers

```
Our class had an adventure      To start the year we decided to
by visiting a historical        have a space adventure.  The
1890 farm.  We saw a home       class was divided into four
that was furnished with         groups, and each group made
all the furniture that a        plans for their space shuttle.
farm family would have.         We planned the food, the
We were able to pet the         equipment, and the lift off.
animals.  There were horses,    Parents have volunteered to
sheep, pigs and chickens.       come in and help with our book
We had a great time!!!          publishing.  Each group will
Our class will write a book     write about their space adventure.
about farms at the turn of
the century.
```

FIGURE 5.3   If you regularly collect anecdotes and children's work, you will easily have enough material for a four-page newsletter for parents.

Try collecting newsletter ideas throughout the year. State home economic extension agencies will probably have some excellent ideas to contribute. See the Appendix following Chapter 11 for additional sources of newsletter material. Commercial newsletters are available that can be used with inserts from your own center to reflect your concerns and news. As you collect interesting comments by the children or complete special projects, make a short note for the newsletter. If you choose a "very important person" each week, include information about that child in the newsletter. If you include articles about individual children, be sure to include each child before the end of the term. When time comes for publication, you will have more than enough news. It is more important to have a newsletter than to worry about its design. If typing isn't practical, write in your neatest script. Subjects that parents will find interesting include nutrition, child development, communication, and activities for rainy days, as well as events specific to your center. A picture drawn by a child to accompany the news is an attractive addition.

Elementary

A newsletter is an excellent curriculum tool in elementary school. Although children in the first grade may not be able to produce their own newsletter, you will be surprised at how well young children can write and edit their news. Make the newsletter an ongoing project, with a center set up to handle the papers and equipment. Assign a group in each subject area to be responsible for the newsletter. Let them collect the news and determine the content and design of the letter. You can have the children develop the newsletter on the computer. Different children could add messages or articles. If you cut and paste, the children can be allowed to type their own copy. Photocopy the master and print it by the most convenient method of duplication.

Middle and Secondary

Although seldom used at this level, the newsletter is an excellent mechanism for secondary students to gain experience in writing, composition, and making page layouts. You receive dual benefits—students learn through the process of doing, and a communication system between school and home is established.

A sophisticated newsletter may be the goal for upper-level students, but the importance of the newsletter as a communication tool should not be overlooked. If producing a sophisticated newsletter is too time consuming, write the newsletter in a simple, informative style (see Figure 5.3). The major objective is communication between the teacher and home. What is the class studying? What assignments are the students expected to

complete? Is there any problem solving being done in class? Which problems seem the most difficult? Are there any parents who would like to contribute to the subject being covered?

The newsletter is a short, practical form of newspaper. It is easily produced on a computer or by a cut-and-paste method and can relate to a smaller and, therefore, more specific group of students. It can address current concerns and interests and can inform a select group of parents of the happenings that affect their children.

Notes and Letters

When a child is doing well, send home an "up-slip" to let the parents know (see Figure 5.4). It is a good idea to buy small sheets of paper with space enough for a one- or two-line note. If you write too much, you may be forced by time limitation to postpone the incidental note, and the positive effect of timeliness is lost.

Letters sent prior to the beginning of school also help establish good communication. They should include significant dates, reminders, and school events (see Figure 5.5).

Many teachers like to use "Good News Notes," happy faces, "Happy Grams," or similar forms periodically to report something positive about each child. The concept behind each of these formats is the same—to communicate with parents in a positive manner, thereby improving both parent-teacher relations and the child's self-concept. Make a concerted effort to send these notes in a spirit of spontaneous sincerity. A contrived, meaningless comment, sent because you are required to do so, will probably be received as it was sent. Preserving good relations requires that the message have meaning.

Newspapers

Most school districts have newspapers, yearbooks, and other school-sponsored publications. These, along with the district newsletter, are important school traditions and effectively disseminate information. Don't stop publishing them,

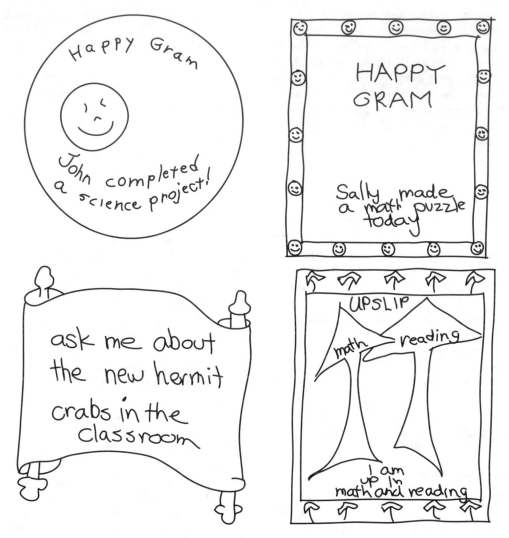

FIGURE 5.4 Happy grams, "upslips," and short notes are appreciated by parents and child.

but always remember that the newsletters that touch on their children are of greater importance to parents. Those most affected by yearbooks are those whose children are pictured in them. Parents most affected by newspapers are those who find articles in them concerning activities in which their children are involved.

Relying solely on newspapers and yearbooks for communicating with parents may promote complacency; some administrators and teachers assume communication is complete because a newspaper comes out periodically and a yearbook is published when seniors graduate. Yearbooks have very little effect on school-home relationships. They arrive after the student's school career ends, they often picture a small segment of the school population, and they are generally the product of a small, select group of students. The majority of students may be omitted or ignored. The school newspaper cannot take the place of individual class newsletters. Parents are more interested in their own children than in school lead-

Dear Parents;

All the teachers and staff at Jefferson Elementary are excited about the beginning of school. Many exciting changes have been made. One new feature is our school's web site. Sue Miller designed a web site so you can now get information about what is happening at Jefferson immediately as well as from the newsletters we will continue to send home.

Everyone responded so enthusiastically to the new Family Resource Room last year that we have decided to expand it in the coming year. We will have a planning meeting on Thursday, September 24 at 10:00 a.m. Call if you are interested in attending.

Don't forget back to school night on Tuesday, September 15. Gather at 7:00 p.m. for refreshments. At 7:45 p.m. parents may go to their children's classrooms to meet with their teachers. We are looking forward to seeing you there.

Summer was a busy time for all the staff. Several teachers went back to school and developed some special projects and curriculum for their classes. Anne Ross, the fourth grade teacher, exchanged with a teacher in New Zealand for a semester. May Hillary toured throughout Europe, visiting child care centers and schools. Both will have a great deal to share with us.

Enjoy the last few days of summer!!! We shall start the school year refreshed and ready to go.

Best wishes,

FIGURE 5.5 Friendly letters sent prior to the opening of school can set the stage for a cooperative and pleasant school year.

ers and star athletes. Newspapers and yearbooks meet different needs and are significant in their own way, but to establish a real, working relationship between parents and schools, the school's publication must concern the parents' number one interest—their own children.

District Newsletter

Many school districts use newsletters to keep the community up-to-date on school events. Often produced by professional public relations firms, they may display excellent style and format and contain precise information, but they may also lack the personal touch and tend to be viewed as a communiqué from the administration. District newsletters do have a place in building effective home-school-community relations, however, and, if these are supplemented by individual class reports (newsletters), parents receive both formal and personalized communication about their children's schooling.

Media

A formal and effective means of reaching parents is through the community newspaper and television and radio stations. Television and radio often make public service announcements. Use these opportunities to inform the community about events at school. Many communities have access to a cable information line that alerts the community to upcoming events. These may include conferences, sports events, musical performances, debates, theater, school board meetings, community meetings, back-to-school nights, and carnivals.

Suggestion Box

A suggestion box placed in the hallway encourages parents to share their concerns and pleasures with the school anonymously. Although this is really a one-way communication system, it effectively tells parents, "We want your suggestions. Let us know what you feel," and encourages them to respond.

Handbooks

Handbooks sent home before the child enters school are greatly appreciated by parents. If sent while the child is a preschooler, the school's expectations for the child can be met early. If given to parents at an open house during the spring term, they can reinforce the directions given by the teacher at that time. Handbooks can help parents new to the area by including information on community activities and associations for families. A district handbook designed to introduce parents to the resources in the area—with special pages geared to each level of student—can be developed and used by all teachers in the district. Moles (1996a) suggests the following handbook inclusions:

- Statement of school goals and philosophy.
- Discipline policy and code.
- Operations and procedures regarding:

    a. grades and pupil progress reports

    b. absence and tardiness

    c. how to inquire about student difficulties

    d. emergency procedures for weather and other events

    e. transportation schedules and provisions for after-school activities

- Special programs at the school such as after-school enrichment or child care programs.
- Parent involvement policies and practices at the school, with items that describe:

    a. "Bill of Rights" for parents

    b. "Code of Responsibilities" for parents

    c. open house and parent-teacher conferences

    d. involvement opportunities, such as volunteer programs, advisory councils, and PTAs

- A calendar of major school events throughout the year: holidays, vacations, regular PTA meetings, report card periods, open houses, other regularly scheduled school-home contacts.
- Names and phone numbers of key school contact people.
- Names and phone numbers of parent leaders (e.g., members of advisory councils, key people in parent organizations, and room parents).
- A tear-off response form allowing parents to ask questions, voice concerns, and volunteer at the school. (p. 9)

In addition, consider the following items when you compile your handbook:

- Procedures for registration
- Invitations to visit the school
- Conferences and progress reports
- Testing and evaluation programs
- Decision-making process, advisory committees, site-based management
- Facilities at the school (cafeteria, clinic, library)
- Special programs offered by the school (band, chorus, gymnastics)
- Summer programs
- Recreation programs
- Associations related to families and children
- Community center

Specialized Handbook

A special handbook related to the child's grade level and academic program can be an effective way to gain parents' cooperation. If it is sent out early in the school term, include the teacher's name and a short autobiography.

A special section related to the curriculum in the child's grade level can be developed by classroom teachers at each level and inserted for children assigned to their classes. This is especially important when the school is changing the manner in which the curriculum is taught. For example, whole-language programs are being used in many schools. Workshops and handbooks describing the benefits of whole language, the methods being used in the classroom, and activities at home that the children can use will help the parents support the program. This is especially important with the writing portion of the program. The development of writing and spelling, from prephonic and invented spelling to conventional spelling, needs to be explained to parents. A handbook that describes the process, along with a workshop where parents can see and be involved in a whole-language project, will increase understanding and cooperation between home and school.

Summer Handbook or Note. If a handbook does not give individualized, personal information, a note from the teacher mailed to the home during the summer will be appreciated by the family and will set the tone for a successful home-school relationship.

✏ TWO-WAY COMMUNICATION

Although one-way communication is important, two-way communication is essential. It is possible only when school personnel meet the children and their parents. The school principals or center directors set the climate of acceptance within their institutions. Their perceptions of the role of the school in communicating with parents permeate the atmosphere, making parents feel either welcome or unwanted.

Increased involvement is necessary for a true partnership. Telephone calls, home visits, parent visits at the school, parent-teacher conferences, and school activities encourage continued parental involvement. Use of the Internet capability on computers allow schools and parents to have immediate opportunities for information exchanges. Visits to the classroom allow parents to become acquainted with their child's educational environment, the other children in the room, and the teacher. Periodic conferences continue the dialogue on the educational progress of the child. Participation in school activities allows parents to become working members of the education team.

Homework Hot Line

The telephone system allows for many inventive ways to serve the student. This includes such services as call-forwarding, taped responses, answering machines, and having people available at the school's telephone number. The traditional use of the telephone requires volunteers or paid professionals to answer the phone at school. Some schools have a hot line open each day after school for students to call when they have questions about homework. If specialists in each academic field are available, the hot-line call may be transferred to the appropriate specialist to answer questions about homework. In individual schools, teachers can leave their assignments with the hot-line specialists so they have the information available for each class. Using call-forwarding, people responding to homework hot-line calls can work out of their homes.

Some communities have the homework hot line connected to local celebrities and others who volunteer for a set number of hours at a special telephone number. Details of individual assignments are more difficult to handle in this type of setup, but it serves well as a public relations format, and general questions about homework may be answered.

Enlist a TV station as a partner in education. Some stations sponsor tutoring programs. Students are encouraged to call designated numbers—such as 555-HELP, 555-PASS, or 555-AIDE—to talk to someone about homework. The station commits funds to hire tutors to answer questions children or parents might have about homework. It also works to have recognizable personalities take turns on the telephone. Watch the tutor service take off if parents and children know that local celebrities are willing to help.

Computer Information Line

Computers can be used in a variety of ways. Each school would have to determine if computers were available to the families in their school area. Families would either own their own online computer or community libraries might give them availability for computer use. A questionnaire could be used to determine if the family has accessibility and if they want to use computers for information access with the school.

E-mail. Individual messages can be used for specific correspondence between the school and the student or the student's family.

E-mails to families whose children have been ill and unable to attend school would help the children keep up with schoolwork. When children are ill it is often difficult for parents to get to the school to get assignments. Use of the computer would give an assignment that could be printed and used by the child.

Background Material and Assignment Explanations. Permanent explanations and discussions of academic assignments could be available on the computer. This would be similar to course work that is done via the computer by many educational institutions of higher education. Although it would be time consuming to set up the programs, they could be easily revised and used again.

Telephone Calls

If it is impossible to visit a parent in person, rely on a telephone call. A telephone call early in the school year produces many benefits from appreciative parents. Beware, however, that most parents will wonder what is wrong when their child's teacher calls. This is quite an indictment of our communication methods; parents are generally contacted only when something is amiss. Change that practice by setting aside a short period each day for making telephone calls to parents. Begin the dialogue on a positive note. Early in the year, calls can include information about who you are, why you are calling, and a short anecdote about the child. If each call takes five minutes and you have 30 children in your class, the calls will consume two and a half hours—a small amount of time for the results you will see. Divide the time into segments of 20 to 30 minutes each evening. Parents also appreciate a note sent home saying you hope to call and asking for a convenient time. A sample letter is shown in Figure 5.6.

Home Visits

Some teachers make the effort to visit their students' homes early in the fall. This may be the only way to reach parents who have no telephone. It is also a rewarding experience for any teacher who can devote the time required. Not all parents are receptive to home visits, however, and some are afraid that the teacher is judging the home rather than coming as a friendly advocate of their child. Take precautions to avoid making the family feel ill at ease. Always let the family know you are coming. It is a good idea to write a note in which you request a time to visit or, possibly, give parents the option of meeting at another place. Once home visits become an accepted part of the parent-involvement program, they become less threatening, and both parents and children look forward to them. Chapter 8 gives suggestions for making home visits successful.

Visits to the Classroom

The traditional visit with parents invited for a specific event works very well in some school systems. In other schools, special events are complemented by an open invitation to parents to participate in ongoing educational programs.

Outside the classroom or just inside the door, hang a special bulletin board with messages for

Dear _____:

    During the school year, I will be making periodic telephone calls to parents of my students. I am able to call on Tuesday evening from 7:00 P.M. to 9:30 P.M. or on Wednesday afternoon from 3:30 P.M. to 5:00 P.M. Could you mark the time that would be most convenient for you?

    Should you want to call me, you will find me available on Thursday evenings from 7:00 P.M. to 9:00 P.M. Feel free to call my home at _____ if you have questions or would like to talk.

    I am looking forward to visiting with you this year.

                                          Best wishes,

_____

Telephone call preference
Tuesday: ❑ 7:00 to 8:00 P.M.   Wednesday: ❑ 3:30 to 4:00 P.M.
                ❑ 8:00 to 9:30 P.M.   ❑ 4:00 to 5:00 P.M.
If none of these times are convenient, please let me know.

FIGURE 5.6   Asking parents when they are available for telephone calls and letting them know when they can call you encourages communication.

parents. It might display assignments for the week, plans for a party, good work children have done, requests for everyday items to complete an art project, requests for special volunteer time, or just about anything that promotes the welfare of the room. Parents can plan and develop the bulletin board with the teacher's guidance.

Participation Visits

Directions for classroom participation are necessary if the experience is to be successful. Parents or other visitors feel more comfortable, teachers are more relaxed, and children benefit more if parents or visitors are given pointers for classroom visits. They can be in the form of a handout or a poster displayed prominently in the room, but a brief parent-teacher dialogue will make the welcome more personal and encourage specific participation.

The best welcome encourages the visitor to be active in the room's activities. Select activities that are easily described, require no advance training, and contribute rather than disrupt. You may want to give explicit directions on voice quality and noise control. If you do not want the parent to make any noise, request that a soft tone be used when talking with students in the room. Or you might want to ask the parent to work in a specific area of the room. Most visitors are happiest when they know what you want.

If it bothers you that some parents tend to give answers to students rather than help the students work out their own problems, suggest the method of instruction you prefer. You might give them a tip sheet for working with students that describes your favorite practices. Making activities simple for "drop-in" participants will keep problems to a minimum. If some parents prefer to sit and observe, don't force participation. As they become more comfortable in your room, they may try some activities. Selecting and reading a story to a child or group, listening to a child read, supervising the newsletter center, playing a game chosen from the game center with a student, supervising the puzzle table, or talking with students about their work are appropriate activities for new volunteers.

Visits by Invitation

A special invitation is sent to parents of a different child each week asking them to visit as "Parents of the Week" or VIPs—Very Important Parents. The invitation, written by the child or teacher, is accompanied by a memo from the administration that explains the objective of the visit. Have the child bring in information about brothers and sisters, favorite activities, and other interesting or important facts about the family. Place a picture of the family on the bulletin board that week. The family could include parents, grandparents, special friends (young or old), and younger siblings. Parents and guests are asked to let the teacher know when they plan to visit.

You could also improve a child's self-concept by making the child "Student of the Week." Not only do the children have a chance to feel good about themselves on their special day, but it also helps children get to know each other better. Feedback from parents after a visit is important. A reaction sheet is given to parents asking them to write their impressions and return it to the school. Comments range from compliments to questions about the school. This process encourages two-way communication.

Student-Parent Exchange Day

An idea similar to the student visiting the parent's place of employment is to have the parent take the place of the student at school. This can be done in several ways. The parent may accompany the student to class and spend the day with the child, or the parent and child may exchange places for the day. Exchanging places for the day works best for an older student who can fulfill some obligation at home or go on a field trip while the parent goes through the student's exact schedule. The parent is responsible for listening to the lecture or participating in the class and doing the homework. The parent learns about the school program, becomes acquainted with the teacher, and is better able to relate to the child's school experience. If the child is young and the school and parent prefer to participate in the school day without the child, the process is possible if the parent hires a baby-sitter or if the school provides a field trip for the children in the class.

Student-Parent-School Exchange

When concerns arise about drugs, alcohol, vandalism, or premarital sex, an enlightening way of having parents interact with students and school personnel is to have the parents visit a school nearby with similar concerns. Parents talk with children they don't know and find out how the students feel about the social issues they face. With the anonymity of parents and students, the discussion becomes more open. This arena can help bring about problem solving and answer some of the students' concerns. Perhaps the students need better after-school facilities to eliminate the attractiveness of misuse of time. Perhaps they want more guidance for their friends so that peer pressure is not so demanding.

Breakfasts

If you have a cooperative cafeteria staff or volunteers who are willing to make a simple breakfast, you can invite parents to an early breakfast. Many parents can stop for breakfast on their way to work. Plan a breakfast meeting early in the fall to meet parents and answer questions. Breakfast meetings tend to be rushed because parents need to get to work, so schedule a series of breakfasts and restrict the number of parents invited to each. In this way, real dialogue can be started. If a group is too large, the personal contact that is the prime requisite of two-way communication is prevented.

✷ ROADBLOCKS TO COMMUNICATION

The goals of those who work with young children are to meet the needs of the children, educate

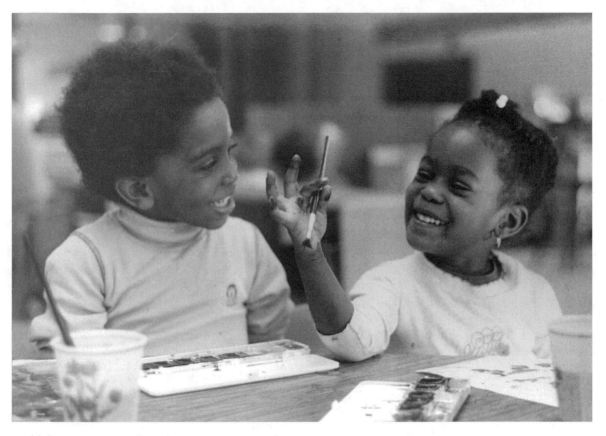

Establish eye contact to show that you are interested

them, and help them reach their potential as children and develop into productive adults. What is the challenge to parents? They have the same goals! Because parents and school personnel have the same goals in mind, it would seem that communication would be quite easy. Such is not the case. There tend to be many roadblocks to good communication between school personnel and parents. Both school personnel and parents set up roadblocks. Some roadblocks are used to protect positions, and others occur because the participants are unable to understand one another's positions.

The roadblocks that hinder effective communication between parents and school personnel are similar to those that affect any communication, but different concerns emerge. Some of the most common parent-and-school roadblocks will be described so we can work to overcome them.

Parent Roadblocks

Parents exhibit roles ranging from inadequacy to abrasive domineering that inhibit their ability to communicate effectively with the schools. Descriptions of some roles follow.

Protector Role

Parents protect their own egos when they overprotect their children. Many parents, often subconsciously, view their children as extensions of themselves. "Criticize my child and you criticize me" is their message. "Are you saying that I did not rear my children correctly?" "Is my child slow in school because I am the parent?" "Is there something that I should have done differently in my childrearing?"

When a parent puts up a shield as a defense against perceived criticism and attack, it becomes very difficult to communicate. When parents are hurt by a child's inability to progress satisfactorily in school, they may withdraw from open, honest communication in an effort to protect their child and their own self-esteem.

A parent's vested interest in the child can be channeled in a positive direction. Effective communication, with positive suggestions for encouraging the child, can help the parent become a partner with the school.

Inadequate-Me Role

Many parents do not feel comfortable talking with school personnel. These parents avoid going to civic events—including events that take place at schools—because they do not feel as if they belong. If parents feel inadequate, they avoid coming in contact with the schools. If they do come, they find it difficult to communicate their desires or feelings to the staff. These parents can benefit from encouragement so that they can contribute and be involved.

Avoidance Role

The avoidance role may include self-assured parents who do not respect the school or the way it treats parents and students. It also includes parents who had a difficult time in school when they were growing up. Perhaps they dropped out of school—the building might bring back bad memories. Schools must reach out to these parents by caring and offering activities and services that the parents need and desire.

Indifferent-Parent Role

It seems more difficult today to be a concerned, involved parent because of financial and time pressures. Although most parents want what is best for their children, some are willing to shift their parental responsibilities to others. The institution where children spend most of their working hours is the school. When children are reared by indifferent parents, their futures can be devastated. If no one cares, why should the children care? Drug abuse, teenage pregnancies, alcohol abuse, truancy, and criminal behavior are evidence that children have indifferent, dysfunctional, or too-busy parents. Early communication with parents can help reverse the trend.

Don't-Make-Waves Role

Many parents are unwilling to be honest in their concerns because they do not want school personnel to take it out on their child. They believe that the teacher or principal might be negative toward their children if they make suggestions or express concerns. This represses communication.

Club-Waving-Advocate Role

Sometimes parents get carried away with their devotion to their children, and they exhibit this through a power play. These advocates often become abrasive in their desire to protect their children or change school policy. These parents are the opposite of the "Inadequate-me" or the "Don't-make-waves" parents. "Club-waving" parents express their concerns through confrontation. Schools must acknowledge these concerns, and change the situation in cases where it is sensible to do so. In addition, give the parents opportunities to be leaders in areas where they can contribute.

School Roadblocks

Many times schools install roadblocks to effective communication without even realizing it. Sometimes they do so intentionally. The stress of educating and working with many children and families, pressure to accomplish many tasks, and the desire to be seen as efficient all get in the way of unhurried, effective communication. The following roles describe some of the roadblocks that hamper communication between home and school.

Authority-Figure Role

School personnel who act as the chief executive officer all too often hinder communication. These teachers and administrators claim to be the authorities, ready to impart information to the parent. They neglect to set the stage for the parent to be a partner in the discussion. If staff members take all the responsibility of running the school without considering the parents' backgrounds and knowledge, there seems to be no reason to communicate. Parents are locked out of the decision-making process. Schools that ignore parents destroy communication between parents and schools.

Sympathizing-Counselor Role

School personnel who focus on the inadequacy of the child in a vain attempt to console the parent miss a great opportunity for communication. Parents want to solve their concerns through constructive remediation or support. Parents and schools both need to focus on the achievements that can be attained through cooperation and collaboration.

Pass-the-Buck Role

Communication stops when school personnel refer the concerns of the parent to another department. "Sara may need help, but we cannot schedule her for tests for five months." "It is too bad that Richard had such a bad experience last year. I wish I could help, but he needs special services." Sometimes parents think the school is deliberately stalling while their child falls further and further behind.

Protect-the-Empire Role

A united, invincible staff can cause parents to think no one cares about their needs. School personnel need to work together and support one another, but they also need to listen to the parent and advocate for the parent as they formulate an educational plan for the student.

Busy-Teacher Role

Perhaps the greatest roadblock to good communication between parent and teacher is time. If you are harried, you do not have time to communicate with your students or their parents. Both teachers and parents need to reduce stress

and set aside time for communication. Reorganize schedules to include on-the-run conferences, telephone calls, and short personal notes to parents and children. Principals and directors might take over the classroom occasionally so teachers could make telephone calls to parents. The principals and directors would get to know the children in the classes and the importance of teacher-parent interaction would be emphasized. Roadblocks can be overcome.

✖ EFFECTIVE COMMUNICATION WITH PARENTS

To achieve effective communication, parents and teachers need to recognize roadblocks to their success. At the same time, they can increase their communication skills by practicing positive speaking, rephrasing, and attentive listening.

When teachers talk with parents, they communicate in many ways—through their words, their body actions, and their manner of speaking. Every contact communicates whether the speaker respects the other person, values that person's input, and is willing to collaborate. The self-fulfilling prophecy works with parents as well as with students. If teachers treat parents as if they are incapable of being partners, the parents will fulfill that prophecy. They will not work with teachers effectively.

Cooley's Looking-Glass-Self

Cooley's (1964) Looking-Glass-Self concept reveals that how you view yourself depends on your perceptions about how others see you. The Looking-Glass-Self contains three phases: (1) *reflection* (parents looking into the mirror), (2) *interpretation* of the reflection (how the parents interpret what they see), and (3) *feeling of pride or mortification*. If, in the second step, parents interpret the reflection as positive, they will, in the third step, feel pride in being able to work with the school to the benefit of their children. If they see disregard and no respect, they will find it difficult to work as partners.

A teacher views parents as either partners or subordinates. The teacher can either help parents feel that they are enablers, empowering them to help their children, or reject the parents.

Effective Communication Skills

Teachers can establish rapport with parents by using effective communication skills. A good partnership, however, takes two partners, so parents also need to work on their skills. Effective communication takes time, is honest, and is open. Good communicators listen, rephrase and check out, and avoid criticizing and acting superior.

Teachers are good communicators when they:

1. Give their total attention to the speaker. They establish eye contact and clearly demonstrate through body language that their interest is focused on what is being said.

2. Restate the parents' concerns. They clarify what has been said and try to discern the speaker's meaning and feeling. They avoid closed responses or answering as a critic, judge, or moralist.

3. Show respect for the other person. They recognize that their concerns, opinions, and questions are significant factors in mutual understanding and communication.

4. Recognize the parents' feelings. How much can you discuss with parents? Perhaps you need to establish a better parent-teacher relationship before you can completely share your concerns for the child.

5. Tailor discussions to fit the parents' ability to handle the situation.

6. Do not touch off the fuse of a parent who might not be able to handle a child's difficulties. They don't accuse; they spend more time with the parent in other communication and conferences.

7. Emphasize that concerns are no one's fault. Teacher and parents have to work on problems together to help the child. They use concerns as forums for understanding one another.

8. Remember that no one ever wins an argument. Calmly, quietly, and enthusiastically they discuss the *good* points of the child before bringing up any concerns.

9. Protect the parents' egos. They don't place blame or make them believe they are to blame for their child's deficiencies. They focus on plans for the future. On the other hand, they give parents credit for their child's achievements.

10. Focus on one issue at a time. They are specific about the child's progress or concerns.

11. Listen. They hear the feeling and meaning of the message, and rephrase and check out the message to be sure that they received it correctly.

12. Become allies with parents.

Parents become partners in the educational process when they:

1. View the teacher as a source of support for their child and themselves.

2. Listen carefully and give total commitment to the speaker.

3. Show respect for the teacher—recognize that the teacher's concerns, opinions, and questions are significant to mutual understanding and communication.

4. Recognize that the teacher has a difficult challenge to meet the needs of all students. They help the teacher succeed.

5. Rephrase and check out understanding of messages during conversations or conferences.

6. Speak openly and honestly about the child.

7. Use concerns as forums for understanding the school and teacher.

8. Become allies with the teacher.

The following sections on positive speaking, listening, reflective listening, rephrasing, and reframing elaborate on each of these communication skills.

Positive Speaking

If your message is positive, the parent is more apt to want to listen. The relationship between teacher and parent is enhanced. A positive statement needs to be accompanied by attentive behavior, good body language, and a warm tone of voice. Add clear articulation, and you have the recipe for effective communication between parent and teacher.

Listening

Listening is the heart of effective communication. Listening is more than hearing sounds. Smith (1986) describes listening as the "basis for human interaction" (p. 246). It is the active process of interpreting, understanding, and evaluating the spoken and nonverbal speech as a meaningful message. Listening, not speaking, is the most-used form of communication. Forty-five percent of verbal communication is spent listening; 30 percent, speaking; 16 percent, reading; and 9 percent writing.

In education, much attention is given to the ability to write, yet there is very little training for listening. Greater understanding and retention of information would occur if an appropriate amount of time were spent on helping people listen effectively. Smith (1986) recommends these steps to improve listening skills:

1. *Be receptive.* Listeners encourage the speaker by being receptive and providing an environment where the speaker feels free to express ideas and feelings.

2. *Pay attention.* Make an effort to concentrate on what is being said.

3. *Use silence.* Communicate that you are listening through attentive behaviors while remaining silent.

4. *Seek agreement.* Look for the broader meaning of the message rather than focusing on isolated facts.

5. *Avoid ambiguity.* Ask questions to clarify, look for main ideas, and focus on intent as well as content.

6. *Remove distractions.* Eliminate daydreaming, remove physical barriers, and delay other important messages to make the climate clear for listening.

7. *Be patient.* Don't rush the speaker. Allow time for the message to be completed.

Teachers and parents communicate when they:

- Listen carefully to the other person.
- Have good eye contact.
- Encourage the speaker using body language and verbal expressions such as "yes."
- Observe the speaker and have a facial expression that shows interest.
- Respond with attentive body language such as leaning forward or touching.
- Can rephrase the substance and meaning of the message they receive from the speaker.

Poor listening is evident if the receiver:

- Has little eye contact.
- Displays a stiff appearance.
- Changes subjects.
- Looks uninterested.
- Is unable to rephrase or interpret the communication properly.

Communicating with Parents Without English Proficiency

Teachers will need to make special efforts to communicate with parents who have difficulty expressing themselves in English. For example, parents whose first language is not English may have difficulty being articulate in English. Parents who are emotionally distraught may not be able to receive the intended message. In these cases it is of even greater importance that teachers have excellent listening skills. They can recognize any miscommunication and strive for clearer understanding.

When parents or teachers listen, they not only increase knowledge and understanding of the message, but they also demonstrate a caring attitude. Listening reduces tension and stress and encourages trust (Center for Family Strengths, 1986).

Open Responses—Closed Responses

An open response encourages communication to continue. Open responses can vary from positive body language demonstrated by a nod of the head or a smile indicating that you wish the speaker to continue, to a verbal response in which you indicate your interest. If a child comes into a home or classroom with a caterpillar in hand ready to display the treasure to mother or teacher, an open response would be a smile, a nod, or a question such as, "Where did you find such a marvelous caterpillar?"

A closed response would be a frown or a comment, "Take that caterpillar away this very minute." What child would dare to explain that the caterpillar was a treasure?

Should a child be a problem to a teacher, the easy response to a question by the parent would be a closed response. "Why does John have trouble with arithmetic?" the parent asks. "If you would help him with his homework, he wouldn't have so much trouble," the teacher responds. The conversation is ended. No one has sought to communicate and find out the best way to handle the situation.

Reflective Listening

Reflective listening is the ability to reflect the speaker's feelings. The listener's response identifies the basic feelings being expressed and reflects the essence of those feelings back to the speaker. Reflective or active listening is used in several parent programs such as the Parent Effectiveness Training

(P.E.T.) (Gordon, 1975), Active Parenting (Popkin, 2002), Systematic Teaching of Effective Parenting (STEP) (Dinkmeyer & McKay, 1989), and Teaching and Leading Children (Dinkmeyer, McKay, Dinkmeyer, & Dinkmeyer, 1992). These programs are described in the next section. The examples illustrate the use of active or reflective listening.

Reflective Listening and Reflective Responses

Reflective listening encourages open responses. A reflective response is effective if the listener recognizes the feelings of the speaker and is able to respond accordingly. The parent asks, "Why does John have trouble with arithmetic?" A reflective response would be, "You are concerned about John's ability to do his arithmetic?" The parent at that point probably would say "Yes."

To practice reflective listening think of the following three steps:

1. Use attending behavior. Make eye contact. Lean forward and be interested.
2. Listen for the feeling behind the message.
3. Respond with a statement of that feeling.

I–You–We Messages

One useful communication skill relies on "I" messages instead of "you" messages. A "you" message places the responsibility on the person receiving the message, and it is often a negative message. With a parent, it might be used in the following way. "If you would just help John with his homework, he would be more successful at school." To change that statement to a more positive "I" message, use words like those described in the following three steps:

1. "When [describe the behavior that is bothering you]."
2. "I feel [state how you feel about the concern]."
3. "Because [describe what you think might happen]."

For example, *"When* John does not finish his homework, *I feel* worried *because* I am afraid he will fall behind and not be able to catch up." Gordon (1975) introduced the "I" message and Dinkmeyer and McKay (1983) and Popkin (2002) use "I" messages in their parenting programs. There are times when a "we" message is more appropriate than an "I" message (Burr, 1990). "When Mary does not finish her homework, we have real concerns because she may fall behind her classmates." By using a "we" message the teacher acknowledges that the parent is also concerned.

Rephrasing

Rephrasing is restating the intent of the message in a condensed version. There are three steps in rephrasing. First, the listener must determine the basic message and the intent of the message. Second, the listener restates the intent of the message. Third, the listener checks out the accuracy of the rephrasing.

When listeners seek to check out or clarify a statement by saying something like, "It sounds as if you feel . . . " or "I'm hearing you say . . . " they are rephrasing the statement. With rephrasing, communicators can avoid misunderstanding the message by checking the accuracy. Confusion and ambiguity in communication are avoided. The interest displayed by rephrasing also shows caring and builds trust (Center for Family Strengths, 1986).

Reframing

Reframing involves taking the sting out of the negative description of a child. When communicating with parents, if your answer reflects your understanding of parents' concerns, the conversation will remain open, but the words you choose can bring either desirable or disastrous results.

A teacher with good intentions and great concern for a child once opened a conference with a parent by referring to the child's "problem" of not staying on task. The antagonized parent struck back: "I think you're obnoxious!" The family was already overwrought by strain and worry over the child. The rest of the conference time had to be devoted to rebuilding a working relationship, allowing no time for productive dialogue about the child and leaving both teacher and parent with emotional scars.

Instead of focusing on the negative aspects of an individual, start with positive comments. Then reframe the child's troublesome quality into an acceptable or even positive trait. Had the teacher started the conference with some friendly remarks and then stated, "I have some concerns about John that we should work on together," the parent might not have responded with such anger.

Examples of phrases that reframe a "problem" as a concern about the child include the following:

Problem	Concern
loud and boisterous	very active
gives others answers	can't help sharing
steals	takes without asking
won't follow rules	has own agenda, or is determined
shy	self-contained
talks too much	likes to share with others
does not pay attention	is preoccupied

It is particularly important in parent-teacher conferences and other communication between parent and teacher to couch the annoying behavior in terms that allow for dealing with it. There may be times, however, when the teacher's concern has reached such proportions that it must be faced squarely and openly. After several fruitless attempts at communicating, it may become obvious that the parent does not recognize that the behavior is hurting the child's progress. In such cases you may have to use more forthright terms. Just beware of the terminology you use. Harsh terms may completely cut off communication.

𝒢𝒢 PARENT EDUCATION PROGRAMS—P.E.T., ACTIVE PARENTING, STEP

Many parent education programs incorporate the resources of childrearing suggestions in Parent Effectiveness Training (P.E.T.) or Systematic Training for Effective Parenting (STEP). Brief excerpts from these programs illustrate the materials and communication techniques each uses.

Parent Effectiveness Training (P.E.T.)

In P.E.T., Gordon (1975) discusses many topics, including active listening, "I messages," changing behavior by changing the environment, parent-child conflicts, parental power, and "no-lose" methods for resolving conflicts. The following excerpt relates to problem ownership and active listening.

> In the parent-child relationship, three situations occur that we will illustrate with brief case histories:
>
> 1. The child has a problem because he is thwarted in satisfying a need. It is not a problem for the parent because the child's behavior in no tangible way interferes with the parent's satisfying his own needs. Therefore, *the child owns the problem.*
>
> 2. The child is satisfying his own needs (he is not thwarted) and his behavior is not interfering with the parent's own needs. Therefore, *there is no problem in the relationship.*
>
> 3. The child is satisfying his own needs (he is not thwarted). But his behavior is a problem to the parent because it is interfering in some tangible way with the parent's satisfying a need of his own. *Now the parent owns the problem.*
>
> It is critical that parents always classify each situation that occurs in a relationship. Which of these three categories does the following situation fall into? It helps to remember this diagram [see Figure 5.7].
>
> When a parent accepts the fact that problems are owned by the child, this in no way means he, the parent, cannot be concerned, care, or offer help. A professional counselor has real concern for, and genuinely cares about, each child he is trying to help. But, unlike most parents, he leaves the responsibility for solving the child's problem with the child. He allows the child to own the problem. He accepts the child's having the problem. He accepts the child as a person separate from himself. And he relies heavily upon and basically trusts the child's own inner resources for solving the problem. Only because he lets the child own his problem is the professional counselor able to employ active listening.
>
> Active listening is a powerful method for helping another person solve a problem that he owns, pro-

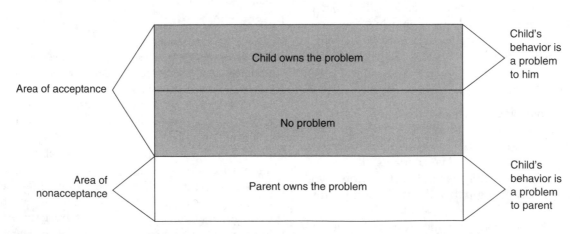

FIGURE 5.7 When the child's behavior is a problem to the parent, the parent owns the problem.
Source: From *P.E.T./Parent Effectiveness Training* (p. 64), by T. Gordon, 1975, New York: Wyden.

vided the listener can accept the other's ownership and consistently allow the person to find his own solutions. Active listening can greatly increase the effectiveness of parents as helping agents for their children, but it is a different kind of help from that which parents usually try to give.

Paradoxically, this method will increase the parent's influence on the child, but it is an influence that differs from the kind that most parents try to exert over their children. Active listening is a method of influencing children to find their own solutions to their own problems. Most parents, however, are tempted to take ownership of their children's problems, as in the following case:

Johnny: Tommy won't play with me today. He won't ever do what I want to do.
Mother: Well, why don't you offer to do what he wants to do? You've got to learn to get along with your little friends. *(advising; moralizing)*
Johnny: I don't like to do things he wants to do, and besides I don't want to get along with that dope.
Mother: Well, go find someone else to play with, then, if you're going to be a spoilsport. *(offering a solution; name-calling)*
Johnny: He's the spoilsport, not me. And there isn't anyone else to play with.
Mother: You're just upset because you're tired. You'll feel better about this tomorrow. *(interpreting; reassuring)*
Johnny: I'm not tired, and I won't feel different tomorrow. You just don't understand how much I hate the little squirt.
Mother: Now stop talking like that! If I ever hear you talk about one of your friends like that again, you'll be sorry. *(ordering; threatening)*
Johnny: (walking away and sulking) I hate this neighborhood. I wish we would move.

Here is how the parent can help the same boy with active listening.

Johnny: Tommy won't play with me today. He won't ever do what I want to do.
Mother: You're kinda angry with Tommy. *(active listening)*
Johnny: I sure am. I never want to play with him again. I don't want him for a friend.
Mother: You're so angry you feel like never seeing him again. *(active listening)*

Johnny: That's right. But if I don't have him for a friend, I won't have anyone to play with, then.
Mother: You would hate to be left with no one. *(active listening)*
Johnny: Yeah. I guess I just have to get along with him someway. But it's so hard for me to stop getting mad at him.
Mother: You want to get along better, but it's hard for you to keep from getting mad at Tommy. *(active listening)*
Johnny: I never used to, but that's when he was always willing to do what I wanted to do. He won't let me boss him anymore.
Mother: Tommy's not so easy to influence now. *(active listening)*
Johnny: He sure isn't. He's not such a baby now. He's more fun, though.
Mother: You really like him better this way. *(active listening)*
Johnny: Yeah. But it's hard to stop bossing him— I'm so used to it. Maybe we wouldn't fight so much if I let him have his way once in a while. Think that would work?
Mother: You're thinking that if you might give in occasionally, it might help. *(active listening)*
Johnny: Yeah, maybe it would. I'll try it.

In the first version, the mother used eight of the "Typical Twelve" categories of responding. In the second, the mother consistently used active listening. In the first, the mother "took over the problem"; in the second, her active listening left ownership of the problem with Johnny. In the first, Johnny resisted his mother's suggestions, his anger and frustration were never dissipated, the problem remained unresolved, and there was no growth on Johnny's part. In the second, his anger left, he initiated problem solving, and he took a deeper look at himself. He arrived at his own solution and obviously grew a notch toward becoming a responsible, self-directing problem solver.[1]

Gordon (1975) clarifies active listening and problem ownership through examples such as these. Parent groups follow up with a parent notebook and discussion within the group. Open discus-

---

[1] From *P.E.T./Parent Effectiveness Training* (pp. 64, 66–68), by T. Gordon, 1975, New York: Wyden.

sion, led by a person knowledgeable about P.E.T., allows parents to apply the methods to their own experiences in childrearing.

Systematic Training for Effective Parenting (STEP)

The STEP program furnishes cassettes, a parent manual, and a leadership manual to facilitate parent meetings. Figure 5.8 is taken from the 1976 parent manual.

Active Parenting

The Active Parenting program is similar to both P.E.T. and STEP in that it is also based on the theories of Alfred Adler and Rudolf Dreikurs. Goals of misbehavior, logical consequences, active communication, exploring alternatives, and family council meetings are described. A handbook and workbook supplement the group meetings and a leader's handbook gives detailed instruction on how the class should be conducted. Each

CHILD'S FAULTY BELIEF	CHILD'S GOAL*	PARENTS' FEELINGS AND REACTIONS	CHILD'S RESPONSE TO PARENTS' ATTEMPTS AT CORRECTION	ALTERNATIVES FOR PARENTS
I belong only when I am being noticed or served.	Attention	**Feeling:** annoyed **Reaction:** tendency to remind and coax	Temporarily stops misbehavior; later resumes same behavior or disturbs in another way	Ignore misbehavior when possible; give attention for positive behavior when child is not making a bid for it; avoid undue service; realize that reminding, punishing, rewarding, coaxing, and service are undue attention
I belong only when I am in control or am boss, or when I am proving no one can boss me!	Power	**Reaction:** tendency to fight or to give in **Feeling:** angry; provoked; as if one's authority is threatened	Active- or passive-aggressive misbehavior is intensified, or child submits with "defiant compliance"	Withdraw from conflict; help child see how to use power constructively by appealing for child's help and enlisting cooperation; realize that fighting or giving in only increases child's desire for power
I belong only by hurting others as I feel hurt. I cannot be loved.	Revenge	**Feeling:** deeply hurt **Reaction:** tendency to retaliate and get even	Seeks further revenge by intensifying misbehavior or choosing another weapon	Avoid feeling hurt; avoid punishment and retaliation; build trusting relationship; convince child that she or he is loved
I belong only by convincing others not to expect anything from me. I am unable; I am helpless.	Display of inadequacy	**Feeling:** despair; hopelessness; "I give up" **Reaction:** tendency to agree with child that nothing can be done	Passively responds or fails to respond to whatever is done; shows no improvement	Stop all criticism; encourage any positive attempt, no matter how small; focus on assets; above all, don't be hooked into pity, and don't give up.

*To determine your child's goal, you must check your feelings *and* the child's response to your attempts to correct him or her. Goal identification is simplified by observing:

FIGURE 5.8 The STEP program guides parents to relate positively with their children by checking the goals of misbehavior.

Source: From *STEP: Systematic Training for Effective Parenting,* by D. Dinkmeyer and G. D. McKay, 1976, Circle Pines, MN: American Guidance Service. Reproduced by special permission of American Guidance Service from *Systematic Training for Effective Parenting* by Don Dinkmeyer and Gary McKay.

Keep records, papers, and anecdotal notes to share during parent-teacher conferences.

session has a corresponding portion of a video that illustrates the child and family issues under discussion.

✆ PARENT-TEACHER CONFERENCES

A parent-teacher conference is a collaborative effort to coordinate the best possible effort for the education of the child in the classroom. It is a time for listening and sharing on the part of the school staff and the parents (Manning, 1985; Moles, 1996a). To accomplish the greatest cooperation between home and school and the greatest benefit for the student, the conference needs to continue the communication between the par-

ent and school, based on agreed-upon goals for the child throughout the year.

Start the school year with a positive interchange between teacher and parent by an early telephone call or a block walk—to initiate the parent-school partnership. A preconference discussion can then be used to set goals and direction for the child during the school year. The goals should reflect that teacher and parent want what is best for the child. The first conference can be a progress and planning session based on those goals.

It is possible to get 100 percent attendance at conferences. In the National Association of Elementary School Principals (1994) discussion of exemplary programs, the Klondike Elementary School in West Lafayette, Indiana, reported a tradition of 100 percent participation at conferences. Rides are provided for parents without transportation. For parents who cannot come to the school, school personnel go to the home or workplace to have the conference. They feel it is worth the extra effort to have high-priority conferences.

Parent-teacher conferences are personal opportunities for two-way communication between parent and teacher or three-way communication among parent, teacher, and student. Parents, as well as teachers, recognize the conference as an excellent opportunity for clarifying issues, searching for answers, deciding on goals, determining mutual strategies, and forming a team in the education of the student. Most schools schedule conferences two or three times a year. How can conferences be as productive as possible and yet nonthreatening to parents, teachers, and students?

Collaborative Conversations

Collaborative conversations can help develop cooperation and resolution of issues. Koch and McDonough (1999), using an example of a young child who hit and bit other children, describe five stages to improve parent-teacher conferences through collaboration, with all parties part of the team.

Stage 1. *Development of trust.* It is essential that a trusting relationship be developed. This can be enhanced prior to the conference at back-to-school nights, home visits, and informal interactions at school.

Stage 2. *Invite.* Extend an invitation that promotes cooperation and involvement. For example: "When would be a good time for us to talk together about Mary? Would you prefer to talk at school or at your home? Is there anyone else involved with Mary who could join us? Between now and the time we meet, let's all notice when Mary expresses her feelings safely" (p. 12).

Stage 3. *Set a mutual goal.* Facilitate or have a facilitator establish a cooperative atmosphere. Focus on the positive actions of the child when she appropriately handled the situation. Come to an understanding of your goal to enhance the positive.

Stage 4. *Listen to all viewpoints and expand understanding.* Allow all participants to express their feelings and ideas. The discussion moves from "identification of and observations about the effects of the problem to a dialogue about the unique outcomes/exceptions and the significance of these for all persons concerned" (p. 14).

Stage 5. *Restate the goal, measure it, and decide what to do about it.*

"Collaborative conversations create an atmosphere filled with possibilities and ideas that enhance the lives of children and the adults that care for them" (p. 14).

Invitations and Schedules

The invitation to attend a conference sets the tone. If it is cordial, shows an awareness of parents' busy lives and obligations, and gives the parents time options for scheduling the conference, the teacher has shown consideration of the parents and a desire to meet with them. Most school systems have worked out procedures for scheduling conference periods. Release time is usually granted teachers. Originally, most conferences took place in the afternoons. Children attended school in the mornings, and classes were dismissed at noon, with conferences between school personnel and parents—usually mothers only—occurring in the afternoon. With the increase in the number of working parents and single-parent families, plus the growing number of fathers becoming more directly involved in their children's education, many schools are scheduling more evening conferences, while retaining some afternoon conferences.

To prepare the schedule, notes are sent to parents asking for their time preference. The formal note should be direct and list specific options for the time and place of the conference. A sample note is found in Figure 5.9. After the responses have been returned, staff members, including teachers in special areas of education, meet to schedule back-to-back conferences for parents with more than one child attending the school.

A telephone call from the teacher to each parent adds a personal touch. These calls, made either before or after the invitation has been sent, may clarify questions and let the parents know they are really welcome.

Notes confirming the exact time and date of the conference should be sent home, whether the parent has been contacted or not. This ensures that both teacher and parent have the same understanding of the conference time. This confirmation note from the teacher to each parent could be personal, or a form could be used (see Figure 5.10).

A personal note might read:

I am looking forward to meeting _____'s parents. I enjoy her contribution to the class through her great interest in _____. The time and date of the conference are _____.

Dear _____ :

We are looking forward to meeting with you and discussing _____ experiences and progress at school. Will you please let us know when a conference would be most convenient for you? Please check the date and time of day you could come.

Thank you,

_____

Teacher or principal's name

Could you give a first and second choice? Please write "1" for your first preference and "2" for your second.

	Afternoon 1 to 4 P.M.	Evening 6 to 9 P.M.
Tuesday, November 12	_____	_____
Wednesday, November 13	_____	_____
Thursday, November 14	_____	_____

Please return by _____

FIGURE 5.9 Send a note home to schedule a conference.

Dear _____ :

Thank you for your response to our request for a conference time about your child's progress. Your appointment has been set for _____ (time) on _____ (day, month, and date) in room _____ .

We have set aside _____ minutes for our chance to talk together. If the above time is not convenient, please contact the office, and we can schedule another time for you.

We are looking forward to meeting with you.

Best wishes,

_____

Teacher

FIGURE 5.10 This note confirms and reminds about conference times.

Private and Comfortable Meeting Place

How often have you gone into a school, walked down the halls, and seen parents and teachers trying to have a private conversation in the midst of children and other adults? To achieve open, two-way communication, parent and teacher need to talk in confidence. Select a room designed for conferences or use an empty classroom, and attach a note to the door so people won't interrupt. Give the parents adult-size chairs so they can be comfortable and on the same level as the teacher. Place a table in front of the chairs so materials, class projects, and the student's work can be exhibited. The parent, teacher, and student (if it is a three-way conference) can sit around the table and talk and exchange information. The room should be well ventilated and neither too warm nor too cold.

Teachers also should be alert to psychological and physical barriers. People conducting interviews often set up such barriers to maintain social distance or imply a status relationship; an executive may sit behind a desk to talk with a subordinate. When teachers set themselves apart from the parents, a barrier is created.

Two-Way Communication in Conferences

"At the heart of effective parent-teacher conferences specifically and the parent-teacher relationship in general are interpersonal communication skills" (Rotter & Robinson, 1986, p. 9). Conditions necessary for effective communication during conferences include warmth—an attitude of caring—shown through attentive behaviors, smiling, touching, and body language. Along with warmth is empathy, the ability to listen and respond in such a way that the parent knows you understand. Respect is key to the success of building a collaborative connection between parent and teacher. If teachers and parents respect each other and enter the conference with a warm, caring attitude, able to listen effectively and understand the other's meanings and feelings, the stage is set for a successful conference (Rotter & Robinson).

Some school administrators and teachers make the mistake of seeing parent-school communication as the school informing the parent about the educational process, rather than as a two-way system. During a conference the teacher should spend only about half the time speaking. If teachers recognize the conference as a sharing time, half the burden has been lifted from their shoulders. They can use half the time to get to know the parent and child better.

Have you ever had a conversation with a friend who seemed miles away in thought? During conferences, communicators need to believe that what they have to say is important to the listener. Body language can reflect feelings contrary to the spoken word, causing the verbal message to be misunderstood or missed altogether. It is important to be aware of what you are communicating. If you are rushed, pressured, or concerned about your own family, you will have to take a deep breath, relax, and concentrate on the conference.

Just as some physical gestures communicate distraction or lack of interest, so does some body language convey your interest and attention to parents' concerns. Use appropriate, attentive behavior to signal your interest.

1. *Eye contact.* Make sure you look at the person as you communicate. Failure to do so could imply evasion, deception, or lack of commitment.
2. *Forward posture.* Leaning forward creates the image of interest in what is being said. Be comfortable but do not slouch, which can indicate that the whole process is boring or unimportant.
3. *Body response.* A nod in agreement, a smile, and use of the body to create an appearance of interest promote empathy. If you act aware and interested, you will probably become interested. If you do not, perhaps you are in the wrong profession.

Listening has been known to be an effective tool of communication since the early 1960s when Rogers affected methods of psychological counseling with his concept of reflective listening.

Earlier in this chapter we saw how the concept has been extended and reinterpreted in the day-to-day world of teaching parents and children. Gordon (1975) talked about the language of acceptance and the use of active listening as essential for improved parent-child relationships. Whether called "active" (Gordon), "effective" (Dinkmeyer & McKay, 1989), "responsive" (Chinn, Winn, & Walters, 1978), or "reflective" (Rogers, 1983), this kind of listening works. It helps open up the communication process.

Understandable Language

Specialized language gets in the way of communication. Although medical terminology is familiar and efficient for a doctor, it often sounds like a foreign tongue to a patient asking for an explanation of a diagnosis. Each year new terms and acronyms become common language in the schools, but they freeze communication when used with people not familiar with the terms. Imagine a teacher explaining to a parent that the school has decided to use the SRA program this year in second grade, but the first grade is trying whole language. Or one who says, "I've been using behavior modification with Johnny this year, and it has been very effective, but with Janet I find TA more helpful." Jargon can create misunderstanding and stop communication.

Sometimes terms have meaning for both communicators, but the meanings are not the same. Hymes (1974) declared that lack of communication, superficial communication, and "words and vocabulary, without friendship and trust and knowledge, get in the way of understanding" (p. 33).

> Look, for example, at "progressive education." Use those words and you have a fight on your hands. People get emotional, and wild charges fly. Yet parents will be the first to say, "Experience is the best teacher"—and there you have it! Different words, but a good definition of what progressive education stands for. (Hymes, 1974, p. 33)

Practice

To achieve the ability to listen reflectively and respond in a positive manner, practice until it becomes natural. You can practice alone, but it is more effective if you can role-play the conference. Having an observer present provides both practice and feedback. Teachers can choose a typical case from among their records or invent a hypothetical one. For example:

> Andy, a precocious third-grade child, spends most of the class period doodling ideas in a notebook. Although he completes his assignments, Andy takes no pride in his work and turns in messy papers. Special enrichment centers in the classroom do not attract him. Andy participates positively during recess and in physical education and music.

Each participant in the role play has basic information: the child's sex, grade assigned, and background. Assign one participant to act as the parent, another as the teacher. The third member of the team observes the interaction between the parent and teacher to check on the following:

1. Reflective listening
2. Attentive behavior (eye contact, forward posture, etc.)
3. Sensitivity to parents' feelings
4. Positive language
5. Cooperative decision making

Because no two teachers or parents are identical, there is no prescribed way to have a conference. The dialogue will be a constant flow, filled with emotions as well as objective analysis. You can prepare yourself, however, by practicing good reflective listening and positive communication. Look forward to sharing together.

Preparation for the Conference

Two types of preparation will set the stage for a successful conference. The first, an optional program, involves training teachers and parents for an effective conference. The second is essential— analyzing the child's records, current performance and attitude, and relationship with peers, and gathering examples of work along with recent standardized test results.

Preconference Workshops and Guides

Workshops for parents, teachers, or a combination of both are fruitful. A discussion of what makes a conference a success or a calamity can bring forth an enormous number of tips for both parents and teachers. If parents and teachers form small groups, many ideas will emerge that can be recorded on the board for discussion later by the total group. Encourage parents to ask questions about their part in conferences. Clarifying objectives and expectations will help parents understand their responsibilities. Parents and teachers attending a workshop together can learn the art of reflective listening and communication. Role-playing during conferences can elicit discussion. Many participants will see themselves in the roles portrayed and will attempt to find alternative methods of handling conference discussions. Films that illustrate common communication problems can also be used as starters for discussion.

At the close of the workshop, handouts or conference guides may be distributed to the participants. The guide should be designed with the school's objectives in mind. Parents can be told what to expect in the school's report and what the school expects from them. If your school does not schedule preconference workshops, put the handout in a newsletter and send it home to the parents before the conference. Questions in the conference guide should be those the school would like answered and also ones the parents might be interested in knowing. Typical questions include the following:

1. How does your child seem to feel about school?
2. Which activities does your child talk about at home?
3. Which activities seem to stimulate your child's intellectual growth?
4. How does your child spend free time?
5. Is there anything that your child dreads?
6. What are your child's interests and hobbies?

Some schools might also include questions about current concerns:

7. What concerns do you have about drugs and alcohol?
8. What kinds of support or collaboration would you like from the school to help your family?

A similar memo suggests questions the parents might want to ask:

1. How well does my child get along with other children? Who seem to be my child's best friends?
2. How does my child react to discipline? What methods do you use to promote self-discipline and cooperation?
3. Does my child select books at the proper reading level from the library?
4. Does my child use study periods effectively?
5. Are there any skills you are working on at school that we might reinforce at home?
6. Do you expect me to help my child with homework?
7. Are there any areas in which my child needs special help?
8. Does my child display any special interests or talents at school that we might support at home?
9. Does my child seem to be self-confident, happy, and secure? If not, what do you think the home or school can do to increase my child's feelings of self-worth?

Supplying questions before the conference is helpful in preparing parents, but it can also limit questions that develop naturally. In addition, if these questions are strictly adhered to during conferences, they can limit the scope, direction, and outcome of the conference.

Teacher Preparation

Throughout the school year teachers should make a practice of accumulating anecdotal records, tests, workbooks, art projects, and papers that represent both academic and extracurricular areas. Folders created by students, an accordion file, or a file box or cabinet can store the papers until conference time. Students may then compile a notebook or folder of samples of their work to share with their parents during conferences. If the file is worked on periodically throughout the term, papers can be placed in chronological order, thus illustrating the progress in each subject. The child's work is an essential assessment tool.

Standardized tests that reveal the child's potential compared with actual performance level are useful in tailoring an education program to fit the student. With this information, parents and teachers can discuss whether the student is performing above or below potential. Parents and teachers can use the information to plan for the future.

One word of caution on the use of standardized tests: these tests are not infallible. One child might not feel well on the day of testing, another might freeze when taking tests. Standardized test results should be used to supplement informal assessment tools such as class papers, notebooks, class observation, and informal tests, but not to replace those tools.

If standardized test results and your informal assessment are congruent and the child scores high on aptitude tests and shows moments of brilliance in class but consistently falls short on work, you can be fairly certain that the child is not working up to ability. If the child scores low but does excellent work in class, observe closely before deciding that the child is under too much pressure to achieve. In that case, the test may not indicate the child's true potential. Should the child score low on the test and also show a high level of frustration when working, you may want to make plans to gear the work closer to the child's ability. The standardized test, used as a backup to the informal assessment, can help teachers and parents plan the child's educational program.

Congruent Beliefs About the Child

Have you ever had a disruptive child in a class only to discover that the child was retiring and well behaved during Scouts? Sometimes the disparity makes one wonder if it is the same child. It is difficult to discuss a child on common ground if the parents' and teacher's perceptions of the child are completely different. Teachers and parents may need to compare their perceptions of the child. It is often meaningful to have students sort their own views so the perceptions of teacher, parents, and student can be compared.

Conference Membership

When children are taught by more than one teacher or have contact with numerous specialists (such as a speech teacher or physical therapist), including all professionals involved with the child is appropriate and requires cooperative planning. Beware of the effect on the parent, however, because a ratio of four professionals to one parent may be awesome and foreboding. If special care is taken to assure parents that all specialists are there to clarify and work with the teacher and parent as a team, the cooperative discussion and planning can have worthwhile results.

An alternative plan allows the parent to talk individually with each involved specialist. In some schools the homeroom teacher reports for all the specialists, but personal contact with each person involved with the child's education is more satisfying to the parents. If time is short, the entire group could meet with the parents once in the fall and assure the parents they will be available whenever the parents have a concern.

Consider including the child in the conference. Who is better equipped to clarify why the child is doing well or needs extra help? Who has more at stake? Preschoolers make less sustained conference members, but as soon as the child becomes interested in assessment and evaluations and recognizes the goal of parent-teacher conferences, the teacher should consider including the child in the process. Initially, the child may attend for a short portion of the conference, but as interest and attention span increase, the child might be present for the entire conference. If portions of the conference need to be conducted without the child present, have a supervised play area available. If older students are included as members of the team, issues can be clarified and goals set. The student is part of the discussion and helps in setting realistic goals.

Bjorklund and Burger (1987) describe a four-phase process for collaboration with parents. *Phase 1,* scheduled early in the year, sets the stage with an overview of when conferences will take place, techniques for observation of the children, and a detailed account of the curriculum based on developmental goals. During this phase both teachers and parents are encouraged to consider the developmental goals of the program. *Phase 2* is based on the goals. Parents, teachers, and administrators meet and set priorities using observation, testing, anecdotal records, and work samples. Two to four goals are given priority for each child. In *Phase 3,* observations, anecdotal records, checklists, and rating scales are collected for review.

Phase 4 involves the child. The teacher sends a progress report home in which all the developmental areas are reviewed. A guide for the conference is also sent, with three questions that parents should discuss with the child before the meeting. These are: (a) What do you like best about school? (b) Who are some of the special friends you like to play with at school? (c) Are there any things at school you would like to do more often? "The teacher begins the progress conference by sharing examples of the child's growth through anecdotes which describe some of the child's best skills or characteristics. This leads into a discussion of the three questions with the child" (Bjorklund & Burger, 1987, p. 31). The conference promotes a good self-image for the child by emphasizing the child's positive growth.

Student-Teacher-Parent Conferences

Many schools have conferences that give the task of deciding about objectives and goals to stu-

dents. The advantage of this approach is that it empowers students to be responsible for their own learning. The conference planning involves the teacher, any special professionals, and the student. In a private setting, the teacher and student decide what the student is going to accomplish.

When conference time arrives, the student and teachers meet in advance to decide what they will talk about at conference time and what they will put in the portfolio to share with the parents. These conferences involve more planning with the student than the traditional conference. At conference time, the student leads the discussion of what has been accomplished, what needs to be worked on, and what the future goals are. The concept behind this conference is similar to the Individualized Education Plan in that plans are made for individual students, but the pupil is more responsible for determining the objectives and goals.

Some schools organize student-teacher-parent conferences into a participatory situation with four sets of parents and children meeting at the same time. Each set discusses the child's achievements and goals. The teacher enters the discussion whenever a parent or child has questions or comments, or when the teacher has a reason for participating in their conference. At some point during the session, each set of parents and students include the teacher in their discussion.

Different issues arise with this change in the format of the conference. With this type of conference, the child and parents are responsible for its success. Teachers must have good organizational and leadership skills so that the student has established goals and direction before the conference. During the conference the teacher will not have the opportunity to monopolize the discussion, but the student and parents must take the teacher's responsibility seriously if the conference is to be successful.

Congruent Conferences

Conferences go more smoothly when the teacher and parents have congruent expectations about

Conferences require that the teacher use attentive behavior, be sensitive to parents' feelings, and use positive language and reflective listening as the parent and teacher collaborate together in decision making.

the performance of the child. If the child is an excellent student and both teacher and parents are pleased with the evaluation, it is easy to accept the report. If the child has a disability and both teacher and parents recognize the disabling condition, they can work together to plan an appropriate program for the child.

Too often the outward signs of good marks and pleasant personality and behavior fail to uncover how the child feels and whether the teacher can make the educational experience more satisfying and challenging. In working with a successful student, parents and teachers may fail to communicate about the child's potential and the need to have a good self-concept. Special interests of the child, friends, reading preferences, experiences, and needs are important for the teacher to know. Bring the child into the decision-making process. Together, the parents, teacher, and child can plan activities that will encourage growth and improve

self-concept. Let these parents and children communicate, too.

Situation

Julie is one of those students every teacher loves to have in class. She is enthusiastic, stays on task, completes her work, and never causes a disturbance in class. A quiet, attractive girl with her long brown hair pulled back in a ponytail, Julie always does the correct thing. She is polite to everyone and avoids fighting or taking sides when others are arguing.

Mrs. Collins relaxed in her chair as she prepared for the conference with Julie's parents. What an easy conference, she thought. I really don't have to talk with Julie's parents because she fits into the routine, is well adjusted, and is progressing nicely. As she looked up, she saw Mrs. Rivers, Julie's mother, standing outside the door. She rose to greet her and led her into the room, offering her a chair. As they sat side by side, Mrs. Collins remarked, "It is really good to see you, Mrs. Rivers. I enjoy Julie in class, and she is having no problems. Here are some of the papers I have collected. You can see that she completes her work and does a good job. I wish all my students were like Julie."

After looking over the papers, Mrs. Rivers looked up and said, "It is nice not to have to worry about Julie. I wish that Anne were as conscientious. I'm dreading that conference. I've really enjoyed having you be Julie's teacher."

Mrs. Rivers and Mrs. Collins glanced at Julie's papers and leaned back, satisfied.

"Look at the time; we finished in 10 minutes," Mrs. Rivers said. "You have five minutes to spare. Have a good day."

"You have a good day, too," the teacher said as she escorted Julie's mother to the door.

1. What did the conference accomplish?

2. Could there be a problem? How does Julie feel?

3. What should Mrs. Rivers and Mrs. Collins consider as they think about Julie? Does Julie feel good about herself? Is she a class leader? Does she get along well with the other children?

4. What does she enjoy doing the most? Is there anything that might make her school career even better?

Situation

"Welcome, Mrs. Alene, we are so pleased to have Joel with us this year," said Joel's preschool teacher, Mr. Better, greeting the boy's mother.

"He's just so happy to be here," Mrs. Alene said. "He was a little anxious at first, but you have made him feel welcome."

"I'm pleased Joel is beginning to feel comfortable. I noticed that he is interacting with the other children more—he played on the jungle gym today. His coordination is improving, and he is much more outgoing than he was three weeks ago when he first started. Let me share some of his paintings and some stories we have recorded. He illustrated this story. Look at the detail. What a great imagination!"

Mr. Better and Mrs. Alene looked at the papers together.

"What does Joel enjoy doing at home?" Mr. Better asked.

"He becomes very involved in building with his Lego set," Mrs. Alene said. "He loves to have us read him stories. We share stories together each afternoon and in the evening before he goes to bed. I try to limit his television viewing, though he does get to watch *Sesame Street* and *Mister Rogers* occasionally."

"Does he have any children to play with in his neighborhood?"

"There are no four-year-old children, but Bobby, who lives down the street, is in kindergarten, and he plays with Joel about three times a week."

"I'll bet they play hard, too!" Mr. Better said, and then turned to the current class activities.

"Our theme for this month is the sun," he said. "We're studying about shadows, reflections, and how the sun helps flowers to grow. These are some of the collages we have made. As you can tell, a lot of the pictures were made by tearing the paper, but we are also working on cutting. Let me show you how we are having him hold his scissors. Do you think you can help him with this at home? I'll be sending home activity suggestions and notes that let you know what we are doing at school."

"Thank you," Mrs. Alene said. "That way, I'll be more able to help Joel at home if he needs it."

"Why don't you go into the observation room and watch him for a while before you leave," Mr. Better said. "Don't forget that you can observe anytime, and you might want to volunteer to help in the preschool.

Joel's mother looked surprised and answered, "I hadn't thought about that, but it might be enjoyable."

"What haven't we covered? Do you have any questions that we neglected to discuss?" Mr. Better asked. After a pause, he added, "It was nice to be able to share with you about Joel's experiences here. Be sure to call if you have any concerns or if something is happening at home that we should know about. We want to keep in touch."

"I enjoyed talking with you. I can see why Joel enjoys school so much. Goodbye," Joel's mother answered as she walked toward the observation room.

1. What was effective in this conference?
2. Did the mother get to share enough?
3. What would you suggest to make it better?

Situation

Benny, a charming seven-year-old with big brown eyes, curly black hair, and a sparkling smile seemed older and larger than most children his age. When he came into the classroom before school started, he always went up to Miss Allen and told her about what was going on in his neighborhood. The stories were usually about fights, guns, hold-ups, gangs, and anger. There was reason to believe that he was relating what he had actually witnessed or heard. Benny lived with his father; his mother had disappeared several years earlier and, although Benny knew she was still alive, he had no contact with her. At one period in Benny's life, he lived in a cardboard box. Life had not been easy for this child, who had experienced much change and abuse.

When school starts, Benny is unable to stay on task. He seems to crave attention, whether it be from sharing, describing a story in the author's chair, or acting out. His primary method of obtaining attention is through acting out. He speaks out of turn, takes pencils from other children, and shoves and pushes. Because he is large for his age, he can hurt another child with a shove.

One day, Benny threatened an aide working in the classroom by suggesting that his older sister would beat her up. Timeout does not help because he does not oblige, but he does seem to be threatened by a trip to the office. The school year is in its fourth week and there have been no parent-teacher conferences.

1. What would you suggest the teacher do to obtain parent collaboration?
2. Do you believe that parent-school cooperation is feasible? Why or why not?

3. What could you do as a teacher to help Benny become a productive child?
4. Would a conference that included Benny and his father be a good idea? Why or why not?
5. If you believed that Benny comes from an abusive home, would you change your approach? Why or why not?

Preconference Preparation

Before the day of the conference, and throughout the reporting period, you, as the teacher, prepare by getting to know the student, conducting ongoing assessment, and developing a portfolio. Before the conference, review the child's history, family situation, successes, and concerns. Depending on what records are kept by the school, try to learn about the student's educational experience. Review the papers in the current portfolio so that you can know the student's growth or delay that has occurred under your guidance.

Try to have three- to five-minute individual conferences with each child to talk about what you are going to cover in the conference. Determine if there is anything that the child would like to see included, thus providing you insight into the child's thoughts. If you recognize the child's thoughts as important you increase the child's respect for self and belief in the teacher or a caring ally.

The Day of the Conference

During the conference, review your objectives, use effective communication skills, discuss concrete examples of work, and plan together.

Clear Statement of Objectives

Some objectives may be universal; others will be specific for the individual conference. Use the following objectives as a guide:

1. To gain a team member (the parent) in the education of the child.
2. To document the child's progress for the parent.

3. To explain the educational program you are using as it relates to the individual child.

4. To learn about the environment in which the child lives.

5. To allow the parents to express feelings, questions, and concerns.

6. To get a better understanding of the expectations the parent holds for the child.

7. To set up a lasting network of communication among parent, teacher, and child.

8. To establish cooperative goals for the education of the child.

Recognition of the Parent as Part of the Team

After you have made sure the room is comfortable, two-way communication will be uninterrupted, and you are ready to listen and be responsive to the parent, it is easy to recognize the parent as a part of the educational team. Parents arrive at conferences as experts on their children's history, hobbies, interests, likes and dislikes, friends, and experiences. You, as the teacher, can gain a great deal of knowledge and understanding of the child from the parents.

The Conference

Begin the conference in a relaxed, positive manner. Besides being adept at reflective listening, you need to listen intuitively to determine if parents have problems within their homes or are themselves emotionally immature. Such problems make it difficult for the child to have the home support needed for educational success. When indicated, invite other professionals, such as the school social worker or principal, to the conference to support and help the family and child. You can be more understanding of the child's needs if you understand the child's home (Grissom, 1971).

Why do parents enter into parent-teacher conferences with apprehension? Some are worried because they want the best for their child but do not know how to achieve it. They are unsure of themselves in the discussion and might be threatened by jargon. If parent and teacher can throw away their usual roles during the conference and view it as a meeting place for the exchange of ideas and information and a chance to support each other, both can enter into the conference with enthusiasm and confidence.

Relax before conference time. It is important to establish a cooperative climate. If the teacher is relaxed and poised, parents will be able to relax, too, and the climate for communication will be improved. Meyers and Pawlas (1989) recommend developing a form to use for record keeping for planning as well as keeping records for future conferences. The teacher is able to focus on one or two predetermined issues and keep records of the collaboration. Multiple concerns can be overwhelming; time does not allow all issues to be resolved. When determining the issues to be discussed, however, parents should have the option of helping determine the agenda. Perhaps they have a concern that is not known by the teacher. They can either share their concerns by sending back an information sheet suggesting what they would like to discuss, or during the conference the teacher can encourage them to bring up their concerns or comments.

Sandwich Approach

Use the sandwich approach when you plan a conference (Manning, 1985). Start the conference with pleasant and positive items. If you have negative comments or concerns to be discussed, bring them up during the middle of the conference. Always end with a positive summary, spend time planning with parents, and make a pleasant comment about the child.

Team Membership

Explain to the parents that all participants in the conference are members of a team looking at the progress of the child and working together to benefit the child. How can *we* help the child who is having a difficult time? How can *we* enrich the program for the child who is accelerated? How can *we* get the child to do the task at hand? How can *we* promote self-esteem? If the teacher and parents work as a team to answer these questions, the conference will be far more productive than if the teacher simply dictates answers to the parents. Here are some tips that will help parents feel they are part of the team:

- Know the parent's name. Do not assume that the child and parent have the same last name. Look in the record for the correct name.
- Ensure the privacy of the conference.
- Know the time limitations.
- Do not use terminology that may have meaning for you but not the parent.
- Do not refer to organizations, forms, tests, materials, or ideas by their initials or acronyms. Do not assume that everyone knows what the initials or acronyms mean.
- Have some questions about and show interest in the child.
- Remind parents that they may ask questions at any time and you will be pleased to explain anything that is not clear.
- Begin on a positive note. Start by praising an accomplishment of the child or a contribution the child has made to the class.
- Review your file and know enough about the child before the parent arrives that the parent can tell you have taken a personal interest in the child's welfare.
- Keep on the subject: the child's schooling and development.
- Encourage the parents to contribute. Allow parents to talk for at least 50 percent of the time.
- Show that you understand the parent by checking periodically during the conference. For example, you might ask, "Would you agree with this?" or "Do you have suggestions to add about this?"
- Make note of an idea suggested by a parent, but do not get so involved in writing that you lose the flow of the conversation.

- Maintain eye contact.
- Use attentive behaviors—that is, lean forward, look interested, and nod when in agreement.
- Do not ignore a parent's question.
- Be honest, yet tactful and sensitive, to the parent's feelings.
- Base your discussion on objective observation and concrete examples of work.
- Deal in specifics rather than generalities whenever possible.
- Evaluate needs and select methods of remediating deficiencies.
- Evaluate strengths and select methods of enriching those strengths.
- Plan educational goals together.
- Clarify and summarize the discussion.
- Make plans to continue the dialogue.

Concrete Examples of Child's Work and Behavior

Both parent and teacher are interested in the child's accomplishments. By making objective observations of the child's classroom behavior, with anecdotal notes collected in a loose-leaf notebook, throughout the reporting periods, the teacher documents the child's social as well as intellectual achievements. Anecdotal records of significant behaviors are especially valuable for conferences with parents of young children. Papers and tests may not be available, so the anecdotal records become tools for evaluating the child's social, intellectual, and physical progress. In the case of children with behavioral problems, it is also important to be able to cite specific incidents rather than vague generalizations about disturbances.

The accumulated examples of the child's work with a few words from the teacher also illustrate to parents what their child is doing. It is not necessary to state when a child has not progressed, for that will be obvious. If another child has made great progress, that too will be evident from the samples collected. Consider asking parents if they have come to the same conclusion as you when comparing early and subsequent papers.

Some teachers supplement papers and anecdotal records with videotapes of children in the classroom. Although time consuming, a film or video report is enjoyable for parents and encourages interaction between parent and teacher on the child's classroom participation.

Bringing concrete examples to the conference illustrating the child's work may prevent a confrontation and allows parent and teacher to analyze the work together. Include anecdotal records and samples of the child's work in comparison with expected behavior at that age level. In preschool this may include fine-motor control, large-muscle activities, art, and problem solving. For school-age children examples may include papers, artwork, projects, work in academic subjects, tests, notebooks, workbooks, and anecdotal records. It is also helpful to parents for the teacher to collect a set of unidentified "average" papers. If parents want to compare their child's work with that of the "average" child, they have a basis for this comparison.

Whatever the level of the child's performance, the parent and teacher need to form a team as they evaluate the child's educational progress and work together for the good of the child.

Use the conference form recommended by Meyers and Pawlas to keep a record. Parents and teacher—and student, if in attendance—decide on goals, highlights or accomplishments, and plans for the future. All attendees should read and sign the conference form and retain a copy.

Postconference Plans

After the conference, write a note thanking the parents for their participation. Later, in a follow-up telephone call, let the parents know how the conference plans are being implemented and how the student is participating. Each contact increases the parent-school collaboration.

A checklist may be used for self-evaluation, as shown in Figure 5.11. If you are able to answer yes to these questions, you are ready to have productive parent-teacher conferences.

Dealing with Angry Parents

What do you do when an upset and angry parent confronts you? Most professionals face such a situation at one time or another. Margolis and Brannigan (1986) list seven steps to help you control the volatile situation and allow the parent to regain composure. If you understand the dynamics of anger, you can engage in reflective listening. As a result, you can redirect the wrath and empathize with the parent. The steps include the following:

1. Remain calm and courteous, and maintain natural eye contact through the barrage. After the parents have expressed their anger, usually dominated by emotion, ask them to repeat their concerns so you can understand the situation better. The second time around, the statements are usually more comprehensible and rational.
2. Use reflective listening and give reflective summaries of their statements. You can explore the content of their messages later, but during this stage attempt to establish a more relaxed and trusting atmosphere.
3. Continue with reflective listening, and ask some open-ended questions that allow them to talk more as you gain greater understanding.
4. Keep exploring until you have determined what the underlying critical issues are. Do not evaluate, and do not be defensive.
5. After the issues have been fully explored, rephrase and summarize, including points of agreement. Check to see if your summary of their concerns is correct. Offer to let them add to what you have summarized. When you clearly define the concerns, they often seem more manageable.
6. Margolis and Brannigan (1986) point out that by now, listening has been used to build trust and defuse the anger. You are more likely to understand the problem from the parent's perspective. "When steps one through five are followed in an open, sincere, and empathetic manner, disagreements frequently dissolve and respect emerges"

Conference Checklist

Yes	No	Did You
❏	❏	1. Review information about the child's family? Did you know the parents' last names? Were you aware of the child's educational experience?
❏	❏	2. Prepare ahead by collecting anecdotal records, tests, papers, notebooks, workbooks, and art materials from the beginning to the end of the reporting period?
❏	❏	3. Provide book exhibits, displays, or interesting reading for parents as they waited for their conferences?
❏	❏	4. Make arrangements for coffee or tea for parents as they waited for their conferences?
❏	❏	5. Prepare your room with an attractive display of children's work?
❏	❏	6. Welcome the parents with a friendly greeting?
❏	❏	7. Start on a positive note?
❏	❏	8. Adjust your conference to the parents' needs and levels of understanding?
❏	❏	9. Have clear objectives for the conference?
❏	❏	10. Say in descriptive terms what you meant? Did you avoid educational jargon and use of initials?
❏	❏	11. Listen reflectively?
❏	❏	12. Keep the communication lines open? Were you objective and honest?
❏	❏	13. Avoid comparing students or parents? Did you discuss other teachers only if it was complimentary?
❏	❏	14. Check your body language? Were you alert to the parents' body language?
❏	❏	15. Plan the child's educational program together?
❏	❏	16. Summarize your decisions? Did you make a record of your agreements and plans?
❏	❏	17. Begin and end on time? If you needed more time, did you set up another appointment?
❏	❏	18. Follow up with a note and a telephone call?

If you had the student lead the conference, in addition to the above

Yes	No	Did You
❏	❏	1. Work with the student to develop goals and objectives?
❏	❏	2. Encourage the student to achieve his/her goals and objectives?
❏	❏	3. Have the student prepare a portfolio with projects, papers, research, tests, and other achievements?
❏	❏	4. Have practice sessions in which the student developed the ability to explain objectives and progress? (Students may work with partners and/or other peers.)
❏	❏	5. Make yourself available to discuss the student's progress with the family during the conference period?

FIGURE 5.11 A checklist reviews important conference practices.

(p. 345). If such is not the case, go back and allow free exploration again.

7. Use a systematic problem-solving approach to any issues that remain unresolved. The steps in collaborative problem solving include: (a) understand each other's needs and the resources available to help satisfy those needs, (b) formulate a hypothesis that might solve the problem, (c) brainstorm other solutions, (d) combine ideas and solutions to create new solutions, (e) together, develop criteria to judge the solutions, (f) clarify and evaluate solutions, and (g) select the most likely solution. At the end of the confrontation, the result should satisfy both educator and parent.

Situation

"I've never come to a school conference without having to wait 45 minutes to talk with you. Then, when I get in, you rush me, never let me ask questions, and just tell me how poorly Mary is doing. I know that Mary is doing poorly! I have my hands full just trying to go to work and feed my four children. Can't you do something to help Mary? Do you care?" Mary's father breathlessly expressed his anger and frustration.

"Hold on, Mr. Wimble," Mr. Bush said. "You're responsible for Mary, not me. She does poorly because she doesn't pay attention; she's more interested in her friends than in school, and she cuts class. I can work with students who come to school ready to learn. I just don't have the strength or the patience to take on your daughter until she changes her attitude."

"I waited 45 minutes to hear that?" Mr. Wimble asked. "What's going on here? No wonder Mary skips school. Where's the superintendent's office? I need to talk with your supervisor." Mr. Wimble stalked out of the room.

1. How could Mr. Bush respond in a manner to reduce Mr. Wimble's anger?

2. What kind of interaction should take place to promote problem solving?

3. Is there anything Mr. Bush can do to help this situation?

4. What can Mr. Wimble do to help resolve his daughter's problems?

5. What responsibility does Mary have?

Making a Contract—Parent-Teacher Communication

Most teachers have experienced working with children who do not stay on task, daydream, act out in class, or seem to be wasting their potential. Parents of these children are usually just as concerned as the teacher. In a contract arrangement, the parents are empowered to get involved in the child's school behavior. In an effort to increase the student's positive participation in school, teachers and parents have an ongoing communication system that acknowledges how the child does in school. Parents and teachers work together to establish the goals and parameters of the contract. Usually a note is sent home each day detailing how the student performed at school. This includes schoolwork as well as classroom behavior. The parents reinforce the positive behavior and help diminish the negative. By communicating each day, parents and teachers form a team to help the child become successful in school, by focusing on the goals of the contract—which includes schoolwork as well as behavior.

Kelley (1990) describes a home-based reinforcement method in her book on school–home notes. It is based on behavioral theory and is similar to the contract method. This approach is beneficial for children who are disruptive, do not stay on task, or are not performing up to their abilities. The school–home note or daily report card is an intervention method that requires the participation of parents as well as teachers. Together they collaborate on problem solving and determine their approach. Each day the teacher completes a simple form and sends it home, letting the parents know how the child behaved and participated in class that day. The parent follows up with consequences. It is important that the consequences fit and that they have the desired result. "The goals in any contingency management system are to reinforce appropriate behavior (so as to increase its frequency) and to ignore or punish inappropriate or unacceptable behavior (so as to decrease its frequency)" (p. 16).

If the school–home contract or notes are not working, the teachers and parents should meet again and revise their plan.

✍ DEALING WITH CONCERNS THROUGHOUT THE YEAR

The following principles (Franklin, 1993) will help facilitate good home-school communication as issues emerge throughout the year.

1. Approach the parents at every meeting with the assumption that you have a common goal—a good environment for the child to learn and develop.

2. Try to facilitate the best in the parent, just as you support and try to develop the best potential in the child.

3. Avoid confrontation and defensive responses. Model working together as partners.

4. Assess your motives before giving negative feedback to parents. Why are you telling this to the parent? What do you hope will come out of the exchange? Will it help the child's learning? Do you expect a positive outcome?

5. Avoid setting yourself up as an authority figure with parents. Work toward establishing a partnership with the parents. Respect the parents' knowledge of their child and ask them to share information with you. Parents and teachers can learn from each other and provide different perspectives.

6. Try to avoid judging the parent, just as you hope they are not focused on evaluating you.

7. Give a careful and thoughtful response to parent concerns. Be available and unhurried in your interaction.

8. There are no typical responses from parents. They are as different from one another as teachers are from each other. Be an active listener, and remain open to different perspectives.

✍ SUMMARY

Effective communication between parents and schools allows parents to become partners in education. Communication includes speaking, listening, reflection of feelings, and interpretation of the meaning of the message. If the message sent is not correctly interpreted by the receiver, then miscommunication has occurred. It can be overcome by rephrasing and checking out meanings. Talking is not the most important element in communication. The way a message is spoken and the speaker's body language account for 93 percent of the message.

It is essential for schools to have good communication with families. One-way communication describes the method that schools use when they offer parents information through newsletters, newspapers, media, and handbooks. Two-way communication allows parents to communicate with school personnel through telephone calls, home visits, classroom visits, and school functions. It continues through the year with classroom visits and participation, back-to-school nights, parent education groups, school programs, projects, workshops, PTA carnivals, exchanges, and a suggestion box.

Parents and schools both put up roadblocks to communication. Parent roadblocks include the following roles: protector, inadequate-me, avoidance, indifferent-parent, don't-make-waves, and club-waving advocate. Roadblocks put up by schools include the following roles: authority-figure, sympathizing-counselor, pass-the-buck, rotect-the-empire, and busy-teacher.

Effective communication and trust building between parent and educator are important. The areas of communication that can be developed include positive speaking, listening, reflective listening, rephrasing, reframing, and attentive behavior. P.E.T., STEP, and Active Parenting all include communication with an emphasis on reflective or active listening in their parent education format.

Parent-teacher conferences are the most common of two-way exchanges. Conferences can be effective if educators and parents prepare for them in advance.

Teachers need to make parents feel welcome; materials and displays should be available. Two-way conversations will build cooperation and trust. Teachers can develop expertise in conducting conferences by relating to the parents, developing trust, and learning from them about the child. A checklist is included to analyze the effectiveness of the conference.

The chapter includes suggestions for dealing with angry parents and how to deal with concerns parents may raise throughout the year.

⤬ SUGGESTED CLASS ACTIVITIES AND DISCUSSIONS

1. Develop a simple newsletter, a note to parents, and a detailed newsletter.
2. Practice speaking positively. Develop situations in which a child has average ability, has a learning disability, or is gifted. Role-play the parent and the teacher. Make the interaction focus on positive speaking. Then reverse your approach and become negative in your analysis of the child. How did you feel during each interchange?
3. Practice listening. Divide the class into groups of three. One person is the speaker, another is the listener, and the third is the observer. Exchange roles so each person in the group gets to play each role. Have each person select a topic of interest, from something as simple as "my favorite hideaway" to something as serious as "coping with death in my family." Each person tells a story; the listener listens and then repeats or rephrases the story. The observer watches for body language, attentive behavior, interest, and correct rephrasing. A checklist is an excellent way to make sure the observer watches for all elements of listening.
4. Visit a school and obtain a copy of the school's newsletter. Analyze it. Does it communicate with parents effectively? How would you improve it?
5. Consider your beliefs and value system. What beliefs might be blocks to communication with parents, particularly those with a different value system?
6. Brainstorm in class for words to use in rephrasing. For example, what words could you use to describe a child who hands in sloppy work?
7. Role-play the parent putting up roadblocks to communication.
8. Role-play the roadblocks that schools put up that hinder communication.
9. Sit in on a staffing or a parent-teacher conference. Observe the parents' and the educators' interaction.
10. Compose situations that need constructive, positive answers. Make up several answers that would be appropriate for each situation.

6 Collaborative Leadership— Working with Parents

A leader is best
When people barely know that he exists
Not so good when people obey and acclaim him
Worst when they despise him
Fail to honor people,
They fail to honor you,
But of a good leader, who talks little
When work is done, his aim fulfilled
They will all say, "we did this ourselves."

Lao-tze, ancient Chinese philosopher

Education makes a people easy to lead, but difficult to drive; easy to govern, but impossible to enslave.

Brougham, 1828

In this chapter on collaborative leadership you will find procedures that will enable you to do the following:

- Use collaborative leadership skills as you work in site-based or community management, charter schools, classroom management, cooperative education, or parent involvement and parent education.
- Describe types of leadership.
- Cite research that supports parent involvement and parent education.
- Plan and develop a needs assessment.
- Organize the format of a meeting.
- Recognize roles that develop in participation in meetings.
- Select the meeting format that meets the needs of the participants.
- Select appropriate topics for meetings.
- Evaluate meetings.

Have you ever attended a meeting where every-one was accepted and encouraged to participate and the objectives of the meeting were accomplished? Each person participated in the meeting and, as a result, developed higher self-esteem and had the opportunity to be a part of a productive group. A well-led parent group or school team is representative of such a meeting and accomplishes its goals by including parents and, in the process, educating all and clarifying and responding to questions and concerns.

Leadership ability is a skill that helps in all facets of human interactions. School professionals find it essential whether they are parent educators, principals, or teachers. Principals, always the educational leaders in their buildings, are being asked to provide more leadership in community or collective collaboration in site-based management of schools. Teachers need leadership skills to encourage problem solving and critical thinking, and to set the stage for learning. In addition, teachers are being asked to serve on site-based or community-based committees. In group decision making, leadership skills are essential to accomplish the goals or objectives of the group. As you read this chapter which focuses on parent education, expand your thinking to visualize how good collaborative involvement and leadership can be used in classrooms, family meetings, professional meeting, and group activities.

✌ FAMILY INVOLVEMENT

Family involvement offers the professional an exciting opportunity to work with highly motivated, interested adults. Whether involved in a site-based, collaborative decision-making team, as a participant in their child's education, or in a parent education program, parents usually are highly motivated. If the parents have attended parent education classes after the birth of their first child, the educator usually will find two concerned and committed parents, ready to gain information that will help them in the first months of their baby's life. If educators work with parents of pre-

school children, they will find parents who have several years of on-the-job training—experience that will help them build their knowledge base. In either case the parents will have concern for the well-being of their children and family. Two elements necessary for effective learning—interest and need—will be present.

Parents, as adult learners, bring with them many of the ingredients of a stimulating, productive learning environment. Their interest and need make it easy to develop topics that are important to the membership. The background and experience of the parents provide rich educational material, an opportunity for sharing expertise and knowledge, and an impetus for self-directed learning. Parent involvement groups should be carefully monitored to make sure that all levels of expertise are allowed to flourish. It is up to the leaders to provide an accepting, risk-free environment, involve the parents in planning, provide relevant materials and knowledge, and devise appropriate delivery systems (such as group discussions, simulations, role-playing, and experts).

✌ DEVELOP COLLABORATIVE LEADERSHIP SKILLS

Good collaborative leadership skills are beneficial in many areas of life. Whether it be the home, school, or the wider arena of the community, information on group leadership and processes is very useful. Students of all ages can participate in a family meeting, and those in intermediate middle school and high school often have presentations about a project they have developed. They learn from the organization and design of the presentation, the research and background information needed to prepare, and the presentation.

Professionals and/or classroom teachers who can support and motivate the group can accomplish the goals of the group without undermining the responsibilities of the participants. The style of the leader will be determined by the individual's training and personality as well as the makeup of the group. Group management can be enhanced by collabo-

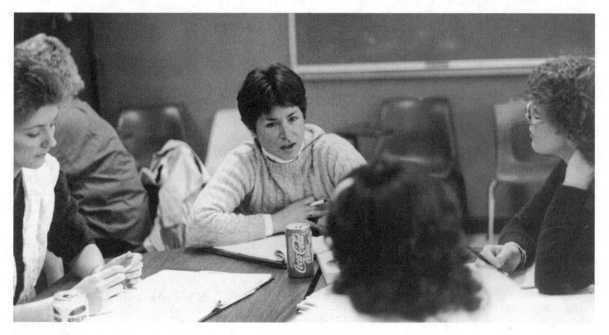

Leaders emerge from the group if they have not been formally elected or selected.

rative leadership training sessions where members of the group can be introduced to group methods, curriculum, and resources. It helps if participants have a basic understanding of group processes and communication, whether the group is being led by students, parents, principals, or professionals.

The leadership role in site-based or community management usually falls to the principal. Principals, along with teachers, must collaborate with parents and other community members to establish the management and objectives of the school. Using a collaborative approach proves to be very effective.

Collaborative Decision Making in Site-Based Management

In collaborative decision making, the principal is usually the leader. Because the approach is collaborative, the designated leader should be a facilitator, one with information and background material that can be used by the entire group. The leader also should be aware that those on the committee have much to share and must be willing to encourage interaction.

The California School Leadership Academy focuses on influencing principals to become better instructional leaders in their schools (Marsh, 1992). Through leadership training they have been able to influence instructional leadership in the schools. In particular, ideas and attitudes changed among educators and the community. With increased partnership among teachers, parents, special educators and administrators, the need for more leadership increased.

Leadership skills go beyond administrators to those with whom they work. In site-based management, members of organizing committees who understand group dynamics, growth, and leadership responsibilities will be more effective than those who flounder trying to develop meaningful and effective group decision making.

✒ PARENT EDUCATION

Leadership in parent education may be viewed along a continuum (Figure 6.1) that ranges from a lay leader, a nonprofessional with little training, to a knowledgeable expert trained to expedite

Parent leader with no training	Parent leader with leadership training	Parent leader with a structured curriculum	Parent leader with professional support	Professional leader with parent support	Professional teacher

FIGURE 6.1   Continuum of leaders in parent education.

group processes, a professional who lectures as an authority. As you begin a parent education program, keep in mind that groups can be organized in different fashions. A trained professional should not dominate the group with specific, didactic teaching, nor should the lay group be left without direction.

The use of lay leaders—parents leading their own groups—encourages parents to be actively involved. Because educational growth and positive change are what is wanted in parent education groups, active involvement is highly desired. More change will occur if the parent formulates some of the educational suggestions and acts upon the information. Parents are more able to develop ways of handling parent-child relationships if they develop their expertise from their own research and interact with other members of the group. This does not mean excluding experts in the field. At times it is necessary to have an authority give background material. After the information is received, however, parents need to discuss and act upon it themselves.

This chapter describes various types of meetings and group processes as a guide in the development of new parent-group programs. The programs discussed here range from those led by the unskilled person without curriculum guides, on the left of the continuum in Figure 6.1, to the authoritative meeting on the right. At the center of the continuum is the parent education group that is most appropriate for achieving parental self-determination, attitudinal change, competence, and educational gains—that of parent leadership with professional support. Descriptions of programs that illustrate each of the types include:

1. Unstructured meetings with no goals, curriculum, or trained leader.

2. Meetings led by lay leaders to get comments, solve a problem, study an issue, or become better acquainted.

3. Meetings led by lay leaders who follow a curriculum devised by professionals, such as Active Parenting, Parent Effectiveness Training (P.E.T.), and Systematic Training for Effective Parenting (STEP).

4. Meetings called by a parent or a professional that involve members and respond to their concerns with professional support. In the case of site-based management, the professional (principal) involves members of the committee and leads them to a consensus or a decision by majority vote.

5. Meetings called and led by a professional, with participation by lay members.

6. Meetings called, led, directed, and controlled by the professional, with members of the audience as observers only.

The aims of traditional parent education are furthered in the recent restructuring trend and collaborative decision making in public education. Parent involvement includes shared goal setting and decision making (Comer, 1988; Seeley, 1989; Swick, 2001). Encouraging parents to be involved calls for active parent collaboration that includes the parents in "mutual accountability. . . . This brings a power into the relationship that supersedes the power of bureaucratic control" (Seeley, p. 48). Belief in the autonomy of parents inspires the promotion of their decision-making abilities and allows them to be full partners in the education process.

Although parent involvement programs differ in their underlying structure—some are led by professionals, others by lay leaders—they are similar in their goal of developing parent participation in their children's education and development (Moles, 1996a, 1996b; Swick, 1983, 2001; U.S. Department of Education, 1994).

Effectiveness of Parent Involvement

Swick describes a statewide evaluation framework that can be used for parent education (Swick, Varner, & McClellan, 1991). An example of a controlled design is the research by Tebes, Grady, and Snow (1989), who had parents of 630 children selected randomly and assigned to experimental and control groups. Four skills were studied: (a) empathic responding level I, or the ability of the parent to respond to the child's feelings with understanding; (b) empathic responding level II, or the ability to respond empathetically to the child when the parent is disturbed by the behavior of the child; (c) facilitation of alternatives in decision making; and (d) facilitation of consequences, or being able to develop appropriate consequences. The findings supported the premise that education could help parents respond empathetically and develop decision-making behavior for parents of adolescents.

In a study of 34 parents, research supported the evaluation that both low-income parents and middle-income parents benefit from parent education. An evaluation of a parenting program showed significant improvement in both groups. Using a practical parenting program, a three-phase approach adapted from the Boys Town Family Home Program, the study included initial assessment of the family followed by an eight-week training program involving two-hour group meetings, weekly assignments, and frequent phone contact. They continued the program in the third phase with telephone contact and a parent support group. Their results showed parent attitudes and problem-solving skills improved significantly after the parent education. The parent education included both didactic-method and experiential involvement as well as group and individual intervention (Thompson, Grow, Ruma, Daly, & Burke, 1993). This study, based on only 34 parents, needs to be replicated with a larger sample.

Powell (1986) reviewed research including Parent Effectiveness Training, behavioral, and Adlerian programs. Although there was evidence of some change in parent attitudes, the research was not consistent and the results seemed to differ according to the assessment tool and income level of participants. Continued research will build the base needed to evaluate parent programs (see Graziano & Diament, 1992; Knapp & Deluty, 1989; Mischley, Stacy, Mischley, & Dush, 1985; Noller & Taylor, 1989; Webster-Stratton & Hammond, 1990).

✌ NEEDS ASSESSMENT

Before you begin a parent education program—and periodically during the program—you should determine the interests and needs of the community. First, meet with a group of parents representative of the diverse ethnic and socioeconomic levels within the community. Jot down the ideas or questions that concern and interest them. A brainstorming session is an ideal mechanism for eliciting many ideas. To facilitate the session, distribute a handout of the problems from Gallup polls and other surveys.

Once you have developed your basic list of interests and concerns, give it to a trial group and ask them to add new ideas and concerns. Next, construct a needs-assessment tool listing possible topics or formats for parents. Disseminate the questionnaire to adults in the school or center community. Finally, choose from the questionnaire those items that received the most requests and develop a program to meet the needs of the community.

Be sensitive to minorities and single parents and incorporate their responses to such needs and desires into the parent program. "Among the parents who indicate greatest need for help . . . are the single parents and parents from minority races" (Yankelovich, Skelly, & White, 1976, p. 120).

The Appalachia Educational Laboratory has designed a comprehensive needs assessment to determine curriculum for a parent education course for television (Coan & Gotts, 1976). Parents of children in 186 classrooms in 26 schools in 10 states were surveyed. From the answers to the needs assessment, six factors were clustered and factored: family care, child growth and development, child management, self as parent, treating your child like a person, and baby care. This needs assessment is illustrated at the end of this chapter and can be used as a guide when you construct an instrument for your locality.

Developing Items for a Needs Assessment

According to a 2001 Phi Delta Kappa/Gallup poll, respondents were asked to choose the biggest problems that schools and communities face. Fifteen percent of the respondents felt the lack of discipline and 15 percent saw the lack of financial support and funding as two of the biggest problems. Other choices recognized as problems included fighting/violence/gangs (10 percent), overcrowded schools (10 percent), and the use of drugs and dope (9 percent). The difficulty in obtaining high-quality teachers rounded out the list with 6 percent (Rose & Gallup, 2001). In 2000, the Phi Delta Kappa/Gallup poll also included overcrowded schools, concern about standards, and crime and vandalism. Current issues such as bullying and peer pressure could be added. After a few suggestions, lists can be generated by parents for use in developing their own needs assessment. Suggestions are meant to help generate ideas and should not restrict the needs recognized by the parents, however. Concerns are selected on the basis of what the current group of parents indicates as their greatest needs, with the final selection of interests and concerns based on individual needs of each group.

If you are working with parents of young children, include some of the items from the Ap-

palachia Educational Laboratory needs assessment in Appendix A at the end of this chapter when you establish your initial list.

Needs assessments at the individual small-group level can be less formal:

1. Brainstorm ideas for concerns and interests.
2. Collect as many ideas as your group can generate.
3. Show the group a similar list that might provide inspiration for other ideas to add to their list.
4. Form buzz groups, and let the participants discuss the lists.
5. Let the members list their choices in order of importance.
6. Generate your programs for the year from the group responses.
7. If a new issue arises that concerns most of the group, find a space or add a session to cover the important topic.

Needs assessments are necessary when new programs are developed, as well as when established parent groups reassess their needs. Less formal assessments are used frequently by ongoing groups.

Interest Finders

If a parent group is already established, members may use a number of informal methods to indicate their interests. These range from brainstorming among the members to soliciting suggestions in a question box.

Brainstorming

For a brainstorming session, choose a recorder and encourage all members to contribute ideas for programs. A list of past successful programs may be distributed. Write ideas on a chalkboard or white board, or on a transparency on an overhead projector. Caution members not to judge any suggestions as good or bad—all suggestions are valid at this point. After all suggestions are listed, have members choose in writing three to six ideas that interest them most. Develop your program from the interests that receive the most votes (or are most frequently mentioned). If the group has difficulty thinking of items, you may be able to generate responses by having participants complete statements such as these:

My greatest concerns are. . . .

My greatest happiness comes from. . . .

If I had three wishes, I would. . . .

If I could eliminate one problem from my home, it would be. . . .

Questions that concern me about my child's education are. . . .

Questions that concern me about my child's development are. . . .

As a parent I hope to be. . . .

Annoyance Test

An annoyance test is relevant for parents. The leader writes the following on a chart, blackboard, or white board:

My children annoy me when they. . . .

I annoy my children when I. . . .

The parents then list points under each, and the results are tabulated. The four or five most popular topics may then be discussed in subsequent meetings (Denver Public Schools, n.d.).

Open-Ended Questions

Parent groups can solicit requests for a wider knowledge of the community and possible ways for parents to become more involved in schools and the community. The leader asks parents to respond to such topics as:

- What do I want to know about my school?
- What do I want to know about my community?
- What would I like to do about my school and/or community?

Questionnaires

Develop a questionnaire, such as *Test Your Know-How as a Parent,* that will bring out differences in opinions in the group and show where interests and room for learning occur.

Question Box

Some parents are hesitant to make suggestions in an open meeting. They might feel more comfortable dropping questions and comments into a box that is available throughout the year.

During early planning it may also be advisable to let the members anonymously write their ideas on a small sheet of paper. Parents may be concerned about alcohol and other drugs, for example, but hesitate to mention that lest they reveal they have that problem in their homes.

Development of Objectives

After the group's interests have been assessed, the program is developed. Within most programs, at least two aspects should receive attention: the content of the meeting and the changes in behavior and attitudes of the participants. Table 6.1 illustrates how objectives in these two areas are intertwined. Social and emotional objectives are as important as content objectives. Table 6.1 is merely an example of how these areas are related in one program.

Most parents know when they want help with parenting skills, although reticent parents may need special encouragement. When a new family is formed and the first baby comes home to live, parents are intensely interested in knowing how to care for the baby. An opportune time for parent education is before the birth and during the child's first three years of life.

Parents are also ready for sharing information during the child's preschool years. Parent education and preschool programs bring the professional and the parents together to share concerns and experiences.

During the child's school-age years, parent education programs that focus on learning activities, building family strengths, and concerns specific to the group are beneficial. There is also

TABLE 6.1 Choose any or all of the content aspects of this chart. Then decide what objectives you want to accomplish related to the chosen issues. For example, in dealing with social problems, the program represented in this table chose drugs/alcohol and violence as necessary topics and determined that all the behavioral objectives were relevant.

Content Aspects of the Objectives	Behavioral Aspects of the Objectives					
	Use of Facts and Materials	Familiarity of Resource Materials	Decision Making and Critical Thinking	Influence of Values on Perceptions of Daily Living	Improved Communication and Interpersonal Relations	Development of Sensitivity to Social Problems
Home and the School						
1. New classroom teaching methods	X	X				
2. Home-school relationships						
3. Children's developmental levels	X	X				
4. Parent involvement					X	
Child Development						
1. Growth						
a. Physical	X	X	X			
b. Mental	X	X				
c. Social	X	X				
d. Emotional	X	X				
2. Behavior and misbehavior	X	X				
3. Individual differences						
a. Special children (gifted or learning disabled)	X	X		X	X	
b. Diagnosis						
c. Building self-concept	X	X				
4. Sexuality						
a. Sex education	X	X				
b. Bias-free education						X

Scope-and-sequence chart (columns are grade/level indicators; no column headers appear on this page).

Topic					
Family Relations					
1. Communication	X	X		X	
2. Interpersonal relations					
3. Sibling rivalry	X			X	
Social Problems					
1. Drugs/alcohol	X	X	X	X	X
2. Violence	X	X	X	X	X
3. Smoking					X
4. Stress					X
5. Living with change					X
Enrichment Activities of Childhood					
1. Creativity/exploration, imagination, music, art			X		
2. Computer use			X		
3. Literature and reading					
4. Influence of television					
Mental and Emotional Health					
1. Values					
2. Self-understanding					
Living in a Democracy					
1. Decision making	X	X		X	
2. Responsibilities					
3. Moral values	X	X		X	X
4. Critical thinking					

growing interest in parent education at the secondary level. Worries about drugs, alcohol, misbehavior, and suicide cause parents to look for help. At parent education meetings they may share issues, talk about common problems, become united in their efforts, and become aware of resources available to help them. Parents want parent education when they feel the need for it. It is important at that time to offer programs that speak to their concerns and allow them to have input into the agenda. Parents need to share, ask questions, and be a part of the decision-making process.

HOW PARENTS LEARN BEST

Parent educators facilitate the learning experience for parents. They design the program and the environment so that the parent is an active participant in the delivery of knowledge. Parents and parent-substitutes will be more apt to become involved in the learning process and thereby change their attitudes more easily if:

- A positive climate is established.
- Risk is eliminated.
- Parents are recognized as having something worthwhile to contribute.
- Parents are actively involved in their own education.
- The curriculum addresses their concerns and needs.
- Parents discover the need for change on their own.
- Respect and encouragement are present.
- Real situations and analogies are used to bring theories to life.
- Positive feedback is used.
- Different approaches (role-playing, short lectures, open discussion, debates, brainstorming, workshops) allow them to learn to use a variety of techniques.

- Different approaches use a variety of sensory experiences (sight, sound, touch, taste, and smell).
- Problem solving and analysis enable the learner to continue learning beyond the personal contact.
- The topic is relevant.
- Parents are considered part of the learning-teaching team.

You may have noted that the way parents learn best can apply to students, professionals, or even young children. Most everyone learns better when it is a positive environment with relevant material.

GROUP DISCUSSIONS

Most meetings involve group discussion, which can range from the use of open discussion as the total meeting format to a short discussion after a formal presentation.

The following examples, an informal discussion plan and a problem-solving format, illustrate two uses of group discussions. The first focuses on the informality of the process, and the second requires prior development of expertise and a resolution of the issue.

Informal Discussion Plan

A. Stems from interest or needs of group.

Example: How can parents be more involved in their child's school?

B. Establishes goals and objectives.

   1. Goal—parental involvement.

   2. Objectives

      a. To determine why parents do not feel comfortable coming to school.

      b. To encourage parents to participate in schools.

c. To initiate a plan for getting parents involved.

d. To suggest activities in which parents can be involved.

C. Provides for informal group meetings.

1. Allows parents to speak freely.

2. Emphasizes the clarification of feelings and acceptance of ideas.

3. Encourages participation.

4. Includes keeping a record of suggestions.

D. Selects and analyzes relevant information that emerges during the discussion.

E. Outlines a plan for action, if the group desires.

Problem-Solving Format

A. Recognition of the problem—state the hypothesis.

1. The problem should be selected by the group and reflect its needs and interests.

Example: Does violence on television impact our children and cause more violence in the country?

2. The leader writes the question or problem for discussion on a chart, chalkboard, or white board.

B. Understanding the problem—discuss the nature of the problem.

Example: Is television viewing a problem and, if so, why?

C. Data collection—gather a wide range of ideas and determine which are relevant.

1. Prior development of expertise—identify resources and read before meeting.

2. Nonjudgmental acceptance—accept and record comments and ideas from participants.

D. Analysis of the problem.

1. Focus on the subject so that it can be discussed thoroughly by participants.

2. Establish criteria for evaluation of a solution.

3. Keep participants focused on problems.

E. Conclusion and summary.

1. Suggest solutions.

2. List possible conclusions.

3. Seek an integrative conclusion that reflects the group's goals and thinking.

F. Appropriate action.

1. Develop a timetable.

2. Determine a method of accomplishing tasks.

3. Delegate tasks.

LEADERSHIP TRAINING

Lay leaders benefit from having guidelines to follow in developing their leadership skills. The leader's goal is to establish an environment that facilitates and guides members in achieving the objectives.

Leaders establish a model for behavior by their (a) participation, (b) acceptance of criticism, (c) nonevaluative comments, (d) willingness to deviate from preplanned procedures, (e) ability to listen with understanding and to capture and reflect feelings, (f) comments that clarify, and (g) method of expressing their own feelings (Gardner, 1974).

Group members can participate more effectively if they are aware of their rights and responsibilities within the group. A handout on communication skills, given to members early in the school term, helps eliminate problems and encourages a relaxed, productive group (Figure 6.2). Use the handout as a guide. This handout, along with a description of group roles (Table 6.2, p. 250), will enable group members to grow into productive participants in group interaction. As a leader, it is your responsibility to share these communication tips with the group membership.

CRITERIA FOR GROUP COMMUNICATION

1. Come to the meeting ready to ask questions and share your ideas.

2. Once your ideas and thoughts are given to the group, do not feel compelled to defend them. Once shared, they become the group's property to discuss and consider. Clarify meaning if it would help the group proceed, but don't feel responsible for the idea just because you suggested it.

3. Speak freely and communicate feelings. Listen to others with consideration and understanding for their feelings.

4. Accept others in the interchange of ideas. Allow them to have opinions that differ from yours. Do not ignore or reject members of the group.

5. Engage in friendly disagreements. Listen critically and carefully to suggestions others have to offer. Differences of opinion bring forth a variety of ideas.

6. Be sincere. Reveal your true self. Communicate in an atmosphere of mutual trust.

7. Allow and promote individual freedom. Do not manipulate, suppress, or ridicule other group members. Encourage their creativity and individuality.

8. Work hard, acknowledge the contributions of others, and focus on the objectives of the group's task.

FIGURE 6.2   Criteria for group communication.

General Qualifications

The following pointers emphasize the leader's personality, interpersonal relationships, and skill in handling group discussions:

A. Leader's personality

1. Ability to think and act quickly. The leader may need to change plans on the spur of the moment.

2. Ability to get along with others, be well liked, and not have a tendency to "fly off the handle."

3. Respect for the opinions of others. The leader should be a good listener and avoid telling others what to think.

4. Willingness to remain in the background. Instead of voicing opinions, ask questions and guide but do not dominate.

5. Freedom from prejudice.

B. Leader's knowledge and skills

1. Knowledge of the discussion method. The leader must know the purpose and the procedure agreed upon if the meeting is to be successful.

2. Knowledge of the opinions of authorities on the subject so that conclusions will be based on evidence rather than on the leader's opinion.

3. Skill in asking questions. The leader should present questions that bring out the opinions of others. Use questions to avoid hasty decisions or the acceptance of conclusions not based on good evidence. Throwing out a question to the group can help the leader avoid expressing personal opinions. The following suggestions give examples of how to handle certain situations that may arise in a discussion:

a. To call attention to a point that has not been considered: "Has anyone thought about this phase of the problem—or about this possible solution?"

b. To evaluate the strengths of an argument: "What reasons do we have for accepting this statement?"

c. To get back to causes: "Why do you suppose a child—or a parent—feels or acts this way?"

d. To question the source of information or argument: "Who gathered these statistics that you spoke of?" or "Would you care to identify the authority you are quoting?"

e. To suggest that new information has not been added: "Can anyone add a new idea to the information already given on this point?"

f. To register steps of agreement or disagreement: "Am I correct in assuming that all of us agree [or disagree] with this point?"

g. To bring a generalizing speaker down to earth: "Can you give us a specific example?" or "Your general idea is good, but I wonder if we can't make it more concrete. Does anyone know of a case . . . ?"

h. To handle the member who has "all the answers": "Would your idea work in all cases?" or "Let's get a variety of opinions on this point."

i. To bring an individual back to the subject: "I wonder if you can relate your ideas to the subject we are discussing?"

j. To handle a question directed to the leader:

(1) If the leader knows the answer but does not wish to be set up as an authority, the question can be redirected to the group.

(2) The leader can quote from resource material and ask for additional opinions.

(3) If the leader is a specialist in the area, occasional questions may be answered.

(4) The leader can say, "I don't know. Who does? Shall we research this?"

k. To cut off a long-winded speaker: "While we're on this point, let's hear from the others" or "Shall we save your next point until later?"

l. To help the members who may have difficulty expressing themselves: "I wonder if I am interpreting you correctly—were you saying . . . ?" or "Can we tie in what you are saying with our subject something like this . . . ?"

m. To encourage further questions: "I'm glad you raised that question. Can anyone answer?"

n. To break up a heated argument: "I'm sure all of us feel strongly about this. Would some of the rest of you care to express opinions?"

o. To be sensitive to body language of the group, watch for people who want to speak and bring out their contributions.[1]

Leaders do not have to be superhuman, charming, physically attractive people. Leaders initiate, plan, guide, and build group norms; give support; challenge; and encourage group growth. In building the group norms, special attention should be paid to the feelings of people in the group.

1. Each person is respected, listened to, and recognized.

2. The meeting is a safe place to be; no one will be ridiculed or put down.

---

[1] Adapted from "Pointers for Discussion Group Leaders," in *Parent Education and Preschool Department Leadership Handbook*, by Denver Public Schools (n.d.), Denver: Denver Public Schools.

3. Feelings are important, and the expression of feelings helps the group solve problems.

4. Feelings may be discussed.

5. The participants and leader are encouraged to be objective. (Adapted from Denver Public Schools, n.d.)

Leaders who show a caring attitude are most effective. They offer protection, affection, praise, and encouragement as well as friendship. But caring is not enough. The effective leader is there to give support, explain, and clarify if needed.

USING TECHNOLOGY

The increased use of communication through the Internet allows parents, leaders, teachers, and students to interact online. The process allows participants to respond to each other. Currently, body language is not available to increase understanding of the messages sent to and fro; however, the availability and the convenience of flexible time schedules and immediate discussion makes Internet communication a viable option. This is especially true for those parents who live a distance from the school or meeting place and for those whose work schedule or children at home make it impossible for them to attend meetings.

E-mail. E-mail may be used to communicate with the opportunity for an immediate response. It can be used to give information and to receive parent responses and questions.

Web Sites. Schools can develop Web sites that communicate with parents about the happenings at school. Emergencies can be explained; school assignments may be posted and explained; and extensions that include articles about educational ideas and procedures for improving academic achievement may be available. Articles that concern education and child development can be placed on the Web site for the parents or students

to read. If the school has had some difficulty with bullying and rejection of some students by others, information from the school can help set up programs and encourage both parents and the school to work on the concerns.

Although this chapter primarily concerns face-to-face meetings, for those parents who have been excluded from meetings because of time schedules, the Internet expands their opportunities to be involved with the school.

ESTABLISHING A POSITIVE ATMOSPHERE

Icebreakers

To create an accepting, warm atmosphere, get-acquainted activities help people relax and become involved in the group. These icebreakers range from introductions of the person to the right to mixers during breaks.

While Members Gather

Signature Sheets. Make a form before the meeting that includes statements about people. Following each statement is a signature blank. These sheets can be made specifically for the group or can be broad enough to be used in any group. The kinds of signature sheets are not limited—create original ones. As the group arrives, give one to each participant. Encourage mixing and meeting new people. By the time the period is completed, the members will have an opportunity to meet and talk with a large number of people. A typical signature sheet is shown in Figure 6.3A. Figure 6.3B illustrates another design for a signature sheet.

Bingo Card. Give each member a card that contains 12 to 25 squares, as shown in Figure 6.4. Ask members to fill each blank with a signature. Signatures may not be repeated. This encourages interaction with all members.

A variation of the bingo card includes a letter within each square. Find someone whose name begins with that letter. Check the roster ahead of

Find people who meet the qualifications listed below and have them sign their names.

1. Find someone who is wearing the same color clothes as you. ——————————————————

2. Find someone who has the same color eyes as you. ——————————————————————

3. Find someone who has the same number of children as you. ———————————————————

4. Find someone who lives in the same area as you. ————————————————————————

5. Find someone who has a child the same age as yours. ————————————————————————

6. Find someone who likes to go hiking. ————————————————————————————

7. Find someone who plays the piano. ———————————————————————————————

8. Find someone who has the same hobby as you. ———————————————————————————

9. Find someone who has lived in this state as long as you have. ————————————————————

10. Find someone who was brought up in the same area you were. ————————————————————

FIGURE 6.3A Use a get-acquainted activity such as a signature sheet at the beginning of a meeting.

WHEEL OF FRIENDSHIP

FIGURE 6.3B During the next few minutes you are to find people who have the same attributes as you. Have them sign their names in the wheel of friendship between the wheel spokes.

247

I watch television regularly.	I enjoy reading.	I have more than two children.	I like to dance.	My favorite color is orange.
I have dark hair.	I like to go shopping.	I enjoy skiing.	I enjoy hiking.	I enjoy biking.
I have red hair.	I have blonde hair.	I have brown eyes.	I have blue eyes.	I have a son.
I have two children.	I live near here.	I have lived in this area for more than one year.	I enjoy music.	I enjoy helping in school.
I exercise regularly.	I have a daughter.	I have a brother.	I have a sister.	I work outside the home.

FIGURE 6.4 Find a person who can sign the squares. When you have completed an entire line, you can call "Bingo!" Bingo games can use initials or attributes of the members of the group.

time and use the members' initials in the squares. A third variation is similar to the signature sheet that asks for the signature of someone who fulfills the attribute.

Who Am I?   Attach a piece of paper with the name of a famous person to the back of each person. Members go from person to person asking questions until they determine who they are. Questions must be phrased so that a yes or no answer is adequate. Variations include changing the famous person to an event, an animal, or an educational statement.

Scrambled Name Tags.   Make up name tags with letters out of order, for example, Ilaehs (Sheila). Have the members try to figure out each name as they talk with each person. Obviously, this has to be done at the first or second meeting, before the group becomes acquainted.

After Members Are Seated

Dyad Introductions.   Have members talk to each other in pairs with the idea that they will introduce each other. You may give specific instructions, for example, to ask the number of children in the family and what the member expects from parent education, or you may leave the discussion completely up to the two individuals. Following the discussion, go around the room and have members introduce their partners.

It is interesting to have the dyad discuss memory questions such as something the partner remembers that happened before the age of five or the person's happiest experience. This activity can be used later in the year as well as at the beginning. Allow members to introduce themselves. Topics they might use include the following:

My secret hiding place was. . . .

As a child I liked to . . . best.

Summertime was. . . .

If I had my wish, I would be. . . .

What I liked best about school was. . . .

What I remember about walking or riding the bus home from school was. . . .

I've Got a Secret. After people have become acquainted, ask each participant to write a secret on a piece of paper. (Be sure that the person does not mind having the secret revealed.) Place the pieces of paper in a bag, and as they are drawn and read, group members try to guess who has that secret.

Activities that promote good relations and allow members to get acquainted are limited only by the planner's imagination. The chairperson or leader may be in charge of this part of the program or may delegate the responsibility to a number of persons charged with the task of discovering new means of interaction.

🙰 GROUP ROLES

Group members should be given descriptions of group roles to help them identify their participatory roles or roles they would like to develop (see Table 6.2). Within each group, roles emerge that are functional and task-oriented, that move the group forward; others are group-sustaining, expressive and maintain the group; and still others that are negative and dysfunctional, and reduce the effectiveness of the group.

Roles emerge within groups and influence the interactive process. A *role*, defined as the behavior characteristic of a person occupying a particular position in the social system, influences the actions of the person and the expectations of others toward that person. Parent groups (in this text) are the "social system"; members of the group expect certain norms or standards of behavior from the perceived leader of the group. These role expectations are projected in members' role behavior toward the leader. Likewise, the leader's own interpretation of the role influences the resulting role behavior or role performance. Should members of the group hold different expectations of behavior for the leadership role from those held by the occupant of that role, interrole conflicts may arise (Applbaum, Bodaken, Sereno, & Anatol, 1979; Berger, 1968; Biddle & Thomas, 1979; Borchers, 1999). For these reasons, it is beneficial to discuss or clarify standards and duties of roles within a group.

Role continuity is easier to obtain in parent education groups with ongoing memberships. Parents are encouraged to participate for at least two years. New officers and leaders, already familiar with the standards of the group, may be elected in the spring and be ready to take over leadership in the fall. Although this system ensures greater continuity than the establishment of a new group each year, the returning members must be careful to be flexible, open to new ideas, and sensitive to the desires of new members.

Early in the year a session may include a discussion of roles and group dynamics. Role-playing is an excellent mechanism for clarifying role behavior. If group members are aware of the effects that roles have on the functioning of a group, they will not fall into dysfunctional roles as readily. By discussing group dynamics with the group before establishment of role patterns, group production is often increased (Beal, Bohlen, & Raudabaugh, 1962).

A leader can deter or eliminate the problem of domination or withdrawal by group members if members are aware of roles and how each member of the group can influence the group's functioning, either positively or negatively. Most people do not want to be viewed as dysfunctional members and will, therefore, refrain from acting in ways that are detrimental to group interaction. I have used this technique of discussing roles in parent groups and classes for many years and have found that the group discussion and the role-playing of group roles greatly enhance the productivity of the group.

This knowledge will encourage some members, but it can also inhibit others who worry about which role theory they are enacting. Although this is a possible negative result of a discussion of group roles, role definition can benefit the total group in the elimination of one common problem in groups—domination of the discussion by a few participants. It is also beneficial to reticent communicators to learn that they can become productive group members despite the inability to express themselves. Asking questions, being an active listener, and being a positive member of the group are shown to be valuable contributions to a well-functioning discussion group. When balanced out, the positive aspects of discussing group roles overshadow the negative ones. One word of caution, however—do not wait until a problem has become obvious before discussing dysfunctional roles. That would embarrass and alienate the person who has been a negative contributor. It is best to handle such a problem through the leadership techniques discussed on pp. 243–246.

✑ DYNAMICS OF ROLES WITHIN GROUPS

Observation of interaction within groups shows that role behavior influences the cohesiveness and productivity of the group. Observation will be facilitated if analysis of the group is based on role interaction (Table 6.2), wherein behaviors within a group are divided into task, group-building and maintenance, and dysfunctional roles.

Task Roles

The roles related to the task area in Table 6.2 are attributed to members of the group who initiate, question, and facilitate reaching the group's goals or objectives.

Group-Building and Maintenance Roles

The roles related to group-building or maintenance are attributed to members of the group who support and maintain the cohesiveness, solidarity, and productivity of the group.

Dysfunctional or Individual Roles

The roles in this area are attributed to members who place their own individual needs, which are not relevant to group goals, above group needs. These individual goals are not functional or productive to group achievement, but if such members are brought into the group process, they can become contributing participants.

Members of groups generally do not fit into only one role category. Members may participate in a task role and switch to a maintenance role with the next action or comment. For example, Helen is anxious about absenteeism and suggests that the group might improve attendance by organizing a car pool. May responds by suggesting a telephone network to contact members. Helen welcomes the

TABLE 6.2 Role interaction. Both task and maintenance roles are necessary for effective group participation.

Task Roles	Group-building or Maintenance Roles	Dysfunctional Roles
Initiator-leader	Encourager	Dominator
Information giver	Harmonizer	Aggressor
Information seeker	Listener	Negativist
Clarifier	Follower	Playboy
Questioner	Tension breaker	Blocker
Asserter	Compromiser	Competitor
Energizer	Standard setter	Recognition Seeker
Elaborator	Observer	Deserter
Orientor	Recorder	
Opinion giver	Gatekeeper	
Opinion seeker		
Summarizer		

idea, "Good thought, May. We might be able to start right away." Helen, within the space of two minutes, has initiated an idea, acting in a task-oriented role, and has then supported May's contribution with a group-building or maintenance statement. There may be moments when members lapse into a dysfunctional role, but as long as the mix of interaction remains primarily positive and productive, the group will be effective.

✒ ROLE DESCRIPTIONS

The following role descriptions are based on Beal and colleagues (1962); Benne and Sheets (1948); Borchers, 1999; and King (1962).

Task-Oriented

Task roles are the roles that initiate and keep the group discussion meaningful and ongoing.

Initiator-leader: Initiates the discussion, guides but does not dominate, contributes ideas or suggestions that help move the group forward.

Information giver: Contributes information and facts that are from authoritative sources and are relevant to the ongoing discussion.

Information seeker: Asks for clarification or expansion of an issue from additional relevant, authoritative information.

Clarifier: Restates the discussion of an issue so that points are made clear to the group and relationships between ideas are clear.

Orientator: Refocuses the group discussion

Questioner: Asks questions about issues, requests clarification, or offers constructive criticism.

Asserter: States a position in a positive manner; may take a different point of view and disagree with opinions or suggestions without attacking them.

Energizer: Stimulates and facilitates the group to action and increased output and problem solving.

Elaborator: Expands an idea or concept; brings out details, points, and alternatives that may have been overlooked.

Orientator: Takes a look at the group's position in relation to the objectives of the meetings and where the discussion is heading.

Opinion giver: States own opinion on the situation, basing the contribution on personal experiences.

Opinion seeker: Requests suggestions from others according to their life experiences and value orientation.

Summarizer: Brings out facts, ideas, and suggestions made by the group in an attempt to clarify the group's position during the meeting and at the conclusion.

Group-Building and Maintenance Roles

Group-building or maintenance roles help the group develop and maintain the existence and quality of the group. The first six roles will emerge within the group; the last four are appointed or elected maintenance roles.

Encourager: Supports, praises, and recognizes other members of the group; builds self-confidence and self-concept of others.

Harmonizer: Mediates misunderstandings and clarifies conflicting statements and disagreements; adds to the discussion in a calming and tension-reducing manner.

Listener: Is involved in the discussion through quiet attention to the group process; gives support through body language and eye contact.

Follower: Serves as a supportive member of the discussion by accepting the ideas and suggestions of others.

Tension breaker: Uses humor or clarifying statements to relieve tension within the group.

Compromiser: Views both sides of the question and offer solutions or suggestions that moves group to a position which fits conflicting viewpoints.

The following four roles are appointed or elected positions:

Standard setter: Sets standards for group performance; may apply standards as an evaluative technique for the meeting.

Observer: Charts the group process throughout the meeting and uses the data for evaluation of group interaction.

Recorder: Records decisions and ideas for group use throughout the meeting.

Gatekeeper: Regulates time spent and membership participation during various parts of the program; keeps communication open and the meeting on schedule.

Dysfunctional Roles

Dysfunctional roles interfere with achievement of the goals of the group.

Dominator: Monopolizes the meeting and asserts superiority by attempting to manipulate the group.

Aggressor: Shows aggression toward the group in a variety of forms, for example, attacks ideas, criticizes others, denigrates others' contributions, and disapproves of solutions.

Negativist: Demonstrates pessimism and disapproval of suggestions that emerge within the group; sees the negative side of the issue and rejects new insights.

Playboy: Refuses to be involved in the discussion and spends time showing this indifference to the members by distracting behavior, for example, talking to others, showing cynicism, making side comments.

Blocker: Opposes decision making and attempts to block actions by introducing alternatives that have already been rejected.

Competitor: Competes with other members of the discussion group by challenging their ideas and expressing and defending his or her own suggestions.

Recognition seeker: Needs recognition and focus on himself or herself.

Deserter: Leaves the group in spirit and mind but not in body; doodles, looks around the room, appears uninterested, and stays aloof and indifferent to the group process.

✌ PRODUCTIVE GROUPS

In productive groups, members of the group are both active and productive.

1. Members listen and pay attention to one another.
2. Members discuss the subject at hand.
3. Everyone's ideas and suggestions are welcomed.
4. Everyone has a chance to state his or her views.
5. The group uses its agenda as a guide for discussion
6. One or two members are appointed to summarize the discussion and to see that everyone has had a chance to speak.
7. Members know and use problem-solving steps.
8. Members are clear about group decisions and committed to them. (MSU Extension, 1999, p. 5)

Less productive groups often do the following:

1. Members do not listen and everyone tends to talk at the same time.
2. The discussion jumps from one idea to another.
3. Some members' ideas don't seem to count, so they feel that they don't belong.
4. One or two members do all the talking
5. The agenda is not clear and there is no written guide for discussion.
6. No one summarizes or checks to see if everyone who wants to speak has actually spoken. Discussions go on and on until people get tired.
7. No order is followed for identifying and solving problems.
8. Decision making is muddy and people are not committed to the plan. (MSU Extension, 1999, p. 5)

Role-Playing Group Roles

Early in the formation of a group, members can benefit from a session in which they role-play task, maintenance, and dysfunctional roles while discussing an issue of high interest. This exercise will illustrate to members how role performance can support or destroy a group. It is practical to arrange seating in two concentric circles, allowing the inner circle to discuss an issue in light of the roles assigned, whereas the outer circle observes and analyzes the roles being demonstrated. The session will be humorous, with members enthusiastically playing dysfunctional roles, but it should end with the understanding that each member is important to the effectiveness of the group process.

Observer

Analytical observation of group interaction reveals patterns that are not always obvious to the casual observer. A systematic observation can pinpoint problems and illustrate strengths to the members. One simple technique for analytical observation is the construction of a discussion wheel. A diagram of the participants is made, with names or numbers reflecting individual members. If the participants are sitting in a circle, the diagram would be similar to the one in Figure 6.5.

As members speak, the observer uses arrows to record the direction of each interaction. An arrow pointed toward the center indicates that the communicator is speaking to the group; an arrow pointed from one member to another represents a statement made to an individual rather than to the group (Beal et al., 1962). A glance at Figure 6.5 shows that Ralph did not make any suggestions; he had either withdrawn from the group or lacked its supportive encouragement. Most members contributed to the group process, rather than making side comments to individual communicators. As interaction continues throughout the meeting, the observer can make cross marks on the arrows to reflect duplication of communication, eliminating an overabundance of lines in the observation circle (Figure 6.6).

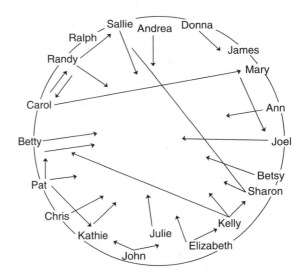

FIGURE 6.5 Group interaction recorded on an observation wheel.

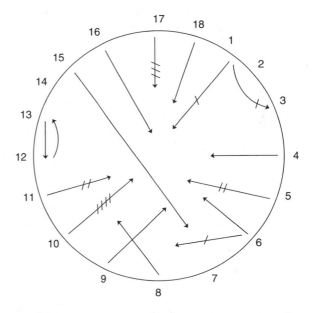

FIGURE 6.6 Group interaction is anonymously recorded on an observation wheel. Each time a person speaks, a mark is added to the interaction line. In this manner, one can see how often and to whom each participant communicates.

Topic: _____   Date: _____

Group: _____

	Check along the continuum.

1. Was the meeting of interest to you?

Very much	Some	Very little

2. Did you receive any pertinent ideas that will be helpful to you?

Many ideas	Some	No ideas

3. Did the group participate and seem involved in the meeting?

Very involved	Some	No involvement

4. Did the meeting give you any new insights, or did you change any of your attitudes as a result of the meeting?

New insights	Some	No effect

5. Were you encouraged to contribute as much as you wanted?

Participation encouraged	Neutral	Left out

6. Did the leader respond to the needs of the group?

Good leadership	Neutral	No leadership

7. Was there adequate preparation by the members?

Excellent preparation	Some	Poor preparation

8. Were group members encouraged to participate?

Strong	Average	Poor

9. Was there enough time for discussion?

Too much	Just right	No time

10. Was the atmosphere conducive to freedom of expression?

Safe environment	Neutral	Felt threatened

11. Do you have any suggestions for improvement?

12. What were the strong points of the meeting?

13. Comments:

You do not need to sign this sheet.

FIGURE 6.7 A meeting evaluation form lets you know exactly how the participants viewed the program.

End-of-Meeting Evaluations

Evaluations are used effectively by many groups to see if the needs of the group are being met. Because every group is somewhat different, evaluations should be constructed to meet the needs of the group and should be based on the goals and objectives of the meeting. Sample evaluations are helpful, however, to guide the group in its development of evaluative methods that work for that particular group. The example in Figure 6.7 may be adapted to any group's needs.

✌ TYPES OF MEETINGS

Meetings can range from formal lectures to informal buzz sessions. In parent groups, informal meetings are used most often to reinforce the active involvement that proves so critical to understanding concepts and changing attitudes. The formal meeting has its place, however, if the group needs a specialist to give an organized background lecture on a specific topic. Figure 6.8 illustrates types of meetings that can be used as needs, time, space, subject, and resources dictate. On the right are meetings that are the most informal and require active involvement by the

participants; in the center is the panel meeting; on the left is the most formal lecture where the only audience participation is listening to the speaker. Although each type of meeting has its place in parent group meetings, the informal meeting elicits more participation by group members—a necessary ingredient for attitude clarification, learning, and change.

✌ ARRANGEMENTS FOR MEETINGS

All parent-group meetings require certain procedures, regardless of the meeting format. Parents need to feel physically and emotionally comfortable at every meeting, whether formal or informal. To ensure this, the person in charge of the meeting should do the following for all meetings:

1. Check the meeting room to be sure the temperature is appropriate, the ventilation and lighting are adequate, and the room is large enough to accommodate the group.
2. As members or guests arrive, make them feel welcome. Greet them, offer name tags, and suggest that they have refreshments, look at a book

FIGURE 6.8 Types of meetings range from the informal on the right to very formal on the left.

Formal	Informal
Lecture	Brainstorming
Lecture-forum	Roundtable
Symposium	Concentric circles
Audio	Buzz sessions
Audiovisual	Workshop
Book review	Dyad interaction and feedback
Debate	Role-playing
Colloquy	Dramatization
Panel	

display, or participate in an icebreaker activity before the meeting begins. Call members or guests by name as soon as possible.

3. Have refreshments available before the meeting, during the break, or at both times. A 15-minute refreshment period before the meeting gives latecomers an opportunity to arrive before discussion commences. It also sets a relaxed tone and gives members a forum for informal interaction.

4. As participants arrive, involve them in an informal discussion through an icebreaker activity. Get-acquainted activities are important, but choose an appropriate one. For meetings where few people know one another, it may prove beneficial to use a signature sheet or the dyad-introductions technique of asking the entire group to form into pairs, with each partner introducing the other one to the group.

5. In large groups where icebreakers are not appropriate, the participants can respond to group questions—where they live, what they do, how many children they have, what their interests are, and so on. Responses to the questions (by a show of hands or verbal answers) help the speaker know more about the audience to be addressed, and audience members feel they have been recognized.

6. After the group feels comfortable, the meeting can commence. Open discussion is part of all but the most formal or informal meetings, so it is important that all group leaders are able to conduct discussion sessions. Debates, panels, audiovisual aids, buzz sessions, workshops, role-playing, book reviews, dramatizations, and observations can precede open discussion. The leader should gauge the time and conclude the meeting.

7. After the presentation and discussion (or question-and-answer session), thank the presenters and give appropriate recognition for their contributions.

8. Announce any specific instructions necessary for the next meeting before the group disperses.

The descriptions of the types of meetings that follow are compiled from my experiences with parent education and information found in Applbaum et al. (1979), Denver Public Schools (n.d.),

and Kawin (1970). Resources that support the curricula are found in the Appendix at the end of this text.

Roundtables (Open Discussions)

Although not the most informal meeting available, the roundtable is a true open discussion, the mainstay of group interaction (see Figure 6.9). It is used to complement most meetings, for example, panels, symposiums, role-playing sessions, or buzz sessions. The roundtable discussion is also used for decision-making meetings and parent councils.

In a roundtable discussion all members are encouraged to participate throughout the meeting. Care must be taken to promote good communication among all members of the group. To facilitate good group interaction, leaders should keep in mind the following suggestions from the Denver Public Schools:[1]

1. Have a clear understanding of the topic as defined by the group.

2. Obtain materials.

3. Get a general knowledge, through reading, to be able to direct and add to the contributions from the group.

4. Be sure to plan an introduction that will stimulate interest of the group.

5. Prepare a logical, progressive list of questions to start the ball rolling and keep it moving.

6. Keep the discussion on track; keep it always directed, but let the group lay its own track to a large extent. Don't groove it narrowly yourself.

7. Be alert to adjust questions to needs of group— omit, change, reword.

8. Remember—the leader's opinion doesn't count in the discussion. Keep your own view out of it. Your job is to get the ideas of others out for airing.

---

[1] From *Parent Education and Preschool Department Leadership Handbook,* by Denver Public Schools (n.d.), Denver: Denver Public Schools.

FIGURE 6.9 The roundtable is the basic open discussion group.

9. If you see that some important angle is being neglected, point it out; "Bill Jones was telling me last week that he thinks. . . . What do you think of that?"

10. Keep spirits high. Encourage ease, informality, good humor. Let everybody have a good time. Foster friendly disagreement. Listen to all ideas with respect and appreciation, but stress what is important, and turn discussion away from what is not.

11. Take time every 10 minutes or so to draw loose ends together; "Let's see where we've been going." Be as fair and accurate in summary as possible. Close the discussion with a summary—your own or the secretary's.

12. Call attention to unanswered questions for future study or for your reference back to speakers. Nourish a desire in group members for continuing study and discussion through a skillful closing summary

Problems that could emerge in a roundtable meeting include domination of the discussion by one or two members, withdrawal from the group and side discussions by two or three people, or lack of preparation by the membership. Good leadership makes it possible to avoid these pitfalls. If the leader is prepared for the meeting and if members come to the meeting prepared, have relevant experiences, or have background expertise on the subject, the meeting can be a most effective means of changing attitudes and educating members. It allows all members to contribute and become involved in discussion, clarification of issues, and decision making.

Arrangements Before the Meeting

1. Select a topic for open discussion and announce it to the membership.

2. Provide members with materials and bibliography.

   a. Duplicate and distribute background information on the topic through a distribution system or at a meeting before the roundtable.

   b. Select members to read relevant material before the meeting.

   c. Come to the meeting well prepared and ready to guide but not dominate.

3. Review the "Arrangements for Meetings" section (pp. 255–256) and make appropriate preparations.

Setup

1. Arrange chairs in a circle or semicircle or around tables so that all participants can see each other and eye contact is possible.

2. Check the room for comfort—ventilation, lighting, and heat.

Procedure

1. The leader starts the meeting with a thought-provoking question or statement of fact. Throughout the discussion, the leader tries to keep the meeting from wandering. Before the meeting, the leader has prepared a list of questions or statements that may keep the discussion moving forward.

2. During the meeting the leader avoids dominating the discussion. Instead, the leadership role brings others into the discussion, helps clarify, and keeps the meeting on the topic.

3. The leader summarizes at the conclusion.

4. If the members want to take action on the conclusions, the leader should call for appropriate action, help the group make plans, and assign tasks.

Appropriate Topics

1. Learning activities that work
2. Behavior and misbehavior
3. Influence of television on children
4. Rivalry between brothers and sisters
5. Problem solving
6. Bullying in the schools
7. Helping children cope with terrorism

Concentric Circles

The concentric-circle arrangement is a variation of the open discussion or roundtable meeting. Instead of one circle, there are two, one inside the other, with everyone facing the center. The dialogue among members is similar to that of the open discussion, only the smaller circle within the larger circle contains the communicators at first (Figure 6.10). Divide the group so that the smaller group has 6 to 12 people. The members of the smaller group discuss the issue; those in the larger group listen to the discussion. After a designated time of 5 to 10 minutes, the meeting is opened to the entire group. If you have 24 to 30 people, with people who are reticent to speak out in a large group, the concentric circle will help solve the problem. Those within the inner circle form a small group with which to interact. This arrangement precipitates more discussion from them and succeeds in getting the total group interested in the discussion. Those sitting in the outer circle are required to listen, but the statements, questions, and ideas offered usually promote their interest as they listen. This method is surprisingly effective in getting groups to discuss. By the time the discussion is opened up to the entire group, many ideas have emerged.

Setup

1. Arrange chairs with one large circle on the outside and a smaller circle within the larger circle.

2. Review the "Arrangement for Meetings" section (pp. 255–256) and make appropriate preparations.

FIGURE 6.10 Concentric circles encourage those who might not participate freely to get involved.

Procedure

1. The leader of the total group may request a volunteer leader for the inner circle, or the leader may take that role.

2. The session is started with a statement or question to promote interest and dialogue.

3. The inner circle discusses the topic, using a small-group, open-discussion format. The outer circle listens. At the end of a designated period, for example, six minutes, the discussion may be opened to all in the room. At that time the leader continues to control the meeting but not dominate it.

4. For variation, reverse the roles. Those in the outer circle move to the inner circle and have the opportunity for more-involved discussion,

while those from the outer circle listen to this discussion. A separate issue or different questions concerning one issue may be used for each group in its discussion.

Appropriate Topics

1. How to build self-esteem in children
2. What to expect of two-, three-, four-, or five-year-olds
3. Problem solving
4. Living with change
5. Positive uses of television
6. Courses and workshops that could be offered at school
7. Issues and concerns of children

Buzz Sessions

Buzz sessions are an excellent means of eliciting participation from all members of the group. They must be small enough to allow interaction among all participants. The smallest session consists of two people, and the maximum size should be six to eight. This makes it possible for all members to have the chance to express their opinions easily. Even in a large group, the audience can divide into smaller groups and discuss. The latter is called a 6–6 discussion, with six people discussing for six minutes. Because the session time is limited, it does not allow thorough examination of issues, but it does bring forth ideas from all involved in a very short period of time—an objective that is not accomplished in an open discussion with a large group.

Setup

1. Up to 24 people.
   a. Arrange chairs in circle or semicircle.
   b. When the smaller group session is to begin, six people turn their chairs together to form their group. It is also possible for a group to move to another area for a quieter meeting.

2. Large auditorium.
   a. If people are seated in rows, three people turn around and discuss with three people behind them.
   b. Use some other technique to form groups of six throughout the auditorium.

Procedure

1. Buzz sessions may be formed at the beginning of the meeting, or they may be initiated later. The leader announces the formation of buzz groups either by proximity of chairs, a common interest in specific discussion areas, or by a mechanism to distribute members, such as counting off one through six and having those with common numbers form a group.
2. Each group chooses a leader and a recorder.
3. The topic is introduced to the group for discussion, and people are encouraged to participate much as they would in any other small-group discussion.
4. The recorder keeps relevant thoughts ready to report back to the larger group. In the smaller meeting (24 people), each group might have the time to give a short report to the total group. In an auditorium 6–6 meeting, it might not be possible to have everyone report back. Allow a specific number of groups that indicate interest in doing so to report back to the total audience.

Appropriate Topics

1. Home-management tips
2. Feelings about childrearing
3. Discipline
4. Moral values
5. Vacation ideas
6. Solving problems around home
7. Issues concerning school
8. Decisions that should be made concerning education

Brainstorming Sessions

Brainstorming is a unique method of active interaction by all members of the group. It promotes interchange, encourages lateral thinking, and facilitates expansion of thought. In brainstorming sessions, all contributions are accepted. Everyone is encouraged to suggest ideas and solutions. The participants may add to, combine, or modify other ideas, or they may introduce something new. There are no value judgments on the quality of suggestions. Osborn (1957) suggested that the "average person can think of twice as many ideas when working with a group than when working alone" (pp. 228–229).

The free and open brainstorming session provides an environment that facilitates the production of a variety of ideas from the participants. Members who are reticent about contributing during an open discussion because they are not sure their ideas are worthy have a guaranteed-safe environment in which to contribute during brainstorming. Quantity of ideas is the object. Later, the ideas may be analyzed, judged as to quality, and reduced to selected items. The brainstorming technique, therefore, is excellent for stimulation of diversified thought and solutions to issues and problems. It also reinforces the socioemotional aspects of a group by accepting the contributions of all people freely.

Setup

1. Arrange chairs in a circle if the group has fewer than 30 members. A small group allows for more interaction.
2. Brainstorming may be used in a larger group with an auditorium arrangement of chairs. In that case, the entire group has difficulty participating, but the mechanism is effective for bringing forth a quantity of ideas and thoughts.

Procedure

1. The brainstorming session requires a leader and a recorder.
   a. Appoint a recorder or ask for a volunteer.
   b. Appoint a leader or assume the leadership role.
2. The leader begins the brainstorming session by explaining the rules and emphasizing that all contributions are wanted and accepted. Even if ideas seem unusual, all members should contribute. Ideas should be interjected as they occur.
3. The topic or issue is explained to the group.
4. The session is opened to contributions from the group.
5. The recorder writes on a board or piece of paper all the ideas that come from the group.
6. After a selected amount of time—4, 6, or 10 minutes, depending on the issue and the flow of ideas—the group may turn to analyzing all the suggestions and pulling out the ones that seem to answer the issue or problem best.
7. A summary of the solutions and ideas gained from brainstorming is reported by the leader.
8. If this is an action meeting, plans for action should be identified at this time.

Appropriate Topics

1. Ideas to solve problems—for example, subjects for meetings, summer activities
2. How to get your child to study (or eat or go to bed)
3. Creative activities
4. Exploring your environment
5. Nutrition
6. Ways to improve relations at the school
7. Summer offerings for families

Workshops and Centers

Workshops are a superb means of achieving involvement by members. Most useful for demonstrating programs and curricula, they can be also used as an effective means of explaining procedures, illustrating the learning process, and developing understanding. The major ingredient in

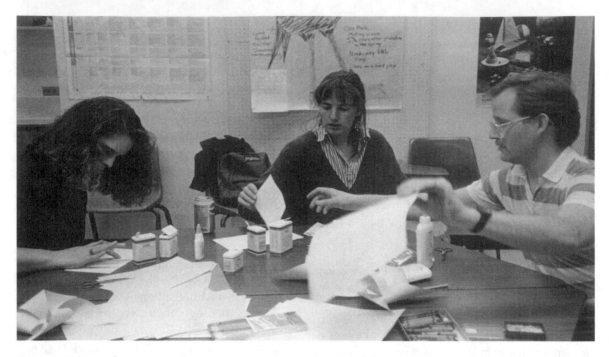

Center activities or buzz groups give everyone an opportunity to participate.

a workshop is active participation by members, whether through making puzzles and toys, working on mathematics, painting, modeling with clay, editing a newspaper, composing music, writing poetry, or planning an action.

Although often confused with workshops, centers are different in that they do not require participants to be actively involved in the project. Centers allow subgroups of the membership to gather simultaneously in various areas of the room, where they might see a demonstration, hear an explanation of an issue or program, or watch a media presentation. If time allows, more than one center may be visited. The variety of centers is limited only by the imagination and productivity of the planning group. The advantages of this diversified meeting are (a) it reduces group size and thus promotes more interaction and allows individual questions; (b) participants are able to select topics of interest to them; and (c) tension and anxiety of the presenters are reduced because of the informal format.

Setup

1. Depending on available space, workshops and centers may take place in separate rooms or in one large room with designated areas.

2. Each presenter might have different requirements. The amount of space and number of tables and chairs requested should be set up according to those requirements.

Procedure

1. The chairperson explains the variety of workshops or centers available and procedures to be used.

2. Participants choose a workshop or center. These may be assigned according to several procedures: free choice, numbers on name tags, or preregistration.

3. Participants attend one or more workshops depending on time available. If plans include a time limit for each, the groups proceed from one to the next at a signal.

4. Members may gather together at the close of the meeting, or it may conclude with the final workshop or center.

Appropriate Topics

1. Learning activities
2. Art activities
3. Bookmaking
4. Games and toys
5. Math activities to do at home
6. Science activities to do at home
7. Rainy day activities
8. Leadership training session
9. Writer's workshop
10. Learning to read

Observations and Field Trips

Although observations and field trips can be quite different in their objectives, they are similar in theory and procedure. The active viewing of a classroom, like a visit in the community, encourages the participant to be involved in observing activities. The opportunity to see an activity in process clarifies that process as no written or spoken word can. It is imperative, however, to discuss objectives and points to consider before the field trip or observation. It is also essential to analyze and discuss observations after the visits, to clarify the experience and bring it into focus. Many times the end of a field trip can be the beginning of a new, expanded project for the individual or group.

Arrangements Before Observations or Field Trips

1. Select the time and place for the observation or field trip.
   a. Plan classroom visits in advance. Specific objectives may be discussed prior to the observation.
   b. If the classroom has an observation area, observers can easily watch without disturbing the class. If there is no observation area, those going into the classroom should know the teacher's preferred procedure.
   c. Field trips must be planned and permission for visiting obtained.
2. Participants learn more and receive more satisfaction from field trips if background information and items to be aware of are discussed before the visit.
3. If the members are going to a place different from their regular meeting area, group travel arrangements should be made.

Procedure

1. The leader plans and conducts a previsit orientation.
2. The observation or field trip is completed.
3. Discussion of the experience clarifies the issues and focuses on the learning that has taken place. Many field trips tend to be an end in themselves, but that omits the most important follow-up, where new ideas and greater understanding are generated.

Appropriate Observations and Field Trips

1. In classroom observations, look for the following:
   a. How children learn
   b. Play—child's work
   c. Interpersonal relations
   d. Aggression
   e. Fine- and gross-motor control
   f. Hand-eye coordination
   g. Stages and ages
2. Field trip options include the following:
   a. Children's museums
   b. Art museums
   c. Parks
   d. Special schools
   e. Newspapers
   f. Hospitals

g. Businesses

h. Farms

i. State legislature

Dyad or Triad Interaction and Feedback

During structured programs such as STEP and P.E.T., interludes that allow the audience or participants to clarify, practice, and receive feedback on their interaction with others are beneficial. For example, if parents and teachers were working to improve interaction during a conference, sample statements would allow them to practice listening and other communication skills. If the topic were reflective listening, one member of the dyad or triad would share with the others an aspect or concern. The second person would answer with a reflective listening response. The third then would critique the response. Each member of a triad would have an opportunity to play each role: the speaker, listener, and observer.

Setup

1. Small group (up to 24).

   a. Arrange chairs in a circle, semicircle, or around tables.

   b. Have participants arrange their chairs so that two or three can communicate with each other.

2. Large auditorium.

   a. Start at the beginning of the row and have the aisle person turn and discuss with the person to the right. Dyads or triads can be formed all along each row.

Procedure

1. After a topic has been described or a video shown, stop the program and have the participants form dyads or triads.

2. Have the dyad or triad decide who will be the speaker, the listener, and the observer.

3. Describe a situation or problem that needs to be clarified or solved. Handouts describing situations are effective in large meetings.

4. Have the participants play out their parts.

5. The observer then critiques the statement and response using positive reinforcement as well as suggestions.

Appropriate Topics

1. Communication

2. Behavior and misbehavior

3. Determination of problem ownership

4. Reflective and active listening

5. Natural and logical consequences

Role-Playing

Role-playing is the dramatization of a situation where group members put themselves into designated roles. Role-playing is a very informal type of meeting, similar to presenting a drama, so it can be adapted to a variety of situations. The roles that people play can be initiated by the players, or players can follow a set format or enact a specific situation. In either situation, the people playing the roles are to put themselves into those roles. They are to feel that they are the character in the role and respond with appropriate reactions and emotions. For this reason, spontaneous role-playing is advantageous over the planned drama.

Role-playing can be used to demonstrate a problem or develop participants' sensitivities to a situation. In demonstrating a situation, the group members discuss their feelings and reactions and offer solutions. It is an excellent means for getting many people involved in a situation and is easily used to illustrate parent-child interaction.

In development of sensitivity, role reversal is often used. For example, a teacher plays the role of principal while a principal plays the role of teacher. Not only do participants begin to understand the obligations of the other role, but through their playing of the role they are able to demonstrate their feelings. This clarifies feelings for both parties. Another role-reversal situation that can be used is the parent-child relationship, with one participant playing the child's role and another playing the parent's role. The parent in the child's role develops sensitivity to the child's position.

Participants in role-playing feel free to communicate their feelings and attitudes because they are not portraying themselves. This encourages greater openness and involvement. When group members begin role-playing, they tend to be hesitant to get involved emotionally with the part. After using role-playing for a period of time, hesitancy and reluctance to be involved disappear and people enjoy the opportunity to participate. If the group progresses to a therapeutic enactment, professional counselors should be included and consulted.

Setup

1. Role-playing can be used in a variety of formats: (a) within the circle of participants—the center of the circle is the stage; (b) with chairs arranged in semicircles and the stage at the front—this is appropriate for larger groups; (c) in a large group meeting with an auditorium stage for the actors.

2. If the role-playing is planned for participation by the entire group, allow members to meet first in a circle arrangement and then break into smaller groups after an introduction.

Procedure

1. A short discussion of the topic or situation is introduced by the leader or panel.

2. The situation that will be role-played is introduced. This may be done by (a) volunteers, (b) people selected before the meeting to start the initial role play, or (c) breaking up the total group into groups of four or five, giving each group a topic with an outline of the role situation or a challenge to develop its own role situations.

3. The role can be played in two ways:
   a. It can be done in front of the entire group with members watching and listening to the dramatization and interaction. After the role play, the members use the open discussion method to clarify issues, study the problem, and make decisions.
   b. If the members are divided into smaller groups, it is beneficial to let each group play its roles simultaneously and have each small group discuss the feelings and attitudes that arose while they were playing their roles. After this, the small groups may discuss alternative means, ideas, and solutions.

4. If the small groups have all met and developed specific situations, it is also meaningful to have each group perform its role-playing in front of the full group. Afterward, the larger group may discuss the role-playing openly. Clarification, questions, and solutions are brought forth at this time.

5. The leader thanks those who participated in role-playing.

Appropriate Topics

1. Parent-teacher conferences
2. Behavioral problems
3. Building self-esteem
4. Reflective listening
5. Roles within groups

Dramatizations

Short plays, written by group members or selected from those available from commercial companies, mental health organizations, or social agencies, can be used as springboards to discussions. There is an advantage to using skits composed by members. First, the skit can be kept short with parts that are easy to learn. Second, the action may be specifically related to the group's needs. Third, the preparation of the skit encourages group participants to become actively involved in the process and in the material that is presented.

A variation of the drama can be the use of puppets. Many participants like to use a puppet because it takes away the threat of performing.

Setup

1. Depending on the number of people at the meeting, the room can be arranged as follows:

   a. Use a circle for a small group, with the dramatization performed as a play in-the-round.

   b. If the group is small, chairs may be arranged in a semicircle with the "stage" at the opening. The stage may be raised or on the same level as the group members.

   c. If the group is large, an auditorium arrangement is appropriate. The dramatization can be performed on a stage.

Procedure

1. The leader convenes the meeting and introduces the drama and the cast of characters.

2. The dramatization is presented.

3. Open discussion ensues, which clarifies feelings, emotions, and information presented.

4. The leader thanks the performers.

Appropriate Topics

1. Family violence
2. Handling the stubborn child
3. Rivalry between children
4. Family rivalry
5. Family conferences
6. Communication among family members

Panels

A panel is an informal presentation by four to six presenters who discuss an issue or idea. Panel members come prepared with background material on a selected subject and, seated behind a table or in a semicircle, discuss the subject among themselves. The presentation allows informal interaction and conversation among the members.

The chairperson, although a member of the panel, has different responsibilities from the other members. The chairperson introduces members, presents the topic, and then encourages participation by the other members. Like a leader, the chairperson can clarify, keep the panel focused on the topic, and summarize the closing.

Setup

1. Place a table, or two tables slightly turned toward each other, in front of the audience. Set chairs for the panelists behind the table, allowing members to see and converse with each other easily.

2. Seat the audience or remaining members of the group in a semicircle, with the panel facing them. If the audience is large, auditorium-style seating may be used with a panel presentation.

Procedure

1. The chairperson does the following:

   a. Clarifies the panel procedure to the audience.

   b. Presents the topic for discussion and the relevance of the topic to the group's concerns.

   c. Introduces the panel members.

   d. Starts the discussion with a question or statement. The panelists begin a discussion, freely interacting and conversing with one another.

   e. Asks for questions from the audience. Questions are discussed among panelists.

   f. Summarizes the major points and the conclusions of the panel.

   g. Thanks the panel members for their contributions.

Appropriate Topics

1. Child development—social, intellectual, emotional, and physical
2. New methods of classroom teaching
3. Bias-free education

4. Exceptional children
5. Influence of drugs and alcohol on children
6. Discipline
7. Emotions in children
8. Managing a home with both parents working
9. Nutrition

Colloquies

The colloquy is a panel discussion by an informed or expert panel where members of the audience are encouraged by the chairperson to interject questions or comments during the presentation. This allows information pertinent to the audience's interests to be discussed during the main part of the presentation instead of waiting for a question-and-answer period after the presentation.

A second form of the colloquy includes two sets of panels, an expert panel and a lay panel. The lay panel uses the procedures for a panel discussion. The expert panel gives advice when called upon by the lay panel or when it thinks pertinent information is being overlooked.

Setup

1. For a single panel, place chairs behind tables that are turned so the members of the panel can make eye contact with one another.
2. For two panels—lay and expert—seat the chairperson in the center with one panel on the left and one on the right. Both sets of panel members should be facing slightly toward the center so they can see each other and the audience.

Procedure

1. Single-panel colloquy:
   a. The leader or chairperson explains and clarifies the colloquy procedure to the audience.
   b. The topic for discussion is introduced.
   c. Panel members are introduced.

d. The chairperson offers a stimulating comment or question to start the discussion.
   e. The chairperson encourages free interaction among panel members and takes questions and comments from the audience.
   f. An open forum follows the conclusion of the panel discussion.
   g. The leader summarizes and concludes the meeting.
2. Dual-panel colloquy:
   a. The chairperson explains and clarifies the two-panel colloquy to the audience.
   b. The chairperson introduces the subject for discussion.
   c. The expert and lay panels are presented to the audience.
   d. The leader starts the discussion with a stimulating remark or question.
   e. As expert advice is needed, the second panel is called upon to contribute.
   f. A question-and-answer period follows the presentation, with comments and questions from the audience answered and discussed by both the lay and expert panels.
   g. The chairperson summarizes, thanks the participants, and concludes the colloquy.

Appropriate Topics

1. Dealing with your child's fears
2. Handling stress
3. Drug addiction and alcoholism
4. Helping exceptional children
5. Nutrition

Debates

When an issue is of a pro-and-con nature, a debate is an effective means of presenting both sides. The debate team presents opposing views of a controversial issue.

Setup

1. Place enough chairs for the members of each debate team on either side of a podium or table.
2. Place chairs in a circle for a small audience; if the group is large, use an auditorium formation.

Procedure

1. The question to be debated is announced by the chairperson, and the issue is turned over to the speakers for each side.
2. One speaker for the affirmative begins with a two- to four-minute speech. The next speaker is from the opposing position. The teams alternate until each member has spoken.
3. Rebuttal following each speech is optional, or leaders of both debate teams may conclude the debate section with rebuttals.
4. The chairperson entertains questions from the audience, and the debate teams answer and discuss the issue.

Appropriate Topics

1. Sex education—home or school?
2. Behavior modification versus logical consequences
3. Open education versus traditional education
4. Encouragement toward achievement versus "Don't push my child"
5. Back to basics versus inquiry and/or literacy-based education

Book Review Discussions

Book reviews by group members or experts provide a format that brings out stimulating new ideas or acknowledges expertise. The review may be given by one presenter or several members. An open discussion by the entire group follows.

Setup

1. Place chairs for book reviewers behind a table in front of the group.
2. Arrange chairs for the audience in a circle or semicircle.

Procedure

1. The chairperson tells a little about the book to be reviewed and introduces the book reviewer or book review panel.
2. The book reviewer discusses the author of the book.
3. The book review is given.
   a. If the book is to be reviewed by panel discussion, the group discusses issues and ideas in a conversational format.
   b. One person may give the book review.
   c. Two or three people may each review a portion of the book.
4. After the review, the entire group joins in an open discussion of the book.

Appropriate Topics

1. Values
2. Decision making
3. Building self-concept
4. Communication
5. Divorce
6. Role identification
7. Single parents
8. Refer to the Appendix at the end of this textbook for a list of books

Audiovisual Presentations

Visual stimuli, programmed material, and film presentations can be catalysts for a good open discussion. The audiovisual format is directed toward two senses—hearing and sight—whereas an audio presentation relies solely on hearing. The addition of visual stimuli is beneficial to those who learn better through sight than sound. Accompanying charts, posters, or pictures always help clarify ideas. Films, filmstrips, and video presentations can present information in an interesting and succinct manner.

Techniques

1. Audiotapes and records.
2. Audiovisual:
   a. Filmstrips with records or tapes
   b. Sound films
   c. Videotapes
   d. Slides with running commentary
3. Visual:
   a. Charts
   b. Posters
   c. Chalk drawings
   d. Filmstrips with printed information
   e. Opaque projector images
   f. Overhead projector transparencies
   g. Computers

Arrangements Before the Meeting

1. The teacher or group decides on information needed by members through interest finders.
2. Review and select films, slides, or tapes. (Choose only programs that are relevant, interesting, and presented well.)
3. Choose a member to give a presentation.
4. Reserve films, videos, or tapes, and order equipment—tape or record players, projectors, chart stands, projection carts, extension cords, outlet adapters, screen, and so on.
5. Preview audiovisual and audio materials to be sure of quality and develop questions and comments relevant to the presentation. Do not use audiovisual materials as fillers; use them only as relevant additions to the curriculum.
6. Review the "Arrangements for Meetings" section (pp. 255–256) and make appropriate preparations.

Setup

1. Check and prepare equipment before the meeting. Have film, slides, or filmstrips ready to begin and have charts and posters set up.
2. Arrange chairs so everyone can see the presentation.

Procedure

1. The chairperson introduces the topic and the presenter.
2. The presenter gives background information on audiovisual material and points out important aspects of the showing.
3. After the presentation, the presenter leads an open discussion and question-and-answer period.

Appropriate Topics

1. Foundations of reading and writing
2. Emotional growth
3. Dealing with fears
4. Exceptional children, for example, those with learning-disabilities, autistic, and gifted
5. AIDS
6. Attention deficit disorder
7. Drugs and alcohol
8. Drop-out problems
9. Teenage pregnancies

Symposiums

A symposium is a formal presentation by several speakers on various aspects of a topic. Each symposium presenter develops a specific talk of 5 to 15 minutes in length. The symposium is similar to a lecture, but information is given by several lecturers rather than just one. Its value, to share expert information, is the same.

Setup

1. Place chairs for the presenters behind a table in front of the audience.
2. Chairs for the audience may be in a circle or semicircle for a small group, or auditorium arrangements can be made for a large group.

Procedure

1. The chairperson or leader introduces the symposium speakers.
2. Each presenter gives a talk.
3. The chairperson or leader provides transitional statements between each speaker's presentation.
4. At the end of the presentations, questions directed to a specific speaker or to the entire symposium are entertained by the chairperson. A discussion of questions follows.
5. The chairperson summarizes the main points of the meeting.
6. Symposium presenters are thanked for their contributions.

Appropriate Topics

1. Nonsexist education
2. Single parenthood
3. Gender-role identification
4. Multicultural understanding
5. Consumer education
6. Death and dying
7. Safety in the home (e.g., toys, poison, home arrangement)
8. AIDS
9. Drugs, alcohol
10. Suicide
11. Restructuring schools

Lectures

A lecture is a talk prepared by an expert or lay presenter. No interruptions or questions are allowed during the presentation, but there may be a question-and-answer period afterward. The lecture without a forum following it results in a formal presentation with no interaction between speaker and audience. A lecture forum that includes a period for questions and answers at the end of the address permits some interaction and allows the audience an opportunity to ask questions, clarify points, and make comments.

The lecture is an excellent vehicle for dissemination of specific information. As a result, care must be taken to choose a speaker who not only knows the subject but who also presents unbiased material.

Arrangements Before the Meeting

1. Select a topic and obtain a speaker who is recognized as an unbiased authority.
2. Communicate with the speaker on group interests and needs, time limit for speech, and forum period.
3. Prepare an introduction that is based on the speaker's background and expertise.
4. Review the "Arrangements for Meetings" section (pp. 255–256) and make appropriate preparations.

Setup

1. Place a podium or table at the center of the stage if the audience is large. Place chairs in a circle with a small table in front of the speaker if the audience is small.
2. Check the sound system if the area is large.
3. Obtain a glass and a pitcher of water for the speaker.

Procedure

1. The chairperson introduces the speaker and topic.
2. The speaker gives a talk for a specific period of time.
3. The chairperson conducts a forum for questions with the guest speaker responding to comments and answering questions.

4. The chairperson thanks the speaker, and the meeting is concluded.

Appropriate Topics

1. Money management
2. Specialists, for example, psychiatrist, pediatrician, dentist, nutritionist, obstetrician, special educator, speech therapist, physical therapist
3. How to manage stress
4. Dealing with illness and death
5. Preventive health measures
6. Childhood diseases
7. School finances

Select the meeting format that fulfills your needs and is most appropriate for the topic. Members of the group have responsibilities to themselves and to the group. After a positive group meeting, the participants should feel supportive and supported as well as fulfilled and productive.

✍ SUMMARY

Parent group meetings are among the most efficient and viable forms of parent education. Positive leadership skills are essential to facilitate productive parent groups. Included in this chapter are a description of a needs assessment and a discussion of the formation of parent groups.

Leadership skills and good group interaction can be developed if groups are aware of leadership and group roles. Roles that emerge within groups affect the interaction among participants. A knowledge of task, maintenance, and dysfunctional roles improves the productivity of group interaction through the concerted elimination of dysfunctional roles. An analysis of group discussion illustrates the interaction in process.

Group meetings use a variety of meeting formats, either individually or in combination. The formats include roundtables, concentric circles, buzz sessions, brainstorming sessions, workshops, field trips, dyad or triad interaction and feedback, role-playing, dramatizations, panels, colloquies, debates, book reviews, audiovisual presentations, symposiums, and lectures.

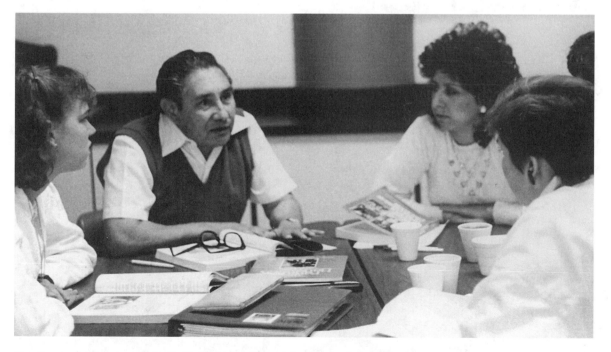

Meeting evaluations can help clarify the strengths and the needs of the group.

Choice of topics for the meetings should fit the interests and needs of the groups.

Evaluations are necessary in ongoing parent groups because they provide a basis for improvement of group interaction and suggestions for the continuing program.

✌ SUGGESTED CLASS ACTIVITIES AND DISCUSSIONS

1. Generate some innovative icebreakers. Try them out on your classmates.
2. Conduct an opening period of a parent meeting. Include icebreakers and interest finders.
3. Make an interaction pattern on an observation wheel. Discuss the interaction pattern.
4. Conduct a needs assessment within the entire class or group. From the results, pick one topic for each of the formats, that is, panel, debate, symposium, workshop, buzz session, and so on. Let each group be responsible for conducting a meeting using these topics and formats.
5. Attend a parent education meeting in your community. Visit with the members. Note how the meeting is conducted, the involvement of the parents, and the feelings of the members. Talk with the director about the goals and objectives of the group. Talk with parents about their desires for the group.
6. Develop a workshop or meeting for parents. Include the objectives of the meeting, questions to be answered, background material on the questions, and a list of additional resources.
7. Attend a board meeting of your district.
8. Attend a parent advisory council meeting.
9. Attend or participate in a site-based or community management meeting.
10. Develop a format for team building in your school.

⧼ Appendix A
Parent Needs Assessment

Dear Parent:

Our Laboratory is preparing a new instructional series for parents. It is called "Education for Effective Parenthood."

Your local school has agreed to help us. Now we need your help. You will find a five-page form with this letter. The form will tell you "what to do." You can help by telling us on the form about your own needs as a parent. If you are married, we hope you will talk with your husband or wife as you give your answers on the form. If you are a single parent, please let us know of your needs from this point of view.

When you finish answering, put your form in the envelope. Then seal it and return it to the school. Do not put your name on the outside of the envelope. We will not tell anyone what you said. We will use your answers to help us plan the "Education for Effective Parenthood" series.

We would like to know your answers. But you do not have to answer. Even if you do not answer, please seal your form in the envelope and return it to the school.

Soon you will hear from the school about the new instructional series. Watch for this news.

Thank you for your help.

Sincerely,

_____

From *Parent Education Needs: A National Assessment Study* (pp. 75–84), by D. L. Coan and E. E. Gotts, 1976, Charleston, WV: Appalachia Educational Laboratory, Inc. (ERIC Document Reproduction Service No. ED132609). *Learning to Be a Better Parent* was developed by E. E. Gotts, D. L. Coan, and C. E. Kenoyer, 1975.

LEARNING TO BE A BETTER PARENT

Name: _____

My city and state: _____

My children's ages (in years): _____

Name of nearest grade school: _____

What to do: First, read what it says below about each thing you might learn more about. Then decide how much you feel you need or want to learn more about that. For example, if you feel you already know all or just about as much as you need or want to know about item 1 under "How children grow and develop," then mark the box *Nothing more at all*. However, if you feel you need or want to learn *more* about that, then you may wish to answer *A little more* or *A lot more*. Put a check mark (✓) in the box under *A lot more, A little more*, or *Nothing more at all* for each question. We are interested in what you feel. You may, of course, feel that you need or want to learn more about some things, and nothing more about others. No one will judge you as a parent, whatever your answers are. If you do not want to answer a question, then leave it blank.

	A Lot More	A Little More	Nothing More at All
A. How children grow and develop			
How much do you feel you need or want to learn more about:			
1. Where you can find out about how children develop.	❏	❏	❏
2. What your child should be able to learn at his age, so as not to "push" your child too much.	❏	❏	❏
3. How children grow into special, one-of-a-kind people.	❏	❏	❏
4. How the world looks and sounds to your child, and how to help her learn about it.	❏	❏	❏
5. How your child's personality is formed.	❏	❏	❏
6. How your child learns to use his body by playing (runs, jumps).	❏	❏	❏
B. Taking better care of your baby			
How much do you feel you need or want to learn more about:			
1. What happens before the baby comes (what to eat; what drugs not to take; how long to wait before having another baby; things that can happen to the baby).	❏	❏	❏
2. How babies learn to talk (what the baby hears; what it learns from what you do and say).	❏	❏	❏
3. Helping the baby feel good (not too warm or cool; enough to eat; food that might upset the baby; giving the baby room to move around).	❏	❏	❏

C. Treating your child like a person

How much do you feel you need or want to learn more about how to:

1. Tell what children are doing by watching them. ❏ ❏ ❏
2. Help your child see and accept his or her own feelings. ❏ ❏ ❏
3. Show love and care to your child. ❏ ❏ ❏
4. Talk with your children about their problems and answer their questions. ❏ ❏ ❏
5. Help your children to behave when they start to fight. ❏ ❏ ❏
6. Help your child learn to get along with family and friends. ❏ ❏ ❏
7. Help your child see why rules are good. ❏ ❏ ❏

D. Talking care of your family

How much do you feel you need or want to learn more about how to:

1. Pick things for the children's bed and for them to wear (so that they last and are easy to take care of). ❏ ❏ ❏
2. Find and take care of a home for your family (how to shop and pay for housing and furniture). ❏ ❏ ❏
3. Pick the right foods and take care of them so they will not spoil (fix meals that are good for your family's health). ❏ ❏ ❏

E. Teaching and training your child

How much do you feel you need or want to learn more about:

1. What ways of teaching will work best with your child (the way you teach; use of books, TV). ❏ ❏ ❏
2. How to control your child by using reward, praise, and correction in a loving way (how to help your children control themselves). ❏ ❏ ❏
3. How to teach your child to be neat and clean and to show good manners. ❏ ❏ ❏
4. How to get your child to go to bed on time (and to rest or take naps). ❏ ❏ ❏
5. How to get your child to change from doing one thing to doing something else. ❏ ❏ ❏
6. How to plan your child's use of TV (picking TV programs; not watching too much TV). ❏ ❏ ❏
7. How to place your chairs, tables, and other things so that your child will have room to play and learn (and keeping some things out of sight so your child will not want them). ❏ ❏ ❏

8. How to feed your child; teach him to feed himself; and make eating fun for your child. ☐ ☐ ☐
9. How to teach your child to dress and undress. ☐ ☐ ☐
10. How to help your child think for herself (choose what she wants to do; make plans). ☐ ☐ ☐
11. How to teach your child to tell right from wrong (to be moral). ☐ ☐ ☐

F. Keeping your family safe and well
How much do you feel you need or want to learn more about:

1. How to keep your child from getting hurt (and how to give first aid). ☐ ☐ ☐
2. How to keep your child well (get shots and have the doctor check your child). ☐ ☐ ☐
3. How to know if something is wrong with your child (is not learning; cannot walk well; cannot see or hear well). ☐ ☐ ☐
4. How to know when your child is sick (has a fever or says he hurts some place). ☐ ☐ ☐
5. How to pick things that are safe to play with. ☐ ☐ ☐
6. How to tell if your child is growing right (body size, height, weight). ☐ ☐ ☐

G. Taking care of things at home
How much do you feel you need or want to learn more about:

1. Making good use of your time (plan your time for child care, housework, school or job, time for yourself and your friends). ☐ ☐ ☐
2. Getting good help with child care (day care, baby sitter, nursery school). ☐ ☐ ☐
3. How your child deals with the way that your family lives (people in the home, what they do together, how they get along). ☐ ☐ ☐
4. Finding help for people who don't take care of their children, or who hurt their children. ☐ ☐ ☐

H. Yourself as a parent
How much do you feel you need or want to learn more about:

1. Your own feelings and habits and how these help or hurt your child care (how they affect your child care). ☐ ☐ ☐

	A Lot	A Little	Not at All
2. Your need to make your child mind you (how your own needs can affect how your child feels about herself, and your child's learning).	❏	❏	❏
3. Why your child will not mind you and how this bothers you (how to get over being upset).	❏	❏	❏
4. How to be sure that you are doing what is best for your child (or your worries about what other people think).	❏	❏	❏

What to do: Just as before, read what it says about each thing from which you can learn. That is, if you think you would enjoy learning about being a better parent from "reading books," then you may wish to answer *A lot* or *A little.* But if you would *not* enjoy learning from "reading books," then mark the box *Not at all.* You may, of course, think that you would like to learn from some things and not from others. Put a check mark (✓) in the box under *A lot, A little* or *Not at all* for each question.

	A Lot	A Little	Not at All
I. How to learn about being a better parent *How much would you like to learn about being a better parent from:*			
1. Reading books.	❏	❏	❏
2. Talking with parents in group meetings.	❏	❏	❏
3. Watching a special TV series.	❏	❏	❏
4. Seeing movies near your home (at a school).	❏	❏	❏
5. Having a person visit your home and talk with you each week.	❏	❏	❏
6. Seeing slides and hearing a person tell about them.	❏	❏	❏
7. Reading about this in magazines or in small newspapers (4 to 8 pages long).	❏	❏	❏
8. Hearing a special radio series.	❏	❏	❏
9. Listening to records or tapes.	❏	❏	❏
10. Playing games that teach you to be a better parent.	❏	❏	❏
J. How to learn about being a better parent *On TV or radio or in the movies, how much would you like to learn from:*			
1. A funny show (humor, comedy, jokes).	❏	❏	❏
2. A talk show with well-known guests and parents.	❏	❏	❏
3. Stories about real people (not humor).	❏	❏	❏
4. Special stories portrayed by actors (not humor).	❏	❏	❏
5. An M.D. (doctor) or other expert.	❏	❏	❏
6. A show that goes into people's homes.	❏	❏	❏

Other Ideas

What else do you think you need or want to learn more about in order to be a better parent? Please print so that your ideas will be easy to read.

_____

_____

_____

_____

_____

Appendix B
Promoting Children's Self-Esteem

Children of all ages need to feel good about themselves, to possess confidence. They need to feel that they can take risks based on their confidence in their abilities. Parents play a major role in their children's development of self-confidence.

This brief description of a parent meeting structured in a center format illustrates how parents can improve their skills.

OBJECTIVES

1. To develop ways of communication between parents and their children that help children develop self-esteem.

2. To practice listening and communication skills that provide positive dialogue between parents and children.

3. To list activities and family practices that help develop a child's self-esteem.

4. To look for and analyze individual strengths of children that can be reinforced by the parents.

PROCEDURE

1. Prepare name tags that say "I AM SPECIAL" with a space for the parent's name on the badge.

2. Prepare an icebreaker that emphasizes self-esteem. One example is a signature sheet that allows participants to have their best achievements listed. Each person interviews another and determines the other person's strongest asset. The second person does the same for the first, listing a strength and signing the sheet.

3. Gather the entire group. Give a 10-minute general introduction to all the participants.

4. Divide the group into small groups. Have participants call off numbers, for example, one through three, depending on the number of centers, and then go to center number one, two, or three. Another way to divide up participants is to use three or four different colors of paper for the name tags. People with the same color name tags gather at the same center. Parents may stay together as a couple or be separated according to the desires of the parents.

Workshop Setup

1. Find a room large enough to allow the entire group to sit auditorium-style. Use this room for the 10-minute introduction to self-esteem and confidence.

2. In another room, prepare three or more center areas. Set up chairs for about eight people at each area. Chairs may be placed in a circle or around a table. Place handouts and materials on the table.

TYPES OF CENTERS

Ideas for centers may be found in the eight books listed under Resources at the end of this Appendix. Other ideas include the following:

A. CENTERS FOR PRACTICING LISTENING SKILLS

1. Prepare a handout that describes reflective listening (see Chapter 5). Have dyads or triads practice reflective listening.

2. Let the group divide into dyads. Ask one member in each group to describe a situation that is important to him or her. Ask another person to listen to the story and then repeat it. Did the respondent interpret the story correctly?

3. Encourage the group to share some activities they do at home to help their children feel confident. List things that deflate their children's egos. Then list statements and activities that might help increase their children's self-esteem.

B. CENTERS TO ENCOURAGE SELF-CONCEPT

Activities may include the following:

1. Family or personal shields that are designed by the participants and include their favorite activities, special abilities, families, and desires.

2. All-About-Me booklets. Have the booklets already made or have instructions for constructing them. Many items may be included. Each page can have a different concept. For example:

   Page 1: Me (draw or write about hair color, eye color, favorite clothing).

   Page 2: My family.

   Page 3: My home.

   Page 4: My pets or favorite toy.

   Page 5: What I like to do best.

   Page 6: My favorite stories.

   Page 7: My favorite _____.

3. Paper sacks decorated on the outside with pictures of how the world sees you and on the inside with your best attributes as you see yourself.

4. A handout of favorite ideas to do with your child during weekends, holidays, or summers. Add a blank sheet with lines for participants to add their ideas. Reproduce this and send home with the child at a later date. The handout may include such things as art ideas, craft ideas, field trip opportunities, collections, drama, or music.

C. WRITING AND BOOKMAKING

1. Books created by the parents or together with the child. Ask parents to bring some snapshots of their children and use them to illustrate the books. Write a story about the snapshots.

2. Simple cinquain poems or free verse describing something that is exciting or beautiful about your child or family. Publish the poetry in the form of a booklet or poster.

RESOURCES

Beane, J., & Lipka, R. (1984). *Self-concept, self-esteem and the curriculum.* New York: Teachers College Press.

Briggs, D. C. (1975). *Your child's self-esteem.* Garden City, NY: Dolphin Books.

Canfield, J., & Wells, H. C. (1976). *100 ways to enhance self-concept in the classroom.* Upper Saddle River, NJ: Prentice Hall.

Coloroso, B. (1994). *Kids are worth It!* Toronto, Ontario: Somerville House.

Frede, E. (1984). *Getting involved: Workshops for parents.* Ypsilanti, MI: The High/Scope Press.

Gardner, H. (1993). *Multiple intelligences.* New York: Basic Books.

Marston, Stephanie (1990). *The magic of encouragement: Nurturing your child's self-esteem.* New York: William Morrow Co.

Rich, D. (1988). *MegaSkills.* Boston: Houghton Mifflin.

Seuss, Dr. (1969). *My book about me.* New York: Beginners Books.

Note: Current articles or books can be selected for specific parent groups.

℘7 School-Based Programs

Education is the great equalizer. All children deserve the opportunity to an education that will allow them to achieve their hopes and visions.

Author

It takes an entire village to educate a child.

African proverb

In this chapter on school-based education you will read about effective parent-school programs. After completing the chapter you should be able to do the following:

☐ Describe the roles that parents have in school involvement.

☐ List the issues related to schools and parents.

☐ Describe how parents can have an active involvement in schools.

☐ Discuss parents as decision makers.

☐ Help reticent parents become involved.

☐ Describe a school where parents are active partners.

☐ Describe the Head Start program and its parent involvement.

☐ Identify programs in which parent involvement is a strong component.

☐ Describe Comer's School Development Program.

☐ Recognize the importance of parent involvement as illustrated by Reggio Emilia.

☐ Identify resources such as the Center on Families, Communities, Schools, and Children's Learning; National Center for Family Literacy; Family Resource Center of America; the Institute for Responsive Education; and the U.S. Department of Education.

☐ Develop activities that strengthen families and parent-school collaboration.

☐ Describe how family resource centers function as a family support system.

☐ Identify the importance of literacy and the development of literacy programs to help overcome illiteracy.

Parents, schools, and society have extremely strong vested interests in the success of students in the schools. Parents want their children to develop into productive, intelligent, mentally healthy young adults. Schools want to provide an environment that facilitates and teaches children as they become educated and successful, fully functioning young adults. Society requires an educated citizenry. These desires have been expressed many times during the past decade. Scores of schools, recognizing the importance of home-school collaboration, have developed special programs that brought about a greater sense of cooperation.

When the first edition of this book was published, although programs for early childhood were evident, it was difficult to find descriptions of schools that were committed to involving parents. Today, a surge toward parent involvement is expressed by many schools and described in a voluminous number of articles. Involvement ranges from offering breakfasts for fathers to recognizing the school as one part of the community that must meet the needs of the family. This would include the following:

1. Implementation of strategies based on the strengths of families and their knowledge of their children.

2. Identification and implementation of preventive strategies that recognize the stresses affecting many families today—financial, emotional, social, and personal—to make the school family-friendly and supportive.

3. Collaboration with community agencies that offer resources for students and families.

4. Exploration of different models that will help schools reach out to families; replication of models that meet the needs of the community and school or development of programs based on community and family needs.

5. Inclusion of parent-school support in preservice classes, and knowledge of resources and parent involvement programs by teachers and administrators (Edwards & Young, 1992).

The forces toward involving parents came from many directions. Parent involvement, however, is not new (see Chapter 2). Head Start included a parent commitment when it was implemented in 1965. Special education programs involved parents in the development of Individualized Education Plans after Public Law 94–142 was enacted in 1975. Hospitals and social agencies developed programs to work with schools to provide children and families with health and diagnostic provisions. Public schools looked toward parent involvement as one method of ensuring student success. The increasing number of child care facilities evoked concern for the child and the need for child care to reinforce the family, not replace it.

SEVEN LEVELS OF PARENT INVOLVEMENT

Parents may be involved with schools on seven different levels, ranging from those who are active educational partners at home and school to those who participate only as recipients of education and support. (See Figure 7.1.)

1. *Parent as an active partner and educational leader at home and at school.* The parent who is actively involved both at home and at school is highly committed. These families want to support their children through active involvement at home as well as in the school. Their roles may end with their commitment to their children or they may also be involved in the second level.

2. *Parent as a decision maker.* The second role goes beyond active involvement to include decision making. These parents may serve on the school board, on a site-based management team, or on an advisory council. With decision making comes the power to affect the offerings and climate of the school. Power and decision making are seen in the use of policy committees, site-based collaborative decision making, advisory task forces, and school boards. The trend toward site-based management, collaborative decision making, and charter schools shows an emerging

Parents are partners with schools on seven levels, including parents as educational leaders, volunteers, and decision makers.

Parent Collaboration With Schools

Parent as an Active Partner and Educational Leader at Home and at School

Parent as a Decision Maker

Parent as an Advocate for the School

Parent Actively Involved as Volunteer or Paid Employee

Parent as a Liaison Between School and Home to Support Homework

Parent as Supporter of the Educational Goals of the School

Parent as a Recipient of Education and Support

FIGURE 7.1   Parents relate to the schools in ways ranging from support of their children's education to decision making.

shift in position. If this trend continues, decision making in public schools will include parents. Charter schools, financed by the public school systems, will continue to increase in numbers with parents acting as the decision makers.

According to the 2000 and 2001 Phi Delta Kappa/Gallup polls, a majority of the public believed charter schools should be exempt from the use of prescribed textbooks (59 percent), use of teachers who were not licensed (57 percent), length of school day (57 percent), length of school year (58 percent), and state testing program (54 percent), but they were opposed to letting charter schools have different curriculum requirements (58 percent). They wanted charter schools to have flexibility but to be accountable (Rose & Gallup, 2001).

3. *Parent as an advocate to help schools achieve excellent educational offerings.* Some parents are primarily involved with the schools as advocates for the school and as fund-raisers. Think of the parent who spends hours setting up the booths for a school fair to earn money to buy computers or some other equipment the school needs. Think of the parent who writes letters to newspapers or administrators supporting school programs or advocates forcefully for educational principles. Advocacy has spurred the development of programs for special education students. Case advocacy, in the hands of individual parents, can give parents the opportunity to state their case and get it resolved to their satisfaction. There are many levels of advocacy and a variety of ways parents can advocate for their children and the concerns they have.

4. *Parent actively involved with the school as a volunteer or paid employee.* Parents who work in the school enjoy a special position there. Through their work they can view the operations of the school, learn about the curricula, and become acquainted with teachers and administrators as friends and colleagues. It is important for the school and parent to have specific guidelines on duties and responsibilities.

They can be a help as advocates for the school in the community.

5. *Parent as a liaison between school and home to support homework and to be aware of school activities.* Parents who act as liaisons between school and home do not become involved in power or advocacy and are most interested in the school as the agency that educates their children.

6. *Parent education.* These parents and the parents in all the previous levels may partake of parent education through classes and/or informal sharing of information. Research shows that fam-

ilies with authoritative parents (rather than permissive or authoritarian) rear children who are better able to succeed in school (Dornbusch, Ritter, Leiderman, Roberts, & Fraleigh, 1987). The way parents raise children, combined with the knowledge of activities that increase skills and concepts needed to learn, helps those children become accomplished. Schools should extend these offerings.

7. *Parent, though not active, supporting the educational goals of the school and encouraging the child to study.* These parents, similar to those who serve as liaisons, are supportive of the schools. Perhaps they are too busy to be involved, or perhaps they do not remember schools with fondness and prefer to keep their distance, but they do not undermine the school's objective to educate their children.

Schools should reach out to these parents and make them feel welcome.

8. *Parent as recipient of education and support from the school.* Schools reach more families than any other agency, and so it becomes expedient to look to schools for support. Parent involvement and family education can help mothers and fathers become better informed and offer support that enables them to strengthen their families. Offerings in the school may include family literacy classes, a crisis nursery, after-school programs for children, a family resource room, clothes and boot exchanges, free breakfasts and lunches for children, as well as parent education. Schools can also serve as referral agencies for community services if families are in need.

If parents can be encouraged to attend classes, knowledge of child development and literacy education may help with their raising their children. For example, knowledge of the importance of language development, based in the first four years of life, is essential for later school success. During parent education classes it has come as a surprise to many parents that talking and reading with their young child are important. This small amount of parent education can help turn a child into a capable student.

Issues and Concerns

As school-based programs look to this complex collaboration between home and school, many issues emerge:

1. Parent-school cooperation in the education of children
2. Power and decision making
3. Advocacy
4. Parent education and strengthening families
5. Family literacy
6. Comprehensive programs to meet the needs of the entire family, including addressing the problems of homelessness, poverty, drugs, and violence
7. Empowerment of families

Society today needs agencies to collaborate and help families grow in strength and ability to survive. With the large number of parents working, all agencies involved with the family (recreation, health, social agencies, businesses, schools, and churches) will need to collaborate to ensure continuity. Employers must reevaluate their structure to allow more part-time, shared, and flexible hours and release time for parents to visit and volunteer in the schools; and they must collaborate with high schools to provide occupational internships. Health agencies also must collaborate with schools. Social agencies can provide support for parents that are unable to provide adequately for their families or that might be neglectful or abusive if they do not have support. Schools cannot be expected to solve all of society's problems and answer all the questions involved in change, but they should work with other agencies and provide education and facilities to help strengthen families.

The emerging family resource centers and the increasing number of schools offering family literacy classes are steps in the right direction. Parents are more able to care for and teach their children if they can read and write themselves. Parents can be more supportive of their children if they can participate in society successfully, earn a living, and provide a home. As Davies (1987) suggests, they are able to be co-productive.

The term *co-production* adds to the concept of school-home partnership. In that partnership students and parents are essential partners with the school as co-producers of education. Education is not something just doled out by the schools. The students, supported by the parents, must be actively involved for education to occur.

SIX TYPES OF INVOLVEMENT

Epstein (1995, 1996) shares a framework of six types of involvement that schools may implement to increase collaboration among schools, families, and community. They are:

1. *Parenting*—Help parents with skills and an understanding of child and adolescent development that enables them to have a home environment that supports learning and school success.
2. *Communicating*—Communicate effectively, school to home and home to school, about children's progress and school programs.
3. *Volunteering*—Involve parents as volunteers with recruitment, training, and flexible schedules available so that parents can be involved.
4. *Learning at Home*—Provide information and activities that parents can use in learning at home, connecting the family and school.
5. *Decision Making*—Include parents in school decisions and governance.
6. *Collaborating with the Community*—Integrate services and resources of the community with the schools to strengthen families, school programs, and children's development and learning. (Epstein, 1996)

Studies on Involvement

Epstein suggests that the six-component framework be used to extend research and knowledge about parent involvement. Studies by her and others revealed there are questions to be answered. One shows that teachers' views of parents are different from parents' views of themselves. The common belief that students want their parents to be uninvolved in middle and secondary schools was challenged when students indicated that they wanted their parents to be more involved and be available for guidance and knowledge about the schools (Epstein, 1996).

Teachers who reach out to parents are more accepting of and more knowledgeable about the families than those who hesitate to be involved with parents. Studies found that teacher practices in their involvement with families were more critical than family background in determining how students progress. "At the elementary, middle, and high school levels, surveys of parents, teachers, principals, and students reveal that if schools invest in practices that involve families, then parents respond by conducting those practices, including many parents who might not have otherwise become involved on their own" (Epstein, 1996, p. 217).

Teachers who involve and work well with parents tend to evaluate the parents without stereotyping them, whether the parents be single or married, educated or lacking in education. When teachers involve parents, they find the parents are helpful. When teachers do not involve parents, they often stereotype single parents and those with less education as not being helpful (Epstein, 1996).

The Center on Families, Communities, Schools, and Children's Learning and the Institute for Responsive Education focus on elementary, middle, and secondary schools in their research and publications. They have guidelines to assist schools in building school-family-community partnerships.

✐ COMER PROCESS

Over 30 years ago in New Haven, Connecticut, the Yale Child Study Center and New Haven Public Schools collaborated to bring change to two public schools. Comer analyzed issues and problems in the schools drawing on his own childhood experiences and his professional background in medicine and psychology. The process Comer used to develop nurturing and successful schools has succeeded and been copied throughout the United States.

Comer's School Development Program (SDP) is based on three principles—consensus, collaboration, and no-fault—needed to develop a climate that allows schools, children, and parents to thrive (see Figure 7.2). In using these principles, school personnel and parents can review aims and concerns without fault being assigned to anyone. Consensus allows discussion, brainstorming for ideas, and decision making without requiring a vote that might cause divisiveness. Collaboration allows the schools, families, and community to move forward to develop a viable, responsive environment for children (Comer, 1997; Comer, Haynes, Joyner, & Ben-Avie, 1996).

The SDP schools focus on child development and positive relationships. The school is empowered to meet the needs of the students through the curriculum, social activities, and teaching methods, while it reinforces the positive aspects of home and builds social networks.

Each school is an ecological system. In order to change children's perceptions and feelings, the interactions in the system must change. How does this change come about? SDP schools are developed through an ongoing process that places the child at the center.

Comer based the framework for school change on Field Theory, Human Ecological Systems Theory, the Population Adjustment Model, and the Social Action Model. The foundation of Comer's framework is illustrated in Figure 7.3, with brief descriptions of the theories behind the school reform. Comer saw that children's behaviors were determined by their environment. Children need to have positive interactions in order to develop physically, socially, and emotionally.

The child-centered environment is facilitated by planning and collaboration between professional

Three principles, consensus, collaboration, and no-fault, are needed to develop a climate that allows schools, children and parents to thrive (Comer, 1996).

and community. To do this, three teams guided by the three guiding principles plan and work to develop a school climate that nurtures the children. The three teams, as shown in Figure 7.4, are:

1. *School Planning and Management Team (SPMT).* The School Planning and Management Team plans and coordinates school endeavors such as curriculum, assessment, and instruction.

2. *Student and Staff Support Team (SSST),* which was first called the Mental Health Team. The Student and Staff Support Team works to prevent concerns from becoming problems and responds to the issues and needs of individual students.

3. *Parent Team (PT).* The Parent Team involves parents at all levels of the school and integrates the school with the community. (Comer, Haynes, & Joyner, 1996; Emmons, Comer, & Haynes, 1996; Haynes, Ben-Avie, Squires, Howley, Negron, & Corbin, 1996)

To develop an SDP school participants must build trust, plan well, empower parents, and continually monitor, assess, and modify as necessary (Haynes et al., 1996, pp. 50–51). For more information, refer to the book by Comer, Haynes, Joyner, and Ben-Avie (1996), *Rallying the Whole Village: The Comer Process for Reforming Education,* or contact the School Development Program in New Haven.

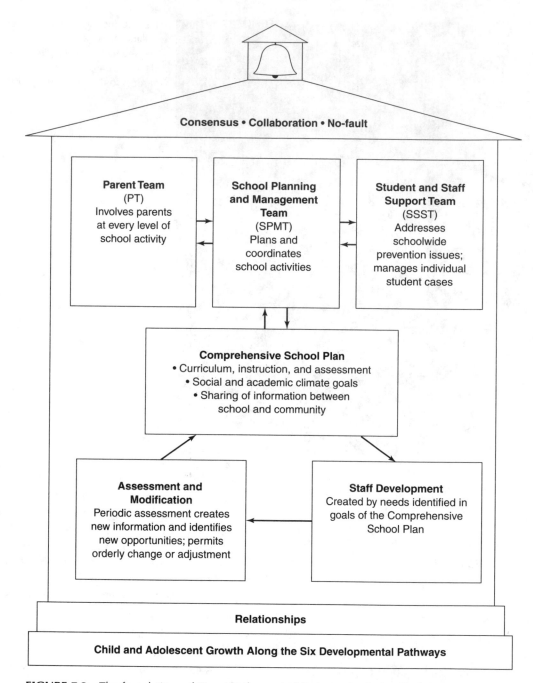

FIGURE 7.2 The foundations of Comer's theoretical framework of school reform.

Source: Reprinted by permission of the publisher from Comer, J. P., Haynes, N. M., Joyner, E. T., & Ben-Avie, M. (Eds.). *Rallying the Whole Village: The Comer Process for Reforming Education.* (New York: Teachers College Press © 1996 by Teachers College, Columbia University. All rights reserved.), Figures 1–1 & 2–1.

Population Adjustment Model
Becker, Wylan, and McCourt (1971)
Hartman (1979)

- Identify populations at risk for developing mental illness.
- Intervene through modifying the environment to promote mental health.

Social Action Model
Reiff (1966)

- Program planning should be a collaborative effort between professionals and community members.
- Professionals should have an integral knowledge of the community in which they are working.

Comer's Theoretical Framework of Child Development

- A child's behavior is determined by his or her interaction with the physical, social, and psychological environments.
- Children need positive interactions with adults in order to develop adequately.
- Child-centered planing and collaboration among adults facilitate positive interaction.
- All planning for child development should be a collaborative effort between professionals and community members.

Comer's Framework Applied
The School Development Program

- Three Guiding Principles
- Three Mechanisms (Teams)
- Three Operations

Field Theory
Lewin (1936)

- Everything an individual knows, feels, and perceives is done in a subjective reality.
- This subjective reality is known as a person's psychological field or life space; only those things present in the life space influence behavior.

Human Ecological Systems Theory
Kelly (1966)

- Behavior is an interaction of human beings with the physical, social, and psychological environments, making behavior adaptive.
- The theory's four principles are:
  — The community is the client.
  — Reduce those community services that maintain the status quo.
  — Strengthen community resources.
  — Plan for change.

FIGURE 7.3 Model of the SDP process.

Source: Reprinted by permission of the publisher from Comer, J. P., Haynes, N. M., Joyner, E. T., & Ben-Avie, M. (Eds.), *Rallying the Whole Village: The Comer Process for Reforming Education.* (New York: Teachers College Press, ©1996 by Teachers College, Columbia University. All rights reserved.). Figures 1–1 & 2–1.

✒ EARLY CHILDHOOD LONGITUDINAL STUDY

Although the Early Childhood Longitudinal Study, Kindergarten Class of 1998–99 (ECLS-K), about early childhood does not specify the contributions of parent involvement versus instruction at school, it does consider the following: age at school entry, health status, home educational experiences, child care histories, and race/ethnicity. The study included more than 1,000 kindergarten classes with over 22,000 children who began kindergarten in the fall of 1998. The 2002 report includes three studies, and further studies will follow the children until the end of their fifth grade. The first two grade reports, *American Kindergartners* and *The Kindergarten Year*, revealed that the children's skills and knowledge

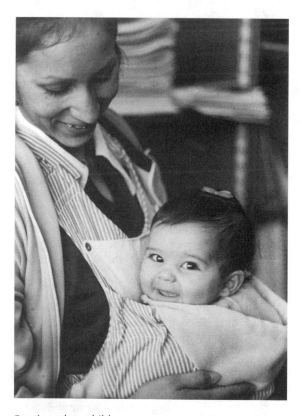

Starting when children are young, teachers need to collaborate with parents.

differ in health status, education in the home, child care, race/ethnicity, and age when they began kindergarten. These first two reports were concerned about the children's kindergarten years. The third report looked at mathematical and reading achievement and skills as they relate to child, family, and school characteristics at the end of first grade. The report also considered how the children's abilities and health when they entered kindergarten related to their approaches to learning, literary, and health at the end of kindergarten and first grade. Both recognition of numbers and recognition of letters were used in the study because they both represent the child's understanding that symbols have meaning.

Are there differences in reading and mathematics abilities between kindergarten and first grade and do they differ in relation to family, child, and school? The relationships examined were (1) proficiency in recognizing letters; (2) being read to at least three times a week; (3) proficiency in recognizing numbers and basic shapes; (4) proficiency in the mathematical concept of relative size; (5) demonstration of a positive approach to learning often or very often; and (6) being in very good to excellent general health.

Figure 7.4 illustrates the levels of achievement at the beginning of kindergarten, in the spring after a school year of kindergarten, and in the spring of the children's first-grade year. When first entering kindergarten, 67 percent had letter recognition; by the end of the year 95 percent knew the letters in the alphabet; and by the end of first grade almost 100 percent were able to recognize letters. Thirty-one percent of the students knew beginning sounds at the beginning of kindergarten and 74 percent were able to recognize beginning sounds by the end of the year. By the end of first grade 98 percent were able to identify beginning sounds. Sight words improved considerably between the beginning of kindergarten, when only 3 percent recognized words and the end of first grade when 83 percent identified words, by sight. Words in context improved to 48 percent by the end of first grade, up from 1 percent in the fall of kindergarten and 4 percent in the spring.

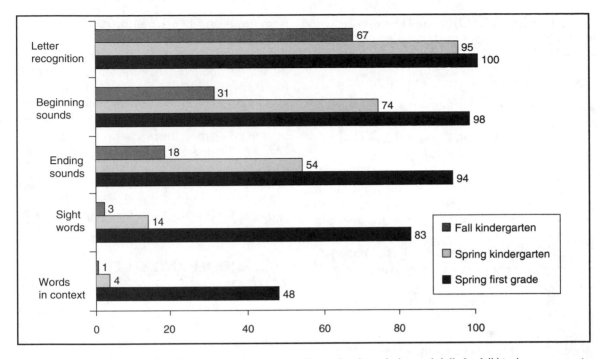

FIGURE 7.4   Percentage of children demonstrating specific reading knowledge and skills for fall kindergarten, spring kindergarten, and spring first grade: 1998–99 and 2000.

Note: Estimates reflect children assessed in English in all three rounds of data collection and who entered kindergarten for the first time in the fall of 1998 and were promoted to first grade in the fall of 1999. The estimates in this report do not exactly match those found in previous reports based on the same data. This report uses a different weight in making the estimates, which is stricter in its response requirements and utilizes a slightly smaller sample of children. For more information, see the Analytic Sample section of this report.

Source: From *Early Childhood Longitudinal Study, Kindergarten Class of 1998–99,* Base Year Public-Use and First Grade Restricted-Use data files, by the U.S. Department of Education, National Center for Education Statistics.

According to the National Center for Education Statistics (2002): Children who recognize their letters, who are read to at least three times a week, who recognize their basic numbers and shapes, and who demonstrate an understanding of the mathematical concept of relative size as they enter kindergarten demonstrate significantly higher overall reading and mathematics knowledge and skills (in terms of an overall scale score) in the spring of kindergarten and the spring of first grade than children who do not have these resources. The same pattern is true for children who frequently demonstrate a positive approach to learning and who are in very good to excellent health as they enter kindergarten. (p. 2)

. . . Differences in children's achievement (as represented by their overall achievement score) by their family's poverty status, race/ethnicity, and school type persist from kindergarten through the spring of first grade. However, children's overall reading and mathematics achievement does not vary by their sex. (p. 1)

. . . By the spring of first grade, females are more likely to be reading and males are more likely to be successful at advance mathematical operations (i.e., multiplication and division). When considering the poverty status of children's families from the kindergarten year, first graders from nonpoor families are more likely to recognize words by sight than first-graders from poor families. The same is true for addition and subtraction. Moreover, about twice as many first-graders from nonpoor families are proficient at understanding words in context and performing multiplication and division as first-graders from poor families. (pp. 1, 2)

Reggio Emilia

Reggio Emilia, located in northern Italy, illustrates the importance of parent involvement in education. In Italy, both municipal and national programs illustrate the belief that young children, infants, toddlers and three- to five-year olds deserve the right to care and education. The 1968 national law that required funding for free public preschool for the three- to five-year olds was followed by one in 1971 that established infant/toddler centers with both national financing and contributions from parents (Gandini, 1993; Hewett, 2001).

The story of parent involvement starts even earlier. After the end of World War II, the first preschool was established by parents who were able to sell a war tank, six horses and three trucks that were left behind when the Germans retreated (Hewett, 2001). "The essential role and intimate involvement of parents in their children's education is, to this day, a fundamental element of the Reggio Emilia Approach" (p. 4).

When authors write about Reggio Emilia and describe the program with no reference to parents, it makes one wonder if they recognize the importance and essential quality that the Reggio Emilia schools have. Malaguzzi, the founder and former director, described it this way: "Our proposition is to consider a triad at the center of education—children, teachers, and families. To think of a dyad of only a teacher and a child is to create an artificial world that does not reflect reality" (Malaguzzi, 1993, p. 9). The inclusive nature of the Reggio Emilia program shows the child as forceful, capable, with strong potential connected to parents and teachers as a participating member of their education. The interaction of children with adults and other children is essential for their development. "Interaction among children affects social, emotional, communicative, and cognitive behavior and development . . . different from those usually reached by children working in isolation" (p. 12).

Hewett (2001) describes the role and image of the learner and the role of the teacher. The child has rights; the child is an active constructor of knowledge; the child is a researcher, and the child is a social being. The teacher is a collaborator and co-learner; the teacher is a guide and facilitator, the teacher is a researcher, and the teacher is a reflective practitioner (pp. 96–98). If you add parent to the roles of the teacher, you will be able to visualize the triad of child, teacher, and parent in the total development of the child.

✏ MIDDLE AND SECONDARY SCHOOLS

Parents seem to reduce their involvement about the time their children reach the fifth and sixth grades, but this need not happen. Middle and secondary schools need to continue the effective methods of communicating with parents.

Five Ideas for Collaborating

Davies (1997) suggests five ideas:

Idea One. Communicate Smarter—Use many ways to get communication across. A good way to start is to provide good news to the parents. Communicate with the reticent parent. Use the radio and newspaper, post notices in laundromats and churches, as well as making use of the telephone, newsletters, home visits, and personal contact.

Idea Two. Friendly School—Make sure the school is friendly, starting with how parents are greeted by secretaries, aides, teachers, and custodians, and continuing on from there.

Idea Three. Reach Out—Go with your message to where parents are: home visits, shopping malls, workplaces, the grocery store, or places of worship.

Idea Four. Enlist Parents and Agencies—Learning does not stop at the schoolhouse door. Enlist others to help with after-school tutoring, home-learning activities, and opportunities for children to talk with others about schoolwork and life.

Idea Five. Help Families with Support—Help with access to health, social services, and counseling centers.

CHARACTERISTICS OF EFFECTIVE COLLABORATION

The characteristics of effective parent-school collaboration at the middle and secondary levels include the following:

1. An open-door policy and climate that respond to parent concerns with excellent communication, an orientation for parents, and a continued relationship. Wheeler (1992) suggests that teachers at the secondary level be assigned a group of students to contact and focus on so that all parents have one person in the school whom they know well.

2. A total teacher commitment, with teachers who are experienced in parent involvement helping new teachers develop their skills and understanding so that they can work well with parents.

3. A practice of setting up conference times based on parents' schedules; making child care available; and offering other educational opportunities available for parent participation.

4. Schools that build the self-esteem of students and parents. They empower parents, work with them from strengths rather than weaknesses, and offer activities and displays that recognize families.

5. Use of the same types of activities that work at the preschool and elementary school level (see Chapter 4). Encouragement for families to visit schools.

6. Schools as the center of the community. Secondary schools have swimming pools more

often than do elementary schools. Theaters, large libraries, gymnasiums, and meeting rooms are also available more often in secondary schools than in elementary schools. If the secondary school becomes a community center, families will have a positive feeling toward the school by the time the children become students there.

7. Help for troubled families with an individual family plan that taps into community resources as well as school offerings to help the family and student handle their difficulties (Stouffer, 1992; Wheeler, 1992).

Late in the 20th century, concern about violence in the schools erupted when children began bringing guns to school and using guns to express their anger. Schools will need to offer a line of defense to help children. Options include counseling, peer counseling, peer resolution, or conflict resolution, and other programs that help children recognize consequences and alternatives. The answers call for community and society involvement in the effort to stem the tide of violence as they work hand in hand with schools.

A WALK THROUGH AN ELEMENTARY SCHOOL

Assume the role of a parent who visits a school committed to the involvement of parents. As you open the school door, you notice a sign that welcomes you. The staff greets you with smiles when you check in at the office. If you want to have a cup of tea or coffee, look through the school's curricula, or read an article, you can visit the family center. There, several parents are developing curriculum material for the school's resource room. One parent is making a game for the third- and fourth-grade classes. Another is clipping curriculum-related articles to be filed for reference. As you sip your coffee, the sounds of young children echo down the hall from the west wing of the building. Parents and their children are arriving for parent education classes or parent-child meetings. The school offers programs for parents of infants, toddlers, and preschool children. Both parents are invited and included in the programs. For those who cannot come during the week, a Saturday session is available. On the fourth Tuesday of every month, the school has a breakfast for students' fathers or friends.

You came to school today to visit your child's classroom, so, after a brief visit in the family center, you walk to your child's room. On the bulletin board outside the door is a welcome notice that shows in detail what the children have been accomplishing. Here the teacher has described the happenings for the week, listed volunteer times for parents, and asked for contributions of plastic containers to be used in making tempera paint prints.

Immediately aware of what is happening in the room, you make a note to start collecting "scrounge materials" for recycling in the classroom. An invitation to an evening workshop reminds you that you have saved next Tuesday evening for that very event. In the space for notes to and from parents, you write a short response to the message you received from the teacher last week.

Also attached to the bulletin board are "Tips for Visiting." These let you know that you can become involved in a classroom activity rather than spend your time passively observing. The teacher smiles and acknowledges your presence but, being involved with the class, continues teaching. The class greeter, a child chosen as a "very important person" this week, comes up and welcomes you. Later, during a center session or break, you have an opportunity to talk with the teacher and your child.

Recruitment of volunteers is under way so you are encouraged—but not forced—to contribute. Flexible hours, designated times, child care services, and a variety of tasks make it easy to share some time in this classroom.

Knowing that the principal holds an open forum each week at this time, you stop by and join a discussion of school policy. Parents are being encouraged to evaluate the "tote bag" home learning activities that have been sent home with children. In addition, plans are under way for an after-school recreation program. The principal will take the comments to the Parent Advisory Board meeting later this week.

As you leave the school, you feel satisfied that this school responds to the needs of both you and your child.

See Figure 7.5 for an illustration of schools reaching out and collaborating with families and communities.

✑ SCHOOL AND CENTER PROGRAMS

As an early childhood educator one might question why parent involvement has suddenly been recognized as important. The tradition of involving parents has been strong in the early childhood profession for years, as exemplified in the parent cooperative movement and carried forth by many child care providers and educators. The following describe programs for early childhood-age children.

School on Saturday

How can it work? In the Ferguson-Florissant School District in St. Louis, Missouri, home and school have joined hands to offer a LINK program, Child Development Centers, a Parents as Teachers program, and a Saturday School. The Saturday School includes two three-hour preschool sessions for four-year-olds on Saturdays throughout the school year. The program has three major objectives:

- To provide an education program that will help four-year-old children succeed in school.
- To involve parents in the education of their children.
- To provide support for families.

These objectives are accomplished by providing the following:

1. Diagnostic screening at the beginning of the school year to establish appropriate goals.

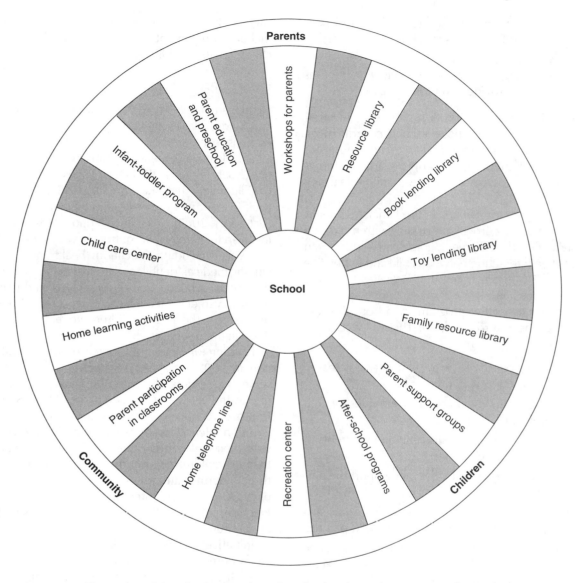

FIGURE 7.5 The spokes of the wheel radiate from the school and reveal opportunities for involving parents, children, and the community.

2. Half-day preschool each Saturday in a public school kindergarten.

3. Opportunities for participation by parents in the preschool. (Parents must participate every four to six weeks as a parent helper in the preschool.)

4. Home visits, one hour each week, with a group of two or three children and their parents.

5. Home activity guides that provide ideas for projects and other activities for the four-year-old child—and younger siblings, if any—to

do at home; these activities foster skills needed for success in school.

6. Consultants in child development, who are available to consider specific concerns as well as provide parent meetings.

Saturday School works! Children gain in intellectual, language, and eye-hand coordination. Parents gain in their ability to communicate with their children, use appropriate reinforcement techniques, and sense a child's learning readiness.

The program reaches out to fathers as well as mothers. The curriculum, dealing with motor coordination development, goes hand in hand with positive interaction between child and father. See Figure 7.6 for an example of activities for father and child.

What can other programs gain from the success of the Saturday School? These aspects seem especially important:

1. Active participation by both parents in teaching their own children.

2. Diagnostic and prescriptive activities for children with disabilities.

3. Observation and participation by parents in a school setting.

4. Guidance and activities that support the parents' efforts.

5. Teacher visits to the home, which establish a team rapport between teachers and parents.

6. Opportunities for the child to experience routine school activities and an enriched curriculum each week.

7. Home-learning activity booklets to be used by parents of children from birth through age three.

The varied approaches of the Saturday School meet many more needs than a program with only one dimension—for example, preschool without the parent component. This was recognized by the district, and although this program was initially funded with federal money, it proved its value and is now financed by the local school district and supplemented with education funds for children with disabilities.

Head Start

Head Start, a federal program with such credibility that funding has continued since 1965, is a comprehensive early childhood program which provides child development programs for low-income, preschool children in the United States, the District of Columbia, Puerto Rico, and the U.S. territories (U.S. Department of Health and Human Services Fact Sheet, 2002). From its inception, Head Start involved the family in its outreach, with spokes of the wheel including education; health care, including medical, dental, and mental health; nutrition; social services; staff development; and parent involvement. Head start makes a significant difference in the lives of children and their parents through these services.

Funding for Head Start increased to $6.5 billion in 2002. This has enabled Head Start to serve approximately 905,000 children. Research indicates that the services of Head Start improve vocabulary, math, and social skills. In addition, Head Start parents are more involved with their children's education. Two thirds read to their children three times a week or more, three fourths attend parent-teacher conferences, and most volunteer in the classroom (U.S. Department of Health and Human Services Fact Sheet, 2002).

Initiatives in the 1990s included Family Service Centers (FSCs), a two-generation approach that attacked problems at adults' and children's levels. Some two-generation programs have been operating since the 1970s. In the 1990s Even Start, New Chance, and Comprehensive Child Development programs joined with the Head Start FSCs to meet the needs of children. Head Start's FSCs provide Head Start programs for children, but also add case managers who assess the needs of the parents by delivering services and making referrals for literacy, employment training, and drug abuse (St. Pierre,

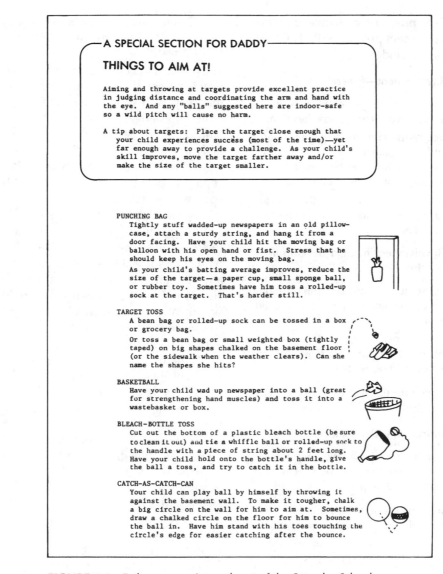

FIGURE 7.6   Fathers are an integral part of the Saturday School.

Source: Reprinted with permission from the Ferguson-Florissant School District, St. Louis, MO.

Layzer, & Barnes, 1995). In 2002, the Head Start initiatives included an Early Childhood initiative with nearly 50,00 Head Start teachers to be trained in the best prereading and language teaching techniques for young children. Other initiatives include an Early Literacy, Early Head Start, Fatherhood, and Research (U.S. Department of Health and Human Services, 2002).

Parent Involvement

In 1998, revised Head Start Performance Standards (HSPS) were implemented. The standards reinforce previous practices of family partnerships. Parent involvement policies HSPS 1304.40 Family Partnerships include:

d. Parent involvement—general

1. Agencies must provide opportunities in policy making, parent involvement, and education.
2. Program settings must be open to parents during all program hours, parents must be welcomed, all parent participation must be voluntary and not a requirement for children's enrollment.
3. Agencies must provide parents with opportunities to participate in the program as employees or volunteers.

e. Parent involvement in child development and education

1. Agencies must include parents in the development of the curriculum and approach to child development.
2. Agencies must provide opportunities for parents to enhance their parenting skills and understanding of child development.

In 1304.51 Management Systems and Procedures the HSPS include:

c. Communication with families

1. Agencies must ensure effective and regular two-way communication between staff and parents. (Epstein, 1998, p. 10)

Previously, Head Start recognized parents as the earliest and most influential teachers of children and recognized the following goals as essential. These goals reinforce the new standards:

1. Maximizing parent participation in the decision-making process in local programs;
2. Increasing parent participation in Head Start classrooms and other activities;
3. Increasing parents' opportunities to participate in activities that they have helped to develop;
4. Insuring that parents are provided the opportunity to work with their children in cooperation with Head Start staff; and
5. Furthering the ability of parents to sustain and build upon Head Start experiences as their children move into Elementary School. (Commissioner's Task Force on Parent Involvement in Head Start, 1987, p. 3)

The thrust of the message from this task force is to enable parents to help themselves. Parents can do this only with more education, more options, more knowledge, greater self-esteem, and more empowerment. Although Head Start parents have had more access to parent involvement than most early childhood programs (with perhaps the exception of parent cooperatives), the task force and standards encourage a more active commitment to ensuring true parent involvement.

Before initiating any parent program, it is wise to ask parents how they perceive their needs. Although needs will change throughout the life of any program, early assessment with periodic review will show the initial needs and the progression of later needs. Develop a needs assessment specific to the population. See Appendix A at the end of Chapter 6.

After Head Start parents complete a needs assessment, plans for parent participation can be devised with better understanding. As parents become more familiar with the program and more sophisticated in their learning, their needs and requests will vary, so provide ongoing assessment by continued use of questionnaires.

In the area of decision making, Head Start programs involve parents at two or three levels: the Head Start Center Committee, the Head Start Policy Committee for the delegate agency, and/or the Head Start Policy Council (for the grantee funded by the federal government). The first is initiated by each center, which should have a committee composed of parents whose children are enrolled.

Head Start, initially conceived with a parent component, has integrated parents into every aspect of its program. Visualize the degree of parent involvement in the Head Start program. On a visit to a typical Head Start class, you will find a teacher and aide surrounded by 12 eager three- and four-year-olds, working, singing, playing, and laughing. Because the center is located in the community it serves, parents usually drop off and pick up their children each day. As they enter the school, teachers and parents exchange pleasant greetings. On some days the parents stay and help.

The teacher may be a college graduate from another neighborhood, but, just as often, the teacher is a local parent who had children enrolled in the Head Start program and/or college degree and who has earned Child Development Associate (CDA) credentials. The aide chats with the parent about something exciting the child did yesterday. The aide, who lives in the neighborhood and also has children, knows the child well. The person responsible for lunch is another community parent. Through a Head Start career ladder, many low-income parents are hired to assist in the program. After lunch, the parent coordinator drops in to check on a child who has been ill. The parent coordinator was chosen by the policy committee because the parents respected and liked this neighbor. This person has succeeded in establishing rapport with and support for the neighbors. Two of the most essential and greatest strengths of the Head Start philosophy are the involvement of parents and the belief that parents can achieve.

Early Head Start

Early Head Start, a program that serves low-income families who have infants and toddlers, was created with the reauthorization of the Head Start Act in 1994. From 68 programs in 1995, it has grown to 635 programs in 2001 that serve approximately 45,000 children. In 2002 and 2003 Early Head Start (EHS) received 10 percent of the Head Start appropriation (Fenichel & Mann, 2001). In January 2001, a national evaluation that covered the first two years of 3,000 children showed that EHS children performed significantly better on cognitive, social-emotional development, and language. In addition, the parents scored higher than the control group on knowledge of infant/toddler development, parenting, and the home environment. It was also found that parents of EHS children were more likely to

go into job training or attend school, and that family conflict declined (Fenichel & Mann).

Families may be served in either center-based or home-based environments, or a combination of the two. Programs need to meet or exceed federal Head Start performance standards (Buell, Hallam, & Beck, 2001). For children from birth to 36 months who are enrolled in out-of-home programs, the EHS standard is a maximum of eight children and a child ratio of 1:4. This standard helps ensure the high-quality care and supportive and nurturing environment that infants and toddlers need.

The Minnesota Early Childhood Family Education Program

The state of Minnesota offers support and information for parents and children, from birth to kindergarten, in 397 school districts and four tribal schools. More than 220,000 participate, and it is available to 98 percent of the parents of young children in the state.

Although there are variances in the program, the most common model is based on a program validated by St. Cloud Seton Hall. It focuses on supporting parents in their parenting roles. Two-hour classes are offered once a week during the morning, afternoon, evening, or on the weekend. Some sessions are offered at lunchtime at workplaces. During the first part of the session, the parents and children are together, participating at learning stations. Parents also observe formal model teaching and informal child-teacher interactions. Afterward, the parents and children separate, with the parents going to a parent education session and the children to a preschool setting. The child development and parenting curriculum in the parent session is determined by the needs of the parents. In addition to these sessions, the programs have resource libraries that include take-home activity kits and books to check out. The program is available for all income levels and all ethnic populations (Goodson, Swartz, & Millsap, 1991; Kristensen & Billman, 1987; National Association & National Diffusion Network, 1993).

Brookline Early Education Project

An excellent example of how the public school system can collaborate with a health organization was the Brookline Early Education Project (BEEP). Brookline Public Schools and Children's Hospital Medical Center in Boston joined to develop a coordinated plan for physical checkups and educational programs for young children up to kindergarten age. Together, the hospital and school supplied a reassuring support system.

Based on the theory that parents are the child's most influential teachers, BEEP had three interrelated components:

1. *Parent Education and Support.* Three levels of support were provided, ranging from frequent home visits and meetings to parent-initiated support. Home visits, parent groups, and center visits were available. When children started in the educational program at 24 months, the parent-staff interaction was centered largely on the child's behavior in school, discussed during conferences based on guided observations. The average number of parent-program contacts during the child's first five years ranged from 87 to 167 (Pierson, Walker, & Tivnan, 1984).

2. *Diagnostic Monitoring.* The children were periodically screened by staff at Children's Hospital Medical Center from the age of 2 weeks until entry into kindergarten. The exam at 2 weeks old was neuralgic; at 3 months there was a physical and developmental exam; at 6, 11, 14, 24, 30, and 42 months there were physical, sensory, and developmental exams. During this five-year period there were two dental screenings and one lead and anemia screening. Health history was completed at age 3 and upon entry into kindergarten (Pierson, Bronson, Dromey, Swartz, Tivnan, & Walker, 1983).

3. *Education and Enrichment.* The 2-year-old children attended weekly play group sessions in the BEEP project center. For the 3- and 4-year-old children, prekindergarten classes took place in Brookline elementary schools. The classes em-

phasized social and mastery skills with a curriculum influenced by the High/Scope program. Follow-up research concludes that school-based early education is effective, especially in the area of reduction of school-related difficulties in the elementary grades (Pierson et al., 1983; Pierson et al., 1984).

The BEEP program, in addition to the three services just described, offered the following:

- A family center
- Consultants
- Library books and pamphlets
- Films and videotapes on child development
- Series of special events—workshops, films, and lectures
- Transportation for parents to BEEP

Figure 7.7 illustrates the extent of involvement of families, school, and a medical center. When schools, maternal and child health, social services, and mental health agencies work together, the family benefits: "Cooperation, communication, and informal advocacy on behalf of young children can enhance prospects for improved quality of life for children" (Pierson et al., 1984, p. 454). Although collaboration between groups may be challenging, "BEEP demonstrates the impact that multiservice preschool programs can have on families" (Hurd, Lerner, & Barton, 1999, p. 76).

Sinai Hospital

In Baltimore, the Sinai Hospital Department of Pediatrics, under the leadership of Dr. Barbara Howard, developed a program to meet the needs of high-risk children (Schorr & Schorr, 1988). Funding was obtained through lead-control and nutrition programs and Head Start. The program offers (a) a preschool program for at-risk children; (b) nutritional meals; (c) a parent program that focuses on nutrition, meal preparation, and child development advice offered by the University of Maryland Cooperative Extension Service; and (d) parent participation in preschool. The three

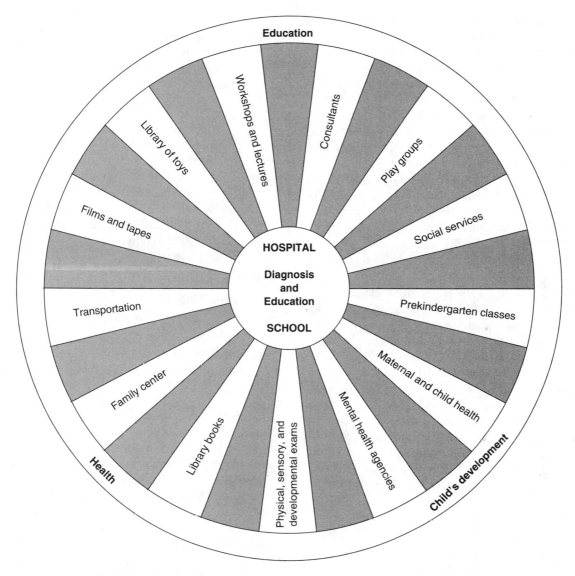

Education

Workshops and lectures

Library of toys

Consultants

Play groups

Films and tapes

Social services

HOSPITAL

Diagnosis and Education

SCHOOL

Transportation

Prekindergarten classes

Family center

Maternal and child health

Library books

Physical, sensory, and developmental exams

Mental health agencies

Health

Child's development

FIGURE 7.7 The hospital and school work together to provide for the child's health, education, and development.

groups—medical, Head Start, and education—join to demonstrate that intervention can be economical as well as effective in reducing the dangers in at-risk families. In the second year of the program, the children showed noticeable improvement and reduced levels of lead in their blood. The parents acquired skills and felt less isolated.

SCHOOL-BASED PARENT INVOLVEMENT

The League of Schools Reaching Out

The League is a national network designed to "increase parent and community involvement in public schools" (Davies, 1990, p. 72). "New relationships among schools, families, and communities must be fashioned to break the link between poverty and school failure" (p. 72). Davies, past president of the Institute for Responsive Education, has been an advocate for greater parent involvement for many years. His work with the Institute for Responsive Education and the Schools Reaching Out project (37 schools) reveals his dedication to helping schools meet the needs of students and families. He recognizes that change will not happen all at once but will occur gradually.

An example of a successful league school is Ellis School in Boston, where the Parent Center made a great change in the school. Parents were given a small classroom for their meetings. They added tables, chairs, a telephone, coffeepot, hot water for tea, and a paid staff of parents, and the Parent Center was ready to begin. Eventually, they: (a) offered ESL classes and GED programs; (b) organized grade-level breakfasts for parents, teachers, and administrators to discuss learning issues and classroom and curriculum concerns; (c) developed a library of books and added toys for the children; (d) served as ombudsmen for parents in their quest for help with housing, health, and social services; (e) organized a clothing exchange and a school store on a cart; and (f) sponsored fathers' breakfasts (Davies, 1990).

The Reaching Out project would not be successful without outreach to parents in the neighborhoods. Ellis School includes Home Visitors based on Moncrieff Cochran and the Family Matters program at Cornell University (see Chapter 8).

Teacher Action Research Teams are a direct way of involving teachers in the reaching-out process. Teacher teams, which may be paid a stipend, usually meet two or three times a month and design a survey, interview colleagues, or develop a program of mini-grants to encourage reaching out to parents (Davies, 1990). Thus, the teachers are the innovators in ways to reach parents.

Parent Involvement in Indianapolis

Parents in Touch is a multifaceted, systemwide parent involvement program in the Indianapolis Public Schools. Developed in 1978 with a grant from the Lilly Endowment, the comprehensive parent involvement program has continued since that time. Among the effective methods used are carefully planned conferences (see Chapter 5), and the following projects (Warner, 1991):

Dial-a-Teacher

Dial-a-Teacher is staffed by two five-member teams consisting of specialists in math, science, language arts, social studies and elementary education, Monday through Thursday from 5 p.m. to 8 p.m. They help students with their homework and answer questions from parents concerning homework. Their aim is to guide students into answering the questions themselves rather than give them the answers.

Homework Hotline

This call-in television program airs on Tuesdays from 5 p.m. to 6 p.m. It is carried on cable and allows students and parents to talk with the television teachers and see the problems worked on a board in the television studio.

Parent Line/Communicator

This computerized telephone system has 140 three- to four-minute taped messages that answer a variety of questions that the parent or student might have about school offerings. It operates 24 hours a day and gives information about policies, programs, parenting skills, adult education, and drugs and alcohol. Sponsored by the Institute for Drug and Alcohol Abuse, there are more than 50 messages about drugs and alcohol. This line is popular; as many as 3,000 calls have been received in one month.

TIPS

Indianapolis also uses materials from other sources. It uses the Teachers Involve Parents in Schoolwork (TIPS) program developed by Epstein (1987b) at Johns Hopkins University. TIPS structures the program so that there is two-way communication, from school to home and from home to school. Parents in Touch offered the

TIPS program in the summer for the second, third, and fourth grades with the activities developed at TIPS.

The Parent Focus Series

This series offers 90 workshops that schools may request, which TIPS will staff during daytime or evening. TIPS uses other agencies to supplement its offerings.

Work-Site Seminars

The Indianapolis School District offers seminars at work sites. These are also supported by the Council of Indianapolis Chamber of Commerce and local businesses, and give parents an opportunity to be involved even though they may have difficulty coming to the school.

Parent Advisory Council

The Indianapolis School District also involves parents in a Parent Advisory Council. Its Title I program, which mandates parent involvement, is supported in its efforts by the TIPS program.

✐ MATH AND SCIENCE ASSOCIATIONS THAT SUPPORT PARENT INVOLVEMENT

The Mathematical Association of America (MAA) and the National Council of Teachers of Mathematics (NCTM) recommend that parents get involved with their children in their success in and enjoyment of mathematics. They suggest that students discuss their classroom activities and what they have learned with their parents. It helps if parents take an active role and

- Provide a place for the student to do homework.

- Participate in parent-teacher conferences.

- Encourage their children to persist—not to do the work for them.

- Engage in activities such as games and puzzles during family time.

- Visit mathematics classes when given the opportunity.

Families are being encouraged to pursue education through many other avenues. Family Math (EQUALS, 1986) and Family Science (Northwest EQUALS, 1988) are two programs that engage families in hands-on science or math at home. The programs support the school's program from kindergarten to eighth grade.

Family Math

The Family Math classes include materials and activities for parents to use while they help their children with mathematics at home. Meetings two to three hours long take place one evening each week for four to six weeks. Children attend the meetings with their parents.

Family Science

An outgrowth of Family Math, Family Science encourages parents and children to work together on day-to-day science using inexpensive materials available in the home. The program's developers hope that minorities and females—traditionally left behind or discouraged from scientific pursuits—will be encouraged to develop their abilities in math and science if they learn about them in a nonthreatening environment.

✐ REACHING ALL FAMILIES

Moles (1996a) describes methods and strategies to reach families that include (1) early fall mailings, (2) home-school handbooks, (3) open houses, (4) school-parent compacts, (5) personal contacts, (6) parent-teacher conferences, (7) home visits, (8) parent liaisons, (9) homework, (10) resource centers, (11) family gatherings, (12) special programs for children with special needs, and (13) positive communication.

Partnership for Family Involvement in Education

Family School Partnership was established to encourage families, local school board governance, administration, teachers, and school staff to form a partnership to affirm the importance in children's learning. They make the following pledge:

- We will share responsibility at school and at home to give students a better education and a good start in life.

- Our school will be welcoming to families; reach out to families before problems arise; offer challenging courses; create safe and drug-free learning environments; organize tutoring and other opportunities to improve student learning; and support families to be included in the school decision-making process.

- Our families will monitor student attendance, homework completion and television watching; take the time to talk and listen to their children; become acquainted with teachers, administrators and school staff; read with younger children and share a good book with a teen; volunteer in school when possible; and participate in the school decision-making process.

- We will promote effective two-way communication between families and schools, by schools reducing educational jargon and breaking down cultural and language barriers and by families staying in touch with the schools.

- We will provide opportunities for families to learn how to help their children succeed in school and for school staff to work with families.

- We will support family-school efforts to improve student learning by reviewing progress regularly and strengthening cooperative actions. (U.S. Department of Education, 1997, p. 12)

In *America Goes Back to School* (U.S. Department of Education, 1997), everyone is asked to care about education and help improve it. One example of improvement in caring was extended learning—caring for and educating children after regular school hours.

Examples of Extended Days

In Seattle, Washington, five Title I schools extended the school day Monday through Thursday from 3:10 to 5:00 p.m. and on Saturday from 9:00 a.m. to 12:00 (U.S. Department of Education, 1997).

In Murfreesboro, Tennessee, nine elementary schools are open from 6:00 a.m. to 7:00 p.m., five days a week, year-round.

Los Angeles operates comprehensive, supervised after-school programs in 24 elementary schools. The program includes tutoring, instruction, academic enrichment, recreation, nutrition, personal skills, and self-esteem development.

✒ TITLE PROGRAMS

Title I

Federal programs funded under several titles also illustrate innovative use of parents as partners in the educational process. Needs assessments, parent advisory councils, conferences, and home-school activities are included in typical programs. Title I programs, active in most state school systems, heavily emphasize parent involvement, recognizing that the parent is the child's first teacher and that home environment and parental attitude toward school influence a child's academic success. A parent-resource teacher is provided to work solely with parents. Parents, paraprofessionals, teachers, and administrators work together to provide support and education for the children. Parents are trained to instruct their children at home and are also involved in the school program.

These successful programs represent the best in curriculum development. Their concern for parent involvement illustrates the significance of parents in the successful education of their children.

If you want to locate these or other programs throughout the United States, call the U.S. Department of Education at 1-800-USA-LEARN, and ask for the most recent publications about families and schools.

Suggestions for change in Title I were included in the 2001 proposal of *No Child Left Behind*. To meet the goal of reducing the achievement gap between disadvantaged and nondisadvantaged students the report proposes maintaining high standards in reading and math and setting high standards in history and science, providing annual assessments in reading and math for third to eighth grades, reporting results of assessments to parents, and increasing flexibility by reducing the poverty threshold from 50 to 40 percent so that more schools can combine their federal money to improve quality. Federal funds would be available for technical assistance and to provide capacity building to schools that need improvement.

If an identified school still has not met adequate progress after two years, the district must implement corrective action and offer public school choice to all students in the failing school.

If the school fails to make adequate progress after three years, disadvantaged students within the school may use Title I funds to transfer to a higher performing public or private school, or receive supplemental educational services from a provider of choice. All nonpublic providers receiving federal money will be subject to appropriate standards of accountability (U.S. Department of Education, 2001, p. 9).

Reading First

A new program, called Reading First, provides funds and tools to states to ensure that all children read by the third grade. The National Reading Panel reported in April 2000 that

> effective reading instruction includes teaching children to break apart and manipulate the sounds in words (phonemic awareness), teaching them that these sounds are represented by letters of the alphabet which can then be blended together to form words (phonics), having them practice what they have learned by reading aloud with guidance and feedback (guided oral reading), and applying reading comprehension strategies to guide and improve reading comprehension. (p. 10)

Title IV

"The purpose of Title IV is to promote parental choice and to increase the amount of flexible funds available to states and school districts for innovative education programs" (p. 18). The proposal promotes charter schools, broadens education savings accounts, expands school choice, consolidates categorical grand programs, and expands private activity bonds to be used for public school construction (p. 19).

✐ HELPING PARENTS WORK WITH THEIR CHILDREN

Warren (1963) listed many excellent ideas for parents to use in working with their children or with the schools. In the introduction she stated:

> You will notice, not one of the methods in this book involves parents taking over the job of teacher. Not one sets the parent to work doing complicated mathematics problems or actually teaching the child to read. That is the teacher's job, and unless you have been trained to teach, educators say, you may do your child more harm than good by trying. (p. x)

Warren was reflecting the beliefs of the time. Since then, change has come to the partnerships between families and schools. This is illustrated by programs' designs as well as the development of compacts.

Compacts

"Learning compacts are pledges that define the expectations and mutual responsibilities of schools and parents as partners in student success" (U.S. Department of Education, 1994, p. 40). In Minneapolis, pledges or covenants are signed by all involved—students, parents or representatives, teachers and other staff members, the superintendent, school board members, and community members. All participants have specific ways in which they can help.

The National Association of State Boards of Education (NASBE, 1991) recommends that parents be involved in decision making on program policy, curriculum, and evaluation. There should be continual communication between parents and schools. Parents should be encouraged to tutor their children at home and have opportunities to observe and volunteer in the classroom. The NASBE report also stresses provisions for the incremental transitions between home and school when the child first enters the public school.

The task force of NASBE suggests inservice training on parent involvement for administrators and teachers. Time for teachers to plan and carry out home visits is recommended. Home activities and materials for parents to use with their children at home should be provided. Local businesses should be encouraged to give parents time off to attend parent-teacher conferences and volunteer in the classroom. Schools should provide leadership in developing family support services in collaboration with existing community agencies. With this strong statement of cooperation between home and school, the task force supports provision of sufficient staff, training, and time to work together (NASBE, 1988).

✌ WORKSHOPS AT SCHOOL FOR PARENTS TO USE AT HOME

A workshop is one vehicle for introducing parents to home-school learning activities. Ann Grimes, a first-grade teacher, invited her students' parents to such a workshop. She greeted them, gave them name tags, and passed out a get-acquainted signature sheet for a signature game (see Figure 6.3 in Chapter 6).

After the signature game, during which parents enthusiastically talked with one another, the make-and-take workshop began. Mrs. Grimes explained the program, its philosophy, and what the school expected of parents. She assured the parents that close, two-way communication helps ensure the program is meeting the needs of the child, parents, and school. If parents were interested in participating in a home-school learning project, she assured them that she would like to work with them as a member of the team.

Mrs. Grimes reminded the parents of how important it is to listen to children, ask open-ended questions, and allow children the opportunity to predict and problem solve. She also reminded the parents that children, like adults, work best when they have a quiet, private work area and a regular time to work.

She stressed that children are expected to enjoy and succeed at home assignments. If a child struggles with more than 20 percent of the projects or problems, the activity selection should be reassessed and new activities better geared to the child's level can be chosen. Many home activities can be recreational and enriching to family life. As she concluded her talk, Mrs. Grimes explained the plans for the evening. Parents were asked to participate in the center activities located in different areas throughout the room. "If you will look at your name tag, you will find a number. Go to that activity first," she instructed the parents.

The centers in the room included games and activities as well as directions on how to play them. Materials and guidelines were also available for activities that parents could make and take home. Some parents played Concentration (Figure 7.8) and made game boards. They found that game boards could be easily made from cardboard, poster board, or a file folder. Mrs. Grimes furnished stickers that the parents could place on the game boards for decoration. To protect the completed board, some parents used the laminating machine, and others spread clear adhesive paper over their work. Each board was different, yet each was based on the same format, that is, squares on which the children placed symbols as they used a spinner or die to tell them how many spaces to move. Some parents wrote letters or numbers on the spaces; others developed cards that children could take as they had a turn. If the spaces were left empty, the board could be used for many skill activities by developing sets of cards for phonics, numbers, or other basic skills. Figure 7.9 illustrates a completed game board that can be used to develop many

PROJECT HOME BASE

AIM: To play a matching game with pairs of cards.

WHY: To practice visual memory, remembering the position of matching cards. To follow rules and take turns are skills used in most games.

MATERIALS: Grocery sack or small cards, five pairs of matching pictures, magazines, sales pamphlets, paste, scissors.

PROCEDURE:

1. Cut pairs of like pictures (10) from magazine and paste on circles cut from paper sacks or cards.

2. Encourage child to talk about pictures and name them. Then, together, place them in pairs.

3. Collect cards, turn them face down, and mix them.

4. Place cards in rows without looking at pictures.

5. Have child pick up one card and turn it over and say what it is. (Repeat the name if the child cannot say the name.) Then choose another card trying for a match. If no match, then both cards are turned over. Say, "That's your turn; now it's my turn."

6. The play continues until all the cards are matched. Count the matched pairs to see who is the winner.

EXTENDING THE CONCEPT:

1. Add more picture cards for pairs.

2. Play game using colors instead of pictures.

3. Use pictures of sets of objects.

FIGURE 7.8 The game of Concentration may be designed, constructed, and played at home or at school.

Source: Project Home Base, Yakima, WA.

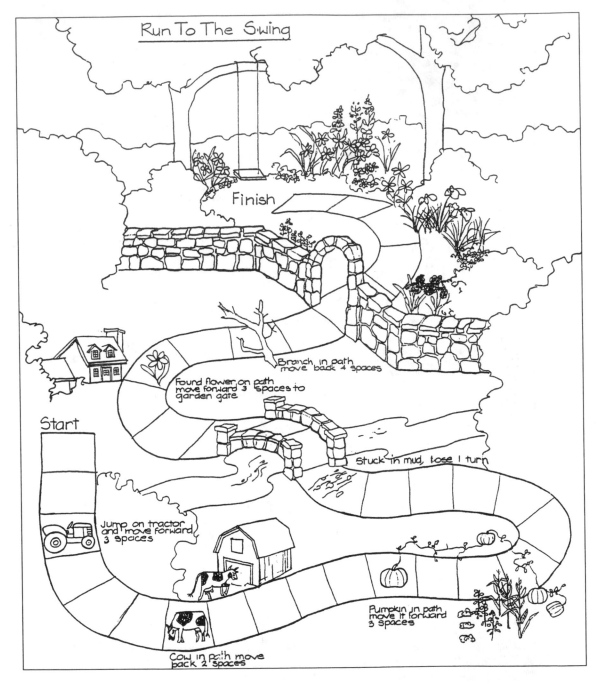

FIGURE 7.9 A "run to the swing" sets the theme for this game board. Children can suggest their special interests, and games can be developed from their ideas.

Source: Artwork by Debra McClave. Printed with permission.

different skills. While some parents were busy with the game boards, others worked on language and math concepts, constructed books, or plied their creativity at the art center.

After a busy two-hour session the group met again, and an animated discussion of the activities began. Two parents volunteered to make canvas tote bags for the class, and another promised to make a silk-screened print of the class emblem on each. They decided the tote bags would be reserved for home-learning adventures. "Please be sure to evaluate the home-learning activities as you use them. And, please contribute your own ideas," encouraged Mrs. Grimes. "I'll keep track of each child's activities on these record sheets. If you have any questions, be sure to write or call me."

After refreshments, the parents began to leave. Some stopped by the table to sign up to volunteer in the program. Mrs. Grimes recognized that she would need help implementing the home-learning program and that she could use help in the room as well. A volunteer training session was planned for the next week; the work toward a productive home-school endeavor had just begun.

Implementation of Home-Learning Activities

Home-learning activities can be useful as enrichment projects, or they can be valuable as a sequential educational curriculum. If they are used to complement learning that is occurring

Children learn at home as well as at school.

simultaneously in the school, it is necessary to monitor the child's work at home and keep track of what is accomplished.

The process varies according to the availability of a parent coordinator. If parent coordinators are available, it will be their responsibility to keep track of the home-learning activities. They can contact parents, make home visits, and report on the progress of each child. It is the teacher's responsibility to advise the parent coordinator about the child's progress in school and recommend appropriate learning activities. If a parent coordinator is not available, a parent volunteer can help with record keeping and provide contact between the parents and the teacher. The following steps are appropriate for either situation:

1. Offer an orientation workshop.

2. Send learning activities home in a tote bag, deliver them personally, or give the responsibility of the delivery system to a parent coordinator.

3. Keep records of activity cards the child has taken home. Make a record card for each child with a space to indicate when each activity went home and a space for response to the activity. This way you will know which activity the child should be given next.

4. Get feedback from parents via notes, reports, phone calls, or visits. Find out their reactions to the activities and their assessments of their child's success.

5. Continue communicating with parents. Include supplemental ideas and activity sheets on a skill that proved difficult for a particular student. Ask parents to reinforce skills up to the too-difficult level. Have them refer to previous activity cards for related projects.

6. Diversify your program to meet the needs of the parents and keep interest levels high.

7. Meet occasionally with parents or make home visits to support the monitoring system.

Communication is a basic ingredient in the success of home-school cooperation. Through talking with parents, you will know whether they consider home-learning activities to be a joy or a threat. You will want to adapt your program according to each parent's desires.

Projects around the home can furnish experiences in math, language, art, music, science, and composition. The process of exploring an idea and carrying it to fruition requires problem solving. The Ferguson-Florissant School District developed a home curriculum to help parents of young children with problem solving (Figure 7.10). Ideas for activities around the home and in the community are restricted only by the imagination.

✐ REACHING RETICENT PARENTS

Parents who do not seem to fit into the "typical" parent role may not be encouraged by the school to take an active role. Are schools willing to open up to the group of parents who need help the most—low-income and minority families? Greenberg (1989) connects the self-esteem of parents with that of the students. If the parents are not valued, the students suffer low self-esteem and do not believe their presence in school is valued. Why should they study and attempt to succeed in school if they are considered second-class citizens?

Which comes first, the parent's involvement in the child's success, or the alienation of and lack of support for the parent, which results in no parental support for the school? Parents who feel good about themselves and who feel validated by the school, participate. This situation is especially true for low-income, minority parents who may be made to feel inferior by school personnel, but it is also true for many middle- and upper-class parents who receive negative feedback on their involvement in the schools.

Families with two parents working and single parents may have difficulty being involved in day-time activities, but this does not mean that they don't care (Moles, 1987, 1996a). They might fit into the level of parents who are actively involved with their children's education at home. Most parents care about their children's progress in

Early Education
Ferguson-Florissant
School District

Lifelong Values
Problem-Solving

Problem-solving is the ability to take what you know and come up with a new solution to a problem. Problem-solving is the foundation that helps children think, reason, and make their own decisions. It enables children to accomplish the goals they choose in life.

One of the ways children learn is by watching and listening to others. As problems crop up in everyday life, by thinking out loud we are modeling problem-solving skills.

Examples:
• "We are having eight people for dinner, and there is only room for six people at the table. I wonder what we should do."

• "We have bird seed but our bird feeder broke. What can we use to build a new bird feeder?"

As you and your child are solving problems together you might ask:

• "Does it work?"
• "What else can I do?"
• "What's going to happen?"
• "How did we do?"

Ways to Encourage Problem-Solving:

1. **Age-appropriate activities and materials**
   Giving children materials that can be used in many different ways helps children understand that there is more than one way to accomplish a task. Materials such as Play-Doh (letting children decide what they want to make with the Play-Doh), blocks (how many different ways can the blocks be used to build with?), and collage materials (paint, scissors, tape, paper, paste) offer opportunities for children to explore, create and experience solving problems. Children are making judgments about size, cause and effect, and special relationships.
   "How can I make the paper stick together?"
   "What happens if I put this block on top?"
   "How can I build a ramp for my cars?"
   "What size does it need to be?"

2. **Take advantage of everyday opportunities**
   The following are just a few examples:

   • You're planning a birthday party—"What can we use to decorate cupcakes for our party? What kind of decorations can we make?"
   • It's time to clean up and your child can't reach the sink to wash his hands. You might ask, "What are you going to do?"
   • You've been to the grocery store and you have a heavy bag of groceries to put away. You ask your child to help but the bag is too heavy for him to pick up. See if your child can think of a different way to get the bag of groceries to the pantry.

FIGURE 7.10 Home activities that help the child learn and solve problems.
Source: Reprinted with permission from the Ferguson-Florissant School District, St. Louis, MO.

3. Time to think and act on their ideas

For children to become successful at solving problems, it's important to give them plenty of time to think and act on their ideas.

It is even more important to accept all ideas. If we don't, they will be afraid to try again. We all learn from our mistakes. Children need that trial-and-error process to learn.

4. Bedtime stories

When reading a bedtime story, ask your child to think of another way the story could end. Ask your child to make predictions about what we think the character will do.

Ways to Encourage Self-Evaluation

Learning is more valuable to children when they evaluate their own performance.

Questions to discuss with children:

1. "What happened?"

2. "Why did or didn't it work?"

3. "What works best?"

4. "What else could you try?"

5. "What would you change?"

When children aren't given the opportunity to solve problems and use materials creatively, they aren't able to take charge of their own learning and make appropriate decisions.

Looking to the Future

Today's problems are very complex. We are concerned about jobs, the environment, and our economy. We need people with creative ideas to help solve these complicated problems.

No one knows what the future holds for our children. But we do know if we help them to make decisions and become independent thinkers and creative problem-solvers, they will be able to handle what the future has in store.

FIGURE 7.10   *continued*

school irrespective of their background and want their children to do well (Epstein, 1987a, 1996; Moles, 1996a). The benefits from parent involvement that most middle-class parents receive cannot be closed to low-income and minority parents. The initiative of involvement by parents must come from the school; the school must reach out to the home.

Child care providers need to "work with the child as a member of a family" (Leipzig, 1987, p. 36). Bring the family together, rather than cause parents to feel inadequate. In all that the teachers do, they need to ask themselves: "Will my interaction, my policies, my way of working, contribute to the growth and dignity of everyone involved?" (p. 37).

Programs That Reach Out to Reticent Families

Parent Involvement Program

New York City provided new incentives to accomplish family involvement. The Parent Involvement Program in the New York City Public Schools needed to change some underlying assumptions to collaborate with parents. The major misleading assumption was that parents did not care; they did. But beyond that, the schools needed to help the parents see how they could collaborate with leadership strategies. Ten factors seemed important in their efforts: (a) leadership from the schools, (b) accessibility—and open lines of communication, (c) time to plan and implement changes, (d) cultural awareness, (e) active teacher roles, (f) continuity, (g) public recognition of those involved, (h) broad-based support, (i) adolescent focus, and (j) recognition of parents as people (Jackson & Cooper, 1992).

Tutoring Sessions

In Indianapolis, schools implemented weekly tutoring sessions, assignment monitoring, and workshops for underachievers that enabled parents to learn how they could help. It also showed parents that the schools cared about them and their children (Hyde, 1992).

Homework Labs

In a suburban school in Illinois, a homework lab was established where children could go two days a week and work with a staff of three teachers who would help them with their homework. In addition, improvement contracts were established that helped structure what the student intended to accomplish (Chapman, 1991).

Empowerment

A research project at Cornell University first worked with parents and later tied parent involvement to the schools. In 1989, the Cornell Empowerment Group described *empowerment* as "an intentional, ongoing process centered in the local community, involving mutual respect, critical reflection, caring, and group participation . . . people lacking an equal share of valued resources gain greater access to and control over those resources" (Cochran & Dean, 1991, pp. 266–267). Working with 160 families, the parent teams helped parents become more confident of their abilities. The group used a series of activities, which included role playing, to help parents feel secure when they became involved with schools. They developed a program titled Cooperative Communication Between Home and School (CCBHS), which included teachers and administrators. Including the school along with the parents provided even more positive attitudes. Parents need to view themselves as worthwhile participants to truly be able to interact with teachers and administrators. School personnel need to respect the parents and recognize their importance as they collaborate. School personnel and parents can be advocates for the children. In this way they work for the greater good of families, schools, and communities.

In Chicago, the ABCs—Alliance for Better Chicago Schools—established a local school council for each of their 540 schools in which "empowerment is clearly established in the minds of the people who are participating in these local school councils, and there is a strong evidence of a positive relationship between empowerment and satisfaction" (Reed, 1991, p. 45).

Perseverance, patience, and true interest in the parent are the most important factors involved in overcoming parents' reticence. Understanding, support, and interest usually will encourage a parent to take that first step toward collaborating with a teacher for the good of the child. In every situation, a few parents may refuse to be involved. Some may have serious social adjustment problems and need professional help in that area. One difficult parent or one bad experience should not destroy the commitment of the home visitor or teacher toward working with others. Teachers should not expect to be 100 percent successful. Do what can be done and acknowledge the impossibility of reaching all parents. Do this with grace, understanding, and no recriminations. Work with the children and involve the parents who want to be involved.

Dunlap (2000) studied family empowerment in a preschool cooperative. Empowerment is a process of adult development, enhanced through participation. "Through involvement with the family component of this preschool, caregivers acquire cultural capital. Over time they translate cultural capital into human capital, or economic gain" (p. 5). The process of developing cultural capital into human capital is the process of empowerment. Dunlap found this can be accomplished without giving up the participant's sense of ethnic identity.

Necessary Communication and Support

If you follow the ideas presented in Chapters 4 and 5, you will probably have no difficulty in communicating with parents. Remember, a call from the teacher or home visitor should not always mean that a child is in trouble. If good communication and support have been established, that call could mean the child is a strong leader or is working hard on a research project.

Involving parents may be difficult because of the following reasons:

1. *Families and parents might be under a lot of stress.* Problems might include lack of money,

illness of a loved one, unemployment, or an argument with a friend. In our fast-paced society many parents are under stress. It is possible that they cannot be actively involved during a time of hardship. They should not be made to feel guilty. Let them know you are supportive and whenever they want to be more actively involved, they may. Keep communication open through telephone calls.

2. *Many hard-to-reach parents feel out of their element whether coming to school or receiving home visitors.* They are unsure of themselves. They do not have confidence in their own ideas, or they believe someone else will not value them. They need their self-esteem and level of trust raised. If they have the time, let them contribute in a small way. Accept their ideas. Enlist their help in an activity at which they will succeed. Build slowly; it takes time to make a change.

3. *The parents do not realize their importance in their child's education.* Many parents, from those in special programs such as Home Start and Head Start to those who live in affluent areas, do not recognize their importance as educators. Starting with parent-teacher conferences or home visits, the teacher needs to reflect that the parent is a true partner. The parents' knowledge about the child is important; they are the best experts on their child. Their interaction with the child is part of the child's education.

4. *The parent believes no one is free of ulterior motives* (Honig, 1979). These parents do not believe that anyone can value their ideas. Trust will build slowly. Find out their goals and help them accomplish them.

5. *Many teachers do not know the parents' interests, strengths, and abilities.* Suggest projects and activities that lend themselves to the capabilities of the parent. In one program where a home visitor was working with an abusive parent, it was suggested that the child was not using the right arm enough. At the next week's class, the home visitor found bruises up and down the child's arm. The parent, who was concerned about the teacher's comment, was "developing" the child's

arm! This may seem extreme, but the response demonstrated the parent's inability to cope with everyday problems and to nurture the child in appropriate ways. The parent actually wanted the child to do well. Some parents cannot work well with their children or help with schoolwork. They become frustrated and angry; the child responds with dejection and hurt. Rather than helping the child, the parent creates a battleground.

Teachers need to develop effective strategies for working with reticent parents. Honig (1979) suggested the use of a 24-hour crisis center with project staff, perhaps psychiatric interns, recruited to give telephone counseling, reassurance, and referrals. In 2002, the need for crisis lines for depressed persons continues to be necessary. There is a national line for those who are depressed or considering suicide: 1-800-SUICIDE (or 1-800-785-2533).

A second idea was a retreat house in the country where families could go to, under the guidance of staff members, discuss and learn as well as have fun. Honig's third suggestion described a workshop where, working together, new trust could be promoted. Family resource centers located in the public schools can be a great assistance to parents at risk and in need of help. Coordinate with the center; use its resources and continue to be supportive of the family.

It is helpful to offer training sessions for parents where techniques and suggestions for working positively with the child are discussed. The STEP and P.E.T. programs give methods for communicating with children (see Chapter 5), using planned programs for parents. Filmstrips and videotapes also illustrate parenting skills and the role of parents as teachers. These resources can serve as guides in setting up sessions on working with children. Parents also learn through modeling. Helping in the classroom can be an effective learning experience. Methods of teaching that permit observation, demonstration, and role-playing prove useful. Parents, like children, learn best through active participation.

Prevention is far better than a cure. That is why it is important to reach reticent parents when their children are young. If parents can be involved from the start, their resistance to programs and partnerships can be reduced or eliminated.

The descriptions of varying kinds of programs and advocacy for children and parents illustrate that different approaches that meet the needs of the individual communities are essential.

PARENT EDUCATION FOR TEENAGERS

A powerful time for reaching new parents and parents-to-be is during adolescence. Although there is a reduction in teenage mothers, the number is still high. In 2000, the birth rate to teenagers decreased to 900,000, having declined for nine straight years. This compares to 1,000,000 who became pregnant in 1991. Overall teenage pregnancies fell 19 percent since 1991. At that time 62.1 per 1,000 teens, aged 15–19, became pregnant; in 2000 48.7 per 1,000 became pregnant.

Using data from 1995, the distribution of results of pregnancy were approximately one in three had abortions, one in seven miscarried, and slightly more than half gave birth, accounting for 13.1 percent of all births in 1995. Of the teenagers who become pregnant, one fourth were married, and one third had a stable relationship. The total number of births to teenagers in 1995 was 512,115. Most were born to females between 15 and 19 years old (499,873), with the older teenagers—those 18 or 19—responsible for 60 percent and those 15 to 17, 38 percent. Teenagers younger than 15 had 12,242 infants, slightly more than 2 percent (Children's Defense Fund, 1998).

According to the National Center for Health Statistics, adolescents 15 to 19 years of age who gave birth in 1995 included 50.1 per 1,000 for Whites, or 1 teenager in 20; 68 percent of these were unmarried. The birth rate for Black teens was 96.1 per 1,000, or almost 1 out of 10—a decline of 17 percent since 1991 (Children's Defense Fund, 1998).

The number of babies born to White teenagers in 1995 was 355,489; to Black teenagers,

139,621; to Asians or Pacific Islanders, 9,038; and Native Americans, 7,967. Four out of five births to teenagers were first births (Children's Defense Fund, 1998).

Factors involved in teenage pregnancies are poverty, low performance in school, and growing up in a single-parent family (more than one and a half to two times higher rates than in two-parent families) (Maynard, 1997). Adolescent mothers are more apt to drop out of school, have dysfunctional families and behavior problems, and live in poverty (Children's Defense Fund, 1998). Lack of education makes assuming financial responsibilities more difficult for the young parent. Additionally, there is a higher mortality rate for baby and mother. Pregnant teenagers often receive inadequate prenatal health care, and their children run a greater risk of being born prematurely, having poor health, having no father in the home, suffering abuse, spending time in foster care, being less successful academically, and becoming pregnant in their teens (Children's Defense Fund, 1997). Infants born to teenage mothers may have neurological problems, mental retardation, low birth weight, or an infectious disease.

These figures point out the large number of young parents, married and unmarried, who need family life or parent education. Over the years, individual school systems have developed excellent family life programs for their students, usually in home economics and sociology classes. Schools are beginning to recognize that human development courses and child care experiences are an essential part of the curriculum. In addition, schools are legally required to allow pregnant girls to attend classes. Title IX of the Education Amendments of 1972 prohibits exclusion of a student from any school receiving federal money on the basis of pregnancy or related conditions.

U.S. Department of Health and Human Services Programs

Programs funded by the U.S. Department of Health and Human Services to promote absti-

nence and help prevent teenage pregnancy and sexually transmitted diseases include:

1. *Abstinence Education Program*—Designed to promote abstinence from sexual activity before marriage.

2. *Community-Based Abstinence Education*—Funded for community-based abstinence education programs.

3. *Adolescent Family Life Program*—Funded for demonstration projects to develop programs to promote abstinence, prevent pregnancies and sexually transmitted diseases, and develop comprehensive health, education, and social services.

4. *Community Coalition Prevention Demonstrations*—Centers for Disease Control and Prevention (CDC) programs have been funded since 1995 to help prevent teen pregnancies. "These projects support coalition of local, public, and private agencies, and organizations in communities with high rates of teen pregnancy in order to develop community action plans, coordinate efforts to reduce teen pregnancy, identify gaps in current programs and services, target existing resources, and design evaluation plans" (p. 1).

5. *Working with Boys and Young Men*—Demonstration programs to ensure that boys and men secure the education and support necessary to postpone fatherhood.

6. *School-Based Prevention*—Centers for Disease Control and Prevention (CDC) works with the Joint Workgroup on School-Based Pregnancy. The JWG gives on-site two-day training sessions to state and local education and health policy makers to educate on how to prevent teen pregnancy. (U.S. Department of Health and Human Services, 2002)

❧ PARENTING SKILLS

Education to bolster parenting skills can be offered through center- or school-based programs, home visitors, or home-center-based programs. Some schools operate child care centers that allow new parents to bring their children to school with them. Having some form of child care is essential for young mothers to continue their schooling (Clewell, Brooks-Gunn, & Benasich, 1989). Bolstered by encouragement and understanding and equipped with knowledge of parenting skills, the young parents are better able to care for their infants.

Teenagers without these opportunities and without positive models in their own homes face the enormous task of childrearing unprepared. Expectations by some young parents for their infant's development are often unreasonable. For example, some teenagers believe that infants should be completely toilet trained by eight months. Understanding and knowledge of child development can smooth the way for effective childrearing. Providing support and mechanisms that allow teenagers to become self-sufficient parents is essential. The problems are evident; teenage parents need special attention, skillful direction, and sensitive support.

Six strategies from the Children's Defense Fund (1998) are:

1. strengthening education and basic skills training for teenagers

2. developing teens' work-related skills through jobs and work experience

3. generating a range of non-academic opportunities for success to help build self-esteem and self-perception

4. offering family life education and life planning counseling that can help teens think about their futures

5. providing comprehensive adolescent health services in a range of settings

6. fostering a national and community commitment to reducing teen pregnancy, with the involvement of caring adults who can provide positive role models, values, and support for teens. (p. 99)

Programs for Young Parents

Teen Outreach Program (TOP) has been implemented in 107 sites in 16 states to address the problems of teen pregnancies and the difficulty of success in school. TOP "works on enhancing teens' competence in decision making, interacting with peers and adults, and identifying and handling their own emotions" (Children's Defense Fund, 1998, p. 100). The program uses four interrelated strategies: youth development, community involvement, learner-centered education, and academic extensions.

In San Francisco and Lawndale, California, Teenage Pregnancy and Parenting (TAPP) programs help teen parents. TAPP coordinates agencies to provide young parents with access to education, health services, and social services. Sixty percent of those enrolled in TAPP continue in school after giving birth, compared with 20 percent of those without its services (Children's Defense Fund, 1989b).

MELD

Minnesota Early Learning Design (MELD), based in Minneapolis, has developed a program for young parents that has been disseminated throughout the United States. That program, started in 1973, was established to strengthen families. From that beginning, it expanded to include New Parents (for first-time parents); MELD Special (for parents of children with special needs); Young Moms; MELD for parents who are deaf; Nueva Familia/La Familia (for Hispanic parents); MELD's Young Dads; and MELD's Young Moms Plus, for parents of three- to six-year-old children. MELD's mission "is to strengthen families at critical periods of transition in parenthood. MELD brings together parents who have similar needs, provides them with pertinent information, and helps them develop into supportive peer groups" (MELD, 1988).

MYM. The MELD Young Moms (MYM) curriculum is based on the philosophy that parents can learn from and support each other. Young moms can cooperate, yet keep their individuality. They can make knowledgeable decisions. Having them meet weekly for two years allows MYM to be a prevention program that helps the young mother and child during the important first two years of life. Schools can sponsor a MELD program. Other possible sponsors include agencies, hospitals, and government agencies (MELD, 1990).

These programs are needed to help teens take control of their lives. Teen pregnancy affects all economic groups of society. For example, two thirds of teen births occur to White teens who are not poor and do not live in large cities. The greatest pregnancy rate, however, is among poor, disenfranchised youth. "There is an established relationship between poverty, limited schooling and life options, and early parenthood" (Children's Defense Fund, 1989b, p. 93).

Agnes, age 15, is pregnant. Her mother is not aware of the impending birth, and Agnes, in tears, confides to her friend at school. Where should she turn? Mary, age 14 and pregnant, wants to marry her boyfriend, Tom, also 14. Tom is still in school. "If I quit," he says, "where will I get a job? Are you sure you want to have the baby?"

Problems and early teenage pregnancies go hand in hand. The young teenager who lives in a city with adequate facilities and programs geared to the young mother is very fortunate. Many public schools now offer special classes for pregnant teenagers and young mothers. Child care is provided while the young mothers attend classes. The programs provide health services and instruction in health care, nutrition, family living, child development, family planning, and homemaking.

Planned Parenthood and public health departments offer additional support systems for the young parent. Health departments are also available to schools as educational resources. Working together, these programs offer the support system needed by young parents.

What Teenagers Need

Young people, boys and girls alike, need to have knowledge and skills to prepare for their roles as adults. The Children's Defense Fund cited five needs that must be met if teenagers are to become successful, functioning adults:

- A good education.
- Nonacademic opportunities for success.

- Opportunities to obtain work-related skills.
- Family life education and assistance with life planning.
- Comprehensive health services. (Children's Defense Fund, 1992b, p. 56)

The second need—nonacademic opportunities—is especially important for students who do not do well in school. They need a chance to feel successful and feel good about themselves. All people need a strong feeling of self and a good self-concept.

The third need—work-related skills—is essential for participation in the job market.

The fourth need—family-life education—helps the child continue to go to school rather than be derailed by parenthood or a sexually transmitted disease.

✑ COMPREHENSIVE SERVICE DELIVERY—FAMILY RESOURCE CENTERS

Real progress toward large-scale comprehensive service delivery is possible only when communities move beyond cooperation to genuinely collaborative ventures at both the service delivery and system level (Melaville & Blank, 1991).

Family Resource Centers

Family resource centers are being developed throughout the United States, and models of centers developed and housed in public schools are increasing. School personnel are becoming increasingly aware that families are the underlying support for the child and that the school must work with both to be successful in the education of the child. The resource centers are based on the following assumptions:

- Families have primary responsibility for children's development and well-being; they need resources and supports that will enable them to fulfill that responsibility effectively.
- Healthy families are the foundation of a healthy society. Families who are unable to

Resource centers offer programs and classes for the parents as well as the children.

promote their children's development ultimately place the entire society at risk.

- Families operate as part of a total system. Children cannot be viewed as separate from their families, nor can families be viewed separately from their communities, their cultural heritage, or the society at large. Decisions made on behalf of children must consider the ways in which these various systems are interconnected.

- The systems and institutions upon which families rely for support must assist families' efforts to effectively raise their children. They must adjust and coordinate their services so as not to hinder families' abilities to maintain positive environments for their children. (Family Support America, 1993a, p. 1)

These centers provide for young parents and mature parents alike. They help the families cope with stress; they offer prenatal classes, child develop-

ment, and parent education to help them with their children; they work to prevent crises; they sponsor drop-in services; and they arrange opportunities for parents to develop support networks. The centers are staffed by empathetic professionals and paraprofessionals. Families are linked with social services that will help them meet their basic needs. The centers focus on families' strengths and respond to parents according to their needs. Typical program components include:

- Life skills training, which can include family literacy, education, employment, or vocational training. It also can include enhancement of personal development skills such as problem solving, stress reduction, and communication.

- Parent information classes and support groups, which provide instruction in child development and opportunities for parents to share their experiences and concerns with peers.

- Parent-child groups and family activities, which provide occasions for parents to spend more time with their children.

- Drop-in time, which provides parents with informal opportunities to spend time with staff members and other parents.

- Information and referral services.

- Crisis intervention/family counseling to respond to parents' special concerns about their children or specific family issues.

- Auxiliary support services such as clothing exchanges, emergency food, and transportation. (Family Support America, 1993c, 1993d, pp. 1–2)

School programs that can serve as models include Connecticut Family Resource Center Program, State of Texas Communities in Schools Program, and State of New Jersey School-Based Youth Services Program. These programs provide a variety of services (Family Resource Coalition, 1993d). Schools that focus on reducing or eliminating substance abuse include Families and Schools Together, Wisconsin; Families Matter, Wilmington, Delaware; and Asian Youth Substance Abuse Project, San Francisco (Family Resource Coalition, 1993b).

Families and Schools Together (FAST)

FAST is a model in Madison, Wisconsin, that illustrates collaboration among schools and other agencies. "Using the school as a hub, FAST brings together families in the same district and creates a community-within-a-community" (Family Resource Coalition 1993b, p. 3). An interesting team approach is used. Each family team works with other family teams, meeting weekly for two months, then monthly for two years. Usually 12 families meet with representatives from the schools and other agencies. The teams have meals, recreation, and parent-child time. They are provided information to support parenting skills and to aid parents with children who are at risk for drug abuse. This enhances community skills and provides alternatives to alcohol and other drugs.

Family and Child Education (FACE)

The Bureau of Indian Affairs, Office of Indian Education desired an integrated program for early

Involvement in activities carry over to home with an incentive to make plans, experiment, read directions, and construct.

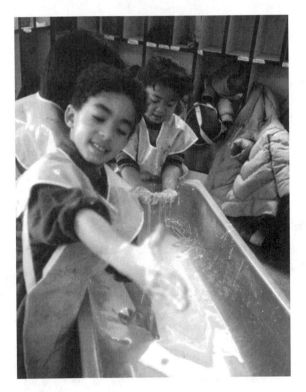

Children get involved in the activities and learn through the process.

childhood parental involvement, birth through third grade. Initiated in 1990, by 2001, the program had served 15,000 persons representing 5,000 families; 1,500 adults obtained employment and 400 adults received their GED. The program grew from 6 sites in 1992 to 32 in 2001.

Three recognized national programs—National Center for Family Literacy (NCFL), the Parents as Teachers (PAT) National Center, and High/Scope Research Foundation—have collaborated in a family education model for these children, birth through grade three. NCFL provides center-based adult education for parents, preschool for three- to five-year-olds, parent education, and time for interaction among family members. PAT provides training for home-based programs with home visits for families with children birth to age three, screening, school and community services, and parent meetings. High/Scope trains

teacher to provide High/Scope curriculum for grades K–3. The Family and Child Education (FACE) training program provides training session and on-site assistance. Through the integration of the three programs, a strong support system of family and child education is implemented for American Indians (National Center for Family Literacy, p. 1).

Programs were developed because of families' obvious need for support to survive and provide the nurturing environment their children need. The National Center for Family Literacy focuses on literacy development for the total family. The Family Resource Coalition is a national coalition of groups who work for resources and provisions to strengthen families. The Education and Human Services Consortium is another coalition interested in connecting families with the services they need. The National Institute on Early Childhood Development and Education is in the Office of Educational Research and Improvement, U.S. Department of Education.

Family Literacy

A study on literacy in the United States, which is to be completed in 2002, will update the figures on literacy that were last compiled in 1992. At that time more than 23 million men and women in the United States were illiterate—unable to read or write. Another 45 million had skills at or below the ninth-grade level (Family Resource Coalition, 1993a).

The federal definition of *family literacy* is as follows:

> Services that are of sufficient intensity in terms of hours and of sufficient duration, to make sustainable changes in a family and that integrate all of the following activities:
>
> a. Interactive literacy activities between parents and their children.
>
> b. Training for parents regarding how to be the primary teacher for their children and full partners in the education of their children.
>
> c. Parent literacy training that leads to economic self-sufficiency.

d. An age-appropriate education to prepare children for success in school and life experiences. (U.S. Department of Health and Human Services, 2000, p. 2)

Parents should engage in interactive literacy activities with their children; learn how to be the primary teacher for their children and to become full partners in their child's education; and become literate to ensure self-sufficient employment. Comprehensive family literacy programs and family-centered literacy programs provide the support that parents need to fulfill their parental roles.

The inability to read and write hinders men and women in fulfilling their role in society, and their roles as parents. Those with children in school have an especially difficult time. Parents who cannot read books their children bring home or notes from school are unable to collaborate effectively with the school for the betterment of their children's education.

In reading about literacy, one finds more written on bilingual education and being literate in English than about literacy for all. Literacy programs should incorporate the person who does not speak English, but there is a great void in the recognition of the many English-speaking adults who cannot read or write.

Young men and women graduate from high school unable to read and write; many other adults drop out of school because of their inability to read and write. Illiterate adults live in a world that expects them to be literate. Employment is difficult; acknowledging their deficiency in the English language is embarrassing. They need adult literacy support as much as the person who does not speak English.

As stated earlier, recognition of the need for adults to be able to read has resulted in federal funding for literacy programs. Family literacy fits into the goals of Title I and Head Start programs. One way the federal government supports family literacy is through Even Start, which links adult literacy programs with a preschool program for parents who need to complete their education and who have children younger than eight.

Nonprofit organizations, workplace literacy programs, and colleges and universities also promote adult literacy. Two major nonprofit associations have made great strides in supporting families. The Family Resource Center in Chicago has spearheaded the move toward more resource centers, whether federally, state, or privately funded. The National Center for Family Literacy received a grant from the Kenan Trust in support of its efforts to promote family literacy through programs and training.

Family literacy includes the total family, rather than just the individual. The criteria for a family literacy program are that it

- Is conceptualized around the needs and concerns of the family in contrast to serving individual family members in isolation.
- Contains an educational component that formally or informally affects the child's literacy or development.
- Contains an educational component for the adult, providing both literacy activities and parenting education to enable adults to attain proficiency in basic skills.
- Includes at least one activity focusing on the exchange of knowledge and information between the adult and the child.
- Is developed based on community needs and participant recommendations. (Family Resource Coalition, 1993d, p. 2)

Family literacy, therefore, has the parent and the child working together. "Activities include side-by-side reading, modeling of child development practices, reading aloud, storytelling, educational field trips, and computer games" (Family Resource Coalition, 1993a, p. 2).

Head Start was targeted to offer family literacy programs by 1992. Its focus on family literacy includes three goals: (a) helping parents realize their own needs and work to overcome their own literacy concerns; (b) helping them increase their access to literacy services, programs, and materials; and (c) supporting them in their role as their child's teacher (Potts, 1992).

The National Center for Family Literacy focuses on building family programs based on the strengths of families rather than on their deficits. It recommends that there should be sufficient duration of literacy programs so that the family is supported enough that it enables success. Literacy programs use methods of teaching adults that have been tested over time. In addition, a whole-language approach is often used, so language is learned in many ways. The curriculum is built around the strengths of families. High-interest, low-vocabulary books that hold their interest are used. Some theories that work for parents who do not speak English may apply to illiterate English-speaking adults, but it remains critical to involve the whole family, or at least the parent and child. They do activities together at school, usually after the parent has had a family literacy class and the child has reached preschool or first grade. Home visits are also used to bring activities and new books to the parents and visit with them on their home territory.

✒ MAKING PROGRAMS HAPPEN

"How can parent programs be started?" This question can be answered from two approaches, both related to financing. Funding can be obtained to establish a parent program, or the individual district, school, or teacher can design a program with or without financial support. This section presents information about funding sources as well as social agencies and other community resources.

Funding

Funding for school-related programs comes primarily from three major sources: (a) government grants, either federal or state, (b) private foundation awards, and (c) local school budgets. A public school's budget is based on local taxes and state distribution of funds. Private schools rely primarily on tuition and private sources to provide their budgets, although they are eligible for some federal grants. Current information on funding and grants can be obtained from your regional Department of Education or Department of Health and Human Services and your state social services or education department.

The most stable funding source for public schools is the local school board. As schools begin to view the parent component as worthwhile or essential, more programs will be implemented and funded through local support. Private foundations also fund special projects for parents and children. Local businesses and foundations are probably the best source of either funds or information about money available in your community.

Most grants have a specified duration, usually three years. If a program is dependent on the extra grant funding, plans must be made for financing after the grant runs out or the program will either deteriorate or disappear. The major importance of grants is the impetus they provide for developing programs, materials, and services. Many programs, now a permanent part of the community, were started on grants.

Try to obtain funding and grants, but if your efforts are not rewarded, consider parent involvement as an integral part of the school program and develop a unique approach to bring about a partnership. Using volunteers in a positive way can help teachers and enable the school to enrich its educational offerings. Volunteers can be an alternative to funding in making programs happen.

Resources and Social Agencies

Collaboration between schools and social agencies helps develop continuity and supply the support that families need. Teachers as well as administrators can make referrals to social services, recreation districts, libraries, and other public agencies. If the school district does not have a list, school personnel may contact the Department of Social Services, United Way, Chamber of Commerce, or other agencies or civic groups to obtain a list of community resources. Check to see if there is a clearinghouse in the area. The telephone book's white pages and Yellow Pages also have listings for the types of services listed here.

Schools and Child Care Centers

- Parent Teacher Association (PTA) or Parent Teacher Organization (PTO) programs.
- Parent education offered by public schools or child care.
- Parent education offered by hospitals and health clinics.
- STEP, P.E.T., and Active Parenting classes.
- Adult education offered by private, nonprofit organizations, the public schools, or through the State Department of Education.
- Alternative education offered through public or private schools.
- Vocational education offered through public schools or Land Grant colleges or universities.
- Agricultural extension divisions—state specialists and county agents (through Land Grant colleges or universities).
- High school equivalency programs.
- Tutoring and homework hotlines provided by schools.
- School social workers and psychologists.
- Testing and special placement for children with disabilities.
- National Education Association (NEA) state organizations and publications.

Libraries

Libraries usually offer the following:

- Weekly story hours for children.
- Talking books, tape recorders.
- Bookmobiles.
- Seminars and discussion groups.
- Opportunity to check out books, paintings, filmstrips, slides, videos, recordings.
- Librarians who can help in selection of books and help find reference materials.

Professional Organizations

Many organizations offer conferences, publications, and meetings. A comprehensive list can be found in the Appendix at the end of the book. It includes such groups as the Association for Childhood Education International, Association for Children with Learning Disabilities, International Reading Association, and the National Association for the Education of Young Children.

Community Services

- Police and fire departments offer educational classes.
- The YMCA and YWCA offer recreational and educational activities.
- Museums may provide a variety of educational experiences.
- Family Resource Clearinghouse and United Way can offer references.
- Alcoholics Anonymous, Al-Anon, and Alateen provide support for alcoholics and families of alcoholics.
- Planned Parenthood provides family planning education.
- Parents Anonymous offers support for parents at risk of abusing their children.
- Salvation Army provides support, food, clothing, and temporary housing.
- Churches have many outreach programs.
- Clothing banks provide clothing for those in need.
- The Red Cross provides training and emergency services.

Health

- Maternal and child health (look in the telephone book under your state or the U.S. government for information).
- Well-baby clinics, pediatric clinics, and local physicians provide examinations and prescriptions for children.
- Lamaze classes for pregnant women and their partners are available.
- La Leche League helps those who want to nurse their babies.

- Mental health associations refer, educate, and provide other services.
- Visiting nurses provide health-care services in homes.
- College and university diagnostic centers may offer health services.

Mental Health

- Mental health and child guidance clinics offer services and information on mental health.
- County mental health clinics offer services.
- Nonprofit emotional support and suicide prevention groups provide support and referrals.
- Battered women's groups provide support and safe houses for abused and homeless women.
- Family therapy and programs on building family strengths help families cope with problems and improve their relationships.
- Colleges and universities offer courses in family and parent education.

Social Services

- County Department of Social Services/State Department of Social Services—Food Stamps and Protective Services—offer various types of support for children and adults.
- Family crisis centers provide a refuge for abused or homeless adults and children.
- Child abuse councils refer children and families for help or remediation.
- National Center for the Prevention of Child Abuse provides education and services.
- Job Corps helps young people obtain training and jobs.
- Refugee services provide support for refugee families.

Reaching Out

It is apparent that families and children (infants to young adults) need supportive environments. Although it has been recognized that those in poverty have special needs, families at all income levels need a sense of community and commitment. Isolation, violence on television and through the Internet, and a sense of alienation affect many of the youth in America. Schools, family resource centers, and families must work together.

If schools and community resources communicate and cooperate with one another, families and children with needs do not have to slip through the cracks.

❧ SUMMARY

School-based programs that involve parents are varied. Efforts are being made to increase literacy and to support families so that all children can be successful in school and life. After describing a walk through a school committed to parent involvement, this chapter explores national efforts and school-based programs.

Parents must be supported in home-school involvement. Teachers should share methods of working with children, organize make-and-take workshops, and develop a home-learning activity program. Teachers must work closely with parents in the development of a home-school program. They should know their students' parents and adapt programs to each family.

Teenage mothers need family life education. Schools and other agencies are responding with programs for the young mother.

Ways to start home-school programs are discussed. Many programs are started with grants. If this monetary support is not available, schools can try to increase personnel support by soliciting volunteers.

School-based programs are diversified, but each type of involvement is essential if the needs of families are to be met.

❧ SUGGESTED CLASS ACTIVITIES AND DISCUSSIONS

1. Visit a Title I program in a public school. Talk with the principal about the parent involvement specifically developed for the program. Or, if you work in a Title I program, develop a family literacy program.
2. Survey three or four schools that have federal funding. How do the schools differ in their approaches

to parent involvement? How are they alike? Are there different responses to the various types of funding, for example, Title I, Title IV-C, Title VII, Follow Through, or Right to Read?

3. Visit schools in different areas and find out how they involve parents. Analyze the different approaches.

4. Design a parent bulletin board that illustrates the various components of the parent program in your classroom.

5. Develop a resource file of games, articles, books, and recycled materials.

6. Develop a workshop in which you have various learning centers—for example, early reading, sorting and classifying, problem solving, creativity, self-esteem, and language development.

7. Make a universal game board and a series of cards to be used with it.

8. Develop activities that parents can use with their children at home.

9. Search the community for resources that can be used in the school. Include specialists, materials, and places to visit.

ℒ 8 Home-Based Programs

To work with a child and not with the parent is like working with only part of the pieces of a puzzle. It would be like a person who put a puzzle together with a thousand pieces, and then as he finished found the center part missing.

Winters, 1988, p. 8

In this chapter you will learn about home-based education, homework, and home-schooling. After completing the chapter, you should be able to do the following:

- List and describe several home-based programs.
- Cite criteria for selection of personnel who offer home-based programs.
- Describe a framework for developing activities to be used in a home-based program.
- Develop a curriculum for a home-based program.
- Cite practices to avoid when working with parents in the home.
- Describe the different levels of homework.
- Develop "homefun" activities.
- Identify the reasons for homeschooling.
- Cite the public's response to homeschooling that supports cooperation between the homeschooler and the school.

The home is the primary educational setting for children. Parents are responsible for nurturing and educating their infants and preschoolers. Some of them share this role with child care centers and schools. They also work with schools by supporting the school's education program and encouraging homework. Some choose to educate their children at home. In this chapter the discussion will center first on children and the home-based offerings that can support the family. Homework or "homefun" is one area where the home is affected by the school when parents are asked to help with homework. How can it be handled satisfactorily? Last, the move toward homeschooling—in which parents take responsibility for their children's entire education—will be considered.

ℒ HOME VISITING

Home visiting originally developed in Europe, especially in England. Help was provided by "friendly visitors," church members, and other nonprofessionals. Florence Nightingale, a nurse recognized for her caring of soldiers during the Crimean War, also was instrumental in promoting health and hygiene in rural areas, villages, and towns. Her efforts led to a school in Liverpool, England, for the training of nurses. She also encouraged health visitors who were not nurses to

Home visitors sometimes provide the only contact a parent has with anyone outside the home.

visit homes in rural areas (Wasik, 1993). "Her dual interests in promoting both professional and paraprofessional home visitors as well as training for home visitors anticipated two of the most significant issues facing the field of home visiting a century later; whether to employ professional or paraprofessional home visitors and what kind of preservice and in-service training home visitors need" (p. 141).

When immigrants from southern and eastern Europe began to come in great numbers to the United States in the latter 1800s, visiting nurses along with settlement houses became part of the response to enculturate the new arrivals into "proper" hygiene and health. As described in Chapter 2, the growth of government intervention and services began in the 20th century. Parent education with parents attending meetings away from their homes became prominent in the

1920s. The trend toward home visiting was renewed after World War II and, since the 1970s, the programs have moved from working with individuals to working with and empowering families. "Over time the home visitor's role has evolved from problem solver, expert, and decision maker, to negotiator, collaborator, and facilitator" (Wasik, 1993, p. 143).

HOME-BASED EDUCATION

Imagine yourself as the parent of two preschoolers living in the country at least a mile from the nearest neighbor. Or pretend that you are a parent in a core-city apartment house. Some parents in urban and suburban areas have no more contact with supportive friends than those isolated by distance in the country. Both urban and rural residents, as the first teachers of their children, need the educational support and knowledge necessary to provide an enriched, positive environment for their children.

Home Start

Head Start added Home Start demonstration programs in 1972, funding 16 Home Start projects from March 1972 until June 1975. The Home Start program differed from Head Start in its location of services and its emphasis on parents as teachers in the home. Although Head Start included parents in decision making and included home visits, Home Start's purpose was to use the home as a base and, through home visitors, help parents to become teachers of their children. The diverse locations of the Home Start programs ensured the implementation of the program among different ethnic and cultural groups and varying social conditions. Although these programs were extremely successful, most were not continued.

Following are some programs still in existence, though there are others for family literacy and for parents of children with disabilities, both center-based and home-based.

PROGRAMS THAT WORK

Numerous approaches have proved effective in a variety of projects throughout the United States. They range from programs specifically designed to educate children and bring good parenting practices into the home to those that provide support for the entire family's health, mental health, housing, income, child development, and education. Summaries of selected programs illustrate the scope and variety of parent involvement in the educational process. Take from them the ideas and procedures that fit your situation.

It is evident, as illustrated by the research cited in Chapter 1, that children's early experiences impact the rest of their lives. Brain development occurs incredibly fast during the first three years. Programs that help parents during these early years have great benefits for the cognitive and language development of these children. Many of these programs developed because of child abuse (see Chapter 10), with a primary goal of reducing abuse and a secondary goal of encouraging parents to develop a nurturing environment, resulting in parent-child attachment and the child's brain development. It is now recognized that a nurturing environment, suggested and encouraged by these programs, not only helps form attachment but also has a direct impact on the development of a child's brain.

The Future of Children (Vol. 9, No. 1, 1999), published by the David and Lucile Packard Foundation, focused on home visiting. The home visiting program models that were described, discussed, and evaluated included the Comprehensive Child Development Program (CCDP); Hawaii Healthy Start; Healthy Families America (HFA); Home Instruction Program for Preschool Youngsters (HIPPY); Nurse Home Visitation Program; and Parents as Teachers (PAT).

Parents as Teachers Program

Programs based in the home often originate in the schools. The spokes from the school radiate out, helping, supporting, and caring about families in the area. One of the most isolated families in an area may be the beginning family that has recently rented or bought its first home. The couple starts on a real adventure after the birth of their first child. These first-time parents, along with established couples having their first child, were selected for the Parents as Teachers Project (PAT) which was developed in four districts in Missouri in the early 1980s and extended to the entire state in 1985. By 1999, the program had expanded to 2,197 sites in 49 states, the District of Columbia, and six other countries serving over 500,000 children. In addition to school districts, PAT is offered by churches, hospitals, socials services, or as part of Head Start, Even Start and Family Resource Centers (The Future of Children, 1999).

PAT program services include four components:

1. Regularly scheduled personal visits by credentialed parent educators who provide information

Young children gain through
verbal interaction as they play and
experiment.

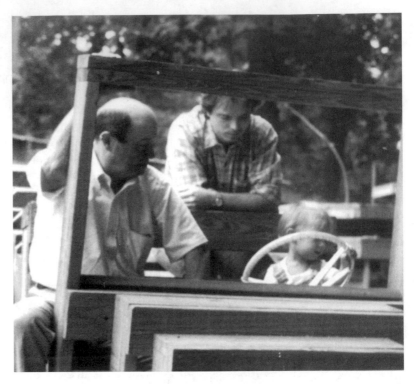

on the child's development, model and involve
parents in age-appropriate activities with the
child, and respond to parents' questions and
concerns.

2. Group meetings in which parents share insights
   and build informal support networks.

3. Monitoring of children's progress by both parents and home visitors to detect and treat any
   emerging problems as early as possible.

4. Linking of families with need community services that are beyond the scope of the program.
   (Winter & McDonald, 1997, pp. 119–145).

Home visits are usually one hour long and are
scheduled monthly, biweekly, or weekly, depending
on family needs and local program budgetary restrictions. For example, while most enrolled families
receive monthly or bimonthly home visits in Missouri, state funds provide for 25 visits per year for
high-needs families—that is, families with one or
more of the following characteristics: teen parents,
single parents, children or parents with disabilities,

low educational attainment, English as a Second
Language, unemployment chemical dependencies,
foster parents, numerous family relocations, high
stress, or involvement with the corrections system
or mental health, health, or social service agencies.
Weekly visits are conducted at the 22 PAT program
sites on Indian reservations which are administered
by the Bureau of Indian Affairs. (*The Future of Children,* 1999, pp. 179–180)

Missouri conducted a school entry assessment
project to study to create a plan where all children come to school ready to succeed. A School
Entry Profile was developed, organized around
seven conceptual areas that reflect dimension of
readiness for school. The "areas identified include symbolic development, communication,
mathematical/physical knowledge, working with
others, learning to learn, physical development
and conventional knowledge. . . . The School Entry Profile is to identify and measure the equities
and inequities of early life experiences known to

promote school success or difficulty. It will be used to identify ways to address those inequities so all children will have access to opportunities that promote school success (Missouri Department of Elementary and Secondary Education, 1999, p. 2).

Research conducted in 1985 on first-time parents validated the parents' positive responses. It showed that children participating in the Parents as Teachers project scored significantly higher on all measures of verbal ability, intelligence, language ability, achievement, and auditory comprehension than did children in a comparison group. The program proved so successful that it was adopted by the Missouri Department of Elementary and Secondary Education for use by 543 school districts throughout the state. Revisions and updating of the PAT curriculum was accomplished in 1996 in addition to development of a Born to Learn curriculum. It was field tested and became standard PAT prenatal to three years curriculum for Missouri in 1999.

In 1987 a National Center on Parents as Teachers was established in St. Louis and continues today. The center offers technical assistance and training. The major goals for participants are not in the teaching of child development—it is expected that the trainees already have knowledge in that area. The five-day training focuses instead on parent empowerment, parent strengths and how to build on them, and a combination of ways to observe parent-child interaction, respond, and demonstrate the curriculum (Winter, 1991).

The programs in Missouri found that first-time parents are usually very receptive to guidance and developed a program for new mothers and infants. Mothers or fathers who do not work outside the home usually have a need to visit and socialize with others as well as a desire to learn how best to raise the child. Contact and support reduce the loneliness of a parent who is solely responsible for an infant. In addition, new parents have no preconceived ideas from their experiences in rearing other children that might conflict with the research design.

Beginning in the third trimester of pregnancy and continuing until the child was three, Ferguson-Florissant School District gave each family the following:

- Information and guidance to help the parents-to-be prepare for the new arrival.

- Information on child development about fostering cognitive, social, motor, and language development. Clearly written handbooks describing what the parents should expect during each phase of development were published. The phases, based on White (1980), were the following:

    Phase 1—birth to 6 weeks

    Phase 2—6 weeks to 3½ months

    Phase 3—3½ months to 5½ months

    Phase 4—5½ months to 8 months

    Phase 5—8 months to 14 months

    Phase 6—14 months to 24 months

    Phase 7—24 months to 36 months (Ferguson-Florissant School District, 1989b)

- Periodic hearing and vision checkups for the children.

- Parent resource center at the school that was available for parent meetings.

- Individualized parent conferences each month.

- Monthly group meetings with other parents.

HIPPY—Home Instruction Program for Preschool Youngsters

The HIPPY program was developed in 1969 at the Hebrew University of Jerusalem in Israel, and it is now used in more than eight countries. The first U.S. programs were established in 1984. In 1999, there were 121 programs serving 15,000 families in 28 states, Guam, and the District of Columbia. The skill areas included are tactile, visual, auditory, and conceptual discrimination, in addition to language development, verbal expression, eye-hand coordination, pre-math concepts, logical thinking, self-concept, and creativity. In 1994, a curriculum for three-year-olds was added with storybooks and activity packets. The program has detailed curriculum design, with each activity illustrated. The material for each year of two years has 9 storybooks, 30 activity packets, 20 manipulative shapes, and weekly instructions for the paraprofessional. A professional coordinates the program, but home visitors are paraprofessionals selected from parents who were in the program. They visit bimonthly or at least 15 times a year to instruct the parents in the use of HIPPY educational materials (*The Future of Children,* 1999). Figures 8.1A and 8.1B illustrate the type of study materials offered to parents in the program.

Healthy Start

Hawaii's Healthy Start is an innovative program that reaches out to families under multiple forms of stress at the time of the birth of an infant. The goals of the program include:

Promote optimal child development

Promote positive parenting

Enhance parent-child interaction

Ensure a health care home and full immunization

Ensure use of community resources including family planning

Prevent child abuse and neglect (State of Hawaii, Department of Health, 1997)

These goals support improved parenting skills, enhancement of child health and development, reduction of family stress, and improved family functioning, as well as prevention of child abuse and neglect.

Families are selected primarily through an early identification process in participating hospitals or by physicians, public health nurses, midwives, and support groups in areas where access to hospital records is unavailable. The risk factors that they consider include: (1) marital status of mother; single, separated, or divorced; (2) partner unemployed; (3) inadequate income or no information regarding source of income; (4) unstable

housing; (5) no phone; (6) education less than 12 years; (7) inadequate emergency contacts; (8) history of substance abuse; (9) late or no prenatal care; (10) history of abortions; (11) history of psychiatric care; (12) abortion unsuccessfully sought or attempted; (13) relinquishment for adoption sought or attempted; (14) marital or family problems; and (15) history of, or current, depression.

Assessment interviews are conducted if 7 of the 15 risk factors cannot be answered from information on medical charts; if 2 of the factors are present; or if any 1 of factors #1, #9, or #12 is present. The assessor scores the answers; those with scores of less than 25 are considered to be at low risk for child abuse; those above, are considered at risk and are offered Healthy Start services.

The home visiting component of the program focused on families that might be at risk for child abuse and neglect as determined by using the Kempe Family Stress Checklist. "Quality of care is defined in two ways: (1) maternal satisfaction with the home visitor and (2) home visitor success in identifying and responding to problems that require intervention" (Duggan et al., 1999, p. 73). Three community agencies took part in the research. They included Child and Family Services (CFS), Parents and Children Together (PACT), and the Healthy Start (HSP) of the Hawaii Family Support Center.

This program is relevant to the discussion of child abuse in Chapter 10 as well as to sound home visitation programs.

Lay home visitors provide supportive services, commencing at birth up to three months, continuing until the child is five. The program begins with level one, weekly visits, progresses to level two, which consists of two visits a month, and completes at levels three and four with monthly or quarterly visits (U.S. General Accounting Office, 1992).

Preliminary research findings (October 1997) conducted by Johns Hopkins School of Medicine found that when compared with nonserved families, the Healthy Start families had the following:

- Mothers achieving higher levels of confidence
- Home environment observed to be better organized

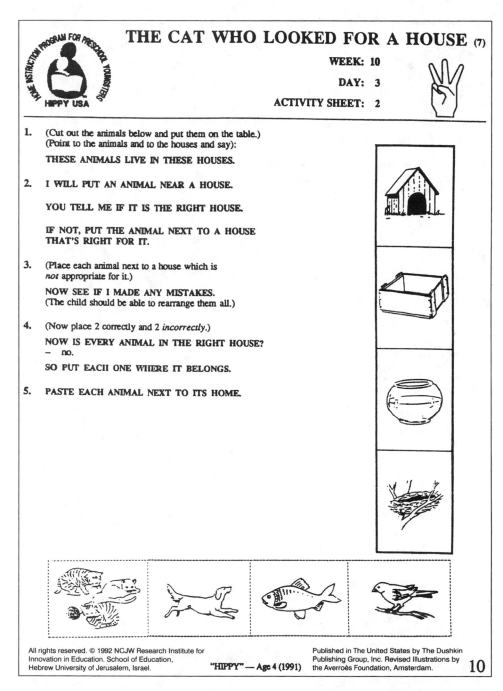

THE CAT WHO LOOKED FOR A HOUSE (7)

HOME INSTRUCTION PROGRAM FOR PRESCHOOL YOUNGSTERS
HIPPY USA

1. (Cut out the animals below and put them on the table.)
   (Point to the animals and to the houses and say):

   THESE ANIMALS LIVE IN THESE HOUSES.

2. I WILL PUT AN ANIMAL NEAR A HOUSE.

   YOU TELL ME IF IT IS THE RIGHT HOUSE.

   IF NOT, PUT THE ANIMAL NEXT TO A HOUSE
   THAT'S RIGHT FOR IT.

3. (Place each animal next to a house which is
   not appropriate for it.)

   NOW SEE IF I MADE ANY MISTAKES.
   (The child should be able to rearrange them all.)

4. (Now place 2 correctly and 2 *incorrectly*.)

   NOW IS EVERY ANIMAL IN THE RIGHT HOUSE?
   — no.

   SO PUT EACH ONE WHERE IT BELONGS.

5. PASTE EACH ANIMAL NEXT TO ITS HOME.

"HIPPY" — Age 4 (1991)

10

FIGURE 8.1A The cat who looked for a house.

Source: Printed with permission. All rights reserved © 1992 NCJW Research Institute for Innovation in Education. School of Education. Hebrew University of Jerusalem, Israel. Published in the United States by the Dushkin Publishing Group, Inc. Revised illustrations by the Averroès Foundation, Amsterdam.

SORTING (3)

WEEK: 10

DAY: 5

ACTIVITY SHEET: 1

(Materials on the table: an empty shoe box, 4 empty cups, 5 coins, 5 stones, toothpicks, 5 bottle caps and paste.)

1. (Sit next to a table.Place the 4 cups and the box with all the other objects in it on the table.)

   IN THIS BOX, THERE ARE MANY DIFFERENT THINGS. THEY ARE ALL MIXED TOGETHER.
   WE WILL ARRANGE THEM.

2. GIVE ME A TOOTHPICK.
   (Place it in a cup.)

   FIND ALL THE TOOTHPICKS AND PUT THEM IN THIS CUP.

   GIVE ME A COIN.
   (Put it in the second cup.)

   PUT ALL THE COINS IN THIS CUP.
   WHAT IS LEFT IN THE BOX?
   – stones and bottle caps.

   GIVE ME ALL THE BOTTLE CAPS.
   (Place them in the third cup.)

   NOW PUT ALL THE STONES IN THE EMPTY CUP.

3. (Put all the objects back in the large container.)

   NOW YOU SORT ALL THE THINGS.

   PUT ALL THE THINGS OF ONE KIND IN ONE CUP.
   (When the child has finished sorting the objects into the four cups, ask):

   WHAT DID YOU DO?
   – I arranged the things.
   – I sorted them
   – I put the _____ together, and the _____ together.

"HIPPY" — Age 4 (1991)

Published in The United States by The Dushkin Publishing Group, Inc. Revised Illustrations by the Averroès Foundation, Amsterdam.

17

FIGURE 8.1B Sorting.

Source: Printed with permission. All rights reserved © 1992 NCJW Research Institute for Innovation in Education. School of Education. Hebrew University of Jerusalem, Israel. Published in the United States by the Dushkin Publishing Group, Inc. Revised illustrations by the Averroès Foundation, Amsterdam.

- Parents engaged in neglectful behavior less often
- Greater acceptance of their children's behavior
- Significantly lower levels of distress
- Significantly fewer reports of abuse and neglect within the first year of life (State of Hawaii, Department of Health, 1997)

Parent-Child Home Program

Parent-Child Home Program (PCHP) is a home-based, family literacy program that relies on positive verbal interaction between the child, two to four years old, and the primary caregiver. Started as a Verbal Interaction Project in 1965, it was in-

Children benefit from guidance offered by home-based educational programs.

corporated in 1982 as the National Center for the Mother-Child Home Program and has continued with its name changed to Parent-Child Home Program. In 1998, there were 29 replications of PCHP in the United States and 10 in other countries. The caregiver may be any adult who has primary nurturing responsibilities for the child. The program is based in the child's home; trained home visitors ("toy demonstrators") come twice weekly for half-hour sessions from the time the child is two until the child is four.

> The program's cognitive curriculum was derived from theories and empirical studies of investigators whose work had influenced the program at its inception. At its core are Vygotsky's links between thought and language (Vygotsky, 1962); Bruner's construct of "instrumental conceptualism," the idea that concept formation is fostered in the two- and three-year-old child through the child's experience with language (Bruner, 1966); and Sigel's (1971) "distancing hypothesis" in which the promotion of representational competence is given tangible meaning through the child's and parent's play focused around books and 3-dimensional toys as representations of reality, besides being intrinsically motivating curriculum materials. (Levenstein, Levenstein, Shiminski, & Stolzberg, 1998, p. 269)

The home visitor demonstrates toys and books in a play session with parent and child. Parenting behavior emphasizing verbal interaction is modeled instead of being taught directly. The parent and child participate as they learn through play. Books and toys are given to the families so that the learning can continue. There are no specific tasks other than enjoying the play and resultant verbal interaction. Guide sheets cover such concepts as colors, shapes, and sizes and such cognitive skills as matching, pretending, and differentiating. The twice-a-week visits to the home are set up at the parent's convenience (Levenstein et al., 1998).

The method, curricula, and delivery of the program include:

- 46 half-hour sessions twice a week spread over seven months each year for two years.

- A guide sheet, a one-page list of concepts, and developmentally appropriate labels for actions or words applied to the toy or book brought by the home visitor to the toddler.

- A 20 item VIP-created instrument called "Child's Behavior Traits," a measure as well as a guide to the child's social-emotional goals.

- A "Parent and Child Together" curriculum of 20 traits that measure and guide positive parent behavior, modeled by the home visitor and achieved by the parent.

- Curriculum materials including 12 illustrated books and 11 toys—with a different set given each year of the two-year program for a total of 46 books and toys, given to the family.

- Parental involvement in the child's play modeled by the home visitor inviting the parent to be involved.

- Home visitor modeling without directly teaching positive response to the child, pleasurable reading to child, encouraging the family's literacy in addition to the child's.

- Sessions arranged at the parent's convenience.

- Program coordinators who are college graduates and work with home visitors to develop necessary nondidactic skills, respect for family privacy and lifestyles, and prepare written reports. (Levenstein et al., 1998)

The goal of the program is to increase the caregiver's interaction with the child in a natural dialogue that enhances and enriches the child's home environment. By training toy demonstrators who are paraprofessionals with a high school education to demonstrate and model their toys without being didactic, the project facilitates relaxed, verbal interaction between parent and child (Levenstein, 1998).

A study (1996) conducted on the Pittsfield, Massachusetts, Parent-Child Home Program (Levenstein et al., 1998) included 123 students who, in 1976–1980, participated as toddlers in the program. The 1976–1980 participants were originally recruited by invitations sent to all parents of children attending Chapter I schools, also termed Title I schools. Those who responded were eligible if they met five of the following eight criteria:

1. Child's IQ score under 100 on the Peabody Picture Vocabulary Test (PPVT)
2. Single-parent family
3. Unemployment of mother
4. Unemployment of father
5. Family receives AFDC payments
6. Parent's education less than 12th grade
7. Family income qualifies for poverty status
8. Older sibling in a Chapter I remedial program (Levenstein et al., 1998)

The study looked at control groups of youngsters who would have been eligible for the Parent-Child Home Program but did not attend. All eligible respondents who were offered the Parent-Child Home Program accepted enrollment.

In a replication of the original MCHP program, high school graduation reached 84 percent for those students who had participated in the program. This is equivalent to the graduation rate among students from middle-income families. Only 15.7 percent of MCHP participants, as compared to 40 percent of the control group, dropped out of school. The MCHP rate was lower than the mean for all Pittsfield students.

PCHP research results show that the program is effective with at-risk parents, but it is not needed for families in which the parents already have strong, verbal interaction with their children. The positive modeling along with books and toys enable at-risk parents to be positive parents.

Homebuilders

An excellent example of collaboration by social agencies is Homebuilders, a group of therapists, social workers, and psychologists who work with families whose children may be taken from them by the courts. Working closely with schools, juvenile court, and other social agencies, Homebuilders works with the total family, helping the

Play, activities, and reading give children opportunities to increase their learning at home.

members overcome their difficulties through counseling, modeling, and other support activities necessary to help them cope.

Established in Tacoma, Washington, Homebuilders has helped 90 percent of the children it has worked with remain with their families. Success has been due to (a) highly motivated families (out-of-family placement was imminent); (b) counseling and support in the family's home; (c) ample time (Homebuilders sometimes spends more than 100 hours with a family); (d) a variety of resources; and (e) a number of ways to help, including practical help, assistance in coping with stress, therapy, assertiveness training, and behavior management. Homebuilders answers a family's crisis call at any time—day, night, or weekends. The workers get satisfaction from seeing the family "pull things together" (Schorr & Schorr, 1988, p. 160).

Portage Project

The Portage Project was developed in 1969 as a home-based, family-centered demonstration program providing service to children with disabilities and their families. The model worked with children from birth to age six and with their families through weekly home visits by a home teacher. The project originally covered 3,600 square miles in south-central Wisconsin. Successful evaluation of the model and validation by the National Diffusion Network led to other areas setting up the program.

Over the years the Portage Project has continued to adhere to the following principles upon which it was based:

1. Intervention for children with disabilities should begin as early as possible. The earlier work begins, the greater the probability of

having a significant effect on the child and the greater the chance that this effect will be maintained over time.

2. Parent/primary caregiver involvement is critical to successful early intervention.

3. Intervention objectives and strategies must be individualized for each child and support the functioning of the family.

4. Data collection is important to reinforce positive change and to make ongoing intervention decisions.

The Portage Project works in collaboration with community agencies to provide comprehensive services to children and families. Referral from individuals and local agencies leads to a play-based assessment conducted by a multidisciplinary team. This process is conducted in the family's home and is designed to provide information on parent-child interaction patterns, parent perceptions, and the developmental functioning level of the child.

If the team, including parents, determines that a child is eligible, the process to develop an Individual Family Service Plan is initiated. This process includes extensive observation and communication with the family. The plan might include weekly home visits by a member of the Portage Project transdisciplinary staff, therapy or counseling from community providers, consultation with child care providers or other caregivers, participation in parent support groups or play groups, or other activities requested by the family.

Typically, one interventionist is the care coordinator for the family and maintains regular communication with other service providers. This interventionist may be an educator, a speech and language therapist, or a motor specialist, but his or her role in working with families is transdisciplinary.

The Portage Project staff has developed materials to support early childhood programs. These materials include the *Portage Guide to Early Education,* developed in the late 1970s and used in the United States and internationally, and *Growing: Birth to Three.*

The *Portage Guide* contains a checklist of 580 developmentally sequenced behaviors for children up to six years old. The behaviors are divided into six areas: infant stimulation, self-help, language, cognition, motor skills, and socialization. Ideas for teaching each of the behaviors are included to assist parents and teachers (see Figure 8.2).

Growing: Birth to Three offers materials to support family-centered interactive intervention. The materials are designed to be used as a package, as each piece contributes to the intervention process. Figure 8.3A describes an On the Move Behavior for children 3 to 6 months, and Figure 8.3B illustrates a Using My Senses Behavior for children 24 to 36 months. The materials are designed to encourage flexibility in working with families as well as a stimulus to expand beyond the specific suggested intervention strategies. A brief description of the components of *Growing* follows:

Ecological Planner

Part I of the *Ecological Planner* suggests guidelines for observation and communication, provides a way to document transactions across time, and offers a selection of formats for individualized intervention planning.

Part II of the *Ecological Planner* is called the *Developmental Observation Guide.* It provides an in-depth, developmentally sequenced series of behaviors that children frequently display from birth through 36 months.

Nurturing Journals

These journals are designed for use by parents or primary caregivers. Each book contains open-ended questions or statements to help parents reflect on the process of parenting.

Interactive Grow Pack

This section represents the heart of interactive intervention. It offers strategies for interactive communication with parents as well as ways to enhance and encourage mutually satisfying interactions between caregiver and child.

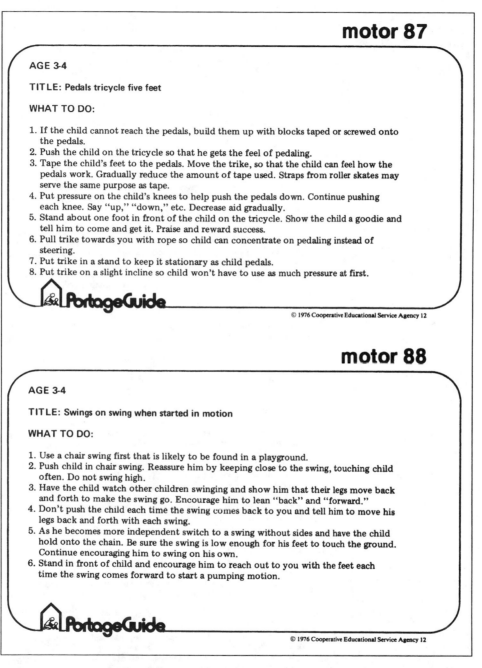

motor 87

AGE 3-4

TITLE: Pedals tricycle five feet

WHAT TO DO:

1. If the child cannot reach the pedals, build them up with blocks taped or screwed onto the pedals.
2. Push the child on the tricycle so that he gets the feel of pedaling.
3. Tape the child's feet to the pedals. Move the trike, so that the child can feel how the pedals work. Gradually reduce the amount of tape used. Straps from roller skates may serve the same purpose as tape.
4. Put pressure on the child's knees to help push the pedals down. Continue pushing each knee. Say "up," "down," etc. Decrease aid gradually.
5. Stand about one foot in front of the child on the tricycle. Show the child a goodie and tell him to come and get it. Praise and reward success.
6. Pull trike towards you with rope so child can concentrate on pedaling instead of steering.
7. Put trike in a stand to keep it stationary as child pedals.
8. Put trike on a slight incline so child won't have to use as much pressure at first.

PortageGuide

© 1976 Cooperative Educational Service Agency 12

motor 88

AGE 3-4

TITLE: Swings on swing when started in motion

WHAT TO DO:

1. Use a chair swing first that is likely to be found in a playground.
2. Push child in chair swing. Reassure him by keeping close to the swing, touching child often. Do not swing high.
3. Have the child watch other children swinging and show him that their legs move back and forth to make the swing go. Encourage him to lean "back" and "forward."
4. Don't push the child each time the swing comes back to you and tell him to move his legs back and forth with each swing.
5. As he becomes more independent switch to a swing without sides and have the child hold onto the chain. Be sure the swing is low enough for his feet to touch the ground. Continue encouraging him to swing on his own.
6. Stand in front of child and encourage him to reach out to you with the feet each time the swing comes forward to start a pumping motion.

PortageGuide

© 1976 Cooperative Educational Service Agency 12

FIGURE 8.2 Two examples from the card deck of the Portage Guide show the types of activities that parents can do with their children at home.

Source: From *Portage Project Readings,* by D. Shearer, J. Billingsley, A. Frohman, J. Hilliard, F. Johnson, & M. Shearer, 1976, Portage, WI: Portage Project.

FIGURE 8.3A On the Move: Three to Six Months. An example of activities from *Growing: Interactions/Daily Routines.*

Source: CESA 5, Portage Project (1998).

ON THE MOVE   J14
Three To Six Months

BEHAVIOR #14:   Maintain Head In Midline When Pulled To Sit
AREA: **On The Move**

Why Is This Important?

When conscious effort is no longer required to maintain head control, the infant can attend to using her eyes, ears, hands, and mouth to explore the world.

Commentary:

I'm using my neck and tummy muscles to keep my head in a straight line with my body when you pull me up to sit. It requires some effort on my part, since these muscles are not yet that strong. With practice I will become stronger.

Information:

The amount of head lag which the child exhibits when pulled to a sitting position is a good indication of progression in the development of head control. At first, her head will lag behind her trunk when she is pulled up; later she will be able to keep her head in line with her trunk. Finally, she will develop enough strength to pull herself up while gripping your hands.

Interactive Activities:

Engaging: When I'm sitting on your lap facing you, place your hands over my shoulders with your fingers can supporting my head and my chin tucked. Hold me firmly so my head doesn't fall back. Slowly lower me slightly backward while you sing or talk to me. Watch to see if I can keep my head in line with my trunk; then bring me up again slowly. Repeat this activity several times while we play together. Caution: don't try this activity unless I can maintain head control while in a supported sitting position.

Expanding: Place me on my back. Grasp my hands and wrists and slowly pull me up into a sitting position. Please do not move faster than my head control allows. When I can keep my head in line with my trunk, pull me up halfway and let me pull myself the rest of the way. I'm getting so strong!

Giving Information: My tummy muscles need to be strong for me to pull myself up into a sitting position. You can help make these muscles stronger by gently rubbing or tickling (if I enjoy this) my tummy. Watch to see if I curl my body into flexion when you stimulate my tummy muscles in this way. Does my head tend to come forward so that my chin tucks down to my chest? Do my legs come up and pull in close to my body? If so, I am strengthening my tummy muscles with this playful activity.

Daily Routine Activities:

Diapering: If I'm in a playful mood after you change my diaper, try to pull me up into the sitting position. See how much I am able to help you. Make sure to smile and praise me for my attempts.

Caution:

Pay attention to the level of head control the child has and do not let her lose head control when you pull her up into a sitting position. It is frightening and potentially harmful to have her head fall back unexpectedly. Be prepared to catch her head when doing "pull to sit" activities.

FIGURE 8.3B Using my Senses: Twenty-Four to Thirty-Six Months. An example of activities from *Growing: Interactions/Daily Routines.*
Source: CESA 5 Portage Project (1998).

USING MY SENSES C41
Twenty-Four To Thirty-Six Months

BEHAVIOR #41: Use Vision Effectively To Guide Hands
AREA: Using My Senses

Why Is This Important?

This behavior alerts the caregiver to the child's ability to effectively use eye-hand coordination.

Commentary:

What was once a complicated task for me, using my vision to guide what my hands do, is now becoming easier. Watch as I learn to put objects in containers, pegs in holes, and work switches on simple busy boxes. Aren't I clever!

Interactive Activities:

Turntaking: The game described in *Playtime* under Daily Routine Activities (see following section) could be lots of fun if we take turns. First, give me a chance to put something in the box, then you take a turn. Pause and wait so that I know it is my turn again.

Daily Routine Activities:

Doing Chores: As you are taking the clothes off the clothesline, you can occupy me by giving me a plastic milk jug or container with a large opening and some clothespins. Show me how to drop the clothespins into the milk jug, and then see if I will do this by myself.

Mealtime: As I begin to use utensils, am I able to scoop up the food, bring my hand all the way to my mouth, and pop it in? This is part of eye-hand coordination. You may need to guide me at first, then slowly let me try on my own.

Bedtime: As we look at a book together, see if I can start to flip the pages of the book by myself. Can I focus on the corner, place my hand on it and, with some help from you, turn the page?

Playtime: Shape boxes are a good way to help me to practice this skill. Find a shape box with 2 or 3 holes, or you may even want to tape up all but one hole at first. Show me how to drop the shapes in the box, then let me try to do this myself. Be sure to clap or praise all my attempts.

Interactions and Daily Routines Books

This collection offers activity suggestions for each skill or behavior listed in the *Developmental Observation Guide.* Activity suggestions are embedded in daily routines, rituals, play, and interactions.

Master Forms Packet

This packet of reproducible forms is designed to assist in family-guided intervention. The forms can be used to document communications and observations, develop a family-generated service plan, and develop intervention suggestions responsive to each individual family being served (CESA 5, Portage Project, 1998).

A Day in the Life of One Home-Based Program

A program initiated in Yakima, Washington, acknowledged the importance of parents as their children's first teachers. Although this home-based program is no longer funded, this article vividly illustrates how home-based programs make a difference in families' lives.

THE WINNING PLAY AT HOME BASE

The Rochas's home, neat and attractive, is modest by almost anyone's standards. A few fall flowers brighten the gravel walk, and a small tricycle that has seen better days lies on its side in the grass announcing the presence of at least one preschooler. From under a bush the family's gray-striped cat lifts an eyelid as a visitor approaches.

Plump, dark-haired Mrs. Rochas responds immediately to the knock, hampered only slightly by her 2½-year-old son, Benjie, who manages to cling to her knee while keeping one finger in his mouth.

"Hi, Jean. Come in," says Mrs. Rochas, with a smile almost as wide as the door she swings open to permit her caller to enter the small living room. As Mrs. Rochas gently eases Benjie back toward his toy collection in the corner, she tells Jean that Margaretta, her daughter who is almost 4, is still napping.

"That's fine, don't disturb her," Jean, a paraprofessional parent-educator, replies before she settles on the davenport and begins pulling some materials from her shopping bag—a stack of index cards, several old magazines, a pair of scissors, and a tube of glue.

The casual banter notwithstanding, some serious business is at hand: Mrs. Rochas is about to undergo a lesson that marks the beginning of her second "school year." She is one of 200 parents in Yakima, a central Washington community of 49,000, who are learning how to teach their own preschool children through Project Home Base, a pioneer early childhood education program. Depending on how well she learns her weekly lessons, she could have a positive and lasting effect on her child's performance in school.

Like many Home Base families, the Rochases were lured to the area from northern California during the previous fall by the promise of better wages in Yakima's fruit industry. Soon afterward they were visited by a representative from the Home Base project, who explained that all parents of children aged 8 months to 4 years in their neighborhood were being given an opportunity for special, federally sponsored training to enable them to help their preschoolers prepare for school. The Rochases were enthusiastic, but even while accepting the invitation, Mrs. Rochas had a number of doubts. Among them, her daughter (then 3 years old) did not always "take to strangers" and Benjie was still

"just a baby." But as the weeks passed and the home-visitor became a familiar and friendly face, the doubts disappeared.

A half hour goes by and Margaretta awakens from her nap. Still sleepy, she enters the living room to find her mother busily engaged in a game of "Concentration." This particular exercise calls for pasting pictures of "like" objects, cut from magazines, onto cards to create a series of pairs. The cards, bearing pictures of various animals and buildings, are then shuffled and placed face down in rows. The game begins with a player picking up a card and trying to match it with a second. If no match results, both cards are returned to their original positions and a second player tries. When all the cards are matched, the player with the most pairs is the winner.

It is important, Mrs. Rochas knows from past experience, that she learn exercises like this one thoroughly before trying them with her children. Then she can become more comfortable in the unfamiliar role of "Teacher."

Before Margaretta plays the game after dinner that day and frequently during the remainder of the week, she will be encouraged to look at the cards and then talk—in complete sentences—about the pictures. As she gains a familiarity changes are made with the objects pictured and the exercise by adding more cards or, to keep the lessons fresh, changing the object of the exercise to matching pairs of colors rather than pictures. It may be just fun to Margaretta, but all the while she is playing, she is acquiring some important skills, including the ability to think logically. She is thus preparing to become a better learner when she enters kindergarten the following year.

Little Benjie, meanwhile, is an important part of the action, too. Before leaving that afternoon, Jean shows Mrs. Rochas how a small hand mirror and a full-length mirror can transform him into "The Most Wonderful Thing in the World."

Examining his face in the mirror, Benjie is helped to identify his most prominent physical characteristic, such as his curly hair, bright brown eyes, and white teeth. Then he tries to figure out what makes him "special," what makes him different from everyone else in his family. He observes that one eyebrow is straighter than the other, and his ears are round. Then there are all the tricky things he can do with his face: he can squint, wrinkle his nose, and pucker his lips. He is encouraged to talk about how a smile is different from a frown. Before the full-length mirror in the bedroom, Benjie studies his posture and imitates various commonplace activities such as eating a hamburger or kicking a football. He and Margaretta look together into the mirror and discover how their appearances are different and how they are alike. The purpose? To help a child realize he or she is special and to feel good and confident about the discovery.

Although the allotted hour has flown by, Jean takes a few more minutes to discuss some new pamphlets on nutritious snacks for children she has brought along from the County Extension Office, and to confirm her appointment for next week.

The exercises for Margaretta and Benjie just described are only two drawn from more than 200 individual "tasks" for various age levels identified and developed by the Home Base staff. Each exercise has a specific goal or aim. Since most learning handicaps in the target population—preschoolers in the Yakima area—relate to language development, Home Base stresses conversations between parents and their children. There is no special significance attached to the activities' sequence. Tasks become more complex as the child's needs and intellectual capacity grow.

Parents are continually encouraged to adhere closely to a number of effective teaching techniques, such as eliciting questions from the learner, asking questions that have more than one correct answer, asking questions that require more than a one-word reply, praising the learner when he or she does well, urging the child to respond according to evidence instead of guesswork, allowing the child time to think out a problem before receiving assistance, and helping him or her to become familiar with the learning situation and materials.

"As we teach parents what to expect from their children in each situation and how to respond to their child's successes or failures, we find that the parents become stronger and more confident in their teaching role," project director Carol Jackson said. "When they understand the necessity for teaching skills like problem solving, they realize the time is well spent."

Home visitor's workday may span from 8:30 to 4, with about an hour spent at each home. It is an emotionally demanding job and requires a valid driver's license, an available vehicle, and vehicle liability insurance. Fortunately, language problems are minimized because several of the home visitors are bilingual. Their services are constantly being used to translate tasks into Spanish and to attend meetings to serve as interpreter for Spanish-speaking parents.

A great deal of role playing is used in the training of parent educators. They try out all of the activities scheduled.

Home Base is not without benefit for the rest of the family, too. "A father told me that being involved in Home Base has made a difference in his wife," reports another of the parent educators. "She's found out she has ability, and she is using it. Her opinion of herself has been greatly improved."

Keeping an otherwise isolated family in touch with the community is another valuable aspect of the Home Base program. "Instead of my feeling alone and all tied up by my problems," a woman told her visitor, "you help by just being a friend that I can talk to once a week."[1] (Hedrich & Jackson, 1977; Popp, 1989)

The Yakima Home Base program illustrated how schools or centers can use the home as a teaching center. The emphasis was on practices that encourage the child's educational growth: (a) learning communication skills, (b) reasoning logically, (c) developing self-concept, (d) becoming nutritionally aware, (e) using developmental activity sequences, (f) employing effective teaching techniques, (g) using easily obtained play materials, and (h) extending new expertise and knowledge about parenting to other members of the family. This program responded to the individual requirements of the community from which it evolved, but many of the techniques of effective parenting and teaching are appropriate for any home-based program.

As the home visitor becomes involved with each family, appropriate activities to accommodate the individual strengths and needs of the family will become apparent. Some home visitors will use suggested and sequential activities for

---

[1] From "Winning Play at Home Base," by V. Hedrich and C. Jackson, 1977, *American Education,* pp. 27–30. Revised by Judy Popp, Early Childhood Director, Project Home Base, Yakima, WA, October 1989.

their teaching curriculum, such as the Portage Program, which is discussed earlier in this chapter. Others will use the commercial books. Another alternative is to develop activities related to the particular interests of the child and parent or the availability of materials. For example, if the parent and child live in the country and have a garden, an entire curriculum project may be developed from the foods that are grown. An illustration of this is shown in the Utah Home Visitor Guide (Figure 8.4). If they live in the city, the environment would lend itself to an examination of types of cars or transportation or building materials, or a visit to the park.

The following guide to developing learning activities would result in the home visitor working with the parent to develop a learning environment based on the interests and availability of materials in or near the home.

FIVE-STEP GUIDE TO LEARNING ACTIVITIES

The Florida Parent Education Program developed by Gordon and his colleagues recommends the following five-step framework in the development of home activities:

Idea

The concept or idea emerges from the child, parent, home visitor, or special interests of the family. What does the family enjoy? Which experiences have been interesting and fun? What collections, toys, or materials are available around the home?

Ideas are also shared among the staff—teachers, other home visitors, and curriculum specialists. When an idea occurs, a memo is jotted down to remind the home visitor of the activity.

Reason

Each idea is used for a reason. The reasons may range from learning experiences to self-concept development. After ideas are collected, examine the skills that can be associated with each. For example, if the child picks a leaf from one of the trees in the neighborhood, start a collection of fallen leaves that can be classified according to size, color, and shape. The child can make texture and outline rubbings of them. You might ask the child how many kinds of trees are represented by the variety of leaves, and instruct the child to put each kind of leaf in a separate pile and count the different kinds. The many learning opportunities available from collecting leaves make this a worthwhile project for as long as the child's interest continues.

Materials

Implementing a reasonable idea requires available materials. Some experiences can be developed around materials commonly found in the home. If the idea requires special equipment and materials, make sure they are easily obtained. One of the main objectives of home visits is to involve the parent as the teacher. If parents do not realize that they have readily available teaching materials or if the learning activities are not furnished for them, part of the parental autonomy and subsequent success of the program is lost.

Action

Follow the child's lead and let the activity develop. If the child chooses something to explore that is different from your plans for the activity, vary your plans, take a detour, and enjoy the inquiry and discovery the child is experiencing. Your ideas may be brought up later or eliminated. Remember the objectives of the learning process. If they are being fulfilled, it does not matter which action brought about the learning.

Extension

Are there other activities related to this idea? If so, expand the action, follow the interest, and extend the learning (Packer, Hoffman, Bozler, & Bear, 1976).

UTAH HOME VISITOR GUIDE
April—1st week

Unit title: Gardens and Vegetables

With the high cost of living, it's important to grow your own fresh vegetables because they are so important in our daily diet. Homegrown vegetables are also healthier (less chemicals and fertilizers) and more nutritious. Families need information on how to store, preserve, and prepare fresh vegetables. Gardening is an excellent learning and sharing experience for families.

Specific objectives:

1. To help parents realize the economical benefits gained through home gardening
2. To give parents help with methods of food preparation and preservation
3. To stress the importance of vegetables to good nutrition

Activities

1. Discussion on growing a garden
   a. Why grow a garden?
   b. How to grow a garden
   c. How to store and preserve food from the garden
   d. Handout on food storage and preserving
   e. How to involve children in gardening
   f. Children will often eat more when they grow the food themselves
   g. Gardening is good exercise and teaches responsibility
   h. Handouts on planting times, spacing, what grows in this area (information from county agents)
2. Choose a garden site
3. Plan a garden
   a. What do you want to grow/like to eat?
   b. How much space, water, and time do you have?
   c. What will grow in your area?
   d. Is this to be a permanent site?
4. If no garden space, use boxes, crates, and flower beds
5. Take fruits and vegetables into home for snack/look, feel, and taste
   a. Cleanliness in handling food
6. Look at seeds and compare or match with vegetable
7. Snack tray of raw vegetables and cottage cheese dip
8. Sprout seeds
9. Plant seeds in plastic bag with wet paper towel
10. Plant seeds in egg carton
11. Grow plants from sweet potato and avocado seeds in water
12. Seed collage
13. Start your own tomato, green pepper, and cantaloupe plants indoors in cardboard cartons
14. Count seeds
15. Pop popcorn
16. Classify vegetables and fruits—cut out pictures from magazines
17. Stories and books
    a. Carrot seed
    b. Turnip seed
    c. Peter Rabbit—Mr. McGregor's Garden
    d. The Little Seed
18. Creative movement—germination and growth of seed
19. Tell parents where to get information and handouts
    a. County extension office
    b. Seed stores
20. Sprinkle grass on wet sponge
21. Print with vegetable or weed leaves
22. Talk about seeds you can eat and eat some for a snack
23. Talk about food that people and animals eat
24. Make a vegetable salad
25. Handouts on vegetables

Follow-up for positive reinforcement:

1. Show seeds—sprouted in bag or planted
2. How do you wash vegetables?
3. What did you decide about your garden?

FIGURE 8.4 The Utah Home Visitor Guide. The unit on gardens and vegetables illustrates how ordinary activities around the home can be used for education.

Source: U.S. Department of Health, Education, and Welfare (1978, pp. 68–69).

Parents can devise a practical educational experience from everyday projects such as planting a garden.

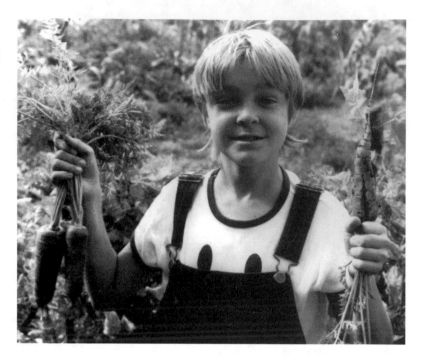

DEVELOPMENT OF A HOME ACTIVITIES FILE

The development of a home activities file depends on the objectives and philosophy of the program. Materials and experiences are based on the home environment, the children's interests, and the parents' enthusiasm. You have an excellent opportunity to involve parents in creating learning activities for their children. You can enable the parents to change through your encouragement and acceptance of their contributions. The idea for a garden described in Figure 8.4 could have originated with a suggestion from a parent.

Throughout the year, home visitors involve parents in teaching their children at home. As the home visitor suggests activities for the child, additional ideas may occur to both the visitor and the parent. In addition, children themselves may elaborate on old ideas or create new activities. The home visitor should bring these ideas back to the office where they can be classified and cataloged. Parents receive a boost if home visitors

recognize their contributions. They will also continue to develop activities for children if they are reinforced. Write down their suggestions and file them for future use or include them in the program for the coming week.

Home Study and Enrichment at Home

Children learn best when they are actively involved. Dr. Joyce Epstein of John Hopkins has developed interactive homework assignments that are easily understood by the parents and are at a level for young children's accomplishments. The idea of home-school cooperation does not mean viewing the parent as a taskmaster intent on forcing the child to learn. Instead, the parent is viewed as a responsive, alert facilitator.

Piaget (1976) insists that learning stems from the active involvement of the person doing the inventing; once invented, the theory or steps are not forgotten. Piaget recommends "the use of active methods which give broad scope to the spontaneous research of the child or adolescent and require that every new truth to be learned be rediscovered or at least reconstructed by the student and not simply imparted to him" (pp. 15–16). Kamii (1985a, 1985b) recommends a Piagetian approach in constructionism. Children construct their own knowledge if given the opportunity.

Experiential activities that afford children an opportunity to learn by discovery are facilitated best in a relaxed, natural, and rich learning environment. The setting can be either in the home or in the community. The steps to developing a home-learning activity, based on Gordon's program in Florida, reflect the use of the natural environment (see p. 344). Most of the summer activities suggested by Saturday School are based on situations and opportunities that emerge or are always present if the parent takes the time to spend a moment with the child (Figure 7.10). Most important is the attitude that learning is possible everywhere for the child.

The home is a learning center. Children learn to talk without formal instruction. They learn as they interact with others and participate in interesting events. Learning tasks at home can and should be intriguing rather than simply difficult. A parent who reads stories to children is actually teaching reading. The development of an interest in and love of reading is the first step toward acquisition of proficient reading skills.

Activities and Resources at Home

Brainstorm for a moment about all the learning opportunities in the home. Record the ideas to use with your students or to share with parents. The following ideas may lead to many more:

- *Art and crafts*. Have tempera paint, watercolors, crayons, chalk, white paper, colored paper, scissors, glue or paste, Play-Doh, and modeling clay available for spontaneous art projects. Draw, paint, make rubbings and collages. Try painting outdoors with water.
- *Read together*. Children begin learning to read at home. To help children with language and reading development, parents need to talk with and read to their infants. Range from nursery rhymes to stories that adults enjoy. Infants hear the voice, develop sensitivity to the sounds, and set out on their way to literacy. The proximity to the reader helps develop trust and attachment.

Continue reading with preschoolers and school-age children. Discover and emphasize the many situations in which children can be engaged in reading and writing.

- *Publishing*. Make a publishing center and include paper, pencils, pens, typewriter or computer, and cardboard for backing of books.

Create poetry, cinquains, haiku, free verse, rhyming, and limericks.

For very young children, transcribe their stories for them and let them illustrate the story or book. If children are older, help them brainstorm ideas for a book or make a history book of their family. Let them write in journals or diaries. Encourage them to write to a relative, pen pal, or friend. Help them edit their work in a cooperative spirit.

Write a cooperative newsletter for the neighborhood or relatives. Make a form with areas for writings by each person or descriptions of each project. Let someone fill in the information.

- *Games*. Take time to play games. The list is long: Concentration, hopscotch, jacks, jump rope, basketball, Ping-Pong, toss a ball, Lotto, Monopoly, Boggle, word or letter Bingo, anagrams, and matching.
- *Backyard science*. Examine the ground for insects and vegetation. Examine bugs with a microscope. Classify leaves by shape, size, and color. Categorize plants or animals.
- *Front yard business*. Have a garage sale and let your child be the cashier.
- *Listening center*. Collect read-along books, and buy tapes or make tapes of the story so the child can listen to the books and read along.

- *Music center.* Have a record player or tape recorder where the child can listen to various types of music. Use the center for singing, moving, and dancing. If you have songs with written words, the activity can also be a reading experience.

- *Communicate.* Talk with each other. Let children describe all the things that are happening. Help them predict and observe by showing interest in their predictions. Make the home a safe place to express feelings.

- *Homemaking activities.* Chores are not chores if you have fun doing them. Cooking is fun and can be used as an intellectual endeavor as well as a functional activity. Practice mathematics by dividing a recipe in half. Research where and how the ingredients were grown.

Activities Away from Home

Trips around and away from home can also be adventures.

- *Take a walk.* Collect water from a stream or puddle. Examine the water through a microscope when you return home. Describe or draw the creatures found in a drop of water.

- *Visit the library.* Go to the library. Help children get library cards if they don't have them. Choose and check out books. If the library has a storytime or program for older children, attending helps make the library a wonderful place to visit.

- *Visit a store.* It can be the grocery store, post office, department store, or hardware store. Before going, make out a shopping list together. Keep it simple. Let the child help with selection and cost of the products.

- *Explore museums.* Art, natural history, historical, or other specialty museums may have pictures or artifacts that lend themselves to artwork at home. To increase observation powers, let the child look for something specific, such as a color or materials. Talk about how the art materials were used or which shapes were selected.

- *Visit historical buildings.* Take along paper, pen, and crayons. Draw the shape of the building. Make a crayon rubbing of the placard that tells about the building's dedication.

- *Visit the airport and bus station.* Watch the people. Imagine where they are going. Count the people who walk by. Find out how the station or airport is managed. Note how many different buses, trains, or airplanes you can see. How are they different from each other? Compare the costs of the different methods of travel.

- *Go to a garage sale.* Determine how many articles you can buy for $5 or $10.

Using intriguing and exciting activities benefits the family in two ways: (a) learning takes place, and (b) the parent-child relationship is enhanced. Parents need to know the importance of a rich home environment; they need to be reinforced for their positive teaching behaviors. Although good times together may be reinforcement enough, schools can help support productive parent-child interaction by encouraging parents, offering workshops, and supplying home-learning activities.

Home-Learning Formulas for the Home Visitor

Each home-based learning has developed its own approach to home learning activities. The Portage Project developed a systematic program for its home visitors that can be used by others. Levenstein's Mother-Child Home Program chose commercial games and books as the basis for verbal interaction between parent and child. HIPPY provides a specific curriculum design with storybooks and activity packets. Some programs focus on giving the families support and encouraging improved parenting skills. Gordon's parent program in Florida devised a method of curriculum development that can be duplicated in any program (Gordon & Breivogel, 1976).

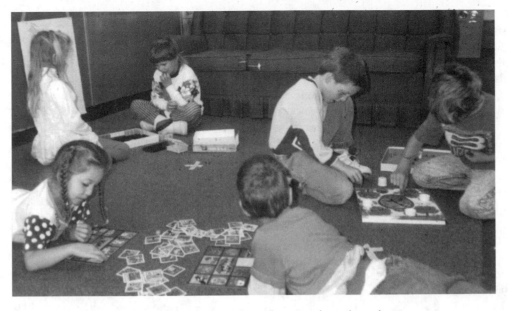

Games and interesting activities can be stimulating homework or "homefun."

As parents and home visitors work together to develop the children's curriculum, the following tips will help.

- Choose an emerging skill that the child has shown an interest in or one in which an interest can be developed.
- Choose some skills that the parent considers important.
- Choose a skill the child needs to learn.
- Choose a developmentally appropriate task that is easily accommodated at home. (U.S. Department of Health and Human Services, 1985)

In the implementation of a home-school program both teachers and parents may develop activities related to individual families, or they may be supported by learning activities developed by commercial companies and school districts. Appropriate learning activities can be purchased or found in the library. Refer to the references and suggested readings in the Appendix at the end of this book for additional de-

velopmentally appropriate activities for young children.

DECIDING ON A HOME-BASED PROGRAM

Before a program is considered, the reasons for and needs of such a program must be examined. The primary goals of home-based programs include the following:

1. To enable parents to become more effective teachers of their children.
2. To support the parents in the roles of caregivers and homemakers.
3. To strengthen the parents' sense of autonomy and self-esteem.
4. To reach the child and family early in the child's formative years.
5. To respond to the family's needs and thus improve the home environment.

The overriding goal of educators is the effect of the program on the child. Desirable results are the child's increased sense of well-being, a more successful educational experience in school, and the realization of the child's potential for optimum development.

Goals for programs vary according to the needs of the area. For instance, an overriding concern in one area may be health; in another, language development; and in still another, nutrition. Although all three are probably important in varying degrees in every home-based program, the intensity of involvement may vary.

Programs that address multiple concerns are more effective than those that focus on one. Families need support in many different ways. A conceptual framework (Ramey & Ramey, 1993) that crosses family, school, and community and impacts the health and development of a child includes:

1. Survival

   - Housing
   - Income
   - Food
   - Clothing
   - Safety
   - Transportation

2. Values and Goals

   - To succeed as a family
   - To do well in school and work
   - To be part of the community

3. Sense of Security

   - Physical
   - Social-emotional
   - Financial

4. Health

   - Physical
   - Mental

5. Social Interaction

   - With family
   - With peers
   - With community

6. Self-esteem

   - Personal competence
   - Academic cognitive competence
   - Social competence

7. Communication

   - Listening skills
   - Speaking skills
   - Reading skills
   - Writing skills

8. Intellectual Skills

   - Everyday living skills
   - Social-emotional skills
   - Academic and work skills (p. 131)

If these goals are achieved, the family, school, and community will be involved.

DECIDING ON A PROGRAM

Schools and centers should consider parent involvement and home-based programs within the framework of their own needs. They should examine all approaches carefully and share a commitment to the child and family before embarking on a home-based program. The following questions can be used as guidelines for choosing a program:

1. Are there children currently in school who could have been helped by early intervention in the home?

2. What can the school do in a home visitation program that cannot be accomplished through other programs?

3. Could early remediation reduce the number of retentions when children go to school?

4. Are there children with disabilities in the area who could be diagnosed and given service before they enter school?

5. Will the preventive program help eliminate later educational problems, offsetting the cost to the public?

6. Will the prevention of later educational problems reduce emotional problems, also offsetting the cost to the public?

7. Are there parents who could be helped by an adult literacy program?

If "yes" is the answer to most of these questions, the next step is to consider the feasibility of a home-based program. The following questions must be addressed:

1. Has there been a thorough assessment of needs to establish community interest in home-based services?

2. Are there *enough* families in the community who are definitely interested and eligible to participate in a program that emphasizes home visits and the role of the parents?

3. Do staff members already have the skills and interests needed to work effectively with parents in their own homes? If not, does the program have, or can it obtain, the considerable training necessary to prepare staff members for their new roles? Is the staff willing to receive such training? Is the staff culturally and linguistically compatible with families to be served?

4. Can transportation needs be met? Public transportation is often an inefficient mode of travel and is not available in many areas. Home visitors need a car to get around quickly, transport materials, and take parents and children for special services needed from local resource agencies.

5. Will the program include family members who are away from home during the day? The answer to this usually involves meetings and home visits in the evenings and on weekends. In some ways, home-based programs require a staff selflessness and dedication that goes beyond the demands of the workload and schedules of center-based services (U.S. Department of Health and Human Services, 1985).

Before a questionnaire or needs assessment is devised, data should be gathered from school files, social service agencies, city surveys, or census reports. Social services will be particularly helpful in determining services and number of children in families. School figures, questionnaires, and surveys will supplement that data so that services can be offered to all those who want or need them. Make every effort to establish a good working relationship with the various agencies. You will need to coordinate your efforts later, and initial communication and rapport are essential to subsequent implementation of the program.

Parents to be served in a home-based program should be actively involved in the initial planning. Many schools and preschool programs have parent advisory councils or citizen advisory councils that can give input on the needs of the community and suggest relevant questions. If a council is not functioning in your area, it may be worth it to start one. You can work through the existing PTO or PTA, or you can establish an entirely new council with the parents you will serve.

The formation or election of the board should be advertised. Parents then have an opportunity to nominate themselves or others, and an election is scheduled to determine who will represent the community on the council. You could advertise the formation of an advisory council by sending notes home with children; explaining the council at meetings of Boy Scouts, Camp Fire Girls, PTA, YMCA, and YWCA; and distributing fliers throughout the community. All nominations should be accepted. If you use a democratic process, you will have to rely on the intelligence of the parents in the selection process.

Distinct advantages to using a democratic selection process rather than appointment to an advisory council include: (a) interest in the program is generated and maintained, (b) the parents feel a sense of self-determination and autonomy, (c) the council becomes a source of relevant information and feedback from those affected, and (d) cooperation between school and parents increases.

Involving Others in the Program

The four components of a Home Start program are (a) education, (b) social services, (c) health services (physical and mental health, dental care, nutrition, and safety), and (d) parent involvement. Although the project will be fully responsible for education and parent involvement, social and health services will need the support of other agencies.

Recruitment of Families

Many families will be identified by existing programs, such as Head Start, schools, and social service agencies. Articles in newspapers about the new home-based program will alert other parents, and fliers can be delivered by students. The most effective method, however, is a door-to-door canvass. Home visitors can go from house to house to chat with parents and explain the program and its benefits. This personal approach seems to encourage parents to participate when a notice through the mail may not. Families new to the area or unknown to social agencies probably will be reached only by a door-to-door campaign.

Published articles can increase parents' interest. Curriculum and child development may be communicated through newsletters as well as personal visits. It is also a good idea to combine the two and give the parent a handout at the end of a home visit.

Selection of Home Visitors

Before selecting home visitors, the choice must be made whether to use professional parent teachers, paraprofessionals, or volunteers. Although the director, coordinator, and special services specialists will probably be professionals, many programs use paraprofessionals or volunteers as the home-visit specialists. Criteria for selection will be determined by the needs of your program.

Five criteria often considered are:

1. Experience, age, and maturity—good judgment and flexibility

2. Race, ethnicity, and culture—key consideration should be to the home visitor who has respect for values and beliefs of other cultures

3. Professional education

4. Gender

5. Helping skills (Wasik, 1993, pp. 143, 147)

Communication Skills

The skills needed for an effective home visitor program also include collaboration and effective communication in which the home visitor is able to

1. Listen empathetically

2. Affirm the family

3. Recognize and affirm the family's strengths

4. Maintain appropriate boundaries

5. Individualize for each family's needs

6. Demonstrate and model effective parenting skills

7. Interpret the purpose of activities and child-parent interactions

8. Problem solve with the parents (Klass, Pettinelli, & Wilson, 1993)

Recruiting

When recruiting paraprofessional home visitors, the available positions should be advertised throughout the community. Announcements must be clear and include the following:

1. *Explanation of the program.*   Explain what your home-based program entails, indicating its goals and objectives.

2. *Job description of the position.*   List the duties and responsibilities, workday schedule, salary range, and benefits.

3. *Qualifications required.*   Indicate whether high school, college, or specific competencies are required.

4. *Equal opportunity employment announcement.* Make a statement of nondiscrimination.

5. *Instructions for applying.* Give instructions on how to apply, whom to contact, and the deadline for application.

The announcement should be posted in public places, such as libraries, schools, stores, and social agencies, such as Head Start. Telephone canvassing will alert many people to the new program. To reach a large population, advertise in the newspaper and distribute fliers. Wide dissemination of information about available positions encourages individuals in the community to become involved and alerts others to the upcoming home-based program.

Visiting Parents at Home

Successful home visitors are flexible and work easily with others. These guidelines will help start home visitors on the road to success.

- Be a good listener.
- Set specific goals for each visit.
- Be flexible.
- Be prompt.
- Realize the limitations of your role.
- Help parents become more independent.
- Dress appropriately and comfortably.
- Be confident.
- Remember that small improvements lead to big ones.
- Be yourself.
- Respect cultural and ethnic values.
- Monitor your own behavior—the parent is observing you.
- Include other members of the family in the visit.
- Bring visitors only when you have the parent's permission.
- Don't socialize excessively.
- Don't impose values.
- Don't talk about families in public.
- Don't expect perfection from the parent.
- Don't ask the parent to do something you wouldn't do.
- Make the parent the focus of your visits. Help develop the parent's role as a teacher.
- Begin working with the parent and child on specific activities immediately. This sets a tone for the home visits, and parents will feel good about their abilities as they see that they can and do teach their children.
- Plan activities around daily routines.
- Make it a habit to discuss the reason for the activity before you or the parent presents it to the child. (U.S. Department of Health and Human Services, 1987)

Home visitors can evaluate their efforts by asking themselves the questions in Figure 8.5 after each visit.

Inservice Training After the Program Has Started

Learning by both the family and the home visitor comes to fruition during the development of the program. During this period, the home visitor responds to the needs, desires, and styles of the parents and children. Close contact with the program's coordinator or trainers supports the home visitor and allows administrators to keep track of what is happening in the field. Reports on each visit, with copies for the home visitor and for the program's administrators or trainers, will enable people from both levels of the program to keep in touch with developments and needs. In doing so, inservice training can be directed to enrich weak areas and clarify procedures.

Small Groups

Throughout the year questions and needs for training will arise. Training sessions are more effective when small groups of home visitors—rather than all members of the program—meet together as needs emerge. The individualized meeting is beneficial because the session has

---

Are YOUR Home Visits Parent-Focused?

• Do you involve the parents in the assessment of the child?	Yes	No
• Do you provide the parent with a copy of the checklist for their own use?	Yes	No
• When you arrive for the weekly home visit, do you direct your attention and greeting toward the parent?	Yes	No
• Do you discuss the previous week's visit and follow up on the weekly activities with the parent?	Yes	No
• Does the parent co-plan the activities for the home visit?	Yes	No
• Do you make sure that the child is sitting beside the parent?	Yes	No
• Does the parent demonstrate EACH new activity?	Yes	No
• Do you review each activity with the parent before presenting it?	Yes	No
• Do you hand all materials to the parent?	Yes	No
• Do you identify and reinforce the parent's teaching strengths?	Yes	No
• When the parent has difficulty, do you intervene with the parent rather than the child?	Yes	No
• Do you let the parent be the primary reinforcing agent?	Yes	No
• Do you help the parent problem solve when problems do arise instead of jumping to the rescue?	Yes	No
• Do you work on activities the parent feels are important?	Yes	No
• Do you ask the parent to provide as many materials as possible?	Yes	No
• Do you give the parent the lead, when appropriate?	Yes	No
• Do you incorporate the parent's ideas into each activity?	Yes	No
• Do you let the parent present new and exciting experiences?	Yes	No
• Do you individualize parent education activities for each parent?	Yes	No
• Do you accept the parent's values?	Yes	No
• Do you involve the parent in evaluation of the home visit?	Yes	No

---

FIGURE 8.5   A self-evaluation form for home visitors.
Source: U.S. Department of Health and Human Services (1987).

been set up especially for the participants, and small numbers allow for a more personalized response by the trainer or coordinator.

Community Resources

Although lists of community resources are given to home visitors early in the program, more definite descriptions and procedures are useful when specific problems arise. During the year, specialists from a variety of community agencies can be invited to share their experiences and knowledge of procedures with the staff. Have them come to training meetings, meet the staff, and answer questions concerning use of their programs.

Program Evaluation

Ongoing evaluations of contacts, visits, and services rendered are essential. Home visit reports give data that can be used to measure progress. If the home visitor systematically completes each report, the administrator will be able to evaluate progress throughout the training period.

Parent Questionnaires

Statements by parents and responses to questionnaires concerning the effect of the program on the child and family are valuable in analyzing the effects of the program. Collect these throughout the program as well as at the completion of the year.

Evaluation is a tool to be used during the development of the program as well as a means to assess accomplishments. Include a variety of evaluations to improve the program and demonstrate its effectiveness.

✵ SCREENING FOR BETTER UNDERSTANDING

As home visitors and parents work with children, they informally assess the child's characteristics and skills. Informal assessments with checklists can be used while the child is playing. It is always best to view the child in a natural setting unrestricted by contrived tasks. A portfolio containing collections of art activities and projects, teacher comments, and the child's comments can aid in assessing the child's development. These kinds of assessment are essential; they provide the parent and teacher with guidelines for developmentally appropriate activities for each child.

Parent educators also need to be able to recognize if families under their guidance need special help. Screening for potential problems in both the developmental status of children and the children's environment—especially if they are growing up in a low socioeconomic area—will help the parent-educator identify problems early and more effectively serve children and their families (Fandal, 1986).

Several instruments are available to screen the developmental progress of children. Two of the most widely used are the Denver Prescreening Developmental Questionnaire (PDQ) and the Denver Developmental Screening Test (DDST).

There are also standardized methods of assessing the home environment of children, such as the Home Screening Questionnaire (HSQ) and the Home Observation for Measurement of the Environment (HOME).

Home Observation for Measurement of the Environment (HOME)

The HOME Inventory (Figure 8.6) is used by schools, child care centers, and other social service agencies to help them determine the quality of the home environment as it relates to the child's development. "Although a child may appear to be developing at a normal rate early in life, the environment begins to either enhance or 'put a lid' on developmental progress within the first year or two" (Fandal, 1986).

The HOME Inventory was developed "to get a picture of what the child's world is like from his or her perspective—i.e., from where he or she lies or sits or stands or moves about and sees, hears, smells, feels, and tastes that world" (Caldwell & Bradley, 1984, p. 8). In addition to the standardized HOME Inventories for birth to three-year-olds and three- to six-year-olds, an inventory for elementary school children is also available.

When using the program, the interviewer should:

- Know the HOME Inventory well before using it.
- Contact the parents and arrange a visit.
- Visit when the child is awake and available.
- Start the interview with friendly, relaxed interaction.

A suggested technique for starting the interview is described by the following statement:

> You will remember that we are interested in knowing the kinds of things your baby (child) does when he is at home. A good way to get a picture of what his days are like is to have you think of one particular day—like yesterday—and tell me everything that happened to him as well as you can remember it. Start with the things that happened when he first

13

HOME Inventory for Families of Infants and Toddlers

Bettye M. Caldwell and Robert H. Bradley

Family Name _____ Date _____ Visitor _____

Child's Name _____ Birthdate _____ Age _____ Sex _____

Caregiver for visit _____ Relationship to child _____

Family Composition _____ (Persons living in household, including sex and age of children)

Family Ethnicity _____ Language Spoken _____ Maternal Education _____ Paternal Education _____

Is Mother Employed? _____ Type of work when employed _____ Is Father Employed? _____ Type of work when employed _____

Address _____ Phone _____

Current child care arrangements _____

Summarize past year's arrangements _____ Other persons present _____

Caregiver for visit _____

Comments _____

SUMMARY

Subscale	Score	Lowest Middle	Middle Half	Upper Fourth
I. Emotional and Verbal RESPONSIVITY of Parent		0-6	7-9	10-11
II. ACCEPTANCE of Child's Behavior		0-4	5-6	7-8
III. ORGANIZATION of Physical and Temporal Environment		0-3	4-5	6
IV. Provision of Appropriate PLAY MATERIALS		0-4	5-7	8-9
V. Parent INVOLVEMENT with Child		0-2	3-4	5-6
VI. Opportunities for VARIETY in Daily Stimulation		0-1	2-3	4-5
TOTAL SCORE		0-25	26-36	37-45

For rapid profiling of a family, place an X in the box that corresponds to the raw score on each subscale and the total score.

14

HOME Inventory*

Place a plus (+) or minus (-) in the box alongside each item if the behavior is observed during the visit or if the parent reports that the conditions or events are characteristic of the home environment. Enter the subtotal and the total on the front side of the Record Sheet.

I. Emotional and Verbal RESPONSIVITY
1. Parent spontaneously vocalized to child twice.
2. Parent responds verbally to child's verbalizations.
3. Parent tells child name of object or person during visit.
4. Parent's speech is distinct and audible.
5. Parent initiates verbal exchanges with visitor.
6. Parent converses freely and easily.
7. Parent permits child to engage in "messy" play.
8. Parent spontaneously praises child at least twice.
9. Parent's voice conveys positive feelings toward child.
10. Parent caresses or kisses child at least once.
11. Parent responds positively to praise of child offered by visitor.
Subtotal

II. ACCEPTANCE of Child's Behavior
12. Parent does not shout at child.
13. Parent does not express annoyance with or hostility to child.
14. Parent neither slaps nor spanks child during visit.
15. No more than one instance of physical punishment during past week.
16. Parent does not scold or criticize child during visit.
17. Parent does not interfere or restrict child more than 3 times.
18. At least ten books are present and visible.
19. Family has a pet.
Subtotal

III. ORGANIZATION of Environment
20. Substitute care is provided by one of three regular substitutes.
21. Child is taken to grocery store at least once/week.
22. Child gets out of house at least four times/week.
23. Child is taken regularly to doctor's office or clinic.
24. Child has a special place for toys and treasures.
25. Child's play environment is safe.
Subtotal

IV. Provision of PLAY MATERIALS
26. Muscle activity toys or equipment.
27. Push or pull toy.
28. Stroller or walker, kiddie car, scooter, or tricycle.
29. Parent provides toys for child during visit.
30. Learning equipment appropriate to age--cuddly toys or role-playing toys.
31. Learning facilitators--mobile, table and chairs, high chair, play pen.
32. Simple eye-hand coordination toys.
33. Complex eye-hand coordination toys (those permitting combination).
34. Toys for literature and music.
Subtotal

V. Parental INVOLVEMENT with Child
35. Parent keeps child in visual range, looks at often.
36. Parent talks to child while doing household work.
37. Parent consciously encourages developmental advance.
38. Parent invests maturing toys with value via personal attention.
39. Parent structures child's play periods.
40. Parent provides toys that challenge child to develop new skills.
Subtotal

VI. Opportunities for VARIETY
41. Father provides some care daily.
42. Parent reads stories to child at least 3 times weekly.
43. Child eats at least one meal per day with mother and father.
44. Family visits relatives or receives visits once a month or so.
45. Child has 3 or more books of his/her own.
Subtotal

TOTAL SCORE

*For complete wording of items, please refer to the Administration Manual.

FIGURE 8.6 Home visitors can use the HOME Inventory to analyze the family's home environment.
Source: Caldwell & Bradley (1984).

woke up. It is usually easy to remember the main events once you get started. (Caldwell & Bradley, 1984, p. 3)

The administration and scoring of each item in the inventory are clearly described in the Administration Manuals, so the interviewer can make correct judgments on the scoring of HOME. For example, see Figure 8.6, Item 4, which states, "Parent's speech is distinct and audible." The score on this item is determined by whether the interviewer is able to understand what the parent says. This item should not be interpreted as meaning that dialect usage mandates a negative score; what is important is whether the interviewer can understand and communicate with the parent.

Home Screening Questionnaire (HSQ)

Coons, Gay, Fandal, Ker, and Frankenburg (1981) recognized the value of an earlier version of the HOME Inventory but were concerned about the length of time needed for a skilled interviewer to make a home visit. They developed a questionnaire, the HSQ, that could be answered by parents. With the cooperation of the authors of the HOME Inventory, items were selected and turned into two questionnaires that correspond to the two HOME scales (for children from birth to three years and those from three to six years of age). Each takes about 15 minutes for a parent to complete.

The questionnaires have been validated as effective screening tools to identify environments that would benefit from a more intensive assessment. "The HSQ Manual gives complete instructions for scoring the questionnaires. As with all suspect screening results, questionable HSQ results should be followed with a visit by a trained home interviewer to assure that the result of the screening test is accurate and that appropriate intervention can be planned" (Fandal, 1986).

✑ HOMESCHOOLING

Homeschooling may be defined as "instruction and learning, at least some of which is through planned activity, taking place *primarily* at home in a family setting with a parent acting as teacher or supervisor of the activity" (Lines, 1991, p. 10). Homeschooling is not new. Many of our nation's early leaders were taught at home. The common school movement began about 1830 and 1840, but it was usual for children to attend for only three months out of the year for three or four years.

The last half of the 19th century saw a greater transformation of schooling. Eighty-six percent of children ages 5 to 14 were attending public schools by 1890 (Carper, 1992). During the 20th century, parents sent their children to public and private schools, and schools became more and more centrally administered. It was not until the 1980s that the increase in homeschooling began to be noticed.

Estimates of the number of children who were being schooled at home in the 1970s ranged from 1,000 to 15,000; in 1983, estimates ranged from 60,000 to 125,000; by 1988 the homeschool "student body" was thought to be 150,000 to 300,000 (Lines, 1991). It increased rapidly in the 1990s—estimates of homeschooled children ranged up to 2 million, but in 1999 the 95 percent confidence interval for the number of homeschoolers was 709,000 to 992,000. Homeschoolers accounted for 1.7 percent of the students in the United States (National Center for Education Statistics, 2001).

In 1999, the Census Bureau's Current Population Survey (CPS) found 790,000 homeschoolers (Bauman, 2001), and the National Center for Education Statistics chose the midpoint of the confidence interval for 850,000 homeschoolers (National Center for Education Statistics, 2001). Children were designated as homeschooled if the parents school them at home and their enrollment in private or public schools is less than 25 hours a week. About four out of five homeschooled (82 percent) were homeschooled and only one out of five (18 percent) also went part time to public or private schools.

Characteristics of Homeschooling and Homeschooled Children

Homeschoolers, when compared to non-homeschoolers, are White, non-Hispanic, and have two parents with higher levels of education (25 percent college graduates compared to 16 percent). One of the parents was not employed full time outside the home. Both boys and girls are homeschooled with slightly more girls. Eighty percent of homeschooled children lived in two-parent households compared to 66 percent of non-homeschoolers. Sixty-three percent of the families had three or more children (National Center for Education Statistics, 2001).

In most cases of homeschooling, the mother is the teacher, and she usually teaches her own children, spending 20–30 hours each week in school activities. There is no one curriculum that parents use, although they can buy curriculum programs from a variety of organizations. Each state also has associations that can help families find materials, supervise tests, grade papers, and find support. (See the Appendix for references for homeschooling.)

Testing for academic achievement and effective development has indicated that most homeschooled children do well in academics. Scores on state-mandated tests indicate that although some score below average, "a large number test above that mark" (Lines, 1996). There also seems to be little risk to their socialization, psychological development, and self-esteem (Lines, 1996; Ray & Wartes, 1991).

The increasing number of homeschools has forced public schools and state legislators to analyze the coordination and cooperation needed between schools and parents who want to educate their children at home. In the past decade proponents have been successful in advocating for homeschools. When there have been court cases, the proponents of homeschooling are able to rely on court decisions and the Bill of Rights (Guterson, 1992).

State legislatures have been responding to parental demands.

All states allow homeschooling. Typically, a state's statutes, through a court ruling, an attorney general opinion, or a regulation that interprets a school attendance law to include homeschooling, consider homeschooling a legitimate option for meeting compulsory education requirements. Because each state regulates homeschooling differently, parents should examine local laws and consult with other homeschoolers before proceeding. In every state, parents must, at a minimum, notify a state or local education agency of their intent to educate their children at home and identify the children involved. (Lines, 1996, p. 1)

Technology—the use of the computer with educational resources, e-mail, and online communication—is becoming an important resource for homeschooled students. Students can research projects on the Internet and communicate with others about their interests (Natale, 1995). The Internet is continually building new avenues, Web sites, and research to offer information to the public. "Traditional publishers, corresponding schools, and dot-com startups are rushing to help overwhelmed parent-teachers offering everything from interactive classes to one-on-one tutoring" (Heurer, 2000, p. 1).

Reasons for Homeschooling

The largest single reason for homeschooling is the belief by the parents that they can give their children a better education at home (48.9 percent). Religious reasons follow (38.4 percent), with a poor learning environment at school ranking third (25.6 percent). Figure 8.7 illustrates the reasons that homeschooling parents gave for homeschooling their children.

School-Parent Cooperation

The next step to help ensure the child's success will be cooperation between the home and school. How can parents and schools accommodate each other? Suggestions include part-time attendance in school by children who are homeschooled (Knowles, 1989; Mayberry, 1989).

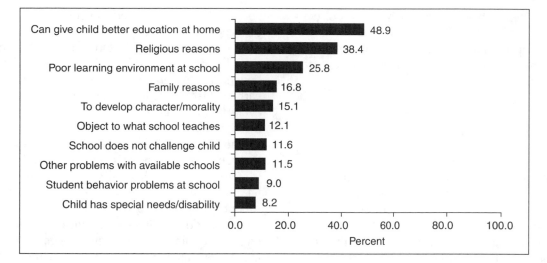

FIGURE 8.7 Ten reasons for homeschooling and the percentage of homeschooled students whose parents gave each reason: 1999.

Note: Percentages do not add to 100 percent because respondents could give more than one reason.

Source: From the *Parent Survey* of the National Household Education Surveys Program, 1999, by the U.S. Department of Education, National Center for Education Statistics.

Two examples of school districts illustrate how schools can respond to the collaboration between public schools and homeschoolers. The Cupertino Union School District in California has given parents options for over 25 years. Parents enroll their child in the district school system, but they educate the child at home. The school receives the revenue from the state, and parents are given curricula, money for books, services, materials, and computer software. Each family has a resource teacher who holds a conference with them monthly, or more often if desired. They also have access to a library of materials and books for homeschooling. They can use the school's supplies and equipment, and children can be enrolled in extended day class (Berger, 1997; Lamson, 1992).

Another example is the San Diego City School District, which offers support to homeschooled children. The school offers a structured curriculum for families to use. Educators are assigned as homeschool teachers who meet with the families on a trimester basis. Families can contact the teacher assigned to them as often as they desire. Parents can take advantage of services, field trips, special education, and counseling, educating their own children with the support of the school district (Dalaimo, 1996).

In collaboration, schools can furnish resources and services for homeschool families. These may include offering the use of resource centers; enrollment in special classes such as music, art, and science; participation of homeschooled parents in school district programs; advisory and facilitating services; inservice workshops; and participation of homeschooled students in extracurricular activities, summer programs, and large group or team activities (Knowles, 1989). "As homeschooling grows, calls will continue for existing public schools to provide services that cannot be provided easily by home-school families themselves—such as advanced courses and extracurricular activities (Bauman, 2001, p. 9).

By allowing the student to be schooled at home, but providing support and an opportunity to participate with other children in activities, the school helps parents achieve their goals of educating their children themselves while giving children opportunities to interact socially with other students. If the child later reenters school, the transition will be easier.

🎗 HOMEWORK

Homework is defined as "tasks assigned to students by school teachers that are meant to be carried out during non-school hours" (Cooper, 1994, p. 2). The U.S. Department of Education's report, *What Works:* Research about Teaching and Learning (1986), emphasized that the home environment and homework are essential for children to reach their full potential (see Chapter 4). Homework varies according to the age of the child. For young children, the home environment, the interaction, and intense work with toys make up the child's learning experience—the home is the child's school and what the child does is homework. As children get older and the location of school goes outside the home, suddenly what they do at home is not considered school unless they bring home an assignment. But the home is still part of the child's learning experiences, and the extra work and advice from school can help make learning richer.

Whether homework should be required for children in early grades is questioned by both parents and educators. The Child Study Movement of the 1890 and early 1900s believed that children should be children and not start school until they were seven. In the mid-1920s to 1940s homework was limited or abolished in New York City, Chicago, and San Diego. Reform of homework rather than elimination was the call after World War II. It should be "moderate in amount, creative in purpose and directed to each child's needs" (Winerip, 1999, p. 30). When the Russians launched *Sputnik* in 1957, the educational system felt challenged and set out to educate the young so that the nation could compete with the Russians. The result was increased homework nationwide (p. 31). The report on education, *A Na-*

tion at Risk, again alarmed the country. In 1986, the report mentioned earlier, *What Works,* stated that homework "worked." Since that time homework has continued to be seen as necessary and beneficial. "Assignments become common as early as first grade, and some schools require it every day. Parents' grumbling is heard across the land" (p. 32).

The article by Winerip describes the success that Chinese parents have in home education. Chinese American children spend an average of 54 minutes each day studying at home. European Americans spend about 6 minutes. "At first and second grade, the Chinese-American families averaged 31 minutes in homework versus 11 for Euro-Americans" (p. 30). Chinese parents also spent working with their children on language. Since their parents spoke Chinese at home, the children were behind in their English. The Chinese parents assigned 15 words each week and by the fourth grade, instead of being behind in English, they were ahead of the European American children (p. 30). Results such as these, even though the work Chinese children do at home is not assigned by the school, make the demand for homework seem worthwhile.

An alternative to homework has been the development of after-school programs where children can do schoolwork under supervision and with the help that they might need. This is especially helpful for families where both parents work.

Home-School Collaboration

The satisfactory use of homework requires communication and planning on the part of the school. Because homework has long been used by schools, many teachers do not see the opportunity or responsibility to communicate with parents about homework. Much greater cooperation and collaboration will occur if a teacher communicates with parents about the importance of homework and finds out how the parents respond to the opportunity to support their child's educational growth through homework. If the school has a stated policy about homework, the parents should know what it is and what their responsibilities are. If the school leaves homework up to individual teachers, each teacher is responsible for communicating with parents about specific requirements for homework in their classes.

Parents should find out: Will there be homework each night? How long should the average amount of homework take? Will the assignments be explained before the student is sent home with them? Will the student understand the assignment? What are the rules and regulations regarding homework? Can homework be made into "homefun," where both student and parent enjoy the challenge?

If parents resent homework, instead of realizing its benefit to the child, it can become a negative experience. Instead of strengthening the family, it can become divisive and fail to strengthen the child's academic achievement. Homework must be handled with care. The teacher should do the following:

1. Send home work that reinforces or enriches what was learned in class. In either case the assignment should be something the child is able to accomplish. Assignments that are short and frequent rather than long and infrequent appear to have a more significant effect on the child's learning (Cooper, 1989).

2. Create meaningful assignments. Homework should not be haphazard busy work; instead, it should be well-planned and well-designed. Clearly explain the homework assignment. If it is new or extension material, review several of the issues or problems so the student knows what is expected.

3. Explain the rules and regulations of homework. Do you take off points for late homework? Is the homework grade figured into the grade for the grading period?

4. Provide a homework form that the student fills out in class that states the assignment, pages, or work sheets that go along with the homework. This could also include a signature line for the parent to sign so that the teacher knows the parent knows about the assignment.

5. Grade all homework personally. Display homework on the bulletin board to show the student that it is recognized and that it is important.

6. Communicate with parents to explain the process and respond to any difficulties that the family may be having with the homework.

7. Teach study skills (Canter & Hausner, 1987; Cooke & Cooke, 1988; Hodapp & Hodapp, 1992; Paulu, 1995; Radencich & Schumm, 1996).

A report by the U.S. Department of Education also emphasizes the need for homework to be well planned. The assignments should relate to the class work and extend the student's learning beyond the classroom. Effective homework assignments do not simply supplement the classroom lesson, they also teach students to be independent learners. Homework gives students experience in following directions, making judgments and comparisons, raising additional questions for study, and developing responsibility and self-discipline (U.S. Department of Education, 1986). Homework provides reinforcement for skills that were learned previously, practice time for developing skills, and an opportunity to "learn in one's own time and style" (Cooke & Cooke, 1988, p. 19).

Homework at Preschool, Elementary, and Secondary School

Homework takes on different dimensions at the preschool, elementary, and secondary levels. At all levels, homestudy or homework can form a bridge between home and school that lets parents know what is happening at school. Homework also can help form a bond between parent and child.

Preschool and Kindergarten

Research results do not support the use of homework for the very young (LaConte, 1981). On the other hand, research does recognize the importance of home-school involvement. A rich home environment provides homestudy. The parent is interested in and involved with the child's activities, and the child does informal study at home and on visits to the store or museum.

Talking and reading together foster the child's development. Selecting television programs and viewing television together, followed by discussion, foster the child's learning and provide interaction between parent and child. Use of home computers, though not a necessity, can give even preschool children a feeling of success when using a self-correcting activity that allows them to be in command. However, the time and length of involvement with computers and television must be monitored, because the most important learning takes place between people. Parents who talk, listen, and read to their children learn a lot about the children's feelings, abilities, and interests.

Preschool teachers or parent educators should focus on the child's experiences at home, take advantage of what is already occurring at home, open the parents' eyes to learning opportunities, and enrich the home experience. If used effectively in positive and supportive ways, homework should build a child's self-esteem (Cooke & Cooke, 1988).

The program or center needs to encourage and support parent-child interaction. Asking parents to read to their children is one form of homework that provides a positive experience for both parent and child and establishes reading as a pleasant and important part of parent-child relationships (U.S. Department of Education, 1986).

Elementary Level

At the elementary school level, the use of assigned homework becomes more defined. The following suggestions for involving the parent with the child's schoolwork are pointed out in *What Works:*

- Some teachers ask parents to read aloud to the child, listen to the child read, and sign homework papers.

- Others encourage parents to drill students on math and spelling and help with homework papers.

- Teachers also encourage parents to discuss school activities with their children and suggest ways parents can help teach their children at home. For example, a simple home activity might be alphabetizing books; a more complex one would be using kitchen supplies in an elementary science experiment.

- Teachers also send home suggestions for games or group activities related to the child's schoolwork that parent and child can play together. (U.S. Department of Education, 1986, p. 19)

If the parent is too busy or is unable to help with the home task, dissension may develop between parent and child. The use of a telephone network (see Chapter 4) to assist the child with homework can help eliminate the awkward situation that arises when the child does not know how to do the assignment and the parent is embarrassed by not knowing how to do it, either.

The computer also offers an extension of the school. If teachers are requiring homework, they should take the time to include assignment explanations and resources if they are needed to complete the homework assignment. If the necessary information is too difficult to put on the school Web site, in telephone messages, or if it is not available on the many sites that have plans and examples, the teacher should save the assignment for an in-class exercise.

Categories of Homework

Traditional homework for elementary and secondary students falls into three categories: practice, preparation, and extension (LaConte, 1981).

Practice is the most common type of homework: A skill learned at school is repeated. "Some homework assignments are intended to provide that students renew, practice and drill material that has been learned at school" (Hong & Milgram, 2000, p. 5). LaConte recommends that practice drills be limited to the classroom and homestudy be individualized. "The most effective kind of practice assignment asks the student to apply recently acquired learning in a direct and personal way" (p. 9). The able student becomes bored with repetition; the poor student will probably ignore the assignment. Thus, the more able students are usually given more and more homework while those who need individualized work either do not do the homework or are not assigned the work. If the teacher limits practice drills to the classroom, assignments can be adjusted according to individual needs and differences. However, *What Works* reports on one study that reveals that when low-ability students do just one to three hours of homework per week, their grades are as high as those of average students who do no homework (U.S. Department of Education, 1986).

Preparation is the assignment of material to be used to lay the groundwork for the next lesson. "Homework is also sometimes used to prepare, in advance, material to be learned" (Hong & Milgram, 2000, p. 5). These assignments should be imaginative and challenging and should include more than assigning a chapter to read. Conducting interviews, doing research, gathering information, or developing an original idea could enrich the child's learning experience (LaConte, 1981). Preparation assignments are not appropriate for young children unless you involve the parents, however. An appropriate example would be a "sound walk." Parent and child walk around their neighborhood, and the child makes a list of all the sounds they hear.

Extension is an individualized approach to homestudy that takes the student beyond the traditional classroom assignment. This homework fosters a creative approach to learning and is usually reserved for older children. Younger children would need their parents' help with a project or research. Homework is "intended to provide students with opportunities to amplify, elaborate, and enrich previously learned information" (Hong & Milgram, 2000, p. 5). Children's whole approach to learning could be labeled extension. They have to reach and grow from the very first day of birth (and even before). The only thing that has not been required is a report on their learning.

Time Spent on Homework

Parents are spending more time with their children and their homework. In a 1986 Gallup Poll,

34 percent spent no time with their oldest child with homework; in a comparable poll in 1997, only 13 percent spent no time. Not only were fewer parents spending no time, those who helped were spending more time. Thirty-nine percent responded that they spent five hours or more each week helping their oldest child with homework, as compared with only nine percent in 1986 (Rose, Gallup, & Elam, 1997).

Although it is easy to believe that homework always helps children, some of the research does not completely reinforce that belief. The average scores compared to the time spent on mathematics in grades four, eight, and twelve, showed an average of 15 minutes to an hour raised the scores for grades four and grades eight. Spending more than an hour did not. Fourth graders who spent more than an hour had lower scores than those spending no time. The explanation is not given, but one guess could be that those spending more than an hour had previous difficulty with math concepts. Figures 8.8A and 8.8B illustrate the findings. Grade 12 students spending an hour on homework resulted in the best scores. In the fourth grade, spending one hour on homework resulted in the highest scores.

A booklet by the U.S. Department of Education's Office of Educational Research and Improvement states that many educators suggest the following amount of homework. You will notice that 15 minutes a day produced the highest math scores for both grade four and grade eight. For children in primary grades, 20 minutes a school day is effective; from fourth through sixth grades, 20 to 40 minutes; and seventh through ninth, up to two hours. Varying these amounts is positive for some students, and parents should talk with the teacher if their child has too much or too little homework (Paulu, 1995).

How Can Parents Help?

Children of all ages can be helped with their homework. The following tips may be provided to parents by their teacher. However, teachers should recognize that parents who live in crowded quarters may not be able to provide a

Mathematics

The Nation's Report Card (home)

Major Findings

- At grades 4 and 8, a moderate amount of homework time–15 and 45 minutes depending on grade level– is associated with a higher average score on NAEP. Fourth-graders who spent an hour or more on homework had lower scores than their peers who did not do homework.
- At grade 12, however, there was no statistically significant difference in the performance of students spending any time between 15 minutes and one hour or more on mathematics homework. Twelfth-graders who reported spendin no time on homework had lower scores than their peers who did homework.

FIGURE 8.8A   Average mathematics scores by students' report on time spent daily on mathematics homework at grades 4, 8, and 12: 2000.

Source: From *2000 Mathematics Assessment* (2001) by the National Center for Education Statistics, National Assessment of Educational Progress (NAEP) Institute of Education Services, U.S. Department of Education. Table *77—2000 NAEP Mathematics Report Card. http://nces.ed.gov/nationsreportcard/ mathematics/results/homework.asp*

positive environment for homestudy. A staffed study hall for after school might be essential. For homework, parents can help by providing the following:

1. Set up a specific place to study that is
   a. Well lighted.
   b. Quiet, but not too isolated.

   c. Comfortable, with appropriate chair and table.
   d. Equipped with materials—paper, pencils, pens, erasers, pencil sharpener, clock, typewriter and/or computer.

2. Set aside a regular time for homework, or make a schedule for the week so that parents or children can fill in activities, study periods,

Reading

The Nation's Report Card (home)

Percentage of students reporting on the
amount of time spent doing homework
each day, 1992–2000

	'92	'94	'98	'00
More than one hour	15	15	16	16
One hour	28	30	31	29
One-half hour	39*	39*	43	43
Do not do homework	2	3*	2	2
Do not have homework	16*	13*	8	10

* Significantly different from 2000.

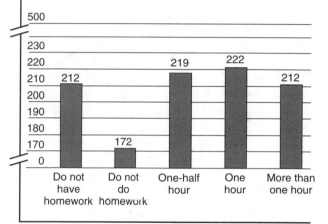

- Fourth-graders who did not not do their homework scored lowest.
- Fourth-graders who reported doing homework for one-half hour or for one hour per day outscored their peers who reported doing more than one hour of homework daily.
- The percentage of fourth-graders who said they do not have homework assigned to them declined from 16 percent in 1992 to only 10 percent in 2000.

FIGURE 8.8B Time spent on homework—grade 4.

Note: Percentages may not add to 100 due to rounding.

Source: From *1992–2000 Reading Assessments,* by the National Center for Education Statistics, National Assessment of Educational Progress (NAEP) Institute of Education Services, U.S. Department of Education. *http://nces.ed.gov/nationsreportcard/reading/results/homework.asp*

dinner time, recreation, and bedtime for each school day.

3. Be supportive and give appropriate help. Parents should not do their children's homework, but parents can engage in problem solving with them, guide them, and help them over the rough spots.

a. Consider the child's learning style. Does the child learn best through seeing, hearing, or manipulating the material?

b. Talk about the assignments. Does the child understand the homework? What does the child need in order to complete the work?

c. Help the child structure the time and assignment, and help the child get started. Recognize that the responsibility for completing the homework belongs to the student.

4. Show interest in and encourage the child's efforts.

5. Be a parent who is both loving and firm.

6. Refer the child to a homework hotline or Web site to get an explanation of the assignment if needed.

7. Contact the teacher if further help is needed (Canter & Hausner, 1987; Cooke & Cooke, 1988; Hodapp & Hodapp, 1992; Paulu, 1995; Radencich & Schumm, 1996).

Hong and Milgram (2000) state that the setting for homework should be determined by the learner's preferences and the conditions under which the student learns best. For example, some learners find background music helpful. Parents may adjust the study area to the child's preference of temperature, lighting, and sound. "It has been clearly established that higher academic achievement and improved attitude result from tailoring the learning experiences to the cognitive and personal social characteristics of the learner" (p. 17).

Conclusion

Because many homes have computers connected to information services and data banks, access to cable television classes, and videotapes and videodisks, the home is now widely recognized as a place where schoolwork can be supplemented and reinforced. Home-based education has many facets and will diversify and increase in the future. Methods may vary, but the home is still a primary educator of children.

❧ SUMMARY

Home-based education, initiated in the 1960s, saw continued and increased use in the 1980s, 1990s, and the 21st century. Programs developed include Parents as Teachers, Home Instruction Program for Preschool Youngsters, and Homebuilders, which joined earlier programs such as Portage Project, Parent-Child Home Program (Verbal Interaction Project), Parent and Child Centers, and home-based programs.

If the school is interested in developing a home-based program, it should (a) show a need for the program, (b) involve others in planning, (c) develop a par-

ent advisory council, and (d) decide on a program format.

Home-learning activities to be used by the home visitor and the family can be obtained through development of individualized activities, commercial offerings, or activities developed by demonstration programs. Use materials that are readily available to the parents, because the parent is the primary teacher in the home-based program. The focus in a home-based program is on the parent interacting with and teaching the child after the home visitor is gone.

Screening instruments may be selected to guide teachers in their work with parents and children and to serve as a basis for referrals for more thorough evaluation.

Homeschooling has emerged as a growing option for parents and children.

Concern about excellence in education has brought added emphasis on homework and the question of what amount shows the greatest benefit. The report *What Works* emphasized the need for homework to supplement the school curriculum. Preschool children need a rich learning environment in the home—their "homework." Homework for older students includes practice, preparation, and extension.

❧ SUGGESTED CLASS ACTIVITIES AND DISCUSSIONS

1. Discuss the type of parent-child interaction that best promotes the child's emotional and intellectual growth.
2. Brainstorm home situations that would be positive experiences for children.
3. Itemize household equipment that can be used as home learning tools. How would you use each?
4. Write role-playing opportunities based on families in several different home situations.
5. Discuss the guidelines related to home visits.
6. Discuss value systems that may vary from your own. How can you work with parents and refrain from infringing on their beliefs? Discuss.
7. Compare the strengths and weaknesses of home-based, center-based, and home/center-based programs.

9 Working with Parents of a Child with Disabilities

Jo Spidel
Eugenia H. Berger

All about me may be silence and darkness, yet within me, in the spirit, is music and brightness, and color flashes through all my thoughts.

Helen Keller, 1957

If our American way of life fails the child, it fails us all.

Buck, 1991

In this chapter on working with parents of children with exceptionalities you will find information and procedures that will enable you to do the following:

- Summarize the development of special education in the United States.
- Cite legislation that supports the needs of children with disabilities.
- Develop an Individualized Education Program (IEP) and an Individualized Family Service Plan (IFSP).
- Describe the types of students for whom special education should be provided.
- Cite the parents' rights in school and parent deliberations.
- List the levels-of-service continuum that provides placement options for students with exceptionalities.
- Discuss special concerns that must be met when working with parents of children with disabilities.

Jo Spidel, M.Ed., was a professional advocate for special education for more than 25 years. She taught, presented papers on, and wrote about special education. Certifications included Learning Disabilities, Behavior Disorders, Mental Retardation, and Director of Special Education. Fifteen years were devoted to teaching in public schools, the last position at Northwest High School in Wichita, Kansas. In addition to teaching, she developed and directed an in-house school for adolescent patients in a psychiatric, drug, and alcohol abuse hospital and served as a case manager for Kansas Elks Training Center for the Handicapped.

Parents are the most significant influence in the life of a child with exceptionalities. Children, raised in proximity to parents or surrogate parents for the first five years of their lives, form emotional attachments, and bonding is established. When children begin school, their parents share them with teachers and peer groups. As they grow older, children are also affected by the community, but parents continue to influence and shape their development.

Teachers would be wise to listen to parents to learn about the child's background and to discuss concerns. Teachers will gain respect and cooperation from parents if they are willing to share objectives and goals for the child. If teachers allow the parents to accept some responsibility for the child's learning and share knowledge of teaching principles and methods of tutoring, the effectiveness of the learning experience can be doubled.

This chapter gives parents and regular classroom teachers techniques that can be used effectively with children with exceptionalities. There are many ways to solve problems, communicate with parents, and teach these children. The methods presented here have been proven effective. Take from them those ideas that will work for you.

✑ DEVELOPMENT OF SPECIAL EDUCATION

Many labels have been placed on children with exceptionalities. One need only review titles of institutions for those with mental illness, retardation, or other mental or physical disabilities to find such descriptions as *imbecile, lunatic, crazy,* and *insane.* Such words are indicative of people's perceptions of the problem of exceptionality. Parents and professionals have voiced concern over and made efforts to correct such misconceived labels, most of which have been replaced by the term *exceptional.* The word is used to describe those who are different in some way from the majority of whatever group they belong to—adults, children, or youth. *Special education* refers to instruction specifically designed to meet the special needs of children with exceptionalities (Hallahan & Kauffman, 1997).

Parents need to accept and encourage their children.

At the middle of the 20th century, the term *special education* commonly referred to the education of those who were mentally retarded. Since then, the term has properly become recognized as more open and inconclusive. Children who have certain traits or disabilities or a combination thereof are encompassed by special education: giftedness; mental retardation; physical, neurological, or emotional disabilities; social maladjustment; speech and language impairments; hearing and visual impairments; learning disabilities; and developmental disabilities. It is significant that the condition of the child was once the labeling factor. The trend now is to label according to the educational needs of the child and to refer to the child first and the exceptionality second—"a child with a disability" rather than "a disabled child." "Use of the phrase *with disabilities* signifies that we think of the person first; the disabling condition is only one characteristic of an individual, who has many other characteristics" (Hallahan & Kauffman, 1997, p. 29).

Throughout history there have been many tales of cruel and inhumane treatment of people with exceptionalities. Recalling the story of *The Hunchback of Notre Dame* quickly brings to mind these cruelties. The Spartans were known to force parents to abandon imperfect babies by exposing them to the elements (Greenleaf, 1978). There are instances, in very early history, however, of people who were more humane toward those who were different. Hippocrates, who lived around 400 B.C., believed that emotional problems were caused not by supernatural powers but by natural forces. Plato (375 B.C.) defended those with mental disabilities as not being able to account for their deeds as normal people could. They, therefore, required special judgment for their criminal acts. The temples built by Alexander the Great provided asylum for mentally ill persons. In 90 B.C. Asclepiades made the first attempt at classifying mental illness, advocating humane treatment of those with the illness. In A.D. 100, Aretaeus described mania and melancholia. Acceptance did not arrive immediately, however, and mistreatment of those too "different" persisted.

The period of A.D. 1450 to 1700 was an especially difficult time for those who were mentally ill and people with other exceptionalities. Belief in demonology and superstition resulted in persecution of those who were mentally ill, retarded, or developmentally disabled, and those with any other form of exceptionality. John Locke, concerned about harsh discipline, cultivated the "blank tablet" concept of the newborn's mind to overcome the popular belief that a child was born full of evil ideas. He advocated that children be given empathic understanding (Cook, Tessier, & Armbruster, 1987).

Jean Jacques Rousseau stressed the importance of beginning the child's education at birth. He believed that strong discipline and strict lessons were inappropriate conditions for optimal learning. He advocated that children should be treated with sympathy and compassion as humans in their own right (Cook et al., 1987).

In the late 1700s Jean Marc Gaspard Itard (1775–1838) sought new methods to teach those with mental retardation. He was a physician and an authority on diseases of the ear and education of the deaf. He found a boy in the forest of Auvergne, France, naked and apparently without upbringing, whom he attempted to raise and educate. Influenced by the teachings of Rousseau and Locke, Itard believed that learning came through the senses and that all people could develop the ability to learn if given adequate stimulation. He produced behavioral changes in the boy, Victor, but was unable to teach him to talk or to live independently. Itard believed he was a failure, but his methods were followed, which began a movement in treatment and education that had a profound effect on the development of special education. Edouard Sequin (1811–1880), a student of Itard's, was much impressed by Itard's work. Sequin emigrated to the United States in 1848 and promoted the European style of residential institution (Hallahan & Kauffman, 1997; Reinert, 1987).

The residential schools and asylums that were built in the United States were very much like those in Europe during the 19th century. The first American residential school for those who were deaf was established in 1817 at Hartford, Connecticut, by Thomas Hopkins Gallaudet (1787–1851). Most early schools avoided severely disabled students or those with multiple disabilities and worked only with those who were deaf, blind, or retarded. Those with more serious disabilities were often not eligible for admission to any school. Private schools were often expensive, and state-operated schools were often limited in their facilities (Hallahan & Kauffman, 1990). This left parents with the nearly total responsibility of caring for their children who were exceptional at home.

Perkins School for the Blind, founded in Watertown, Massachusetts, was the first school for people without sight. Samuel G. Howe (1801–1876) proved that those who were blind could be taught when Laura Bridgemen, who was blind and deaf, was educated (Hallahan & Kauffman, 1997). Seeking education for his daughter who was deaf and blind, Helen Keller (1880–1968), Arthur H. Keller consulted many doctors. Dr. Alexander Graham Bell advised him to write to Anagnos, the director of the Perkins Institution. It was from this institution that Anne Mansfield Sullivan came to teach Helen, when Helen was almost seven years of age (Keller, 1991). The fame of the successful life of this person with disabilities did much to persuade parents and professionals that, indeed, persons with disabilities could be educated.

It was not until the beginning of the 20th century that community-based programs for children with exceptionalities began to appear. Gallaudet College, the only college for those who were deaf, started a teacher training program in the 1890s. In 1904, summer training sessions for teachers of children who were retarded began at the Vineland Training School in New Jersey. The community-based programs, however, often became "sunshine" rooms, in which such activities as arts and crafts were pursued, with little attempt to educate the children. In some cases expecta-tions were unrealistic and disappointment in the programs ensued. Few parents or professionals were optimistic about educating those who were exceptional (Hallahan & Kauffman, 1990).

The Binet-Simon Scale of Intelligence, translated and revised by Goddard, was cited in 1904 by the National Education Association as a useful test for children with disabilities, especially those with mental retardation. It was used to determine the degree of retardation and, it was hoped, to guide individualized instruction. Thus began an era of testing that lasted well into the latter part of the 20th century. The validity of testing has been questioned, but it continues to be a tool for determining exceptionality and a factor in placing children in special education programs.

Novelist Pearl S. Buck's frank and open discussion of her child and how she learned to accept her child's disability reached many parents (Buck, 1991). Her urging helped spur the massive movement to provide educational services for people with disabilities.

Educators from Europe who immigrated to the United States during World War II also affected the education of persons with disabilities. Marianne Frostig, a psychiatric social worker and rehabilitation therapist, trained in the United States as a psychologist and worked with children who were retarded, delinquent, or learning disabled (Hallahan & Kauffman, 1990). Alfred A. Strauss and Laura Lehtinen published *Psychopathology and Education of the Brain-Injured Child,* a text that influenced special education.

Others who have contributed to and influenced the special education movement include Samuel A. Kirk (1989), known for his work on the Illinois Test of Psycholinguistic Abilities, and Barbara Bateman, who developed a linguistic approach to learning problems of disabled people.

The Association for Retarded Citizens (ARC), previously the National Association for Retarded Children was chartered in 1950 and became active in influencing state legislatures and Congress. In 1957, along with other organizations, it supported such important legislative action as the federal establishment of national programs in

Can you tell which is the child with disabilities?

the field of special education and governmental support of research and leadership training in mental retardation. In 1963 support was extended to other people with exceptionalities—except for people who were gifted, who did not receive support until 1979. The Bureau of Education for the Handicapped was established in 1966.

Another influence on the special education movement was the rehabilitation of World War II and Korean War veterans. Research into and efforts toward rehabilitation have carried over into the areas of working with people who are exceptional. For example, with expanded programs for mobility and occupational training, it was found that those who were blind or deaf did not have to be isolated and dependent upon fate. This philosophy spread to children's programs, and many schools began integrating children who were blind and deaf into regular classes for part of the

day while separating them for the rest of their studies in a resource room with a special teacher.

The Kennedys, a powerful and influential family with a daughter with a disability, have done much to help the cause of people with disabilities. They established the Joseph P. Kennedy Jr. Foundation—a multimillion-dollar effort in support of those with mental retardation. The foundation's main objectives are "the prevention of mental retardation by identifying its causes and improving means by which society deals with its mentally retarded citizens" (The Foundation Center, 1990). It supports research, special projects, consulting services, technical assistance, conferences, and seminars. Thus, parents, educators, and influential families reinforce the growing concern of all parents of children with disabilities: that their children should have opportunities to develop to their highest potential.

Children with disabilities are served in a variety of ways related to their needs. The Individuals with Disabilities Education Act Amendments of 1997 emphasizes the practice of using the regular classroom for the child with disabilities if it is possible to provide it as the least restrictive environment. The act, known as IDEA 97 or P.L. 105-17, provides education rights for children with disabilities.

❧ LEGISLATION FOR PEOPLE WITH DISABILITIES

Legislation for people with disabilities has been developing since the 1960s. With each new law or amendment to existing legislation, the programs for children and adults with disabilities have become more encompassing. During the 1960s parents organized effective groups that became vocal and attracted enough attention to result in legislation for their children with disabilities. In 1971 the Pennsylvania Association for Retarded Children (PARC) won a landmark case against the Commonwealth of Pennsylvania. It was a decision based on the 14th Amendment, which assures all children, including those with disabilities, the right to a free and appropriate education. Decisions such as this one led to the passage of other important laws.

Vocational Rehabilitation Act of 1973, Section 504

Section 504 of the Vocational Rehabilitation Act of 1973, which relates to nondiscrimination under Federal Grant, P.L. 93-112, required that "no otherwise qualified handicapped individual in the United States shall, solely by reason of his handicap, be excluded from the participation in, be denied the benefits of, or be subjected to discrimination under any program or activity receiving Federal financial assistance" (29 U.S.C. § 794). At the time, Section 504 specifically applied to discrimination in employment. The Rehabilitation Act Amendments of 1974 extended cover-

age to all civil rights, including education, employment, health, welfare, and other social services programs.

Under Section 504, all recipients of Department of Education funds which operate public elementary and secondary programs must provide a ["Free Appropriate Public Education"] to each qualified individual with a disability who is in the recipient's jurisdiction, regardless of the nature or severity of the person's disability.

Since the legislation was passed, there has been confusion about implementation and compliance of the regulations. In the past few years, the Office of Civil Rights has issued policies and rulings which clarify many issues.

A person is considered disabled under the definition of Section 504 if the individual:

1. Has a mental or physical impairment which substantially limits one or more of such person's major life activities;

2. Has a record of such impairments; or

3. Is regarded as having such an impairment.

Major life activities include functions such as caring for one's self, performing manual tasks, walking, seeing, hearing, speaking, breathing, learning, and working. When a condition does not substantially limit a major life activity, the individual does not qualify for services under Section 504.

Much confusion also exists regarding the relationship between Section 504 and special education laws and regulations. It must be emphasized that Section 504 falls under the management of regular education. Students who have disabilities, but who do not qualify for special education, may still be eligible for accommodations under Section 504.

Section 504, which covers a broader range of disabilities than the special education law, also requires public schools to provide students with a free appropriate public education and, in addition, ensures that students with disabilities are afforded an equal opportunity to participate in school programs. A student who is found to be disabled under Section 504 should be served by the resources provided through regular education. The exception to this standard would be a student who has been determined eligible as disabled under the Individuals with Disabilities Education Act (IDEA). Such a student could receive special education services under IDEA and accommodations required under Section 504 of the Rehabilitation Act of 1973.

For students with disabilities, this means that schools may need to make special arrangements so that the students have access to the full range of programs and activities offered. Some students may need access to the curriculum which can be provided by using a computer or an electronic communication device. Other students may need technology to provide physical access to the school facilities.

For example, a student who needs a wheelchair lift on a school bus to get to school must be provided with this technology. Other examples of modification which might be required under Section 504 include installing ramps into buildings and modifying restrooms to provide access for individuals with physical disabilities. (*Families Together,* 1993, p. lv.xxv)

The Americans with Disabilities Act

The Vocational Rehabilitation Act of 1973 was made more comprehensive by the Americans with Disabilities Act of 1990. In it, child care centers were designated as public accommodations which must be available to all who desire to use them. They must serve all children, including those who are disabled, unless (a) the child is a direct threat to self or others, (b) the facility cannot provide child care without it being an undue burden, or (c) the child care center would have to change the services it provides.

The act prohibits discrimination on the basis of disabilities in such areas as employment, transportation, public accommodations, travel, communications, and activities of state and local government. It covers businesses with 15 or more employees, housing providers covered by federal fair housing regulations, public accommodations, transportation companies, those engaged in broadcasting or communications, and state and local governments.

The act specifically defines discrimination, including various types of intentional and unintentional exclusions; segregation, inferior or less effective services, benefits, or activities; architectural, transportation, and communication barriers; failure to make reasonable accommodations; and discriminatory qualifications and performance standards.

Actions that do not constitute discrimination include unequal treatment unrelated to a disability or that result from legitimate application of qualifications and performance standards necessary and substantially related to the ability to perform or participate in the essential components of a job or activity.

The act stipulates that the Architectural and Transportation Barriers Compliance Board will issue minimum accessibility guidelines. Other regulations will be issued by the attorney general, the U.S. Equal Opportunity Commission, the secretary of Housing and Urban Development, the secretary of Transportation, the Federal Communication Commission, and the secretary of Commerce.

The act does not repeal Sections 503 and 504 of the Vocational Rehabilitation Act of 1973, and all regulations issued under those sections remain in full force.

Enforcement procedures include administrative remedies, a private right of action in federal court, monetary damages, injunctive relief, attorney's fees, and cutoff of federal funds (New Jersey State Federation, 1989).

Employers are required to provide reasonable accommodations to enable employees with disabilities to perform essential job functions, unless the employer can prove it will cause undue hardship. This act increases the opportunities for the transition of students from education to the working community.

Education for All Handicapped Children Act of 1975—P.L. 94-142

The most far-reaching and revolutionary legislation related to education was P.L. 94-142, the Education for All Handicapped Children Act of 1975. All people between the ages of 3 and 18 must be provided free and appropriate public education (FAPE). The term *appropriate* means suited to the disability age, maturity, and past achievements of the child and parental expectations. The education must be in a program designed to meet the child's needs in the least restrictive environment (Section 504 Regulations). This means that the child will be placed in the classroom that will benefit the child the most. If the student would benefit more from a regular classroom, the child is to be placed there.

The terms *mainstreaming* and *inclusion* have become synonymous with placing children with disabilities into the regular classroom. However, meeting the child's needs in the *least restrictive environment* can also refer to moving the child with disabilities out of a regular classroom into a resource room or self-contained special education room. The law requires diagnosis and individualization of the educational program. This is encompassed in the Individualized Education Program (IEP) (Section 504 Regulations). Teachers, special teachers, administrators, parents, and others who are concerned with the child's education are involved in the development of the IEP. If appropriate, the child is also included. Finally, the law provides for a hearing that can be initiated by the parents if they do not agree with the diagnosis of the child, the placement, and/or the IEP. This is "due process," and it is the responsibility of the school to inform the parents of their rights.

Amendments of 1983—P.L. 98-199

The Education of the Handicapped Act Amendments of 1983, P.L. 98-199, extended fiscal authorization for federal aid to state and local school systems through 1987; improved reporting and information dissemination requirements; increased assistance to children who are deaf and blind; provided grants for transitional programs; and expanded services for children from birth through five years of age (*Congressional Record*, 1983).

Amendments of 1986: Infants and Toddlers with Disabilities—P.L. 99-457

The Education of the Handicapped Act Amendments of 1986, P.L. 99-457, established statewide,

comprehensive, coordinated, multidisciplinary, interagency programs of early intervention services for infants and toddlers with handicaps and their families (*Congressional Record,* 1986). This law addressed easily recognized needs of the very young with disabilities.

However, there are many conditions that are not immediately recognized, so services early in life may be delayed for those with genetic conditions associated with mental retardation, congenital syndromes associated with delays in development, sensory impairments, metabolic disorders, prenatal infections (AIDS, syphilis, cytomegalic inclusion disease), and low birth weight. There are also concerns for infants whose parents are developmentally delayed, have severe emotional disturbances, or are 15 years or younger.

Parents or caretakers may have difficulty finding the programs and services they need to help them care for these young children. These services are provided through the Department of Education in each state, so the first contact should be through the local school. Another group that may be able to offer information about services for rural families is:

American Council on Rural Special Education (ACRES)
Kansas State University
2323 Anderson Avenue, Suite 226
Manhattan, Kansas
785-53-ACRES
http://www.ksu.edu/acres/

ACRES' goals foster quality services and education for individuals with disabilities who live in rural America.

P.L. 99-457 provided for public supervision at no cost (except where federal and state laws allow), meeting the needs of handicapped infants and toddlers, family training, counseling, special instruction, physical therapy, stimulation therapy, case management, diagnosis-qualified personnel, and conformation with the Individualized Family Service Plan.

Individuals with Disabilities Education Act: IDEA—P.L. 101-476

This federal law—formerly the Education for All Handicapped Children Act, P.L. 94-142—mandated that all children receive an education regardless of the severity of their disability.

1. The term *handicapped child* was changed to the *child with disabilities* because it was recognized that the children are handicapped by the limitations placed on them rather than by their abilities. The child has a disability, which may not be a handicap, depending on the situation.

2. All children with disabilities will have an education that is individualized to meet their needs. This is written in an Individualized Education Program (IEP) for children 3 to 21, and in an Individualized Family Service Plan (IFSP) for infants and toddlers (Utah Parent Center, 1997).

3. "A child with a disability should receive education in an environment that promotes interaction with nondisabled peers to the maximum extent appropriate to that student's need" (Utah Parent Center, 1997, p. 11).

4. "Parents are part of the team to help make decisions and decide on the child's education program" (Utah Parent Center, 1997, p. 11).

IDEA (P.L. 101-476) mandated that all children up to 21 years old receive an education regardless of the severity of their disability. IDEA was divided into nine parts. Part B spoke to the students, preschool and school-aged—3 through 21. Part H (changed to Part C in IDEA 97) related to the education of infants and toddlers—birth to age 3. Although alike in many ways, the differences include

IDEA requires that special education be provided to all who need it.

"zero reject" in Part B. It required that there be no exclusion of children aged 3 through 21, and public school systems are responsible for including all these children in an educational program, regardless of the extent or the kind of disability.

Part H for infants gave discretion to the states to develop a program that best serves the needs of infants and toddlers. Each state determines which agency can work most effectively with parents and their infants and toddlers. States utilize different agencies such as the Departments of Education, or Health and Human Services.

IFSP

In the birth-to-three program, the student and the family have an Individualized Family Service Plan (IFSP) written to serve both student and family. "One of the requirements for the IFSP is to document family concerns, resources, and priorities and to provide the family with services, consistent with members' preferences, so the family can increase its capacity to meet the child's special needs" (Turnbull & Turnbull, 1997, p. 24).

IEP

From ages 3 through 21, the student has an Individualized Education Program (IEP). The school district is responsible for serving or seeing that children aged three to five are served in preschools. The primary focus of the IEP is the education of the student, although the family may receive some services. The outline for the IEP review meeting is illustrated in Figure 9.1.

✍ INDIVIDUALS WITH DISABILITIES EDUCATION ACT AMENDMENTS OF 1997—P.L. 105-17

An amended IDEA was reauthorized in June 1997 and went into effect on July 1, 1998. IDEA 97 was organized into four parts: (A) general provisions; (B) school-aged and preschool—3- to 5-year-olds; (C) infants and toddlers, birth through 2; and (D) support. In 2002, a portion of IDEA, Parts C and D, was up for reauthorization. Part B has permanent authorization.

Recommendations for Reauthorization

In the reauthorization by Congress, the Council for Exceptional Children felt the following issues should be addressed:

1. Amount of paperwork required by special education teachers

2. Need for an increase of federal expenditures per pupil from the current 17 percent to 40 percent for full funding for B,C, and D, with permanent funding for C, infants and toddlers

3. Discipline—if a child with disabilities violates school discipline code not related to the disability, the discipline should be applied consistent with the discipline for a child without disabilities, but no child should be denied appropriate education if discipline has a suspension of more than 10 days or expulsion

4. An increase in qualified special education teachers so children are taught by certified special education teachers (Council for Exceptional Children, 2002)

The National Council on Disability (NCD) had similar recommendations, but focused more on monitoring and enforcement. In its paper *Individuals with Disabilities Education Act: Where Do We Stand,* 2002, the NCL identified four critical areas:

1. *Monitoring and enforcement.* The discussion of monitoring and enforcement included standards, technical assistance, accountability and enforcement.

2. *Funding.* NCD recommended that "Congress adopt mandatory funding in keeping with the original commitment from the Federal Government to fund 40 percent of the per pupil cost of special education" (p. 7).

3. *Discipline.* It was recommended that "current discipline requirements be carefully examined and simplified where possible, without eliminating any protections for students with disabilities. No cessation must remain an absolute requirement by law" (p. 8).

Outline for an IEP Review Meeting

I. Introductions

Introduce the individuals present.

II. Purpose of the Meeting

State the purpose of the meeting and indicate to everyone, including the parent(s), that each person is a part of the IEP team and all exchanges of ideas, questions, and comments are welcome.

III. Process for the Meeting

Explain the process that will be used for reaching consensus and closure on issues.

IV. IEP

A. Participants

Record the names of participants indicating their attendance at the meeting. If a student who is age 14 or older does not attend, indicate steps taken to determine student's preferences and interests.

B. Present Level of Educational Performance and Needs

For a student who is age 14 or older, identify the Post School Transition Outcome in each of the designated areas. Consider the student's strengths and needs in relation to the identified transition outcomes. Identify the child's/student's strengths and prioritized needs in each functioning area on the basis of the results of the assessments (cognitive, social/emotional/adaptive behavior, physical, sensorimotor, communicative, educational, and transition/life skills/career). Consider the critical academic, key component, and access skills needed for success within the general curriculum. In the case of a child who is an English Language Learner (Limited English Proficient), consider the language needs of the child, as such needs relate to his/her IEP. List any additional concerns of the parent(s) for enhancing the child's/student's education.

C. Summary of Transition Services (for students 14 and older)

Refer to the student's identified post school transition outcomes. Identify the projected date of graduation or program completion and the document the student is expected to receive at completion. Develop a statement, or a list, of the student's course of study related to the identified transition outcomes. Include required courses, elective, and modified or specially designed courses and experiences. Determine needed transition services and/or interagency linkages for each area as appropriate for the student's needs. (Required for students beginning at age 16). If the student will turn 20 during this IEP period, inform parent(s) and student of any transfer of rights at Age of Majority/Consent and document.

D. Goals and Objectives

1. With the exception of the initial IEP, review and document progress toward completion of the previous goals and objectives.
2. Identify annual goals to be measured by achievement of objectives/benchmarks. Goal(s) should reflect standards/key components/access skills.
3. Identify the baseline for each short-term instructional objective/benchmark.
4. Identify objective criteria, evaluation procedures and schedules for determining whether each short-term instructional objective/benchmark has been accomplished.

E. Early Childhood Transition Plan

Complete the Early Childhood Transition Plan if the child is age three to six.

FIGURE 9.1 Outline for an IEP review meeting.

F. Special Education and Related Services
1. Identify the specific special education and related services which will be provided and the amount of each service.
2. Identify the projected starting date and anticipated duration of services.
3. Describe how parent(s) will be informed of the child's/student's progress toward annual goals and objectives.
4. Determine if the child/student is eligible for services beyond the regular school year (ESY)
5. Determine if the child/student requires special transportation.
6. Determine if the child/student requires a communication plan. (Required for child/student with hearing disabilities.)
7. Determine if the child/student requires a literacy modality plan. (Required for child/student with vision disabilities.)
8. Determine if the child/student requires a behavior plan.
9. Determine if the child/student requires assistive technology services and/or devices.
10. Determine if any adaptations, modifications, or accommodations are necessary for the child/student to participate in the general education curriculum, including the language needs of the child/student.
11. Determine the necessary accommodations and modifications in the administration of the state and district assessments for the child/student to participate. If they will not participate, describe the compelling reason(s). Describe the expanded/alternate assessment system that will be used. (Does not apply to early childhood).

G. Recommended Placement in the Least Restrictive Environment
Determine the settings in which special education and related services will be provided.

H. Consent for Placement
If it is the initial meeting to determine eligibility, obtain the signature(s) of the parent(s) for placement of their child in special education.

Give the Parent(s) a Copy of the IEP.

FIGURE 9.1   *continued*

4. *Overrepresentation.*   Overrepresentation is based on concerns about students from diverse backgrounds being placed incorrectly in special education. "NCD recommends that the law support the Office of Special Education and Rehabilitative Services in the Department of Education to expand its initiatives to serve non-English speaking groups and/or people with limited English proficiency and create culturally appropriate training materials" (p. 8).

Development of the Individualized Education Program (IEP)

The development of an Individualized Education Program illustrates the goals that schools and parents want for their children with disabilities. Determination of the child's eligibility and disability is illustrated in Figures 9.2A and 9.2B.

All children with disabilities receiving any type of special education services must have an Individualized Family Service Plan (birth to three years of age)

IEP
Eligibility and Disability — Page 1

Date of Meeting

_____   _____   _____
Legal Name of Child/Student   Child/Student ID   Date of Birth

Determination of Eligibility and Disability

Have sufficient and appropriate evaluations been completed, documented, and considered to determine the child's /student's current level of functioning, achievement performance, and educational needs? ☐ Yes ☐ No

If no, obtain additional information and reconvene the meeting.

Can the child/student receive reasonable educational benefit from general education alone? ☐ Yes ☐ No

Is the child's/student's performance due to the lack of instruction in reading or math? ☐ Yes ☐ No

For the child/student whose primary language is other than English, is limited English acquisition the primary cause of the child's/student's learning problems? ☐ Yes ☐ No

If any response is yes, terminate the meeting.

If no, does the child/student have a disability as defined in the State Rules for the Administration of the Exceptional Children's Education Act? ☐ Yes ☐ No

If no, complete recommendations for general education and terminate the meeting.

If the child/student has a disability, the disability is: *(If more than one disability is determined, the primary disability should be identified with a "1," the secondary disability with a "2.")*

☐ Significant Limited Capacity

☐ Significant Identifiable Emotional Disability

☐ Perceptual or Communicative Disability

☐ Hearing Disability (requires communication plan)

☐ Vision Disability (requires literacy plan)

☐ Speech/Language Disability

☐ Preschool Child with a Disability

Physical Disability:

☐ Traumatic Brain Injury

☐ Autism

☐ Other Physical Disability

Multiple Disabilities:

☐ Deaf-Blind

☐ Multiple Disabilities with Cognitive Impairment

Complete the appropriate checklist for determination of each disability selected.

REQUIRED FOR ELIGIBILITY MEETING ONLY.

FIGURE 9.2A Determination of eligibility and disability.

Source: From *Recommended Standard Forms for Colorado's Special Education Process.* Denver, CO: Colorado Department of Education.

IEP
Eligibility and Disability

Date of Meeting

_____   _____   _____
Legal Name of Child/Student   Child/Student ID   Date of Birth

Determination of Disability

DEFINITION: A preschool child with a disability shall be three through five years of age and shall, by reason of one or more of the following conditions, be unable to receive reasonable benefit from general education: *physical impairment, vision impairment, hearing impairment, significant limited intellectual capacity, emotional disability, perceptual or communicative disability, or speech/language disability.*

Criteria for a preschool child being unable to receive reasonable benefit from general education shall be:

☐ A substantial discrepancy between the child's performance and behavior as compared to children of a comparable age.

☐ or is eligible by variance from standard criteria according to the following rationale:

_____

_____

_____

_____

_____

_____

_____

_____

_____

NOTE: For a preschool child who qualifies according to one of the categorical conditions listed in this definition, complete the identification form for the appropriate disability.

A child aged three through five who would otherwise qualify according to one or more of the categorical conditions, but for whom the category cannot be appropriately determined may qualify for preschool special education if multiple sources of information are utilized and if such child meets one or more of the following criteria: *(check those that apply)*

☐ A child who ranks in the seventh percentile or below on a valid standardized instrument, or the technical equivalent, in standard scores (76 if the mean is 100 and the standard deviation is 16), or standard deviations (1.5 standard deviations below the mean) in one or more of the following areas of development: cognition, communication, physical, and/or psychosocial.

☐ A child with an identifiable condition known through empirical data to be associated with significant delays in development.

☐ In extraordinary cases when a standardized score cannot be determined, a child may be determined disabled based on the informed opinion of the evaluation team, which includes the parent(s), and with documentation of the rationale for the inability to obtain a standardized score.

FIGURE 9.2B   Determination of disability.

| Legal Name of Child/Student | Child/Student ID | DOB | Date of Meeting |

Recommended Placement in the Least Restrictive Environment
(Special Education Instructional Setting)

Check all settings which were considered (first column) and all settings in which
special education and related services will be provided (second column)

Considered   **Selected**

☐ Early Childhood Integrated Setting
    (designed primarily for children without disabilities)   ☐

☐ Early Childhood Special Education Setting
    (designed primarily for children with disabilities, and housed in   ☐
    regular school buildings or other community-based settings)

☐ Multiple Settings   ☐

☐ Home   ☐

☐ Itinerant Services Outside the Home   ☐

☐ Separate School
    (public or private day schools designed specifically for children   ☐
    with disabilities)

☐ Residential Facility
    (residential schools, or residential medical facilities on an   ☐
    in-patient basis)

<u>Of those special education instructional settings selected,
place an asterisk (*) by the primary setting.</u>

Provide justification for placement decision:

FIGURE 9.2C Recommended placement.

or an Individualized Education Program (3 through 21) prepared especially for them. It must be the product of the joint efforts of members of a child study team, which must include items (i) through (v) of the following:

MEMBERS OF THE IEP TEAM

(i) parents of the child with a disability;

(ii) at least one regular education teacher of the child if the child is participating in the regular classroom environment;

(iii) at least one special education teacher, or where appropriate, at least one special education provider of such child;

(iv) a representative of the local educational agency who is (I) qualified to provide, or supervise the provision of, specially designed instruction to meet the unique needs of children with disabilities; (II) knowledgeable about the general curriculum; and (III) knowledgeable about the availability of resources of the local education agency;

(v) an individual who can interpret the instructional implications of evaluation results, who may be a member of the team described in clauses ii through vi;

(vi) at the discretion of the parent or the agency, other individuals who have knowledge or special expertise regarding the child, including related services personnel as appropriate; and

(vii) whenever appropriate, the child with the disability. ([Section 614(d) (1)(B)] as cited in National Information Center for Children and Youth with Disabilities [NICHYC], 1998)

→ The Individualized Education Program (IEP) as well as the Individualized Family Service Plan (IFSP) should accomplish the following:

• The IEP meeting serves as a communication vehicle between parents and school personnel, and enables them, as equal participants, to jointly decide what the child's needs are, what services will be provided to meet those needs, and what the anticipated outcomes may be.

• The IEP process provides an opportunity for resolving any differences between parents and school personnel concerning the special education needs of a child with a disability; first, through the IEP meeting, and second, if necessary, through the procedural protections that are available to the parents.

• The IEP sets forth in writing a commitment of resources necessary to enable a child with a disability to receive needed special education and related services.

• The IEP is a management tool to help ensure that each child with a disability is provided special education and related services appropriate to the child's special learning needs.

• The IEP is a compliance and monitoring document that may be used by authorized monitoring personnel from each governmental level to determine whether a child with a disability is actually receiving the free appropriate public education agreed to by the parents and the school.

• The IEP serves as an evaluation device for use in determining the extent of the child's progress toward meeting the projected outcomes. (Utah Parent Center, 1997, pp. 26–27)

Many requirements must be met when dealing with the child with disabilities. The IEP should be reviewed periodically, but not less than annually, to determine if progress toward the goals is advancing as expected and to reevaluate and assess the program. Administrators and teachers must be aware of all procedures that the schools are responsible for administering. These procedures include the following types of subjects: definitions, opportunity to examine records, independent educational evaluation, prior notice, parent consent, procedures when parent refuses consent, content of notice, formal complaint resolution, impartial due-process hearing, reasonable attorney's fees, impartial hearing officer, appointment of hearing officer, access rights, records, children's rights, and more.

Rights and Responsibilities for Parents—IDEA 97

IDEA 97 addressed the participation of parents in the development of their child's program. It states

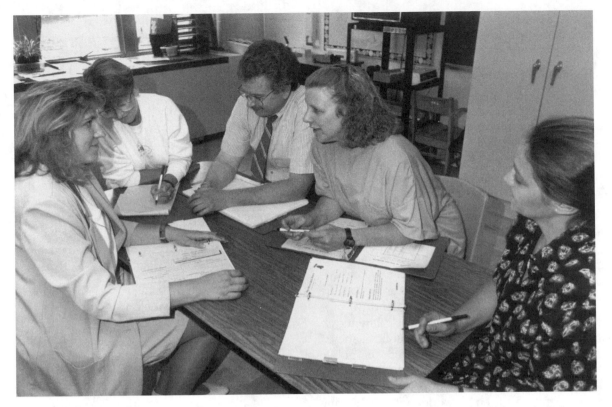

An IEP or IFSP meeting is a time to discuss the child's plan. Whenever feasible, the child should be included.

that the Local Education Agency (LEA) or the State Education Agency (SEA) will ensure that parents are members of any group that makes decisions on the educational placement of their child. Parents can examine all records and participate in meetings regarding the evaluations, placement, and the free and appropriate public education that the child will receive. Specifications include:

- Public agencies must notify parents when the agencies propose or refuse to initiate or change the identification, evaluation, or educational placement of the child or the provision of free appropriate public education (FAPE) to the child.

- Parents have the right to inspect and review all records relating to their child that a public agency collects, maintains, or uses regarding the identification, evaluation, or educational placement of the child or the provision of FAPE to the child.

- Parental consent is required before a child may be evaluated for the first time.

- Parents have the right to obtain an independent educational evaluation (IEE) of their child.

- Parental consent is required for a child's initial special education placement.

- Parents have the right to challenge or appeal any decision related to the identification, evaluation, or educational placement of their child or the provision of FAPE to their child. (PEAK Parent Center, 1997)

Rights and Responsibilities Added in 1997

IDEA 97 added rights that require more parent involvement in the decision-making process. Additional responsibilities require parents to inform the public agency of placement change and request for due process. These rights and responsibilities include (1) input during evaluation; (2) participation in the group that makes decisions regarding eligibility; (3) decision making regarding their child's educational placement; (4) informed consent for their child to be reevaluated; (5) participation in all meetings with regard to identification, evaluation, and educational placement of their child as well as the provision of FAPE for their child; and (6) progress reports and revisions of the IEP. Parents are responsible for (1) notifying the public agency if they plan to remove their child from the public agency for placement in a private school at public expense, and (2) notifying the public agency if they intend to request a due-process hearing (PEAK Parent Center, 1997).

Notification.   There are also procedural safeguards that require written notification to parents prior to any proposed action. The notification must be in the parents' native language or preferred mode of communication—for example, Braille or sign language. There is protection of the child's rights when parents cannot be located.

Mediation.   If disagreements arise, a mediation system employing a qualified, impartial mediator must be available. Parents may be required to attend a mediation meeting.

FAPE.   Free appropriate public education (FAPE) is available to all children, including those who have been expelled or suspended, but it is not available to youth incarcerated in adult correctional facilities unless they have been previously identified as needing special education.

Developmental Delay.   The developmental delay category, previously used for placement of children three to five years old, was recognized as appropriate for those three to nine and was therefore extended to cover that age group.

Charter Schools.   Charter schools, new since the original IDEA, were included in the provisions. They must follow the same guidelines as other publicly funded schools.

Discipline

IDEA 97 maintains the "stay-put" provision of IDEA, but there was a clarification stating that schools can take disciplinary action, including changing the child's placement to an appropriate interim alternative educational setting or suspending the child from school. Following are disciplinary actions for certain offenses.

1. If a child with a disability brings a weapon to school or to a school function, the child may have alternate placement or suspension for the same amount of time that a child without a disability would have been subject to in a disciplinary action, but not more than 45 calendar days.

2. If a child with a disability knowingly possesses or uses illegal drugs or sells or solicits the sale of a controlled substance at school or at a school function, the child may be subject to discipline the same as the child who brings a weapon to school.

3. If a child with a disability violates a school rule other than the previous two, the child would be disciplined the same as a child without a disability, but for no longer than 10 days.

The interim, alternative educational setting is determined by the IEP team and must allow the student to continue in the general curriculum. No later than 10 days after the disciplinary action, the local educational agency must develop an assessment plan to address the behavior if a behavioral intervention plan had not already been drawn up. If the child already has a behavioral intervention plan, the IEP team will meet to review and modify the plan as needed (National Information Center for Children and Youth with Disabilities [NICHCY], 1998).

IDEA 97: Placement—Inclusion—Least Restrictive

IDEA 97 continues the expectation that a general education classroom be considered first when determining a child's placement; however, the term *inclusion* was not used in IDEA 97. To ensure that programs serve children with disabilities consistent with this consideration, IDEA 97:

- reinforces the expectation of the former IDEA that the general education classroom be considered first for the student's placement along with the aids and supports that could assist the student to be successful there.

- specifies that the assessment yield information that will enable the student to be involved in and progress in the general curriculum or, for preschool children, to participate in appropriate activities.

- requires that IEPs must now state how the student's disability affects involvement and progress in the general curriculum (in the discussion of "present level of educational performance").

- requires that annual, measurable goals, including benchmarks/objectives, be related to helping the child be involved and progress in the general curriculum. [See Figures 9.3A and 9.3B.]

- requires the IEP to state the "supplementary aids and services" needed by the student and the "program modifications or supports for school personnel" so that the student can be involved and progress in the general curriculum and participate in extracurricular and other nonacademic activities.

- requires IEP teams to consider positive behavioral intervention strategies and supports for students whose behavior impedes their own learning or that of others.

- requires that the IEP include an "explanation of the extent, if any, to which the child will not participate with nondisabled children in regular class" and in extracurricular and nonacademic activities.

- adds the regular education teacher to the IEP team as a required member.

- requires that the IEP state how the parents will be regularly informed of the student's progress toward the annual goals (as often as parents of other students receive progress reports).

- allows local districts to use IDEA funds to support students in general education classrooms without concern that students without disabilities might also benefit. (PEAK Parent Center, 1997)

≈≈ POSITIVE COLLABORATION OF PARENTS AND SCHOOL

Through collaborating with one another, parents and school professionals have the opportunity to:

- secure a full understanding of the student's needs and strengths

- take into account the observations of parents and others (including educators) as they develop that understanding

- ensure that the evaluation is useful to and used by the student's teachers and other involved professionals and by the family as they work together to provide a free appropriate public education. (Turnbull & Turnbull, 1997, p. 21)

≈≈ STUDENTS WHO ARE GIFTED AND TALENTED

Students who are gifted and talented have the potential for superior performance. This can include intellectual achievement, special aptitudes, or creative thinking and performing abilities.

The Gifted and Talented Children's Education Act, P.L. 95-561, gave states and local education agencies financial incentives to identify and educate students who are gifted and talented, provide inservice training, and conduct research (Heward & Orlansky, 1988). None of the federal legislation has mandated educational opportunities for children who are gifted. Approximately 30 states mandate educational opportunities for youngsters who are gifted, and other states have legislation

Administrative Unit Name	Date of Meeting

Legal Name of Child/Student	Child/Student ID	Date of Birth

INDIVIDUALIZED EDUCATION PROGRAM (IEP)

TYPE OF MEETING *(check one box only)*

Eligibility Meeting   **IEP Review**

☐ Initial   ☐ Triennial   ☐ Review*   ☐ Annual   ☐ Additional Meeting*

* Required for change in disability, significant change
in placement, or exit

Specify purpose: _____

DATES OF MEETINGS *(complete both dates)*

Date of Next Eligibility meeting _____   Date of Next IEP Review Meeting _____
    (on or before)   *(month/day/year)*   (on or before)   *(month/day/year)*

CHILD/STUDENT AND FAMILY INFORMATION	**Prior to Meeting**	**After Meeting**
District of Residence (if BOCS)		
Home School		
School of Attendance		
Unit/Facility of Attendance (if out-of-district)		
Primary Disability, if Any *(from IEP – Eligibility, Page 1)*		
Secondary Disability, if Any *(from IEP – Eligibility, Page 1)*		
Primary Special Education Instruction Setting *(from IEP – Setting, Page 1)*		

Grade _____ Age _____ Gender: Male _____ Female _____

Race/Ethnicity: American Indian _____ Hispanic _____ Asian _____ White _____ Black _____

Primary Language/Mode of Communication in the Home _____
    Name of Questionnaire/Test Used _____ Date _____

Primary Language/Mode of Communication of the Child/Student _____

If the primary language is other than English, then the child's/student's English language proficiency must have been evaluated prior to the special education referral. It is recommended to also evaluate the child's/student's proficiency in his/her primary language.

Name of Instrument _____ Date _____

Proficiency Level	English	Primary Language
Listening (all grades)		
Speaking (all grades)		
Reading (from 2nd grade on)		
Writing (from 2nd grade on)		
Child's/Student's Parent(s)		

Address _____

Telephone Numbers _____
      Home   Work   Home   Work

Is there an educational surrogate parent?   ☐ Yes   ☐ No

REQUIRED FOR ALL MEETINGS.   MAY BE COMPLETED PRIOR TO THE MEETING.

FIGURE 9.3A Individualized Education Program (IEP).

Source: From *Recommended Standard Forms for Colorado's Special Eductaion Process*. Denver, CO: Colorado Department of Education.

Date of Meeting

Legal Name of Child/Student	Child/Student ID	Date of Birth

Goals and Objectives

With the exception of the initial IEP, the committee must review and document progress toward completion of the child's/student's previous goals and objectives prior to the development of new goals and objectives.

Annual Goal to be Measured by Achievement of Benchmarks (#): (Write goals about standards/key components/access skills.)

_____

_____

Short-term Instructional Objectives/Benchmarks	Criteria and Evaluation Procedures to be Used (i.e., formal/informal measures, observations, recorded data, work samples, etc.)	Schedule for Achievement of Objective		Progress (Not Evident, Not Yet Proficient, Proficient, or Advanced) *		Does objective need to be carried over to new IEP, modified, or is it no longer appropriate? (C, M, or N/A)
		Beginning Date	Target Completion Date	Date	Proficiency	
(#)						
Baseline:						
(#)						
Baseline:						
(#)						
Baseline:						

* Not Evident: Skill/behavior rarely or never is demonstrated, even with sufficient prompts or cues.
Not Yet Proficient: Skill/behavior is demonstrated inconsistently, even with frequent prompts or cues.
Proficient: Skill/behavior is demonstrated consistently over time with only occasional prompts or cues.
Advanced: Skill/behavior is generalized (demonstrated in different settings or environments) and transferable (adapted to different contexts) with no prompts or cues.

GOALS AND OBJECTIVES REQUIRED FOR ALL CHILDREN/STUDENTS FOR ALL MEETINGS.
MUST USE GOALS AND OBJECTIVES FOR TRANSITION — PAGES 1A–D.
SHOULD COMPLETE THE EARLY CHILDHOOD TRANSITION PLAN IN ADDITION TO THIS PAGE FOR PRESCHOOL.

FIGURE 9.3B Goals and objectives.

permitting establishment of such classes (Karnes & Marquardt, 1997).

The Jacob K. Javits Gifted and Talented Students Education Act of 1988 was followed by the Jacob K. Javits Gifted and Talented Education Act of 1992. In 1998 the Javits Act was the only federal funding earmarked for gifted education. Funding not earmarked for gifted education may be used to benefit students who are gifted. In funding for children with disabilities, meeting the child's needs is required, but children with gifts and talents do not have legislation that requires support. The purpose of the federal acts is to encourage rich education for gifted and talented students and to have special programs broadened and expanded into the regular classroom (Boren, 1994).

✆ DEFINITIONS OF DISABILITIES OR EXCEPTIONALITIES

The following descriptions of children with exceptionalities as defined in IDEA (34 Code of Federal Regulations, Section 300.7) clarify those who need special programs. If a student in a classroom fits into any of the following categories, special services should be provided.

1. Autism—A developmental disability significantly affecting verbal and nonverbal communication and social interaction, generally evident before age 3, that adversely affects educational performance.

2. Deafness—A hearing impairment so severe that a child is impaired in processing linguistic information through hearing, with or without amplification, which adversely affects educational performance.

3. Deafness-Blindness—Simultaneous hearing and visual impairments, the combination of which causes such severe communication and other developmental and education problems that a child cannot be accommodated in special education programs solely for children who are deaf or for children who are blind.

4. Hearing Impairment—An impairment in hearing, whether permanent or fluctuating, that adversely affects a child's educational perform-

ance but is not included under the definition of "deafness."

5. Mental Retardation—Significantly subaverage general intellectual functioning existing concurrently with deficits in adaptive behavior and manifested during the developmental period, which adversely affects a child's educational performance.

6. Multiple Disabilities—Simultaneous impairments (such as mental retardation and blindness or mental retardation and orthopedic impairment), the combination of which causes such severe educational problems that the child cannot be accommodated in a special education program solely for one of the impairments. The term does not include children with deafness-blindness.

7. Orthopedic Impairment—A severe orthopedic impairment that adversely affects a child's educational performance. The term includes impairments caused by a congenital anomaly (e.g., clubfoot or absence of a limb), impairments caused by disease (e.g., poliomyelitis or bone tuberculosis), and impairments from other causes (e.g., cerebral palsy, amputations, or fractures or burns that cause contractures).

8. Other Health Impairment—Having limited strength, vitality, or alertness, due to chronic or acute health problems—such as a heart condition, tuberculosis, rheumatic fever, nephritis, asthma, sickle cell anemia, hemophilia, epilepsy, lead poisoning, leukemia, or diabetes—that adversely affects a child's educational performance. According to the Office of Special Education and Rehabilitative Services' clarification statement of September 16, 1991, eligible children with Attention Deficit Disorder may also be classified under "other health impairment."

9. Emotional Disturbance

    a. A condition exhibiting one or more of the following characteristics over a long period of time and to a marked degree and that adversely affects educational performance: (1) an inability to learn that cannot be explained by intellectual, sensory, or health factors; (2) an inability to build or maintain satisfactory interpersonal relationships with peers and teachers; (3) inappropriate types of behavior or feelings under normal circumstances; (4) a general pervasive mood of unhappiness or depression; or (5) a tendency to develop physical symptoms or fears associated with personal or school problems.

b. The term includes children who have schizophrenia. The term does not include children who are socially maladjusted, unless it is determined that they have an emotional disturbance.

10. Specific Learning Disabilities—A disorder in one or more of the basic psychological processes involved in understanding or in using language, spoken or written, that may manifest itself in an imperfect ability to listen, think, speak, read, write, spell, or to do mathematical calculations. The term includes such conditions as perceptual disabilities, brain injury, minimal brain dysfunction, dyslexia, and developmental aphasia. The term does not include children who have learning problems that are primarily the result of visual, hearing, or motor disabilities, of mental retardation, of emotional disturbance, or of environmental, cultural, or economic disadvantage (NICHCY, 2002b).

11. Speech or Language Impairment—A communication disorder, such as stuttering, impaired articulation, a language impairment, or a voice impairment, that adversely affects a child's educational performance.

12. Traumatic Brain Injury—An acquired injury to the brain caused by an external physical force, resulting in total or partial functional disability or psychosocial impairment, or both, that adversely affects educational performance. The term does not include brain injuries that are congenital or degenerative, nor does it include brain injuries induced by birth trauma.

13. Visual Impairment, Including Blindness—A visual impairment that, even with correction, adversely affects a child's educational performance. The term includes both children with partial sight and those who are completely blind (NICHCY, 1997).

Visually impaired children and youth shall be identified as those whose limited vision interferes with their education and/or developmental progress. Two divisions for the visually impaired shall be made:

"Partially Sighted" indicates some type of visual problem has resulted in a need for special education;

"Low vision" generally refers to a severe visual impairment, not necessarily limited to distance vision. Low vision applies to all individuals with sight who are unable to read the newspaper at a normal viewing distance, even with the aid of eyeglasses or contact lenses. They use a combination of vision and other sense to learn, although they may require adaptations in lighting or the size of print, and sometimes, braille;

"Legally blind" indicates that a person has less than 20/2000 vision in the better eye or a very limited field of vision (20 degrees at its widest point); and

Totally blind students learn via braille or other non-visual media.

Visual impairment is the consequence of a functional loss of vision, rather than the eye disorder itself. Eye disorders which can lead to visual impairments can include retinal degeneration, albinism, cataracts, glaucoma, muscular problems that result in visual disturbances, corneal disorders, diabetic retinopathy, congenital disorders, and infection.

Attention-Deficit Disorder—Attention-Deficit/Hyperactivity Disorder

A policy developed in the 1990s resulted in children with attention-deficit disorder (ADD) or attention-deficit/hyperactivity disorder (AD/HD) being classified under Other Health Impairment, making them eligible to receive special education and related services. Other Health Impairment is defined as "having limited strength, vitality, or alertness, including a heightened alertness to environmental stimuli, that results in limited alertness with respect to the educational environment, that is due to chronic or acute health problems such as asthma, attention deficit disorder or attention deficit hyperactivity disorder, diabetes, epilepsy, a heart condition, hemophilia, lead poisoning, leukemia nephritis, rheumatic fever, and sickle cell anemia; and adversely affects a child's educational performance" (NICHCY, 2001). A federal policy issued by the Office of Special Education and Rehabilitative Services, U.S. Department of Education, September 16, 1991, specified that a child no longer needs to be labeled as having a specific learning disability or as being seriously emotionally disturbed to receive special education services. Under the policy, a child who is identified as having ADD or AD/HD to the extent that it adversely affects education "performance" can now be served.

Symptoms that are a sign of AD/HD are (a) problems with paying attention, (b) being very active (called hyperactivity), and (c) acting before thinking (called impulsivity). Three types of AD/HD are

- inattentive type, where the person cannot seem to focus on a task or activity
- hyperactive-impulsive type, where the person is very active and often acts without thinking
- combined type, where the person is inattentive, impulsive, and too active

A Brief Look at Autism, Learning Disabilities, and Mental Retardation

Autism

Characteristics.   Children will vary in intelligence, abilities, and behaviors. Some do not speak, whereas others have limited language that may include repeated phrases. Autistic children have difficulty with abstract concepts, have a limited range of interests, a small range of topics, and commonly have unusual responses to sensory information such as lights, loud noises, and some textures of food or fabrics. The NICHCY (2001) described the following characteristics of autism:

- Communication problems (e.g., using and understanding language)
- Difficulty in relating to people, objects, and events
- Unusual play with toys and other objects
- Difficulty with changes in routine or familiar surroundings

- Repetitive body movements or behavior patterns. (p. 2)

Recommendations.   The autistic child responds best in a predictable and consistent program.

> Behavior and communication problems that interfere with learning sometimes require the assistance of a knowledgeable professional in the autism field who develops and helps to implement a plan which can be carried out at home and school.... Students learn better and are less confused when information is presented visually as well as verbally. Interaction with nondisabled peers is also important, for these students provide models of appropriate language, social, and behavior skills. To overcome frequent problems in generalizing skills learned at school it is very important to develop programs with parents, so that programs of learning activities, approaches, and experiences can be carried over into the home and community. (NICHCY, 2001, p. 2)

Learning Disabilities

Characteristics

1.   Children with learning disabilities are primarily intact children. They are not primarily visually impaired, hearing impaired, environmentally disadvantaged, mentally retarded, or emotionally disturbed. In spite of the fact that these children have adequate intelligence, adequate sensory processes, and adequate emotional stability, they do not learn without special assistance.

2.   Children with learning disabilities show wide discrepancies of intra-individual differences in a profile of their development. This is often shown by marked discrepancies in one or more of the specific areas of academic learning or a serious lack of language development or language facility. These disabilities may affect the child's behavior in such areas as thinking, conceptualization, memory, language, perception, reading, writing, spelling, or arithmetic.

3.   The concept of deviation of a child with learning disabities implies that the child deviates so markedly from the norm of the child's group as to require specialized instruction. Such special-

ized instruction required for these children may be of value to other children. However, the population to be served with special education funds authorized for children does not include children with learning problems that are the result of poor instruction or economic or cultural deprivation. (Kearns, 1980)

Signs of Learning Disabilities.   Learning disabilities are generally recognized when the child enters school and specific learning tasks are expected. Watch for the difference between what a child accomplishes in school and what that child should be able to do given the child's intellect and ability. There is no one sign that says that the child has a learning disability.

Silver and Hagin (2002) describe and discuss learning disorders, research, and the various curriculum designs used to help students develop. Planning for students requires an understanding of the factors that affect them including cognitive, emotional, social, neuropsychological, and educational. "Learning disorders are complex conditions. The characteristics vary from person to person and from stage to stage in the development of an individual. . . . People responsible for educational planning with learning disabilities must understand these differences and provide for them appropriately" (p. 218).

Identification of the problems that disable a child's learning need to be analyzed by a specialist, but if a child has several of the following problems, then a learning disability should be considered by the parent or teacher. Clues include the following:

- may have trouble learning the alphabet, rhyming words, or connecting letters to their sounds;
- may make many mistakes when reading aloud, and repeat and pause often;
- may not understand what he or she reads;
- may have real trouble with spelling;
- may have very messy handwriting or hold a pencil awkwardly;
- may struggle to express ideas in writing;
- may learn language late and have a limited vocabulary;

- may have trouble remembering the sounds that letters make or hearing slight differences between words;
- may have trouble understanding jokes, comic strips, and sarcasm;
- may have trouble following directions;
- may mispronounce words or use a wrong word that sounds similar;
- may have trouble organizing what he or she wants to say or not be able to think of the word he or she needs for writing or conversation;
- may not follow the social rules of conversation, such as taking turns, and may stand too close to the listener;
- may confuse math symbols and misread numbers;
- may not be able to retell a story in order (what happened first, second, third; or
- may not know where to begin a task or how to go on from there. (NICHCY, 2002b p. 3)

Tips for Teachers and Parents

1. Learn as much about learning disabilities as you can. (See resources in the Appendix.)
2. Recognize the child when he or she works hard or does well. Give positive feedback.
3. Recognize the child's strengths and interests. Find out how the child learns best. Give the child opportunities to use his or her talents and strengths.

Tips for Teachers

1. Review the student's records and ask specialists about the best method for working with the child. This may include
   a. give students more time to take tests
   b. break tasks into smaller units
   c. provide directions verbally and in writing (NICHY, 2002b)
   d. have a peer or classroom assistant take notes or write answers on a test
   e. provide tutors in order to individualize teaching
   f. provide audio-taped textbooks

g. provide supplementary video materials that relate to the classroom topic

For students who have listening difficulties, allow them to use a tape recorder or to borrow notes. For students who have difficulty writing, furnish a computer with specialized software that recognizes speech, and let the student use grammar checks and spell checks on a computer.

2. Teach study skills, organizational skills, and learning strategies. Study various ways to assess a student's learning so that students with learning disabilities can show what they have learned.

3. Communicate and become partners with the parents.

Tips for Parents

1. Give your child with learning disabilities the opportunity to excel or just enjoy activities outside the classroom such as dancing, music, sports, or computers. Give your child opportunities to participate in areas of interest or/and talent. Encourage friendships with children whom they meet in these activities.

2. Help your child learn through areas of strengths. Talk with your child's teacher and observe for yourself how the child learns best. Establish a special place where the child can do homework and prioritize its importance.

3. Meet other parents who have children with learning disabilities. Share concerns and successes with others as well as advice and emotional support.

4. Help develop an educational plan for your child with the school. Establish a positive working relationship and communicate regularly with your teacher, discuss questions, and exchange information about successes and progress (NICHCY, 2002b).

Mental Retardation

Mental retardation is diagnosed by determining (1) the ability of a person's brain to learn, think,

solve problems, and make sense of the world (called intelligence quotient [IQ] or intellectual functioning); and (2) whether the person has the skills he or she needs to live independently (called adaptive behavior, or adaptive functioning) (NICHCY, 2002a).

The average score of an IQ test is 100, but those classified as mentally retarded score 70 to 75 or below. To look at the skills needed to live independently, the child is compared to others of the same age. The adaptive skills are (a) daily living skills, dressing, using the bathroom, and feeding oneself; (b) communication skills—understanding what is said and being able to respond; and (c) social skills with adults, friends, and family (NICHCY, 2002a).

More than 614,000 children with mental retardation, ages 6 through 21, have need for special education. "One out of every 10 children who need special education has some form of mental retardation" (NICHCY, 2002a, p 3).

Tips for Parents

• Learn about mental retardation in order to give your child the help he or she needs.

• Encourage your child to be independent, learning daily care skills such as dressing, grooming, eating, and using the bathroom.

• Give your child chores, but make the chores one in which she or he can be successful. Use them as teaching tools. For example, in setting the table have the child count out the number of napkins. Give the child one task at a time and help when assistance is needed.

• Praise, praise, praise when the child has worked hard and accomplished the task. Give feedback and build your child's abilities.

• Have your child join in outside activities such as scouts, sports, and recreational activities.

• Work with the school and your child's teacher. Apply what he or she is learning at school with activities at home and in the community (NICHCY, 2002a).

• Volunteer in the classroom or in another classroom. See how the teachers work with the children. Contribute to the success of the class by cooperating with the teacher.

Tips for Teachers

- Learn as much as you can about mental retardation. Check with organizations such as NICHCY and the Council for Exceptional Children. (See resources in the Appendix.)
- "Recognize that you can make an enormous difference in this student's life! Find out what the student's strengths and interests are, and emphasize them. Create opportunities for success" (NICHCY, 2002a, pp. 5–6).
- "Be as concrete as possible. Demonstrate what you mean rather than just giving verbal directions. Rather than just relating new information verbally, show a picture. And rather than just showing a picture, provide the student with hands-on materials and experiences and the opportunity to try things out" (NICHCY, 2002a, pp. 5–6).
- "Break longer, new tasks into small steps. Demonstrate the steps. Have the students do the steps, one at a time. Provide assistance as necessary" (NICHCY, 2002a, pp. 5–6).
- Have an IEP which will give the educational goals for the child. Check with the special education teacher for effective ways of teaching this student (NICHCY, 2002a).
- Work with the parents; make a partnership for the welfare of the student.

Learning Is Hard

For years, the popular philosophy has been that we could best motivate young people in pleasing and attractive settings. The lesson would stimulate interest, be fun, and be relevant to the learner. Because students enjoyed doing it, they would be willing to learn. This is an excellent theory, and there is no quarrel with its premise. However, we have produced some youths who have not met their potential because, in real life, work is not always pleasing and for children with disabilities it is even more of a challenge to achieve.

Work involves diligence, tenacity, endurance, sacrifice, discipline, and repetition. It requires deep concentration and dedication. Work is *not* always fun. It is often boring! Most of us spend our lives doing work. We are willing to make this sacrifice not only for the extrinsic values of status, income, and fringe benefits but also for the intrinsic values of self-worth, dignity, and contribution to society. Some of our children have become confused because they were given the impression that life should be fun and games. It is not, and we need to set them straight. Work is work.

Children with disabilities often work harder and longer to accomplish what other children do easily and quickly. It is not always easy for them to accept this. It is hard for parents to refrain from expecting the school and the teacher to lighten the load, to expect less because the child has a disability. But this deprives the child of the feeling of accomplishment, of striving for and reaching full potential. The Individualized Education Program provides for the appropriate level of accommodation. Use this tool effectively to ensure that all exceptional children are given the opportunity to reach their goals.

Just as the parent feels warmth and joy at the progress of a child with a disability, so will the professional whose help and guidance leads to better family relations, improved schoolwork, and an ability to participate in life more fully for the child with a disability. It is a worthy and mighty undertaking.

✍ CHILD FIND PROJECT

Concern about reaching parents and their children with disabilities resulted in the federal funding of the Child Find Project. In this program: "All children with disabilities residing in the State, including children with disabilities attending private schools, regardless of the severity of their disabilities, and who are in need of special education and related services are identified, located, and evaluated and a practical method is developed and implemented to determine which children with disabilities are currently receiving needed special education and related services" (NICHCY, 1998).

Child Find is designated to locate children with disabilities using any feasible methods available such as door-to-door surveys, media campaigns, dissemination of information from the schools, and home visits by staff and/or volunteers (Lerner, Mardell-Czudnowski, & Goldenberg, 1987). Figure 9.4 summarizes the special education process starting from Child Find or other referrals to the placement and evaluation team meeting.

In recent years other names such as Count Your Kid In and Make a Difference have been used to designate this type of program. In many cases this program is funded by both federal and state governments. Preschool screenings have been very successful in finding children in need and informing parents that help is available.

Evaluation

When parents believe that their child needs special assistance, or if a child is identified through Child Find, the subsequent evaluations must be evaluated in a fair and unbiased manner. Parents must be informed and must give their consent to have the original evaluation. For initial evaluations:

- Notice must be provided to evaluate a child, and informed consent of parents must be obtained.
- No single procedure shall be the sole criterion for determining eligibility.
- The child must be assessed in all areas of suspected disabilities.
- Determination of eligibility shall be made by a team of qualified professionals and the child's parents. Children are not eligible if the only deciding factor is a limited English proficiency or a lack of math or reading instruction. (National Association of State Directors of Special Education, 1997)

Figure 9.5 illustrates the special education cycle. For insight and a detailed discussion of the major issues in education for children with disabilities see *Free Appropriate Public Education: The Law and Children with Disabilities* (Turnbull & Turnbull, 1998). The text discusses the law as well

A Summary of the Special Education Process	
Childfind/Referral	Referral of child for diagnosis may be formal or informal; may come from parent or from others.
Assessment/Diagnosis	Multidisciplinary, non-biased comprehensive battery of tests. (Complete re-evaluation for classification required every 3 years.)
Classification (includes parent)	Team reviews assessment/diagnostic data and classifies for special education based on test results. Parent signature required.
IEP Meeting (includes parent)	Individualized Educational Plan developed by team. Must be updated yearly, but team or parent may request as needed. Parent signature required.
Placement (includes parent)	Team decides placement based on the IEP. Parent signature required.
Evaluation Team Meeting	Team evaluates child's total special education program and (includes parent) progress at least yearly. (Teacher evaluates daily as child works on short-term objectives.)

FIGURE 9.4 A summary of the special education process.
Source: Utah Parent Center, Salt Lake City, UT.

FIGURE 9.5 The special education cycle.
Source: Utah Parent Center, Salt Lake City, UT.

as the zero reject principle, nondiscriminatory evaluation, individualized appropriate education, least restrictive environment, procedural due process, and parent participation.

Reaching Infants and Toddlers with Disabilities

The importance of development while a child is an infant or a toddler is increasingly recognized. All children require a nurturing and positive environment beginning at birth. The importance of attachment and brain development was discussed in Chapter 1. Recently developed brain-scan techniques have made it possible to see how synapses and connections develop during the first

years of life. If this is a critical time for children without disabilities, one can immediately recognize how important it is for a child with a disability. This is a period in which great change and remediation can be made.

Child Find, discussed in the previous section, is one method of reaching parents of infants or toddlers with disabilities. Health agencies, doctors, visiting nurses, and hospitals are important sources in finding infants who need services.

✒ PART C OF IDEA 97

Part C of the Individuals with Disabilities Education Act Amendments of 1997 focuses on infants and toddlers with disabilities. An at-risk infant or toddler is an individual younger than three who would be at risk of experiencing substantial developmental delay if early intervention services were not provided to the individual. Each state sets up its own program, but the program is expected to have the following:

1. A comprehensive child-find system, including a system to make referrals to service providers.

2. An Individualized Family Service Plan, including service coordination.

3. A comprehensive, multidisciplinary evaluation of the infant or toddler with a disability.

4. A family-directed identification of the needs of each family with an at-risk infant or toddler to assist the child's development.

5. A public awareness program that focuses on early identification of infants and toddlers with disabilities. This emphasizes that hospitals and physicians need to be provided with information about the services so that parents will know about their availability.

6. A comprehensive system of personnel development. Qualified personnel include special educators, speech-language pathologists and audiologists, occupational therapists, physical therapists, psychologists, social workers, nurses, nutritionists, family therapists, orientation and mobility specialists, and pediatricians and other types

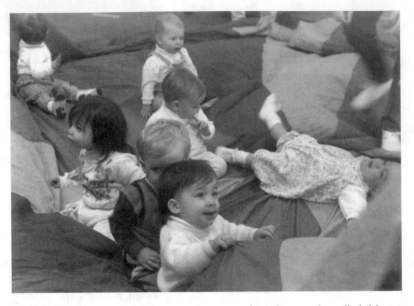

Play and interaction with others are important for infants and small children.

of physicians. Part C also includes the training of paraprofessional and primary referral sources—recruitment and retention of early education service providers; early intervention providers, fully and appropriately qualified to provide early intervention; personnel to work in rural and inner-city areas; and personnel to coordinate transition services for infants and toddlers to preschool or other appropriate services. Nothing prohibits the use of paraprofessionals and assistants who are appropriately trained and supervised, and states were given three years to develop the qualified staff.

These services are provided at no cost to families, except where federal or state law provides for a system of payment by families, including a schedule of sliding fees.

Identifying the Infant and Toddler with Disabilities

The phrase *infant or toddler with a disability* means any child under three years of age who needs intervention services because the child is at risk of substantial developmental delays if intervention is not provided to the child. The areas of delay may be in cognitive development, physical development, communicative development, social or emotional development, adaptive development, or a diagnosed physical or mental condition that would probably cause developmental delay (National Association of State Directors of Special Education, 1997).

Conditions that are associated with significant delays in development include:

- chromosomal conditions (such as Down syndrome, Fragile X)
- congenital syndromes or conditions (such as spina bifida)
- sensory impairments (such as hearing or visual impairments)
- metabolic disorders (such as PKU or lactic acidosis)
- prenatal and/or perinatal infections or conditions (such as AIDS, CMV, or exposure to toxic substances)
- significant medical problems (such as cerebral palsy)

- babies weighing less than 1,200 grams (less than 2 lbs., 10 oz.)

- postnatal conditions (such as attachment disorder) (Colorado Department of Education, Early Childhood Initiatives, the Arapahoe Early Childhood Network, PEAK Parent Center, the Colorado Consortium of Intensive Care Nurseries, 1997, p. 3)

ꕥ THE INDIVIDUALIZED FAMILY SERVICE PLAN AND FAMILY SURVEY

The Individualized Family Service Plan (IFSP) differs from the IEP in format because it is designed to focus on programs for infants and young children. IDEA 97 places preschoolers under the school system and does not differentiate between preschooler programs and elementary and secondary programs, which leave the IEP as the format to decide on the child's program. If it appears that a family would benefit from services, it seems appropriate to continue to use the IFSP for that family as was indicated in previous IDEA legislation. Each state may make its own determination. The intent is the same—to serve individuals with disabilities. The IFSP gives attention to family concerns and needs as well as services for the child.

The IFSP is designed to be flexible, family-focused, and unintrusive for families. It includes the following elements:

1. A statement of the infant's or toddler's present levels of attainment in physical or motor, sensory, cognitive, communication, social-emotional, and adaptive development. The law requires that this statement be based on objective criteria acceptable to both parent and provider.

2. A statement of the family's resources, priorities, and concerns related to enhancing the development of the child with special needs and/or related to broader family issues.

3. A statement of the major outcomes expected for the child and family, including how and when the team will evaluate whether progress is being made and whether changes or updates in outcomes or services are needed.

4. A statement of specific supports and services necessary to meet the unique strengths and needs of the infant/toddler and family, including options and a variety of all community supports and services available.

5. A statement describing the environments in which services will be provided and the location of services.

6. Dates when services will start and how long services will be used.

7. The name of the service coordinator. This person is responsible for seeing that the IFSP is carried out and coordinating the process among all involved parties.

8. The steps to be taken to support the child's transition to home, community, or preschool services, if appropriate. (Colorado Department of Education et al., 1997, p. 7)

The IFSP is evaluated once a year, and the family is provided a review of the plan at six-month intervals or more often, if appropriate, based on the infant's and family's need.

Procedural Rights for Infants and Toddlers

Each state has flexibility in how it sets up Part C for Infants and Toddlers, IDEA 97. Most programs should have the following components:

First, a program should have *multidisciplinary evaluations*. A team consisting of the family and two or more qualified professionals looks at how the child is doing in the following areas: physical or motor, sensory, cognitive, communication, social-emotional, and adaptive development. This evaluation is the procedure used to determine initial and continuing eligibility for services.

Second, an *Individualized Family Service Plan* (IFSP) is needed, consisting of a team of people, including family members, who jointly plan supports and services and identify resources that will meet the family's concerns and priorities about the child's development. This plan is documented.

Other components include a *service coordinator*, who works with the family to identify resources, supports, and services and coordinates agencies and people involved. Parents are given *prior notice* about any changes that service providers want to make, and parents are given the chance to say "yes" or "no" to those changes.

Information, both written and spoken, will be given in the child's native language or, if that is impossible, will be translated orally or by another mode of communication so that parents understand the information. Parents have the right to accept or deny service and must have *informed consent. Confidentiality* is ensured by keeping private any information about the child and the family. Parents will have *access to records* with the ability to change incorrect information.

Support and services are provided in a *natural environment,* the environment typically used for children who are the same age but do not have disabilities. Parents will also have *access to services,* helped by the service coordinator.

Parents may use an *appeals process* to resolve any disagreements they have with providers. The appeals process can involve mediation and due process. Finally, *mediation* will be used to find a solution satisfactory to all involved in the dispute. Due process is employed in resolving complaints. (Colorado Department of Education et al., 1997).

ᔕᔕ CHILDREN WITH DISABILITIES IN HEAD START AND CHILD CARE

In 1974, with the passage of the Community Services Act (P.L. 96–644), Congress stipulated that 10 percent of Head Start's enrollment must be children with disabilities. Head Start developed procedures and policies to answer the needs of these children by offering individualized and appropriate education.

The Local Education Agency (LEA) is responsible for ensuring that services are provided to children with disabilities three to five years of age, but it is not responsible for providing all services. IDEA's policy is to ensure that all children with disabilities beginning at least by age three have the right to a free, appropriate education in either public or private institutions. This includes Head Start and private child care facilities. Head Start facilities were directed to use IDEA's definition of children with disabilities. Changes in IDEA 97, discussed earlier in this chapter, also pertain to Head Start.

The coordinator of services for children with disabilities must have a plan containing (1) procedures for timely screening; (2) procedures for making referrals to the LEA for evaluation; (3) procedures to determine whether there is a need for special education and related services for a child as early as the child's third birthday; (4) provisions to ensure accessibility of the facilities and appropriate special furniture, equipment, and materials as needed; and (5) transition of children into Head Start from infant/toddler programs and into appropriate placement following Head Start.

The disabilities service plan must include options to meet the needs and take into consideration the strengths of each child based upon the IEP so that a continuum of services available from various agencies is considered.

Eligibility requirements are similar to those cited in the discussion of IDEA 97, with the addition of developmental delays. These include health impairment, hearing impairment, orthopedic impairment, visual impairment including blindness, learning disabilities, autism, and traumatic brain injury. The developmental delays are in physical development, cognitive development, communicative development, social-emotional development, or adaptive development as discussed in IDEA 97's Part C for Infants and Toddlers.

Parent Involvement in Head Start

Parents must be involved in the program for their child. The Head Start staff must:

1. support parents of children with disabilities entering from infant/toddler programs

2. provide information to parents on how to foster their child's development

3. provide opportunities for parents to observe large-group, small-group, and individual activities described in their child's IEP

4. provide follow-up assistance and activities to reinforce program activities at home

5. refer parents to groups of parents of children with similar disabilities who can provide peer support

6. inform parents of their rights under IDEA

7. inform parents of resources that may be available from the Supplemental Security Income (SSI) Program, the Early and Periodic Screening, Diagnosis and Treatment (EPSDT) Program, and other sources as well as assist them with initial efforts to access such resources

8. identify needs (caused by the disability) of siblings and other family members

9. provide information that might help prevent disabilities among younger siblings

10. build parents' confidence, skill, and knowledge in accessing resources and advocating to meet the needs of their children (Federal Register, 1993, p. 5509)

⁓ PARENT-SCHOOL PARTNERSHIPS

Helping the Young Child Develop

Infants and toddlers need opportunities to interact with the environment, including parents and others who respond to their cues. Developmental delays need special consideration, but very young children, in particular, benefit from a nurturing and responsive home or child care center. Individual concerns for such things as autism, Fragile X, and Down Syndrome need to be addressed in relation to appropriate intervention. Because there is not enough space in this text to include all the information and recommendations, the care provider should contact the Special Education Early Childhood program and the parent center for children with disabilities in their home state. Call or write the National Information Center for

Communication between teacher and parent is essential.

Children and Youth with Disabilities (NICHCY). (See the Appendix for references.) NICHCY can furnish information on each area of the child's disability and can also furnish the names of other references.

Children ages three to five should attend a good, developmentally appropriate class that has supplemental intervention that meets the needs of each child. They need an appropriate nurturing environment where language, movement, creativity, and discovery support their physical, social-emotional, and cognitive development.

Communicate with the Child

Communication is how children learn their language, and they must be given opportunities to practice that skill. Talk naturally so the child can understand and develop language. When your child talks, listen. How do you feel when you talk to someone who will not listen to what you are saying? Most adults don't waste time talking to people who do not listen to them. Children don't either. If you want your children to express themselves, let them initiate conversations and respond by giving them your attention.

Give Praise and Encouragement

Praise reinforces learning and behaviors, and encouragement helps children continue working. Let children know when you are pleased with what they are doing. We all work for rewards, and praise is one of the most important rewards you can give. Be patient with children. It takes many trials and many errors to learn skills. Adults forget over the years how it was to be a child. If the situation gets out of hand and you become impatient or angry, leave the situation, do something else, and come back to it when you are in control of yourself.

Never Compare

Don't compare your children with others. Allow for individuality. Every child is different, with special characteristics that make up his or her personality and no one else's.

Offer Enrichment Activities

Help increase your children's knowledge by taking them to places such as zoos, libraries, or airports. Use television as a learning tool by selecting appropriate programs, viewing them together, and discussing them afterward. Another learning experience that is often overlooked is the family mealtime. Sharing experiences, talking about interesting subjects, and improving conversational skills can happen around the dining table.

Encourage Play

Play is as important for children with disabilities as it is for children without. It is especially important for children who are deaf or blind. These disabilities do not interfere with the natural phenomenon of learning about the world and growing and developing while doing so. Activities that are appropriate for normal babies are appropriate for the infant with disabilities, too. Clapping hands, cooing, playing peek-a-boo, and cuddling are necessary and helpful. Provide the baby or small child with objects to grasp. Firm cushions may be used for crawling babies. Rock children back and forth or play with them on a swing so they will have the experiences needed to develop. Babies and small children must have the opportunity to think, experiment, investigate, and learn about their environment. Of course, infants should never be left unsupervised.

Read and Talk Together

Read to your children, have them read to you, and listen to them read. Let them tell you about what they have been reading. Magazines, newspapers, comics, and books can all be used to increase a child's knowledge and reading ability.

For school-age children add the following:

Develop Good Work Habits

Set the stage for good homework habits. A well-lighted place to study that is quiet, with room for books, pencils, and papers, helps. Schedule regular home study.

Get Sufficient Rest

Set a bedtime and stick to it. Children need a lot of rest to be able to do good mental work. Rest is necessary for proper growth.

Attend School Regularly

See that your child attends school regularly and on time. Visit with teachers to learn how your child is getting along in school and listen to what they have to tell you about your child.

✍ HOW PARENTS CAN HELP THE SCHOOL-AGE CHILD AT HOME

For teachers and parents alike, the goal is to have all children reach their full potential. Students with disabilities may need extra help at home to keep up their schoolwork. Special tutoring by someone outside the family might be very effective. If the parents are planning to work with their child, the following suggestions should help guide them.

What Parents Can Do

Know your child. You are your child's first teacher and often know better about his or her capabilities than anyone else. Communicate your hopes and plans to your child's teacher.

Actively participate in your child's school. Treat all students and other members of the school community with respect (Educational Resources Information Center, National Library of Education, Office of Educational Research and Improvement, U.S. Department of Education, 1996, p. 32).

First, Visit with the Teacher

Explain that you want to help your child at home with schoolwork. Ask the teacher to explain the material the class will be covering and how assignments should be done. Try to get a time schedule for assignments if your child doesn't already have one.

Set a Definite Time for the Child

Set a time to work with your child. Go over the day's experiences and listen to how your child felt about them. Discuss how the assignments can be completed and turned in on time.

Monitor Progress

Keep a record of the assignments handed in and the scores received, so you can tell how your child is doing in school. If the grades are low or you do not understand them, visit with the teacher to find out exactly what the teacher expects.

Promote Success

Your child will be more likely to succeed in home-school collaboration if you do the following:

1. Use a pleasant, firm approach that says, "Yes, this must be done, and we'll do it as quickly and pleasantly as we can."

2. Set up a reward system. Few of us will work hard at a job we do not receive satisfaction from or get paid for. Your praise and approval are the students' pay for a job well done. If they get scolded all the time, they are unlikely to want to work for another scolding.

3. Make sure your child has time for work, play, and rest. There has to be some work, play, and rest in everyone's life. If we do too much of one, the other two will suffer. Parents are the best ones to determine how to keep this balance.

Parents may be the most important force in seeking the correct educational placement for their children. It is important that they are aware of the various ways their children may be served. Different labels for placement may exist in different regions. The *interrelated classroom* is a popular term for a classroom in which children are placed according to their level of academic achievement rather than according to their diagnosed disabilities.

Parent Involvement in the Classroom

In addition to an advocacy role, parents should also take an active role in the education of their children. Parent involvement in the classroom is an asset that is often overlooked or mismanaged. The parent is involved in planning the IEP and has the right of input and due process. Although parents are aware of these rights, many probably do not feel self-assured enough to fully capitalize on them. They rely on the teacher, the administrator, or the psychologist to keep them informed of what they, as parents, should be doing. Many parents believe the teacher, or some other person in an authority role, knows what is best and that it is up to that person to decide whether the parent can be of assistance. The counterpart is the teacher who fears parent involvement, perhaps because of misconceptions or a bad experience. Thus, there may be a lack of communication or overt action that prevents application of an influential force—the parents—for the education of the student with disabilities.

An Example of Parent Involvement

Precise Early Education for Children with Handicaps (PEECH) involves parents by offering conferences, group meetings, home visits, classroom observations, and a lending library, as well as by being receptive to their questions and suggestions. This program integrates children with disabilities in a classroom with children who have no special education needs. The children, ages three to six, attend the program half a day, five days a week (National Dissemination Association & National Diffusion Network, 1993).

Merle Karnes, director of the project, emphasizes the importance of family involvement and the necessity of skillful staff interaction with parents. She finds that parents are interested in their children with disabilities and want to learn how to work with them. Karnes offers the following advice to the professional educator working with these parents.

To ensure success in your work with parents, give specific directions and objective feedback on their contributions. Respect them as individuals and be flexible in responding to their needs and value systems. If parents are included in decision making, if the program makes sense to

them, if their goals and values are compatible with those of the school, if they are approached as individuals and are convinced that you, the professional, are interested in helping them, they will join you in developing their abilities and contributing their time.

Parents can work effectively in the classroom, and they will extend their newfound understanding to other members of the family. They may become so knowledgeable and skillful that they can reach out to help other parents of children with disabilities.

How Parents Can Tutor at Home (School-Age Children)

Tutoring is one of the most effective and necessary tools in education. It requires understanding another's rate of learning and being responsive to feelings and moods.

The cassette recorder is one of the most valuable instruments available in helping the student learn at home or at school. With a recorder, parents (in this case, the tutors) can put exactly what they want in a lesson and determine its format. This means that parents can adapt the lesson to the student's level and develop it in a way that will be most beneficial to the student. A set of headphones further enhances the learning situation.

The cassette recorder is excellent for recording spelling words and for having children take spelling tests as they would in a classroom. If the children can read the words, have them record the words on the tape and take them as in a spelling lesson. When the students listen to the words, they automatically monitor the sound of the word, the inflection, and the phrasing. Corrections are made unconsciously as the mind corrects errors that the ear hears.

The cassette recorder is also valuable for taping messages to family members. It is particularly useful for giving directions. Instructions on how to set a table, mix pudding, or make a bed can be recorded on tape to give a child valuable experience in learning to follow directions.

Another important use is letting children record a reading lesson on the tape and then asking them to correct their own errors. A chart of the time, number of words read, and errors made can be kept to show progress.

Suggestions for Putting Lessons on Cassettes

1. Make the length of your lesson five minutes shorter than the period you want the lesson to last. This gives flexibility for handling interruptions.

2. Arrange the tasks sequentially. Check the order by doing the lesson once yourself.

3. Speak more slowly than your normal rate of speech. Children with learning disabilities do not process words and thoughts as quickly as most people do. Check to see if children know what the tape is saying by asking them to repeat what they hear. Be careful not to ask if they understand the information. They may think they do, but testing may reveal they don't.

4. Include a set of questions at the end of the taped lesson for immediate review of the material. This is also helpful for the teacher with students who have missed reading lessons or lectures.

A Few Things to Remember

When teaching children with disabilities, teachers and parents should follow these suggestions:

1. Encourage correct responses—wrong responses have to be relearned.

2. Use tests as learning instruments. More learning takes place when tests are answered and corrected soon after being given.

3. Learning occurs more effectively when more channels of learning are involved. Involving the visual and hearing channels is more effective than involving just vision or just hearing.

4. Putting what has been learned into action through verbal or physical reaction increases the learning experience.

5. Learning is reinforced by repetition, that is, reviewing often at first and then again at varying intervals.

6. Begin with concrete items and move gradually to teaching abstract concepts.

7. When teaching motor skills, always begin with large-muscle activities and gradually switch to fine-muscle activities.

✍ COMMUNICATION BETWEEN PROFESSIONALS AND PARENTS OF CHILDREN WITH DISABILITIES

Teachers may be confronted with dispirited parents experiencing considerable doubt, confusion, and anxiety about their child with a disability and their reactions to her. A troubled parent may enlist the help of a teacher to discuss problems that are related to a child's performance at school or other, more personal concerns that bear a relationship to the child. A parent's inability to cope effectively with a child is often a motivating factor in seeking help. (Seligman, 2000, p. 9)

It takes skill, tact, and ingenuity for a professional to communicate with people who have different needs. Mistakes to avoid include "talking down" to the parents, assuming an understanding exists where in fact none may, and using jargon or technical language.

Parents react differently and sometimes unpredictably to the birth or the diagnosis of a child with a disability. Reactions are a result of feelings; parents may experience frustration, hurt, fear, guilt, disappointment, ambivalence, or despair. For the professional to work effectively with parents of children with disabilities, there must be an ability to recognize these feelings and a willingness to honor them (Chinn, 1984; Chinn et al., 1978).

It is usually easier for the professional to view the child with a disability objectively than it is for the parents. The professional deals with the child on a day-to-day basis or only occasionally, whereas the parents deal with the child before and after school and on weekends. Parents of a child with a severe disability may be faced with a lifetime of caring for the child. There is a need to offer parents relief from the constant care that is often required. Foster parents, substitute grandparents, and knowledgeable volunteers are becoming more available to give these parents helpful breaks (Chinn, 1984; Chinn et al., 1978).

Parents are receptive to open and direct communication. Messages should be clear and in language the parents can understand. The teacher or professional will deal with a wide variance of language efficiency, so they should acquaint themselves with the parents' backgrounds. The professional should also be receptive to clues from the parents to determine if the message is being received and accommodated as intended. Ask a leading question to let the parents express their understanding of the topic being discussed. You might be surprised to find the interpretations are different from what you intended.

The professional should include the support and consultation of the medical and theological professions if the parents exhibit a need for these services. Be aware of the agencies and organizations that assist parents and professional workers in the local community as well as national organizations.

Communication Sources

Although two-way communication is essential, important tips and information can be relayed to parents through books, newsletters, personal letters, and charts. These can be used in conjunction with a conference, or they can be separate forms of communication.

Sources for learning more about communicating with parents include Turnbull and Turnbull's *Families, Professionals, and Exceptionality: A Special Partnership* (1997, 3rd ed.), and Turnbull and Turnbull's *Parents Speak Out: Then and Now* (1985, 2nd ed.). *Two-way Talking with Parents of Special Children, A Process of Positive Communication* (Chinn et al., 1978) is a book that discusses in-depth communication, semantics, transactional analysis, stroking, family interactions, and

transactions. Case studies may be read in *Case Studies about Children and Adolescents with Special Needs* (Halmhuber & Beauvais, 2002) and *The Parental Voice* (Holzberg & Walsh-Burton, 1996). Both books describe the trials and concerns of individuals who have a variety of disabilities.

Mullins (1987) chose 60 books written by parents of children with disabilities and analyzed them for issues and concerns that were prominent in their lives. Parents of children with disabilities paint a picture of parenthood as one with "exceptional parenting, with its attendant special problems, pain, and pleasure" (p. 31).

Although the authors of the books presented their concerns in a variety of ways and used different approaches, the same four themes were repeated: (1) realistic appraisal of the disability, (2) extraordinary demands on families, (3) extraordinary emotional stress, and (4) resolution.

1. The parents who wrote the books were realistic about the disabilities. Many shared their manner of coping and information about their child's disability. Mullins pointed out Jablow's (1982) book about her child with Down syndrome, Parks's (1982) discussion on the autistic child, and the Turnbulls' book *Parents Speak Out* (1985).

2. Rearing a child with a disability affects the whole family, and in much greater depth than one that has not had a child with a disability can imagine. Some siblings worry that they might have a child with a disability themselves. They also have to share a greater amount of their parents' time and may find the obligation of caring for the child overwhelming. Parents have greater difficulty deciding on the best way to handle the child with a disability, and many marriages fail. The books show that parents use creative ways to handle the challenge, but having a child with a disability places "extraordinary demands on the physical and financial resources of the family" (Mullins, 1987, p. 31).

Concerns included inaccurate or ambiguous diagnosis in which families have had to search for the answers to their concerns. A great deal of insensitivity to the parents was exhibited by some professionals who worked with them. Some parents had to work for years to get their children placed in appropriate schools. On the other hand, parents were forever grateful for professionals who were helpful and caring.

3. Parents express emotional ambivalence and grieve for the ideal child they did not have. Children may also wish for what could have been. Sometimes parents blame themselves for their child's disability. Parents who live with a child who has a degenerative condition are under constant stress about the future. These intense emotional concerns, joined with the physical and financial stress on the family, have an extraordinary effect on family life.

4. After gaining insights and living with their child with a disability, most parents believe their lives were "enriched and made more meaningful" by their child (Mullins, 1987, p. 32).

5. Visit the *http://www.fathersnetwork.org* for expressions of feelings about being the father of a children with disabilities.

Additional Ways to Reach Parents

Newsletters

Use a newsletter to offer tips for parents. There are things that all parents can do to help their children in school that are important to parents of both children with disabilities and without.

Letters

Letters are another effective means of communicating an idea or message to parents. Letters should state the concern, then present methods or suggestions for dealing with or changing the situation, include any guidelines or datelines that are pertinent, and finally, end with a conclusion and an offer for assistance if needed.

There are as many ways to write the message you wish to convey as there are teachers. Each will need to adapt the contents to the concerns of the situation.

Reaching Out with Programs

When parents are confronted with the task of rearing a child with a disability, they need both emotional support and specific information. One program for fathers of infants with disabilities illustrates an innovative way to reach out to parents (Delaney, Meyer, & Ward, 1980). The first step is the establishment of attachment between father and infant. The second step is the development of parenting qualities in the father. This ability is acquired when the father is able to read cues and understand the baby's behavior. The cues and behavior patterns of a child with a disability may not be the same as those of a typically developing infant. If misinterpreted by the parents, a certain behavior may confuse and frustrate the parents, causing them eventually to withdraw from meaningful relationships. The end result may be that the attachment process between parent and child is disturbed.

The program for fathers and infants offered a support group, provided time for father-child interaction, offered appropriate childrearing information, and fostered awareness of community resources. The class met each Saturday (Delaney, 1980). The class used the following

> *Sharing,* 10:00 to 10:15 a.m. schedule (Delaney, et al 1980). During the sharing period, fathers discuss their observations of their children, developing camaraderie among the participants. This period may also be used to bring up questions about the topic of the day.
>
> *Music and exercise,* 10:15 to 10:45 a.m. Fathers join in song and rhythm exercises with their infants. Songs that greet are followed by songs pertaining to parts of the body, action songs, recorded music for dancing, and relaxing songs (lullabies and tender music) to bring the period to a pleasant end.
>
> *Zingers,* 10:45 to 11:00 a.m. Fathers discuss zingers, which were distributed at the previous class so they could discuss them during

the week and come to class ready for a lively discussion. Many zingers are controversial, others are thought-provoking—for example, "the average American middle-class father spends 39 seconds per day with his children" or "parents should respond to a baby every time he or she cries" (p. 11).

Snack, 11:00 to 11:15 a.m. Two fathers volunteer to bring snacks for the group each Saturday. Snacks must be nutritionally sound and appropriate for infants.

Guest speaker—child/family development, 11:15 to 11:55 a.m. In an informal presentation, a professional able to relate to the fathers shares expertise and knowledge about a variety of subjects, for example, physical therapy, health, nutrition, special education, and group care.

Preview, 11:55 a.m. The last five minutes focus on the issues to be covered the next week. This program illustrates how a small amount of time spent with parents of exceptional children can bring understanding and support. Although it is not meant to be a substitute for counselors and professionals in the health field, it serves as a model for reaching parents of exceptional children.

The state of Washington continues to have an emphasis on fathers and their children with disabilities. The *http://www.fathersnetwork.org* web site shares information on fathers and their children.

✣ PARENTAL REACTIONS TO DISABILITIES

Parents of a child with a disability typically go through a series of steps or stages in dealing with their concerns. First, they become aware of and recognize the basic problem. Then they become occupied with trying to discover a cause and later begin to look for a cure. Acceptance is the last stage (Chinn, 1984; Chinn et al., 1978). The usual progression to acceptance may vary, but most parents experience guilt and grief before they reach acceptance and compassion.

Parents' Initial Response

Denial

Parents who deny the existence of a child's disability feel threatened. Their security is uncertain, and they are defending their egos or self-concepts. This is a difficult reaction for the professional to deal with. Time, patience, and support will help these parents see that much can be gained through helping children with disabilities realize their potentials.

Projection of Blame

A common reaction is to blame the situation on something or someone else—the psychologist, the teacher, the doctor. Often parents' statements begin with "If only . . . " Again, patience, willingness to listen to the parent, and tact will help the professional deal with a potentially hostile situation.

Fear

The parents may not be acquainted with the cause or characteristics of the disability. They may have unfounded suspicions or erroneous information, which causes anxiety or fear. Information, in an amount that the parent can handle, is the best remedy for fear of the unknown. A positive communication process helps the professional judge the time to offer additional information.

Guilt

Parents' feelings of guilt—thinking they should have done something differently or believing the disability is retribution for a misdeed—are difficult to deal with. The professional can help by encouraging guilt-ridden parents to channel their energies into more productive activities after genuine communication has been established.

Grief

Grief is a natural reaction to a situation that brings extreme pain and disappointment. Parents who have not been able to accept their child as having a disability may become grief-stricken. In such a case it is necessary to allow the parents to go through a healing process before they can learn about their child and how the child can develop.

Withdrawal

Being able to withdraw and collect oneself is a healthy, necessary response. It is when one begins to shun others, avoid situations, and maintain isolation that it becomes potentially damaging.

Rejection

There are many reasons for rejection and many ways of exhibiting it. It may be subtle, feigning acceptance, or it may be open and hostile. Some forms of rejection are failing to recognize positive attributes, setting unrealistic goals, escaping by desertion, or presenting a favorable impression to others while inwardly rejecting the child.

Acceptance

Finally, the reaction of parents may be acceptance that the child has a disability—acceptance of the child and of themselves. This is the goal and realization of maturity. The parents and the child can then grow and develop into stronger, wiser, and more compassionate human beings (Chinn, 1984; Chinn et al., 1978).

Although parents may have some of these feelings, one of the most important components in handling their feelings is the knowledge that there are things they can do to help their child. When parents are able to focus on the positive and able to design a program that will enable their child to develop to full potential, they have a challenge and an answer to the crisis that they may have felt initially. Too often, professionals and friends respond with sympathy rather than suggestions for ways to face the future and meet the challenges.

Students Speak Out

The National Council on Disability (2002) asked youth to respond to questions about their school experiences in IDEA. The questions included were

1. When you think about your years in school, what comes to mind about special education and related services?

2. If your school was reluctant to provide special education services because of financial concerns, which services were disputed? Did you receive the services that you IEP team said you needed?

3. If the discipline procedures under IDEA need to be clearer, how would you change the way the discipline policy is explained to students and their parents?

4. How could schools do a better job before students leave high school to help you and other young people with disabilities prepare in areas such as: Employment, Transportation, Housing, Managing my finances, Health care, Independent living, Connecting to resources in my community, and/or Postsecondary (college or vocational) education? (pp. 8–9)

One student wrote the following:

I have been out of school for 2 years and my years in school were a nightmare for my family and me. I ended up not graduating because in November of my last year in school I was in a bad traffic accident and in the hospital for three months. During that time my school dropped me from the roles because I was "truant" (even though they knew where I was). By the time I could go back to school (I was on life support for two months) my family and I decided I did not have enough time left to get the credit I needed. One of the biggest problems faced was the school had problems with me having a lot of health problems, which forced me to miss a lot of school. When I was a senior they insisted my mom send me for exams even though I had a very high fever. She did and I went to sleep during the exams and was in the hospital for a month with pneumonia. I was never a discipline problem and the supports I needed were fairly minor but the school constantly fought my mom on everything. I hated school and did not care if I graduated or not. On the transition end, the only choice I was given as a work opportunity was washing dishes in a fast food place. (p. 9)

Another student had a more positive experience:

I am a 12-year-old who has been diagnosed with Chronic Fatigue Syndrome (CFS) and Postural Orthostatic Tachycardia Syndrome (POTS). I am currently finishing the 6th grade and have been ill with these illnesses for most of my life. By the 3rd grade I was unable to attend school at all and my parents worked with the school to have me classified as Other Health Impaired so that I could receive services under the IDEA. The problem that they had initially was that my test scores showed that I was at the high end of my ability, even though my education was being severely affected by the illness. . . . I have been very fortunate in my school system because once my eligibility was accepted the CSE has been very supportive. They have been very open to our suggestions and those of the tutor to services that may benefit me, and have stuck by my IEP in following through with services. My parents have had to maintain an active role and remind the school of things we needed, such as extra textbooks, or use of a word processor, but the school has accommodated when reminded. Individual teachers have been our great allies and our worst enemies. If they try to understand my illness and limitations they bend over backwards to help me out. But some teachers have been totally unwilling to teach me via a tutor. They will not grade my work and resist modifying my workload. We have been fortunate to be able to find ways to work around these situations. . . . Most of my teachers have been willing to offer help in modifying and consolidating the workload to a manageable level for me to complete. (pp. 11–12, 17)

The difference in feelings between these two students shows how increased positive communication can help significantly.

✂ PARENTS SHARE THEIR FEELINGS

Suzanne Crane is the mother of a child with a disability. She has shared her feelings and thoughts about this so that others may benefit from her experiences.

Having a handicapped child was not what we expected. I remember the feelings likened to having run into a brick wall, the heartbreak of having a broken doll and no one able to fix her. The uncertainties were even more of a struggle due to fragmented medical care and follow-up on her development. We were told of the absolute and immediate necessity of finding special help for her and then sent home with no guidance as to who and where we could turn to for this help. However, through community support and the efforts of other parents we were able to secure services for our child. I do not believe our daughter would be walking or talking now if we hadn't persevered in this. She presently is 7 years old and being served by special education in the public school system. However, I will always crusade for the infants, toddlers, and preschoolers with special needs and their families who are faced with the overwhelming situation of no help available.

I feel that we are more like other families than set apart. I have seen other children accept her with open arms, bridging the gap. Our daughter's celebrative spirit, her love for music, her essence have affected us, her parents, and our second child in positive ways. She has shaped our perspective on the world and life. She has taught us to be happy. We hope that her future will enhance her internal spirit and allow her to be accepted by others. (Crane, 1986)

In 1994, Crane offered an update on her child:

My daughter is now 15, a friendly, outgoing young lady with much promise. She will be able to live semi-independently in the community. It is my hope that her future will be happy and fulfilling. Our family focus is on vocational skills, community work experience, and supportive community living. (Crane, 1994)

Parents of Twin Boys with Cerebral Palsy Share

Bruce and Kelly Stahlman did not expect their twins to be born 3 months early at 28 weeks gestation.

BRUCE'S LETTER:

Relativity.

Whenever we discuss speed or velocity (an object's speed and its direction of motion), we must specify precisely who or what is doing the measuring . . . each observer feels stationary and perceives the other as moving. Each perspective is understandable and justifiable. As there is symmetry between the two space-dwellers, there is, on quite fundamental grounds, no way of saying one perspective is "right" and the other "wrong." Each perspective has an equal claim on truth. (Greene, 2000, p. 28)

Special needs kids weren't visible during the 60s and 70's when I progressed through public school. Once in while, you'd see bus No. 16 making an afternoon run, shorter than all the other buses and rumored to be carrying retards. We didn't really understand what that meant, of course, any more than we understood what it meant to be Negro or Jewish or Communist. We gave no thought, shallow otherwise, to what having a disabled sibling or child might imply.

They'd always been out there, unseen, hidden away by parents and convention, probably ashamed or afraid. More likely out of exhaustion and confusion from having nowhere to turn, no one to help and no one to empathize out of personal experience.

Mike's brother, Tom, had Down's Syndrome. Strong as an ox, he was never without his beloved tinker toy wheel on the end of a coat hanger. We'd always see him while playing cards in Mike's basement. There was a sense of loss, years later, when I heard Tom had passed away. I wish I'd known him better.

Rob was transformed from a cocky high school student to a drooling semi-vegetable in the span of a boating accident. He'd play cards, too, but he was unintelligible most of the time and he moved so slowly. His parents got divorced. I lost track of Rob in short order.

That pretty much covers my formative experience with disabilities. So it's fair to say I wasn't overly prepared for the arrival of our second and third sons, Mark and Eric, 28-week preemies. One alone would have been a shock, two crossed the line into farce. It started with an extended stay in the Intensive Care Nursery. When Eric, the younger twin, finally arrived home he sported a newly repaired heart, apnea monitors, oxygen tanks, and joined his brother in fussing most every night due to their inability to consume enough calories. Sleep deprivation was the worst because it precipitated a cascade of dysfunctionality throughout the house.

I could go on and on. Cerebral palsy is a complicated disorder. Both boys have gastrointestinal tubes for feedings, a regimen of medications and supplements to help with everything from muscle spasm to bowel movement, and a fleet of assistive devices. Hospital trips for specialist review, surgeries, botox injections, and an endless stream of therapist and nursing assistants invading our privacy have become something of a routine that's emotionally draining yet monotonous. A sales professional by training, my wife has become an expert at navigating the private and public health care systems out of necessity, an educational consultant out of conviction and an advocate out of desire.

It would have flatly been impossible to survive this institutionalized anarchy any other way than by simply growing into it, over the years, one day at a time. In the process, the twins have gone from premed thesis material to become our sons with rich, individual personalities, idiosyncrasies and foibles just like "normal" kids. While we wish for them more than is presently possible, we take great pride in their many and significant accomplishments: Eric babbling away at dinner and sitting by himself in his red rocker; Mark learning to use his talker; Eric driving his power chair and endlessly playing and rewinding the Lion King with a remote controller all by himself, and Mark laughing hysterically whenever his older brother gets in trouble. We love them as any parent loves his children. We love reading at bedtime, tickling and teasing, going to a baseball game and swimming. And Eric's Make-A-Wish trip to Give Kids the World Village and Disney World in Florida to meet his favorite Radio Disney DJ was one of the most inspirational events of my life.

People in the disability community threw us a lifeline early on by acting as guides through the maze of public services access. It's beyond astonishing that the richest society on earth makes people traverse a gauntlet to receive even the most basic services. It's worse when you realize how many more get no help or respect from agencies purportedly designed for that purpose. In the process, my politics have changed from conservative to liberal. Both my wife and I have served in various charitable capacities to give something back to the community because it's important to remember you're in a lifeboat with others.

Our oldest son, Jay, gets a lot of credit. I assume he's been impacted in ways I can't comprehend, but mainly for the good. He produced a video of his brothers and spent a day in a wheel chair for a school project last year, something that would never have occurred to me when I was his age.

Our marriage has become stronger over the years as we've grown with the family. My wife is fond of saying life is what you do every day. That's true, but I could certainly live without changing my ten-year-olds' diapers, administering tube feeds, doing the "clean and jerk" whenever they need to be moved and watching Barney tapes for the umpteenth million time and counting. This last point is particularly heinous—no parent should be made to endure Barney for ten years without receiving a Congressional medal.

The emotions, surgeries, finances, the life overall certainly isn't what I'd expected or planned. Does God work in mysterious ways? Probably. Do I put more stock in theology vs. philosophy? Depends on the day. Are Mark and Eric better off than Chinese, Bosnian, or Rwandan kids with CP? Unquestionably. Do other people see it that way? I guess it's relative.

Bruce R. Stahlman
Littleton, Colorado
September 26, 2002

Kelly follows with a letter which she hopes will clarify the relationship between parent and teacher and help teachers understand parents better.

A letter to teachers, current and future:

As a mother of twins with cerebral palsy, I want to thank you for taking the time and making great efforts to care for my children. Without you I would be lost.

Next, I would like to explain, one by one, some of my actions and reactions. Please be patient.

First. After reading the vignette "Story" in the book, *Changed by a Child,* I finally understood why I keep telling you the same story over and over and over. The vignette talks about the excruciating details that I need to convey, because it is all still so real and so raw to me. That, like a spider spinning its web, retelling my story allows me to connect my old life to this new, overwhelming reality.

My story is the vehicle that makes the trip of survival and allows me to cope with the present.

Second. In caring for children with disabilities, a large part of the care is emotional, so the teacher/parent relationship is, by definition, also emotional. We are both investing all that we can into my children, yet we frequently seem to be at odds. Please work WITH me. Give careful consideration to the information that I bring to the table, because it comes as the result of sweat and tears. It is also my role in your system, as a parent, to push the envelope, to be looking ahead, and to be asking for everything that I can to support my child. I will still be here when I am 80 and they are 50, and we shall still be "doing the best we can."

Third, Asking "how are things going" at the start of our meetings gives necessary information. My sleep, the children's health, and life overall will be things that affect our conversation and how effectively I am able to communicate.

Last, never forget that I am grateful for all that you do. It becomes tiring to always say thank you, because that is the nature of our life. In fact, one of the blessings of a disability is that it frequently brings out the best in others. I never forget a kindness, even years later, but it still gets old saying "thank you" as a way of life. Nevertheless, THANK YOU.

Kelly Stahlman
Mother 3 sons, Jay, 13,
Mark and Eric, 10 year
twins with cerebral palsy
due to prematurity

A FEW JEWELS FROM THE STAHLMAN FAMILY SURVIVAL SKILLS

Why me?
Why not me?
Ignorance is bliss; knowledge is power.
Kids with disabilities take much longer to go to the next stage. They wear you out.
Patience and endurance are required, with lots of support!
In some ways it gets easier; in some ways it gets harder, and in some ways it just gets different as you go through stages and ages.
God never gives you more than you can handle. He did at our house! The miracle is to watch God's grace at work in the midst of all the chaos.

My kids teach the art of being with the gift
of presence, the miracle of doing, and the
priority of having.
No matter where you are, someone is
better off and someone is worse off.
Equipment is the quintessential mixed
blessing:
It can be social barrier which prevents the
community from seeing the child/person, a
management nightmare and just plain
awkward while being vital to the child's
participation in life. My greatest nightmare
is that Eric and Mark will learn the low
expectation of observing life instead of
participating in it.[1]

FOR FRIENDS OF THE HANDICAPPED

Blessed are you who take the time
To listen to difficult speech
For you help me to know that
If I persevere, I can be understood.
Blessed are you who never bid me to
"hurry up"
Or take my tasks from me and do them
for me,
For I often need time rather than help.
Blessed are you who stand beside me
As I enter new and untried ventures,
For my failures will be outweighed
By the times I surprise myself and you.
Blessed are you who asked for my help
For my greatest need is to be needed.
Blessed are you who understand that
It is difficult for me
to put my thoughts into words.
Blessed are you who never remind me
That today I asked
the same question twice.
Blessed are you who respect me
And love me just as I am.[2]

---

[1]Reprinted by permission from Bruce and Kelly Stahlman
(2002).

[2] Reprinted by permission from Ann Landers (1986), author
unknown; News America Syndicate.

✒ CONCERN FOR THOSE WHO WORK WITH CHILDREN WITH DISABILITIES

Burnout

Burnout is a term applied to the loss of concern
and emotional feeling for people you work with
or live with (Maslach, 1982). Both teachers and
parents experience burnout. It is felt most when
what you are trying to do seems unproductive, or
you may think you have few alternatives that
would change or improve the course of events.
This frustration can lead to a feeling of being
trapped. It can happen to any teacher and any
parent. The obligations of teaching and parenting are similar. Both are in an authoritarian role
and are responsible for setting up the child's program. Balancing the student's needs with time
constraints, the mechanical constraints of running a classroom or a home, and the constraints
of the personal needs of the authoritarian figure
is a role for a magician. Indeed, when parents
and teachers are successful, the result does seem
to be magical. Both teacher and parent know,
however, that their success was produced by
hard work, good planning, cooperation, and
perseverance.

Those who set high standards and aim for
perfection are sometimes more likely to experience burnout, as are those who feel a need to be
in control. Feelings of anger, guilt, depression,
self-doubt, and irritability are symptoms of
burnout. When these occur, take a hard look at
what is really going on and what needs to be going on. Are you neglecting yourself? Are the
things you want to do essential? Do some things
need to be changed? Learn to accept the fact
that change can occur. Be willing to give yourself
and others credit where credit is due. Build in
rewards so that you and others feel good about
what you are doing. Always have some goals
that are short-term and accessible. Nothing feels
better than success. This is one of the best methods to combat burnout. Remember, burnout is
reversible.

Depression and Suicide

People who parent or work with exceptional children need to know that these children are in a high-risk group for depression and suicide. Children with learning disabilities are particularly at risk because of the frustration they often encounter in trying to learn. Children with giftedness often find it difficult to feel comfortable in the school and home environment.

Parents and teachers must recognize the child's symptoms of depression and impending suicide and be willing to take appropriate action. Generally, the child will be depressed or irritable, lacking enjoyment in usually pleasurable activities. Changes in weight, appetite, or eating habits may be signals. Sleeplessness, hyperactivity, loss of energy, or fatigue are also signals that something is wrong. Loss of self-esteem and feelings of inadequacy or decreased ability to concentrate should alert teachers and parents to a very real need for help. Thoughts of death or suicide should not be taken lightly. Recognize these as very serious symptoms and get professional help. Mental health centers and public schools have programs for crisis intervention and can give guidance and help in a time of need.

✑ RIGHTS AND SERVICES AVAILABLE TO PARENTS

Many parents of children with exceptionalities are unaware of the rights they have and the services available to them. The Buckley Amendment, described here, is a right for all parents, but it is especially important for parents who have children with disabilities.

Family Educational Rights and Privacy Act (FERPA)—The Buckley Amendment

The Buckley Amendment, written for all citizens, greatly affected record keeping for people with disabilities. Please refer to page 000 in Chapter 11 for a description of FERPA.

How to File a Complaint of Discrimination

No one enjoys being a complainer. Most of us do not enjoy confrontations. But every U.S. law was written because someone cared enough to speak up and work to get the law passed. Then the legislature built in procedures for citizens to protect their rights. If parents and friends of the disabled do not stand up for these rights, they will be lost. Whenever discrimination occurs, it hurts not just the people involved, but our nation as well. Complaints should be directed first to the person in charge. If a satisfactory conclusion is not reached, take the complaint to the next higher level of responsibility. Follow the chain of command. If this is not satisfactory, then contact the Regional Office of Civil Rights for your area. The following items are important to include in a complaint:

- Your name and address (a telephone number where you can be reached during business hours is helpful, but not required).

- A general description of the person or class of people injured by the alleged act or acts (names are not required).

- The name and location of the institution that allegedly committed the discriminatory act or acts.

- A description of the allegedly discriminatory act or acts in sufficient detail to enable the individual or organization you are addressing to understand what occurred, when it occurred, and the basis for the alleged discrimination (based on race, color, national origin, sex, handicap, or age). (U.S. Department of Education, July 2000 p. ii)

✑ MASLOW'S HIERARCHY OF NEEDS

When schools become involved with parents, it is wise to list the basic needs that must be satisfied before parents can effectively assist in the education of their children with disabilities. Coletta (1977) elaborates on Maslow's hierarchy of needs in *Working Together: A Guide to Parent Involvement.*

How does Maslow's hierarchy apply to these children? When teachers or administrators work with parents, it is helpful if they understand the parents' feelings, motivations, and concerns. Maslow's hierarchy of needs serves as a guide to this understanding. Parents who are poor and struggling to provide the necessities of life have different views of their problems from those of affluent parents. That is, physiological needs such as food and shelter must be satisfied before individuals can attend to higher order needs such as success and fulfillment. All parents' love and concern for their children will be the same. Therefore, all parents—regardless of economic standing—must be treated with dignity and respect.

The various levels of Maslow's hierarchy are discussed in the following sections.

Physical Needs

The needs for sustaining life—nourishment, protection from the elements, and sexual activity—are physical. There must be protection from the cold, wind, and rain, which usually means a shelter, such as a house, and clothing. There must be food, and to be effective, it must be nourishing. There is a need for companionship and sexual activity.

Psychological Needs

People need to feel secure. It is important to know that you will awake each day to go to a job. It is difficult to handle change, conflict, and uncertainty. It is important to reduce these frustrations. Much emphasis is placed on norms and rules, which results in little flexibility at this level.

Emotional Love and Belonging

At this level there is a need to feel a part of a group where you are accepted, wanted, loved, and respected. When these needs are met or satisfied, then there can be love, respect for others, and consideration for or helpfulness to others.

When these needs are not met, there may be self-defeating, attention-getting behaviors, such as suspicion and aggression.

Self-Esteem

Basic needs must be met before the need for self-esteem can be satisfied. When you are regarded as valuable and competent by others, you have self-esteem. Growth in awareness of self-worth leads to less dependence upon another's judgment of one's worth. The key for the professional is to find ways to help parents see themselves as worthwhile contributors to their children's education.

Fulfillment

This is referred to as self-actualization and is achieved only after the previous levels have been reached. The person strives for self-development, directs energies toward self-established goals, and takes risks willingly.

This hierarchy of needs is applicable to children, teachers, and administrators as well as to parents. It is wise to note where we and the people we would like to help are in the hierarchy. If there is an understanding of needs, then our expectations and suggestions for helping may be more valid.

✑ SUMMARY

Parents, teachers, and other professionals are effective forces in influencing the life of the exceptional child. It is important that all be able and willing to work together for the benefit of the child with disabilities. Special educational terms, once crude, have been replaced with more inclusive educational terms.

During the 20th century the special education movement grew, and in 1971 the Pennsylvania Association for Retarded Children (PARC) won a court case against the Commonwealth of Pennsylvania affirming the right of all children to a free and appropriate education. This includes children with disabilities. The Vocational Rehabilitation Act of 1973, the Education of All Handicapped Children Act of 1975

(Public Law 94–142), the Education of the Handicapped Act Amendments of 1983 (Public Law 98–199), Americans with Disabilities Act, Individuals with Disabilities Act, and IDEA 97 are some of the far-reaching laws passed in the last quarter of the century.

From the Education of All Handicapped Children Act of 1975 to IDEA 97 (P.L. 105–17), and reauthorization, the Individualized Education Program (IEP) and the Individualized Family Service Program (IFSP) have been instrumental in addressing the needs of children with disabilities. They are plans developed by the parents, the child, teachers, administrators, special teachers, psychologists, and any others involved with the child's education. The plans assure a continuum of services, appropriate to age, maturity, handicapping condition, achievements, and parental expectations. The child or student with a disability includes those with autism, deafness, deafness-blindness, hearing impairments, mental retardation, multiple disabilities, orthopedic impairments, other health impairments (including ADD), emotional disturbances, learning disabilities, speech or language impairments, traumatic brain injury, and visual impairments. For children three to nine years old, developmental delays are also used for placement. IDEA 97 also provides for due process-the right to a hearing—if parents disagree with the educational placement.

Parents have been effective forces in securing this legislation. Parents should and do have an important role in the life and education of their exceptional children. The parent's role begins as one of nurturing in the home but can become an effective force in the school as the parent supports the teacher at home as a tutor or at school as a volunteer.

℘ SUGGESTED CLASS ACTIVITIES AND DISCUSSIONS

1. Write a brief review of the development of special education.
2. Describe in your own words what "least restrictive" means.
3. List and describe briefly the 13 categories of exceptional students.
4. A *staffing* refers to the meeting that takes place when an exceptional student's IEP is developed or changed. Who is included on the IEP team? What are their responsibilities?
5. *Mainstreaming and inclusion* are terms used quite frequently. Read carefully about them and write in your own words what you think they mean.
6. List ways that the general classroom can adapt to and support a child with a disability.
7. Study the legislation that has developed for children with disabilities. How has it progressed? List changes.
8. Using Maslow's hierarchy of needs, assess yourself and five acquaintances. Try to select people in different professions. Use this as background material for a general class discussion to increase awareness of these needs.
9. Choose one of the problems a parent of an exceptional child may encounter and describe how you as a professional would try to help that parent.

10 The Abused Child

Children who live through years of assault, degradation, and neglect bear emotional scars that can last for years. We all pay the price of their suffering.

Besharov, 1990, p. 2

Then there is the pain. A breaking and entering when even the senses are torn apart. The act of rape on an eight-year-old body is the matter of the needle giving because the camel can't. The child gives, because the body can, and the violator cannot.

Angelou, 2002, p. 76

In this chapter on child abuse and neglect, you will learn about recognizing and intervening in cases of child abuse and neglect. After completing the chapter you should be able to:

- Acknowledge the moral responsibility and legal requirement that teachers and school personnel have to report suspected maltreatment of children.
- Identify ways schools can help ameliorate the crisis of child abuse and neglect.
- Describe when and how abuse of children was identified and brought to the attention of the public.
- List and describe the characteristics that may indicate child abuse of preschool, elementary, and secondary students.
- Identify types of abuse—physical, emotional, and sexual.
- Identify neglect, and differentiate between neglect and poverty.
- List the psychological characteristics of abused children.
- Describe possible characteristics of the abusive parent.
- List guidelines for interviewing children and parents about abuse.
- Recognize the danger of violence in the schools and the importance of working to eliminate it.
- Discuss the climate of the school and school offerings that would help abusive families.

What is child abuse? According to the Child Abuse Prevention and Treatment Act of 1974, or P.L. 93–247 (1977), it is

> The physical or mental injury, sexual abuse, negligent treatment or maltreatment of a child under the age of 18 by a person who is responsible for the child's welfare under circumstances which indicate that the child's health or welfare is harmed or threatened thereby. (p. 1826)

RESPONSIBILITY TO REPORT

School personnel and child care staff members have more than a moral responsibility to report suspected abuse. Laws in each state require them to report it (Besharov, 1990, 1994; Horton & Cruise, 2001). Some states identify categories of school personnel such as teachers, psychologists, or administrators; others have a general category of school personnel. Four categories of professional-mandated reporting are medical, legal, and human service professionals, and educators (Lowenthal, 2001). No states require proof of the abuse before reporting, and the reporters must report if they have suspicions of maltreatment. Teachers, child care professionals, and others who report in good faith are immune from legal action.

Schools are essential agencies in the reduction of the national crisis of child abuse and neglect. Recommendations from the U.S. Advisory Board

It is difficult to see and understand this kind of physical abuse against children.

Source: Courtesy of Barton D. Schmitt, M.D., C. Henry Kempe National Center for Prevention and Treatment of Child Abuse and Neglect.

on Child Abuse and Neglect (1990) illustrate the national crisis:

> The Board has concluded that child abuse and neglect in the United States represents a national emergency.
>
> The Board bases this conclusion on three findings: 1) each year hundreds of thousands of children are being starved and abandoned, burned and severely beaten, raped and sodomized, berated and belittled; 2) the system the nation has devised to respond to child abuse and neglect is failing; and 3) the United States spends billions of dollars on programs that deal with the results of the nation's failure to prevent and treat child abuse and neglect.
>
> Not only are child abuse and neglect wrong, but the nation's lack of an effective response to them is also wrong. Neither can be tolerated. Together they constitute a moral disaster.
>
> All Americans share an ethical duty to ensure the safety of children. Protection of children from harm is not just an ethical duty: it is a matter of national survival.
>
> Although some children recover from maltreatment without serious consequences, the evidence is clear that maltreatment often has deleterious effects on children's mental health and development, both short- and long-term.
>
> Although most victims of serious and fatal child abuse are very young, to regard older children and adolescents as invulnerable to the severe consequences of abuse and neglect is a mistake.
>
> All Americans should be outraged by child maltreatment. (pp. vii–viii)

The responsibilities are great, and an affirmative response by schools is vital to the well-being of thousands of children throughout the United States. Because of required school attendance and an increase in the use of child care centers, caregivers and teachers have an expanded opportunity for contact with families and children. These professionals work closely with children and families over extended periods. In so doing, they are also the people most able to detect and prevent abuse and neglect.

School has not always been recognized as an important agency in the detection of child abuse. At one time it was believed that most cases of child abuse involved infants who are vulnerable to serious injury or death. But it is now recognized that older children are also victims. More than 70 percent of the children who are abused or neglected may have contact with schools or child care centers. Through Home Start, Head Start, and private and public preschool programs, it has become easier to detect abuse of two- to six-year-olds. Increasingly, the detection and prevention of child abuse and neglect is recognized as a concern and responsibility of the schools. Denver Public Schools (1998), under the topic "legal responsibilities," states that "suspicion or knowledge of abuse/neglect must be reported to the Denver Department of Social Services (DDSS) Child Abuse Hotline or the Police depending on the situation. School personnel have a legal and moral obligation to make a report if child abuse or neglect is suspected. *No one within the school district has the authority to veto reporting.* If it is necessary for school personnel to examine a student for evidence of physical abuse, two adults should be present during the examination."

Abuse and neglect include many degrees and varieties of neglect, physical abuse, emotional abuse, and sexual abuse. The effect on the child differs by age and development, degree of intensity, duration, the relationship between abused and abuser (Steele, 1986), and the intervention that the child receives.

Physical abuse that causes permanent damage to a child is generally easy to recognize and evokes outrage. The damage to a child's psychological development is more difficult to recognize and assess. Unpredictable parental behavior gives the child a "sense of insecurity and difficulty trusting other human beings" (Steele, p. 285). Parents who lack appropriate parenting behavior exhibit inconsistent caregiving; they most often learned their parenting methods during their own formative years when they were themselves neglected or abused.

Besharov (1994) recommends that better information and education on reporting responsibilities is needed in order to encourage more accurate and more complete reporting. "Training efforts should be both expanded and improved.

Professional education programs should sensitize all child-serving professionals to the occurrence of child abuse and neglect, and should instruct them in how and when to report" (p. 143).

The U.S. Advisory Board on Child Abuse and Neglect (1991) made 27 recommendations for responding to this crisis. Recommendation D–4a refers to Child Protection and the Schools as follows:

Strengthening the Role of Elementary and Secondary Schools in the Protection of Children

The Federal Government should take all necessary measures to ensure that the nation's elementary and secondary schools, both public and private, participate more effectively in the prevention, identification, and treatment of child abuse and neglect. Such measures should include knowledge building, program development, program evaluation, data collection, training, and technical assistance. The objective of such measures should be the development and implementation by State Educational Agencies (SEAs) in association with Local Educational Agencies (LEAs) and consortia of LEAs, of:

- Inter-agency multidisciplinary training for teachers, counselors, and administrative personnel on child abuse and neglect;

- Specialized training for school health and mental health personnel on the treatment of child abuse and neglect;

- School-based, inter-agency, multidisciplinary supportive services for families in which child abuse or neglect is known to have occurred or where children are at high risk of maltreatment, including self-help groups for students and parents of students;

- Family life education, including parenting skills and home visits, for students and/or parents; and

- Other school-based inter-agency, multidisciplinary programs intended to strengthen families and support children who may have been subjected to maltreatment, including school-based family resource centers and after-school programs for elementary and secondary school pupils which promote collaboration between schools and public and private community agencies in child protection. (p. 164)

Both public and private schools are considered essential to the child protection system and have responsibilities to effectively provide for the children who attend schools.

The school professionals must consider legal considerations (mandated reporting), ethical considerations (confidentiality), and moral considerations (commitment to the child's well-being) (Horton & Cruise, 2001). When a professional reports suspicions of maltreatment, "families may move away from the school or at least cancel their children's participation in any counseling relationships" (p. 55). The parents may feel that their belief and trust in the school has been destroyed. Reporting, however, may prevent severe physical injury, psychological harm, or inadequate nourishment and health care. "On a case-by-case basis, reports may protect children from severe physical injury or even death. Psychological suffering may be lessened and dysfunctional patterns interrupted. Families may get needed services" (p. 56).

The school must serve as a defense against child abuse in three basic ways: (a) as a referral agency to child protection agencies—reporting suspected abuse is required by law; (b) as an educational institution offering parent education, family-life education, and home visitations to adults and students; and (c) as a support system for families and as a collaborator with other agencies in providing a total protection system.

✍ BACKGROUND

Child abuse and neglect have been social phenomena for centuries. Childhood is described by deMause (1988) in a history of child abuse. The child was considered property of the father to be worked, sold, loved, or killed as the father willed. The child had no rights (Crosson-Tower, 2002; Gelles & Lancaster, 1987; Helfer & Kempe, 1987; Nagi, 1977). "The notion that parents have the right to rear children as they see fit, in the privacy of their home, is a deeply rooted tradition in American history" (Vondra & Toth, 1989, p. 18).

Actions that would be called child abuse today were overlooked or considered to be the parent's right to discipline.

In the 1800s it was common for children to work 12 hours a day under the threat of beatings. They were cheap and useful laborers. Children "continued to be the property of their parents who could choose to beat them, neglect them, or send them out to work" (Crosson-Tower, 2002, p. 4). It was not until 1874, in New York City, that the first case of abuse was reported. It involved a nine-year-old girl, Mary Ellen, who was beaten daily by her parents and was severely undernourished when found by church workers. Because there were no agencies to deal with child abuse, the workers turned to the American Society for the Prevention of Cruelty to Animals.

One year later the New York Society for the Prevention of Cruelty to Children was organized (Fontana & Besharov, 1979; Lazoritz, 1990). The Children's Division of what is now the American Humane Association began addressing the issues in 1878 (American Humane Association, 1998). There were other early indications of growing concern for children. A paper published in 1888, for example, discussed acute periosteal swelling in infants, which can indicate injury (Nagi, 1977). National groups such as the Child Study Association of America and the National Congress of Parents and Teachers were formed. Mounting concern over working conditions and care of children culminated in 1909 in the first White House Conference on Children, which resulted in the 1912 legislation establishing the Children's Bureau.

In recent years, widespread concern over and protective action for the child at risk of maltreatment has become a mandate to schools, and medical care agencies have recognized the prevalence of children who are abused. This relatively recent overwhelming concern resulted in the nearly unanimous passage of the federal Child Abuse Prevention and Treatment Act of 1974.

What transpired between 1913 and recent decades to focus attention on the child at risk? Dr. John Caffey, a radiologist, began collecting data that indicated child abuse in the early 1920s, but he was not supported in his beliefs by his associates. Thus, it was not until after World War II that he published the first of several studies relating to fractures in young children (American Humane Association, 1978; Elmer, 1982). Caffey's first medical paper, written in 1946, reported the histories of six traumatized infants and questioned the cause of their injuries. In it he reported that fractures of the long bones and subdural hematomas occurring concurrently were not caused by disease (pp. 163–173).

Dr. Frederick Silverman, who had been a student of Caffey's, followed in 1953 with an article that indicated that skeletal trauma in infants could be the result of abuse (American Humane Association, 1978; Elmer, 1982). Reports began appearing more frequently (Altman & Smith, 1960; Bakwin, 1956; Fisher, 1958; Silver & Kempe, 1959; Woolley & Evans, 1955), but it was an article by Kempe, Silverman, Steele, Droegemueller, and Silver (1962), "The Battered-Child Syndrome," that brought national attention to the abused child. The authors began their article with the following charge to physicians:

> The battered-child syndrome, a clinical condition in young children who have received serious physical abuse, is a frequent cause of permanent injury or death. The syndrome should be considered in any child exhibiting evidence of fracture of any bone, subdural hematoma, failure to thrive, soft tissue swellings or skin bruising, in any child who dies suddenly, or where the degree and type of injury is at variance with the history given regarding the occurrence of the trauma. Psychiatric factors are probably of prime importance in the pathogenesis of the disorder, but knowledge of these factors is limited. Physicians have a duty and responsibility to the child to require a full evaluation of the problem and to guarantee that no expected repetition of trauma will be permitted to occur. (Kempe et al., p. 17)

The article described the status of child abuse in the nation and pointed out the effectiveness of X-ray examinations in determining abuse. The term *battered* came from the description of bruises, lacerations, bites, brain injury, deep body

When X-rays became available, doctors began noticing recurring breaks that revealed abuse.

Source: Courtesy of Barton D. Schmitt, M.D., C. Henry Kempe National Center for Prevention and Treatment of Child Abuse and Neglect.

injury, pulled joints, burns and scalds, fractures of arms, legs, skull, and ribs, and other injuries that resulted from beating, whipping, throwing the child about, or slamming the child against something. Fontana (1973b) described battering by parents as follows:

Parents bash, lash, beat, flay, stomp, suffocate, strangle, gut-punch, choke with rags or hot pepper, poison, crack heads open, slice, rip, steam, fry, boil, dismember. They use fists, belt buckles, straps, hairbrushes, lamp cords, sticks, baseball bats, rulers, shoes and boots, lead or iron pipes, bottles, brick walls, bicycle chains, pokers, knives, scissors, chemicals, lighted cigarettes, boiling water, steaming radiators, and open gas flames. (pp. 16–17)

National Response

The term *battered* and the picture it evoked aroused the nation. By 1967, all 50 states had legislation to facilitate the reporting of child abuse. There was, however, no provision for the coordination of procedures, nor was there a standard definition of abuse and neglect. Other conditions that precluded standardized reporting included the inconsistent ages of children covered by law, hesitation of professional and private citizens to report cases, different systems of official record keeping, and varied criteria on which to judge abuse.

National Center on Child Abuse and Neglect

The National Center on Child Abuse and Neglect (NCCAN) was created in 1974 by P.L. 93–247. The NCCAN disseminates information through the Clearinghouse on Child Abuse and Neglect. Call or write the NCCAN Clearinghouse using the information listed in the Appendix that follows Chapter 11.

After the establishment of NCCAN, regional centers on child abuse were funded. Their purpose was to conduct research to determine the cause of child abuse and neglect, its identification and prevention, and the incidence of child abuse in the nation. Reporting of child abuse and neglect has been conducted by a variety of organizations. From 1973 until 1986 the American Association for Protecting Children (now the American Humane Association) supplied data on abuse and neglect. The National Committee for the Prevention of Child Abuse did a survey of the 50 states in 1991. At that time, NCCAN established the National Child Abuse and Neglect Data System

(NCANDS) to be responsible for providing comprehensive data on abuse and neglect.

Reports by states have always been voluntary. Each state develops its own procedures for analyzing and reporting, but because it is important to have data that is useful throughout the United States, NCANDS provides forms for states to use. These forms ask for report source; number of investigations; number of children by disposition; victim data that includes the type of maltreatment, age, gender, and ethnicity; number of victims from each home; number of victims removed from homes; number of victims for whom court action was initiated; number of victims who died; number of victims and families who received additional services; and the relationship of the victim to the perpetrator (U.S. Department of Health and Human Services, Children's Bureau, 1998).

✑ EXTENT OF CHILD ABUSE AND NEGLECT

In 2000, child protection agencies (CPA) throughout the United States reported to the National Child Abuse and Neglect Data System (NCANDS). Out of approximately five million children there were three million referrals identified, with 62 percent needing to be "screened in" and 38 percent, "screened out." "Screened-in referrals alleging that a child was being abused or neglected received investigations and assessment to determine whether the allegations of maltreatment could be substantiated" (National Child Abuse and Neglect Data System [NCANDS], 2002, p. 1).

Of these referrals, 879,000 children were identified as victims of maltreatment. The maltreatment categories include neglect, physical abuse, sexual abuse, medical neglect, and psychological or emotional maltreatment. The largest category was neglect, including medical neglect, with almost two thirds (63 percent) being neglected.

Figure 10.1 compares the incidence of child maltreatment in 1990, 1996, and 2000. As shown in Figure 10.1, in addition to the 63 percent who

were neglected, 19 percent were physically abused, 10 percent were sexually abused, and 8 percent were emotionally abused (NCANDS). The other maltreatment in the 1990 and 1996 reports includes abandonment, congenital drug addiction, and threats.

Who Are the Victims?

The largest percentage (51 percent) of maltreated children were White. One fourth or 25 percent were African American, whereas 15 percent were Hispanic. American Indian/Alaska Natives were responsible for 2 percent of maltreated children, whereas Asian/Pacific Islanders account for 1 percent (NCANDS, 2002).

As children grow older, the victimization rate reduces. Children birth to three years of age account for 15.7 victims per 1,000, whereas youths 16 to 17 years of age account for 5.7 victims per 1,000 of children.

Rates for neglect and emotional and physical abuse were similar for males and females, with 11.2 for males and 12.8 for females per 1,000 children. This changes for sexual abuse, with 1.7 victims per 1,000 for female children and 0.4 victims per 1,000 for males. There were more than four times as many female victims of sexual abuse as male victims (NCANDS, 2002). The incidence of neglect and medical neglect decreased with age, but physical, sexual, and emotional abuse increased with the child's age. Of children who were sexually abused, 10 percent were under 4 years of age and 36 percent were older than 12 (U.S. Department of Health and Human Services, Children's Bureau, 1998).

Who Are the Abusers?

Most of the victims (84 percent) were abused by their parents. Mothers were responsible for 32 percent of the physical abuse and 47 percent of the neglect.

Nonrelatives were the perpetrators of 29 percent of sexual abuse. Fathers acting alone were responsible for 22 percent, whereas other relatives

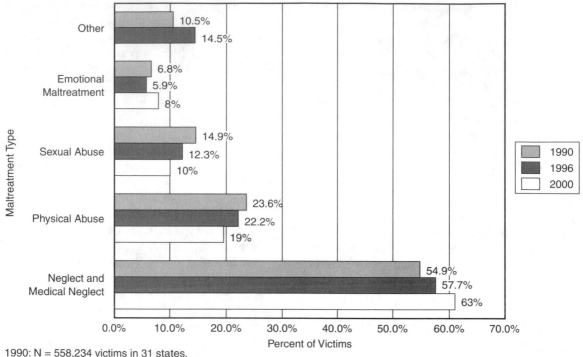

1990: N = 558,234 victims in 31 states.
1996: N = 572,943 victims in 31 states.
2000: N = 879,000 victims in 31 states.

FIGURE 10.1 Types of maltreatment, 1990, 1996, 2000.

Neglect, as manifested in deprivation of necessities, is the most frequently reported form of abuse and neglect.

Sources: From *Child Maltreatment, 1996: Reports from the States to the National Child Abuse and Neglect Data System,* by the U.S. Department of Health and Human Services, Children's Bureau, 1998, Washington, DC: U.S. Government Printing Office.

Summary of Key Findings from Calendar Year 2000, by the U.S. Department of Health and Human Services, Children's Bureau, Administration on Children, Youth and Families, National Child Abuse and Neglect Data System (NCANDS), retrieved May 22, 2002, from *http://www.calib.com/nccanch/prevmnth.scope/ncands.cfm*

accounted for 19 percent of sexual abuse. Most sexual abuse was committed by someone who continued to be near the child, placing the child at high risk for repeat attacks.

Perpetrators of maltreatment are defined by most states as parents and other caregivers including other relatives, foster parents, and babysitters. Females account for 60 percent of the perpetrators, and males, 40 percent. Median age of perpetrators was 34 for males and 31 for females (NCANDS, 2002).

Fatalities of the Young

Young children are most at risk for fatal attacks. In 2000, 1,200 children died of abuse or neglect, a rate of 1.71 victims per 100,000 children. Of these, 44 percent were infants. Eighty-five percent of the fatalities were for children under six years of age. The large increase in fatalities in early childhood appears to be the consequence of better reporting (NCANDS, 2002). The figures in Table 10.1 have slightly different age categories, but the incidence of fatalities of the young

TABLE 10.1   Child fatality victims by sex and age, detailed case data component (DCDC).

Age Group	Child Sex		Totals
	Male	**Female**	
0–3	128	106	234
	(74.4%)	(78.5%)	(76.2%)
4–7	23	21	44
	(13.4%)	(15.6%)	(14.3%)
8–11	15	4	19
	(8.7%)	(3.0%)	(6.2%)
12 and over	6	4	10
	(3.5%)	(3.0%)	(3.3%)
Totals	172	135	307
	(100.0%)	(100.0%)	(100.0%)

Note: Over 76 percent of fatalities occurred to children three or younger.

Source: From *Child Maltreatment, 1996: Reports from the States to the National Child Abuse and Neglect Data System*, by the U.S. Department of Health and Human Services, Children's Bureau, 1998, Washington, DC: U.S. Government Printing Office.

are evident. Seventy-six percent were infants under the age of three. Infants and young children are much more vulnerable to fatal injuries than older children because their skull, muscles, and bones are in the early stages of development.

Shaken Baby Syndrome

Parent educators and teachers should discuss shaken baby syndrome with parents and those who care for infants, because violent shaking is extremely dangerous for infants and young children. Children under two have undeveloped neck muscles, and sudden motion can result in the brain pulling away and tearing blood vessels and brain cells. The force with which an angry person might shake a child is five to ten times greater than if the child had simply fallen (American Humane Association, 2001).

Even pushing a young child on a swing is cause for concern. Is the baby able to hold its head upright? Is the head bobbing back and forth? If it is, the jarring of the brain might cause injury. Tossing a baby in the air results in jarring and should be avoided. Shaken baby syndrome appeared in medical literature about 1972 and has since been recognized as a cause of injury or death for young children. Shaking can cause subdural hemorrhage, brain swelling, and damage that may result in developmental delays, mental retardation, blindness, paralysis, hearing loss, or death (American Humane Association, 2001). Parents should play with their children, but they should never shake them, either in play or in anger.

Incidence of Child Abuse

Although some may believe the incidence of abuse is exaggerated, doctors who see children every day believe that child abuse occurs more often than the data indicate and that statistics reveal merely the tip of the iceberg (Fontana, 1973b; Gelles & Lancaster, 1987; Green, 1988). Fontana, a pediatrician who works with abused children, believes that one or two children are killed and thousands are permanently injured by their parents each day in the United States. He states, "In New York City two children per week die at the hands of their care providers" (Green, 1988, p. 10).

It was not until the 1980s that people began to realize the extent of sexual abuse. The lingering aftermath of being sexually abused was not previously acknowledged by the medical community. There were 150,000 confirmed cases of child sexual abuse reported in 1993 (Finkelhor, 1994). Adults who suffered sexual abuse as children have begun to report their plight and seek help.

The story is clear: There is a great deal of child abuse and neglect in our society. For many, violence has become an accepted mode of behavior. Sexual abuse is increasing. Television often depicts violence and force as the normal way of life. Physical punishment has long been condoned and is sanctioned by schools in many states as an alternative to other forms of discipline. The long acceptance of physical abuse makes its detection and control more difficult.

Response by Schools

> It is very important to distinguish between willful neglect and a parent's or caretaker's failure to provide necessities of life because of poverty or cultural norms. (U.S. Department of Health and Human Services, 1992, p. 2)

Schools can be part of the child abuse and neglect prevention system when they identify families that have difficulties due to poverty or cultural norms. The school can provide clothing exchanges, free breakfasts and lunches, and educational support for families at risk of abuse and neglect because of poverty. The school can offer workshops to help families understand the importance of nurturing their children. It can help parents who do not speak English by offering interpreters and educational opportunities. Positive interactions in the classroom where each child has a partner—someone to help them feel a part of the classroom—can reduce children's isolation and depression.

Besharov (1990) wrote a book, *Recognizing Child Abuse*, to help professionals recognize child abuse. There is concern that the flood of unsubstantiated claims makes it difficult to care for the children who are being abused. Child protection agencies are overwhelmed with reports. Families wrongly accused can go through a very traumatic experience. For example, Besharov points out that reasonable corporal punishment, such as spanking a child, should not be reported, but a suspicious injury or a "forceful assault to the head of a child of any age is so dangerous that it is usually considered 'unreasonable'" (p. 67). Consider whether the injury was accidental—the intent of the parent or other person—and the condition of the child. Refer to *Recognizing Child Abuse* for detailed information. When in doubt, you must report.

Communication with Families

Just as there are varieties and levels of abuse and neglect, there should be variations in the school's interaction with parents. Child care workers and school personnel who want to help an abused child must exercise good judgment. Their first response may be to want to call the parent to determine how the injury occurred. In the case of violent abuse, the child may be in danger of being permanently injured or killed. Calling the family to discuss the problem not only fails to help the family but also may precipitate more abuse. In addition, the family may become alarmed and move away. Then the child may be abused for many more months before a new school or center detects the problem. *With serious abuse, do not call the parents or try to handle the situation by yourself. Contact the appropriate authorities immediately.*

If you are working with a child you think might be enduring physical punishment at home, but who is disruptive in class, it is better to have a conference and discuss the situation. Offer appropriate discipline ideas, such as timeouts or restrictions on free time or television viewing, and continue communication with the parents. Include the child in the conference. A contract between parents, child, and teacher might be helpful. Merely calling and talking with the parent about misbehavior at school may result in the child being severely punished.

When the problem appears to be neglect rather than abuse, as when a child comes to school hungry or inappropriately dressed, a supportive visit or call to the family is in order. The school can provide emotional support and food and clothing. Working *with* parents shows them they are not alone with their overwhelming problems. If providing services is beyond the capability of the school, or if the family needs professional help, social services should be called.

CATEGORIES OF MALTREATMENT

Factors in Child Abuse

Three factors are almost always present for child abuse to occur. The first is parents or caregivers who have the potential to abuse. The second is a child the parents regard as different. The third factor is a stress situation that brings on a crisis.

According to Helfer and Kempe (1987), abusive parents or caregivers tend to acquire the potential to abuse over many years. These people usually had deprived childhoods. They lacked a consistent, loving, nurturing environment when they were young. They have a poor self-image, and their mates are passive and do not or cannot give their spouses the emotional support they need. The family probably has isolated itself; the parents have no support system from neighbors or community. Because few of them understand child development, they have unrealistic expectations of their children.

Such parents are most likely to abuse children they consider different. Child abuse also occurs against a child who actually is different from the norm—for example, a child with hyperactivity or mental retardation or another disability.

Before the abusive act occurs, there is a precipitating event—one that does not directly cause the specific act against the child, but a minor or major crisis that sets the stage for the parent to lose control. This crisis may be physical (e.g., a broken washing machine) or personal (e.g., spouse desertion, a death in the family). With these three factors the stage is set. The parent or caregiver loses control and abuses the child (Helfer, 1975).

NEGLECT

Child neglect occurs when there is failure to care for the child's basic needs. This type of maltreatment is reported most often (see Figure 10.1). Physical neglect is the area most frequently identified, but there are also emotional and educational neglect. Parents may not be indifferent. Instead, they may not recognize the importance of medical care or a developmental environment, or they may be incapable of furnishing them.

Physical neglect refers to the parents' failure to provide the necessities—adequate shelter, care and supervision, food, clothing, and protection. Neglect is the most common type of child abuse, accounting for more than half of maltreatment. The child shows signs of malnutrition, usually is irritable, and may need medical attention. The child often goes hungry and needs supervision after school. The parents are either unable or unwilling to give proper care. Neglect is often the result of the parent's inability to supply necessary care in 90 percent of those cases reported. Insufficient income is cited as the greatest cause of neglect (Cupoli & Sewell, 1988; Horton & Cruise, 2001).

Physical neglect may include medical neglect, abandonment, and not allowing a runaway to return home. When a child is abandoned, it represents renunciation and total rejection of the child by the parent.

Educational neglect occurs when parents permit chronic truancy, fail to make sure their child attends school, or fail to tend to any special educational needs of the child. Both medical neglect and educational neglect result in the child's inability to develop fully.

Emotional neglect includes refusal to provide psychological help if the child needs it, exposure of the child to abuse of someone else (e.g., spousal abuse in the child's presence), and permission for use of drugs and alcohol by the child

(U.S. Department of Health and Human Services, 1992).

Parents may be psychologically unavailable to the child, ignoring their child's need for comfort. Instances of failure to thrive may be the result of emotional neglect (Brier, Berliner, Bulkley, Jenny, & Reid, 1996).

❧ PHYSICAL ABUSE AND NEGLECT

The *physically abused* child shows signs of injury—welts, cuts, bruises, burns, fractures, or lacerations. Educators should be aware of repeated injuries, untreated injuries, multiple injuries, and new injuries added to old.

Multiple maltreatment often occurs in a child who suffers abuse or neglect. Although emotional maltreatment can be isolated, instances of physical abuse or neglect usually are accompanied by emotional abuse.

Recognizing Physical Abuse

Although many bruises and abrasions are accidental, others give cause for the teacher to believe that they were intentionally inflicted. Bruises are the most common symptoms of physical abuse. Other symptoms include welts, lumps, or ridges on the body, usually caused by a blow; burns, shown by redness, blistering, or peeling of the skin; fractured bones; scars; lacerations or torn cuts; and abrasions.

Head Start personnel are given guidelines with four criteria for identifying abuse of the preschool child. These guidelines are useful for detection of abuse in children of any age. The first is location of the injury. As illustrated in Figure 10.2, bruises on the knees, elbows, shins, and—for the preschool child—the forehead are considered normal in most circumstances. "If these bruises were found on the back, genital area, thighs, buttocks, face or back of legs, one should be suspicious" (U.S. Department of Health, Education and Welfare, 1977, p. 67).

The second criterion is evidence of repetition of injury. A significantly large number of bruises or cuts and injuries in various stages of healing should be suspect. There are instances, however, when repetition could be accidental: the child could be accident-prone, so the correlation between the injury and an explanation of its cause—the fourth criterion, described later—needs to be kept in mind.

The third criterion is the appearance of the injury. If it is obvious that the bruise, cut, or burn was inflicted by an object, such as a belt, stick, or cigarette, the teacher or caregiver should suspect abuse.

The fourth criterion is the correlation between the injury and the explanation given by the child or the parent. The accident as described should be likely to produce the resultant injury. For example, could round burns shaped like cigarettes be caused by the child playing too near the stove?

Parents who were victims of maltreatment as children are more likely to resort to abuse when confronted with other risk factors (Horton & Cruise, 2001).

In ascertaining the extent of suspected physical abuse, the teacher should not remove any of the child's clothing. That should be done only by such personnel as a nurse or doctor who would undress a child as part of their professional responsibilities.

After reviewing the four criteria and checking school policy—the suspicious placement of injury, the severity and repetition of injuries, evidence of infliction by an object, and inconsistent explanation (or consistent if the child reports the abuse)—the educator must report a suspected injury to the appropriate authorities.

❧ EMOTIONAL ABUSE

Compared to physical neglect and abuse, it is more difficult to identify *emotional neglect and abuse,* defined as a "pattern of behavior that can seriously interfere with a child's positive emotional development" (American Humane Association, 1992c). Parents of emotionally abused children are usually overly harsh and critical. They withhold love and acceptance and do not

Cigarette burns on the hands or body, puncture wounds, scald marks, and bruises are easily recognizable signs of physical abuse.

Source: Courtesy of Barton D. Schmitt, M.D., C. Henry Kempe National Center for Prevention and Treatment of Child Abuse and Neglect.

Front view

Normal bruising areas

Front and back views

Suspicious bruising areas

FIGURE 10.2 Comparison of typical and suspicious bruising areas.

Note: The bruises children receive in play are depicted on the left. The bruises on the right would not normally happen in everyday play.

Source: From *Child Abuse and Neglect: A Self-Instructional Text for Head Start Personnel,* by the U.S. Department of Health, Education and Welfare, Head Start Bureau and Children's Bureau, 1977, Washington, DC: U.S. Government Printing Office.

give the child either physical or verbal encouragement and praise. Although they expect performance, they do not support the child's endeavors. Physical abuse damages a child's body, and emotional abuse damages a child's psyche. "Children who are constantly shamed, terrorized, humiliated, or rejected suffer at least as much if not more than if they had been physically assaulted" (p. 1). Patterns can include the following:

- Terrorizing
- Continued rejection of the child
- Refusal to provide needed nurturance

- Refusal to provide help for a child's psychological problems
- Lack of needed mental or physical stimulation
- Forced involvement with drugs, criminal activities, and other corruptive forces (American Humane Association, 1992b)

Chapter 1 discusses the importance of attachment during the first years of life. Spitz (1945) reported on children who developed marasmus—progressive emaciation—and died from lack of nurturing. These are obvious cases of emotional abuse, but children who are not nurtured and who live in an emotionally insecure environment may show signs of low self-esteem, slow educational growth, and insecurity.

Egeland (1988) reported on the Minnesota Mother-Child Project, a longitudinal study that worked with at-risk children and their families. In the 267 families, 44 children were identified as maltreated during their first two years of life. The researchers assessed four maltreatment groups: physical abuse, neglect, verbal rejections, and psychological unavailability at 12, 18, 24, 41, and 54 months. The infancy period was examined in relation to attachment, the "relationship that the infant develops a sense of trust and confidence" (p. D-12). The children were followed through the periods until they were in school. At each level it was apparent that psychological unavailability affects the child's development, self-esteem, and confidence. The children who were neglected (psychological unavailability) displayed greater problems in attention. They were

> . . . uninvolved, reliant, lacking creative initiative, and having much more difficulty comprehending the day-to-day schoolwork than children in the control group. They were impatient, disrespectful, expressed anxiety about their schoolwork and were more likely to make irrelevant response in the classroom. . . . On the individual scales, the neglected children were rated as anxious, withdrawn, unpopular, aggressive, and obsessive-compulsive. Not only did they present far more problems than children in the control group, but they also presented more problems than children in the physical abuse group. (p. D–15)

The difficulty of identifying psychological unavailability and emotional neglect makes it doubly difficult for the schools to respond to the concern. It also is impossible for teachers to overcome a student's childhood devoid of emotional security. However, there are incidents and examples of teachers who have had a positive effect on children who were emotionally neglected.

> I don't think my fourth-grade teacher, Mr. Evans, had any idea what an impact he had on my life. He was my father's opposite and taught me much about

how men could be. He was consistent and concerned while my father was drunk or ignoring me. He praised me while my father criticized. He prized my mind and my accomplishments; my father cared only about abusing my body. I learned a great deal from that teacher about who I was and that I was an important person. I think I became a teacher myself to be like him, so that I could make a difference for some other child. (Tower, 1992, p. 57)

Teachers have a great deal of power over how the students in their classes feel about themselves. Children's self-confidence and self-esteem can be either enhanced or diminished. They can either feel good about themselves or view themselves as incapable, unlikable people.

﷯ SEXUAL ABUSE

Sexual abuse is defined under the Child Abuse Prevention and Treatment Act (CAPTA) as:

- the employment, use, persuasion, inducement, enticement, or coercion of any child to engage in, or assist any other person to engage in, any sexually explicit conduct or simulation of such conduct for the purpose of producing a visual depiction of such conduct; or

- the rape, and in cases of caretaker or interfamilial relationships, statutory rape, molestation, prostitution, or other form of sexual exploitation of children, or incest with children. (NCCAN, 2001, p. 2)

Keep in mind that although the child might be forced to cooperate, he or she is (by legal definition) not capable of giving consent (Hagans & Case, 1988, p. 21).

Categories of sexual abuse include:

1. *Incest.* Physical sexual activity between members of the extended family.

2. *Pedophilia.* Sexual preference by an adult for prepubertal children.

3. *Exhibitionism.* Exposure of genitals to someone of the opposite gender.

4. *Molestation.* Fondling, touching, masturbation, or kissing child, especially on breast and genital areas.

5. *Sexual intercourse (statutory rape).* Includes penile-vaginal intercourse, fellatio (oral-genital contact), and sodomy (anal-genital contact).

6. *Rape.* Sexual intercourse or attempted sexual intercourse without consent.

7. *Sexual sadism.* Infliction of bodily harm for sexual gratification.

8. *Child pornography.* Photographs, videos, or films showing sexual acts featuring children. An estimated 300,000 children are involved in child pornography.

9. *Child prostitution.* Children in sex acts for profit. (Kempe & Kempe, 1984)

Sexual conduct becomes abuse when activities are instigated through trickery or force with the instigator—one who has caretaking relations with the child or has age and maturational advantage over the child. The situation includes a perpetrator who has a power advantage over a child and breaks the rule of consensuality (Finkelhor, 1994).

Abuse may be categorized as contact and noncontact sexual abuse. Contact includes touching sexual parts of a child's body or having the child touch parts of the sexual partner's body which may include penetration (into the vagina, mouth, or anus) and nonpenetration. Nonpenetration contact involves fondling, kissing, or touching sexual parts of the body by either the child or the partner.

Noncontact sexual abuse may involve exhibitionism, voyeurism, or the making of pornographic materials, and may also include verbal harassment (Finkelhor, 1994).

Sexual abuse is difficult to detect. About 80 percent of the offenders are known to the family or are family members. The victims are most often girls (77 percent) ranging from infants to adolescents (U.S. Department of Health and Human Services, Children's Bureau, 1998).

Although historically most societies have had taboos against such behavior, sexual abuse and incest have always existed. But sexual abuse generally has been concealed, mythicized, or ignored. Not until the late 1970s and early 1980s did its existence become realistically recognized. Even then, most people gathering information on the problem believed that, as in reported incidents of other kinds of child abuse, only the tip of the iceberg had been revealed.

Incest and other sexual abuse occurs in all socioeconomic groups, and therefore, teachers in all schools or child care settings should be aware of the indicators. Sexually abused children often exhibit some of the following physical and behavioral characteristics (Krugman, 1986; Riggs, 1982):

Physical Signs
- Bruises or bleeding in external genitalia or anal area
- Uncomfortable while sitting
- Difficulty walking
- Pregnancy
- Torn, bloody, or stained underclothing
- Sexually transmitted disease

Behavioral Signs
- Appetite disorders
- Phobias
- Guilt
- Temper tantrums
- Neurotic and conduct disorders
- Truancy
- Suicide attempts
- Confides with teacher or nurse that he or she has been sexually mistreated
- Reports by other children that their friend is being sexually mistreated
- Displays precocious sexual behavior and/or knowledge
- Unwilling to change for gym

- Withdrawn, engages in fantasy
- Depressed, sad, and teary-eyed
- Confused about own identity
- Frequent absences justified by male caregiver or parent
- Acts out in a seductive manner
- Reluctant to go home
- Young child regresses to earlier behavior by thumb-sucking, bed-wetting, difficulty in eating, sleeping, and fear of the dark
- Older child turns to drugs, tries to run away, and has difficulty doing schoolwork

Concern about sexual abuse has steadily risen because of its deleterious effects on the child and, later, the adult. Psychological and emotional reactions are common. Children feel trapped, confused, betrayed, and disgraced. They may have fears, phobias, somatic complaints, mood changes, anxieties, hysterical seizures, multiple personalities, or nightmares. They may become prostitutes, self-mutilating, or suicidal. At school they may show developmental lags, communication problems, and apparent learning deficiencies (Finkelhor, 1986; Krugman, 1986; Ryan, 1989; Wodarski & Johnson, 1988).

After a 15-year increase (from 1977 until 1992), substantiated cases of child sexual abuse have declined from 149,890 substantiated cases in 1992 to 103,600 cases in 1998, a 31 percent reduction. There may be a variety of reasons for this. Public awareness, prevention programs, incarceration of offenders, and treatment programs may have had an effect on the reduction of incidence of abuse (Jones & Finkelhor, 2001).

Boys and girls have similar responses to sexual abuse, both long term and short term, including fears, sleep problems, and distractedness (Finkelhor, 1990). The differences show boys are less symptomatic when evaluated by teachers and parents, but the same when evaluated by themselves. Whereas boys may act out more aggressively, girls may act more depressed.

Children who are being sexually abused often go through five phases: (a) secrecy; (b) helplessness; (c) entrapment and accommodation; (d) delayed, conflicted, and unconvincing disclosure; and (e) retraction (Summit, 1983). To understand a child's predicament, one must understand the helplessness the child feels in responding to the adult who is more physically powerful and supposedly more knowledgeable. The adult first approaches the child with the need for secrecy: "Everything will be all right if you do not tell. No one else will understand our secret." "Your mother will hate you." "If you tell, it will break up the family." "If you tell, I'll kill your pet." "If you tell, I'll spank you."

Whatever the secret, the child is in a no-win position. The child fears being hurt if he or she tells the secret. When the child does tell, the reaction is often disbelief. "Unless the victim can find some permission and power to share the secret and unless there is the possibility of an engaging, non-punitive response" the child may spend a life of "self-imposed exile from intimacy, trust and self-validation" (Summit, 1983, p. 182).

The teacher or child caregiver who suspects sexual abuse must report those suspicions—social service and child protection agencies are established in every state.

The teacher's role is a supportive one. Continue to have normal expectations for the child, keep a stable environment for the child, and do not make the child feel ostracized or different. Treat the child with understanding, be sensitive to the child's needs, and help build the child's self-esteem. Several programs have been developed to help the child develop defenses against personal abuse (see the Appendix following Chapter 11).

Reviewers and teachers have asked for more help in responding to a child who shares about an abusive situation. An article by Austin (2000) gives suggestions to help teachers respond to a sexually abused child. The topics include:

- Remain calm and reassuring. Speak quietly; do not panic.

- Take the child to a private place like the nurse's office.
- Position yourself at the child's eye level.
- Speak on the child's level. Use language the child understands.
- Listen intently.
- Take the child seriously.
- Obtain only the information necessary to make a report.
- Do not put words in the child's mouth.
- Do not use words that the child has not already used. (Don't use words describing the sex that are not in the child's vocabulary.)
- Allow the child to have feelings.
- Reassure the child that the abuse is not his or her fault.
- Start your conversation with general open-ended questions and allow the child to tell the story without interrupting.
- Do not condemn the abuser.
- Let the child know that he or she is not alone and that you are willing to help.
- Do not touch the child without permission.
- Tell the truth—do not make promises you will not be able to keep.
- Tell the child about the process, that others will be told about the abuse.
- Thank the child for confiding in you.
- Help the child devise a safety plan if abuse occurs again. Have the child tell someone immediately—a reliable person at home or a teacher or school professional.
- Assure the child that she or he will remain with someone safe until authorities come. Do not allow the child to return to the home of the abuser. (pp. 4–5)

✖ BULLYING AND VIOLENCE IN SCHOOLS

"Bullying refers to repeated, unprovoked, harmful actions by one child or children against another" (Bullock, 2002, p. 130). Bullying can be physical or emotional. The emotional bullying includes be-

ing teased, threatened, taunted, called names, or having negative rumors started about one. Equally devastating is being rejected and excluded from other groups of children (Banks, 1997; Bullock, 2002; Garrity, Baris, & Porter, 2000).

Physical bullying can include hitting, pushing, rough and intimidating actions, a quick jab, or a head shoved into a locker (Bullock, 2000; Garrity et al., 2000). There is a difference between girl bullying and boy bullying. Boys use more physical along with verbal aggression, whereas girls add social intimidation to verbal aggression.

Two types of victims are chosen by the aggressor. One is the passive victim who seems to be helpless and unable to fight back. Afraid and alone, the child is an easy victim of the aggressor. The victim may convey his or her vulnerability through body language.

The second type of victim is the child who is a provocative victim. This child is impulsive, acts without thinking, and responds to the attack by fighting back (Bullock, 2002; Garrity et al., 2000). "Soon the bully has far more children on his or her side and the victim feels even more helpless. When a scene such as this plays itself out day after day, the victimized child grows more miserable, desperate, and incapable of handling the situation. If the cycle has grown this serious, it will not turn itself around without adult help" (Garrity et al., p. 7).

Bullies tend to be children whose parents use physical discipline; these children strike back physically to handle problems. They may break school rules and are oppositional to authority (Banks, 1997). Bullies enjoy dominating others; they also have little empathy for others. As mentioned, boy bullies usually have physical strength that helps them dominate others. Girls use their ability to control other girls through intimidation and exclusion.

Is it time for schools to provide programs that reduce the incidence of emotional violence? Is it time to recognize the emotional damage that is done to children by children? Is it time to recognize that bullying and rejection are more than opportunities to learn how to handle aggression?

Are bullying and violence against a child more than a part of growing up? Could bullying be classified as psychological and physical abuse?

Awareness of Abuse, Child to Child

Another area of concern that has been evident in schools and playgrounds for many years, but which is most often overlooked as a process of growing up, is degradation of one child by another whether it is defined as bullying or teasing. Research by the Family and Work Institute, conducted from October to December 2001, found that the issue of being teased or gossiped about in a mean way within the past month reached 67 percent. The study cannot say which came first, the being hurt or hurting, but 68 percent of those who were gossiped about or teased in the past month turned around and did the same to others. Sixty-one percent of the Colorado students in the study had been rejected or ignored, and 32 percent had been bullied (Galinsky & Salmond, 2002).

"Many kids believe that insensitivity and meanness can be triggers for more harmful kinds of violence" (p. 15). The study involved students, 5th through 12th grades. More children are bullied, hit, kicked, shoved between 5th and 8th grade than high school where there is more gossip and students are more often teased. Programs designed to reduce devastating experiences for children in school need to be implemented in schools. Action steps to end violence include:

1. help to establish norms where differences are not put down but are celebrated

2. work toward the creation of a civil society where there is more caring and respect

3. improve the relationships that children have in all aspects of their lives—at home and at school

4. include young people's views of how to end violence in violence prevention efforts

5. establish, invest in, and evaluate violence prevention efforts, as well as positive youth development efforts (Galinsky & Salmond, 2002, pp. 57–63)

6. do *not* victimize the child who has already been bullied and victimized

Can Teachers Make a Difference?

Teachers are extremely important to a child's feeling adequate, competent, and cared for. One way teachers can lose this and add to a child's insecurity is by using children as scapegoats in a class. They control the rest of the class by focusing on one or two children who are targeted for discipline and negative reinforcement. This author has observed classrooms in which teachers cause emotional abuse in their efforts to control the classroom. Teachers can have an attitude toward a child that fosters prejudice and discrimination against that child by the child's classmates. They do not recognize that they are, in effect, emotionally abusing the child. Their actions are not occasional disciplinary decisions; they are caused by a repeated pattern as described by James Garbarino, executive director of the Erikson Institute, "the chronic pattern that erodes and corrodes a child . . . that persistent, chronic pattern of behavior toward a child" (American Humane Association, 1992c, p. 2).

Garbarino was speaking about parents and children, but this chronic pattern is also damaging when it is used in the schools. An occasional loss of control by parents (or teachers) does not indicate emotional abuse. Human beings may lose control and say hurtful things, but the person who consistently destroys a child's self-esteem is the one who is being extremely hurtful to the child and is emotionally abusing the child.

Programs to Combat Bullying and Violence in Schools

The National Education Association Professional Library has published teacher guides to prevent bullying and sexual harassment. The one for students kindergarten through grade three is titled *Quit It*. Educational Equity Concepts, Inc., Wellesley College Center for Research on Women, and the NEA Professional Library cooperated in producing the teacher's guide which discusses procedures and activities in detail (Froschi, Sprung, & Mullin-Rindler, 1998).

The second guide, *Bullyproof: A Teacher's Guide on Teasing and Bullying,* was developed for fourth- and fifth-grade students and was a joint publication of the Wellesley College Center and NEA Professional Library (Stein, 1996). One activity illustrates an example of a letter written to the person who is bullying. Lesson 8, which is one or two class sessions, is titled "What Are Your Rights" and is a review and discussion of sexual harassment and relevant laws. Lesson 10 is an action alert, and allows the students to brainstorm to answer how to end bullying and teasing among the students. The guides include materials, a teacher's guide, and many references (Stein & Sjostrom, 1996).

The third guide, titled *Flirting or Hurting? A Teacher's Guide to Student-to-Student Sexual Harassment in Schools,* gives examples and discussion points to clarify what sexual harassment is and what can be done if a student thinks he or she is being harassed (Stein & Sjostrom, 1994).

✏ CORPORAL PUNISHMENT IN SCHOOLS

Does there seem to be an element of inconsistency in our work to eliminate abuse in the schools with the policy of corporal punishment still in place in many schools? Every industrialized country in the world prohibits school corporal punishment except the United States, Canada, and one state in Australia (Center for Effective Discipline, 2000, July). In 2000, 27 states in the U.S. had banned corporal punishment. The paddle is the primary instrument of physical discipline in the schools that still had corporal punishment. In the United States 365,058 students were physically punished in the 1997–1998 school year. Mississippi (10.1 percent punished) and Arkansas (9.2 percent punished) had the greatest use of corporal punishment in schools. Texas had the largest number of students (81,373) paddled in one year, ac-

cording to data released in 2000 (Center for Effective Discipline, 2000, July).

Zigler noted that "the widespread acceptance of physical abuse as an appropriate disciplinary technique implicitly condones the physical abuse of children" (Green, 1988, p. 10). "Not only can children be injured, but the practice perpetuates the cycle of child abuse. . . . Children abused at school as well as at home further incorporate the message that violence is the only way to ensure compliance with rules laid down by another individual or group of individuals" (Tower, 1992, p. 56). Although we have made considerable progress since the 1700s and 1800s when child labor was rampant, our cultural values, socialization patterns, and resultant discipline still support the use of physical force with children.

The National Committee for Prevention of Child Abuse adopted the following policy statement in 1983:

> Since corporal punishment in schools and custodial settings contradicts our national policy dedicated to the eradication of child abuse from our society, and since appropriate disciplinary alternatives can be made available, we will work toward the elimination of corporal punishment in the schools and toward the adoption of alternatives to corporal punishment. (Green, 1988, pp. 9–10)

More than 40 national organizations have policies that oppose corporal punishment in the schools. Among them are the American Academy of Pediatrics, American Association for Counseling & Development, American Bar Association, American Medical Association, American Psychiatric Association, American Psychological Association, American Public Health Association, Association for Childhood Education International, Council for Exceptional Children, National Association for the Advancement of Colored People, National Association of Elementary School Principals, and the National Association of School Nurses, National Association of School Psychologists, National Association of State Boards of Education, National Congress of Parents and Teachers, National Education Association, and the National Mental Health Association.

In 2002, 27 states had banned corporal punishment. They included Alaska, California, Connecticut, Hawaii, Illinois, Iowa, Maine, Maryland, Massachusetts, Michigan, Minnesota, Montana, Nebraska, Nevada, New Hampshire, New Jersey, New York, North Dakota, Oregon, Rhode Island, South Dakota, Utah, Vermont, Virginia, Washington, West Virginia, and Wisconsin. Many cities in states that have not abolished corporal punishment have abolished the practice in their schools. In general, schools have been alarmingly slow to join the national movement to reduce abuse—a movement that began in the 1960s and has continued into the 21st century. Thus, schools perpetuate the use of force to discipline children. In addition, schools that use ridicule, fear, and ostracism to discipline children may cause emotional abuse in the classroom (Krugman & Krugman, 1984).

The reasons to abandon corporal punishment rest on the beliefs that corporal punishment

- Discourages the development of internal controls by the child.
- Is not a necessary form of discipline.
- Shows that inflicting pain is permissible.
- Eliminates discussion and positive communication between child and adult.
- Causes children to try not to get caught and to avoid punishment through devious behavior.
- Increases the child's aggression.
- Shows a lack of respect for the child as a human being.

Nineteen nations have abolished corporal punishment: American Samoa, Austria, Belgium, Britain, Denmark, Fiji, Finland, France, Germany, Holland, Ireland, Italy, Kenya, Namibia, New Zealand, Norway, Poland, Portugal, Romania, Russia, South Africa, Spain, Sweden, Switzerland, Thailand, Tobago, Trinidad, Turkey, Zambia, and Zimbabwe, (Center for Effective Discipline, 2000). Poland was the first to abolish it in 1783 (End Violence Against the Next Generation, n.d.). There is a move in Europe to put an end to all corporal punishment in both home and school.

WHO REPORTS MALTREATMENT CASES?

Cases of child maltreatment are reported by both nonprofessionals and professionals. Educators have become much more aware of their responsibility, and most reports come from this group (16 percent in 1996), as shown in Figure 10.3. Professionals—including educators as well as law enforcement, social services, and medical personnel—made 52 percent of the reports. Friends and family members reported 25 percent of the cases (U.S. Department of Health and Human Services, Children's Bureau, 1998). As Figure 10.3 illustrates, 12 percent of the reports were made anonymously and 8 percent were classified as "other"; both probably contain some of the same groups.

Situations related to teachers and schools are described in *Child Abuse and Neglect: A Shared Community Concern* (U.S. Department of Health and Human Services, 1992). Two examples follow.

REPORT

When Cindy was 8 years of age, her teacher called Child Protection Services (CPS). Cindy was the only child in her family who wore old, tattered clothing to school and was not given the same privileges and opportunities as her brothers and sisters. The other children were allowed to join in after-school activities; however, Cindy was not allowed to participate in any outside activities. Cindy became very withdrawn at school. She stopped speaking in class and would not engage in play activities with her classmates. Her academic performance declined rapidly. Finally, Cindy became incontinent and had "accidents" in class.

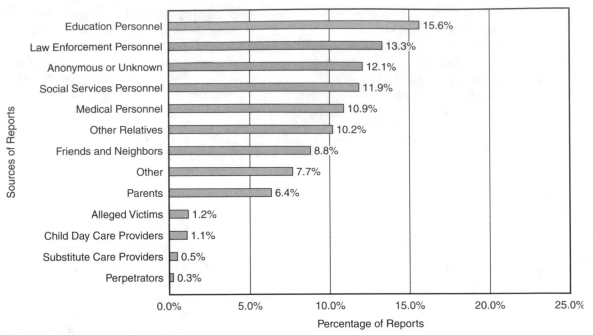

N = 1,490,340 reports from 42 states.

FIGURE 10.3 Sources of child abuse and neglect reports.

Education personnel make up the largest single source of child abuse and neglect reporting.

Source: From *Child Maltreatment, 1996: Reports from the States to the National Child Abuse and Neglect Data System,* by the U.S. Department of Health and Human Services, Children's Bureau, 1998, Washington, DC: U.S. Government Printing Office.

REASONS

The reasons the teacher reported this case to CPS were:

- Serious differential treatment of one child in the family.
- Marked decline in academic performance and class participation.
- Incontinence.

REPORT

Susan, aged 7, was in her first-grade class when her teacher noticed that she had difficulty sitting and had some unusually shaped marks on her arm. Susan was sent to the school nurse to be examined. The nurse noted approximately 12 linear and loop-shaped marks on her back and buttocks. These marks ranged in length from 6 to 10 inches. The nurse believed that the marks were inflicted by a belt and belt buckle. The marks were purple, blue, brown, and yellow, indicating that the bruises were sustained at different times. Susan said she did not know how she got the bruises. The nurse spoke with the principal, who called CPS.

REASONS

The school principal reported this case to CPS because:

- The child had sustained a physical injury.
- The bruises were inflicted at different times, perhaps days apart. (Even if the bruises had been inflicted at one time this case should still be reported. The fact that the bruises were in different stages of healing raises greater concern for the child's safety.)

- The nurse's clinical opinion was that the injuries were inflicted by a belt and belt buckle. (U.S. Department of Health and Human Services, 1992)

Indicators that a child has the potential need for protections is described in Box 10.1.

BEHAVIORS AND ATTITUDES OF PARENTS AND CHILDREN THAT MAY INDICATE CHILD ABUSE

Specialists working with child abuse (Fontana, 1973a; Helfer & Kempe, 1987) have also developed some guidelines to help educators determine the existence of child abuse. The following are modified from publications by Head Start, the U.S. Department of Health and Human Services, and the American Humane Association.

The Child of Preschool Age

1. Does the child seem to fear his or her parents?
2. Does the child miss preschool or the child care center often?
3. Does the child bear evidence of physical abuse? Are there signs of battering, such as bruises or welts, belt or buckle marks, cuts, or burns?
4. Does the child exhibit extreme behavior changes? Is the child very aggressive at times and then fearful, withdrawn, and/or depressed?
5. Does the child have sores, bruises, or cuts that are not adequately cared for?
6. Does the child come to school inadequately dressed? Does the child look uncared for?
7. Does the child take over the parent role and try to "mother" the parent?
8. Does the child seem to be hungry for affection?

The Child of Elementary School Age

1. Does the child exhibit behavior that deviates from the norm? Is the child (a) aggressive, destructive, and disruptive or (b) passive and withdrawn? The first may be a child who is shouting for help, demanding attention, and striking out, whereas the second may be out of touch with reality, remote, submissive, and subdued, but crying for help in another way.
2. Does the child miss classes, or is the child often tardy? Does the child come to school too early and stay around after hours? In the first instance, the child's behavior suggests problems at home. In the second, the child may be pushed out in the morning and have nowhere to go after school.
3. Does the child bear evidence of physical abuse? Are there obvious signs of battering: bruises, belt or buckle marks, welts, lacerations, or burns?
4. Does the child lack social skills? Is the child unable to approach other children and play with them?
5. Does the child have learning problems that cannot be diagnosed? Does the child underperform? If intelligence tests show average academic ability and the child is not able to do the work, there may be problems at home.
6. Does the child show great sensitivity to others' feelings? Does the child get upset when another person is criticized? Abused children often have to "mother" their abusive parents, and some are overly sensitive to the feelings of others.
7. Does the child come to school inadequately dressed? Is the child unwashed and uncared for? These may be signs of neglect.
8. Does the child seem tired or fall asleep in class?
9. Does the child appear undernourished? Does the child attempt to save food? Is there real poverty in the home, or do the parents not care?
10. Does the child seem to be afraid of his or her parents?

Box 10.1

INDICATORS OF A CHILD'S POTENTIAL NEED FOR PROTECTION

	Physical Indicators	*Behavioral Indicators*
Physical Abuse	• unexplained bruises (in various stages of healing), welts, human bite marks, bald spots • unexplained burns, especially cigarette burns or immersion burns (glove like) • unexplained fractures, lacerations or abrasions	• self destructive • withdrawn and aggressive—behavioral extremes • uncomfortable with physical contact • arrives at school early or stays late as if afraid to be at home • chronic runaway (adolescents) • complains of soreness or moves uncomfortably • wears clothing inappropriate to weather, to cover body
Physical Neglect	• abandonment • unattended medical needs • consistent lack of supervision • consistent hunger, inappropriate dress, poor hygiene • lice, distended stomach, emaciated	• regularly displays fatigue or listlessness, falls asleep in class • steals food, begs from classmates • reports that no caretaker is at home • frequently absent or tardy • self destructive • school dropout (adolescents)
Sexual Abuse	• torn, stained or bloody underclothing • pain or itching in genital area • difficulty walking or sitting • bruises or bleeding in external genitalia • venereal disease • frequent urinary or yeast infections	• withdrawal, chronic depression • excessive seductiveness • role reversal, overly concerned for siblings • poor self esteem, self devaluation, lack of confidence • peer problems, lack of involvement • massive weight change • suicide attempts (especially adolescents) • hysteria, lack of emotional control • sudden school difficulties • inappropriate sex play or premature understanding of sex • threatened by physical contact, closeness
Emotional Maltreatment	• speech disorders • delayed physical development • substance abuse • ulcers, asthma, severe allergies	• habit disorders (sucking, rocking) • antisocial, destructive • neurotic traits (sleep disorders, inhibition of play) • passive and aggressive—behavioral extremes • delinquent behavior (especially adolescents) • developmentally delayed

Source: From *Guidelines for Schools to Help Protect Abused and Neglected Children,* by the American Association for Protecting Children (n.d.), Denver, CO: American Humane Association. Adapted in part from *Early Childhood Programs and the Prevention and Treatment of Child Abuse and Neglect,* by D. D. Broadhurst, M. Edmunds, and R. A. MacDicken, 1979, The User Manual Series, Washington, DC: U.S. Department of Health, Education and Welfare.

Scalded and battered, these children were victims of child abuse.

Source: Courtesy of Barton D. Schmitt, M.D., C. Henry Kempe National Center for Prevention and Treatment of Child Abuse and Neglect.

The Secondary-Level Student

Most of the traits just mentioned are relevant to detection of abuse in the middle school and high school student, but there are additional signs to watch for in the upper levels. In addition to evidence of physical abuse, neglect, truancy, and tardiness, the older student may experience the following:

1. Does the student have to assume too much responsibility at home?

2. Does the parent expect unrealistic and overly controlled behavior?

3. Does the student have difficulty conforming to school regulations and policies?

4. Does the student have problems communicating with his or her parents?

5. Does the student have a history of running away from home or refusing to go home?

6. Does the student act out sexually?

7. Does the student lack freedom and friends?

🐛 BEHAVIORAL AND PSYCHOLOGICAL CHARACTERISTICS OF THE CHILD IN SCHOOL

The largest group of children who chronically act out in the classroom is not a group with psychotic or cognitive impairments, but children with behavior disorders. Hochstedler categorizes three disorders: attention-deficit disorder, conduct disorder, and adjustment disorder (Sandberg, 1987). Although disorders do overlap, each disorder needs an individualized analysis to determine the appropriate intervention plan. *In each case, however, it is harmful to punish and make the child feel even more inadequate.* In conduct disorders the "alarming process is fueled by punishment approaches, when what is needed is to hold the child responsible for his/her destructive behavior without branding the child 'bad'" (p. 11). Acting out is a coping mechanism used by children who do not have an appropriate response repertoire.

Children with attention-deficit disorder (ADD) are found in almost every classroom. These children do not seem to be able to stay on task, concentrate, or complete their assignments. Children who are hyperactive probably have ADD, but it is not necessary to be hyperkinetic or hyperactive to be unable to concentrate and sit still. Every teacher has experienced the child who disrupts the room, fails to progress, and is constantly distracted, going from the assigned task to watch another child, flitting from one task to another and, thus, failing to progress in the academic program. Some of these children may have too much energy, or they may be hyperactive. ADD is distinguished by poorly organized, haphazard, and nongoal-directed activities. It is 10 times more likely to happen to a boy than to a girl.

In addition, without early intervention, ADD is a precursor to more intense problems. Hochstedler observed that "the pattern we see over and over with ADD children in the early years is their inability to pay attention and behave properly, followed by parents and teachers viewing the child as bad or unacceptable" (Sandberg, 1987, p. 10). This hurts the child's self-esteem and leads to a worsening of the condition. If these patterns continue, the child may become conduct disordered, a child who breaks rules and is "calloused toward the needs and rights of others" (p. 10).

Conduct-disordered children are at risk of developing adult personality disorders. A comprehensive intervention plan that limits the acting-out behavior needs to be developed. Multiple factors may affect the child. Some of these factors are child abuse, family violence, adoption, divorce, and harsh discipline. The child may live in a family with an antisocial lifestyle, or the parents may be engaged in criminal activity. The factors related to each child need to be addressed by the therapist (Sandberg, 1987).

Adjustment disorder is connected to either single or multiple traumatic events that affect the child. The treatment and prognosis for success varies with the social-emotional condition of the child. Children who do not have persistent psychiatric and social impairment may be helped by therapy and by talking through the critical event to help them understand and resolve their pain.

"A significant body of child abuse research suggests that child abuse precipitates disorders in children" (Sandberg, 1987, p. 12). Teachers should not assume child abuse is present just because the child has attention deficiencies. However, the school must be "involved with identifying and remediating assorted problems, including child abuse, that severely jeopardize a child's opportunity to learn" (p. xvi). It is important for teachers to help the child learn appropriate behaviors at an early age. They should use disciplinary methods that help the child learn self-control rather than discipline that is actually punishment. Classrooms should give support and continuity to children. They should provide special help for children with learning deficiencies, use special education services to help socially and emotionally deficient children get the help they need, and above all else, make sure these children do not feel inadequate.

How can teachers accomplish this? Teachers need parent volunteers or aides in the classroom plus a support system to meet the needs of each child and make sure that each child has more successes than failures.

Halperin (1979) cites practical guidelines for teachers to follow in identifying the child who needs attention. He cautions against jumping to conclusions, however. Marks on a body may come from many circumstances. "Only when school personnel have gathered substantial information on the family and its internal functioning are they in a position to assess if a child is being maltreated at home" (p. 67).

Educators who bear in mind that children are unique, may respond to the same treatment in opposite ways, and display a wide range of behaviors will be cautious in labeling a child.

When educators recognize Halperin's clues for children who need attention, whether or not there is any suspicion of maltreatment, they will be doing a great service to all children in their classrooms. Individualization of the academic program as well as individualization for emotional needs will result in a well-rounded educational program for each child. As the teacher gets to know a child better and responds to the child with needed praise or reinforcement, as well as with an individualized curriculum, the result will be improved education. The following descriptions are modified from Halperin (1979).

Aggressive Child

Typical Characteristics

Defiant

Domineering

Blames others

Possible Reasons for Actions

Little self-esteem

Cannot control impulses

Unhappy

Little self-discipline

Show-Off

Typical Characteristics

Extremely extroverted

Answers questions without knowing the answer

May appear hyperactive

Wants to be center of attention

Possible Reasons for Actions

Masks insecurity

Little attention at home

Shows off to compete for praise and love

May be Attention Deficit Disorder (ADD) or Attention Deficit Hyperactive Disorder (ADHD)

Disobedient Child

Typical Characteristics

Purposely breaks rules

Impolite and insolent

Struggles against authority

Possible Reasons for Actions

Unhappy

Disobeys to get attention

Models parental attitude toward authority

Inconsistent discipline at home

Prefers punishment to indifference

Has internalized feelings of worthlessness

Child Who Lies, Cheats, and Steals

Typical Characteristics

Tells lies

Cheats in games and on tests

Steals from stores, classmates, others

Possible Reasons for Actions

Lies to escape punishment

Wants to get away with action without being caught

Gains attention

Little supervision at home

Actions of dishonesty are condoned at home

Child Nobody Likes

Typical Characteristics

Sullen

Depressed

Jealous

Blames others for acts

Frequently absent

Possible Reasons for Actions

Little warmth from parents

Unable to establish healthy relationship with others

Lives an isolated life

Not fond of self

Poor self-concept

May be bullied and not able to handle it

Unkempt Child

Typical Characteristics

Soiled clothes

Unkempt hair and body

General lack of care in work

Possible Reasons for Actions

Lack of adult supervision and concern

Poor self-image

Fearful Child

Typical Characteristics

Anxious

Uneasy

Emotionally unstable

Possible Reasons for Actions

Neurotic family life

Harsh punishment from caregivers

Unpredictable home environment

Afraid of bullying or violence in the school

Shy Child

Typical Characteristics

Fearful in contacts with others

Sits quietly with lowered head

Seldom defends self

Seldom expresses self

Possible Reasons for Actions

Lacks encouragement and acceptance at school

Excessively critical parents

Fears failure

May share same timid characteristics as parents

Withdrawn Child

Typical Characteristics.

Isolates self

Appears tense, nervous, and unhappy

Easily discouraged and frustrated

Abandons tasks if they prove difficult

Possible Reasons for Actions

Unsatisfactory experiences in past

Unsatisfactory experiences at school

Excessive demands from parents

Frequently lacks love, affection, and praise

Parents may be unpredictable and unable to establish relationships

Emotionally Unstable Child

Typical Characteristics

Volatile and unpredictable

Attitude toward life is negative

Appears agitated, worried, or preoccupied

Possible Reasons for Actions

Little attention or affection

Inadequate supervision or psychological support at home

Under tremendous pressure

Low-Achieving Child

Typical Characteristics

Short attention span

Withdrawn from classroom activities

Disobedient and disruptive

Rarely completes assignments

Possible Reasons for Actions

Brain damage

Physically neglected

Medical problems

Educational neglect

If these characteristics and causes are kept in mind when working with children, along with the realization that typical factors may not affect a particular child, the educator can adapt the educational program to the needs of the child.

With the increase of violence in the schools, children who have needs should be identified. Programs that help children become increasingly and positively involved, as well as programs that help children see alternatives to rage, must be a part of the schools. These include learning how to resolve conflicts with peers, handle anger, recognize consequences, and seek alternatives to violence.

The development of the ability to make friends as well as the ability to control anger begins at a young age—preschool. At an early age some children need guidance in the appropriate way to interact with classmates. Children continue to need support throughout their school years.

Teachers are very powerful in their influence on children. They can make children into scapegoats by ridiculing them before classmates. It is better to help children develop the skills they need to interact with others and give them opportunities to be positive participants than it is to shame them into obedience.

The opportunity to raise a child's self-esteem will often improve the child's behavior. It is a safe beginning.

২৯ WHY DO ABUSE AND NEGLECT CONTINUE TO HAPPEN?

The National Center on Child Abuse and Neglect identified the following factors to determine which contribute to ongoing abuse and neglect of children.

- *Family income.* Children who come from families with incomes below the poverty level are seven times more likely to be abused than those at a higher income level.

- *Gender.* A child's gender has no effect on whether the child is neglected. However, girls are more likely to be abused than boys. The rate of sexual abuse is three times higher for girls than for boys.

- *Family size.* Children in families with four or more children are more apt to be neglected or abused.

- *Race or ethnicity.* There was no significant difference among children of different ethnic groups.

- *Type of community.* Abuse and neglect occur in rural, suburban, and urban communities (U.S. Department of Health and Human Services, 1992).

- *Exposure to violence.* Personal experience, and exposure to media reports, television programs, and movies exposes the child and the school to excessive violence.

২৯ CHARACTERISTICS AND RISK FACTORS OF ABUSIVE PARENTS

Three approaches for understanding abusive parents have been investigated: the psychological model, the sociological model, and the parent-child interaction model.

In the psychological model, lack of empathy distinguishes the abusive parent. In the sociological model, cultural attitudes toward violence, social stress, family size, and social isolation are factors that relate to child abuse. Prevention and treatment based on the sociological model focus on the effect the community and society have on the family. Environmental stress is a sociological risk factor in abuse of children. Stress from poverty or in the workplace may cause anxiety in parents, and they may lash out at their child.

In the parent-child interaction model, the parents lack skill in interacting with their children, disciplining them, and teaching them appropriate behavior (Wiehe, 1989). Parents may have had inadequate exposure to positive parenting and lack information on child development. If raised by maladaptive parents or if raised with cultural beliefs that are compatible with mistreatment, the parent may not be capable of adapting to the child's needs. "Just as beliefs about child development and behavior arise from prior experience, parenting skills and strategies must be learned at some time in an individual's life" (Iverson & Segal, 1990, p. 42).

The U.S. Department of Health and Human Services (1992) discusses parents who are more likely to abuse their children:

> Parents may be more likely to maltreat their children if they abuse drugs or alcohol (alcoholic mothers are three times more likely and alcoholic fathers are eight times more likely to abuse or neglect their children than are nonalcoholic parents); are emotionally immature or needy; are isolated, with no family or friends to depend on; were emotionally deprived, abused or neglected as children; feel worthless and have never been loved or cared about; or are in poor health. Many abusive and neglectful parents do not intend to harm their children and often feel remorse about their maltreating behavior. However, their own problems may prevent them from stopping their harmful behavior and may result in resistance to outside intervention. It is important to remember that diligent and effective intervention efforts may overcome the parents' resistance and help them change their abusive and neglectful behavior.
>
> Children may be more likely to be at risk of maltreatment if they are unwanted, resemble someone the parents dislike, or have physical or behavioral traits which make them different or especially difficult to care for.
>
> - *Family interactions.* Each member of a family affects every other member of that family in some way. Some parents and children are fine on their own, but just cannot get along when they are together, especially for long periods of time. Some characteristics commonly observed in abusive or neglectful families include social isolation and parents turning to their children to meet their emotional needs.

> - *Environmental conditions.* Changes in financial condition, employment status, or family structure may shake a family's stability. Some parents may not be able to cope with the stress resulting from the changes and may experience difficulty in caring for their children. (U.S. Department of Health and Human Services, 1992, p. 5)

The National Center on Child Abuse and Neglect suggests these guiding principles:

- Child maltreatment is a family problem. Consequently our treatment efforts must focus on the family as a whole as well as the individual family members. Treatment must be provided to abused and neglected children as well as their parents. Unless children receive the support and treatment for the trauma they have suffered, they may suffer permanent physical, mental, or emotional handicaps, and as adults they may continue the cycle of abuse with their own family or other children. In addition, abused and neglected children are more likely than other children to have substance abuse problems.

- Although we cannot predict with certainty who will abuse or neglect their children, we do know the signs indicating *high risk.* People at high risk include parents who abuse drugs and alcohol, young parents who are ill-prepared for the parenting role, families experiencing great stress who have poor coping skills and have no one to turn to for support, and parents who have difficulty with or who have not developed an emotional bond with their infant. We need to be alert to these and other high risk indicators and offer assistance, support, counseling, and/or parent education to families "at risk" before their children are harmed.

- Families "at risk" may be most receptive to help soon after the birth of their first child.

- Child sexual abuse prevention programs aimed at school-aged children appear to be useful in helping children avoid sexually abusive situations and to say no to inappropriate touch by adults. However, prevention programs must be carefully examined and selected. These programs must be responsive to the learning capacities and developmental stages of the children involved. Inappropriately designed programs may frighten young children or fail to teach them what they can do to protect themselves.

- Volunteers can be very effective with some abusive and neglectful parents—especially with those parents who are experiencing stress, who have been emotionally deprived, and who lack knowledge of child development and effective parenting skills. Volunteers must be carefully screened, trained, and supervised.

Clearly, if we are going to stop child abuse and neglect and help the child victims and their families, we all must work together. Efforts must occur at the Federal, State, and local levels. (U.S. Department of Health and Human Services, 1992, pp. 10–11)

The following behavioral characteristics can help the professional determine the likelihood of abuse or neglect:

1. Do the parents fail to show up for appointments? Do they stay away from school? When they come to school, are they uncooperative and unresponsive?

2. Do the parents have unrealistically high expectations for themselves and their child? Do the parents describe the child as "different" or "bad"?

3. Do the parents have expectations for the child that are inconsistent or inappropriate for the child's age?

4. Do the parents become aggressive or abusive when school personnel want to talk about the child's problems?

5. Do the parents isolate themselves? Do they know other parents in the school? Are they known by other parents?

6. Do they lack knowledge of child development and the child's physical and psychological needs?

7. Do the parents report that they were abused or neglected as children?

8. Do the parents refuse to participate in school events?

9. Do the parents ignore the child and avoid touching?

10. Do the parents show little interest in the child's activities or concern for the child's well-being?

ROOTS OF VIOLENCE

In a book *Ghosts from the Nursery: Tracing the Roots of Violence,* the authors give compelling evidence of the importance of a caring environment for the infant and young child, and the effects of being abused or neglected. It is especially important to have a rich, loving environment for the child prenatal until five years of age. "When environmental experiences early in life cause noradrenaline levels to be too high and serotonin levels too low, the result, in the presence of later emotional triggers, may be impulsive violence" (Karr-Morse & Wiley, 1997, p. 44).

Children who are ignored or physically mistreated are at risk. The effects of abusive early experiences without intervention or change put the child at risk, unable to trust others or feel connected. The book chronicles the life of Jeffrey, a young man on death row, who grew up in a sterile, disorganized family, with one short period of a caring foster family. His reactions were impulsive and at the age of 16 he killed another. A youth who is neglected or abused has a 53 percent increased likelihood of being arrested and a 38 percent increased likelihood of the arrest being for a violent crime (p. 262). Violence breeds violence.

Jeffrey wrote the following in August 1996:

> Everybody has to deal with anger. . . . When I get mad, I borderline up there, then I follow my impulses . . . . If I can't control my impulses, then I do things that I regret later. . . . I do follow my impulses. . . because that was the way I learned to survive when I was little. (p. 152)

School-age children also show their fear, concern, and sadness through drawings that reveal the violence they have encountered. "With education and support, adults can recognize children's aggressive or withdrawn behavior, or their dulled emotions, as symptoms of posttraumatic stress disorder" (Osofsky & Fenichel, 1996, p. 7).

These children need special support from the school professionals.

Infant and Toddler Exposure to Abuse

It is often believed that infants and toddlers do not remember their exposure to violence. Infants and toddlers are not able to remember the details of their life when they were one or two years old, but the impact is still there. "In fact, infants and young children can be overwhelmed by their exposure to violence, especially—as is likely to be the case with very young children—when both victims and perpetrators are well-known and emotionally important to the child and the violence occurs in or near the child's own home" (Osofsky & Fenichel, 1996, p. 7). Factors that relate to the severity of the exposure to violence include *intensity* (a killing versus a pushing); *proximity* (if the child is in close vicinity to the violence); *familiarity* (if the victim or perpetrator is known by the child); *developmental status* (ability to cope with the violence); and *chronicity of exposure* (if the child is exposed to violence again and again). "It is likely that experiencing violence repeatedly over the years may be devastating to the social and emotional development of young children, who learn, from what they see, that violence is a usual and acceptable way to respond to other people" (p. 8). Infants and toddlers exhibit the same type of symptoms that adults and older children exhibit. They reexperience the violence, a traumatic experience, by numbing their response and avoidance of the remembrance and signs of hypervigilance and hyperarousal (Zeanah & Scheeringa, 1996).

Brain Damage Risk Linked to Child Abuse and Neglect

Research at the McLean Hospital identified four types of brain abnormalities related to child abuse and neglect. The abnormalities caused are permanent; the solution is elimination of abuse and neglect.

- *Limbic irritability:* The limbic system, a network of brain cells that "controls many of the emotions and drives for survival. The McLean researchers found evidence that abuse may cause disturbances in electrical impulses as limbic nerve cells communicate, resulting in seizures or significant abnormalities on an EEG, a diagnostic test that measures brain waves" (McLean Hospital, 2000, p. 2).

- *Arrested development in the left hemisphere:* Studies show that there is deficient development in the left brain of abused persons, which may contribute to depression and the increased risk of memory impairment.

- *Deficient integration between the left and right hemispheres:* "In abused children the corpus callosum was smaller than in healthy children" (p. 2).

- *Increased vermal activity:* "The researchers theorize that the abused patients had higher vermal activity in order to quell electrical irritability within the limbic system. They hypothesize that the cerebellar vermis helps to maintain emotional balance, but that trauma may impair this ability" (p. 3).

The researchers examined animal studies and came to the following conclusion: "We know that an animal exposed to stress and neglect early in life develops a brain that is wired to experience fear, anxiety and stress. . . . We think the same is true of people" (p. 3).

Children, Youth, and Gun Violence

More than 20,000 children and youth under age 20 are killed or injured by guns each year, the second leading cause of death of young people ages 10 to 19 (Behrman, 2002). Children exposed to gun violence often experience psychological disturbances that include sleep distortion, withdrawal, and posttraumatic stress disorder (Garbarino, Bradshaw, & Vorrasi, 2002). "Studies suggest that children exposed to gun violence at home, at school, in the community, or through the media can experience negative psychological effects including posttraumatic stress, poor school performance, increased delinquency, risky sexual behaviors, substance abuse, and desensitization to violence. All of these effects can make child and youth more prone to violence themselves" (*The Future of Children*, 2002, p. 1). The four strategies to reduce gun violence include

- reducing children's unsupervised exposure to guns;
- engaging communities and straightening law enforcement;
- changing the design of guns (requiring safety features and personalizing guns); and
- limiting the flow of illegal guns to youth. (Reich, Culross, & Behrman, 2002)

✑ WHY IS THERE ABUSE?

Children learn parenting patterns from their parents (Iverson & Segal, 1990). With few exceptions, abusive parents experienced some form of maltreatment when young (Steele, 1986). These parents did not have a childhood that allowed them to become independent, productive, functioning adults. Generally they had to disregard their own needs and desires for the wishes of an authority figure. They were unable to develop inner controls and looked to outside figures for direction. Such parents also exhibit dependence on others in their search for love and affection. They are still affected by maternal deprivation. Their parents were their only models. "Learned patterns of abusive parenting are transmitted from parent to child and are replicated by the child upon becoming a parent in his/her own right" (Bavolek, 1989, p. 99). These practices include:

1. *Inappropriate expectations.* Abusive parents often perceive the child's abilities to be greater than they are. Parents expect children to take on responsibilities that are not appropriate for their ages. These parents may have expectations such as toilet training the child at 6 to 12 months, talking by age 2, and taking on house-

keeping chores at an early age. Young or inexperienced parents, who do not know child development, may interpret an infant or toddler's appropriate behavior as stubbornness and rebellion. Combine this with a belief that physical punishment will help the child behave, and you have the conditions for abuse. Children in these families develop a poor self-concept, and feel incapable, unacceptable, and worthless (Bavolek, 1989; Hamilton, 1989).

2. *Lack of empathy.* Abusive parents often did not experience loving care when they were growing up, so they do not have a model to follow. They cannot change their own personality traits until they receive the support and love they need. These parents usually have dependency needs and are unable to empathize with their children. The child's basic needs are ignored. Such parents may justify cruel and abusive behaviors under the guise of teaching and guiding their children. Mothers who were brought up by uncaring, inattentive mothers will tend to mother their own children in the same way. Their children grow up with a low sense of self-esteem and inadequate identity (Bavolek, 1989; Hamilton, 1989; Steele, 1986, 1987).

3. *Belief in physical punishment.* Abusive parents often believe that physical punishment is necessary to rear their children without spoiling them. This is a common belief in the United States, but abusive parents go to extremes and believe that babies and children should not be allowed to get away with anything. They punish to correct perceived misbehavior or inadequacy on the part of their child. The child does not live up to expectations and is considered "bad." The parents think they have the moral duty to correct their child's behavior any way they choose.

4. *Parent-child role reversal.* In these abusive families, children are looked upon by the parents as providing the love and support that the parent needs. The parent is like a needy child, so the child must play the role of the adult. If the child is able to take on some of the parental roles, abuse may be avoided, but only at the expense of the child's normal development. This is destructive to

children—they do not go through normal developmental stages, do not develop their own identities, and see themselves as existing to meet the needs of their parents (Bavolek, 1989; Hamilton, 1989).

5. *Social isolation.* Social isolation is recognized by most child abuse researchers as a factor that perpetuates neglect and abuse. Either the absence of social support or inability to accept any support has the same effect. The abusive family isolates itself, attempts to solve its problems alone, and avoids contact with others. Isolation is a defense against being hurt and rejected. Although abusive parents may act self-sufficient and sure of themselves, they are dependent, frightened, and immature. Cross-cultural research indicates that child maltreatment occurs less often in cultures with multiple caregivers, including extended families (Hamilton, 1989).

6. *Difficulty experiencing pleasure.* In other abusing families, the parents do not enjoy life. Their social relationships are minimal and unrewarding. They do not feel competent, have difficulty planning for the future, and do not trust their own performances. Children in these families exhibit similar behavior.

7. *Intergenerational ties.* Although a history of maltreatment and lack of parenting skills set the scene for more neglect and abuse, the "majority of maltreated children do not maltreat their own children" (Hamilton, 1989, p. 38). According to Vondra and Toth (1989), one third of the maltreated are abusive to their children (p. 13). If abuse and neglect are viewed in a broad sense, however, an alarming number of parents did not receive adequate parenting or develop a positive attachment to their parents and other loved ones and thus have a difficult time providing the kind of environment that nourishes and cares for a child adequately (Steele, 1986).

The American Association for Protecting Children, a division of the American Humane Association, has developed a flier that briefly describes parental attitudes, the child's behavior, and the child's appearance. This flier succinctly focuses on the highlights of the foregoing discussion.

Schools may purchase this flier from the American Humane Association for a nominal fee and distribute it to staff and teachers. The flier is illustrated in Box 10.1 on page 438.

≫ DEVELOPMENT OF POLICIES

School districts and child care centers need to develop the policies and training programs vital to successful child abuse intervention. If there is no policy, the teacher should see the school nurse, psychologist, director, counselor, social worker, or principal, depending on the staffing of the school. Even in a school district with a policy statement, each school or child care center should have one person who is responsible for receiving reports of child abuse. Making one person responsible results in greater awareness of the problem of abuse and facilitates reporting. It is also helpful to establish a committee to view evidence and support the conclusions of the original observer. A written report contains the details of the situation as illustrated in Figure 10.4

All states require reporting of suspected child abuse. Evidence of violent physical abuse must be reported immediately. If school officials refuse to act, you should call social services, law enforcement, or a family crisis center. The person making the report should have the right to remain anonymous. When reporting in good faith, the person reporting is protected by immunity described in state legislation. Colorado law, for example, specifically states: "Any person participating in good faith in the making of a report or in a judicial proceeding held pursuant to this title shall be immune from any liability, civil or criminal, that otherwise might result by reason of such reporting" (Denver Public Schools, 1992).

Needs Assessment

Schools and child care centers first must determine the prevention and protection delivery systems that are already available in the community. They should consider social service departments, child protection teams, child welfare

Denver Public Schools   **Attachment #1**

CAR983

CHILD ABUSE REPORT TO THE DENVER DEPARTMENT OF SOCIAL SERVICES
Division of Services for Families, Children and Youth

Student ID# _____

Name of Child _____ Date of Birth _____ Sex _____

Address _____ State _____ Zip _____

Parent/Guardian Name _____

Address _____ State _____ Zip _____ Telephone Number _____

1. Nature and extent of the child's injuries or evidence of neglect or molestation:

2. Child's account of how incident occurred:

3. Describe any evidence of previous known or suspected abuse or neglect to the child or the child's siblings:

4. Names and addresses and relationship of the person(s) responsible for the suspected abuse or neglect, if known:

5. Name, address, telephone number of school and name and position of the person making the report:

6. Date, time of call to Crisis Hotline and/or Denver Police Department, and person taking call:

7. Other Concerns:

_____
(Date)   (Signature)   (School)

FOR OFFICE USE ONLY

Date _____   Child Protection Team Worker _____

Disposition: _____

_____

FIGURE 10.4   Child abuse report to the Denver Department of Social Services.
Source: Denver Public Schools (1998).

449

agencies, law enforcement, juvenile court system, Head Start, child care centers, hospitals, clinics, public health nurses, mental health programs, public and private service groups, fund-raising agencies such as United Way, and service organizations that might be unique to their community.

Following assessment of the community, the schools and child care centers have to determine their roles in an integrated approach to abuse and neglect. Communication lines must be kept open at all times. A representative of the schools should serve on the child protection team. One role that is mandated is identification of abuse and neglect. Other roles will be individualized according to the needs of the community, the resources in the schools and child care centers, and the commitment of the personnel.

Policy

Child abuse is found in all socioeconomic groups in the United States, so all school districts must be prepared to work with interdisciplinary agencies in the detection and prevention of this national social problem.

Policies should be written in compliance with the requirements of each state's reporting statute, details of which may be learned by consulting the state's attorney general. Because reporting is required in all states, the policy should include a clear statement of reporting requirements. The policy should also inform school personnel of their immunity and legal obligations. Dissemination of the policy should include the community as well as all school employees. Not only is it important that the community realize the obligation of the school or child care center to report suspected abuse or neglect, it is vital that the community becomes aware of the extent of the problem.

HOW TO TALK WITH CHILDREN AND PARENTS

Care must be taken in talking with or interviewing children or parents. The conversation should take place in a private, relaxed, and comfortable atmosphere. Children should not feel threatened, nor should they be pressed for information or details they do not want to reveal. Parents should be aware of the school's legal obligation to report suspected neglect and abuse. If they believe the school is supportive of the family, the interaction between parents and school will be more positive. Tower (1992) provides some guidelines:

When Talking with the Child

Do:

> Make sure the interviewer is someone the child trusts.
>
> Make sure the educator is the most competent person in the school to talk with children.
>
> Conduct the interview in private.
>
> Sit beside the child, not across a table or desk.
>
> Tell the child that the interview is confidential, but that child abuse and neglect must be reported.
>
> Conduct the interview in language the child understands.
>
> Ask the child to clarify words or terms that are not understood.
>
> Tell the child if any future action will be required.

Don't:

> Allow the child to feel "in trouble" or "at fault."
>
> Disparage or criticize the child's choice of words or language.
>
> Suggest answers to the child.
>
> Probe or press for answers the child is unwilling to give.
>
> Display horror, shock, or disapproval of parents, the child, or the situation.
>
> Pressure or force the child to remove clothing.
>
> Conduct the interview with a group of interviewers.
>
> Leave the child alone with a stranger (e.g., a CPS worker).

When Talking with the Parents

Do:

Select the person most appropriate to the situation.

Conduct the interview in private.

Tell the parents why the interview is taking place.

Be direct, honest, and professional.

Tell the parents the interview is confidential.

Reassure the parents of the support of the school.

Tell the parents if a report has been made or will be made.

Advise the parents of the school's legal responsibilities to report.

Don't:

Try to prove abuse or neglect; that is not an educator's role.

Display horror, anger, or disapproval of parents, the child, or the situation.

Pry into family matters unrelated to the specific situation.

Place blame or make judgments about the parents or child.

❧ PROGRAMS TO PREVENT ABUSE

Parent Education

Parent education can be delivered in high school, provided by hospitals when parents have their first child, offered through adult education, or provided by social services. The STEP, Parent Effectiveness Training, and Active Parenting courses have been effective. Building Family Strengths programs reinforce the positive aspects of a family. Specially designed programs are also appropriate.

Caring Programs

Home visitation programs have demonstrated that early intervention is effective. First-time parents are especially receptive to help from visiting nurses or nonprofessionals who model, support, and help them with their infant (Justice & Justice, 1990). Programs that have been developed to offer this support include the Prenatal/Early Infancy Project in Rochester, New York, the AVANCE Parent-Child Education Program in San Antonio, Texas, the Pre-School Intervention Program in Bloomfield, Connecticut, MELD in Minnesota, the State of Missouri's Parents as Teachers program, and Hawaii's Healthy Start (see Chapter 8). The emphasis in the last three programs—MELD, Parents as Teachers, and Healthy Start—is broader than home visitations for parenting skills, but the programs include these areas and demonstrate that larger groups can benefit from a national response. In Great Britain, newborns and their parents are visited by public health nurses. Although the parents do not have to accept the visit, most do, and after the initial visit there are follow-ups with periodic assessments of intellectual, emotional, and physical development.

The Community Caring Project

A joint project of the Center and the Junior League of Denver (C. Henry Kempe National Center for the Prevention and Treatment of Child Abuse and Neglect, n.d.) is based on the concept of intervention and was developed after Kempe and others found that home visitations for at-risk parents could prevent abuse. It provides support and parenting skills to new mothers. These mothers, selected from four hospitals in the Denver area, are matched with a community volunteer who offers assistance, modeling, and education to new mothers.

The Caring Program is an offshoot of programs developed by researchers at the University of Colorado Medical School. Mothers who are at high-risk for abnormal parental practices (following observations made during and after labor and delivery) are offered special programs. When identified as high-risk, the family receives a pediatric follow-up by a physician, lay health visitor, and/or public health nurse.

Support Offered by Schools

The position statement by the American School Counselor Association supports programs to help eliminate child abuse. The association hopes to provide children with coping skills; help teachers understand abuse; provide continuing counseling to the child and the family; and offer workshops for parents that focus on handling anger, parenting skills, and methods of discipline other than corporal punishment (American School Counselor Association, 1988). Some of the school-based programs include life skills training, socialization skills, problem solving, and coping skills (Tower, 1992).

If the public were aware of how essential it is for teenagers who have not received these skills at home to be able to learn and model life skills, there would not be the demand to eliminate these types of courses. Although academic basics (reading, writing, and arithmetic) are essential, the focus away from life skills could be detrimental to the next generation. Offering of workshops or courses on conflict resolution, consequences of actions, and seeking alternatives should be recognized as essential. It should be possible for schools to provide all the needed academic skills as well as the necessary skills for parenthood, self-protection, and life skills.

Many schools are developing family resource centers, as described in Chapter 7. Offerings for parents who are no longer students include parent education and family literacy.

Programs After Abuse Is Recognized

Professionals who work with the abusive parent must first understand themselves and their values so they can come to peace with their feelings toward abuse and neglect of children. To help the family, professionals should not have a punitive attitude toward the parents. It may help to remember that many abusive or neglectful parents are rearing their children the same way they were reared. It is a lifelong pattern that must be broken (Bavolek, 1989; Reppucci, Britner, & Woolard, 1997; Steele, 1987; Vondra & Toth, 1989).

Although the parents may resist intrusion or suggestion, they desperately need help in feeling good about themselves. They need support, comfort, and someone they can trust and lean on. They need someone who will come when they have needs. Instead of criticism, they need help and assurance that they are worthwhile. Because they are unable to cope with their child, someone must help them understand the child without shaming them. Parents need to feel valuable and adequate.

Parents Anonymous

Parents Anonymous (1985) is a self-help program that gives parents the chance to share their feelings with others who have had similar experiences. Parents can use Parents Anonymous (PA) and its crisis-intervention hotlines without fear of public disclosure. The members help each other avoid abuse by providing the opportunity to talk out problems. Groups generally have two leaders—a chairperson and a sponsor. The chairperson is chosen from the parent group. The sponsor, not an abuser, is often a mental health worker who facilitates the group's growth. PA believes that abuse happens because parents have unresolved issues about their own childhood, stressful current problems and unmet needs, and a precipitating crisis that brings about the abuse. The goal of Parents Anonymous is to prevent abuse (Post-Kammer, 1988). Positive ways of behaving and relating to others are learned as they work through their pain and anger about the past (Holmes, 1982).

Community Help

Help from social services or nonprofit organizations may include treatment that is offered by parent-aides, homemakers, and health visitors (Hamilton, 1989). The helper may serve as an advocate for the family to get the extra assistance it needs. This might include family therapy (Pardeck, 1989), assertiveness training, and Building Family Strengths programs. These programs try to bolster the positive elements in the family and eliminate the destructive elements. "Treatment may require in-depth, long-term therapy and a lot of permanent social support systems" (Hamilton, 1989, p. 41).

Many abusive parents want help. When they reveal their desires, they indicate that they want another parent to help them develop childrearing skills through modeling and friendship. Professionals can give them psychiatric help and other support, but because these parents may have missed a childhood with nurturing parents, their greatest need is the opportunity to have an active experience with a nurturing model. The importance of bonding and of a close relationship between parent and infant has been recognized as necessary for the child's emotional and physical growth. Severe deprivation can result in failure to thrive and marasmus (Skeels & Dye, 1939; Spitz, 1945). Failure to develop close and trusting bonds as infants and children results later in parents who need special help in learning to relate to their own child. These parents are still looking for someone to mother them. The supportive help of another parent can function as a nurturing model for both parent and child.

Preschool Settings

Youngsters who have been abused adapt in two ways, according to Pearl (1988). They either internalize and overcontrol their behavior, or they externalize and undercontrol their actions. Children in the first category will be easy to overlook—their behavior is often fearful, withdrawn, depressed, and shy. The externalized child will demand attention, be aggressive, and act out (Pearl, 1988; Steele, 1986). Both types of children have low self-esteem. Aggressive, externalized children see themselves as unlovable and bad. The withdrawn child tries to please but feels little pleasure. Abused children will scan their surroundings often, avert their eyes, and stare away to avoid eye contact. Preschool teachers can help both types of children if they:

1. Use a quiet clear voice
2. Have good eye contact

3. Stand near the child when giving directions
4. Use body language that says the same thing as the oral message
5. Give directions that tell the child the appropriate behavior using specific instructions
6. Set limits and have expectations for behavior
7. Accept all feelings, but be consistent with behavioral expectations (Pearl, 1988)

INTERVENING IN SEXUAL ABUSE

Programs that help children say "No" to sexual abuse have been developed throughout the nation. (Some of these programs are listed in the Appendix at the end of this book.) Teachers and social services personnel who use the methods suggested in these programs need to be careful to ensure that the child does not become fearful, however (Binder & McNiel, 1987).

Programs for preschool children should avoid causing children to become fearful of every stranger. An example of a program that works well is the Safe Child Personal Safety Training Program. Safe Child uses a scripted videotape curriculum for training teachers and parents, with segments for children ages 3 through 10. It demonstrates role-playing techniques and teaches basic life skills such as communication, assertiveness, problem solving, and decision making.

Young children need to know how to respond. Programs should be experientially based. Teaching children the concepts of safety from abuse is not as effective as teaching them the skills they need to prevent the abuse. In the program Safe Child, the children practiced the preventive skills and were taught to resist "unwanted touch, even in the face of bribery, emotional coercion, rejection, and intimidation" (Kraizer, Witte, & Fryer, 1989, p. 25). The study suggests:

1. Preschool children did as well as older children in the program, so prevention education should begin in preschool.
2. Prevention programs should give the information needed and nothing more. Labels of

good and *bad* need not be used, nor the suggestion that someone they love might hurt them.

3. Evaluation of the programs should continue.

4. Children with very low self-esteem may not respond to the program. Ten percent of the children did not benefit from this program.

A government pamphlet shares tips to parents concerning sexual abuse. See Figure 10.5 for suggestions on how to listen and talk to children, how to choose a child care center, and what to do if you think your child may have been abused.

Another concern of sexually abused children is their need for concerned intervention. The intervention should address the issue and help the child overcome feelings of unworthiness. The high rate of victims becoming victimizers also makes it necessary to work with children who have been sexually abused so they will not victimize others. An alarming finding is the number of young sexual abusers—20 percent of sexual abusers are adolescents. Victims tend to become victimizers. Ryan (1989) cites studies suggesting that as many as 80 percent of adult sexual abusers were abused themselves as children.

Checklist for Schools and Centers

- Does the school have a policy on reporting child abuse and neglect?
- Did the school do a needs assessment that shows the resources in your area and the status of child abuse and neglect in the school district?
- Does the school or center coordinate activities and resources with other social agencies?
- Does the school or center hold periodic meetings for improved communication and coordination among agencies?
- Does someone in the school district serve on the child protection team?
- Does the school or center have a training program?

- Do parents feel welcome in the school?
- Does the school or center have a parent education program for parents of preschoolers?
- Does the school or center have a parent education program for parents of infants and toddlers?
- Is the PTA or any other parent group involved with the school or center in a meaningful way for parents?
- Is there a parent resource room in the school?
- Do parents feel welcome to visit the school?
- Is there regular contact with parents, the teacher, and the school or center? Do the teachers have frequent communication with parents when there is something good to report?

Rights of the Child

The U.S. Advisory Board on Child Abuse and Neglect (1993), using statements (shown in italics) taken from the United Nations Convention on the Rights of the Child (United Nations, 1989), declares the following rights for the child:

Respect for the inherent dignity and inalienable rights of children as members of the human community requires protection of their integrity as persons.

Children have a right to protection *from all forms of physical or mental violence, injury or abuse, neglect or negligent treatment, maltreatment or exploitation, including sexual abuse, while in the care of parent(s), legal guardian(s) or any other person who has the care of the child, including children residing in group homes and institutions* (art. 19, 1).

Children have a right to *grow up in a family environment, in an atmosphere of happiness, love and understanding* (preamble).

The several Governments of the United States share a profound responsibility to ensure that children enjoy, at a minimum, such protection of their physical, sexual, and psychological security.

The several Governments of the United States bear a special duty to refrain from subjecting children in their care and custody to harm.

Listen and Talk to Your Children

Perhaps the most critical child sexual prevention strategy for parents is good communication with your children. This is not only challenging to every parent but also can be difficult, especially for working parents and parents of adolescents.

☐ Talk to your child every day and take time to really listen and observe. Learn as many details as you can about your child's activities and feelings. Encourage him or her to share concerns and problems with you.

☐ Explain to your children that their bodies belong only to them alone and that they have the right to say no to anyone who might try to touch them.

☐ Tell your child that some adults may try to hurt children and make them do things the child doesn't feel comfortable doing. Often these grownups call what they're doing a secret between themselves and the child.

☐ Explain that some adults may even threaten children by saying that their parents may be hurt or killed if the child ever shares the secret. Emphasize that an adult who does something like this is doing something that is wrong.

☐ Tell your child that adults whom they know, trust and love or someone who might be in a position of authority (like a babysitter, an uncle, a teacher or even a policeman) might try to do something like this. Try not to scare your children—emphasize that the vast majority of grownups never do this and that most adults are deeply concerned about protecting children from harm.

Choosing a Preschool or Child Care Center

Although the vast majority of this nation's preschools and child care centers are perfectly safe places, recent reports of child sexual abuse in these settings are a source of great concern to parents.

☐ Check to make sure that the program is reputable. State or local licensing agencies, child care information and referral services, and other child care community agencies may be helpful sources of information. Find out whether there have been any past complaints.

☐ Find out as much as you can about the teachers and caregivers. Talk with other parents who have used the program.

☐ Learn about the school or center's hiring policies and practices. Ask how the organization recruits and selects staff. Find out whether they examine references, background checks, and previous employment history before hiring decisions are made.

☐ Ask whether and how parents are involved during the day. Learn whether the center or school welcomes and supports participation. Be sensitive to the attitude and degree of openness about parental participation.

☐ Ensure that you have the right to drop in and visit the program at any time.

☐ Make sure you are informed about every planned outing. Never give the organization blanket permission to take your child off the premises.

☐ Prohibit in writing the release of your child to anyone without your explicit authorization. Make sure that the program knows who will pick up your child on any given day.

If You Think That Your Child Has Been Abused...

☐ Believe the child. Children rarely lie about sexual abuse.

☐ Commend the child for telling you about the experience.

FIGURE 10.5 Child sexual abuse prevention: tips for parents.

Source: U.S. Department of Health and Human Services, Administration for Children, Youth and Families, National Center on Child Abuse and Neglect, 1986, Washington, DC: U.S. Government Printing Office. Reprinted with permission.

Children have a right to be treated with respect as individuals, with due regard to cultural diversity and the need for culturally competent delivery of services in the child protection system.

Children have a right to *be provided the opportunity to be heard in any judicial and administrative pro-ceedings* affecting them (art. 12), with ample opportunity for representation and for provision of procedures that comport with the child's sense of dignity.

The duty to protect the integrity of children as persons implies a duty to prevent assaults on that integrity whenever possible. (p. 84)

☐ Convey your support for the child. A child's greatest fear is that he or she is at fault and responsible for the incident. Alleviating this self-blame is of paramount importance.

☐ Temper your own reaction, recognizing that your perspective and acceptance are critical signals to the child. Your greatest challenge may be to not convey your own horror about the abuse.

☐ Do not go to the school or program to talk about your concern. Instead, report the suspected molestation to a social services agency or the police.

☐ Find a specialized agency that evaluates sexual abuse victims—a hospital or a child welfare agency or a community mental health therapy group. Keep asking until you find a group or an individual with appropriate expertise.

☐ Search for a physician with the experience and training to detect and recognize sexual abuse when you seek a special medical examination for your child. Community sexual abuse treatment programs, childrens' hospitals and medical societies may be sources for referrals.

☐ Talk with other parents to ascertain whether there are unusual behavior or physical symptoms in their children.

☐ Remember that taking action is critical because if nothing is done, other children will continue to be at risk. Child sexual abuse is a community interest and concern.

> Finally, do not blame yourself. Sexual abuse is a fact in our society. Many individuals who molest children find work through employment and community activities which give them access to children. The vast majority of abuse occurs in situations where the child knows and trusts the adult. Do your homework well, but remember a community and national consciousness is needed before we can stamp out sexual molestation in our society.

We encourage photocopying or reprinting this information.

☐ Make sure that your children know that if someone does something confusing to them, like touching or taking a naked picture or giving them gifts, that you want to be told about it. Reassure them and explain that they will not be blamed for whatever an adult does with them.

Observe Physical and Behavioral Signs

Children who may be too frightened to talk about sexual molestation may exhibit a variety of physical and behavioral signals. Any or several of these signs may be significant. Parents should assume responsibility for noticing such symptoms including:

☐ Extreme changes in behavior such as loss of appetite.

☐ Recurrent nightmares or disturbed sleep patterns and fear of the dark.

☐ Regression to more infantile behavior such as bedwetting, thumb sucking, or excessive crying.

☐ Torn or stained underclothing.

☐ Vaginal or rectal bleeding, pain, itching, swollen genitals, and vaginal discharge.

☐ Vaginal infections or venereal disease.

☐ Unusual interest in or knowledge of sexual matters, expressing affection in ways inappropriate for a child of that age.

☐ Fear of a person or an intense dislike at being left somewhere or with someone.

☐ Other behavioral signals such as aggressive or disruptive behavior, withdrawal, running away or delinquent behavior, failing in school.

GPO : 1986 O - 498-594

FIGURE 10.5 *continued*

❧ SUMMARY

The wave of child abuse cases reveals a phenomenon that is not new. Child abuse has been with society since very early times, but it was not recognized as a problem until the second half of the 20th century, and no concerted effort was made to stem the crisis until the 1960s.

Legislation requires schools to report cases of abuse and neglect. Schools work with children more than any other agency, so they need to be in the forefront in preventing child abuse.

The chapter defines and describes child abuse and neglect—physical, sexual, and emotional. It includes characteristics of families who tend to be abusive, ways to identify the abused or neglected child, and psychological characteristics of abusive parents and abused children. Points useful for interviewing the child and/or parents are given.

The recognition of the incidence of abuse has increased since the early reports and Kempe's article on the battered child. The chapter includes a discussion of what precipitates abuse, and typical characteristics of abusers.

Greater concern for gun control and reduction of violence in schools, communities, and media is recognized throughout the nation.

School district policy and responsibility are described and illustrated by a typical policy statement. Ways schools can work to help potentially abusive parents are discussed. Recognition of and response to the problem by financial support from the school, parent education groups, school curricula, resource rooms, crisis nurseries, and/or parent-to-parent support groups are necessary.

✑ SUGGESTED CLASS ACTIVITIES AND DISCUSSIONS

1. Attend a meeting of the Child Protection Council or similar group. What is the composition of the council—for example, doctors, educators, social workers, or a judge? How does the wide spectrum of specialists show the need for cooperation among agencies working with families?
2. Discuss the signs that teachers may observe in suspected child abuse and neglect cases.
3. What are the steps teachers should take if they suspect child abuse or neglect?
4. Develop a policy for dealing with child abuse and neglect in a hypothetical school.
5. Talk to teachers about how they feel about reporting child abuse. What policies do they follow in reporting suspected child abuse or neglect cases?
6. Identify and describe the local community agencies that help parents learn parenting skills.
7. Identify and describe the agencies in the local community that counsel victims and perpetrators of child abuse.
8. Investigate the manner in which the courts handle child abuse and neglect cases. How do they manage out-of-home placements? Which rights are guaranteed the parents?
9. Make a list of guidelines for identifying maltreated children. Base your discussion on Halperin's descriptions of these children. What are some ways a teacher can support maltreated children?
10. Visit a school and determine what action the teachers and administrators take to reduce and prevent bullying and school violence.

11 Rights, Responsibilities, and Advocacy

G. R. Berger

Eugenia Hepworth Berger

Who advocates for the children? If it is not the parents, it must be someone in the community—teachers, coaches, neighbors. A child's ability to grow and develop is not only a responsibility of parents and community, it also is essential for the survival of the culture and society.

America has an undeniable stake in the economic well-being of families with children. Families with an adequate income are better able to provide the emotional and intellectual, as well as physical, care children need to become healthy, productive adults. Failure to prevent poverty and address the economic needs of families will inevitably lead to other social ills—more crime and delinquency, more teenage childbearing, more unhealthy babies, more failure in school, more substance abuse and mental illness, more child abuse and neglect, and lower productivity among the working-age population.

National Commission on Children, 1991, p. 80

In this chapter on rights and responsibilities you will study the customs and judicial decisions that will guide you and enable you to:

- Cite the Bill of Rights and other amendments to the U.S. Constitution, as well as administrative laws, that form the basis for rights in schools.
- List rights that students and parents have under the Family Educational Rights and Privacy Act (Buckley Amendment).
- Cite the rights of students related to freedom of speech, expression, and press; suspension and due process; search and seizure; flag salute and Pledge of Allegiance; religion; racial and sexual discrimination; disability issues; corporal punishment; text selection; and use of languages other than English.
- Discuss the responsibilities students have in their roles as members of the school community.

- 📖 Develop a school behavior code.
- 📖 Develop an advocacy program.
- 📖 Describe advocacy in other countries.
- 📖 Describe the power of advocacy and collaboration.

With rights come responsibilities for parents, children, educators, and society. Could mutual recognition of privileges and obligations provide guidelines for productive dialogue between schools and families? Today the school and the family, two of our most important social institutions, face a challenge to provide what is best for the child.

🐚 ORIGIN OF PARENTS' AND CHILDREN'S RIGHTS

Parents have long been recognized as having guardianship rights over their biological children. Parents of adopted children are guaranteed those same rights, which can be terminated only by court action or voluntary relinquishment. At the same time parents have responsibilities to their children. They have the right and responsibility to socialize their children; choose and provide health services for them; discipline and rear them; choose whether they will be educated in private or public schools; and give them care, shelter, and nourishment. It is only when they ignore or misuse these responsibilities that authorities have the right to intervene.

The rights and responsibilities of parents are derived from the U.S. Constitution and its amendments, social customs, legislation, and opinions of state and federal courts. Customs as well as law have influenced the manner in which a child's rights are viewed. Basic to this view are two assumptions: (a) children need to be protected and taught until they are mature enough to make wise decisions, and (b) parents can be trusted to protect children's rights (Caldwell, 1989) and care and provide for their children.

But all one has to do to see that parents do not always protect and provide for their children is to look at history (Chapter 2) and current child abuse (Chapter 10). As far back as the 15th century there was concern in Britain for the protection and rights of children. The government could

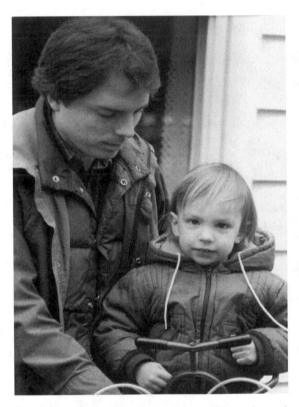

The rights that guard this parent and child are derived from the U.S. Constitution, the Bill of Rights, social customs, legislation, and rulings of state and federal courts.

intervene if the family did not act properly in rearing their children. The concept of *parens patriae* became a part of British custom and law, embodying the state's right to intervene for the child because ultimately the state is the child's parent (Caldwell, 1989; Hawes, 1991).

The founders of the United States were concerned about protecting people's rights when they wrote the Constitution and the first 10 amendments. The basis for legal rights in the United States are the Bill of Rights (the first 10 amendments to the Constitution) and the 14th Amendment. The 1st Amendment states: "Congress shall make no law respecting an establishment of religion, or prohibiting the free exercise thereof; or abridging the freedom of speech, or of the press; or the right of the people peaceably to assemble, and to petition the Government for a redress of grievances." Thus, all citizens, including parents and their children, are guaranteed freedom of religion, freedom of speech, the right to assemble peacefully, a free press, and the right to petition for redress of grievances.

Constitutional Law

The Constitution forms the framework that guides the federal government. Each state also has its own constitution. Rights are prescribed by the federal Constitution and by individual state constitutions. The U.S. Constitution and the Supreme Court hold precedence over lower courts and states. Some powers, such as education, are delegated completely to the states. According to the 10th Amendment of the Constitution: "The powers not delegated to the United States by the Constitution, not prohibited by it to the States, are reserved to the States respectively, or to the people." Education was not included as a responsibility of the federal government and was designated as an obligation and right of the individual states.

The federal Constitution provides basic rights that are common throughout the United States. "Constitutions are adopted by the people, statutes by legislatures, regulations by agencies, and the common law is created by courts" (Imber & van Geel, 2000, p. 4). Because regulations and laws vary from state to state, people concerned about their rights should check the state constitu-

tion, common law, and rules and regulations in their state. State legislatures delegate authority to school boards who must conform to the "limitations of relevant constitutional provisions, statutes, regulations and common law" (p. 5).

Statute Law

The legislative branch of government enacts statutes that affect individual rights. These laws extend from the U.S. Congress to state legislatures, down to county or city governments, and may be reviewed by the courts to determine their constitutionality.

The state constitution usually provides for the establishment of the public school system. The structure and operation of the school system are provided, revised, and supplemented by legislative enactment of education statutes (Valente, 1987) The federal statutory laws that provide funding to schools and prohibit discrimination are also significant (Imber & van Geel, 2000).

Most state legislatures have statutes that

- Establish and dissolve local school districts and boards
- Determine the selection process, responsibilities, and duties of the local board of education
- Designate the requirements for public school teachers and administrators to be qualified for school positions
- Determine who is eligible and who must attend schools
- Prescribe the curriculum that must be offered
- Specify requirements for high school graduation
- Establish regulations for discipline
- Determine and/or create funding for education
 (Adapted from Imber & van Geel, 2000)

Court Law

Court decisions handed down by judges at the federal, state, or local level are called court law, common law, or case law. The Supreme Court is the highest court in the land, and its decisions are binding on all lower courts. For example, in June 2002 a Supreme Court decision allowed vouchers to be used by parents or guardians who want their child to attend a school administered by a religious organization. Other court decisions are binding only within their jurisdiction.

Administrative Law

Regulations and rules of federal and state agencies also affect the rights of parents and families. The *Federal Register* publishes the regulations of federal administrative agencies. Check in your state for specific regulations guiding your rights as a parent or teacher.

Rights vary, depending on the rights and authority of the courts and administrative agencies. The Supreme Court has jurisdiction over the nation, but federal courts, state courts, and local courts have jurisdiction over their own areas. Check with the attorney general's office or ask your legal counsel to find out the laws and regulations in your state.

✎ PARENTS' RIGHT TO SELECT THEIR CHILD'S EDUCATION

Parents' right to choose and guide their children's education is substantiated by several court decisions. In 1923 the *Meyer v. Nebraska* decision ruled that parents have the right to teach their own children.

In 1925 it was ruled that parents have the right to choose parochial rather than public schools to teach their children. The Supreme Court in *Pierce v. Society of Sisters of the Holy Name* (1925) ruled that an Oregon law requiring children to attend public school was unconstitutional. The requirement for an educated citizenry could be met by acceptable private schools, whether parochial or secular, as well as public schools. On November 7, 1922, Oregon had adopted a Compulsory Education Act. The Society of Sisters was an Oregon corporation estab-

lished in 1880 that cared for orphans, established schools and academies, and educated students primary through junior college. When the Act was passed, parents removed their children from the private schools causing a loss of income and property to the Society. The 14th Amendment states, "nor shall any State deprive any person of life, liberty, or property, without the due process of law." The court ruled that the 14th Amendment guaranteed them protection against the loss of their property without due process of law. "It declared the right to conduct schools was property, and that the parents and guardians, as part of their liberty, might direct the education of their children by selecting reputable teachers and places" (Imber & van Geel, 2000, p. 18).

All states have compulsory attendance laws. Children usually must start school at the age of 6 or 7 and attend until they are 16 or 17. Parents are responsible for seeing that their children attend school. All states have free public schools. Children must attend them, or their parents must provide acceptable and approved schooling at home or in a private school. The number of children who are receiving their education at home has been increasing.

A few exceptions to school attendance have been approved by the courts. In *Wisconsin v. Yoder* (1972), the Supreme Court ruled in favor of Amish parents—Messrs. Yoder, Miller, and Yutzy in Green County, Wisconsin—who refused to send their children to school after they completed the eighth grade. The Amish religion emphasizes a life separate from worldly influences. The parents did not object to their children learning basic reading, writing, and mathematics because basic education is necessary for them to be able to read the Bible and work on the communal farms.

They did object, however, to their children attending school until age 16. In high school, their children would learn values that conflict with Amish religious beliefs. Secondary schools are based on competitiveness, self-achievement, and success, quite different from the cooperative, simple life of the Amish. The adolescent years are viewed as formative years that could influence young adults and take them away from the ways of the church. Amish children did not need to learn modern science, claimed the parents; their work on their farms could be taught at home in their own shops under the supervision of the Amish.

Chief Justice Warren E. Burger delivered the majority opinion that Wisconsin's compulsory attendance laws were invalid for the Amish. The decision was based primarily on the 1st Amendment, which states: "Congress shall make no law respecting an establishment of religion, or prohibiting the free exercise thereof."

Justice William O. Douglas wrote a dissenting opinion, arguing that if a child "is harnessed to the Amish way of life by those in authority over him or if his education is truncated, his entire life may be stunted and deformed." A mature child "may well be able to override the parents' religiously motivated objections."

Two concerns were at issue: the free exercise of religious beliefs and the need and right of states to have an educated citizenry. In cases where both of these issues are resolved, the courts may find in favor of the parents as they did in the Yoder case. In 1980, in an Ohio case, *Nagle v. Olin,* the Yoder provision prevailed. In this case a father wanted to send his daughter to Kopperts' Korner, an Amish school that did not meet state standards. The school was the only one close enough to the family's home that met the family's religious beliefs. Although the father was not Amish, the court found in favor of him because the school met his religious needs (Lines, 1982a).

Other cases have not met the Yoder test. In *State v. Faith Baptist Church* (1981) the Nebraska high court rejected a request for exemption from compulsory education. In *State v. Shaver* (1980) a North Dakota court found that, though the religious beliefs were sincere, attending public school did not preclude free exercise of those beliefs. In North Carolina, Peter Duro refused to send his children to school because he believed his children's religious beliefs would be undermined by secular humanism, and exposure to beliefs contrary to theirs. The Duros, Pentecostals, were not

Parents are responsible for seeing that their children attend school, but there are a variety of alternatives— public, private, parochial, and charter schools, as well as homeschooling.

members of an established, self-sufficient community as the Amish were, nor had the children attended school for eight years as the Amish children had, so the courts ruled against Duro. The state overrode the parent's request. In situations such as these, both concerns must be addressed: the need for an educated citizenry and established religious tenets that might be undermined by the school (LaMorte, 2001; Schimmel & Fischer, 1987).

Public Money for Private Schools

The 1990s saw the use of public money to support students in private schools as well as a growing number of other alternatives to public schools.

Private schools have been a legally recognized alternative to public education since 1925 *(Pierce v. Society of Sisters of the Holy Name),* but the public and the courts had resisted the use of tax money to support private schools. This changed in 2002.

On June 27, 2002, the Supreme Court by a vote of 5 to 4 issued a ruling that vouchers, which use taxpayer money, can be used by parents or guardians to send their children to private (secular or religious) schools. The case concerned a school-voucher program in Cleveland, Ohio. The ruling came after a challenge to a six-year-old voucher program in Cleveland which allowed low-income children a $2,250 voucher to attend private schools.

Opponents to the use of vouchers to attend religious schools argue that they violate the 1st Amendment which guarantees a separation of church and state. The opinion written by Chief Justice Rehnquist said that the voucher program did not breach the 1st Amendment because it offers private choice by the parents rather than payment directly to the religious schools. The parent is able to choose whether to send the child to private, charter, a school outside their district, magnet, or religious school.

The Road to Use of Vouchers

Several states passed legislation in the mid-1990s to permit vouchers to be used at public or private schools. These allow parents to use public money in the form of vouchers to pay tuition at private schools. Opponents of the voucher system claim that the system is unfair, that it would hurt people financially who are not well-to-do, and that it would ruin the public school system. Supporters of the voucher system think the public school system has failed and should be competitive or should be replaced. The voucher system allows parents to choose the school in which they enroll

Charter schools have flexibility in school procedures at the same time that they have public school financial support.

their child. That could be a private school or a public school in or outside the family's attendance district.

In *Zobrest v. Catalina Foothills School District,* the Supreme Court ruled in a 5–4 vote that public schools could use a public employee to provide sign-language interpretation for a student attending a religious school ("The Supreme Court's Decisions of Note," 1993).

Charter Schools

A public school alternative to the voucher system, charter schools, gives parents greater choice in the type of school they have in their community. Charter schools allow parents to help plan the school, determine the curriculum, and select teachers with the expectation that the school will be more responsive to the parents and community.

Homeschooling

Another trend is for parents to educate their children at home. Chapter 8 discusses homeschooling in more detail. Although parents have no constitutional right to educate their children at home, state law can determine the regulations for home education or refuse to allow home education.

Most states permit parents to teach their own children, but the states have varied requirements. To learn of current regulations, contact your state's Department of Education.

STUDENT RECORDS—OPEN RECORD POLICY

In 1974 Congress passed the Family Educational Rights and Privacy Act (FERPA), or the Buckley Amendment, which gives parents of students younger than 18 and students 18 and older the right to see and control their school records, except for information placed in the file before January 1, 1975. These records, including health files, grades, school records, and other documents concerning the person and kept by the school, must be available within 45 days of the request.

Directory information is given to newspapers and others who request it unless the parents or person over 18 years old request that their name or the child's name be removed from the directory information list. Directory information includes the student's name, address, telephone number, place and date of birth, dates of attendance, degrees and

The Buckley Amendment (Family Educational Rights and Privacy Act) gives the parents of these children the right to see their school records.

awards, participation in recognized activities of the school, height and weight if the student is a member of an athletic team, and the most recent previously attended educational agency. Parents who do not want their child's address and telephone number known should request that the school take their child's name off the list.

Privacy Procedures

1. Schools must permit eligible students or parents to inspect student records.
   a. The teacher's grade book is to be shared only with a substitute teacher. It is exempt from inspection.
   b. Schools must provide an explanation of records when requested by parents or students.
   c. Records may be destroyed before a request, but once a request has been made, the records may not be destroyed until the parent or eligible student has seen them.
   d. Psychiatric or treatment records may be available only to a medical doctor who can review them for the parent or eligible student.
   e. If parents are unable to come to school, the school should send the records to them. The school may charge a reasonable amount for making copies, but not for the time spent preparing and obtaining the records.
2. Schools must let parents or eligible students correct misleading or false information.
   a. If the school administrator agrees with the parent's or student's request, the official may remove questionable data.
   b. If the official refuses to change or remove the questionable information, a hearing may be requested. This hearing must take place within a reasonable time, although the law does not specify a deadline. Parents and students may bring a lawyer or friend to present evidence for them. Both sides may present evidence at a meeting presided over by an impartial hearing officer. If the decision is against the parents,

they may insert a written statement about why they disagree with the information.
3. Schools must inform eligible students and parents of their rights to record disclosure and privacy.
4. Schools must obtain written permission from parents or eligible students before giving information to others, with the following exceptions:
   a. School officials and teachers with a legitimate educational interest.
   b. Federal and state officials for use in an audit or evaluation of state- or federal-supported programs.
   c. Accreditation associations doing accreditation work.
   d. Financial aid officials seeking information for processing financial aid requests.
   e. Administrators of another school district to which the student is transferring. Parents and eligible students have the right to review the file before it is processed.
   f. People doing research, if the individuals are not identified.
   g. Officials responding to emergencies in which the information is necessary to protect the health of the student.
5. No information about a student may be kept secret.

If these requirements are met, eligible students and their parents can be sure that student records are accurate and that the records are not used for any purpose other than those stated above without their approval (Berger & Berger, 1985).

Situation

Melissa had not done well in her second-grade class. Her parents thought the teacher did not appreciate Melissa's talents because she had difficulty staying in her seat and refraining from talking to her neighbors.

When they moved to another school district, the teacher had Melissa sit in a carrel to help her concentrate on her work and avoid talking when she was supposed to be studying. Mrs. Jones, Melissa's mother, was furious. "Why should she be isolated from the rest of the children?" she complained to her husband. "This is going to ruin her self-confidence. I won't stand for it! I am going to make an appointment with the principal."

The following week both Mr. and Mrs. Jones were sitting in the principal's office waiting to talk. "May we see Melissa's record?" asked Mr. Jones. "What is in there that would make her teacher segregate her from the rest of the class on the first day of school?" The principal responded, "It will take several days to obtain her record. I also would like to talk with her teacher to find out why she separated her from the rest of the class. We have a wonderful school here; teachers work hard and are devoted professionals. I am sure there was a reason. Did Melissa have trouble at her former school? Ask the secretary to set up another appointment for you. I'm sure we can straighten this out and give you a satisfactory explanation."

1. What rights do Melissa's parents have?
2. Why do you think the teacher separated Melissa from the rest of the class?
3. What should happen next?

ℬℯ RIGHTS AND RESPONSIBILITIES OF STUDENTS AND PARENTS

Students and their parents have rights and responsibilities while the child is attending school. This section includes a discussion of these rights and responsibilities. Because laws change and vary, you should check the most recent law in your state if a specific incident occurs within your district.

Free Speech and Expression

The 1st Amendment provides that "Congress shall make no law . . . abridging the freedom of speech or of the press; or the right of the people peaceably to assemble. . . . " Students have the right, therefore, to express themselves, verbally or symbolically (armbands, symbols on clothing,

salutes), even if their position is in disfavor. They have the responsibility, however, to not slander another or disrupt the operation of the school. Misconduct in the guise of free expression need not be tolerated. Student rallies may have prescribed times and places. Students do not have the right to commandeer the school and intrude on the rights of others (Valente, 1987).

Freedom of Expression

The landmark decision on freedom of expression came in 1969 during the Vietnam War. In *Tinker v. Des Moines Independent Community School District* (1969) the Supreme Court ruled that students had the right to expression while they were at school: "It can hardly be argued that either students or teachers shed their constitutional rights to freedom of speech or expression at the schoolhouse gate."

The case involved a protest against the Vietnam War. The petitioners, John F. Tinker, Christopher Eckhardt, and Mary Beth Tinker, were among a group of adults and students who held a meeting at the Eckhardt home. They determined that they would wear black armbands during the holiday season commencing December 16, 1965, to protest the war in Vietnam. The parents, who were Quakers, supported their children's actions. The school administrator heard of the plan and instituted a rule that students who wore black armbands would be asked to remove them and, if they refused, would be suspended (Schimmel & Fischer, 1987).

The students refused to remove their armbands and were subsequently suspended. Their parents protested the suspension and took the case to court. Both the U.S. District Court and the 8th U.S. Circuit Court of Appeals found in favor of the schools, stating that their action prevented a disturbance. When the Supreme Court wrote its decision, the justices emphasized that schools must have the right "to prescribe and control conduct in the schools," but to prohibit an expression of opinion, the school must show that it substantially interfered with "appropriate discipline in the operation of the school." The Court found that there was no evidence that it interfered "with the school's work or with the rights of other students to be secure or left alone" (Fischer, Schimmel, & Kelly, 1999, p. 173). The passive use of armbands was not disruptive in this situation. The principal had put the suspension policy in place because he opposed the students' action, not because he feared a disturbance.

The threat of a disturbance influences court decisions. In *Guzick v. Drebus* (1971) Guzick, a student at Shaw High School in East Cleveland, Ohio, wore a button that was a symbol against the Vietnam War. Shaw High School, with a ratio of 70 percent Black and 30 percent White students, had a long-standing rule against wearing symbols and buttons because they had promoted racial disturbances. The court ruled against Guzick in this case because of the danger of a racial disturbance in the school.

Gang activity has caused concern about students wearing clothes or colors to school to signify their allegiance to a gang. Would this be considered freedom of speech? In *Olesen v. Board of Education of School District No. 228* (1987) the courts found that dress in this case was not "speech" protected by the 1st Amendment but was individualization or membership in a group, and schools could restrict the displaying of gang apparel because of student safety. If the wearing of certain colors or clothes might cause disruption of the schools, then barring their display probably would be found to be reason for prohibiting those clothes or colors.

Search and Seizure

The 4th Amendment states:

> The right of the people to be secure in their persons, houses, papers, and effects, against unreasonable searches and seizures, shall not be violated, and no warrants shall issue, but upon probable cause, supported by oath or affirmation, and particularly describing the place to be searched, and the persons or things to be seized.

The idea that children do not leave their constitutional rights at the schoolhouse gate, expressed in *Tinker v. Des Moines Independent Community School District* (1969), means that school personnel need probable cause before they search lockers or individuals. *Irby v. State of Texas* (1988) set forth the principle that school officials who want to search a child or the child's locker must have a reason. "Under ordinary circumstances, a search of a student by a teacher or other school official will be justified at its inception when there are reasonable grounds for suspecting that the search will turn up evidence that the student has violated or is violating either the law or the rules of the school" (Kierstead & Wagner, 1993). In this case officials had reason to believe the student possessed marijuana. A Supreme Court ruling in *New Jersey v. T.L.O.* (1985) states that "first, one must consider whether the 'action was justified at its inception,' . . . second, one must determine whether the search as actually conducted 'was reasonably related in scope to the circumstances which justified the interference in the first place'" (Kierstead & Wagner, 1993, p. 76).

Testing for Drugs

A decision by the Supreme Court issued on June 27, 2002, expanded the right for schools to randomly test students for drug use if the students participate in extracurricular activities. The school district began random drug tests for students who wanted to participate in extracurricular activities such as Future Farmers of America, playing chess, band, choir, and Academic Teams (Greenberger, 2002; Holland, 2002). This expanded a ruling in 1995 that allowed random testing of high school athletes. Lindsay Earls, an Oklahoma honor student, was subjected to a random drug test when she was a sophomore in high school. Two students and their parents challenged the testing, stating that it violated their 4th Amendment protection against unreasonable searches. The Supreme Court rejected their case 5–4, In the ruling, Justice Clarence Thomas stated that testing of students "is a reasonably effective means of addressing the school district's legitimate concerns in detecting and preventing drug use" (p. 2A). Opponents based their arguments on invasion of privacy. Others have argued that students participating in extracurricular activities such as music activities and debating are less likely to use drugs than students who do not participate. Yet, *all* students who participate can be randomly tested.

Freedom of the Press

The Supreme Court case *Hazelwood School District v. Kuhlmeier* (1988) has affected schools' supervisory capacity over publications. Until that time the governing theory was that a school could regulate the grammar and technical quality of a newspaper produced in connection with a high school journalism class, but that it could not remove articles because they might be controversial or unpopular. The *Hazelwood* case involved a Journalism II class producing a newspaper that had traditionally been reviewed by the principal before publication. In 1983 the principal rejected two stories, one on pregnancy and one on divorce. The principal felt that the students in the article on pregnancy were identifiable, and printing the story was an invasion of privacy. In the one on divorce, a student complained about her father's behavior without the father having an opportunity to respond.

The trial court upheld the principal's action, stating that his deletions were "legitimate and reasonable" based on invasion of privacy issues. A federal appeals court reversed that, holding that a journalism class newspaper is a public forum for students and not just an academic project and therefore deserved the protection of the 1st Amendment (Fischer et al., 1999; Schimmel & Fischer, 1987). The Supreme Court decision placed the newspaper as a curriculum project connected to academics, thus the principal could oversee the work. Justice Byron R. White wrote the majority opinion: "A school need not tolerate speech that is inconsistent with its basic education mission, even though the government could not censor similar speech outside the school."

Suspension and Due Process

The 14th Amendment guarantees the right to due process for all citizens—"nor shall any State deprive any person of life, liberty, or property without due process of law." When a student is suspended, the act affects the parents' rights as well as the child's. An early case concerning due process—*Dixon v. Alabama State Board of Education* (1961)—involved college students who were expelled or placed on probation after they staged a sit-in at a lunch counter. The students had not been given a hearing or notice of the charges against them. The court established the right to notice and to a hearing before suspension or expulsion.

A landmark case, *Goss v. Lopez* (1975), resulted from a disturbance at a school lunchroom in Ohio during the winter of 1971. Seventy-five students were suspended. In Ohio, a principal could suspend students for up to 10 days if parents were notified within 24 hours and told the reason for the suspension. To get a hearing, the parents or students had to appeal. Nine students, including Dwight Lopez, filed a lawsuit in federal district court citing the lack of due process. The court ruled in favor of the students, and the school administration appealed to the U.S. Supreme Court. The Supreme Court also found in favor of the students, holding that students are entitled to a public education and that right could be taken away from them only after due process. The Court used the same principle as the one in *Tinker*. Students "do not shed their constitutional rights at the school house door."

Students who are suspended for a short time (up to 10 days) must be given (a) notice of the charges, (b) an explanation of the charges and reasons for the suspension, and (c) an opportunity to explain their side of the situation. The Supreme Court opinion recognized that formal, adversarial proceedings would take too much of the school's time, but "effective notice and informal hearing permitting the student to give his version of the events will provide a meaningful hedge against erroneous action" (Fischer et al., 1999; Schimmel & Fischer, 1987, p. 251).

Students who present a danger to the school can be removed immediately. In the *Goss v. Lopez* decision, the court addressed short suspensions, stating that longer suspension or expulsions may require more formal hearings. The Supreme Court has not addressed the procedures for longer suspensions, but notice, the right to counsel, presentation of evidence, and cross-examination of witnesses should be permitted in any such hearing. The student and parents should also have a statement of findings, conclusions, recommendations, and the right to appeal (Fischer et al., 1999; Schimmel & Fischer, 1987).

Valente (1987) points out that brief in-school sanctions do not require prepunishment hearings. Nor does *Goss v. Lopez* apply in corporal punishment cases (*Ingraham v. Wright,* 1977) because corporal punishment does not require a student to miss school. "The student's right to demand an *open hearing* is not settled" (Valente, 1987, p. 307).

Flag Salute and Pledge of Allegiance

Students do not have to salute the flag or say the Pledge of Allegiance if it violates their religious beliefs. In *West Virginia State Board of Education v. Barnette* (1943), Jehovah's Witnesses parents objected to their children being required by state law to salute the flag. The U.S. Supreme Court found in their favor. Children did not have to salute the flag if the salute violated their beliefs or values.

The decision that students do not have to salute the flag has since been extended to cases in which a person objects as a matter of conscience. In a Coral Gables, Florida, high school, a student objected to having to stand during the Pledge of Allegiance as a matter of conscience. The Florida court found in favor of the student: "Standing is an integral portion of the pledge ceremony and is no less a gesture of acceptance and respect than is the salute or the utterance of the words of allegiance" (Fischer et al., 1999, p. 206).

Other cases have reaffirmed that students cannot be required to say the Pledge of Allegiance or stand during the pledge. A New York honor student refused to pledge allegiance because he did not believe there was freedom and liberty for all. Although the school board had offered to let him leave the room or stand up during the pledge, he preferred to remain seated. The act of standing was an affirmation. "Therefore, the alternative offered plaintiff of standing in silence is an act that cannot be compelled over his deeply held convictions. It can no more be required than the pledge itself" (Fischer et al., 1999, p. 207).

Racial Discrimination

The 14th Amendment states:

All persons born or naturalized in the United States, and subject to the jurisdiction thereof, are citizens of the United States and of the State wherein they reside. No State shall make or enforce any law which shall abridge the privileges or immunities of citizens of the United States; nor shall any State deprive any person of life, liberty, or property, without due process of law, nor deny to any person within its jurisdiction the equal protection of the laws.

The *Brown v. Topeka Board of Education* (1954) decision on racial discrimination in 1954 set the stage for implementing racial equality in the schools. The U.S. Supreme Court stated:

Today, education is perhaps the most important function of state and local governments. Compulsory school attendance laws and the great expenditures for education both demonstrate our recognition of the importance of education to our democratic society. It is required in the performance of our most basic public responsibilities, even service in the armed forces. It is the very foundation of good citizenship. (p. 493)

Congress enacted the Civil Rights Act of 1964 as an instrument to eliminate continued discrimination. Recipients of federal funds, including schools, must meet its guidelines to receive government support. Title VI of the act states

. . . that no person in the United States shall, on the grounds of race, color, or national origin, be excluded from participation in, be denied the benefits of, or be otherwise subjected to discrimination under any program or activity receiving Federal financial assistance from the Department of Education. (Civil Rights Act, § 601 [1964])

A "recipient under any program to which this part applies may not, directly or through contractual or other arrangements, on the basis of race, color, or national origin" engage in the following discrimination practices (*Federal Register*, 1990, p. 30918). Because most schools receive federal financial support and are therefore recipients, they must abide by these regulations and cannot:

1. Deny an individual any service, financial aid or other benefit provided under the program;
2. Provide any service, financial aid or other benefit to an individual which is different or is provided in a different manner from that provided to others under the program;
3. Subject an individual to segregation or separate treatment in any matter related to his receipt of any service, financial aid or other benefit under the program;
4. Restrict an individual in any way in the enjoyment of any advantage or privilege enjoyed by others receiving any service, financial aid or other benefit under the program;
5. Treat an individual differently from others in determining whether he satisfies any admission, enrollment, quota, eligibility, membership or other requirement or condition which individuals must meet in order to be provided any service, financial aid or other benefit provided under the program;
6. Deny an individual an opportunity to participate in the program through the provision of services or otherwise afford him an opportunity to do so which is different from that afforded others under the program. . . .
7. Deny a person the opportunity to participate as a member of a planning or advisory body which is an integral part of the program;
8. . . . Utilize criteria or methods of administration which have the effect of subjecting individuals to discrimination because of their race, color, or national origin, or have the effect of defeating or substantially impairing accom-

plishment of the objectives of the program as respect individuals of a particular race, color, or national origin. (*Federal Register*, 1990, pp. 30918–30919)

Schools must not, therefore, separate students based on race, determine services for students using methods that in effect discriminate against a student, or in any way discriminate against students based on race, color, or national origin.

Situation

Rex came to school ready to learn. He was an African American child with poor but interested parents. The first day the teacher assigned him to a seat in the back of the room. She was pleased that he seemed alert and smiled at her a lot, but she was sure that he would probably need a lot of help, and she had 32 children in her class already. "Why did they have to assign another student to me in the middle of the year? Don't they know that I have as much as I can handle?"

She assigned him to the polar bear group. Everyone in the room knew that was the low group, but Miss Barton thought Rex would be better off there than in the other groups.

During reading groups, Rex read unhesitatingly and with great expression. When Miss Barton asked him questions, he was able to describe the plot and the ending of the story. "He seems to be ready for a higher group, but I think I will keep him in this group until I really find out," thought Miss Barton.

During math Rex raised his hand ready to answer questions, but Miss Barton did not call on him. "I want to give him time to adjust," she said. This continued for the first two weeks that Rex was in the classroom, but by the third week, he no longer smiled; he no longer raised his hand; he no longer wanted to attend school; and his parents worried that something was terribly wrong. They called the school and made an appointment with Miss Barton.

1. Do you think the parents were right in asking for an appointment?
2. Why did Miss Barton continue to ignore Rex?

When this child gets involved in extracurricular sports, Title IX will ensure that she has an opportunity to participate.

3. How can Miss Barton turn the situation around?

4. What should Rex do to help his school experience?

Sex Discrimination

Title IX of the Educational Amendments of 1972 provides that "no person in the United States shall, on the basis of sex, be excluded from participation in, be denied the benefits of, or be subjected to discrimination under any program or activity receiving Federal financial assistance" (U.S. Department of Education, n.d.).

The Office for Civil Rights based in the Department of Education enforces the laws that apply to elementary, secondary, and postsecondary schools. In 1975 a federal regulation required schools to examine their programs to see if discriminatory policies were in effect. Military schools, religious organizations where the regulations are at variance with religious beliefs, and single-sex colleges are exempt. Other than these, educational institutions receiving federal funds cannot "assign students to separate classrooms or activities, or prevent them from enrolling in courses of their choice, on the basis of sex. This includes health, physical education, industrial arts, business, vocational, technical, home economics, music and adult education courses" (U.S. Department of Education, n.d., p. 1).

Educational institutions that receive federal funds cannot do the following:

1. Exclude students of one sex from participation in any academic, extracurricular, research, occupational training or other educational program or activity.

2. Subject any student to separate or different rules of discipline, sanctions or other treatment.

3. Apply different rules of appearance to males and females (for example, requiring males to wear their hair shorter than females).

4. Aid or perpetuate discrimination against any person by providing significant assistance to any agency, organization, or person which discriminates on the basis of sex in providing any aid, benefit, or service to students.

5. Assign pregnant students to separate classes or activities, although schools may require a student to obtain a physician's certificate as to her ability to participate in the normal educational program or activity so long as such a certificate is required of all students for other physical or emotional conditions requiring the attention of a physician.

6. Refuse to excuse any absence because of pregnancy or refuse to allow the student to return to the same grade level that she held when she left school because of pregnancy.

7. Discriminate against any person on the basis of sex in the counseling or guidance of students or the use of different tests or materials for counseling unless such different materials cover the same occupation and interest areas and the use of such different materials is shown to be essential to eliminate sex bias.

Exceptions include:

1. In music classes, schools may have requirements based on vocal range or quality, which may result in all-male or all-female choruses.

2. In elementary and secondary schools, portions of classes that deal exclusively with human sexuality may be conducted in separate sessions for boys and girls.

3. In physical education classes or activities, students may be separated by sex when participating in sports where the major purpose or activity involves bodily contact (for example, wrestling, boxing, rugby, ice hockey, football, and basketball).

4. Students may be grouped in physical education classes by ability if objective standards of individual performances are applied. This may result in all-male or all-female ability groups.

5. If the use of a single standard to measure skill or progress in a physical education class has an adverse effect on members of one sex, schools must use appropriate standards that do not have such an effect. For example, if the ability to lift a certain weight is used as a standard for assignment to a swimming class, application of this standard may exclude some girls. The school would have to use other, appropriate standards to make the selection for that class. (U.S. Department of Education, n.d., pp. 1–2)

Children with Disabilities

Section 504 of the Rehabilitation Act of 1973 provides that "no qualified handicapped individual shall, on the basis of handicap, be excluded from participation in, be denied the benefits of, or otherwise be subjected to discrimination under any program or activity receiving Federal financial assistance" (U.S. Department of Education, 1980, pp. 30937–30938). The Education for All Handicapped Children Act of 1975, P.L. 94-142, ensures that children with disabilities have an appropriate public education. Amendments of 1986, P.L. 94-457, extend the concept to preschool children. The Individuals with Disabilities Education Act

(IDEA), P.L. 101-476, and Individuals with Disabilities Education Act Amendments 1997 (IDEA 97), P.L. 105-17, clarified requirements and increased parent involvement in the education choices for their children. The child is to be educated in the least restrictive environment—one that fits the child's needs. An Individualized Education Program or Individualized Family Service Plan, developed by professionals and parents, protects the child's interest. Refer to Chapter 9 for more complete information.

Corporal Punishment

Although parents may object to corporal punishment, schools do not always honor their request. Punishment must not be harsh and excessive. If it is, teachers and administrators may be subject to civil and criminal liability. In 23 states, however, corporal punishment was still allowed in 2000 (Center for Effective Discipline, 2000). The court decision of *Ingraham v. Wright* (1977) upheld corporal punishment as a means of control in public schools, so schools in most states have the right to use corporal punishment on children without hearings or other components of due process.

Situation

Melvern was late for school that day. When he swaggered into class, he grinned at his buddy across the room, made a motion with his hand, and began to go to the teacher's desk. The teacher greeted him by telling him that his work was late and would not count. "Sorry," said Mr. Beller, "if your work had been here at 9:00 a.m. I would have accepted it, but it is now 9:20, and you'll just have to take the consequence. This just might change your grade from a C to a D. I'm afraid you won't be able to go out for the track team."

Melvern glared at Mr. Beller, threw down his book, kicked at his desk, and made inaudible comments under his breath. "To the office this minute, Melvern, I will not tolerate that kind of behavior. This is your third offense in this class. Mrs. Markam will handle the physical punishment."

Children who come to class speaking a language other than English need to be in a classroom that encourages and accommodates them.

1. Did Mr. Beller handle the situation correctly?
2. How do you evaluate Melvern's response?
3. Should physical punishment be allowed in the schools? Does it help control the school?
4. Is corporal punishment allowed in the state where you reside?
5. Are there any offenses that you think might require corporal punishment? Why?

Rights of Non-English-Speaking Students

In 1965, the Elementary and Secondary Act supported bilingual education for students who do not speak English. This was followed in 1974 by a Supreme Court decision in *Lau v. Nichols* that children who could not speak English did not have equal educational opportunity if they did not receive education in their own language. In this case, 1,800 ethnic Chinese children in San Francisco attended classes conducted in English. The parents contended that the children were discriminated against because no classes were provided that would benefit them. The Supreme Court agreed and stated that schools must take affirmative action and provide classes for students who do not speak English by providing bilingual education or English as a Second Language programs. The court did not offer regulations concerning language programs and left the decision of provisions up to the states.

Situation

Kim Sung came into the fourth-grade classroom. She had arrived just the week before from Venezuela, where her family had lived for the last 10 years. She was a lovely young lady with dark hair and beautiful eyes. She could speak Spanish and Chinese fluently, but she had no experience with English. The teacher, Miss Zingle, had not expected to have a student this term who could not speak English, and she could not speak Spanish or Chinese. By using body language she was able to direct Kim to a seat in the back of the classroom. As soon as Kim was seated, Miss Zingle continued to tell the class what the assignment was. School progressed slowly for Kim. She sat there unable to understand what was going on, and wondering if she were behaving correctly.

1. How could Miss Zingle have handled the situation differently?
2. What would be the best arrangement and learning situation for Kim?
3. What could a teacher and classmates do to help Kim adjust to the new surroundings?
4. What could Miss Zingle have done to help Kim that first day?

Selection of Texts

In general, schools choose text materials to achieve their educational objectives and goals. When parents object to the use of particular books, the courts make decisions based on each individual circumstance and how the book relates to the school's objectives. Courts determine the constitutionality of a position; legislatures may set curriculum requirements to be achieved by public schools. Private schools and early childhood centers that are not connected to the public school system have autonomy in text selection. However, it is wise for both public and private schools to include parents in book selection to prevent later disagreements.

Obscenity is not protected by the 1st Amendment, but the Supreme Court has not defined the term definitively. When the issue over a book or other media becomes so heated that it ends up in court, the court will judge whether it lacks serious literary, artistic, political, or scientific value and if it is obscene because it appeals to prurient interests (*Miller v. California,* 1973). Whether it is obscene will be judged by contemporary, local community standards.

✍ DEVELOPING CRITERIA TOGETHER

Only when parents and teachers work together does the opportunity for optimum education exist. A delineation of three levels of involvement for home and school will clarify and help establish procedures that support positive home-school interaction:

1. Development and periodic review of a code of rights and responsibilities for each class, school, or local school district.

2. Election of and active involvement with a parent or citizen advisory council.

3. Implementation of the educational program in a classroom community.

The first two levels can be accomplished by administrators and parents working together; however, individual classrooms can develop codes and advisory councils as well. The third level of teacher-parent involvement is that essential area where the benefits of positive relationships most make a difference—the classroom. The teacher-child-parent relationship nourishes the opportunity for learning. The clarification of issues and development of codes, a two-way communication system, and advisory councils are but means of supporting direct involvement with the classroom and its most important member, the child.

Development of a Code

An opportunity for participating in a democratic decision-making process exists in the formation of a school or classroom code. If parents and students join school staff in developing a code for their class or school, both rights and responsibilities are learned through a democratic process. *The Rights and Responsibilities of Students: A Handbook for the School Community* (U.S. Department of Health, Education, and Welfare, 1979) suggests a model code and a procedure for implementing a code. Recommended steps include:

1. *Identification of the level of interest.* Determine the interest in and awareness of codes with a questionnaire or informal survey of the school community. Include teachers, administrators, students, parents, and interested community residents. If there is a lack of understanding of the purpose of a code, you must launch an awareness campaign to explain the code, its benefits, and why it is needed.

2. *Research.* Background information on the current rules and regulations should be gathered before writing a code. Samples of codes from other schools or states, legal groups, professional associations, and civil liberty organizations are helpful in the process. Key issues that need to be addressed in your individual area should be identified.

3. *Formulation of a draft code.* The actual writing of the code needs to be done by a committee of parents, teachers, students, and administrators. Include the regulations that are important for your school and community. If guidance is needed, base your draft on the samples obtained.

4. *Feedback.* After the code is drafted, distribute copies or publish the document in the

newsletter. Schedule an open forum or ask for written comments on the code. The responses will reveal questions and areas of confusion or vagueness, which will guide revisions of the draft.

5. *Approval and implementation.* The code should be approved by the student body as well as the school staff. If the code is being developed for the entire district, the school board should review and approve the code. Their support is essential for implementation. At the preschool level the students will not need to approve the code, but their parents should be involved, and discussion of rules and regulations with the children is appropriate.

6. *Review.* Each year the student body or governing committee should review the code. If needed, items may be revised. The review makes the code relevant to the current student body and is a learning as well as a decision-making process.

The three levels of involvement—the code, the parent advisory council, and the classroom—strengthen a school-home partnership. The parent advisory council is discussed in more detail in Chapter 4; good classroom relations are discussed in Chapters 4, 5, and 7. The code can be developed on a formal level in the entire school district, or individual teachers may modify it and use it in an informal way in their classrooms.

✣ CHILD ADVOCACY

Child advocacy becomes an emotional involvement in the lives of children, a caring, a recognition of need, and a willingness to do something about that need. On both a personal level (micro) and a social level (macro), the opportunity for advocacy is ever present for teachers. It is there when the teacher assesses the children's abilities and life situations. How can children be protected so that they grow into productive adults? How can children be enabled to achieve their potential?

Was there a sudden realization of children's need for protection that caused the Child's Rights Movement and Civil Rights Movement? No, as described in this text, through the ages there have been movements to help the child, although sometimes the answers seemed to remove children's rights rather than help them. Asylums for children during the Roman days, for example, were intended to save children from death or disfigurement. Locke's plan to take children from their parents to train and educate them, though harsh, was meant to help the children survive and become productive adults.

Rights, in the form of the doctrine *parens patriae,* were established in law and custom in Britain as early as the 15th century. Parents were not allowed to treat their children in any manner desired because the state could "exercise 'paternal rights' when evidence existed that parents were jeopardizing the welfare of their minor offspring" (Caldwell, 1989, pp. 4–5). This custom followed the settlers to the colonies.

The *Body of Liberties* passed in the American colonies in 1641 provided that youths 16 and older could be put to death if they cursed or smote their parents. The youths had some protection, however. If there was evidence that the parents were extremely harsh and cruel, it could be demonstrated that the youth were forced to act that way to save themselves (Hawes, 1991). The youths had the responsibility to obey their parents, but the government could intervene if the parents were not raising their children properly.

The family was a very strong unit in the colonies, and survival required that each person contribute to the welfare of the family. Most families lived on farms that required numerous chores to manage the production of food and other provisions. Children obeyed their parents, and parents had responsibilities to the children. In spite of the importance of the family, *parens patriae* allowed the state to intervene in the family on behalf of the child. "In the colonial world the concept of *parens patriae* was so pervasive that it scarcely received comment" (Hawes, 1991, p. 6).

As the nation developed and grew, beliefs about childhood changed. Rousseau, Locke, Pestalozzi, and Froebel had developed philosophies based on the child as a developing person who needed nurturance and care. Their beliefs influenced the notion of childhood in America. During the 1800s Elizabeth Peabody and Henry Barnard brought over and campaigned for the Froebelian concept of education in the United States. In the late 19th century, G. Stanley Hall began his studies on children, and children began to be viewed relative to their development.

Community-based services for children were established between 1890 and 1920. Lightner Witmer's psychological clinic was started in 1896. The National Committee for Mental Hygiene was founded in 1909. Other associations for young people were formed, such as the Young Women's Christian Association (1906), Camp Fire Girls (1910), and Girl Scouts (1912). To deal with problem adolescents, the juvenile courts were started in Chicago and Denver about 1899. The visiting teacher movement began in 1906. The National Federation of Settlements was formed in 1912 (Levine & Levine, 1992). Family interests, governmental activities, and new organizations illustrated the strong feelings for children at the turn of the century.

Concern about children and how they should be reared continued throughout the 20th century. The Civil Rights Movement and the rights of people with disabilities focused on fair and equal treatment in the 1960s, and both movements continued to work for equality into the 1990s.

Currently the Children's Defense Fund, headed by Marion Edelman, advocates vehemently for children's rights. Other associations—such as the Center on Families, Communities, Schools and Children's Learning; Family Resource Coalition; Institute for Responsive Education; National Association of Elementary School Principals; National Center for Family Literacy; and National Parent and Teacher Association—work to provide equal educational opportunities for children of all abilities, ethnicity, and gender.

Government agencies such as social services and mental health agencies continue to provide services for those who are at risk and in need. Although we seem concerned, the United States does not rank high in health or social services for children. For example, about eight million American children do not have health care (American Bar Association Presidential Working Group on the Unmet Legal Needs of Children and Their Families, 1993). How does the United States compare with other nations in child advocacy?

A Sleeping Giant: The Child Advocate

Children have neither the skills nor the power to advocate for themselves. It rests with parents and teachers to recognize their needs and advocate for them. The issues of the 1990s vividly illustrate why children need advocates. The growing demand for child care, along with increases in poverty, homelessness, and reports of incest and child abuse, shout to the public. These social problems need a great deal of action to overcome the obstacles that children face. But children also need advocates at a personal level. Many children who come to child care centers or schools lack self-esteem. They need advocates—individual teachers who may be able to help such children feel important and wanted. Advocacy is needed at all levels; both teachers and parents must stand up for the children. If they do not, who will?

As a group, parents of students with disabilities have been particularly successful advocates for their children's education. Strong parental involvement resulted in passage of P.L. 94–142 (The Handicapped Children Act of 1975) and has continued since that time. The 1986 amendments in P.L. 99–457 include education for very young children and provisions for an Individualized Family Service Plan (IFSP) similar to the Individualized Education Program (IEP) of P.L. 94–142. In 1997 the Individuals with Disabilities Education Amendments of 1997, P.L. 105–17 (IDEA), and the reauthorization in 2002 strengthened the rights of children with disabilities and participation in decision making by parents. (See Chapter 9 for additional information.)

No one can escape the responsibility of being an advocate; parents are their child's first advocates.

Levels of Advocacy

Advocacy can be approached on the case or class level, at administrative or legislative levels, or on the public level.

Case or Class Action

Advocates may work with individual cases or in class actions. The individual or case advocate works on behalf of a specific child. The class or social advocate works for a whole group of children who need special or basic services (e.g., the Children's Defense Fund works for child rights; the Pennsylvania Association for Retarded Children began advocacy for the rights of children with mental retardation). Lay advocates must obtain the necessary services and help. When legal issues and court cases are involved, legal counsel from a lawyer, a professional advocate, is needed. The Family Leave Bill, which languished but was finally passed by Congress and signed into law by President Clinton, is an example of the persistence demanded of those who advocate for families.

Administrative or Legislative Levels

Advocates can bring change at the administrative and legislative levels. The advocate may work toward change in regulations and guidelines at the administrative level, or toward change in the laws through legislative advocacy (Goffin & Lombardi, 1988).

Advocacy on the Public Level

Individuals work together and separately to advocate on the public level. Most successful advocacy requires a broad-based approach, whether it is achieved through the responses of many individuals, the advocacy work of professional organizations, or the lobbying efforts of political action committees. The issue of child care affects many people: parents, children, grandparents, employers, schools, and society as a whole.

Youngsters who go through a troubled childhood—abusive, poverty-stricken, or the like—become adults who are unable to hold a job, who use alcohol or other drugs to mask their pain, or who serve time in prison. In the long run, adequate and fulfilling child care is very cost effective.

✎ THE CHILD ADVOCATE

An advocate is a parent, teacher, or citizen—alone or in a group—who speaks or acts on behalf of a child's welfare. The advocate must grasp the needs of the child, the resources available within the school system, and the alternative resources outside the school system. Advocates may be involved at any of three levels:

1. *Personal*—advocate on a personal level for an individual child or a group of children.
2. *Private*—advocate for a cause in the private sector.
3. *Public*—advocate in a group, as one of many advocating for political change or legislation; advocate for a child through the courts; or advocate for a cause in the public sector. (Goffin & Lombardi, 1988)

Working as an Advocate on a Personal Level

The most common kind of advocacy is one that many teachers and parents do every day. If parents and teachers look upon positive intervention that helps children live full and meaningful lives as advocacy and recognize that children cannot advocate for themselves, they will accept the responsibility and challenge of advocacy as a necessary role. Individual advocates who work for children in their own child care programs or classrooms can have a huge effect on children's lives.

No one can escape the responsibility of being an advocate, whether as a parent, classroom teacher, friend, or child care worker. If everyone who works or lives with a child would assume the important role of an advocate for the child, the lives of all children would be changed for the better.

Child care is also affected by personal advocacy. About one third of children in the United States are cared for in their own homes or in the homes of others. More than half of all children are cared for at school; many are latchkey children before and after school and in the summer.

If working parents have the opportunity to use grandparents, other relatives, neighbors, and friends for child care, it is important that the community offer parent support, education, enrichment, and recreation to help these caregivers provide an excellent environment that will benefit the children. This can be addressed at the grass-roots level. Private agencies can help, as can churches, recreation districts, and schools. They may provide crisis child care, parent education, and drop-in child care. Parents who provide their own care could also benefit from this community support, as could child care centers. Children are the responsibility of country and community as well as parents.

Parents and teachers can advocate on a personal level in the following ways:

- Provide a stimulating, appropriate environment so the child can play and work productively.
- Advocate for a child in a classroom or for their own children.
- Spend time with children, listening to what concerns or interests them.
- See that children are in educationally and socially appropriate classes.
- Seek out interesting excursions and activities that will benefit the child.
- Determine the best facilities for a child who needs special help.
- Take time to give proper care to their own children.

- Report physical and sexual abuse.
- Become an ombudsman and share resources with or develop resources for a parent who is neglectful because of lack of resources.
- Share information about good childrearing practices.
- Communicate with the teacher if you are a parent, and with the parents if you are a teacher.
- Attend meetings and speak out on issues (for example, the school board, child care institutions, PTA, League of Women Voters).
- Become active in professional organizations (for example, the local affiliate of the Association for the Education of Young Children, the National Association for the Education of Young Children, or the National Council on Family Relations).
- Write and contact your legislator about upcoming legislation.

What Is a Personal Advocate's Role?

Situation

Joyce, a small child with big brown eyes and a pixie haircut that frames her face, is usually an outgoing, pleasant child. She has many friends and is a leader during class and at recess. But for the past four weeks, she has come to school with a worried look on her face and has avoided the other children during recess. Instead of participating in class, she sits and stares. Her teacher has reacted to her lack of class participation by hav-

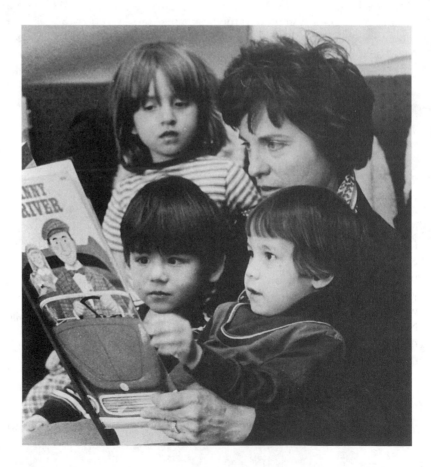

Parents, teachers, concerned citizens, and child care workers must serve as advocates for children.

ing her stay in during music class in an attempt to get her to finish her work.

"I don't know what has gotten into you," Miss Lerch complains. "I used to be able to depend on you, but you have become so lazy lately. You'll never learn if you don't get busy. If you don't straighten out, I'll have to send you to the principal and contact your parents."

1. Is Miss Lerch advocating for Joyce?
2. What could she do to help Joyce?
3. Should she communicate with Joyce's parents?

On a personal level, the classroom teacher can advocate every day for all the children in the classroom.

Situation

One day, Robbie came to school with his hair uncombed and his clothes torn and dirty, but with a smile on his handsome face. Miss Eller knew his mother had died the previous spring and his father was out of work but doing his best to get the children to school.

"Am I late?" Robbie asked as he rushed into the room. "Dad told me that if I didn't hurry I would be late for class."

"You are fine, Robbie," Miss Eller responded. "In fact, you are 15 minutes early—just in time for a snack in the lunchroom. Have you looked at the weekly class organization board? You are in charge of lunch count and taking the money to the office this week. I know you will do a good job. Robbie, I talked with your father yesterday and he said it would be all right if you stayed after school tonight, because I have a special treat for you. I won't tell you what it is right now, but if you do your work well today, I know you will be pleasantly surprised. Now, off with you. Go to the lunchroom with this note. They will give you a snack."

1. Did Miss Eller advocate for Robbie?
2. Was it appropriate for her to call Robbie's father?
3. Do you think the morning snack was a good idea? Why?

4. What do you think the after-school surprise is going to be?

Qualifications for Personal Advocates

Essentially what qualifies a person to be a good child advocate is the intrinsic quality of being truly motivated to help children. The help must be systematic, knowledgeable, and thorough. The advocate must be committed to finding out all the needs of the child or children being helped. Although it is time consuming and difficult, advocacy, when supported by the best available data, is helpful to the community, parents, and schools.

✇ PREPARING FOR ADVOCACY

To be a successful advocate, one needs to be knowledgeable about the case at hand. The Child Care Employee Project has developed curriculum to be used with persons to help them develop their advocacy skills. These are some of the suggestions to better prepare advocates for long-term advocacy:

- Know about the history of child care, child abuse, and the rights of children.
- Recognize the process of social change—how change happens and the history of change in the nation.
- Recognize the effect that social and economic conditions and the organization of society have on the advocate and other families and children.
- Become aware of the effect that technology, power, class, and race have on families in a given society.
- View children as the future of society and as a protected class, with children of all races and classes having needs.
- View child care in a positive light, as a profession with ethical guidelines and practices.
- Identify and use resources in the community, state, and nation. (Whitebook & Ginsburg, 1984)

Procedure

Teachers advocate for their students when they see that the children's needs are met. At times, this seems to be just part of the role of a teacher. At other times, objectives and preparation must be established to advocate effectively.

To achieve their objectives, advocates must systematically study and proceed with a sound foundation. They first list the needs of the child and justify these needs by making certain they have been professionally determined. They read the literature and speak to experts in the field so that their views are supported by reputable observations. Good advocates make sure their positions are based not on their own beliefs alone but on the true needs of the child, the group of children, and society at large.

The following guidelines describe the steps to take when working on an individual advocacy case.

1. *Know your facts.* Be sure they are correct. Find out: Who? What? Where? When? and Why?

2. *Know the rights* of the child, the parent, or other parties in the case. Contact an advocacy organization or lawyer if you have any questions.

3. *Know the policy* and/or procedures that relate to the problem. Get it in writing; don't accept just a verbal version.

4. *Keep accurate notes.* Document as much evidence as possible. Date everything.

5. *Discuss various options* with the child or parents you are assisting. Do not tell the young person or parent what to do. Rather, let the people you are helping choose the option and course of action that is wisest and that they are willing to live with.

6. *Never go alone* (except in unusual circumstances) to a meeting with officials. Take the young person, the parent, or another concerned person with you.

7. *Keep to the point* when meeting with officials. Be firm but not antagonistic and keep focused on the problem and the need to resolve it. Steer clear of personality conflicts.

8. *Follow channels.* Don't go over someone's head without first talking to that person about the problem. It is wise to let the person know you are dissatisfied with the result of your meeting and that you intend to go to the next person in authority.

9. *Send a letter,* if appropriate, to indicate your understanding of what took place at a meeting with officials or administrators. (Fernandez, 1980, p. 83)

National Advocacy

Three prime areas that can be addressed by advocates are child abuse and neglect, child care, and education. Education may include parent education, brain development, attachment, Goals 2000, and being ready to learn. Quality in child care centers and early education is discussed in this chapter. See Chapter 10 for child abuse and neglect.

The National Center for Early Development & Learning and the Frank Porter Graham Child Development Center compiled research on child care centers. This research gives child care advocates information that is useful as they advocate for improved child care. Contact the Centers in Chapel Hill, North Carolina, or the U.S. Department of Education for more information.

The following studies emphasize the importance of quality child care.

- The Center's survey found that quality in child care centers around the country is often mediocre. For example, of more than 400 centers studied in four states, only 8 percent of infant classrooms and 24 percent of preschool classrooms were of good or excellent quality. Ten percent of preschool programs and 40 percent of infant programs were rated as having poor quality (Cost, Quality, and Child Outcomes Study Team [CQO], 1995).

- A significant correlation exists between program quality and outcomes for children. Outcomes related to quality include cooperative play, sociability, creativity, ability to solve social conflicts, self-control, and language and cognitive development (CQO, 1995; Frede, 1995; Love, Schochet, & Meckstrom, 1996; NICHD Early Childhood Research Network, 1996).

- Research suggests that education of staff is positively related to quality of care. However, two recent studies found that only a small percentage of teachers in child care programs have a bachelor's degree or higher (CQO, 1995; National Institute of Child Health and Human Development [NICHD] Early Childhood Research Network, 1996).

- Child care center staff turnover is high, ranging from 25 to 50 percent a year. This means that children are constantly adapting to new caregivers and administrators are constantly orienting and training staff.

- Child care center staff compensation, including wages and benefits, is exceptionally low, with child care staff among the lowest paid of all classes of workers in the United States.

- Research suggests that quality is important for all children, regardless of family income level (CQO, 1995; Love et al., 1996; NICHD Early Childhood Research Network, 1996).

Advocacy for Child Care and Education

Steps can be taken to improve the quality of child care. They include the following policy changes:

- Strengthen standards and regulations for child care programs.

- Require initial and ongoing training for staff working in child care programs.

- Recruit and retain more highly educated and skilled staff.

- Continue efforts to inform parents about the importance of good-quality child care and its effects on children.

- Provide funds sufficient to support the costs of high-quality child care. (National Center for Early Development & Learning, 1997)

The quality of care in centers and other child care settings must be excellent for young children to receive nourishing and nurturing care and be ready to learn when they attend public or private schools. Children's readiness to learn is a goal that is ever present.

Goals 2000

The National Education Goals Panel (1991) developed goals to be achieved by 2000. These goals, a joint statement by the president and governors of the United States, February 26, 1990, were passed by Congress as amended (with the addition of Goals 4 and 8) on March 21, 1994.

Working toward achievement of the goals requires advocacy on the part of families, schools, and community. The goals continue to be goals worth reaching.

Goal 1—All children in America will start school ready to learn.

Goal 2—The high school graduation rate will increase to at least 90 percent.

Goal 3—American students will leave grades 4, 8, and 12 having demonstrated competency in challenging subject matter, including English, mathematics, science, history, and geography; and every school in America will ensure that all students learn to use their minds well, so they may be prepared for responsible citizenship, further learning, and productive employment in our modern economy.

Goal 4—The nation's teaching force will have access to programs for the continued improvement of their professional skills and the opportunity to acquire the knowledge and skills needed to instruct and prepare all American students for the next century.

Goal 5—U.S. students will be first in the world in science and mathematics achievement.

Goal 6—Every adult American will be literate and will possess the knowledge and skills necessary to compete in a global economy and exercise the rights and responsibilities of citizenship.

Goal 7—Every school in America will be free of drugs and violence and will offer a disciplined environment conducive to learning.

Goal 8—Every school will promote partnerships that will increase parental involvement and participation in promoting the social, emotional, and academic growth of children.

The final goal recognizes the major tenet of this text: parents as partners are necessary ingredients in educational success. These goals relate to learners ranging from very young children to young adults. They are a challenge not only to parents, but to the entire nation.

Help Parents Become Advocates and Active Partners in the Schools

How can professionals ensure that parents will feel empowered and become involved? The following suggestions are adapted from a book on community mobilization from the Families and Work Institute (Dombro, O'Donnell, Galinsky, Melcher, and Farber, 1996).

- If you provide ongoing support to parents from the beginning—showing respect, using a buddy system, encouraging them to ask questions, and introducing them into the school program—you will promote feelings of competence and empowerment. The parents will be more comfortable and confident and will see how they can contribute.

- Help parents see that they are important as part of the organization. Parents come to the table with different skills and experiences. "When parents define roles with which they are comfortable, they are more likely to be

effective and remain involved in the process" (Dombro, et al., 1996).

- Parents have unique skills, but you can offer them training and workshops to develop their skills and leadership potential.

- Recognize that parents have limited time. If possible, reimburse them for expenses such as transportation or try to assist with their transportation needs so they can participate. Provide child care to permit parents with younger children to attend meetings. Reach out to single parents with their special needs and help them get "representation in the political process" (Dombro et al., 1996).

If you include parents as partners in the education process, you are advocating for them and their children.

Steps to Take for Public Advocacy

These are the basic steps involved in advocacy at the public level:

1. *Write federal officials.* Individual letters written by constituents are more effective than form letters with many signatures. You can also use e-mail and telephone contact. Send letters about national issues and legislation to:

   President of the United States—The White House, Washington, D.C. 20500.

   Representatives—The Honorable *(name)*, U.S. House of Representatives, Washington, D.C. 20515.

   Senators—The Honorable *(name)*, U.S. Senate, Washington, D.C. 20515.

   For representatives' telephone numbers, call the Capitol switchboard, 202-224-3121.

2. *Talk with and write to state legislators.* On the state level, write or call the following:

   Your state representative

   Your state senators

Work with your representative before the assembly or legislature meets if you or your group has a bill that you want introduced.

3. *Get involved before elections.* Campaign for legislators who agree with your position on child care, families, and children.

4. *Stay involved after elections.* After an election, invite elected officials to meet with your organization.

5. *Join professional organizations in your region.* For example, the National Association for the Education of Young Children, the Council for Exceptional Children, the National Association for Children with Learning Disabilities, your local Association for the Education of Young Children, and National Council on Family Relations. (Addresses are in the Appendix.)

6. *Get firsthand experience.* Visit child care centers, homeless shelters, schools, and other facilities.

ᘔᘓ FACTS ON CHILDREN AND FAMILIES

Facts can be used by persons to advocate for improvement in children's lives and conditions.

Population

- In 2002 there were 288 million persons in the United States, an increase of nearly 33 million persons over the 1990 population count. Sixty percent of the increase was natural, birth over death; immigration was responsible for the remaining 40 percent (Kent & Mather, December 2002).

- In 2000 there were 72,293,812 children in the United States. This is a 14 percent increase over the population of children in 1990 (*KIDS COUNT*, 2001).

- Twenty-eight million or 25.5 percent of the nonfamily householders live alone (U.S. Census Bureau, 2000a).

Poverty

- The poverty rate for everyone in 2000 was 11.3 percent. Thirty-one million were poor (U.S. Census Bureau, 2000d).

- The poverty rate for Hispanic families with a mother and no husband was 41.4 percent; Hispanic families with a father and no mother poverty rate was 17 percent (U.S. Census Bureau, 2000b).

- The poverty level in 2000 for a family of four was $17,603 and for a family of three, $13,738 (U. S. Census, 2001).

- In 2000, 49.8 percent of families headed by women were below the poverty level of $13,738 (U.S. Census, 2000).

- In 2000 child poverty stood at 16.2 percent, downward since its peak in 1993 of 22.7 percent.

- Children make up 37 percent of the poor but only 26 percent of the population.

- Children from poor families are at higher risk for poor health, inadequate maternal care, and poor education experiences. They are more prone to die in childhood, score poorly on standardized tests, drop out of school, fall victim to violence, and continue the poverty cycle (Levit, Terman, & Behrman, 1997).

- A child is born into poverty every 36 seconds in the United States (Children's Defense Fund, 1998).

- Sixty percent of all children in poverty are White, but 90 percent of children in poverty for the long term are African American (Corcoran & Chaudry, 1997).

- Long-term poverty for children was greatest for African American children; 29 percent were in poverty for 10 or more years and half were in poverty for 5 years. By comparison, 1 percent of Whites were poor for 10 or more years and 6 percent for 5 years (Corcoran & Chaudry, 1997).

- Children who live in extreme poverty or who are in poverty for long periods suffer the most. If the poverty occurs during early childhood, the consequences are more severe than if it occurs in their later years (Brooks-Gunn & Duncan, 1997).

- In young families—those with parents under 30, single or married—the poverty rate doubled from 20 to 41 percent between 1973 and 1994, as their median income plunged 330 percent (Children's Defense Fund, 1998).

- Between 1975 and 1995 cash welfare program spending increased from $40 billion to $95 billion. Expenditures on Aid to Families with Dependent Children (AFDC), however, decreased by 8 percent over the same period in spite of a 19 percent increase in the number of children. This was followed by elimination of ADFC by the Personal Responsibility and Work Opportunity Reconciliation Act of 1996. It was replaced with Temporary Assistance for Needy Families (Levit et al., 1997). This new program, TANF, has time limits on benefits and reduced food stamps for recipients with children. Some five million families saw their food stamp benefits drop an average of $36 a month in 1998 (Children's Defense Fund, 1998).

Young Parents

- An infant is born to a teenager every minute of the day in the United States.

- There were 505,000 births to mothers ages 15 to 19 in 1996; 75 percent of those were to unmarried teenagers.

- Parents who are young are more often poor. They make up the largest proportion of families living in poverty. Forty-one percent of children in young families are in poverty. (Children's Defense Fund, 1998)

Working Parents

- Of married women who have children under six and are living with their husbands, 68 percent are employed outside the home (Bianchi & Spain, 1996).

- One in five fathers cares for preschool-age children while the mother works (Casper, 1997).

- Fathers have increased the time that they spend with their children (Bond et al., 1998).

- Enrollment in nursery school increased from less than 8 percent in 1970 for children three to six years of age, to 28 percent by 1998 (Population Reference Bureau, AmeriStat, 2000).

Single-Parent Families

- The percentage of children living in two-parent families in the United States declined from 76 percent in 1990 to 68 percent in 1999, whereas the percentage of children in one-parent families increased from 20 to 27 percent.

- The increase in percentage of births to single unmarried mothers increased from 5 percent in 1970 to 14.2 percent in 1975, and from 18 percent in 1980 to 32.8 percent in 2001.

- The increase of single mothers in the workforce went from 4 percent in 1970 to 8 percent in 2000. (Population Reference Bureau, AmeriStat, 2000)

Homelessness

- Over three million persons (men, women, and children) were homeless in 2001 (National Law Center on Homelessness and Poverty, 2002a).

- Data on homeless showed that

    40% are families with children

    67% are single-parent families

    22% have mental disabilities

    20% work

    4% are unaccompanied children

Of these

50% are African American

35% are White

12% are Hispanic

2% are Native American

1% are Asian (Adapted from National Law Center on Homelessness & Poverty, 2002a, Overview, p. 1)

- Homeless people lack a support network—families and friends—that could help them through a crisis. Becoming homeless also takes them away from whatever network they may have established with former neighbors, friends, churches, or communities.

- Compared to children in higher income families, poor children have triple the risk of lead poisoning, a poisoning that causes neurological damage (Children's Defense Fund, 1998).

- In 1992, 55 percent of two-year-olds in the United States were immunized. This increased to 78 percent in 1996 (Children's Defense Fund, 1998).

- Three million teenagers—about one in four of those who are sexually active—are infected with sexually transmitted diseases each year (Children's Defense Fund, 1998).

- The United States ranked 18th in the world in infant mortality (Children's Defense Fund, 1998).

- Forty percent of programs for infants and 10 percent of preschool programs are rated as poor in quality (CQO, 1995).

- Child care centers have high turnover in staff, ranging from 25 to 50 percent a year (National Center for Early Development & Learning, 1997).

- Every nine seconds a child drops out of school (Children's Defense Fund, 1998).

- 93 percent of White students, 89 percent of Black students, and 62 percent of Hispanic students complete high school (Children's Defense Fund, 2001).

- 31 percent of fourth-grade students are at or above the proficient reading level (Children's Defense Fund, 2001).

- Almost 7 million children, 5 to 14 years of age, care for themselves without supervision (Children's Defense Fund, 2001).

- Children in foster care increased from 262,000 children in 1982 to 568,000 in 1999. Almost one third were in foster homes with relatives (Children's Defense Fund, 2001).

- The care for children under three was

27% parent care

27% relative care

22% center care

17% family child care

- The care for preschoolers was

21% family child care

30% child care centers

42% care by a relative

6% care for child at work (Adapted from Casper, 1997)

Violence

- Juvenile crime peaks between 3 and 7 p.m., endangering nearly five million latchkey children (Children's Defense Fund, 1998).

- In 1996 there were 969,000 substantiated cases of child abuse or neglect out of 3.1 million reports (Children's Defense Fund, 1998).

- On the average, one child or teen is killed with a gun every two and a half hours. Ten children die each day from gunshot wounds (Children's Defense Fund, 2001).

- Children incarcerated in adult prisons are five times more likely to be sexually assaulted, eight times more apt to commit suicide, and twice as likely to be sexually assaulted by staff as those who serve time in a juvenile facility (Children's Defense Fund, 1998).

✍ ADVOCACY FOR CHILDREN AROUND THE WORLD

Europe has been a leader in advocacy for children. The Council of Europe has been active since after World War II, 50 years of work, many of it concerned with children and their rights. European states also adopted the United Nations Convention on the Rights of the Child and there is movement in recognizing the need for rights for children.

> The concept of Ombudsman—the representative of the people—may still be new in Ireland, but in Sweden an Ombudsman was first appointed in 1809. In 1919 Finland adopted the idea but it was not until after 1954, when Denmark established an Ombudsman's Office, that the idea of an Ombudsman started to attract world-wide attention. (Office of the Ombudsman, 1998, p. 2)

European Network

A European Network of Ombudsmen for Children (ENOC) reports on the achievements of the nations in Europe. This includes Austria, France, Lithuania, Norway, Russia (Volgograd), Belgium, Georgia, Macedonia, Poland, Sweden, Catalonia, Hungary, Madrid, Portugal, Denmark, Iceland, Northern Ireland, and Romania. Some nations, such as Norway, Sweden, and Finland, have had ombudsman systems for many years. Other countries, having adopted the United Nations Convention on the Rights of the Child, are developing their children's ombudsman program.

In Norway the system was created by national legislation. In Finland the ombudsman is the legal aspect of the Mannerheim League for Child Welfare, a private advocacy group, and in Israel the ombudsman is under the direction of the Jerusalem Children's Council (Rauche-Elnekave, 1989). In Sweden, it was run by Radda Barnen (Save the Children), a large, private organization until 1993, when Sweden established an Office of Children's Ombudsman (Mork, 1998; Rauche-Elnekave, 1989). In each of these coun-

tries, in addition to working on behalf of individual children, the ombudsmen work toward betterment for groups of children and answer general complaints.

Norway

Norway and Sweden have highly developed systems of ombudsmanship—a comprehensive child advocacy office. Norway's involvement with families reaches back several centuries. In 1621 a Norwegian law required parents to find a useful occupation for their children. If the children were found idle, public guardians would take over the responsibility of the parents. Now Norway has one of the first national ombudsman programs for children—the Ombudsman for Children office, established in 1981 (Flekkoy, 1989). "The Ombudsman for Children is by law regarded as an independent, non-partisan, politically neutral which neither the national Assembly nor the Government have the power to instruct" (Barneombudet, 2000, p. 1).

The Ombudsman for Children advocates for children's education based on international conventions, including the United Nation's Convention on the Rights of the Child. Children have rights to education, rights in education, and rights through education. The rights to education include: (1) the right of refugees to obtain education without regard to the length of their stay in the country or their legal status; (2) the right to a religious and moral education (Norway has a state church); and (3) the right to come and go to school without extra costs—"right to go to school in the closest environment" (Hauge, 1998, p. 53).

The rights in education provide for quality of education with stimulating education and child care. These rights also include the right to be protected from bullying or abuse by teachers, with the right to complain and to have the situation resolved in a "secure procedure" (p. 53).

The rights through education include participation and democracy. Schools have a dialectic process leading to democracy and school development with input from the children.

The ombudsman has particularly focused on:

- *Environment:* learning environment, environment of labor to increase opportunities of growth and learning, directly and indirectly.

- *Participation:* children's competence, participation in school-democracy and in the community.

- *Equality:* equal access to schooling and to quality in education by means of participation (p. 54).

The ombudsman, in order to see that rights of children are established, needs to persuade those in power to recognize and respond to the children's rights, needs, and interests (Hauge, 1998).

Save the Children Norway established the Children Centre for Prevention of Child Sexual Abuse. At the first World Congress against Commercial Sexual Exploitation of Children which was held in Stockholm, August 1996, the Norwegian Ombudsman for Children and Save the Children Norway started a project for identifying child pornography, the pedophile network, and other methods used by criminals in the exploitation of children (Save the Children, 2000).

A free Children's Powerline was established in 1989 in order for children to be able to reach the office easily. Evidence of its use are the 23,200 calls and 500 e-mails to the Powerline in 2000. Replies are put on Ombudsman Web pages and on Tex-TV (Barneombudet, 2000).

Sweden

The Office of Children's Ombudsman, referred to in Swedish as Barnombudsmanner (BO), was established in Sweden in 1993 and followed the United Nations Convention on the Rights of the Child (Children's Ombudsman, 1998) for the purpose of ensuring children's rights. "The Ombudsman has the task of ensuring that the Rights of the Child [are] respected, as well as promoting good formative condition, a good psychosocial environment and a good standard of child safety" (Mork, 1998, p. 21).

Sweden is concerned about the children who come from homes where they are at risk. The debate continues: Should children be separated from biological parents or stay with them and live in a home detrimental to the child? Concern is shown for children whose parents are severe drug addicts, alcoholics, mentally ill, or mentally retarded. The question remains: "Shall we sacrifice them in order to satisfy grown-ups' need to have children? Have children no human rights of their own?" (Ronstrom, 1989, p. 127).

The main issues that the Ombudsman focuses on include

- Information, implementation, and application of the United Nations Convention on the Rights of the Child

- Children in situations such as sexual abuse and bullying where they may be subject to harm

- Public activities that cover safety of children and young people

- Legal, political, and social conditions for children (Adapted from The Children's Ombudsman, 1998, p. 3).

The Children's Ombudsman can start with an individual case and interpret the case based on the UN Convention from a Swedish point of view "in order to give greater prominence to principles which could form the basis for different standpoints, recommendations and proposals for change" (The Children's Ombudsman, 1998, p. 2).

Finland and Israel

In Finland and Israel, the ombudsman works alone, dealing with complaints and problems that individual children have. In Israel, the organization Working Group on Children's Rights includes all faiths, including Jewish, Muslim, and Christian children, and works for all children, including those in preschool and those who are children of prisoners (Rauche-Elnekave, 1989; Utriainen, 1989).

Hungary

Hungary's office of Ombudsman was established June 30, 1995. Its work with children includes:

- Direct consultations with individual children
- Telephone hotline
- Community meetings with groups of children
- Correspondence

The office influences policy at the national and local level and also monitors the implementation of the UN Convention on the Rights of the Child. Most of its work has been with school systems and local and municipal government.

The themes in 2001 and 2002 were

- Protection from all forms of violence
- Sexual exploitation
- Children in institutions
- Disabled children
- Education—closing down of schools (Centre for Europe's Children, 2002a)

Austria

The Federal Youth Welfare Act of 1989 was established through child welfare legislation. By 2002, each of the nine provinces had an Ombudsman for Children and Youth. Each office is in direct contact with children and young people: "We provide information and give advice, we mediate between them and the parents or other professionals. We try to represent their interest, to find amicable solutions. We help them to solve their problems" (Centre for Europe's Children, 2001b, p. 3).

Changes for children and young persons in Austria include

- School mediation
- Improved protection for victims of violence and abuse, including a network against sexual violence
- A safety card to help them say "No"
- Youth helps youth

- UN Convention on the Rights of the Child booklet on what parents should know (Adapted from Centre for Europe's Children, 2001b, pp. 4–5)

France

The Ombudsman for Children was established March 6, 2000, as an independent agency vested with authority to defend and promote children's rights as defined by law or an international agreement such as the UN Convention of the Rights of the Child (Centre for Europe's children, 2001a).

The office has a fourfold mission: It reviews individual cases and intervenes when regular procedures have not been adequate to protect the children; it identifies dysfunctions in services that affect the rights of children in hospitals, schools, institutions, and prisons; it promotes children's rights and organizes campaigns, information for children, and training for professionals who do not have sufficient information on rights of children; and it is responsible for ensuring that children's views are heard.

The office has established a Web site accessible to children. In the first 10 months it was contacted 49,000 times. In addition, the office received approximately 4,000 letters over a period of 16 months, with 922 of them concerned with individual complaints. Its report to the European Network of Ombudsman for Children states: "The Ombudsman for Children has become a widely respected authority as regards the protection of children's rights and the benefits of the Office are now unanimously recognized" (Centre for Europe's Children, 2001a, p. 6).

Latin America

Although Latin American countries do not have an Office of Ombudsman for Children, children's rights are advocated by either a broader ombudsman office or a commissioner for human rights. Honduras has a National Commissioner for Human Rights Office. Costa Rica has an Ombudsman Office for the Inhabitants of the Republic. Guatemala has an Ombudsman Office for the

Rights of the Child within the Human Rights Ombudsman Office. In Colombia, within the Defensoria del Pueblo there is a delegate for Children, Women, and Seniors. Panama has an office of a General Ombudsman. Ecuador and Peru have Commissioners of State that include a defender of children. The National Commission of Human Rights includes Coordination of Woman, the Child and the Family in Mexico (Centre for Europe's Children, 2001d). Latin America has begun to recognize the special needs and rights of women and children, but much greater development needs to accomplished.

Ombudsmanship

The United Nations Convention on the Rights of the Child has made a strong impact on the development of programs concerned about children's rights and the need to be protected. The need for protection range from slavery and sexual violence, to provision of a home and nourishment. The European Network of Ombudsmen for Children (ENOC) is working to end all corporal punishment of children in Europe. ENOC states: "Hitting children is disrespectful and dangerous. Children deserve at least the same protection from violence that we as adults take for granted for ourselves?" (Centre for Europe's Children, 2001b, p. 3). What a giant step it would be if the same practices could be considered and implemented throughout the world.

✑ SUMMARY

Rights and responsibilities of parents, students, and professional educators are explored in this chapter. Criticisms of schools make cooperation between home and schools even more essential than in previous times.

Rights and responsibilities of parents and students are expressed on the following topics: suspension and expulsion, speech and expression, flag salute and Pledge of Allegiance, racial discrimination, sex discrimination, students with disabilities and special education, corporal punishment, and the Buckley Amendment on open-record policy.

Three levels of involvement between home and school help clarify and delineate procedures that support positive home-school relationships. These include (a) development and periodic review of a code of rights and responsibilities for each class, school, or local school district; (b) election of and active involvement with a parent or citizen advisory council; and (c) implementation of the educational program in a classroom community. Development of a code involves identification of interests, research and gathering of background material, formulation of a draft code, feedback, approval, implementation, and review.

Parents and teachers must advocate for children's rights. This can be accomplished by organizing, planning, and advocating for a more caring and healthy environment. Parents and schools working together can provide a wholesome, intellectually stimulating, and challenging environment for families and children.

The chapter closes with a review of ombudsman practices in selected countries.

✑SUGGESTED CLASS ACTIVITIES AND DISCUSSIONS

1. What is free speech? How are the boundaries defined? Discuss.
2. What rights do parents and students have to see school records?
3. Discuss the concept that rights are also accompanied by responsibilities.
4. How have schools responded to the need to eliminate racial discrimination? Investigate the changes that have occurred in schools in your area because of affirmative action.
5. Contact a school in your area and find out what alternative programs exist.
6. Develop a plan for advocating that your school district reach the Goals 2000 Educate America goals for education in the United States.
7. Follow the legislative action in your state, choose a bill that you strongly support, and advocate for its passage.
8. Brainstorm and come up with a list of needs that should be addressed by an advocate or advocacy groups.
9. Research the status of the United Nations Convention on the Rights of the Child in the United States.

Appendix
Resources for Home and School Programs

A resource center or library is necessary for effective school-based and home-based programs. Compile references that discuss the issues of communication, child development, health, and other topics concerning parents. Collect books, pamphlets, magazines, and media materials that cover the many aspects of working with parents. This appendix lists resources for a basic parent education program.

Books form a basis for reference in a resource center, but pamphlets and short articles are practical for parent groups. Refer to the section on organizations that furnish free or inexpensive pamphlets to obtain materials that can be loaned on a wide scale. The size of a handout or pamphlet is less intimidating than a large book to busy parents. In addition, books are expensive; you cannot have copies for everyone.

Buy books for a basic library, but supplement them with pamphlets and copies of articles (abiding by copyright regulations). Government publications generally can be duplicated freely. Permission to make copies of articles from professional magazines can usually be obtained by writing the publisher. After copies of articles are duplicated, staple each into a file folder or back each with a piece of construction paper. Mark the folder with the name of the resource center. Classify and file the articles for easy retrieval and subsequent loan. With reference books, pamphlets, and articles you can plan and develop many diverse parent meetings.

For current information about the availability of materials, write to the National Maternal and Child Health Clearinghouse and the Superintendent of Documents. Telephone the U.S. Department of Education at 800-USA-LEARN. Look under publication sources in this appendix for addresses of additional resources. For a complete listing of new books available, check *Books in Print* under subject titles, such as child development. This reference may be found in your public library. It lists books that are currently available, but you will have to determine whether a book is appropriate.

ASSOCIATIONS CONCERNED WITH PARENT INVOLVEMENT

Items marked with an asterisk (*) have parent involvement as their major focus.

American Association of School Administrators
1801 North Moore St.
Arlington, VA 22209
703-528-0700
AASA has publications, such as *Home/School/Community Involvement, Partnerships: Connecting Schools and Community,* a video, and pamphlets that relate to parent involvement.

ASPIRA Association, Inc.
1444 I St. NW, #800
Washington, DC 20005-2210
202-835-3600
ASPIRA works toward socioeconomic development of Puerto Ricans and Latinos/Latinas. To this end it has included publications and technical assistance on working with Hispanic communities.

Association for Childhood Education International
The Olney Professional Building
17904 Georgia Ave., #215
Olney, MD 20832
301-570-2111
ACEI is a professional organization that publishes a journal, *Childhood Education;* a research journal; and books concerning children, education, and parent involvement.

**Bush Center in Child Development
and Social Policy**
Yale University
310 Prospect St.
New Haven, CT 06511
The Bush Center conducts research, publishes, and holds conferences.

Carnegie Corporation of New York
437 Madison Ave.
New York, NY 10022
212-371-3200
(Publications: PO Box 753, Waldorf, MD 20604)
Carnegie Corporation studies issues and public policy concerning the needs of the nation. In 1994, it produced *Starting Points: Meeting the Needs of Our Youngest Children.*

**Carnegie Foundation for the Advancement
of Teaching**
555 Middlefield Rd.
Menlo Park, CA 94025-3443
650-566-5100
The Carnegie Foundation produces research and papers on education.

Center for Law and Education
1875 Connecticut Ave. NW
Washington, DC 20009
202-986-3000
The center has released a publication titled *Urgent Message: Families Crucial to School Reform* which emphasizes family involvement in schools.

Center for the Future of Children
David and Lucile Packard Foundation
300 Second St., #200
Los Altos, CA 94022
The center publishes books on special subjects such as children and poverty, children and divorce, critical issues for children, and special education. The publications are free.

***Center on Families, Communities, Schools, and
Children's Learning**
Johns Hopkins University
3505 North Charles St.
Baltimore, MD 21218
Joyce Epstein of Johns Hopkins University and others from Boston University, Institute for Responsive Education, Temple University, Wheelock College, Yale University and Michigan State University focus on research, dissemination projects, newsletters, and publications. Send a letter to Johns Hopkins to receive their newsletter or e-mail them at info@ncrel.org.

Children's Defense Fund
122 C St. NW, #400
Washington, DC 20001
CDF advocates for children and families, especially those who are poor and powerless. Each year it publishes books and pamphlets of data on the welfare of children in the United States.

Council of Chief State School Officers
One Massachusetts Ave. NW, #700
Washington, DC 20001
202-408-5505
CCSSO is a nationwide organization of professionals who head departments of public education. It maintains a resource center on educational equity, providing guidelines for state action to help at-risk children succeed.

*Families and Work Institute
330 Seventh Ave., 14th Floor
New York, NY 10001
212-465-2044
The institute focuses on research and publications that support workplaces, families, and communities. It published *Rethinking the Brain* in 1997, a book about infants and young children.

*Family Resource Coalition
801 G St. NW
Washington, DC 20001
202-393-2100
The coalition disseminates information on family programs and policies. The National Resource Center for Family Support Programs was established to provide a database of family support programs.

*The Home and School Institute
1500 Massachusetts Ave. NW
Washington, DC 20005
202-466-3633
This nonprofit association founded in 1984 by Dorothy Rich focuses on families and parents. Training, workshops, and publications are offered to help parents and families become more successful. HSI has trained many Chapter I participants and teachers.

*Institute for Responsive Education
21 Lake Hall
Boston, MA 02215
617-373-2595

IRE conducts research and field projects to promote parent collaboration with schools. Don Davies has written many articles on advocacy and parent involvement. One project of IRE—Schools Reaching Out—has involved schools across the nation in working for school-home cooperation. Articles, pamphlets, reports, and books such as *Building Parent-Teacher Partnerships: Prospects from the Perspective of the Schools Reaching Out Project* are available.

International Reading Association
800 Barksdale Rd.
PO Box 8139
Newark, DE 19714-8139
302-731-1600

The IRA is a professional organization that focuses on reading instruction. It has recognized the importance of parents in the reading process and has developed book lists, brochures, and other publications to support the family's involvement in the child's reading success.

National Association of Elementary School Principals
1615 Duke St.
Alexandria, VA 22314-3483

NAESP offers a newsletter for principals to send home to parents. It also publishes standards for programs for early childhood and elementary education.

National Association of Partners in Education
901 N. Pitt St., #320
Alexandria, VA 22314
703-836-4880

To NAPE, "partners" encompasses all who can work to help students. This includes parents as well as businesses, community groups, and volunteers. The association offers handbooks and information on obtaining volunteers and creating partners.

National Association of Secondary School Principals
1904 Association Dr.
Reston, VA 20191-1537
703-860-0200

NASSP includes parent involvement in its materials and discussions of a variety of educational issues.

National Association of State Boards of Education
1012 Cameron St.
Alexandria, VA 22314
703-684-4000

The NASBE has issued several outstanding publications including *Caring Communities; Partners in Educational Improvement: Schools, Parents and the Community;* and *Right from the Start.*

National Center for Children in Poverty
Columbia University, School of Public Health
154 Haven Ave.
New York, NY 10032
212-304-7100

This center focuses on poverty and its effects on children.

National Center for Education in Maternal and Child Health
2000 15th St. N, #701
Arlington, VA 22201-2617
703-524-7802

Information on maternal and child health is available from the center.

*National Center for Education Statistics
1990 K St. NW
Washington, DC 20006
202-502-7300

*National Center for Family Literacy
Waterfront Plaza, #200
325 West Main St.
Louisville, KY 40202-4251

The center provides training and materials to individuals and organizations that want to help adults become literate.

National Center for the Study of Corporal Punishment and Alternatives
Temple University
1301 W. Cecil B. Moore Ave.
253 Ritter Annex
Philadelphia, PA 19122
215-204-6091

The center researches the effects corporal punishment has on children and aims to prove that corporal punishment should be replaced with other forms of discipline.

*National Coalition of Title I Parents
National Parent Center
Edmonds School Building
14th St. NW
Washington, DC 20005

The National Coalition is a parent advocate organization that works with Chapter I. It provides information, training, and technical assistance to schools and parents.

**National Commission on the Education
of Migrant Children**
1501 Broadway, #403
New York, NY 10036
212-840-1801

The commission's area of concern is the education of migrant children.

National Community Education Association
3929 Old Lee Hwy., #91
Fairfax, VA 22030
703-359-8973

NCEA supports community involvement in education from kindergarten through the grade 12. Publications are available through a mail-order catalog.

National Conference of State Legislatures
1560 Broadway, #700
Denver, CO 80202-5140
303-830-2200

The office is a clearinghouse on state policy issues, including those pertaining to children and families.

National Education Association
1201 16th St. NW
Washington, DC 20036
202-833-4000

NEA, a national policy and advocacy organization, publishes articles, pamphlets, and books on parent involvement in education.

National Maternal and Child Health Clearinghouse
500 Fishers Lane
Rockville, MD 20857
703-356-1964

The center distributes current publications on maternal and child health, covering such topics as pregnancy, nutrition, chronic illness, and disabilities. A publications catalog is available.

*National Parent and Teacher Association
135 South LaSalle St.
Chicago, IL 60674-1927
312-549-3253

PTA connects parents with teachers. It is active throughout the nation, advocating and supporting school-home collaboration. A single copy of many of the association's pamphlets can be obtained free.

National Urban League
120 Wall St.
New York, NY 10005
212-558-5300

The league advocate for Blacks and other minorities in employment, housing, education, social welfare, and other issues of concern. Its Parent Involvement Project works with parents of African American students.

Partnership for Family Involvement in Education
800-USA-LEARN

The U.S. Department of Education has established a partnership with schools, organizations, and parents to foster excellence in education. In addition to telephoning the number above, you may write the partnership in care of the department.

Society for Research in Child Development
University of Michigan
505 East Huron, #301
Ann Arbor, MI 48104-1522

The society publishes excellent research reports on all facets of child development.

U.S. Department of Education
400 Maryland Ave. SW
Washington, DC 20202

A series on "Helping Your Child" offers suggestions on helping your child succeed in school, early childhood education, reading and so forth. These suggestions can be obtained by calling 1-800-USA-LEARN. In addition, addresses and telephone numbers are given for resources for families and caregivers.

Zero to Three Infants, Toddlers, & Families
2000 M St. NW, #2000
Washington, DC 20037-3306
202-638-1144

Zero to Three focuses on infants and toddlers to three years of age with training programs, publications, and technical assistance.

RESOURCES FOR PARENTS AND TEACHERS OF CHILDREN AND YOUTH WITH DISABILITIES

Children and Adults with Attention Deficit Disorder

8181 Professional Pl., #201
Landover, MD 20785
302-306-7070

The group aids families with children with attention-deficit disorder by providing advocacy and education.

Council for Learning Disabilities

PO Box 40303
Overland Park, KS 66204

CLD is a professional organization with educational material and information on learning disabilities.

Council on Exceptional Children

1110 N. Glebe Rd., #300
Arlington, VA 22201-5704
1-800-224-6830

CEC is a professional organization that advocates for children with disabilities.

ERIC Clearinghouse on Disabilities and Gifted Education

Office of Special Education and Rehabilitative Services
Switzer Bldg., 3132
Washington, DC 20202-2524
800-328-0272 or 202-205-8241

ERIC provides information on 17 specialized areas, including early childhood and elementary education and special education. Many of its publications are free; others are available on microfiche in college libraries or can be bought from ERIC. ERIC has a pocket guide to federal help for individuals with disabilities.

International Dyslexia Association (Orton Dyslexia Society)

8600 La Salle Rd.
Chester Building, 382
Baltimore, MD 21286
800-222-3123 or 410-296-0232

The society offers conferences, resources, and publications on dyslexia. There are branch groups that meet across the nation.

Learning Disabilities Association of America

4156 Library Rd.
Pittsburgh, PA 15234
412-341-1515

LDA has chapters across the nation to assist professionals and parents concerned about learning disabilities. It holds conferences and offers publications and film rental.

National Council on Disabilities

1331 F St., NW, #850
Washington, DC 20004
202-272-2004

NCD furnishes information, referrals, educational programs, legislative advocacy, and publications.

National Information Center for Children and Youth with Disabilities

PO Box 1492
Washington, DC 20013-1492
800-695-0285 or 202-884-8200

NICHCY is a clearinghouse of information on disabilities of children, birth to age 25. It offers free information searches, referrals, and technical assistance.

National Institute of Child Care and Human Development

U.S. Department of Health and Human Services
31 Center Dr.
Building 31, Room 2A32, MSC-2420
Bethesda, MD 20892-2425

Office of Special Education and Rehabilitative Services

U.S. Department of Education
Washington, DC 20202

The two preceding entries are federal offices that provide support and information to parents of children with disabilities.

Recording for the Blind and Dyslexic

The Anne T. MacDonald Center
20 Roszel Rd.
Princeton, NY 08540
800-424-8567 or 800-221-4792 or 609-452-0606

RFB&D serves those with verified visual or learning disabilities that limit their ability to read. A free library of books on audiocassettes from fourth grade through postgraduate work is available.

Talking Books—National Library Service
Library of Congress
1291 Taylor St. NW
Washington, DC 20542

Talking books, magazines, and four-track tape recorders can be borrowed by those who establish eligibility.

PROGRAMS HELPFUL IN DEVELOPING PARENTING SKILLS

Numerous formats have been developed to help parent educators teach parenting skills. These range from books to audio and videocassettes. The following selections illustrate the types of programs available.

American Guidance Service, (n.d.). *Systematic training for effective parenting.* Circle Pines, MN.

American Guidance Service (AGS) publishes a number of programs including Early Childhood STEP by Dinkmeyer, McKay, and Dinkmeyer.

The seven sessions address understanding young children, building self-esteem, communicating, helping young children learn to cooperate, effective discipline, and nurturing emotional and social development. Available materials include a manual, *Parenting Young Children*; a videocassette; a leader's manual; and discussion guidelines. AGS also offers these sets:

STEP/Teen—Systematic Training for Effective Parenting of Teens

TIME—Training in Marriage Enrichment

Responsive Parenting

Strengthening Stepfamilies

PREP for Effective Family Living—Preparenting materials for students in marriage and family-living classes

Bradshaw, J. (1996). *Bradshaw on the family: A new way of creating solid self-esteem.* Deerfield, FL: Health Communications.

Bradshaw emphasizes emotional health and the development of self-esteem.

Cooperative Educational Service Agency 5. (1977). *Portage guide to early education.* Portage, WI: Author.

This program includes 580 developmentally sequenced behaviors packaged in a kit with a manual and card file. The Portage project was originated to design programs and serve preschoolers who were at risk developmentally. It has been expanded to use these offerings for all parents. It distributes books including *Portage Home Teaching Handbook, A Parent's Guide to Early Education,* and *Get a Jump on Kindergarten.*

Cooperative Educational Service Agency 5. (1993). *Growing: Birth to three.* Portage, WI: Author.

The program focuses on family-centered interaction. The *Interactive Growing Pack* illustrates strategies for interactive communication between caregiver and child. This is supported by books that suggest activities for the skills that are based on typical routines within the family.

Dinkmeyer, D., McKay, G. D., Dinkmeyer, J. S., & Dinkmeyer, D., Jr. (1992). *Teaching and leading children.* Circle Pines, MN: American Guidance Service.

This book is addressed to child care professionals, but it includes information and practices on communication, discipline, encouragement, "I" messages, and the practices included in their works for parents. The 1992 work is a good compilation of their work, so it is worthwhile for both parent leaders and parents, as well as child care workers.

Dinkmeyer, D., McKay, G. D., & McKay, J. L. (1987). *New beginnings: Skills for single parents and stepfamily parents.* Champaign, IL: Research Press.

New Beginnings helps single-parent families and stepfamilies develop their families' self-esteem. Included in the book are discussions of relationships, communication, decision making, discipline, and new parenting methods, as well as practical suggestions for activities that will enhance the family. In addition they provide information on troubled teen parents and raising nonviolent children.

Faber, A., & Mazlish, E. (1995). *How to talk so kids will listen and listen so kids will talk.* New York: Simon & Schuster.

Workshops are developed around sessions on (a) helping children deal with their feelings, (b) engaging cooperation, (c) alternatives to punishment, (d) encouraging autonomy, (e) praise, (f) freeing children from playing roles, and (g) final review. An available kit includes a chairperson's guide, participant's workbook, and reading material.

Faber, A., & Mazlish, E. (1998). *Siblings without rivalry: How to help your children live together so you can live too.* New York: Avon.

Workshop material includes this book, a chairperson's guide, and a participant's workbook. Sessions are (a) helping children deal with their feelings about their siblings, (b) keeping children separate and unequal, (c) siblings in roles, (d) when the kids fight, (e) problem solving, and (f) a final review.

Frede, E. (1984). *Getting involved: Workshops for parent effectiveness.* Ypsilanti, MI: High/Scope Press.

Frede developed workshops to be used by leaders in parent education programs. There is a wide range of programs, based on attitudes toward learning, play, language, reading, writing, math, science, TV, and problem solving. The book was developed through a federal grant, which means workshops can be reproduced.

Gordon, T. (2000). *The proven program for raising responsible children: 30th anniversary edition.* New York: Crown.

Gordon uses active listening, "I" messages, and a "no-lose" method in his program for parents. The program has helped many parents communicate with their children. (See Chapter 5.)

Parents as Teachers National Center. (n.d.). *Parents as teachers.* St. Louis, MO: Author.

The Parents as Teachers program has been instituted throughout Missouri and has been extended across the United States. Sixty Bureau of Indian Affairs will implement the program. The center offers training and materials. Write to 22287 Ball Dr., St. Louis, MO 63146.

Popkin, M. H. (2002). *Active parenting now.* Marietta, GA: Active Parentisim.

This parent education format contains new 2002 videotapes for six sessions, a *Parent's Guide, Leader's Guide,* and PowerPoint transparencies supporting the program. The six video sessions may be used without a leader, at home, or in a large-group presentation.

Popkin has also written guides for different age groups, such as *Parenting Your 1–4 Year Old: Parents' Workbook,* and *Active Parenting Now for Parents of 5 to 12 Year Olds.*

FAMILY-SCHOOL RELATIONS

Barbour, C., & Barbour, N. H. (2000). *Families, schools, and communities: Building partnerships for educating children.* Upper Saddle River, NJ: Merrill/Prentice Hall.

A text concerning home, school, and community influences on children's lives.

Bern, R. M. (1993). *Child, family and community.* New York: Harcourt & Brace.

Bern writes of the child, family, and community, focusing on child development.

Brim, O. G., Jr. (1965). *Education for child rearing.* New York: Free Press.

Brim wrote this classic on parent education for the Russell Sage Foundation in the 1950s. The material is still relevant for professionals concerned with parent education. The appendix includes the history of education for childrearing. The main body of the book discusses the nature and aims of parent education, influence of parent on child, causes of parent behavior, and methods for education programs.

Cataldo, C. Z. (1987). *Parent education for early childhood: Concepts and program content for the student and practicing professional.* Ann Arbor, MI: Books in Demand.

Cataldo's comprehensive book on parent education in the schools emphasizes early childhood and families.

Chinn, P. C., Winn, J., & Walters, R. H. (1978). *Two-way talking with parents of special children: A process of positive communication.* St. Louis, MO: C. V. Mosby.

This book contains an excellent discussion of the communication process and its importance in education. It is no longer being distributed, but may be available in your library.

Coleman, J. S., & Schneider, B. (Eds.). (1996). *Parents, their children, and schools.* Boulder, CO: Westview Press.

This book studies the family and its effect on student outcomes. It includes parent involvement, structure of families, academic achievement, and inequality.

Comer, J. P. (1999). *Child by child: The Comer process for change in education.* New York: Teachers College Press.

Comer explains his program and the process for making education work for all children.

Comer, J. P. (1999). *Waiting for a miracle: Why schools can't solve our problems—and how we can.* New York: Dutton.

Comer describes his childhood and his parents' influence on his later accomplishments. He uses this background to discuss what needs to be done for and with families for all children to have an opportunity to succeed.

Comer, J. P., Haynes, N. M., Joyner, E. T., & Ben-Avie, M. (1996). *Rallying the whole village: Comer's process for reforming education.* New York: Teachers College Press.

Comer and others involved in the Comer process describe how the changes were made in a school. Emphasis is on empowering parents and no-fault, collaborative decision making.

Curran, D. (1989). *Working with parents.* Circle Pines, MN: American Guidance Service.

Curran's book joins the STEP program from the American Guidance Service with a book that gives suggestions for working with parents.

Gestwicki, C. (1991). *Home, school and community relations: A guide to working with parents* (2nd ed.). Albany, NY: Delmar.

This parent-home book emphasizes communication and working with parents of preschool children.

Honig, A., & Wittmer, D. S. (1992). *Prosocial development: Caring, helping, and cooperating. A resource guide for parents and professionals.* New York: Garland.

The authors focus on the social development of young children, with a guide for both parents and professionals.

Honig, A. S. (1996). *Behavior guidance for infants and toddlers from birth to three years.* Little Rock, AR: Southern Early Childhood Association.

Hymes, J. L. (1974). *Effective home-school relations.* Sierra Madre, CA: Southern California Association for the Education of Young Children.

This easily read book discusses elementary school parents and the schools.

Kagan, S. L. (1998). *The care and education of America's young children: Obstacles and opportunities. Ninetieth yearbook of the National Society for the Study of Education.* Chicago: University of Chicago Press.

Includes information about the education of America's children, policy, and a discussion of the issues of parent partnerships.

Kawin, E. (1969). *Basic concepts for parents: Parenthood in a free nation.* West Lafayette, IN: Purdue University.

Kawin's series of books includes *Basic Concepts for Parents, Early & Middle Childhood,* and *Later Childhood & Adolescence.* All are designed for parent education courses. These well-written guides stress the responsibilities of raising children in a democracy. Even though the copyright date is 1969, the title listed above is still in print.

Kroth, R. L. (1997). *Strategies for communicating with parents of exceptional children.* Denver, CO: Love.

The title depicts the theme of the book, but many of the ideas can be used with parents of most other children as well.

Larrick, N. (1983). *A parent's guide to children's reading* (5th ed.). New York: Westminster Press.

Teachers and administrators can give this inexpensive paperback to parents to guide them in home activities. Written first in 1958, this classic book is as good as ever. It is out of print, but libraries should have it.

Lerman, R. L., & Ooms, T. J. (Eds.). (1993). *Young unwed fathers: Changing roles and emerging policies.* Philadelphia: Temple University.

Very little has been written about unwed fathers. This book helps to clarify various issues such as the public debate on welfare reform, paternity and child support, and family values.

McCaleb, S. P. (1994). *Building communities of learners.* New York: St. Martin's Press.

McCaleb stresses that partnership cannot be successful until the teachers and schools develop a community of learning with respect for both teachers and parents.

Procidano, M. E., & Fisher, C. B. (Eds.). (1992). *Contemporary families: A handbook for school professionals*. New York: Teachers College Press.

This book discusses issues concerning families today. It includes chapters on dual-wage families, single parents, stepfamilies, minority families, vulnerable children, and families in stress.

Rich, D. (1998). *Megaskills in school & life: The best gift you can give your child* (Rev. ed.). Boston: Houghton Mifflin.

Includes many ideas and activities you can use with children to help them develop self-esteem and positive attitudes.

Stone, J. G. (1987). *Teacher-parent relationships*. Washington, DC: National Association for the Education of Young Children.

This 40-page booklet focuses on teacher-parent relationships in child care programs and preschools.

Swap, S. M. (1993). *Developing home-school partnerships*. New York: Teachers College Press.

Swap suggests three paths to partnership. The first is a limited partnership; the second builds a comprehensive program; and the third includes restructuring schools for partnership.

Swick, K. J. (1992). *An early childhood school-home learning design: Strategies and resources*. Champaign, IL: Stipes.

Swick discusses children's need for continuity and support from everyone around them. Swick relates his discussion to the realities of today's society and the child's world.

Swick, K. J., & Graves, S. B. (1993). *Empowering at-risk families during early childhood*. Washington, DC: National Education Association.

Working with families of young children can help empower these families to accomplish the tasks and establish the self-esteem necessary to be a healthy family.

Turnbull, A. P., & Turnbull, H. R. (Eds.). (1990). *Parents speak out: Then and now* (2nd ed.). Upper Saddle River, NJ: Merrill/Prentice Hall.

Parents who are also professionals write movingly of their experiences with their children with mental retardation, autism, or other disabilities.

Turnbull, A. P., & Turnbull, H. R. (2000). *Families, professionals, and exceptionality: A special partnership*. Upper Saddle River, NJ: Prentice Hall.

The Turnbulls understand the position of both the family and the professional. The book includes many approaches and suggestions on developing partnerships.

Turnbull, H. R., & Turnbull, A. P. (2000). *Free appropriate public education: The law and children with disabilities*. Denver, CO: Love.

CHILDREARING

American Academy of Pediatrics Staff. (1991). *Caring for your adolescent: Ages 12 to 21*. Elk Grove, IL: Author.

These books on school-age children and adolescents discuss issues that arise during important phases of childrearing.

American Academy of Pediatrics Staff. (1995). *Caring for your school-aged child: Ages 5 to 12*. Elk Grove, IL: Author.

Ames, L. B. (1992). *Raising good kids: A developmental approach to discipline*. New York: Dell.

Ames has written excellent books about children for many years. This book relates discipline to the developmental age of the child, an important concern. Although it is out of print, it should be in libraries.

Anselmo, F. (1995). *Early childhood development: Prebirth through age eight* (2nd ed.). Upper Saddle River, NJ: Merrill/Prentice Hall.

This text discusses the first year of life extensively, followed by year one to three and concluding with the early school years, ages four through eight.

Bear, G. (1997). *Children's needs II: Development problems and alternatives* (3rd ed.). Bethesda, MD: National Association of School Psychology.

A beneficial book if one is looking at special needs of children and searching for alternatives to use to help these children.

Berk, L. E. (1996). *Child development* (4th ed.). Boston: Allyn & Bacon. A comprehensive child development text.

Black, J. K., & Puckett, M. B. (1996). *The young child: Development from prebirth through age eight* (2nd ed.). Upper Saddle River, NJ: Merrill/Prentice Hall.

This text divides the child's ages into six phrases. In each it covers physical, motor, psychosocial, cognitive, language, and literacy development.

Bowlby, J. (2000). *Attachment.* New York: Basic Books.
Bowlby, J. (1990). *Secure base.* New York: Basic Books.

Bowlby's wide expertise on attachment makes these books excellent contributions to early childhood.

Brazelton, T. B. (1994). *Touchpoints—the essential references: Your child's emotional and behavioral development.* Reading, MA: Addison-Wesley.

Brazelton's descriptive style enables inexperienced parents to recognize the 'points' that occur in childrearing.

Brazelton, T. B. (1994). *Touchpoints: Your child's emotional and behavioral development, the essential reference.* Reading, MA: Addison-Wesley.

Brazelton writes about emotional and behavioral development.

Brazelton, T. B., & Greenspan S. (2000). *The irreducible needs of children: What every child must have to grown, learn and flourish.* Cambridge, MA: Perseus.

Touchpoints and the irreducible needs of children are discussed in the first chapter of this book. *Irreducible* is a strong word that describes the important of a nurturing early childhood.

Comer, J. P., & Poussaint, A. F. (1992). *Raising black children.* New York: Plume Books.

This is a practical book on childrearing for Black parents. The format uses questions and answers to cover the material. The book is good for parents and professionals of all ethnic backgrounds.

Faber, A., & Mazlish, E. (1982). *How to talk so kids will listen and listen so kids will talk.* New York: Avon.

Faber, A., & Mazlish, E. (1988). *Siblings without rivalry: How to help your children live together so you can live too.* New York: Avon.

Two mothers who studied with Haim Ginott continue his emphasis on effective communication.

Faber, A., & Mazlish, E. (1990). *Liberated parents, liberated children: Your guide to a happier family.* New York: Avon.

Fraiberg, S. H. (1996). *The magic years: Understanding and handling problems of early childhood.* New York: Simon & Schuster.

This classic book concentrates on infancy through six years of age. Emotional issues that arise during this period are discussed in an easily read and understandable manner. Issues include imagination, reality, sex education, and development of a conscience. Fraiberg's book is an excellent book for parents.

Gerber Library. (1982). *500 questions new parents ask.* New York: Dell.

Ginott, H. G. (1976). *Between parent and child.* New York: Avon.

Ginott emphasizes reflective listening and open communication lines as necessary ingredients to productive child-parent relationships. Ginott's message is still clear, years after his death: Learn to listen to your child, and respond accordingly.

Ginott, H. G. (1982). *Between parent and teen-ager.* New York: Avon.

The author writes in a style that promotes understanding on the part of parent and teenager. Open communication establishes an understanding that allows parent and teenager to develop a process of cooperation and/or coping behavior.

Ginott, H. G. (1993). *Teacher & child.* Upper Saddle River, NJ: Merrill/Prentice Hall.

This excellent book helps teachers effect positive student-teacher relationships.

Greenberg, M. E. et al. (Eds.). (1993). *Attachment in the preschool years: Theory, research, and intervention.* Chicago: University of Chicago Press.

Attachment is an important development in the young child's growth.

Leach, P. (1995). *Children first: What society must do— is not doing—for children today.* New York: Random House.

Leach, P. (1997). *Your baby and child from birth to age five*. New York: Knopf.

The book discusses the stages of development in children up to five years old. Leach gives very clear and specific guidance about questions related to children. It has proved to be a most helpful and popular book for new parents.

Neifert, M. E. (1987). *Dr. mom*. New York: New American Library–Dutton.

Dr. Mom is a practical, comprehensive book on day-to-day childrearing written by an M.D. It includes a section on childhood illnesses.

Schmitt, B. D. (1991). *Your child's health: The parents' guide to symptoms, emergencies, common illness*. New York: Bantam.

Schmitt concentrates on the child's health including emergencies, trauma, behavior problems, medicines, immunization, and common illnesses of the newborn.

Spock, B. (1996). *A better world for our children: Rebuilding American family values*. Chicago: Contemporary Books.

This book discusses family values, an important part of childrearing.

Spock, B., & Packer, S. (1998). *Baby and child care* (7th ed.). New York: New American Library.

Spock's classic on childrearing covers everything from health to discipline. It became a best seller because it is an excellent book to answer parents' questions about health as well as child care. Material in this book is easily understood and relevant to questions parents ask. This type of book helps parent groups in the search for answers to specific problems. It can be used as a discussion starter.

Turecki, S. (1995). *Normal children have problems too: How parents can understand and help*. New York: Bantam.

This book covers a very important point—understanding children who do not seem to have problems. It should be helpful to parents raising children.

Turecki, S., & Tonner, L. (1985). *The difficult child*. New York: Bantam.

Turecki and Tonner focus on understanding the child's behavior. Even though Turecki is a child psychiatrist, he experienced the problems of raising a difficult child, so the book is based on both professional training and life experiences. Brazelton endorses the book as a real contribution to parents.

U.S. Department of Health and Human Services. Washington, DC: U.S. Government Printing Office.

Send for the most recent publication list from the government and order a series of booklets on childrearing. Include these in your resource library for parents. The booklets are clear and concise. Titles include:

Infant Care/El cuidado el su bebe

Prenatal Care

Your Child from 1 to 6

Your Child from 1 to 3

Your Child from 6 to 12

Your Child from 3 to 4

White, B. L. (1995). *Raising a happy, unspoiled child*. New York: Simon & Schuster.

White, B. L. (1996). *The first three years of life* (Rev. ed.). Upper Saddle River, NJ: Prentice Hall.

White divides the first 36 months into 7 developmental stages. Within each stage he gives a comprehensive discussion of intellectual, emotional, and physical development. The book also includes advice on childrearing based on social learning theory and appropriate toys and materials that enrich the child's world.

White, B. L. (1997). *Educating the infant & toddler*. San Francisco: Jossey-Bass.

White is a specialist in the growth of young children, especially from infancy to three years of age.

Zigler, E. F. (1993). *Children in a changing world: Development and social issues*. Pacific Grove, CA: Brooks-Cole.

Zigler has been active in the early childhood field and has many publications. There is a study guide that goes with the text.

FAMILIES: RAISING CHILDREN IN THE UNITED STATES

Bradshaw, J. (1996). *Bradshaw on the family: A new way of creating solid self-esteem* (2nd ed.). Deerfield Beach, FL: Health Communications.

Bradshaw describes in more depth the concepts he presents in the television series of the same title. He discusses the family as a rule-bound system, identifies dysfunctions within the family, and suggests ways to improve the functioning of the family.

Brazelton, T. B. (1992). *Working and caring.* Reading, MA: Addison-Wesley.

Brazelton, a pediatrician, used case studies to develop the issues of working while caring for children. Juggling work and child care is difficult, and Brazelton tries to help parents with the problems of doing both.

Building Family Strengths Project. (1986). *Building family strengths.* Lincoln: University of Nebraska.

The University of Nebraska Building Family Strengths Project developed a program based on family research that focuses on strengths instead of weaknesses. A trainer's manual, a facilitator's manual, and activity cards are available for use in training sessions. A series of books, compiled from conferences of the same name, are also available.

Children's Defense Fund. (2001). *The state of America's children: 2001.* Washington, DC: Author.

This is but one of numerous publications of the Children's Defense Fund that analyzes the position of children and their families in the United States. The information is updated regularly, and the source is valuable for those working in and advocating for children's services.

Galinsky, E. (1987). *The six stages of parenthood.* Reading, MA: Addison-Wesley.

Galinsky divides parenthood into six stages, commencing before the child's birth and lasting through the child's departure from the home. Parenthood has stages just as children have stages of development. They are (a) image-making stage, when images are formed and preparations are made before the birth; (b) nurturing, the period of infancy and attachment; (c) authority; (d) interpretive, preschool to adolescence; (e) interdependent, teen years; and (f) departure.

Salk, L. (1992). *Familyhood: Nurturing the values that matter.* New York: Simon & Schuster.

Schorr, L. B., & Schorr, D. (1989). *Within our reach: Breaking the cycle of disadvantage and despair.* New York: Doubleday.

This interesting book is filled with examples of at-risk children who have been helped by programs. The thesis is that children can achieve and become productive adults when given help to break the bondage of poverty and disadvantage.

Schorr, L. B. (1997). *Common purpose: Strengthening families and neighborhoods to rebuild America.* New York: Anchor Books/Doubleday.

Schorr discusses human services, social problems, community development, and public welfare.

Check the associations listed at the beginning of the Appendix for foundations, centers, and associations—such as The Future of Children of the David and Lucile Packard Foundation, and the Annie E. Casey Foundation—that provide information on families. Both the Future of Children, who publish books on a variety of current topics concerning children, and Annie E. Casey, which provides *KIDS COUNT,* furnish complimentary copies of their publications.

FATHERS

Greenberg, M. (1985). *The birth of a father.* New York: Continuum.

Greenberg based his book on his own experience with fatherhood as well as studies on parenthood. He encourages fathers to get involved with their children.

Grisold, R. L. (1993). *Fatherhood in America: A history.* New York: Basic Books.

Grisold writes about the changing roles of fathers.

Hewlett, B. S. (Ed.). (1992). *Father child relationships: Cultural and bio-social contexts.* New York: Aldine De Gruyter.

This book contains a compilation of articles on the father and child and their interactions and relationships.

Lamb, M. E. (Ed.). (1996). *The role of the father in child development* (3rd ed.). New York: Wiley.

Based on research and studies on children, articles were selected from many authorities in the field. They conclude that fathers are important to the psychological development of children.

LaRossa, R. (1996). *The modernization of fatherhood: A social and political history.* Chicago: University of Chicago Press.

This book provides a comprehensive history of fatherhood.

Levine, J. A., Murphy, D. T., & Wilson, S. (1993). *Getting men involved: Strategies for early childhood programs.* New York: Scholastic.

This is a hands-on guide to help teachers involve fathers and other men in nurturing and educating children.

Pruett, K. D. (2000). *Fatherneed: Why father care is as essential as mother care for your child.* New York: Free Press.

Pruett looks at the nurturing role that a father can develop as a parent.

THE STEPPARENT

Burns, C. (1986). *Stepmotherhood: How to survive without feeling frustrated, left out, or wicked.* New York: Harper Trade.

This book recognizes the concerns of the stepmother and points out ways to cope with adapting to a new family.

Everett, C. A. (Ed.). (1997). *Understanding stepfamilies: Their structure and dynamics.* Binghamton, NY: Haworth Press.

Everett used a global approach to study the structure and dynamics of families, assessment and intervention, and parent-child interaction.

Gardner, R. A. (1985). *The boys and girls book about stepfamilies.* Cresskill, NJ: Creative Therapeutics.

This book deals with children's concerns about the difficult transition of moving into a stepfamily.

Gardner, R. A. (1992). *Boys and girls book about divorce* (reprint of 1983 ed.). New York: Aronson.

This book was reissued because it helps boys and girls understand the situations arising from their parents' divorce.

Kelly, P. (1995). *Developing healthy stepfamilies: Twenty families tell their stories.* Binghamton, NY: Haworth Press.

The book describes the ways stepfamilies adjust to their new roles, as told by 20 stepfamilies.

Levin, I., & Sussman, M. B. (1997). *Stepfamilies: History, research, and policy.* Binghamton, NY: Haworth Press.

The text integrates different disciplines and cultures in the study of stepfamilies.

Visher, E. B., & Visher, J. S. (1989). *Old loyalties, new ties: Therapeutic strategies with stepfamilies.* New York: Brunner/Mazel.

Written for both therapists and stepfamilies, this book presents an overview of stepfamily research and intervention methods, followed by chapters focused on the difficulties stepfamilies have in integrating and establishing their identity.

Visher, E. B., & Visher, J. S. (1991). *How to win as a stepfamily* (Rev. ed.). New York: Brunner/Mazel.

The Vishers, recognized authorities on stepparenting, write about positive methods to mold a successful stepfamily.

Visher, E. B., & Visher, J. S. (1996). *Therapy with stepfamilies.* New York: Brunner/Mazel.

Understanding therapy will help to understand stepfamilies. If you are working with stepfamilies in need of therapy, refer to a specialist.

DIVORCE AND THE SINGLE PARENT

Ackerman, M. J. (1996). *Does Wednesday mean mom's house or dad's? Parenting together while living apart.* New York: Wiley.

Ackerman recognizes a realistic situation in the separation of parents after divorce. How can this be handled to the benefit of the children?

Benedek, E. P., & Brown, C. F. (1995). *How to help your child overcome divorce.* Washington, DC: American Psychiatric Association.

The APA writes to help parents respond to their children during the difficult period after divorce. What kinds of activities and feelings are helpful?

Burns, A., & Scott, C. (1994). *Mother-headed families and why they have increased.* Hillsdale, NJ: Erlbaum.

This book includes historical, demographic, and theoretical discussion of motherhood. The authors look at motherhood through a global and historical perspective.

Cherlin, A. J. (1992). *Marriage, divorce, remarriage* (Rev. and enl. ed.). Cambridge, MA: Harvard University Press.

This book does not solve all the problems of divorce, but it does analyze the trends of families in the United States by discussing social change and social thought.

Gardner, R. A. (1991). *Parents' book about divorce* (2nd ed.). Cresskill, NJ: Creative Therapeutics.

Gottman, J. (1993). *What predicts divorce?* Hillsdale, NJ: Erlbaum.

This text, based on Gottman's research on marital process and marital dissolution, includes the discussion of three typologies of marriage—validating, volatile, and avoiding—and the negative behaviors that produce dissolution of the marriage.

Gottman, J. (1995). *Why marriages succeed or fail.* New York: Pocket Books.

Gottman's book is organized into three parts: (1) marital satisfaction and styles, (2) marital conflict, and (3) ideas for improving marriages.

Gottman, J. (2000). *Seven principles of marriage.* New York: Crown.

The title describes the contents of Gottman's most recent book.

Stevenson, M. R., & Black, K. N. (1996). *How divorce affects offspring: A research approach.* Boulder, CO: Westview.

More work is focusing on divorce's effects on children.

Wallerstein, J., & Blakeslee, S. (1996). *Second chances: Men, women, and children a decade after divorce.* Boston: Houghton Mifflin.

Wallenstein and Blakeslee did a follow-up of the families they interviewed 10 years earlier. There are interesting findings about the different responses and issues concerning divorce.

Wallerstein, J., & Kelly, J. B. (1996). *Surviving the breakup: How children and parents cope with divorce.* New York: Harper and Row.

DISCIPLINE—BEHAVIOR OR MISBEHAVIOR

Bettelheim, B. (1988). *A good enough parent: A book on childrearing.* New York: Vintage.

Bettelheim, a psychoanalytical theorist, wrote this book based on the emotional needs of the child.

Cherry, C. (1982). *Please don't sit on the kids: Alternatives to punitive discipline.* Belmont, CA: Fearon Teaching Aids.

Cherry, C. (1985). *Parents, please don't sit on the kids: Guide to nonpunitive discipline.* Belmont, CA: Fearon Teaching Aids.

Cherry, author of many excellent children's books, offers workable alternatives to punitive discipline.

Dreikurs, R. (1974). *Discipline without tears.* New York: Dutton.

Dreikurs uses a system of consequences based on Adlerian psychology with the result that children become responsible for their actions. Logical and natural consequences related to children's behavior form a basis for discipline and guidance.

Dreikurs, R. (1991). *The challenge of parenthood.* New York: Dutton.

The phrase *logical consequences* brings to mind Dreikurs, so books that reveal his work in the area of discipline always supply excellent background material on the subject of consequences.

Dreikurs, R., & Grey, L. (1990). *Logical consequences: A new approach to discipline.* New York: Dutton.

Dreikurs, R., & Soltz, V. (1987). *Children: The challenge.* New York: Dutton.

The four goals of misbehavior—attention, power, revenge, and inadequacy—are discussed, as are the use of consequences. His book supports parents in their development of guidelines for children's behavior.

Gordon, T. (1991). *Discipline that works: Promoting self discipline in children at home and school.* New York: Dutton.

Gordon is another name that has been recognized as an expert for many years. Self-discipline is a necessity for children.

Nelsen, J. (1996). *Positive discipline.* New York: Ballantine Books.

Nelsen's step-by-step approach for both parents and teachers combines the best of Adler, Dreikurs, and others about how to promote children's long-term development. She focuses on self-discipline, responsibility, and cooperation. Her recommendations are both sensible and sensitive, and she raises many thought-provoking questions.

Nelsen, J. (1997). *Positive discipline for blended families*. Rocklin, CA: Prima.

Samalin, N., & Jablow, M. M. (1998). *Loving your child is not enough: Positive discipline that works*. New York: Viking Penguin Books.

This easily read book starts with suggestions on how to avoid battles and goes on to discuss positive and consistent guidelines to deal with discipline issues.

Simon, S. B., & Olds, S. W. (1991). *Helping your child find values to live by*. New York: Values.

Values clarification and understanding one's own motives and attitudes helps in the development of responsibility. Children learn to examine problem solving and develop their own system of values.

Swick, K. (1985). *Parents and teachers as discipline shapers*. Washington, DC: National Education Association.

A small book written specifically for the NEA library. It is a practical guide for teachers and parents.

Swick, K. (1991). *Discipline: Toward positive student behavior*. Washington, DC: National Education Association.

Swick addresses discipline, student behavior, and classroom management.

Unell, B. C., & Wyckoff, J. (1984). *Discipline without shouting or spanking*. Deephaven, MN: Meadowbrook. (Distributed by Simon & Schuster.)

This small book gives specific responses to common behavior problems during the preschool years.

HEALTH AND NUTRITION

American Academy of Pediatrics. (1999). *American Academy of Pediatrics guide to your child's nutrition*. Evanston, IL: Author.

American Academy of Pediatrics. (1993). *Making peace at the table and building healthy eating habits for life*. New York: Villard Books.

These references were produced by the academy and contain the knowledge and approved practices of that prestigious organization.

Boston Children's Hospital Staff. (1987). *The new child health encyclopedia*. New York: Dell Books.

This encyclopedia answers many of parents' common questions about illness, childhood diseases, and preventive health care.

Endres, J. B., & Rockwell, R. E. (1993). *Food, nutrition, and the young child* (4th ed.). Upper Saddle River, NJ: Merrill/Prentice Hall.

This practical book examines nutrition and dietary guides and standards. It focuses on the role of nutrition in early childhood programs and provides basic concepts about food and nutrition, suggestions for menus, methods of interrelating curriculum, basic nutritional concepts, and suggestions for working with parents.

Feingold, B. F. (1985). *Why your child is hyperactive*. New York: Random House.

Although parent groups must keep in mind the controversies surrounding Feingold's theories, they might also like to discuss his ideas about food and hyperactivity.

Samuels, M., & Samuels, N. (1991). *The well child book: A comprehensive manual of baby care from conception to age four* (Rev. ed.). New York: Summit Books.

The Well Child Book, a popular book on health and staying well, was revised to give up-to-date information on health.

U.S. Department of Health and Human Services and U.S. Department of Education, Washington, DC.

These agencies furnish many booklets concerning health and nutrition. Write to the Consumer Information Center, Pueblo, CO 81002 for a copy of the *Consumer Information Catalog*. Educators, libraries, consumers, and other nonprofit groups that wish to receive 25 copies of the quarterly catalog on consumer information may get on the mailing list. Articles and booklets cover information from 30 federal agencies. More than half of these articles are free. The following reference is typical of the offerings:

Food and Drug Administration. *Fruits and vegetables: Eating your way to 5 a day—613 E*. Pueblo, CO: Consumer Information Center.

A guide to better diet with information about the nutritive value of fruits and vegetables and how to get them into your diet.

CHILD ABUSE
Sexual Abuse

Adams, C., & Fay, J. (1992). *Helping your child recover from sexual abuse.* Seattle: University of Washington Press.

Parents have found this to be a valuable book because it offers an approach to use in preventing the sexual abuse of their children.

American Academy of Pediatrics Staff and C. Henry Kempe. National Center on Child Abuse and Neglect. (1994). *The visual diagnosis of child physical abuse.* Denver, CO: Author.

Finkelhor, D. (1986). *A sourcebook on child sexual abuse.* Beverly Hills, CA: Sage.

Finkelhor, D. (1994). Current information on the scope and nature of child abuse. *The Future of Children: Sexual Abuse of Children 4*(2), 31–53.

Finkelhor is respected as one of the foremost authorities on sexual abuse. This issue of *The Future of Children* is devoted to the study of sexual abuse of children. Copies of these issues are provided free of charge from the circulation department of the foundation located at 300 Second Street, Suite 200, Los Altos, CA 94022.

Finkelhor, D., & Ormrod, R. (2000, June). Characteristics of crimes against juveniles. *Juvenile Justice Bulletin.* Washington, DC: Office of Juvenile Justice and Delinquency Prevention.

Another excellent report that may be obtained from the Office of Juvenile Justice.

Hagans, K. B., & Case, J. (1988). *When your child has been molested: A parent's guide to healing and recovery.* Lexington, MA: Lexington Books.

Hagans discussed child sexual abuse in the United States as well as counseling for the child and family relationships.

Herman, J. L. (1997). *Trauma & recovery: The aftermath of violence.* New York: Basic Books.

Judith Herman writes about post-traumatic stress disorders and their treatments.

Herman, J. L. (2000). *Father daughter incest.* Cambridge, MA: Harvard University Press.

This book analyzes sexual abuse based on clinical experiences with incest victims.

PHYSICAL ABUSE AND NEGLECT RESOURCES

Antler, S. (Ed.). (1982). *Child abuse and child protection: Policy and practice* (reprint). Silver Springs, MD: National Association of social workers

This reprint of a book published by social workers contains a series of articles pertaining to child abuse, ranging from the definition of the problem to strategies for dealing with the violence. It discusses treating the abused and the abuser as well as protection the child protective worker.

Crossom-Tower, C. (2002). *Child abuse and neglect* (5th ed). Boston: Allyn Bacon.

This text has been revised five times and is a comprehensive book on child abuse and neglect.

Fontana, V. J. (1989). *Somewhere a child is crying.* New York: New American Library.

Fontana, V. J., & Besharov, D. J. (1995). *Maltreated child: The maltreatment syndrome in children, a medical, legal, and social guide* (5th ed.). Springfield, IL: Charles C. Thomas.

Fontana, V. J., & Moalman, V. (1992). *Save the family, save the child: What we can do to help children at risk.* New York: New American Library.

Fontana's experience in the field of child abuse have made his books interesting reading.

Green, M. R. (Ed.). (1981). *Violence and the family.* Boulder, CO: Westview Press.

An American Association for the Advancement of Science symposium formed the basis for this book. It includes material not found in other texts such as television viewing, family style, and cultural differences.

Horton, C. B., & Cruise, T. K. (2001). *Child abuse and neglect.* New York: Guilford Press.

A comprehensive book on child abuse and neglect. Covers historical and current information.

Kempe, C. H., & Helfer, R. E. (Eds.). (1987). *The battered child* (4th ed.). Denver, CO: Kempe National Center.

Kempe and Helfer were pioneers in the field of child abuse. Their books are excellent references.

Lowenthal, B. (2001). *Abuse and neglect.* Baltimore: Brookes.

The book provides information for teachers and schools to use in setting up child abuse and neglect programs.

Straus, M. M. (1994). *Beating the devil out of them: Corporal punishment in American families.* New York: Lexington Books.

Straus defines corporal punishment as punishment that does not inflict physical harm, but he goes on to denounce it because it is destructive to the child.

U.S. Department of Health and Human Services, Office of Human Development Services. (1979). *A curriculum on child abuse and neglect.* Washington, DC: U.S. Government Printing Office.

U.S. Department of Health and Human Services, Office of Human Development Services. (1979). *Leader's manual.* Washington, DC: U.S. Government Printing Office.

The agency has published an enormous amount of excellent material on child abuse and neglect. This leader's manual is a comprehensive text on teaching others about child abuse and neglect.

U.S. Department of Health and Human Services, Office of Human Development Services. (1980). *Child abuse and neglect: A self-instructional text for Head Start personnel.* Washington, DC: U.S. Government Printing Office.

This text is excellent for anyone who works in a child care center or school. It is easily used, self-correcting, and easily read.

BULLYING AND VIOLENCE

The Future of Children. (2002, summer/fall). Children, youth, and gun violence. *The Future of Children 12(2).*

This volume, published by the David and Lucile Packard Foundation, has a collection of ten articles on violence, ranging from guns and violent crimes, cost and effects of gun violence on children, to an analysis and recommendations on children, youth and gun violence. The address to request a complimentary copy is 300 Second Street, Suite 200, Los Altos, CA 94022, or on the web site at http://www.futureofchildren.org.

Garrity, C. Baris, M. & Porter, W. (2000). *Bully proofing your child: A parent's guide.* Longmont, CO; Sopris West.

Bully-Proofing Your School (Elementary) and *Bully-Proofing Your School (Middle School)* are also published by Sopris West. Each offers practical ideas on ways of reducing bullying and ways to help the child respond.

Olweus, D. (1993). *Bullying at school.* Oxford, England: Blackwell.

Olweus wrote about aggression in the schools in 1978. One of the first to point out bullying in the schools, his book and program are classics in the field of reducing bullying.

Osofsky, J. D. & Fenichel, E. (eds.) (1996). *Islands of safety: Assessing and treating young victims of violence.* Washington, DC: Zero to Three.

The volume speaks to young children and how violence can affect their lives, ranging from an evaluation of posttraumatic symptomatology in infants to a discussion of young children who witness domestic violence.

Poland, S., & McCormick, J. S. (2000). *Coping with crisis: A quick reference.* Longmont, CO: Sopris West.

The reference is written for schools to help them prepare and cope with the crisis of violence that may occur in the schools.

Slaby, R. G., Roedell, W. C. Arezzo, D. & Hendrix, K. (1995). *Early violence prevention: Tools for teachers of young children.* Washington, DC: National Association for the Education of Young Children.

The statement, "patterns of violence develop early and last long," (p. 2) illustrates the importance of early childhood. This volume addresses this issue and has 14 chapters on developing an environment for children that ranges from the physical environment, materials, cooperative activities to helping children with aggressive tendencies.

Stein, N., & Sjostrom, L. (1996). *Bullyproof: A teacher's guide on teaching and bulllying for use with fourth and fifth grade students.* Washington, DC: Wesley College Center for Research on Women and NEA Library.

This joint publication of Wellesley and the NEA Profession library is detailed and instructive with lessons to be used in classes. The children get involved in a discussion of bullying and harassment.

Stein, N., & Sjostrom, L. (1998). *Flirting or hurting: A teacher's guide to student-to-student sexual harassment in schools (grades 6 through 12).* Washington, DC: NEA Professional Library.

The issues of flirting and abusive actions are discussed and suggestions are given for reducing the occurrences.

Suckling, A., & Temple, C. (2002). *Bullying: A whole school approach.* Philadelphia: Jessica Kingsley.

Some of the most successful programs have focused on the climate of the entire school in the reduction of bullying. This book speaks to that process.

Sullivan, K. (2000). *The anti-bullying handbook.* Melbourne: Oxford University Press.

The book discussion ranges from school discipline, aggression in children, to prevention and behavior modification.

CHILDREN WITH DISABILITIES

Finnie, N. R. (1995). *Handling the young cerebral palsied child at home* (2nd ed.). New York: Plume Books.

This comprehensive book has descriptive pen drawings that describe ways of caring for the child with cerebral palsy (or other children who have physical disabilities). It is a practical reference for parents and other caregivers.

Miller, N. B. (1994). *Nobody's perfect: Living and growing with children who have special needs.* Baltimore: Brookes.

The book describes four stages of adaptation—adaptation, surviving, searching, and settling in. It continues with separating. The discussion then focuses on strategies for successful adaptations.

Sullivan, T. (1995). *Special parent, special child.* New York: Jeremy P. Tarcher/Putnam Books.

The author, blinded at birth by too much oxygen fed into his incubator, starts the book by talking about his mother. Upon his realization of the experience she had had rearing him, he traveled throughout the United States and talked with families who had children with disabilities. The book is based on the families' experiences.

Tracy, A. M., & Maroney, D. I. (1999). *Your premature baby and child.* New York: Berkley Books.

This is a manual for parents who have premature infants. It covers coming home, medical concerns including lungs, brain, eyes, and ears, and other issues on the child's growth and development.

ADVOCACY

The following organizations form a base from which to obtain information on legal rights, responsibilities, and advocacy. Because addresses and telephone numbers change with regularity, some will be outdated. Check with your library for the yearly update on associations and organizations in the United States if you find an address has changed.

Center on Children and the Law

American Bar Association
740 15th St. NW, 9th Floor
Washington, DC 20005-1009
202-662-1720

The center has information and books on children's rights. In 1993 it published *America's Children at Risk: A National Agenda for Legal Action.*

Children's Defense Fund

25 E St. NW
Washington, DC 20001

Long-range advocacy of children was the goal of the Children's Defense Fund when founded in 1974. It has since monitored areas of education, child care, health, and juvenile justice. The agency works with individuals, agencies, and community groups and supplies information on the condition of children in the United States.

Child Welfare League of America

440 First St. NW
Washington, DC 20001
202-638-2952

The league, a privately supported organization with 376 affiliate groups, works for the benefit of dependent and neglected children and their families. It also published *Parenting Curriculum* by Grace C. Cooper for adolescent mothers.

Institute for Responsive Education

Northeastern University
21 Lake Hall
Boston, MA 02215
617-373-2595

Founded in 1973 to assist citizen involvement in educational decision making, the institute believes that parents and the community, in collaboration with school officials and teachers, can make a difference. To promote parent and community involvement in the schools, the institute publishes a quarterly journal, *Citizen Action in Education.*

National Coalition of ESEA Title I/Chapter I Parents

1541 14th St. NW
Washington, DC 20005

The federal Title I program has made great strides in involving parents in the education of their children. Its findings and suggestions are appropriate for parents and schools in any economic area. Currently called Chapter I, the coalition supports Chapter I parents as well as others. The organization established the National Parent Center.

National PTA

330 N. Wabash Ave., #2100
Chicago, IL 60611-3690
312-670-6782

The PTA is the oldest organization devoted to improving relations between home and school on behalf of children. Founded in 1897, this organization has fluctuated in the acceptance of its role as the spokesperson for parents and teachers, but has consistently furnished educational information through the following publications: *PTA Today, PTA Communique,* and pamphlets on parent education, juvenile protection, safety, parent-teacher relationships, and improving education in schools.

National School Boards Association

1680 Duke St.
Alexandria, VA 22314
703-838-6722

This association, founded in 1940, furnishes information on curriculum development and legislation that affects education and school administration. School board members are familiar with its publications: *Insider's Report,* a weekly newsletter, and the *American School Board Journal,* a monthly journal. These publications are also informative for parents concerned about schools.

National School Volunteer Program

701 N. Fairfax St., 320
Alexandria, VA 22314

Volunteers have made great strides in opening schools to parent involvement. They have state groups, some of which give six training sessions to volunteers. Homemakers, professionals, and young people are typical volunteers.

CHILDREARING AND PARENT EDUCATION

The following organizations and government agencies publish periodicals, pamphlets, and booklets that can be used for a parent resource center. Articles range from prenatal care to adolescent motherhood. Write to them for current publications lists. The addresses listed here were current at the time of publication. Check the *Encyclopedia of Associations* at the public library to determine whether an address has changed.

Alexander Graham Bell Association for the Deaf

3417 Volta Pl. NW
Washington, DC 20007-2778
202-337-5220

American Academy of Child and Adolescent Psychiatry

3615 Wisconsin Ave. NW
Washington, DC 20016-3007
202-966-7300

American Academy of Pediatrics
141 Northwest Point Blvd.
Elk Grove Village, IL 60007-1098
847-434-4000

American Alliance for Health, Physical Education, Recreation, and Dance
1900 Association Dr.
Reston, VA 21091
202-429-5131

American Association for Adult and Continuing Education
1200 19th St. NW, #300
Washington, DC 20036
202-429-5131

American Foundation for the Blind
11 Penn Plaza, #300
New York, NY 10011
212-502-7600

American Home Economics Association
1555 King St.
Alexandria, VA 22314

American Humane Association
63 Inverness Dr. E
Englewood, CO 80112
303-792-9900

American Library Association
50 East Huron St.
Chicago, IL 60611
312-944-7298

American Montessori Society
281 Park Ave. S, 6th Floor
New York, NY 10010
212-358-1250

American Speech-Language-Hearing Association
10801 Rockville Pl.
Rockville, MD 20852
800-638-8255

ARC (formerly Association for Retarded Citizens)
1010 Wayne Ave., #650
Silver Springs, MD 20910
301-565-3842

Association for Childhood Education International
The Olney Professional Building
17904 Georgia Ave., #215

Olney, MD 20832
310-570-2111

Association for Children with Down Syndrome
4 Fern Pl.
Plainview, NY 11803
516-933-4700

C. Henry Kempe National Center for Prevention and Treatment of Child Abuse and Neglect
1825 Marion St.
Denver, CO 80205
303-864-5252

Child Welfare League of America
440 First St. NW, #310
Washington, DC 20001
202-638-2952

Children and Adults with Attention Deficit Disorder
8181 Professional Pl., #201
Landover, MD 20785
301-306-7070

Children's Defense Fund
25 E St. NW
Washington, DC 20001
202-628-8787

Clearinghouse on Child Abuse and Neglect Information
320 C St. SW
Washington, DC 20447
703-385-3206

Council for Basic Education
1319 F St. NW, #900
Washington, DC 20004-1152
202-347-4171

Council for Exceptional Children
1110 N. Glebe Rd., #300
Arlington, VA 22201-5704
800-224-6830

Department of Education
Washington, DC 20202-0498

Education Commission of the States
707 17th St., #2700
Denver, CO 80202-3427
303-299-3600

EPIE Institute
103-3 W. Montauk Hwy.
Hampton Bay, NY 11946
516-728-9100

**ERIC Clearinghouse on Elementary and Early
    Childhood Education (ERIC/EECE)**
University of Illinois at Urbana–Champaign Children's
    Research Center
51 Gerty Dr.
Champaign, IL 61820-7469
800-583-4135

Family Resource Coalition
200 S. Michigan Ave., #1600
Chicago, IL 60604

Family Service Association of America
11700 W. Lake Park Dr.
Milwaukee, WI 53224

**High/Scope Educational Research
    Foundation**
600 North River St.
Ypsilanti, MI 48198-2898
734-485-2000

Home and School Institute
1500 Massachusetts Ave. NW
Washington, DC 20005
202-466-3633

Institute for Responsive Education
Northeastern University
21 Lake Hall
Boston, MA 02215
617-373-2595

International Reading Association
PO Box 8139
800 Barksdale Rd.
Newark, DE 19714-8139
302-731-1600

La Leche League International
1400 Meadem
Schaumburg, IL 60168-4079
847-519-7730

Learning Disabilities Association of America
4156 Library Rd.
Pittsburgh, PA 15234-1349
412-341-1515

Mental Health Materials Center
PO Box 304
Bronxville, NY 10708
914-337-6596

**National Association for the Education
    of Young Children**
1509 16th St. NW
Washington, DC 20036-1426
202-232-8777

National Association of Partners in Education
901 N. Pitt St., #320
Alexandria, VA 22314
703-836-4880

National Black Child Development Institute
1101 15th St. NW, #900
Washington, DC 20005
202-833-2220

National Congress of Parents and Teachers
330 N. Wabash Ave., #2100
Chicago, IL 60611-3690

**National Council on Child Abuse
    and Family Violence**
1155 Connecticut Ave. NW, #400
Washington, DC 20036
202-429-6695

National Council on Family Relations
3989 Central Ave. NE, #550
Minneapolis, MN 55421
763-781-9331

National Education Association
1201 16th St. NW
Washington, DC 20036
202-833-04000

National Institute of Mental Health
6001 Executive Blvd., Room 8184, MSC-9663
Bethesda, MD 20892-0662
301-433-4513

National Maternal and Child Health Clearinghouse
5600 Fisher Lane
Rockville, MD 20857
703-356-1964

National Mental Health Association
1021 Prince St.
Alexandria, VA 22314-2971
703-684-7722

National School Boards Association
1680 Duke St.
Alexandria, VA 22314-3493
703-838-6722

National School Volunteer Program
16 Arlington St.
Boston, MA 02116

Pacer Center (education on children with disabilities)
8161 Normandale Blvd.
Minneapolis, MN 55437-1044
952-838-9000

Parent Advocacy Coalition for Educational Rights
4826 Chicago Ave. S
Minneapolis, MN 55417-1098

Science Research Associates
259 E. Erie St.
Chicago, IL 60611

Southwest Educational Development Laboratory
211 E. Seventh St.
Austin, TX 78701
512-476-6861

Stepfamily Association of America
650 J St., #205
Lincoln, NE 68508
800-735-0329

Stepfamily Foundation
333 W. End Ave.
New York, NY 10023
212-877-3244

Superintendent of Documents
U.S. Government Printing Office
Washington, DC 20402
   Check the Children's Bureau, Administration for Children, Youth and Families, Department of Health and Human Services, and the Department of Education for publication lists pertaining to children and families.

CENTERS AND ASSOCIATIONS CONCERNED WITH CHILD ABUSE

American Humane Association
63 Inverness Dr. E.
Englewood, CO 80112

C. Henry Kempe National Center for Prevention and Treatment of Child Abuse and Neglect
1825 Marion St.
Denver, CO 80218

National Clearinghouse on Child Abuse and Neglect Information, Department of Health and Human Services
330 C St. SW
Washington, DC 20447
703-385-7565
800-394-3366

National Committee for Prevention of Alcoholism and Drug Dependency
12501 Old Columbia Pike
Silver Springs, MD 20904-6600
301-680-6719

Parents Anonymous
675 W. Foothill Blvd., #220
Claremont, CA 91711-3416
909-621-6184
800-421-0353

Additional 800 numbers

HIV/AIDS
800-342-AIDS
800-344-SIDA (in Spanish)
800-AIDS-TTY (access for persons with hearing impairment)

Narcotics Anonymous
800-COCAINE

National Alliance for the Mentally Ill
800-950-6264

YMCA/YWCA, YMHA/YWHA
800-USA-YMCA

SUPPORT FOR PARENT INVOLVEMENT IN READING

American Library Association Publications Order Department
50 E. Huron St.
Chicago, IL 60611
312-944-7298

Children's Book Council
Attn: Publication List
12 West 37th St., 2nd Floor
New York, NY 10018-7480
212-966-1990

International Reading Association
800 Barksdale Rd.
PO Box 8139
Newark, DE 19714-8139
302-731-1600

Reading Is Fundamental
Publications Department
1825 Connecticut Ave. NW, #400
Washington, DC 20009
202-289-3226

INTERNET CONNECTIONS[1]

American Academy of Pediatrics
http://www.aap.org

American Library Association
http://www.ala.org/parents/index.html

50 great sites from the American Library Association
http://www.ssdesign.com/parentspage/greatsites/50.html

AskERIC (Educational Resources Information Center) askeric@askeric.org
http://www.aspensys.com/eric

Children's Defense Fund
http://www.childrensdefense.org

Council for Exceptional Children
http://www.cec.sped.org

Internet Public Library: Reference Center
http://www.ipl.org/ref

Library of Congress
http://www.loc.gov

National Center for Family Literacy
http://www.famlit.org

National Coalition for Parent Involvement in Education
http://www.ncpie.org

National Early Childhood Technical Assistance
http://www.nectas.unc.edu

National Information Center for Children and Youth with Disabilities
http://www.nichcy.org

National Rehabilitation Information Center
http://www.naric.com/naric

Public Broadcasting System
http://www.pbs.org/

Zero to 3
http://www.zerotothree.org

MAGAZINES AND JOURNALS

Magazines and journals are important because they contain relevant and up-to-date information. Most of the following can be found in public libraries. Some are published by professional organizations, others by businesses. Have them delivered to your home by subscribing to them or by joining the professional organization that publishes them.

Black Child Advocate
National Black Child Development Institute
1023 15th St. NW, #600
Washington, DC 20005
Concerned primarily with public policy related to Black children, this monthly magazine also includes articles on curriculum and other subjects related to the development of the Black child.

Child Care Information Exchange
PO Box 3249
Redmond, WA 98073
This magazine focuses on the concerns and issues that affect directors of child care centers.

Child Development
Society for Research in Child Development
University of Michigan
3131 South State St., #302
Ann Arbor, MI 48101-1623

---

[1] (If the Internet address does not work, try searching through http://www.google.com.)

This professional journal is concerned with research related to various topics in child development.

Childhood Education
Association for Childhood Education International
The Olney Professional Building
17904 Georgia Ave., #215
Olney, MD 20832

Assorted articles about educating young children. Materials and activities that encourage optimal development in children are included. Many articles pertain to theory and educational philosophy.

Children Today
Children's Bureau
Administration for Children, Youth and Families
Office of Human Development
Superintendent of Documents
U.S. Government Printing Office
Washington, DC 20402

This government magazine includes a wide selection of articles on children, birth through adolescence. The articles range from mental health, education, child care, health, and children with disabilities to social services and crime prevention.

Child Welfare
Child Welfare League of America
440 First St. NW
Washington, DC 20001-2085

Contains both research and applied articles related to children and examines social services and policies as well as practical implementation of programs for children.

Early Childhood Education Journal
Kluwer Academic/Human Sciences Press
Kluwer Academic Publishers
Journals Department, Distribution Center
101 Phillips Dr., Assissippi Park
Norwell, MA 02061

This magazine is for those who work with young children: child care workers, preschool teachers, and others. It includes articles, research reviews, and activities for young children.

Early Childhood Today
Scholastic Inc. Office of Publications
2931 East McCarty St.
PO Box 3710
Jefferson City, MO 65101

This journal, published eight times a year, has articles on children and an activity plan pullout.

Exceptional Children
Council for Exceptional Children
1110 North Glebe Rd., #300
Arlington, VA 22201-5704

The journal for the CEC contains articles about special education and children with exceptionalities. It provides information on materials, books, films, and legislation.

The Future of Children
David and Lucile Packard Foundation
300 Second St., #200
Los Altos, CA 94022

The foundation publishes two volumes each year that address current issues concerning families and children. The foundation provides these very well researched and written journals free to those who order them.

Gifted Child Quarterly
National Association for Gifted Children
1707 L St. NW, #550
Washington, DC 20036

This is the journal for the National Association for Gifted Children. It focuses on various issues and research concerning children who are gifted and their education.

High/Scope Resources
The High/Scope Press
600 North River St.
Ypsilanti, MI 48198-2898

The High/Scope Educational Research Foundation publishes a newspaper that describes the most recent publications from High/Scope. It also includes articles and discussion of early childhood from a High/Scope position.

Journal of Research in Childhood Education
Association for Childhood Education International
The Olney Professional Building
17904 Georgia Ave., #215
Olney, MD 20832

A scholarly journal published twice a year, the magazine's focus is on advancing knowledge and theory of the education of children, infancy through early adolescence.

Pre-K Today
Scholastic Inc.
PO Box 513
Dalton, MA 01227-0513

Pre-K is a magazine about young children. Scholastic also publishes educational materials for students.

The Single Parent
Parents Without Partners
1560 South Dixie Hwy., #510
Boca Raton, FL 33432

Parents Without Partners publishes a journal concerned with special problems and issues confronting the single parent.

Young Children
National Association for the Education
  of Young Children
1509 16th St. NW
Washington, DC, 20036-1426

In keeping with the organization's goals, NAEYC publishes *Young Children*, geared to teachers and parents of children from birth to eight years. It includes a wide selection of articles related to childrearing, professional objectives, and education.

Bibliography

Achord, B., Berry, M., Harding, G., Kerber, K., Scott, S., & Schwab, L. O. (Eds.). (1986). *Building family strengths*. Lincoln: Department of Human Development and Family, University of Nebraska.

Adams, R. L. (1991). *Great negroes: Past and present* (Rev. 3rd ed.). Chicago: Afro-Am.

Ahlburg, D. A., & De Vita, C. J. (1992). New realities of the American family. *Population Bulletin, 47*(2), Washington, DC: Population Reference Bureau.

Ainsworth, M. D. (1973). The development of infant-mother attachments. In B. M. Caldwell & H. N. Ricciuti (Eds.), *Review of child development research*. Chicago: University of Chicago Press.

Allen, M. L., Brown, P., & Finlay, B. D. (1992). *Helping children by strengthening families*. Washington, DC: Children's Defense Fund.

Altman, D. H., & Smith, R. L. (1960). Unrecognized trauma in infants and children. *Journal of Bone and Joint Surgery, 42A*(1), 407–413.

Amato, P. R. (1994). Life-span adjustment of children to their parents' divorce. *The Future of Children: Children and Divorce 4*(1), 143–164.

American Association for Protecting Children. (n.d.). *Guidelines for schools to help protect abused and neglected children*. Denver, CO: American Humane Association.

American Association of School Administrators. (1991). *America 2000: Where school leaders stand*. Arlington, VA: Author.

American Bar Association Presidential Working Group on the Unmet Legal Needs of Children and Their Families. (1993, July). *America's children at risk: A national agenda for legal action*. Washington, DC: The ABA Center on Children and the Law.

American Humane Association. (1978). *National analysis of official child neglect and abuse reporting*. Denver, CO: Author.

American Humane Association. (1992b, July). *Fact sheet: Shaken baby syndrome*. Englewood, CO: Author.

American Humane Association. (1992c, October). *Fact sheet: Child abuse and neglect data*. Englewood, CO: Author.

American Humane Association. (1998). *Children's division*. Englewood, CO: Author.

American Humane Association (2001). Fact sheet: Shaken baby syndrome. Retrieved December 6, 2001, from *http://www.americanhumane.org/children/factsheets/shake.htm*

American Institute for Research. (1994). *Educational innovation in multiracial contexts: The growth of magnet schools in American education*. Palo Alto, CA: U.S. Department of Education.

American School Counselor Association. (1988). The school counselor and child abuse/neglect prevention. *Elementary School Guidance & Counseling, 22*(4), 261–263.

Anastasiow, N. (1988). Should parenting education be mandatory? *Topics in Early Childhood Special Education, 8*(1), 60–72.

Anderson, R. C., Hiebert, F. H., Scott, J. A., & Wilkinson, I. A. G. (1985). *Becoming a nation of readers: The report of the Commission on Reading*. Champaign, IL: Center for the Study of Reading.

Angelou, Maya (2002). *I know why the caged bird sings*. New York: Random.

Annie E. Casey Foundation. (2001). *Kids count data book, 2001*. Baltimore: Author.

Annie E. Casey Foundation (2002a). *Kids count data book, 2002*. Baltimore: Author

Annie E. Casey Foundation (2002b). *Kids count pocket guide*. Baltimore: Author.

Applbaum, R. L., Bodaken, E. M., Sereno, K. K., & Anatol, K. W. E. (1979). *The process of group communication* (2nd ed.). Palo Alto, CA: Science Research Associates.

Asher, L. J., & Lenhoff, D. R. (2001). Family and medical leave: Making time for family is everyone's business. *The Future of Children: Caring for Infants and Toddlers, 11*(1), 115–121.

Aries, P. (1962). *Centuries of childhood.* New York: Vintage Books.

Austin, J. S. (2000). When a child discloses sexual abuse: Immediate and appropriate teacher responses. *Childhood Education, 77*(1), 2–5.

Bakwin, H. (1956). Multiple skeletal lesions in young children due to trauma. *Journal of Pediatrics, 49*(1), 7–15.

Ballantine, J. H. (1999/2000, winter). Figuring the father factor. *Childhood Education, 76*(2), 140–145.

Banks, J. A. (1991). *Teaching strategies for ethnic studies* (5th ed.). Boston: Allyn & Bacon.

Banks, J. A. (1997). *Teaching strategies for ethnic studies* (6th ed.). Boston: Allyn & Bacon.

Barbour, N. H., & Seefeldt, C. (1993). *Developmental continuity across the preschool and primary-grades.* Wheaton, MD: Association for Childhood Education International.

Barneombudet. (2002). The ombudsman for children in Norway. Retrieved June 29, 2002, from *http://www.barneombudet.no/html/english/factsheet.html*

Barton, P. E. (2002, January). Raising achievement and reducing gaps. Retrieved February 5, 2002, from *http://www.negp.gov*

Bassuk, E. L. (1991). Homeless families. *Scientific American, 264*(6), 66–74.

Bassuk, E., & Rubin, L. (1987). Homeless children: A neglected population. *American Journal of Orthopsychiatry 57*(22), 279–285.

Bauman, K. J. (2001, August). *Home schooling in the United States: Trends and Characteristics.* Washington, DC: U. S. Census Bureau Population Division.

Bavolek, S. J. (1989). Assessing and treating high-risk parenting attitudes. *Early Child Development and Care, 42,* 99–111.

Beal, G., Bohlen, J. M., & Raudabaugh, J. N. (1962). *Leadership and dynamic group action.* Ames: Iowa State University.

Becker, H. J. (2000, Fall/Winter). Who's wired and who's not: Children's access and use of computer technology. *The Future of Children: Children and Computer Technology 10*(2), 44–75.

Bell, R. Q., & Harper, L. V. (1980). *Child effects on adults.* Lincoln: University of Nebraska Press.

Benne, K. D., & Sheets, P. (1948). Functional roles of group members. *Journal of Social Issues, 4*(2), 41–49.

Berck, J. (1992). No place to be: Voices of homeless children. *Public Welfare, 5*(2), 28–33.

Berger, E. H. (1968). *Mature beginning teachers: Employment, satisfaction, and role analysis.* Unpublished doctoral dissertation, University of Denver.

Berger, E. H. (1996a). Don't leave them standing on the sidewalk. *Early Childhood Education Journal, 24*(2), 131–133.

Berger, E. H. (1996b). Communication: The key to parent involvement. *Early Childhood Education Journal, 23*(3), 179–183.

Berger, E. H. (1997). Home schooling. *Early Childhood Education Journal, 24*(3), 205–208.

Berger, E. H. (1998). Reaching parents through literacy. *Early Childhood Education Journal, 25*(3), 211–215.

Berger, E. H., & Berger, G. R. (1985). Parents and law: Rights and responsibilities. In L. Sametz & C. S. McLoughlin (Eds.), *Educators, children and the law.* Springfield, IL: Charles C. Thomas.

Berliner, D. (1987, May). Parents can be great summer tutors. *Instructor,* 20–21.

Berrueta-Clement, J. R., Schweinhart, L. J., Barnett, W. S., Epstein, A. S., & Weikart, D. P. (1984). *Changed lives: The effects of the Perry Preschool Program on youths through age 19. (Monograph of the High/Scope Educational Research Foundation,* No. 8). Ypsilanti, MI: High/Scope Press.

Besharov, D. J. (1990). *Recognizing child abuse.* New York: Free Press.

Besharov, D. J. (1994). Responding to child sexual abuse: The need for a balanced approach. *The Future of Children: Sexual Abuse of Children, 4*(2), 135–155.

Bianchi, S. M., & Spain, D. (1996). Women, work, and family in America. *Population Bulletin, 51*(3). Washington, DC: Population Reference Bureau.

Biddle, B. J., & Thomas, E. J. (1979). *Role theory: Concepts and research.* Melbourne, FL: Robert E. Krieger.

Bigner, J. J. (1985). *Parent-child relations.* New York: Macmillan.

Billingsley, A. (1992). *Climbing Jacob's ladder.* New York: Simon & Schuster.

Binder, R. L., & McNiel, D. E. (1987). Evaluation of a school-based sexual abuse prevention program: Cognitive and emotional effects. *Child Abuse and Neglect, 11*(4), 497–506.

Binkley, M. R. (1988). *Becoming a nation of readers: What parents can do.* Lexington, MA: D. C. Heath.

Bjorklund, G., & Burger, C. (1987). Making conferences work for parents, teachers, and children. *Young Children, 42*(2), 26–31.

Bloom, B. S. (1964). *Stability and change in human characteristics*. New York: Wiley.

Bloom, B. S. (1981). *All our children learning*. New York: McGraw-Hill.

Bloom, B. S. (1986). The home environment and school learning. In Study Group of National Assessment of Student Achievement, *The nation's report card*. Washington, DC: U.S. Department of Education. (ERIC Document Reproduction Service No. ED279663)

Blow, S. E., & Eliot, H. R. (1910). *The mottos and commentaries of Friedrich Froebel's mother play*. New York: D. Appleton.

Board on Children and Families. (1995). Immigrant children and their families: Issues for research and policy. *The Future of Children: Critical Issues for Children and Youth 5*(2), 72–89.

Bodrova, E., & Leong, D. J. (1996). *Tools of the mind: The Vygotskian approach to early childhood education*. Upper Saddle River, NJ: Merrill/Prentice Hall.

Bogolub, E. B. (1995). *Helping families through divorce: An eclectic approach*. New York: Springer.

Bond, J. T., Galinsky, E., & Swanberg, J. E. (1998). *The 1997 national study of the changing workforce*. New York: Families and Work Institute.

Borchers, T. (1999). Small group communication: Roles in groups. Retrieved August 28, 2002, from *http://www.abacon.com/commstudies/groups/roles.html*

Boren, S. (1994). *Education of the gifted and talented reauthorization fact sheet*. Washington, DC: (ERIC Document Reproduction Service Nos. ED371526 and EC303113).

Bossard, J. H. S., & Boll, E. S. (1966). *The sociology of child development*. New York: Harper and Row.

Bower, T. G. R. (1982). *Development in infancy* (2nd ed.). San Francisco: W. H. Freeman.

Bowlby, J. (1966). *Attachment*. New York: Basic Books.

Bowlby, J. (1982). *Maternal care and mental health*. New York: Schocken Books.

Bowlby, J. (1988). *A secure base*. New York: Basic Books.

Boyer, E. L. (1991). *Ready to learn: A mandate for the nation*. Princeton, NJ: The Carnegie Foundation for the Advancement of Teaching.

Boyer, E. L. (1995). *The basic school: A community for learning*. Princeton, NJ: Carnegie Foundation for the Advancement of Teaching.

Brazelton, T. B. (1987). *Working and caring*. Reading, MA: Addison-Wesley.

Brazelton, T. B., & Greenspan, S. I. (2000). *The irreducible needs of children: What every child must have to grow, learn, and flourish*. Cambridge, MA: Perseus.

Brazelton, T. B., & Greenspan, S. I. (2001). The irreducible needs of children. *Young Children, 56*(2), 6–14.

Brazelton, T. B., & Yogman, M. W. (1986). *Affective development in infancy*. Norwood, NJ: Ablex.

Bredekamp, S. (Ed.). (1987). *Developmentally appropriate practice in early childhood programs serving children from birth through 8* (expanded ed.). Washington, DC: National Association for the Education of Young Children.

Bredekamp, S., & Rosegrant, T. (1992). *Reaching potentials: Appropriate curriculum and assessment for young children* (Vol. 1). Washington, DC: National Association for the Education of Young Children.

Brier, J., Berliner, L., Bulkley, J. A., Jenny, C., & Reid, T. (1996). *The APSAC handbook on child maltreatment*. Thousand Oaks, CA: Sage.

Bright, J. A. (1994). Beliefs in action: Family contributions to African-American student success. *Equity and Choice, 10*(2), 5–3.

Brim, O. (1965). *Education for child rearing*. New York: Free Press.

Broderick, C. B. (1993). *Understanding family process: Basics of family systems theory*. Newbury Park, CA: Sage.

Bronfenbrenner, U. (1979). *The ecology of human development*. Cambridge, MA: Harvard University Press.

Bronfenbrenner, U. (1986). Ecology of the family. Research perspectives. *Developmental Psychology, 22*, 723–742.

Brook-Gunn, J., & Duncan, G. J. (1997). The effects of poverty on children. *The Future of Children: Children and Poverty, 7*(2), 55–71.

Brougham, Lord. (1828). Speech to the House of Commons. In B. Evans (1978), *Dictionary of quotations* (p. 193). New York: Avenel Books.

Brown v. Topeka Board of Education, 347 U.S. 483 (1954).

Bruckey, S. (Ed.). (2000). *Children of poverty*. New York: Garland.

Bruner, J. S., & Greenfield, P. (1996). *Studies in cognitive growth*. New York: Wiley.

Bryson, K. (1996, October). Household and family characteristics. March, 1995. *Current Population*

Reports (P20–488). Washington, DC: Bureau of the Census.

Buck, P. S. (Reprint, 1991). *The child who never grew.* Cutchogue, NY: Buccaneer Books.

Buell, M. J., Hallam, R. A., & Beck, H. L. (2001, May). Early Head Start and child care partnerships: Working together to serve infants, toddlers, and their families. *Young Children, 56*(3), 7–12.

Bullock, J. R. (2002). Bullying among children. *Childhood Education, 78*(3), 130–133.

Burr, W. R. (1990). Beyond I-statements in family communication. *Family Relations, 39*(3), 266–273.

Butts, R. F., & Cremin, L. A. (1953). *A history of education in American culture.* New York: Holt, Rinehart and Winston.

Byrne, G. (1997, October). Father may not know best, but what does he know? *Population Today 15*(10), 1–3.

C. Henry Kempe National Center for the Prevention and Treatment of Child Abuse and Neglect. (n.d.). *Kempe Center programs.* Denver, CO: Author.

Caffey, J. (1946). Multiple fractures in long bones of infants suffering from chronic subdural hematoma. *American Journal of Roentgenology, 56,* 163–173.

Caldwell, B. (1968). The fourth dimension in early childhood education. In R. Hess & R. Bear (Eds.), *Early education: Current theory, research, and action.* Chicago: Aldine.

Caldwell, B. M. (1989). Achieving rights for children: Role of the early childhood profession. *Childhood Education, 66*(1), 4–7.

Caldwell, B. M. (1991). Continuity in the early years: Transitions between grades and systems. In S. L. Kagan (Ed.), *The care and education of America's young children: Obstacles and opportunities. Ninetieth Yearbook of the National Society for the Study of Education.* Chicago: University of Chicago Press.

Caldwell, B. M., & Bradley, R. H. (1984). *Administration manual: Home observation for measurement of the environment.* Little Rock: University of Arkansas.

Calhoun, A. W. (1960). *A social history of the American family* (Vols. 1–3). New York: Barnes & Noble.

California Task Force on School Readiness. (1988). *Here they come: Ready or not.* Sacramento: California Department of Education.

Candoli, I. C. (1991). *School systems administration: A strategic plan for site-based management.* Lancaster, PA: Technomic.

Canter, L., & Hausner, L. (1987). *Homework without tears.* New York: Harper and Row.

Carlson, C. I. (1992). Single-parent families. In M. E. Procidano & C. B. Fisher (Eds.), *Contemporary families: A handbook for school professionals.* New York: Teachers College Press.

Carlson, M. (2002, January). Developing self and emotions in extreme social deprivation. In panel: The effect of emotions: Laying the groundwork in childhood. Retrieved February 5, 2002, from *http://www. lcweb.loc.gov/loc/brain/emotion/Carlson*

Carnegie Corporation of New York. (1994). *Starting points: Meeting the needs of our youngest children.* New York: Author.

Carper, J. C. (1992). Home schooling: History and historian: The past and present. *The High School Journal, 75*(4), 252–257.

Carroll, L. (1968). *Through the looking-glass and what Alice found there.* New York: St. Martin's Press.

Casanova, U. (1987, May). Parents can be great summer tutors. *Instructor,* 20–21.

Casper, L. M. (1997, November). Who's minding our preschoolers? Fall 1994 (Update). *Current Population Reports* (P70–62). Washington, DC: Bureau of the Census.

Casper, L. M., & Bianchi, S. M. (2002). *Continuity & change in the American family.* Thousand Oaks, CA: Sage.

Casper, L. M., & Bryson, K. R. (1998, March). Co-resident grandparents and their grandchildren: Grandparent maintained families. Washington, DC: Population Division, U.S. Bureau of the Census. Retrieved April 2, 2002, from *http://www. census.gov/population/www/documentation/ twps0026.html*

Cataldo, C. Z. (1987). *Parent education for early childhood.* New York: Teachers College Press.

Center for Effective Discipline (2000, July). *Facts about corporal punishment.* Retrieved January 14, 2003 from *http://www.stophitting.com/disatschool/ facts.php*

Center for Family Strengths. (1986). *Building family strengths: A manual for facilitators.* Lincoln: University of Nebraska.

Center for the Future of Children, The David and Lucile Packard Foundation. (1995). The Future of Children. *Critical Issues for Children and Youth, 5*(2).

Centre for Europe's Children. (2001d, March 30) Latin America. Retrieved June 29, 2002, from *http:// www.ombudsnet.org/ombudsmen/RestOfWorld/ LatinAmerica/LatinAmerica.htm*

Centre for Europe's Children. (2001a, December 13). Annual report on the activities of the French ombudsman for children/Defenseur des enfants. Retrieved June 29, 2002, from *http://www. ombudsnet. org/Ombudsmen/France/Activities_00_01.htm*

Centre for Europe's Children. (2001b, December 13). Austrian report for the annual meeting of ENOC. Retrieved June 29, 2002, from *http://www.ombudsnet. org/Ombudsmen/Austria/austria.htm*

Centre for Europe's Children. (2001c, December 13). Standards for human rights. Retrieved June 29, 2002, from *http://www.ombudsnet.org/WhatsNew.htm*

Centre for Europe's Children. (2002, April 4). History of the office. Retrieved June 29, 2002, from *http:// www.ombudsnet.org/ombudsmen/Hungary/ hungary.htm*

CESA 5, Portage Project. (1998). *Growing: Interactions/Daily routines.* Portage, WI: Author.

Chambliss, R. (1982). *Social thought.* New York: Irvington Press.

Chapman, W. (1991). The Illinois experience: State grants to improve schools through parent involvement. *Phi Delta Kappan, 72*(5), 355–358.

Child Abuse Prevention and Treatment Act of 1974. (1977). *United States Code, 1976, The Public Health and Welfare, Section 5101* (Vol. 10). Washington, DC: U.S. Government Printing Office.

Children's Ombudsman in Sweden. (1998). Children's ombudsman in Sweden report. Retrieved June 29, 2001, from *http://www.bo.se/eng/engelsk.asp*

Children's Defense Fund. (1989). *A vision for America's future.* Washington, DC: Author.

Children's Defense Fund. (1992). *The state of America's children, 1991.* Washington, DC: Author.

Children's Defense Fund. (1997). *The state of America's children: Yearbook 1997.* Washington, DC: Author.

Children's Defense Fund. (1998). *The state of America's children: Yearbook 1998.* Washington, DC: Author.

Chinn, P. C. (Ed.). (1984). *Education of culturally and linguistically exceptional children.* Reston, VA: Council for Exceptional Children.

Chinn, P. C., Winn, J., & Walters, R. H. (1978). *Two-way talking with parents of special children: A process of positive communication.* St. Louis, MO: C. V. Mosby.

Citizens for Parental Rights v. San Mateo County Board of Education, 124 Cal. Reptr. 68 (1975).

Civil Rights Act of 1964, 42 U.S.C. 601, 78 Stat. 252; 2000d. Cited in the *Federal Register, 45*(92).

Clark, R. M. (1983). *Family life and school achievement.* Chicago: University of Chicago Press.

Clewell, B. C., Brooks-Gunn, J., & Benasich, A. A. (1989). Evaluating child-related outcomes of teenage parenting programs. *Family Relations, 38*(2), 201–209.

Coan, D. L., & Gotts, E. E. (1976). *Parent education needs: A national assessment study.* Charleston, WV: Appalachia Educational Laboratory. (ERIC Document Reproduction Service No. ED132609).

Cochran, M., & Dean, C. (1991). Home-school relations and the empowerment process. *Elementary School Journal 91*(3), 261–269.

Coleman, J., Campbell, E. Q., Hobson, C. J., McPartland, J., Mood, A. M., Weinfeld, F. D. et al. (1966). *Equality of educational opportunity.* Washington, DC: U.S. Government Printing Office.

Coleman, J. S. (1987). Families and schools. *Educational Researcher, 16*(1), 32–38.

Coleman, J. S. (1994). Family involvement in education. In C. L. Fagnano & B. Z. Werber (Eds.), *School, family and community interaction: A view from the firing lines.* Boulder, CO: Westview Press.

Coleman, J. S. (1997). *Redesigning American education.* Boulder, CO: Westview Press.

Coleman, J. S., & Schneider, B. (Eds.). (1993). *Parents, their children and schools.* Boulder, CO: Westview Press.

Coletta, A. J. (1977). *Working together: A guide to parent involvement.* Atlanta, GA: Humanics Limited.

Colorado Department of Education, Early Childhood Initiatives, The Arapahoe Early Childhood Network, PEAK Parent Center, & The Colorado Consortium of Intensive Care Nurseries. (1997). *From one parent to another.* Denver, CO: Author.

Comenius, J. A. (1967). *The great didactic of John Amos Comenius* (M. W. Keatinge, Ed. & Trans.). New York: Russell & Russell. (Original work published 1657.)

Comer, J. P. (1988). Educating poor minority children. *Scientific American, 259*(5), 42–48.

Comer, J. P. (1997). *Waiting for a miracle.* New York: Dutton.

Comer, J. P., & Haynes, N. M. (1991). Parent involvement in schools: An ecological approach. *The Elementary School Journal, 91*(3), 271–277.

Comer, J. P., Haynes, N. M., & Joyner, E. T. (1996). The school development program. In J. P. Comer, N. M. Haynes, E. T. Joyner, & M. Ben-Avie (Eds.), *Rallying the whole village: The Comer process for reforming education* (pp. 1–26). New York: Teachers College Press.

Comer, J. P., Haynes, N. M., Joyner, E. T., & Ben-Avie, M. (Eds.). (1996). *Rallying the whole village: The*

Comer process for reforming education. New York: Teachers College Press.

Commissioner's Task Force on Parent Involvement in Head Start. (1987). *Final report: Commissioner's task force on parent involvement in Head Start.* Washington, DC: U.S. Department of Health and Human Services, Office of Human Development Services, Administration for Children, Youth and Families, Head Start Bureau.

Congressional record. (1983). 98th Congr., Vol. 129, pt. 24: 33310–33329, 98–199.

Congressional record. (1986). 99th Congr., Vol. 132, pt. 125: H7908–H7912, 457.

Consortium for Longitudinal Studies. (1983). *As the twig is bent.* Hillsdale, NJ: Erlbaum.

Cook, R. E., Tessier, A., & Armbruster, V. B. (1987). *Adapting early childhood curricula for children with special needs* (2nd ed.). Upper Saddle River, NJ: Merrill/Prentice Hall.

Cooke, G., & Cooke, S. (1988). Homework that makes a difference in children's learning. Personal communication.

Cooley, H. C. (1964). *Human nature and the social order.* New York: Schocken Books.

Coons, C. E., Gay, E. C., Fandal, A. W., Ker, C., & Frankenburg, W. K. (1981). *Home Screening Questionnaire.* Denver, CO: JFK Child Development Center.

Cooper, H. (1989). *Homework.* New York: Longman.

Cooper H. (1994, Summer). *Homework research and policy: A review of the literature.* Center for Applied Research and Education Improvement. Retrieved June 21, 2002, from *http://education.umn.edu/carei/Reports/Rpractice/Summer94/homework.htm*

Corcoran, M. E., & Chaudry, A. (1997). The effects of poverty on children. *The Future of Children: Children and Poverty 7*(2), 40–54.

Cost, Quality, and Child Outcomes Study Team (CQO). (1995). *Cost, quality, and child outcomes in child care centers.* Denver, CO: Department of Economics, University of Colorado at Denver.

Council for Exceptional Children. (2002). Public policy and legislative information. IDEA reauthorization recommendations. Retrieved June 22, 2002, from *http://www.cec.sped.org/pp/*

Crane, S. (1986). Personal communication.

Crane, S. (1994). Personal communication.

Crosbie-Burnett, M., & Giles-Sim, J. (1994). Adolescent adjustment and step-parenting styles. *Family Relations, 43*(4), 394–399.

Crosbie-Burnett, M., & Skyles, A. (1989). Stepchildren in schools and colleges: Recommendations for educational policy changes. *Family Relations, 38*(1), 59–64.

Crosson-Tower, C. (2002). *Child abuse and neglect* (5th ed.). Boston: Allyn & Bacon.

Cupoli, J. M., & Sewell, P. M. (1988). One thousand fifty-nine children with a chief complaint of sexual abuse. *Child Abuse and Neglect, 12*(2), 151–161.

Dainton, M. (1993). The myth and misconceptions of stepmother identity. *Family Relations 42*(1), 93–98.

Dalaimo, D. M. (1996). Community home education: A case study of public school-based home schooling program. *Education Research Quarterly, 19*(4), 3–21.

Daresh, J. C. (1986). Effective home-school-community relations for secondary school improvement. *The Clearing House, 59*(7), 312–315.

DaSilva, B., & Lucus, R. D. (1974). *Practical school volunteer and teacher-aide programs.* West Nyack, NY: Parker.

Davies, D. (1987). Parent involvement in the public schools. *Education and Urban Society, 19*(2), 147–163.

Davies, D. (1990). Shall we wait for the revolution? A few lessons from the Schools Reaching Out project. *Equity and Choice, 6*(3), 68–73.

Davies, D. (1997). Crossing boundaries: How to create successful parnerships with families and communities. *Early Childhood Education Journal 25*(1), 73–77.

Day, J. C. (1996a). Population projections of the United States by age, sex, race, and Hispanic origin: 1995–2050. *Current Population Reports* (P25–113). Washington, DC: Bureau of the Census.

De Gaetano, Y., Williams, L. R., & Volk, D. (1998). *Kaleidoscope: A multicultural approach for the primary school classroom.* Upper Saddle River, NJ: Merrill/Prentice Hall.

Delaney, S. W. (1980, March 12–16). Fathers and infants class: A model program. *Exceptional Teacher.*

Delaney, S. W., Meyer, D. J., & Ward, M. J. (1980). *Fathers and infants class: A model for facilitating attachment between fathers and their infants.* Seattle, WA: Experimental Education Unit, Child Development and Mental Retardation Center, University of Washington.

deMause, L. (Ed.). (1974). *The history of childhood.* New York: Psychohistory Press.

deMause, L. (Ed.). (1988). *The history of childhood: The untold story of child abuse.* New York: Harper and Row.

Denver Public Schools. (1998). *Child abuse bulletin.* Denver, CO: Author.

Denver Public Schools. (n.d.). *For VIPs only. Volunteers in public schools.* Denver, CO: Author.

Denver Public Schools, Emily Griffith Opportunity School. (n.d.). *Parent education and preschool department leadership handbook.* Denver, CO: Author.

Derman-Sparks, L., & A.B.C. Task Force. (1989). *Antibias curriculum: Tasks for empowering young children.* Washington, DC: National Association for the Education of Young Children.

Dervarics, C. (2001). Charter school catching on. *Population Today, 29*(6). Washington, DC: Population Reference Bureau.

Deutsch, C. P., & Deutsch, M. (1968). Brief reflections on theory of early childhood enrichment programs. In R. Hess & R. Bear (Eds.), *Early education: Current theory, research, and action.* Chicago: Aldine.

Devaney, B. L., Ellwood, M. R., & Love, J. M. (1997). Programs that mitigate the effects of poverty on children. *The Future of Children: Children and Poverty 7*(2), 88–112.

Dewey, J. (1916). *Democracy and education: An introduction to the philosophy of education.* New York: Macmillan.

Dinkmeyer, D., & McKay, G. D. (1989). *STEP: Systematic training for effective parenting.* Circle Pines, MN: American Guidance Service.

Dinkmeyer, D., McKay, G. D., Dinkmeyer, J. S., & Dinkmeyer, D., Jr. (1992). *Teaching and leading children.* Circle Pines, MN: American Guidance Service.

Dixon v. Alabama State Board of Education, 368 U.S. 930 (1961).

Dombro, A. L., O'Donnell, N. S., Galinsky, E., Melcher, S. G., & Farber, A. (1996). *Community mobilization: Strategies to support young children and their families.* New York: Families and Work Institute.

Dornbusch, S., Ritter, P., Leiderman, P. H., Roberts, D. F., & Fraleigh, M. (1987). The relation of parenting style to adolescent school performance. *Child Development, 58*(5), 1244–1257.

Duggan, A. K., McFarlane, E. C., Windham, A. M., Rohde, C. A., Salkever, D. S., Fuddy, L. et al. (1999). Evaluation of Hawaii's Healthy start program. *The Future of Children: Home Visiting: Recent Program Evaluations, 9*(1),73.

Earls, F. (2002, January). Studying the causes of delinquency and violence. In panel: The effect of emotions: Laying the groundwork in childhood. Retrieved February 5, 2002, from *http://www.lcweb. loc.gov/loc/brain/emotion/Earls.html*

Eddowes, E. A. (1992). Children and homelessness: Early childhood and elementary education. In E. H. Stronge (Ed.), *Educating homeless children and adolescents: Evaluating policy and practice.* Newbury Park, CA: Sage.

Education Commission of the States. (1996). *Bridging the gap between neuroscience and education.* Denver, CO: Author.

Educational Resources Information Center, U.S. Department of Education. (1996, Fall). Inclusion. *ERIC Review, 4*(3).

Egeland, B. (1988). The consequences of physical and emotional neglect on the development of young children. In U.S. Department of Health and Human Services, Children's Bureau, *National Center on Child Abuse and Neglect: Research symposium on Child Neglect,* February 23–25. (D-10–D-21)

Ehrle, J., Adams, G., & Tout, T. (2001). *Who's caring for our youngest children/Child care patterns of infants and toddlers.* Washington, DC: The Urban Institute.

Elam, S. M., Rose, L. C., & Gallup, A. M. (1992). The 24th annual Gallup Phi Delta Kappa Poll of the public's attitudes toward public schools. *Phi Delta Kappan 74*(1), 41–53.

Elkind, D. (1987a). The child yesterday, today, and tomorrow. *Young Children, 42*(4), 6–12.

Elmer, E. (1982). Abused young children seen in hospitals. In S. Antler (Ed.), *Child abuse and child protection: Policy and practice.* Silver Springs, MD: National Association of Social Workers.

Emmons, C. L., Comer, J. P., & Haynes, N. M. (Eds.). (1996). Translating theory into practice: Comer's theory of school reform. In J. P. Comer, N. M. Haynes, E. T. Joyner, & M. Ben-Avie (Eds.), *Rallying the whole village: The Comer process for reforming education* (pp. 27–41). New York: Teachers College Press.

End Violence Against the Next Generation. (n.d.). *Child abuse in schools: A national disgrace.* Berkeley, CA: Author.

Engle, P. L., & Breaux, C. (1998). Fathers' involvement with children: Perspectives from developing countries. *Social Policy Report, 12*(1). Ann Arbor, MI: Society for Research in Child Development.

Epstein, A. S. (1998). Is the High/Scope educational approach compatible with the revised Head Start performance standards? *High/Scope Resource, 17*(2). Ypsilanti, MI: High/Scope Press.

Epstein, J. L. (1986). Parents' reactions to teacher practices of parent involvement. *The Elementary School Journal, 86*(3), 277–294.

Epstein, J. L. (1987a). Parent involvement: What research says to administrators. *Education and Urban Society, 19*(2), 119–136.

Epstein, J. L. (1987b). What principals should know about parent involvement. *Principal, 66*(3), 6–9.

Epstein, J. L. (1994). Theory to practice: School and family partnerships lead to school improvement and student success. In C. L. Fagnano & B. Z. Werber (Eds.), *School, family, and community interaction: A view from the firing lines.* Boulder, CO: Westview Press.

Epstein, J. L. (1995). School/family/community partnerships: Caring for the children we share. *Phi Delta Kappan, 76*(9), 701–712.

Epstein, J. L. (1996). Perspective and previews on research and policy for school, family and community partnerships. In A. Booth & J. F. Dunn (Eds.), *Family-school links: How do they affect educational outcomes?* Mahwah, NJ: Erlbaum.

Epstein, J. L., & Dauber, S. L. (1991). School programs and teacher practices of parent involvement in inner-city elementary and middle schools. *The Elementary School Journal, 91*(3), 289–305.

EQUALS. (1986). *Family math.* Berkeley: University of California.

Erikson, E. (1986). *Childhood and society.* New York: W.W. Norton.

Executive summary: Children, youth and gun violence: Analysis. (2002). *The Future of Children: Children, Youth, and Gun Violence, 12*(2). The David and Lucile Packard Foundation.

Fagnano, C. L., & Hughes, K. N. (1993). *Making schools work: A view from the firing lines.* Boulder, CO: Westview Press.

Families and Work Institute. (1994). *Employers, families, and education: Facilitating family involvement in learning.* New York: Author.

Families together. (1993, Summer). Newsletter. Topeka, KS: Author.

Family and Child Education. (2002). *Family and child education (FACE).* Retrieved May 27, 2002, from *http://www.famlit.org/faqs/faqface.html*

Family Resource Coalition. (1993a). *Family support programs and family literacy.* Chicago: Author.

Family Resource Coalition. (1993b). *Family support programs and the prevention of alcohol and other drug abuse (AOD).* Chicago: Author.

Family Resource Coalition. (1993c). *Family support programs and school readiness.* Chicago: Author.

Family Resource Coalition. (1993d). *Family support programs and school-linked services.* Chicago: Author.

Fandal, A. (1986, February). Personal correspondence. Denver: University of Colorado Medical Center.

Federal register. (1990, May 9). *Part II Department of Education, 45*(92), 30918–30965.

Federal register. (1993, January 21). *Part VI Department of Health and Human Services: Administration for Children and Families, 58*(12), 1304–1305, 1308.

Fehrmann, P. G., Keith, T. Z., & Reimers, T. M. (1987). Home influence on school learning: Direct and indirect effects of parental involvement on high school grades. *Journal of Educational Research, 80*(6), 330–337.

Fenichel, E., & Mann, T. L. (2001). Early Head Start for low-income families with infants and toddlers. *The Future of Children: Caring for Infants and Toddlers, 11*(1), 135–141.

Ferguson-Florissant School District. (1989b). *Parents as first teachers.* Ferguson, MO: Author.

Fernandez, H. C. (1980). *The child advocacy handbook.* New York: The Pilgrim Press.

Fierman, A. H., Dreyer, B. P., Quinn, L., Shulman, S., Courtland, C. D., & Guzzo, R. (1991). Growth delay in homeless children. *Pediatrics, 88*(5), 918–925.

Finkelhor, D. (1986). *A sourcebook on child sexual abuse.* Beverly Hills, CA: Sage.

Finkelhor, D. (1990). Early and long-term effects of child sexual abuse: An update. *Professional Psychology: Research and Practice, 21*(5), 325–330.

Finkelhor, D. (1994). Current information on the scope and nature of child sexual abuse. *The Future of Children: Sexual Abuse of Children, 4*(2), 31–53.

Finkelhor, D., & Ormrod, R. (2000, June). Characteristics of crimes against juvenile. *Juvenile Justice Bulletin.*

Fischer, L., Schimmel, D., & Kelly, C. (1999). *Teachers and the law* (5th ed.). New York: Longman.

Fisher, M. (1933). Parent education. In *Encyclopedia of the social sciences* (Vol. 2). New York: Macmillan.

Fisher, S. H. (1958). Skeletal manifestations of parent-induced trauma in infants and children. *Southern Medical Journal,* 956–960.

Flekkoy, M. G. (1989). Child advocacy in Norway: The ombudsman. *Child Welfare, 68*(2), 113–122.

Fontana, V. (1973a). The diagnosis of the maltreatment syndrome in children. *Pediatrics, 51*, 780–782.

Fontana, V. (1973b). *Somewhere a child is crying.* New York: Macmillan.

Fontana, V. J., & Besharov, D. J. (1979). *The maltreated child: The maltreatment syndrome in children.* Springfield, IL: Charles C. Thomas.

The Foundation Center. (1990). *The foundation directory.* New York: Author.

Fox, S. J. (1988). A whole language approach to the communication skills. In H. Gilliland (Ed.), *Teaching the Native American.* Dubuque, IA: Kendall/Hunt.

Frank, L. R. (Ed.). (2001). *Quotationary.* New York: Random House.

Franklin, C. J. (1993, June). Dealing with concerns throughout the year. Personal correspondence. Colorado Springs, CO.

Frede, E. C. (1995). The role of program quality in producing early childhood program benefits. *The Future of Children: Long-Term Outcomes of Early Childhood Programs, 5*(3), 115–132.

Froschi, M., Sprung, B., & Mullin-Rindler, N. (1998). *Quit it: A teacher's guide on teasing and bullying for use with students in grades k–3.* Washington, DC: NEA Professional Library.

Frost, S. E., Jr. (1966). *Historical and philosophical foundations of Western education.* Upper Saddle River, NJ: Merrill/Prentice Hall.

Furstenberg, F. F., Jr. (1994). History and current status of divorce in the United States. *The Future of Children: Children and Divorce 4*(1), 29–43.

Future of Children, The (1999, Spring/Summer). *Home visiting: Recent program evaluations.* (Vol 9) Los Gatos, CA: The David and Lucile Packard Foundation.

Galinsky, E. (1987). *The six stages of parenthood.* Reading, MA: Addison-Wesley.

Galinsky, E., & Salmond, K. (2002, July). *Youth & violence.* Denver: Colorado Trust and Families and Work Institute.

Gamble, T. K., & Gamble, M. (1982). *Contacts: Communicating interpersonally.* New York: Random House.

Gandini, L. (1993, November). Fundamentals of the Reggio Emilia approach to early childhood education. *Young Children 49*(1), 4–8.

Garbarino, J., Bradshaw, C. P., & Vorrasi, J. A. (2002). Mitigating the effects of gun violence on children and youth. *The Future of Children: Children, Youth, and Gun Violence, 12*(2), 73–85.

Gardner, N. D. (1974). *Group leadership.* Washington, DC: National Training & Development Service Press.

Garrity, C., Baris, M., & Porter, W. (2000). *Bully proofing your child: A parent's guide.* Longmont, CO: Sopris West.

Gelles, R. J., & Lancaster, J. B. (Eds.). (1987). *Child abuse and neglect: Biosocial dimensions.* New York: Aldine de Gruyter.

Gilliland, H. (Ed.). (1988). *Teaching the Native American.* Dubuque, IA: Kendall/Hunt.

Ginott, H. G. (1965). *Between parent & child.* New York: Macmillan.

Ginsberg, E. (Ed.). (1960). *The nation's children* (Vols. 1–3). New York: Columbia University Press.

Goffin, S. G., & Lombardi, J. (1988). *Speaking out: Early childhood advocacy.* Washington, DC: National Association for the Education of Young Children.

Goldman-Rakic, P. (1996). What can neuroscience contribute to education? In Education Commission of the States, *Bridging the gap between neuroscience and education.* Denver, CO: Author.

Gomby, D. S., Larson, C. S., Lewit, E. M., & Behrman, R. E. (1993). Home visiting: Analysis and recommendations. *The Future of Children: Home Visiting, 3*(3).

Gomby, D. S., Culross, P. L., & Behrman, R. E. (1999, Spring/Summer). Home visiting: Recent program evaluations. *The Future of Children, 9*(1), 4–26.

Gonzalez-Mena, J. (1998). *The child in the family and the community* (2nd ed.). Upper Saddle River, NJ: Merrill/Prentice Hall.

Goodson, B. D., & Hess, R. (1975). *Parents as teachers of young children: An evaluative review of some contemporary concepts and programs.* Stanford, CA: Stanford University Press.

Goodson, B. D., Swartz, J. P., & Millsap, M. A. (1991). Working with families: Promising programs to help parents support children's learning. *Equity and Choice, 7*(2–3), 97–107.

Goodykoontz, B., Davis, M. D., & Gabbard, H. F. (1947). Recent history and present status in education for young children. In *National Society for the Study of Education, 46th yearbook, part II.* Chicago: National Society for the Study of Education.

Gordon, I. J., & Breivogel, W. F. (Eds.). (1976). *Building effective home-school relationships.* Boston: Allyn & Bacon.

Gordon, T. (1975). *P.E.T.: Parent effectiveness training.* New York: Wyden.

Goss v. Lopez, 419 U.S. 565 (1975).

Gotts, E. E. (1989, February). *HOPE revisited: Preschool to graduation, reflections on parenting and school-family relations: Occasional paper 28.* Charleston, WV: Appalachia Educational Laboratory.

Governor Romer's Responsible Fatherhood Initiative. (1997). *Colorado fathers' resource guide.* Denver, CO: Author.

Gray, S. W., & Klaus, R. A. (1965). An experimental preschool program for culturally deprived children. *Child Development, 36*(4), 887–898.

Gray, S. W., Ramsey, B. K., & Klaus, R. A. (1982). *From 3 to 20: The early training project.* Baltimore: University Park Press.

Graziano, A. M., & Diament, D. M. (1992). Parent behavioral training: An examination of the paradigm. *Behavior Modification, 16,* 3–38.

Green, F. (1988). Corporal punishment and child abuse. *The Humanist, 48*(6), 9–10, 32.

Greenberg, P. (1989). Parents as partners in young children's development and education: A new American fad? Why does it matter? *Young Children, 44*(4), 61–75.

Greenberger, R. S. (2002, June 28). Supreme Court expands right to drug-test students. *The Wall Street Journal, 239*(126) p. 4.

Greene, B. (2000). *The elegant universe.* New York: Vintage Books.

Greenleaf, B. (1978). *Children through the ages: History of childhood.* New York: McGraw-Hill.

Greenspan, S. (2002, January). Emotional origins of intelligence. Special presentation. Retrieved February 5, 2002, from *http://www.lcweb.loc.gov/loc/brain/emotion/Greenspan.html*

Grissom, C. E. (1971). Listening beyond words: Learning from parents in conferences. *Childhood Education 48*(3), 138–142.

Grossman, S. (1999, Fall). Examining the origin of our beliefs about parents. *Childhood Education, 76*(1), 24–27.

Gruenberg, B. C. (Ed.). (1927). *Outlines of child study.* New York: Macmillan.

Gruenberg, S. (1940). Parent education: 1930–1940. In W. B. Grave (Ed.), *Annals of the American Academy of Political and Social Sciences.* Philadelphia: American Academy of Political and Social Sciences.

Gutek, G. L. (1968). *Pestalozzi and education.* New York: Random House.

Guterson, D. (1992). *Family matters: Why homeschooling makes sense.* New York: Harcourt Brace Jovanovich.

Guzick v. Drebus, 401 U.S. 948 (1971).

Hagans, K. B., & Case, J. (1988). *When your child has been molested: A parent's guide to healing and recovery.* Lexington, MA: Lexington Books.

Hale, J. E. (1994). *Unbank the fire: Visions for the education of African American children.* Baltimore: The Johns Hopkins University Press.

Hale-Benson, J. E. (1986). *Black children: Their roots, culture, and learning styles.* Baltimore: The Johns Hopkins University Press.

Hallahan, D. P., & Kauffman, J. M. (1997). *Exceptional learners: Introduction to special education* (7th ed.). Boston: Allyn & Bacon.

Halmhuber, N., & Beauvais, K. J. (2002). *Case studies with children and adolescents with special needs.* Boston: Allyn & Bacon.

Halperin, M. (1979). *Helping maltreated children: School and community involvement.* St. Louis, MO: C. V. Mosby.

Hamilton, L. R. (1989). Child maltreatment: Prevention and treatment. *Early Child Development and Care, 42,* 31–56.

Handel, G. (Ed.). (1988). *Childhood socialization.* New York: Aldine de Gruyter.

Hanson, R. A. (1975). Consistency and stability of home environmental measures related to IQ. *Child Development, 46*(2), 470–480.

Harris, L., & Associates. (1987). *The American teacher, 1987. Strengthening links between home and school. The Metropolitan Life Survey.* Washington, DC: U.S. Department of Education. (ERIC Document Reproduction Service No. ED289841)

Hauge, E. (1998). Promoting children's interests and rights in education. In Curtis, A. (Ed.), *International Journal of Early Childhood: 50th anniversary issue OMEP, 30*(1), 52–55.

Hawes, J. M. (1991). *The children's rights movement.* Boston: Twayne.

Haynes, N. M., Ben-Avie, M., Squires, D. A., Howley, J. P., Negron, E. N., & Corbin, J. N. (Eds.). (1996). It takes a whole village: The SDP school. In J. P. Comer, N. M. Haynes, E. T. Joyner, & M. Ben-Avie (Eds.), *Rallying the whole village: The Comer process for reforming education* (pp. 42–71). New York: Teachers College Press.

Hazelwood School District v. Kuhlmeier, 484 U.S. 592 (1988).

Hedrich, V., & Jackson, C. (1977, July). Winning play at home base. *American Education, 13*(6), 27–30.

Head Start Family Literacy Project. (2002). Federal definition of family literacy. Retrieved May 27, 2002, from *http://www.famlit.org/headstart/ hsdefine.html*

Helfer, R. E. (1975). *The diagnostic process and treatment programs.* Washington, DC: U.S. Department of Health, Education and Welfare.

Helfer, R. E., & Kempe, R. S. (Eds.). (1987). *The battered child* (4th ed.). Chicago: University of Chicago Press.

Henderson, A. T. (Ed.). (1987). *The evidence continues to grow.* Columbia, MD: National Committee for Citizens in Education.

Henderson, A. T., & Berla, N. (1994). *A new generation of evidence. The family is critical to student achievement.* Washington, DC: National Committee for Citizens in Education.

Hess, R. D., & Holloway, S. D. (1984). Family and school as educational institutions. In R. D. Parke, R. N. Emde, H. P. McAdoo, & G. P. Sackett (Eds.), *Review of child development research: Vol. 7. The family.* Chicago: University of Chicago Press.

Heward, W. L. (1990). *Exceptional children: Introduction to special education.* Upper Saddle River, NJ: Merrill/Prentice Hall.

Heward, W. L., & Orlansky, M. D. (1988). *Exceptional children: An introductory survey of special education* (3rd ed.). Upper Saddle River, NJ: Merrill/Prentice Hall.

Hewett, V. M. (2001, Winter). Examining the Reggio Emilia approach to early childhood education. *Early Childhood Education Journal, 28*(4), 95–99.

Hildago, N. (1994). Profile of a Puerto Rican family's support for school achievement. *Equity and Choice 10*(2), 14–22.

Hill, R. (1960). The American family today. In E. Ginsberg (Ed.), *The nation's children.* New York: Columbia University Press.

Hill, R. B. (1992). Dispelling myths and building on strengths: Supporting African American families. *Family Resource Coalition Report, 12*(1), 3–5.

Hodapp, A. F., & Hodapp, J. B. (1992). Homework: Making it work. *Intervention in School and Clinic, 27*(4), 233–235.

Hodges, J. (1996). The natural history of early non-attachment. In B. Bernstein & J. Brannen (Eds.), *Children, research and policy: Essays for Barbara Tizard.* London: Taylor & Francis.

Holland, G. (2002, June 28). Students who compete subject to drug testing. *Rocky Mountain News,* p. 2A.

Holmes, S. (1982). Parents Anonymous: A treatment method for child abuse. In S. Antler (Ed.), *Child abuse and child protection.* Silver Springs, MD: National Association of Social Workers.

Holzberg, R., & Walsh-Burton, S. (Eds.) (1996). *The parental voice.* Springfield, IL: Charles C. Thomas.

Hong, E., & Milgram, R. M. (2000). *Homework: Motivation and learning preference.* Westport, CT: Bergin & Garvey.

Honig, A. S. (1979). *Parent involvement in early childhood education.* Washington, DC: National Association for the Education of Young Children.

Horn, W. F. (1997, July, August). You've come a long way, daddy. *Policy Review,* No. 84, 24–30.

Horton, C. B., & Cruise, T. K. (2001). *Child abuse and neglect.* New York: Guilford Press.

Howe, W. J. (1988). Education and demographics: How do they affect unemployment rates? *Monthly Labor Review, 111*(1), 3–9.

Hunt, D. (1970). *Parents and children in history.* New York: Basic Books.

Hunt, J. M. (1961). *Intelligence and experience.* New York: Wiley.

Hurd, T. L., Lerner, R. M., & Barton, C. E. (1999). Integrated services: Expanding partnerships to meet the needs of today's children and families. *Young Children, 54*(2), 74–80.

Hyde, D. (1992). School-parent collaboration results in academic achievement. *NASSP Bulletin, 76*(543), 39–42.

Hymes, J. L., Jr. (1974). *Effective home-school relations.* Sierra Madre: Southern California Association for the Education of Young Children.

Hymes, J. L., Jr. (1987). *Early childhood education: The year in review: A look at 1986.* Carmel, CA: Hacienda Press.

Imber, M., & van Geel, T. (2000). *Education law* (2nd ed.). Mahwah, NJ: Erlbaum.

Ingraham v. Wright, 430 U.S. 651 (1977).

Irby v. State of Texas, 751 S.W.2d 670 (p. 1002) [Tex. Ct. App.] 1988).

Iverson, T. J., & Segal, M. (1990). *Child abuse and neglect: An information and reference guide.* New York: Garland.

Jablow, M. M. (1982). *Cara: Growing with a retarded child.* Philadelphia: Temple University Press.

Jackson, B. L., & Cooper, B. S. (1992). Involving parents in improving urban schools. *NAASP Bulletin,* 76(543), 30–38.

Jacobson, S. W., & Frye, K. F. (1991). Effect of maternal social support on attachment: Experimental evidence. *Child Development, 62*(3), 572–582.

John, R. (1988). The Native American family. In C. H. Mindel, R. W. Habenstein, & R. Wright, Jr. (Eds.), *Ethnic families in America* (3rd ed.). New York: Elsevier.

Johnston, J. H. (1990). *The new American family and the school.* National Middle School Association. Macon, GA: Panaprint.

Jones, L., & Finkelhor, D. (2001, January). The decline in child sexual abuse cases. *Juvenile Justice Bulletin.* Washington, DC: Office of Juvenile Justice and Delinquency Prevention.

Justice, B., & Justice, R. (1990). *The abusing family.* New York: Plenum Press.

Kagan, S. L., & Cohen, N. E. (Eds.). (1996). *Reinventing early care & education: A vision for a quality system.* San Francisco: Jossey-Bass.

Kagan, S. L., Moore, E., & Bredekamp, S. (Eds.). (1995). National Education Goals Panel. *Reconsidering children's early development and learning: Toward common views and vocabulary.* Washington, DC: U.S. Government Printing Office.

Kagan, S. L., & Zigler, E. F. (1987). *Early schooling.* New Haven: Yale University Press.

Kamii, C. (1985a). Leading primary education toward excellence: Beyond worksheets and drills. *Young Children, 40*(6), 3–9.

Kamii, C. (1985b). *Young children reinvent arithmetic.* New York: Teachers College Press.

Kaplan, G. P., Van Valey, L., & Associates. (1980). *Census '80: Continuing the factfinder tradition.* U.S. Bureau of the Census. Washington, DC: U.S. Government Printing Office.

Karnes, F. A., & Marquardt, R. (1997, February). Know your legal rights in gifted education. Reston, VA: The ERIC Clearinghouse on Disabilities and Gifted Education, The Council for Exceptional Children.

Karr-Morse, R., & Wiley, M. S. (1997). *Ghosts from the nursery: Tracing the roots of violence.* New York: Atlantic Monthly Press.

Kaufman, H. O. (2001, July). Skills for working with all families. *Young Children 56*(4), 81–83.

Kawin, E. (1970). *A manual for group leaders and participants.* Lafayette, IN: Purdue University.

Kearns, P. (Ed.). (1980). *Your child's right for a free public education: Parent's handbook.* Topeka: Kansas Association for Children with Learning Disabilities.

Kellaghan, T., Sloane, K., Alvarez, B., & Bloom, B. S. (1993). *The home environment and school learning: Promoting parental involvement in the education of children.* San Francisco: Jossey-Bass.

Keller, H. (1957). *The open door.* Garden City, NY: Doubleday.

Keller, H. (1991). *The story of my life: With her letters (1887–1901) and supplementary account of her education including passages from the reports and letters of her teacher, Anne Mansfield Sullivan.* CA: Temecula American Biography Series, Reprint Services Co.

Kelley, M. L. (1990). *School-home notes: Promoting children's classroom success.* New York: Guilford Press.

Kelly, P. (1995). *Developing healthy stepfamilies: Twenty families tell their stories.* New York: Haworth Press.

Kempe, C. H., & Kempe, R. (1984). *The common secret: Sexual abuse of children and adults.* San Francisco: W. H. Freeman.

Kempe, C. H., Silverman, F. N., Steele, B. F., Droegemueller, W., & Silver, H. (1962). The battered-child syndrome. *Journal of the American Medical Association, 181,* 17–24.

Kent, M. M., & Mather, M. (2002, December). What drives U.S. population growth? *Population Bulletin, 57*(6).

Kent, M. M., & Pollard, K. M., Haaga, J., Mather, M. (2001, June). First glimpses from the 2000 U.S. census. *Population Bulletin 56*(2), 3–8.

Kids count. (2001, May 14). Promising progress yet troubling trends face kids in the new millennium. Retrieved April 2, 2002, from *http://www.accf. org/kidscount/Kc2001/kc2001_press.htm*

Kierstead, F. D., & Wagner, P. A., Jr. (1993). *The ethical, legal, and multicultural foundations of teaching.* Madison, WI: Brown & Benchmark.

King, C. E. (1962). *The sociology of small groups.* New York: Pageant Press.

Kirk, S. A. (1989). *Educating exceptional children* (5th ed.). Boston: Houghton Mifflin.

Klass, C., Pettinelli, D., & Wilson, M. (1993). Home visiting: Building linkages. Personal correspondence.

Klaus, M. H., & Kennell, J. S. (1982). *Parent-infant bonding.* St. Louis, MO: C. V. Mosby.

Klein, T., Bittel, C., & Molnar, J. (1993). No place to call home: Supporting the needs of homeless children in the early childhood classroom. *Young Children, 48*(6), 22–31.

Knapp, P. A., & Deluty, R. H. (1989). Relative effectiveness of two behavioral parent training programs. *Journal of Clinical Child Psychology, 18,* 314–322.

Knowles, J. G. (1989, January). Cooperating with home school parents: A new agenda for public schools? *Urban Education, 23*(4), 392–411.

Koch, P. K., & McDonough, M. (1999, March). Improving parent-teacher conferences through collaborative conversations. *Young Children 54*(2), 11–15.

Kontos, S. (1992). The role of continuity and context in children's relationships with nonparental adults. In R. C. Pianta (Ed.), *Beyond the parent: The role of other adults in children's lives.* San Francisco: Jossey-Bass.

Kozol, J . (1991). *Savage inequalities: Children in American schools.* New York: Crown.

Krall, C. M., & Jalongo, M. R. (1998–1999). Creating a caring community in classrooms. *Childhood Education, 75*(2), 83–89.

Kraizer, S., Witte, S. S., & Fryer, G. E., Jr. (1989, September–October). Child sexual abuse prevention programs: What makes them effective in protecting children? *Children Today,* 23–27.

Kristensen, N., & Billman, J. (1987). Supporting parents and young children. *Childhood Education, 63*(4), 276–282.

Krugman, R. D. (1986). Recognition of sexual abuse in children. *Pediatrics in Review 8*(1), 25–30.

Krugman, R. D., & Krugman, M. K. (1984). Emotional abuse in the classroom. *American Journal of Diseases of Children, 138,* 284–286.

Kuhl, P. K. (1996). How babies map their native languages. In Education Commission of the States, *Bridging the gap between neuroscience and education.* Denver, CO: Author.

Kullen, A. S. (1994). *The peopling of America: A timeline of events that helped shape our nation.* Beltsville, MD: Americans All: The Portfolio Project.

LaConte, R. T. (1981). *Homework as a learning experience.* Washington, DC: National Education Association of the United States.

Lamb, M. E. (Ed.). (1997). *The role of the father in child development.* New York: Wiley.

Lamison-White, L. (1997, September). Poverty in the United States, 1996. *Current Population Reports: Consumer Income.* (P60-198). Washington, DC: Bureau of the Census.

LaMorte, M. W. (2001). *School law: Cases and concepts* (7th ed.). Boston, MA: Allyn & Bacon.

Lamson, P. A. (1992). Home schooling: A choice the Cupertino district supports. *The School Administrator, 49*(1), 26–27.

Landers, A. (1986). For friends of the handicapped. (Ann Landers' column, author unknown, News America Syndicate.) In *Special Educational Instructional Paraprofessional Facilitator Program.* Topeka: Kansas State Department of Education.

Language and Orientation Resource Center. (1981). *Indochinese students in U.S. schools: A guide for administrators.* Washington, DC: Center for Applied Linguistics.

Larner, M. (1996). Parents' perspective on quality in early care and education. In S. L. Kagan & N. E. Cohen (Eds.), *Reinventing early care and education: A vision for a quality system.* San Francisco: Jossey-Bass.

Lazar, I. (1983). Discussion and implications of the findings. In Consortium of Longitudinal Studies, *As the twig is bent.* Hillsdale, NJ: Erlbaum.

Lazar, I., Darlington, R., Murray, H., Royce, J., & Snipper, A. (1982). Lasting effects of early education: A report from the Consortium for Longitudinal Studies. *Monographs of the Society for Research in Child Development, 47* (2–3).

Lazoritz, S. (1990). Whatever happened to Mary Ellen? *Child Abuse and Neglect 14*(2), 143–149.

LeDoux, J. (1996, September). *Response. Bridging the gap between neuroscience and education.* Denver, CO: Education Commission of the States.

Lee, S. M. (1998, June). Asian Americans: Diverse and growing. *Population Bulletin, 53*(2).

Leipzig, J. (1987). Parents as partners. *Day Care and Early Education, 15*(2), 36–37.

Lerner, J., Mardell-Czudnowski, C., & Goldenberg, D. (1987). *Special education for the early childhood years.* Upper Saddle River, NJ: Prentice Hall.

Levenstein, P. (1988). *Messages from home: The mother-child program.* Columbus: Ohio State University Press.

Levenstein, P., Levenstein, S., Shiminski, J. A., & Stolzberg, J. E. (1998). Long-term impact of a verbal interaction program for at-risk toddlers: An exploratory study of high school outcomes in a replication of the mother-child home program.

Journal of Applied Developmental Psychology, 19(2), 267–285.

Levine, J. A., Murphy, D. T., & Wilson, S. (1993). *Getting men involved: Strategies for early childhood programs.* New York: Scholastic.

Levine, J. A., & Pittinsky, T. L. (1997). *Working fathers: New strategies for balancing work and family.* Reading, MA: Addison-Wesley.

Levine, M., & Levine, A. (1992). *Helping children: A social history.* New York: Oxford University Press.

Levit, E. M., Terman, D. L., & Behrman, R. E. (1997). Children and poverty: Analysis and recommendations. *The Future of Children: Children and Poverty 7*(2), 40–54.

Lewis, J. K. (1992). Death and divorce: Helping students cope in single-parent families. *NASSP Bulletin, 76*(543), 55–60.

Lines, P. (1991). Home instruction: The size and growth of the movement. In J. Van Galen & M. A. Pitman (Eds.), *Home schooling: Political, historical, and pedagogical perspective* (pp. 9–42). Norwood, NJ: Ablex.

Lines, P. (1996). *Homeschooling.* Washington, DC: Office of Educational Research and Improvement, U.S. Department of Education. (ERIC Document Reproduction Service No. ED965033)

Lines, P. M. (1982a). *Compulsory education laws and their impact on public and private education.* Denver, CO: Education Commission of the States.

Liontos, L. B. (1992). *At risk families and schools: Becoming partners.* Eugene, OR: ERIC Clearinghouse on Education.

Lipsky, D. K., & Gartner, A. (1989). Overcoming school failure: A vision for the future. In F. J. Macchiarola & A. Gartner (Eds.), *Caring for America's children, 37*(2). New York: The Academy of Political Science.

Little Soldier, L. (1985). To soar with the eagles: Enculturation and acculturation of Indian children. *Childhood Education, 62*(2), 185–191.

Locke, J. (1989). *Some thoughts concerning education* (J. W. Yolton & J. S. Yolton, Eds.). Oxford: Clarendon.

Lombardi, J. (1992). Beyond transition: Ensuring continuity in early childhood services. *ERIC Digest.* Urbana, IL: ERIC Clearinghouse on Elementary and Early Childhood Education (ED345867).

Lorence, B. W. (1974). Parents and children in eighteenth century Europe. *History of Childhood Quarterly: The Journal of Psychohistory, 2*(1), 1–30.

Loucks, H. (1992). Increasing parent/family involvement: Ten ideas that work. *NASSP Bulletin, 76*(543), 19–23.

Love, J. M., Schochet, P. Z., & Meckstrom, A. (1996). *Are they in any real danger? Children's well-being.* Princeton, NJ: Mathematica Policy Research.

Lowenthal, B. (2001). *Abuse and neglect.* Baltimore: Brookes.

Lyons, P., Robbins, A., & Smith, A. (1983). *Involving parents in schools: A handbook for participation.* Ypsilanti, MI: High/Scope Press.

Macchiarola, F. J., & Gartner, A. (Eds.). (1989). *Caring for America's children. 37*(2). New York: The Academy of Political Science.

Malaguzzi, L. (1993, November). For an education based on relationships. *Young Children, 49*(1). 9–12.

Manning, B. H. (1985). Conducting a worthwhile parent-teacher conference. *Education, 105*(4), 342–348.

Manning, D. T., & Wootten, M. D. (1987). What stepparents perceive schools should know about blended families. *The Clearing House, 60*(5), 230–235.

Manning, M. L. (1992). Parent education programs at the middle level. *NASSP Bulletin, 76*(543), 24–29.

Margolis, H., & Brannigan, G. G. (1986). Relating to angry parents. *Academic Therapy, 21*(3), 343–346.

Marsh, D. (1992). Enhancing instructional leadership: Lessons from the California School Leadership Academy. *Education & Urban Society, 24*(3), 386–409.

Martin, P. & Widgren, J. (2002, March). International migration: Facing the challenge. *Population Bulletin, 57*(1). Washington, DC: Population Reference Bureau.

Maslach, C. (1982). *Burnout: The cost of caring.* Upper Saddle River, NJ: Prentice Hall.

Maslow, A. H. (1968). *Toward a psychology of being.* Princeton, NJ: D. Norstrand.

Mauldin, T. A. (1990). Women who remain above the poverty level in divorce: Implications for family policy. *Family Relations 39*(2), 141–146.

Mayberry, M. (1989). Home-based education in the United States: Demographics, motivations, and educational implications. *Educational Review, 41*(2), 171–180.

Maynard, R. A. (Ed.). (1997). *Kids having kids: Economic costs and social consequences of teen pregnancy.* Washington, DC: Urban Institute Press.

McCormick, L., & Holden, R. (1992). Homeless children: A special challenge. *Young Children, 47*(6), 61–67.

McLean Hospital. (2000, December). McLean researchers document brain damage linked to child abuse and neglect. Retrieved May 20, 2002, from *http://www.mcleanhospital.org/PublicAffairs/20001214_child_abuse.htm*

McLearn, K. T., Davis, K., Schoen, C., & Parker, S. (1998). Listening to parents: A national survey of parents with young children. (Reprinted from the *Archives of Pediatrics and Adolescent Medicine, 152,* March 1998.) New York: The Commonwealth Fund.

Mead, M., & Wolfenstein, M. (1963). *Childhood in contemporary cultures.* Chicago: University of Chicago Press.

Meadows, B. J., & Saltzman, M. (2000). *Building school communities: Strategies for leaders.* Golden, CO: Fulcrum Resources.

MELD. (1988). *MELD's Young Moms (MYM): Information and support for teen mothers.* Minneapolis, MN: Author.

MELD. (1990). *Blending information and support for parents.* Minneapolis, MN: Author.

Meyer v. Nebraska, 262 U.S. 390, 399 (1923).

Meyerhoff, M. K., & White, B. L. (1986). New parents as teachers. *Educational Leadership, 44*(3), 42–46.

Meyers, K., & Pawlas, G. (1989). Simple steps assure parent-teacher conference success. *Instructor, 99*(2), 66–67.

Michel, G. J. (1996). *Building schools: The new school and community relations.* Lancaster, PA: Technomic.

Middlekauff, R. (1969). Education in colonial America. In J. A. Johnson, H. W. Collins, V. L. Dupuis, & J. H. Johansen (Eds.), *Foundations of American education: Readings.* Boston: Allyn & Bacon.

Miller v. California, 413 U.S. 15 (1973).

Miller, S., Wackman, S., Nunnally, F., & Miller, P. (1988). *Connecting with self and others.* Littleton, CO: Interpersonal Communication Programs.

Mischley, M., Stacy, E. W., Mischley, L., & Dush, D. (1985). A parent education project for low income families. *Prevention in Human Services, 3,* 45–57.

Missouri Department of Elementary and Secondary Education (1999). *School entry assessment project.* Jefferson City, MO: Author.

Moles, O. C. (1987). Who wants parent involvement? Interest, skills, and opportunities among parents and educators. *Education and Urban Society, 19*(2), 137–145.

Moles, O. C. (Ed.). (1996a). *Reaching all families: Creating family-friendly schools.* Washington, DC: U.S. Department of Education, Office of Educational Research and Improvement.

Moles, O. C. (1996b). New national directions in research and policy. In A. Booth & J. F. Dunn (Eds.), *School-family links: How do they affect educational outcomes?* Mahwah, NJ: Erlbaum.

Moody, E. (1775/1972). The school of good manners: Composed for the help of parents in teaching children how to behave during their minority. In D. J. Rothman & S. M. Rothman (Eds.), *The colonial American family: Collected essays.* New York: Arno Press.

Moore, R. L. (1974). Justification without joy: Psychohistorical reflections on John Wesley's childhood and conversion. *History of Childhood Quarterly: The Journal of Psychohistory, 1*(3), 31–52.

Mork, O. (1998). Playing processes—Art processes. In A. Curtis (Ed.), *International Journal of Early Childhood: 50th Anniversary Issue OMEP 30*(1), 20–26.

Morrison, G. S. (1991). *Early childhood education today* (5th ed.). New York: Macmillan.

MSU Extension. (1999). Group effectiveness: Understanding group member roles. Retrieved August 27, 2002, from *http://www.msue.msu.edu/msue/imp/modii/ii719202.html*

Mullins, J. B. (1987). Authentic voices from parents of exceptional children. *Family Relations, 36*(1), 30–33.

Nagi, S. Z. (1977). *Child maltreatment in the United States.* New York: Columbia University Press.

Nagle v. Olin, 415 N.E.2d 279 (Ohio, 1980).

Napier, R. W., & Gershenfeld, M. K. (1981). *Groups, theory, and experience* (2nd ed.). Boston: Houghton Mifflin.

Natale, J. A. (1995, July). Home, but not alone: Home schoolers are linking up with e-mail and on-line classes. *American School Board Journal 182*(7), 34–36.

National Association for the Education of Young Children (NAEYC) & National Association of Early Childhood Specialists in State Departments of Education. (1991). Guidelines for appropriate curriculum content and assessment in programs serving children ages 3 through 8. *Young Children, 46*(3), 21–38.

National Association of Elementary School Principals. (1990). *Early childhood education and the elementary school principal: Standards for quality programs for young children.* Alexandria, VA: Author.

National Association of Elementary School Principals. (1994). *Best ideas from America's blue ribbon schools.* Thousand Oaks, CA: Corwin Press.

National Association of State Boards of Education (NASBE). (1988). *Right from the start*. Alexandria, VA: Author.

National Association of State Boards of Education. (1991). *Caring communities: Supporting young children and families*. Alexandria, VA: Author.

National Association of State Directors of Special Education. (1997). *1997 amendments to the Individuals With Disabilities Education Act*. Washington, DC: Author.

National Center for Early Development & Learning. (1997). *Early childhood research and policy briefs, 1*(1). Chapel Hill, NC: Frank Porter Graham Child Development Center.

National Center for Education Statistics. (2001, March). National Assessment of Educational Progress History—Time spent on homework. Retrieved June 21, 2002, from *http://nces.ed.gov/ nationsreportcard/ushistory/findhomework.asp*

National Center for Education Statistics. (2002). Children's reading and mathematics achievement in kindergarten and first grade. Retrieved May 25, 2002, from *http://nces.ed.gov/pubs2002/kindergarten/ 5.asp?nav=1*

National Center on Child Abuse and Neglect (NCCAN). (2001). Child abuse and neglect state statutes elements. Definitions of child abuse and neglect. Retrieved May 20, 2002, from *http://www.calib. com/nccanch/pubs/stats01/define/indes.cfm*

National Center for Family Literacy (2002). *Family and child education (FACE)*. Retrieved January 11, 2003 from *http://www.famlit.org/faqs/faqface.html*

National Center on Fathers and Families (2002). *Fathering indicators framework; a tool for quantitative and qualitative analysis*. Philadelphia, PA: Author.

National Child Abuse and Neglect Data System (NCANDS). (2002, April). *Summary of key findings from calendar year 2000*. Washington, DC: U.S. Department of Health and Human Services, Children's Bureau, Administration on Children, Youth and Families, National Clearinghouse on Child Abuse and Neglect Information. Retrieved July 9, 2002, from *http://www.calib.com/nccanch/pubs/factsheets/ canstats.cfm*

National Child Abuse Coalition. (1991). *Corporal punishment*. Washington, DC: Author.

National Commission on Children. (1991). *Beyond rhetoric: A new American agenda for children and families*. Washington, DC: Author.

National Commission on Excellence in Education. (1983). *A nation at risk: The imperative for educational reform*. Washington, DC: U.S. Department of Education.

National Council on Disability. (2002, July). Individuals with disabilities education act reauthorization: Where do we really stand? Retrieved August 2, 2002, from *http://www.ncd.gov/newsroom/publications/ synthesis_07-05-02.html*

National Dissemination Association & National Diffusion Network. (1993). *Educational programs that work*. Longmont, CO: Sopris West.

National Education Goals Panel. (1991). *The national education goals report: Building a nation of learners, executive summary*. Washington, DC: Author.

National Information Center for Children and Youth with Disabilities. (1997). *NICHCY documents on disabilities*. Washington, DC: Author.

National Information Center for Children and Youth with Disabilities. (1998). IDEA amendments of 1997. *NICHCY News Digest 26* (Rev. ed.). Washington, DC: Author.

National Information Center for Children and Youth with Disabilities. (2000, February). Reading and learning disabilities. Retrieved on August 7, 2002, from *http://www.nichy.org/pubs/factshe/fs17text.htm*

National Information Center for Children and Youth with Disabilities. (2001, December). Attention deficit/hyperactivity disorder (AD/HD). Retrieved August 7, 2002, from *http://www.nichcy.org/ pubs/factshe/fs19txt.htm*

National Information Center for Children and Youth with Disabilities. (2002a, January). Mental retardation. Retrieved August 7, 2002, from *http:// www.nichcy.org/pubs/factshe/fa8txt.htm*

National Information Center for Children and Youth with Disabilities. (2002b, April). Learning disabilites. Retrieved August 7, 2002, from *http:// www.nichcy.org/pubs/factshe/fs7txt.htm*

National Information Center for Children and Youth with Disabilities, Early Childhood Research Network. (1996). Characteristics of infant child care: Factors contributing to positive caregiving. *Early childhood Research Quarterly, 11*, 269–306.

National Law Center on Homelessness & Poverty. (2002a). Homelessness and poverty in America. Retrieved March 18, 2002, from *http://www.nlchp. org/FA_HAPIA/*

National Law Center on Homelessness & Poverty. (2002b). *McKinney-Vento 2001 reauthorization—at a glance.* Retrieved March 18, 2002, from *http://www. nichp.org/FA_Education/mckinneyGlance.cfn*

National Reading Panel (2000). *Teaching children to read: An evidence-based assessment of the scientific research literature on reading and the implication for reading instruction reports of the subgroups.* Washington, DC: National Institute of Child Health and Human Development.

National Society for the Study of Education. (1929). *Twenty-eighth year book. Preschool and parent education (parts 1 and 2).* Bloomington, IL: Public School Publishing.

New Jersey State Federation. (1989, May). *CEC newsletter.* New Brunswick, NJ: Council for Exceptional Children.

New Jersey v. T.L.O., 469 U.S. 325 (1985).

Newman, F. (1996). Introduction. In Education Commission of the States, *Bridging the gap between neuroscience and education.* Denver, CO: Author.

Newman, L. (1996). Response. In Education Commission of the States, *Bridging the gap between neuroscience and education.* Denver, CO: Author.

Nimnicht, G. P., & Brown, E. (1972). The toy library: Parents and children learning with toys. *Young Children, 28*(2), 110–116.

Noller, P., & Taylor, R. (1989). Parent education and family relations. *Family Relations, 38*(2), 196–200.

Northwest EQUALS. (1988). *Family science.* Portland, OR: Portland State University.

Norton, A. J., & Glick, P. C. (1986). One parent families: A social and economic profile. *Family Relations, 35*(1), 9–17.

Nunez, R. da Costa. (1996). *The new poverty: Homeless families in America.* New York: Plenum Press.

O'Callaghan, J. B. (1993). *School-based collaboration with families.* San Francisco: Jossey-Bass.

O'Connell, M., & Bloom, D. E. (1987). *Juggling jobs and babies: America's child care challenge. Population Bulletin,* No. 12. Washington, DC: Population Reference Bureau.

Office of the Ombudsman (1998). *Information manual.* Retrieved June 29, 2002 from *http://www.ir/gov.ie/ ombudsman/2362156.htm*

Olesen v. Board of Education of School District No. 228, 676 F. Supp. 820 D.C. N.D.III. (1987).

Osborn, A. F. (1957). *Applied imagination.* New York: Scribner's.

Osborn, D. K. (1991). *Early childhood education in historical perspective* (3rd ed.). Athens, GA: Education Associates. P.L. 94–142, Part B of the Education of

All Handicapped Children Act, Title 20 of the United States Code, Sections 1400–1420. Regulations, Title 34 of the Code of Federal Regulations, Sections 300.1–300.754 and Appendix C, IEP Notice of Interpretation.

Osofsky, J. D., & Fenichel, E. (1996). *Islands of safety: Assessing and treating young victims of violence.* Washington, DC: Zero to Three.

Packer, A., Hoffman, S., Bozler, B., & Bear, N. (1976). Home learning activities for children. In I. Gordon & W. F. Breivogel (Eds.), *Building effective home-school relationships.* Boston: Allyn & Bacon.

Papernow, P. L. (1993). *Becoming a stepfamily.* San Francisco: Jossey-Bass.

Pardeck, J. T. (1989). Family therapy as a treatment approach to child maltreatment. *Early Child Development and Care, 42,* 151–157.

Parents Anonymous. (1985). *The program development manual.* Los Angeles: Author.

Parents as Teachers National Center. (2002). What's new. Retrieved September, 2002, from *http://www. patnc.org/forpatprograms-whatsnew.asp*

Parks, C. C. (1982). *The siege: The first eight years of an autistic child with an epilogue, fifteen years after.* Boston: Little, Brown.

Paulu, N. (1995). *Helping your child with homework for parents of elementary and junior high school-aged children.* Washington, DC: Office of Educational Research and Improvement, U.S. Department of Education.

PEAK Parent Center. (1997). IDEA 97 and the tie to the general curriculum. Module 9–1. Colorado Springs, CO: Parent Education and Assistance for Kids (PEAK).

Pearl, P. (1988). Working with preschool aged child abuse victims in group settings. *Child and Youth Care Quarterly, 17*(3), 185–194.

Pennsylvania Association for Retarded Children v. Commonwealth of Pennsylvania, 343 F. Supp. (E.D. Penn. 1972).

Pennsylvania Department of Public Instruction. (1935). *Parent education.* Bulletin 86. Harrisburg: Author.

Pestalozzi, F. J. (1915). *How Gertrude teaches her children.* London: Allen & Unwin.

Pestalozzi, F. J. (1951). *The education of man.* New York: Philosophical Library.

Piaget, J. (1976). *To understand is to invent.* New York: Penguin Books.

Pierce v. Society of Sisters of the Holy Name, 268 U.S. 510 (1925).

Pierson, D. E., Bronson, M. B., Dromey, E., Swartz, J. P., Tivnan, T., & Walker, D. K. (1983). The impact of early education: Measured by classroom observations and teacher ratings of children in kindergarten. *Evaluation Review, 7*(2), 191–216.

Pierson, D. E., Walker, D. K., & Tivnan, T. (1984). A school-based program from infancy to kindergarten for children and their parents. *The Personnel and Guidance Journal, 62*(8), 448–455.

Plato. (1953). *The dialogues of Plato* (4th ed., B. Jowett, Trans.). London: Oxford University Press. (Original work published 1871.)

Popkin, M. H. (2002). *Active parenting now.* Marietta, GA: Active Parenting. Retrieved September 12, 2002, from *http://www.activeparenting.com/xapn.htm*

Popp, J. (1987, October). Personal correspondence. *Revision winning play at first base.* Yakima, WA: Author.

Population Reference Bureau, AmeriStat. (2002). Single mothers still a small fraction of the U.S. labor force. Retrieved March 16, 2002, from *http://www.prb.org/ AmeristatTemplate.cfm?Section=Labor_Employment& template=/Contentmanagement/ContentDisplay.cfn& ContentID=2731*

Post-Kammer, P. (1988). Does Parents Anonymous reduce child abuse? *Education Digest, 54*(3), 33–39.

Potts, M. (1992, March). Strengths model. *National Center for Family Literacy, 4*(1), 5.

Powell, D. R. (1986). Parent education and support programs. *Young Children, 41*(3), 47–53.

Pruett, K. D. (1996). Child development: The difference a dad makes. *Family Resource Coalition Report, 15*(1), 8–10.

Puckett, M. Marshall, C. S., and Davis, R. (1999, Fall). Examining the emergence of brain development research: The promises and the perils. *Childhood Education 74*(1), 8–12.

Radencich, M. C., & Schumm, J. S. (1996). *How to help your child with homework* (2nd ed.). Minneapolis, MN: Free Spirit.

Ramey, C. T., & Ramey, S. L. (1993). Home visiting programs and the health and development of young children. *The Future of Children: Home Visiting, 3*(3), 129–139.

Rauche-Elnekave, H. (1989). Advocacy and ombudswork for children: Implications of the Israeli experience. *Child Welfare, 68*(2), 101–112.

Ray, B. D., & Wartes, J. (1991). The academic achievement and affective development of home-schooled children. In H. Van Galen & M. A. Pitman (Eds.), *Home schooling: Political, historical, and pedagogical perspective* (pp. 43–62). Norwood, NJ: Ablex.

Reed, J. (1991). Grass roots school governance in Chicago. *National Civic Review, 80*(1), 41–45.

Reich, K., Culross, P. L., & Behrman, R. E. (2002, Summer/Fall). Children, youth, and gun violence: Analysis and recommendations. *The Future of Children: Children, Youth, and Gun Violence, 12*(2), 5–23.

Reinert, H. R. (1987). *Children in conflict: Educational strategies for the emotionally disturbed and behaviorally disordered* (3rd ed.). Upper Saddle River, NJ: Merrill/Prentice Hall.

Reppucci, N. D., Britner, P. A., & Woolard, J. L. (1997). *Preventing child abuse and neglect through parent education.* Baltimore: Brookes.

Rich, D. (1988). *Megaskills: How families can help children succeed in school and beyond.* Boston: Houghton Mifflin.

Rich, D., & Mattox, B. (1977). *101 activities for building more effective school-community involvement.* Washington, DC: Home and School Institute.

Riggs, R. C. (1982). Incest: The school's role. *The Journal of School Health, 52,* 365–370.

Rigsby, L. C., Reynolds, M. C., & Wang, M. C. (Eds.). (1995). *School-community connections: Exploring issues for research and practice.* San Francisco: Jossey-Bass.

Rioux, J. W., & Berla, N. (1993). *Innovations in parent and family involvement.* Princeton, NJ: Eye on Education.

Rogers, C. (1983). *Freedom to learn for the '80s.* Upper Saddle River, NJ: Merrill/Prentice Hall.

Ronstrom, A. (1989). Sweden's children's ombudsman: A spokesperson for children. *Child Welfare, 68*(2), 123–128.

Rose, L. C., & Gallup, A. M. (2000). The 32nd Annual Phi Delta Kappa/Gallup Poll of the public's attitudes toward the public schools. *Phi Delta Kappan.* Retrieved July 31, 2002, from *http://www.pdkintl. org/kappan/kpol0009.htm#2a*

Rose, L. C., & Gallup, A. M. (2001). The 33rd annual Phi Delta Kappa/Gallup Poll of the public's attitudes toward the public schools. *Phi Delta Kappan.* Retrieved July 31, 2002, from *http://www.pdkintl. org/kappan/k0109gal.htm*

Rose, L. C., Gallup, A. M., & Elam, S. M. (1997). The 29th annual Gallup Phi Delta Kappa Poll of the public's attitudes toward public schools. *Phi Delta Kappan, 79*(1), 41–56.

Rosenblatt, P. C. (1994). *Metaphors of family systems theory: Toward new constructions.* New York: Guilford Press.

Rotter, J. C., & Robinson, E. H. (1986). *Parent-teacher conferencing: What research says to the teacher.* Washington, DC: National Education Association of the United States.

Rousseau, J. J. (1979). *Emile: Education* (A. Bloom, Trans.). New York: Basic Books. (Original work published 1762.)

Rutter, M. (1981). *Maternal deprivation reassessed.* Harmondsworth, England: Penguin Books.

Rutter, M. (1985). Family and school influences on cognitive development. *Journal of Child Psychology and Psychiatry, 26*(5), 683–704.

Ryan, G. (1989). Victim to victimizer: Re-thinking victim treatment. *Journal of Interpersonal Violence, 4*(3), 325–341.

Reich, K., Culross, P. L., & Behrman, R. E. (2002, Summer/Fall). Children, youth, and gun violence. *The Future of Children, 12*(2), 5–23.

Sandberg, D. N. (1987). *Chronic acting-out students and child abuse: A handbook for intervention.* Lexington, MA: Lexington Books.

Save the Children. (2000). The history of children@risk. Retrieved June 29, 2002, from *http://www. reddbarna.no/english/children_at_risk/history/*

Schimmel, D., & Fischer, L. (1987). *Parents, schools and the law.* Columbia, MD: National Committee for Citizens in Education.

Schlossman, S. L. (1976). Before Home Start: Notes toward a history of parent education in America, 1897–1929. *Harvard Educational Review, 46*(3), 436–467.

Schorr, L. B., & Schorr, D. (1988). *Within our reach: Breaking the cycle of disadvantage.* New York: Doubleday.

Schweinhart, L. J., Barnes, H. V., & Weikart, D. P. (1993). *Significant benefits: The High/Scope Perry Preschool student through age 27.* Ypsilanti, MI: High/Scope Press.

Section 504 Regulations, Title 34 of the Federal Regulations, Sections 104.1–104.61 and Appendix A: Analysis of Final Regulations (29 U.S.C. § 794).

Seefeldt, C. (1985). Parent involvement: Support or stress. *Childhood Education, 62*(2), 98–102.

Seeley, D. S. (1989). A new paradigm for parent involvement. *Educational Leadership, 47*(2), 46–48.

Seligman, M. (2000). *Conducting effective conferences with parents of children with disabilities.* New York: Guilford Press.

Shapiro, I., & Greenstein, R. (1988). *Holes in the safety net.* Washington, DC: Center on Budget and Policy Priorities.

Shaw, D. S. (1992). The effects of divorce on children's adjustment. In M. E. Procidano & C. B. Fisher (Eds.), *Contemporary families: A handbook for school professionals.* New York: Teachers College Press.

Shearer, D., Billingsley, J., Frohman, A., Hilliard, J., Johnson, F., & Shearer, M. (1976). *Portage Project readings.* Portage, WI: Portage Project.

Shields, M. K., & Behrman, R. E. (2000). Children and computer technology: Analysis and recommendations. *The Future of Children: Children and Computer Technology, 10*(2), 4–30.

Shiono, P. H., & Quinn, L. S. (1994). Epidemiology of divorce. *The Future of Children: Children and Divorce, 4*(1), 15–28.

Shipman, V. C., Boroson, M., Bidgeman, B., Gart, J., & Mikovsky, M. (1976). *Disadvantaged children and their first school experiences.* Princeton, NJ: Educational Testing Service.

Shore, R. (1997). *Rethinking the brain.* New York: Families and Work Institute.

Sigel, I. E. (1971). Language and the disadvantaged: The distancing hypothesis. In C. S. Lavatelli (Ed.), *Language training in early childhood education.* Urbana: University of Illinois Press.

Silver, A. A., & Hagin, R. A. (2002). *Disorders of learning in childhood.* New York: Wiley.

Silver, H. K., & Kempe, C. H. (1959). Problems of parental criminal neglect and severe physical abuse of children. *American Journal of Diseases of Children 95,* 528.

Silverman, F. (1953). Roentgen manifestations of unrecognized skeletal trauma in infants. *American Journal of Roentgenology, 69,* 413–427.

Silvern, S. B. (1988). Continuity/discontinuity between home and early childhood education environments. *The Elementary School Journal, 89*(2), 147–159.

Skeels, H. (1966). Adult status of children with contrasting early life experiences: A follow-up study. In *Monographs of the Society for Research in Child Development* (Vol. 31). Chicago: University of Chicago Press.

Skeels, H. M., & Dye, H. B. (1939). A study of the effects of differential stimulation on mentally retarded children. *Proceedings and Addresses of the American Association on Mental Deficiency, 44,* 114–136.

Smith, V. (1986). Listening. In O. Hargie (Ed.), *A handbook of communication skills* (pp. 246–265). Washington Square: New York University Press.

Spidel, J. (1980, March). *Exceptional students in the regular classroom: How we help them learn.* Paper presented at Showcase Kansas, Wichita State University, Wichita, KS.

Spitz, R. A. (1945). Hospitalism: An inquiry into the genesis of psychiatric conditions in early childhood. In A. Freud et al. (Eds.), *The psychoanalytic study of the child* (Vol. 2). New York: International Universities Press.

Spitz, R. A. (1965). *The first year of life.* New York: International Universities Press.

Spock, B. (1957). *Baby and child care.* New York: Pocket Book.

Spodek, B. (Ed.). (1982). *Handbook of research on early childhood education.* New York: Free Press/Macmillan.

St. Pierre, R. G., Layzer, J. I., & Barnes, H. V. (1995). Two generation programs: Design, cost, and short-term effectiveness. *The Future of Children: Long-Term Outcomes of Early Childhood Programs 5*(3), 76–93.

Stahlman, B. R. (2002). Personal communication.

Stahlman, K. (2002). Personal communication.

State of Hawaii, Department of Health. (1997, October). *Innovations in American government recognizes Hawai'i Healthy Start for Program Excellence.* Honolulu: Author.

State v. Faith Baptist Church, 107 Neb. 802, N.W.2d 571 (1981).

State v. Shaver, 294 N.W.2d 883 (N.D. 1980).

Steele, B. F. (1986). Notes on the lasting effects of early child abuse throughout the life cycle. *Child Abuse and Neglect, 10,* 283–291.

Steele, B. F. (1987). C. Henry Kempe memorial lecture. *Child Abuse and Neglect, 11,* 313–318.

Stein, M. R. S., & Thorkildsen, R. J. (1999). *Parental involvement in education: Insights and applications from the research.* Bloomingham, IN: Phi Delta Kappa International.

Stein, N., & Sjostrom, L. (1994). *Flirting or hurting? A teacher's guide to student-to-student sexual harassment in schools (grades 6 through 12).* Washington, DC: NEA Professional Library.

Stein, N. (1996). *Bullyproof: A teacher's guide on teasing and bullying for use with fourth and fifth grade stu-*

dents. Washington, DC: Wesley College Center for Research on Women and NEA Professional Library.

Stendler, C. B. (1950). Sixty years of child training practices. *Journal of Pediatrics, 36*(1), 122–134.

Stevens, J. H., Jr. (1982). Support systems for black families. In J. D. Quisenberry (Ed.), *Changing family lifestyles.* Wheaton, MD: Association for Childhood Education International.

Stinnett, N., & DeFrain, J. (1985). *Secrets of strong families.* Boston: Little, Brown.

Stouffer, B. (1992). We can increase parent involvement in secondary schools. *NASSP Bulletin, 75,* 5–8.

Stronge, J. H. (Ed.). (1992). *Educating homeless children and adolescents: Evaluating policy and practice.* Newbury Park, CA: Sage.

Stronge, J. H., & Helm, V. A. (1991). Legal barriers to the education of homeless children and youth: Residency and guardianship issues. *Journal of Law & Education, 20*(2), 201–218.

Sui, S. (1994). Taking no chances: A profile of Chinese-American family support for school success. *Equity and Choice, 10*(2), 23–32.

Summit, R. C. (1983). The child sexual abuse accommodation syndrome. *Child Abuse and Neglect, 7,* 177–193.

Sunley, R. (1955). Early nineteenth-century American literature on child rearing. In M. Mead & M. Wolfenstein (Eds.), *Childhood in contemporary cultures* (pp. 150–163). Chicago: University of Chicago Press.

The Supreme Court's decisions of note. (1993, July 19–25). *The Washington Post National Weekly Edition,* p. 9.

Swap, S. M. (1990). Comparing three philosophies of home-school collaboration. *Equity and Choice, 63,* 9–19.

Swick, K. J. (1983, April). Parent education: Focus on parents' needs and responsibilities. *Dimensions,* 9–12.

Swick, K. J. (1986). Parents as models in children's cultural development. *The Clearing House, 60*(2), 72–75.

Swick, K. J. (1997). A family-school approach for nurturing caring in young children. *Early Childhood Education Journal 25*(2), 151–154.

Swick, K. J. (1999). Empowering homeless and transient children/families: An ecological framework for early childhood education. *Early Childhood Education Journal, 26*(3), 195–201.

Swick, K. J. (2001). Nurturing decency through caring and serving during the early childhood years. *Early Childhood Education Journal, 23*(2), 131–137.

Swick, K. J., & Manning, M. L. (1983). Father involvement in home and school settings. *Childhood Education, 60*(2), 128–134.

Swick, K., Varner, J., & McClellan, S. (1991, November). *Toward an evaluation framework for statewide parent education.* Paper presented at the meeting of the National Association for the Education of Young Children, Denver, CO.

Swick, K. J., Da Ros, D. A., & Kovach, B. A. (2001). Empowering parents and families through a caring inquiry approach. *Early Childhood Education Journal, 29*(1), 65–71.

Taylor, K. W. (1981). *Parent and children learn together: Parent cooperative nursery schools.* New York: Teachers College Press.

Tebes, J. K., Grady, K., & Snow, D. L. (1989). Parent training in decision-making facilitation: Skill acquisition and relationship gender. *Family Relations, 38*(3), 243–247.

The Children's Ombudsman. (1998). *The children's ombudsman in Sweden.* Retrieved June 29, 2002 from *http://www.bo.se/eng/engelsk.asp*

Thompson, F. (1988). Shelley. In D. C. Browning (Ed.), *Dictionary of quotations and proverbs.* Secaucus, NJ: Chartwell Books.

Thompson, R. W., Grow, C. R., Ruma, P. R., Daly, D. L., & Burke, R. V. (1993). *Family Relations, 42*(1), 21–25.

Thornton, A., & Freedman, D. (1983). The changing American family. *Population Bulletin,* No. 38, 4. Washington, DC: Population Reference Bureau.

Tinker v. Des Moines Independent Community School District, 393 U.S. 503 (1969).

Tizard, J., & Hodges, J. (1978). The effect of early institutional rearing on the development of eight-year-old children. *Journal of Child Psychology and Psychiatry, 19*(2), 99–118.

Tower, C. C. (1992). *The role of educators in the protection and treatment of child abuse and neglect.* Washington, DC: U.S. Department of Health and Human Services, National Center on Child Abuse and Neglect.

Turbiville, V., Umbarger, G. T. III, & Guthrie, A. C. (2000, July). Fathers' involvement in programs for young children. *Young Children, 55,*(4).

Turnbull, A. P., & Turnbull, H. R. III. (1985). *Parents speak out: Then and now* (2nd ed.). Upper Saddle River, NJ: Merrill/Prentice Hall.

Turnbull, A. P., & Turnbull, H. R. III (1997). *Families, professionals, and exceptionality: A special partnership* (3rd ed.). Upper Saddle River, NJ: Merrill/Prentice Hall.

Turnbull, H. R., & Turnbull, A. P. (1998). *Free appropriate public education* (5th ed.) Denver, CO: Love.

Umansky, W. (1983). On families and the re-valuing of childhood. *Childhood Education, 59*(4), 259–266.

United Nations. (1989). *United Nations convention on the rights of the child.* New York: Author

U.S. Advisory Board on Child Abuse and Neglect (1990, August). Department of Health and Human Services: Office of Human Development Services, Child Abuse and Neglect. *Critical first steps in response to a national emergency.* Washington, DC: U.S. Government Printing Office.

U.S. Advisory Board on Child Abuse and Neglect. (1993, April). In Department of Health and Human Services, Administration for Children and Families, *The continuing child protection emergency: A challenge to the nation.* Washington, DC: U.S. Government Printing Office.

U.S. Bureau of the Census. (1991a). *The Census and You, 26*(1). Washington, DC: U.S. Government Printing Office.

U.S. Bureau of the Census. (1991c). *The Census and You, 26*(11). Washington, DC: U.S. Government Printing Office.

U.S. Bureau of the Census. (1991d). *The Census and You, 26*(12). Washington, DC: U.S. Government Printing Office.

U.S. Bureau of the Census. (1995, June). *Who receives child support? Statistical briefs* (SB 95–16). Washington, DC: Author.

U.S. Bureau of the Census. (1997, Spring). Who's minding the kids? Child care arrangements. Retrieved August 22, 2002, from *http://www.census. gov/prod/w2002pubs/p70-86.pdf*

U.S. Bureau of the Census. (1998). Money income in the United States: 1997 (with separate data on valuation of noncash benefits). *Current Population Reports* (P60–200). Washington, DC: U.S. Government Printing Office.

U.S. Census Bureau. (2000a). Current Population Reports (P20-515) and unpublished data. Households, families, sub/families and married couples: 1980 to 2000. Retrieved March 5, 2002, from *http://www.census.gov/prod/2001pubs/statab/ sec01.pdf*

U.S. Census Bureau. (2000b). *Current Population Survey (March 1950–2000). Poverty rates by race and Hispanic origin: 1959 to 2000.* Retrieved March 5,

2002, from *http://www.census.gov/hhes/poverty/ poverty00/povrac00.html*

U.S. Census Bureau. (2000c). *Historical poverty tables*. Retrieved March 18, 2002, from *http://www. census.gov/hhes/poverty/hispov/hispov4.html*

U.S Census Bureau. (2000d). *Income and poverty, 2000*. Retrieved February 25, 2002, from *http:// www.census.gov/hhes/income/income001/prs01/ asc.html*

U.S. Census Bureau. (2000e). *Real median household income holds steady between 1999 and 2000*. Retrieved February 25, 2002, from *http://www.census. gov/hhes/www/img/incpov00/fig01*

U.S. Census Bureau. (2001, April 25). Administrative and Customer Services Division, Statistical Compendia Branch. *Population by race and Hispanic/ Latino status*. Retrieved February 21, 2002, from *http://www.census.gov/statab/www/partla.html*

U.S. Census Bureau (2001, July). *Population briefing, National Population estimates for July, 2001*. Retrieved February 25, 2002, from *http://www.census. gov/popest/data/national/popbriefng.php*

U.S. Census Bureau, U.S. Department of Commerce News. (2001, September 25). *Nations household income stable in 2000. Poverty rate virtually equals record low*. Census Bureau Reports. Retrieved March 16, 2002, from *http://www.census gov/Press-Release/www/2001/cb01-158.html*

U. S. Census Bureau (2002). *Historical poverty tables*. Retrieved December 18, 2002 from *http://census.gov/hhes/poverty/hispoolfamindex.html*.

U.S. Department of Commerce, U.S. Bureau of the Census (2000). *Statistical Abstract of the United States, Education*. Washington, DC: Author.

U.S. Department of Education. (1980, May 9). Establishment of Title 34, Section 504, Rehabilitation Act of 1973, Rules and Regulations. *Federal Register 45*(92), 30937–30938.

U.S. Department of Education. (1986). *What works: Research about teaching and learning*. Washington, DC: U.S. Government Printing Office.

U.S. Department of Education. (1987). *Schools that work: Educating disadvantaged children*. Washington, DC: U.S. Government Printing Office.

U.S. Department of Education. (1991a). *America 2000: An education strategy*. Washington, DC: U.S. Government Printing Office.

U.S. Department of Education. (1991b). *Preparing young children for success: Guideposts for achieving our first national goal*. Washington, DC: Author.

U.S. Department of Education. (1993). *Goals 2000: Educate America*. Washington, DC: Author.

U.S. Department of Education. (1994). *Strong families, strong schools: Building community partnerships for learning*. Washington, DC: Author.

U.S. Department of Education. (1996, October 3). *United States Department of Education news: Riley announces $17 million in support for charter schools*. Washington, DC: Author.

U.S. Department of Education. (1997). *America goes back to school: The partnership for family involvement in education*. Washington, DC: Author.

U.S. Department of Education. (1998a). Partnership for family involvement in education. *Community Update*. Washington, DC: Office of Intergovernmental and Interagency Affairs.

U.S. Department of Education, Office of Intergovernmental and Interagency Affairs. (1998b). America's public opinion on education and budgets. *Community Update*. Washington, DC: Author.

U.S. Department of Education, Office of the Secretary. (2001, February). *No child left behind*. Washington, DC: Author.

U.S. Department of Education, Office for Civil Rights. (n.d.). *Student assignment in elementary and secondary schools and Title IX*. Washington, DC: Author.

U.S. Department of Education, Office of Intergovernmental and Interagency Affairs. (2002, January/February). No child left behind plan becomes law. *Community Update*. Washington, DC: Author.

U.S. Department of Education, Office of Educational Research and Improvement, Office of Educational Technology. (1997). *Parents' guide to the Internet*. Washington, DC: Author.

U.S. Department of Education, Office of Special Education and Rehabilitative Services. (1997, September). *Resource 10–4*. Washington, DC: Author.

U.S. Department of Health and Human Services, Office of Human Development Services. (1985). Administration for Children, Youth and Families, Head Start Bureau. *A guide for operating a home-based child development program*. Washington, DC: U.S. Government Printing Office.

U.S. Department of Health and Human Services, Office of Human Development Services. (1987). Administration for Children, Youth and Families, Head Start Bureau. *The Head Start home visitor handbook*. Washington, DC: U.S. Government Printing Office.

U.S. Department of Health and Human Services, Administration for Children and Families, Administration on Children, Youth and Families, National Center on Child Abuse and Neglect. (1992, March). *Child abuse and neglect: A shared community concern.* Washington, DC: U.S. Government Printing Office.

U.S. Department of Health and Human Services. Administration for Children and Families (2000). *Information memorandum: Family literacy services in Head Start and Early Head Start programs.* Retrieved January 11, 2003 from *http://www.headstartinfo. org/publications/im00/m00_25.htm*

U.S. Department of Health and Human Services, Children's Bureau. (1998). *Child maltreatment 1996: Reports from the states to the National Child Abuse and Neglect Data System.* Washington, DC: U.S. Government Printing Office.

U.S. Department of Health and Human Services (2002). *Head Start promoting early childhood development.* Retrieved January 11, 2002 from *http://www.hhs.gov/news/press/2002pres/head-start.html*

U.S. Department of Health, Education and Welfare, Children's Bureau. (1949). *Your child from 6 to 12.* Washington, DC: U.S. Government Printing Office.

U.S. Department of Health, Education and Welfare. (1962). *Your child from one to six.* Washington, DC: U.S. Government Printing Office.

U.S. Department of Health, Education and Welfare. (1974). *Home Start/Child and family resource programs. Reports of a joint conference—Home Start, child, and family resource programs.* Washington, DC: U.S. Government Printing Office.

U.S. Department of Health, Education and Welfare, Head Start Bureau, Children's Bureau, Administration for Children, Youth and Families, Office of Human Development. (1977). *Child abuse and neglect: A self-instructional text for Head Start personnel.* (Publication No. OHDS 8–31103) Washington, DC: U.S. Government Printing Office.

U.S. Department of Health, Education and Welfare, Office of Human Development. (1978). Administration for Children, Youth and Families; Head Start Bureau. *Partners with parents.* Kathryn D. Hewett et al. for Abt Associates and High/Scope Educational Research Foundation. Washington, DC: U.S. Government Printing Office.

U.S. Department of Health, Education and Welfare, Office of Human Development Services. (1979). *The rights and responsibilities of students: A handbook for the school community.* Washington, DC: U.S. Government Printing Office.

U.S. General Accounting Office. (1992, August). Report to the chairman, Oversight of Government Management Subcommittee, U.S. Senate Committee on Governmental Affairs. *Child abuse: Prevention programs need greater emphasis. Appendix I: Hawaii's Healthy Start program.* Washington, DC: Author.

Utah Parent Center. (1997). *Parents as partners in the IEP process: Information booklet.* Salt Lake City, UT: Author.

Utriainen, S. (1989). Child welfare service in Finland. *Child Welfare, 68*(2), 129–130.

Valente, W. D. (1987). *Law in the schools* (2nd ed.). Upper Saddle River, NJ: Merrill/Prentice Hall.

Vandewalker, N. C. (1971). *The kindergarten in American education.* New York: Arno Press.

Venezky, R. L. (1995). *Read write now: The partners tutoring program.* Washington, DC: U. S. Department of Education.

Vincent, C. E. (1951). Trends in infant care ideas. *Child Development, 22*(3), 199–209.

Visher, E. B., & Visher, J. S. (1979). *Stepfamilies: A guide to working with stepparents and stepchildren.* Secaucus, NJ: Citadel Press.

Vondra, J. I., & Toth, S. L. (1989). Child maltreatment research and intervention. *Early Child Development and Care, 42,* 11–24.

Vygotsky, L. S. (1978). *Mind in society: The development of psychological processes.* Cambridge, MA: Harvard University Press.

Wadsworth, B. (1712/1972). The well-ordered family: Or relative duties. In D. J. Rothman & S. M. Rothman (Eds.), *The colonial American family: Collected essays.* New York: Arno Press.

Walberg, H. F. (1984). Families as partners in educational productivity. *Phi Delta Kappan, 65*(40), 397–400.

Wallerstein, J. (1985). Effect of divorce on children. *The Harvard Medical School Mental Health Letter, 2*(3).

Wallerstein, J. S., & Kelly, J. B. (1980). The effects of parental divorce: Experience of the child in later latency. In A. Skolnick & J. H. Skolnick (Eds.), *Family in transition.* Boston: Little, Brown.

Walsh, M. E. (1992). *Moving to nowhere.* Westport, CT: Auburn.

Wanat, C. L. (1992). Meeting the needs of single-parent children: Schools and parent views differ. *NASSP Bulletin, 76*(543), 43–48.

Warner, I. (1991). Parents in touch: District leadership for parent involvement. *Phi Delta Kappan, 73*(5), 372–375.

Warren, V. B. (1963). *Tested ways to help your child learn.* Upper Saddle River, NJ: Prentice Hall.

Wasik, B. H. (1983, August). *Teaching parent problem-solving skills: A behavioral-ecological perspective.* Paper presented at the American Psychological Association Meeting, Anaheim, CA.

Wasik, B. H. (1993). Staffing issues for home visiting programs. *The Future of Children: Home Visiting, 3*(3), 140–157.

Watson, T., Brown, M., & Swick, K. J. (1983). The relationship of parents' support to children's school achievement. *Child Welfare, 72*(2), 175–180.

Weatherford, J. (1988). *Indian givers: How the Indians of the Americas transformed the world.* New York: Fawcett Columbine.

Weatherford, J. (1991). *Native roots: How the Indians enriched America.* New York: Fawcett Columbine.

Weber, E. (1969). *The kindergarten.* New York: Teachers College Press.

Webster's encyclopedic unabridged dictionary of the English language. (1989). New York: Portland House.

Webster-Stratton, C., & Hammond, M. (1990). Predictors of treatment outcome in parent training for families with conduct problem children. *Behavior Therapy, 21,* 319–337.

Weikart, D. R., & Lambie, D. A. (1968). Preschool intervention through a home teaching program. In J. Hellmuth (Ed.), *Disadvantaged child. Vol. 2: Head Start and early intervention.* New York: Brunner/Mazel.

West Virginia State Board of Education v. Barnette, 319 U.S. 624 (1943).

Westinghouse Learning Corporation & The Ohio State University. (1969). *The impact of Head Start: An evaluation of the effects of Head Start on children's cognitive and affective development.* Springfield, VA: Clearinghouse for Federal Scientific and Technical Information.

Wheeler, P. (1992). Promoting parent involvement in secondary schools. *NASSP Bulletin, 76*(543), 28–35.

White, B. L., Kaban, B. T., Attanucci, J., & Shapiro, B. B. (1973). *Experience and environment: Major influences on the development of the young child* (Vol. 1.) Upper Saddle River, NJ: Prentice Hall.

Whitebook, M., & Ginsburg, G. (Eds.). (1984). *Beyond "just working with kids": Preparing early childhood teachers to advocate for themselves and others.* Berkeley, CA: Child Care Employee Project.

Wiehe, V. R. (1989). Child abuse: An ecological perspective. *Early Child Development and Care, 42,* 141–148.

Wiehe, V. R. (1996). *Working with child abuse and neglect: A primer.* Thousand Oaks, CA: Sage.

Williams, D. L., Jr. (1992). Parental involvement teacher preparation: Challenges to teacher education. In L. Kaplan (Ed.), *Education and the family.* Boston: Allyn & Bacon.

Wilson, M. (1991). Forging partnership with preschool parents: The road to school success begins in the home. *Principal, 70*(5), 25–26.

Winerip, M. (1999, January 3). Homework bound. *Education Life.* New York: New York Times.

Winter, M. (1991, February). An overview and discussion of Parents as Teachers: A parent education project for the state of Missouri. Speech given for First Impressions, Denver, CO.

Winter, M. M. (1999, Spring/Summer). Parents as teachers. *The Future of Children: 9*(1) 179–181.

Winters, D. G. (1988). *Parents: The missing link in education reform.* (Hearing before the Select Committee on Children, Youth, and Families. House of Representatives 100th Congress. November 16, 1987.) Washington, DC: U.S. Government Printing Office.

Winters, W. G. (1993). *African American mothers and urban schools: The power of participation.* New York: Lexington Books.

Wisconsin v. Yoder, 406 U.S. 205, 233 (1972).

Wodarski, J. S., & Johnson, S. R. (1988). Child sexual abuse: Contributing factors, effects and relevant practice issues. *Family Therapy, XV*(2), 157–173.

Wolfenstein, M. (1953). Trends in infant care. *American Journal of Orthopsychiatry, 23*(1), 120–130.

Woolley, P. V., Jr., & Evans, W. A. (1955, June). Significance of skeletal lesions in infants resembling those of traumatic origin. *Journal of American Medical Association,* 539–543.

Yankelovich, Skelly, & White Inc. (1976). *Raising children in a changing society: The General Mills American family report, 1976–1977.* Minneapolis, MN: General Mills.

Youngblade, L. M., & Belsky, J. (1989). Child maltreatment, infant-parent attachment security, and dysfunctional peer relationships in toddlerhood. *Topics in Early Childhood Special Education 9*(2), 1–15.

Zeanah, C. H., & Scheeringa, M. (1996, April/May). Evaluation of posttraumatic symptomatology in infants and young children exposed to violence. In Opofsley, J. D., & Fenichel, E. (Eds.). *Islands of safety: Assessing and treating young victims of violence. Zero to Three, 16*(5), 9–14.

Zill, N. (1996). Family change and student achievement: What we have learned, what it means for schools. In A. Booth & J. F. Dunn (Eds.), *Family-school links: How do they affect educational outcomes?* Mahwah, NJ: Erlbaum.

Index

Abortion advocates/protestors, 82, 83–84
Abraham, 47
Abused/neglected children, 418–420
   associations and centers, 514
   behavior disorders and, 440–443
   brain damage, 446
   bullies, 432–434
   caring programs, 451
   communications with families, 424–425, 450–451
   community help, 452–453
   corporal punishment, in schools, 434–435
   educational neglect, 425
   elementary school children, 437
   emotional abuse, 426, 428–429
   emotional neglect, 425–426
   extent of, 421–425
   factors associated with abuse, 425, 443
   fatalities, 422–423
   history of, 418–419
   incidence of, 423–424
   indicators, 437, 438, 439
      elementary school
         children, 437
      preschool children, 437
      secondary school
         children, 439
   infant exposure to abuse, 446
   National Center on Child Abuse and Neglect
      (NCCAN), 420–421
   national response, 419, 420
   parent education, 451
   Parents Anonymous
      (1985), 452
   parents-at-risk, 14, 443–445
   physical abuse, 426, 427, 428
      resources, 508–509
   physical neglect, 425
   preschool children, 437, 453
   prevention programs, 451–453
   reporting abuse, 80, 416–418, 435–437
   resources, 508–509
   rights of children, 454–455
   school policies, development of, 448–450
   school response, 424, 452
   secondary school children, 439
   sexual abuse, 429–432
      intervention in, 453–454
      prevention tips, 455–456
      resources, 508
   shaken baby syndrome, 423
   support programs, 452
   talking with children and parents, 450–451
   toddler exposure to abuse, 446
   what is, 416
   who the abusers are, 421–422
      parents-at-risk, 14, 443–445
      talking with parents, 451
   who the victims are, 421
      talking with children, 450
   why abuse exists, 447–448
Accommodation, 20
Achord, B., 180
Active Parenting program, 214–215
Activity lending library, 168
Adams, R. L., 138
Adjustment disorder, 440
Adler, Alfred, 215
Administrative law, 462
Advocacy. See Child advocacy; Child advocates
Affluence
   in the 1980s, 81
   poverty. See Homelessness; Poverty
African Americans, 136
   1930-1954, substandard treatment, 69
   1976 study (home environment), 79
   achievements of, 136–137
   child count, 104
   college graduates, 104
   defined, 93
   emancipation of slaves, 54

equal educational opportunity, 76
helpful insights about, 137–139
high school graduates, 103
integration, 69–70
population count, 93, 94
poverty rates, 120, 121, 122
right to vote, 54
segregation, 54, 69–70
slavery, and the Civil War, 49, 53, 54
African history, 40
After-school programs, 7, 107, 154, 156, 157, 177
Ahlburg, D. A., 108
AIDS, 82, 83
Aid to Families with Dependent Children (AFDC), 83
Ainsworth, M. D., 14, 32, 80
Alaska Natives
census 2000, 94
child count, 104
defined, 93
population count, 93, 94
poverty rates, 120, 121
Alcohol, 18, 22, 81, 82
Alexander the Great, 370
Allen, M. L., 124
Altman, D. H., 420
Alumni events, 164
Alvarez, B., 24
Amato, P. R., 114
American Association of University Women (AAUW), 59
American Indians, 130–131
in the 1700s and 1800s, 49–50
1890-1900, 61
census 2000, 94
child count, 104
contributions to civilization, 131
defined, 93
education for, 132
helpful insights about, 132–133
movement west, 132
population count, 93, 94
poverty rates, 120, 121
Americans with Disabilities Act (ADA), 373
Anagnos, 371
Anastasiow, N., 23
Anatol, K. W. E., 250, 257

Ancient societies, 35
Africa, 40
the Americas, 40
Asia, 40
Egypt, 35
Greece, 36–37
Rome, 37–38
Anderson, R. C., 23
Angelou, Maya, 416
Annenberg, Leonore, 52
Annenberg, Walter H., 52
Anshutz, Thomas P., 55
Anti-bias curriculum, 128–129
Applbaum, R. L., 250, 257
Arellano, 134
Aretaeus, 370
Aries, P., 38, 41, 49
Aristotle, 33, 37, 47
Armbruster, V. B., 370
Asclepiades, 370
Asher L. J., 86
Asian history, 40
Asians/Pacific Islanders, 139
census 2000, 94
child count, 104
college graduates, 104
defined, 93
helpful insights about, 140
high school graduates, 103
language diversity, 141, 142
population count, 93, 94
poverty rates, 120, 122
Southeast Asian diversity, 139–140, 141, 142
Assimilation, 20
Attachment. See Human attachment
Attachment behavior, 10
Attanucci, J., 79
Attention-deficit disorder (ADD), 389–390, 440
Attention-deficit hyperactivity disorder (AD/HD), 389–390
Attucks, Crispus, 137
Authoritarian parents, 100, 101
Authoritative parents, 100
Autism, 388, 390

Baby decade (1940-1950), 70
Back-to-school nights, 163–164
Bakwin, H., 420
Balboa, 134

Ballantine, 111
Banks, J. A., 61, 63, 132, 136–137, 433
Bannker, 137
Barbour, N. H., 24–26
Baris, M., 433
Barnard, Henry, 33, 55–56, 57, 478
Barnes, H. V., 23, 297–298
Barnett, W. S., 79
Barton, C. E., 301
Barton, P. E., 85, 86
Bassuk, E. L., 126
Bateman, Barbara, 371
Batiste-Simeon, Jean, 43
Battered children. *See* Abused/neglected children
Bauman, 358, 360
Bavolek, S. J., 448–449, 453
Beal, G., 250, 252, 254
Beane, J., 281
Bear, N., 345
Beauvais, K. J., 405
Beck, H. L., 300
Becker, H. J., 87, 290
Beckwourth, James P., 138
Before-school programs, 7, 107, 154, 156
Behavior disorders, 440–443
   adjustment disorder, 440
   attention-deficit disorder (ADD),
      389–390, 440
   attention-deficit hyperactivity disorder (AD/HD),
      389–390
   conduct disorder, 440
Behaviorism
   1930-1940, 70
   1940-1950, 70
Behrman, R. E., 86, 447, 448, 486
Bell, Dr. Alexander Graham, 371
Bell, R. Q., 35–38, 41
Belsky, J., 15
Benasich, A. A., 318
Ben-Avie, M., 26, 287–288, 289, 290
Benne, K. D., 252
Berck, J., 126
Berger, E. H., 92, 131, 174, 360, 467
Berger, G. R., 467
Berla, N., 23
Berliner, D., 170
Berliner, L., 427
Berrueta-Clement, J. R., 79
Berry, M., 180

Besharov, D. J., 416–418, 420, 425
Bianchi, S. M., 108, 487
Biddle, B. J., 250
Bidgeman, B., 79
Bigner, J. J., 73
Billingsley, A., 138
Billingsley, J., 340
Billman, J., 300
Binder, R. L., 454
Binkley, M. R., 166, 176
Bittel, C., 126, 179
Bjorklund, G., 223
Black Americans. *See* African Americans
Blank, M. J., 319
Blended families, 116
   grandparent maintenance families, 118–119
   helpful insights about, 117–118
   stages of, 116–117
"Block walks," 129, 172
Bloom, B. S., 23, 24, 77, 150
Bloom, D. E., 81
Blow, Susan E., 44, 57
Bodaken, E. M., 250, 257
Bodrova, E., 19
Bogolub, F. B., 115
Bohlen, J. M., 250, 252, 254
Boll, E. S., 38, 46–48
Bond, J. T., 107, 111, 487
Book publishing, 169–170
Books, selection of, 474–475
Borchers, T., 250, 252
Boren, S., 389
Boroson, M., 79
Bossard, J. H. S., 38, 46–48
Bower, T. G. R., 13
Bowlby, J., 10, 12–13, 15, 32, 80
Bowlby study, 12–13
Boyer, E. L., 5, 8, 23, 28, 166
Bozler, B., 345
Bradley, R. H., 356, 357, 358
Bradshaw, C. P., 447
Brain development, 15–16
   abused/neglected children, 446
   children 0-3 years old, 16–17
   emotions, 18–19
   environment, effect of, 18
   heredity and, 18
   intellect. *See* Intellectual
      development

Brain development, *continued*
  language development, 17–18, 30
  nonlinear, 16
  "wiring" or "circuitry," 16
Brannigan, G. G., 229
Brazelton, T. B., 14, 15, 19, 21, 27, 80
Breakfasts with parents, 204
Breaux, C., 111
Bredekamp, S., 19, 25, 29
Breivogel, W. F., 349
Bridgeman, Laura, 371
Brier, J., 427
Briggs, D. C., 281
Bright, J. A., 25
Brim, O., 50, 59, 62, 65, 70–72
Britner, P. A., 453
Broadhurst, D. D., 439b
Broderick, C. B., 7
Bronfenbrenner, U., 8
Bronson, M. B., 301
Brookline Early Education Project, 300
Brooks-Gunn, J., 120, 318, 487
Brougham, Lord, 234
Brown, E., 169
Brown, M., 23, 174–175
Brown, P., 124
Bruner, 336
Bryan, Anna, 60
Bryson, K. R., 96, 119
Buck, P. S., 368, 371
Buckley Amendment, 412, 465
Buell, M. J., 300
Bulkley, J. A., 427
Bullies, 432–434
  resources, 509–510
Bullock, J. R., 433
Burger, C., 223
Burger, Chief Justice Warren E., 464
Burke, R. V., 238
Burr, W. R., 212
Bus trips, 172
Butts, R. F., 79
Byrne, G., 111

Cadogan, William, 45
Caffey, J., 420
Cain, Richard H., 138
Caldwell, B. M., 24, 77, 356, 357, 358,
  461–462, 477
Calhoun, A. W., 55

Calmady, Emily, 51
Calmady, Laura Ann, 51
Campbell, E. Q., 76
Canfield, J., 281
Canter, L., 362, 367
Career day, 170
Caring communities, 4–5
Caring families, 5–6
Caring programs, 451
Caring schools, 4–5
Carlson, C. I., 115
Carlson, M., 13
Carnivals, 166
Carper, J. C., 358
Carroll, L., 192
Cartier, Jacques, 144
Casanova, U., 170
Case, J., 430
Casper, L. M., 119, 487
Cataldo, C. Z., 100
Catholicism
  Counter-Reformation, 41
  religious schools, public money for, 464
  in the Spanish Southwest, 48
Cattell, 60
Census 2000, 93, 94, 96
Challenges, 3
Chambliss, R., 35–37
Chapman, W., 26, 314
Charles II, King, 144
Charter schools, 23, 83, 86, 464, 465
Chaudry, A., 122, 486
Child abuse. *See* Abused/neglected children
Child Abuse Prevention and Treatment Act (CAPTA)
    of 1974, 419
  sexual abuse, definition of, 429
Child advocacy, 476–477
  1970-1980, 78
  Austria, 490
  child care, 483
  European Network of Ombudsmen for Children
    (ENOC), 488, 491
  Finland, 489
  France, 490
  Hungary, 490
  Israel, 489
  Latin America, 490–491
  levels of, 478–479
  national, 482–483
  Norway, 488–489

procedure, 482
public level, 478–479, 484–485
resources, 510–511
Sweden, 489
Child advocates, 477, 479–481
administrative, 478
class actions, 478
legislative, 478
litigation, 478
parents, 484
personal level, 479–480
preparation for, 481
public level, 478–479, 484–485
role of, 480–481
Child care, 6–7
1980s governmental views, 80–81
advocacy, 483
after-school, 7, 107, 154, 156, 157, 177
before-school, 7, 107, 154, 156
during conferences, 176
preschool, 106–107
Child Care Development Fund, 85
Child care providers, 6–7
Child Development Associate (CDA) program, 82
Child count, 104, 106
Child Development Associate (CDA) program, 82
Child Find Project, 393–395
Child labor, 419
Childrearing
attachment. *See* Human attachment
father involvement, 107–110
historical beliefs/practices. *See* Ancient societies;
History; U.S. history
nurturing infants, 8–9, 99
parents posing concerns, 14–15
resources, 501–504, 511–514
working mothers, 107, 110
Children's/students' rights
abused/neglected children, 454–455
code of rights, 475–476
corporal punishment, 434–435, 473–474
disabled children. *See* Disabled children
drug testing, 468–469
flag salute, 470
free press, 469
free speech and expression, 467–468
non-English-speaking students, 474
origin of, 460–461
Pledge of Allegiance, 470
search and seizure, 468–469

sex discrimination, 472–473
suspension from school, 469–470
Child Study Association of America (CSAA), 59
Child study movement, 60
Child support, 112–113
Child welfare, 104–105
Chinese history, 40
Chinn, P. C., 220, 404–405, 407–408
Cicero, 33, 37, 57
Cisneros, 54
City families, 7
Civil War, 53–55
Civil rights
in the 1960s, 78
in the 1980s, 81
Civil Rights Act of 1964, 470
Civil Rights Act of 1965, 78
Civil War
African Americans, and slavery, 49, 53, 54
women, changes for, 54–55
Clark, R. M., 23, 139
Classroom visits, by parents, 202–203
by invitation, 204
participation visits,
203 204
Clewell, B. C., 318
Clinton, President, 479
Coan, D. L., 239, 274
Cochran, Moncrieff, 303, 314
Coffees, with parents, 172
Cognition. *See* Intellectual development
Cohen, N. E., 6
Coleman, J. S., 4, 7, 23, 76
Coletta, A. J., 413
Collaboration, 7, 23, 156, 157
generally. *See* Home-school-community
relationships
homework, 360–361
leadership. *See* Collaborative leadership
parent-teacher conferences, 215–216
school-based programs
effective collaboration, characteristics
of, 293
middle and secondary schools, 292–293
Collaborative leadership, 234
child's self-esteem, promotion of, 279–280
group discussions. *See* Parent education groups:
meetings
Internet communications, 246
knowledge/skills of leader, 244–245

Collaborative leadership, *continued*
 parent involvement, 234
  effectiveness of, 237
 personality of leader, 244
 site-based management, 235
 skills development, 234–235
 training, 243–246
College research centers, 63
Colonial America, 47–48
 families in, 49
Coloroso, B., 281
Columbus, Christopher (Christofor Colombo), 52, 54, 132, 134, 137
Comenius, J. A., 33, 41–42, 46, 57
Comer, J. P., 4, 5, 23, 26–27, 130, 138–139, 237, 282, 287–288, 289, 290
Comer's School Development Program (SDP), 26–27, 286–289
Communication, 192
 abused/neglected children, families of, 424–425, 450–451
 breakfasts with parents, 204
 classroom visits, by parents, 202–203
  by invitation, 204
  participation visits, 203–204
 computer information lines, 202
 conferences
  district or school, 166
  parent-teacher. *See* Parent-teacher conferences
  student-parent-teacher conferences, 221, 222
 Cooley's Looking-Glass-Self, 207–209
 defined, 192
 effective, 207–211
 English as second language parents, 209–210
 handbooks, 200–201
 "happy grams," 197, 198
 home visits, 202
 homework hot lines, 201–202, 302
 Internet, 246
 issues throughout the year, 231
 letters to parents, 197, 199
 listening, 209
  reflective, 210
 media, 200
 messages, 192–193
  I-you-we, 210–211
  positive, 209

 miscommunication, 193
 newsletters. *See* Newsletters
 newspapers, 197–199
 notes, 197, 198
 one-way, 193, 194–201
 parent education programs, 212–215
 parent-teacher conferences. *See* Parent-teacher conferences
 positive speaking, 209
 reframing, 211
 rephrasing, 211
 responses
  closed, 210
  open, 210
  reflective, 210
 roadblocks to, 204–205
  parent roadblocks, 205–206
  school roadblocks, 206–207
 student-parent exchange day, 204
 student-parent-school exchange, 204
 suggestion boxes, 200
 telephone calls, to parents, 202, 203
 two-way, 193–194, 201–204
 "upslips," 197, 198
 visual messages, 193
Community relationship(s). *See* Home-school-community relationships
Community resources
 home-based education, 354
 school-based programs, 323–325
Compacts, 305–306
Compulsory school attendance laws, 462–463
Computer information lines, 202
Computer technology
 impact of, 86–87
Conduct disorder, 440
Conferences
 district or school, 166
 parent-teacher. *See* Parent-teacher conferences
 student-parent-teacher conferences, 221, 222
Consortium for Longitudinal Studies (1983), 79
Constantine, Emperor, 38, 57
Constitutional law, 461
 due process, suspension and, 469–470
 flag salute, 470
 free press, 469
 free speech and expression, 467–468
 Pledge of Allegiance, 470
 racial discrimination, 470–472
 search and seizure, 468–469

Contract arrangements, 230–231
Cook, R. E., 370
Cooke, G., 362–363, 367
Cooke, S., 362–363, 367
Cooley, H. C., 208
Cooley's Looking-Glass-Self, 207–209
Coons, C. E., 358
Cooper, B. S., 26, 314
Cooper, H., 361–363
Corbin, J. N., 288
Corcoran, M. E., 122, 486
Coronado, 134, 137
Corot, Jean-Baptiste, 34
Corporal punishment abuse. *See* Abused/neglected
        children
    in schools, 434–435, 473–474
    spanking, 73
Cortes, 134
Courtland, C. D., 126
Court law, 461–462
Crane, S., 409
Cremin, L. A., 79
Crosbie-Burnett, M., 118–119
Crosson-Tower, C., 419–420
Culross, P. L., 448
Cultural diversity, 87, 129–130
    anti-bias curriculum, 128–129
    caring strategies, 130
    of community, 128
    of Hispanics, 134–135
    of self, 127–128
    of Southeast Asians, 139–140, 141, 142
    working with diverse groups, 127–129, 130
Culture, 129–130
Cupoli, J. M., 426
Curriculum
    anti-bias, 128–129
    developmentally appropriate, 24–26
        National Association for the Education of Young
                Children (NAEYC) position statement, 82
    home-based education. *See* Home-based
        education

Da Gama, Vasco, 54
Dainton, M., 117
Dalaimo, D. M., 360
Daly, D. L., 238
Daresh, J. C., 150
Darlington, R., 77, 79
Da Ros, D. A., 175, 179

DaSilva, B., 188
Dauber, S. L., 23, 26, 150, 153, 166, 170
Davies, D., 23, 150, 162, 286, 293, 303–304
Davis, 22
Davis, K., 29
Davis, M. D., 69, 71
Day, J. C., 94
Dean, C., 314
DeFrain, J., 179
De Gaetano, Y., 129
Delaney, S. W., 406
De Las Casa, Bartoleme, 54
Deluty, R. H., 238
DeMause, L., 38, 419
De Onate, Juan, 135
Derman-Sparks, L., 129–130
Dervarics, C., 86
De Soto, 134
Detachment. *See* Human attachment
Deutsch, C. P., 77
Deutsch, M., 77
Developmental continuity, 23–26
    in the 1970s, 80
Developmentally appropriate curriculum,
        24–26
    National Association for the Education of Young
            Children (NAEYC) position statement, 82
De Vita, C. J., 108
Dewey, J., 63, 66
De Zuniga, Don Manuel Osorio Manrique, 40
Dial-a-Teacher (Indianapolis), 302
Diament, D. M., 238
Dinkmeyer, D., 211–212, 215, 220
Dinkmeyer, D., Jr., 211
Dinkmeyer, J. S., 211
Disabled children
    advocacy groups (1970s), 78–79
    Americans with Disabilities Act (ADA), 373
    attention-deficit disorder (ADD), 389–390
    attention-deficit hyperactivity disorder
        (AD/HD), 389–390
    autism, 388, 390
    Child Find Project, 393–395
    communication sources, 404–405
    definitions of disabilities, 388–389
    discrimination against, 473
        filing of complaints, 412
    Education for All Handicapped Children Act of
        1975 (P.L. 94-142), 373–374, 473
        1983 amendments (P.L. 98-199), 374

Disabled children, *continued*
    1986 amendments (P.L. 99-457), 374
    emotional needs, 413
    Family Educational Rights and Privacy Act
        (FERPA), 412
    fulfillment, 413
    in Head Start, 398–399
    Individualized Education Plans (IEPs). *See*
        Individualized Education Plans (IEPs)
    Individualized Family Service Plans (IFSPs),
        376, 397
    Individuals with Disabilities Education Act (IDEA:
        P.L. 101-476), 375
        1997 amendments. *See* Individuals with
            Disabilities Education Act (IDEA 97)
    infants. *See* Infants and toddlers
    learning disabilities, 389, 390–392
    letters to parents, 405
    Maslow's hierarchy of needs, 412–413
    mental retardation, 388, 392–393
    newsletters for parents, 405
    parental involvement, 401–402
    parental reactions to, 406–407
        shared thoughts/feelings, 408–411
    parental tutoring, 402–403
    parent burnout, 411
    parent depression, 412
    parent suicide, 412
    physical needs, 413
    professional-parent communications, 403–404
    psychological needs, 413
    reaching out programs, 405–406
    resources for parents and teachers,
        497–498, 510
    self-esteem, 413
    special education history, 368–372
    students' thoughts and feelings, 407–408
    teacher burnout, 411
    teacher depression, 412
    teacher suicide, 412
    toddlers. *See* Infants and toddlers
    Vocational Rehabilitation Act of 1973 (Section
        504), 372–373
Discipline
    abusive. *See* Abused/neglected children
    corporal punishment, 434–435, 473–474
    resources, 506–507
Discontinuity, 25–26
Discrimination
    disability, 412, 473

    racial, 470–472
    sex, 472–473
District conferences, 166
District newsletters, 199
Diversity. *See* Cultural diversity
Divorce, 111–112
    economic well-being after, 112–113
    helpful insights about, 112
    resources, 505–506
Dombro, A. L., 485
Dornbusch, S., 285
Douglas, Justice William O., 464
Douglass, Frederick A., 138
Drake, Sir Francis, 144
Dreikurs, Rudolf, 215
Drew, Charles, 138
Dreyer, B. P., 126
Droegemueller, W., 420
Dromey, E., 301
Drugs, 18, 22, 81, 83
Drug testing, 468–469
Drummond, 45
Due process, suspension and, 469–470
Duncan, G. J., 120, 487
Dunlap, 315
Duro, Peter, 463
Dush, D., 238
Dye, H. B., 454
Dysfunctional parents, 100, 101

Earls, Lindsay, 469
Early Childhood Longitudinal Study, 290–292
Early Head Start, 85, 299
Eckhardt, Christopher, 468
Economic well-being
    affluence, in the 1980s, 81
    after divorce, 112–113
    poverty. *See* Homelessness; Poverty
Eddowes, E. A., 179
Edmunds, M., 439b
Education for All Handicapped Children Act of 1975
        (P.L. 94-142), 373–374, 473
    1983 amendments (P.L. 98-199), 374
    1986 amendments (P.L. 99-457), 374
Egeland, B., 430
Egypt, ancient, 35
Ehrle, J., 107
Elam, S. M., 153, 155, 364
Elementary and Secondary Education Act (ESEA), 77, 84
    reformation of, 85

Elementary schools
  abused/neglected children
      indicators, 437
  homework, 362
  newsletters, 197
  a walk-through, 293–294
Eliot, H. R., 44
Elizabeth I, Queen, 144
Elkind, D., 21, 38
Elliott, Robert B., 138
Elmer, E., 420
El Negro, Diego, 137
E-mail, 246
Emmons, C. L., 288
Emotional abuse, 426, 428–429
Emotional development, 18–19, 29
  disabled children's needs, 413
  Erikson's theory, 73
Emotional neglect, 425–426
Engle, P. L., 111
English Language learners
  discontinuity and, 25–26
  parent communications, 209–210
  rights of, 474
Environment
  and brain development, 18
  responsive school
      environment, 24
Epstein, A. S., 79, 299
Epstein, J. L., 5, 7, 23, 25–26, 150, 153–154, 157,
      166, 170, 174, 286–287, 314, 347
Equal educational
      opportunity, 76
Equilibrium, 20
Ericsson, Leif, 134
Ericsson, Thorwald, 134
Erikson, E., 58, 72, 73
Erikson's theory, 73
European Network of Ombudsmen for Children
      (ENOC), 488, 491
Evans, W. A., 420, 430
Exceptional children. *See* Disabled children
  disabled children
      generally. *See* Disabled children
      Individualized Education Plans (IEPs). *See*
          Individualized Education Plans (IEPs)
      Individualized Family Service Plans (IFSPs),
          376, 397
      Individuals with Disabilities Education Act
          (IDEA: P.L. 101-476), 375. *See also*

Individuals with Disabilities Education
      Act (IDEA 97)
  gifted and talented children, 385, 388
Exchanges, 166–167
Exclusion, 4
Exosystem, 8
Extended school services, 154
  after-school programs, 7, 107, 154, 156, 177
  before-school programs, 7, 107, 154, 156

Fagnano, C. L., 23
Fairs, 166
Families, 92
Family and Medical Leave Act (FMLA), 83, 86
Family concept, 48–49
Family Educational Rights and Privacy Act (FERPA),
      412, 464, 465
Family forms/structure, 96–99, 101–102
  blended families. *See* Blended families
  homeless families. *See* Homelessness
  single-parent families. *See* Single-parent families
  two-income families. *See* Two-income families
  two-parent families, 101
  unwed, single-teenage-mother family, 101, 102,
      105, 114
Family households, 95–96, 97, 98
Family involvement. *See* Parent involvement
Family life, stages of, 100
Family literacy, 321–322
Family literacy programs, 83, 123, 177, 322–323
Family Math, 303
Family resource centers, 83, 123, 318–323
Family roles, 99–100
Family School Partnership, 304
Family-school relationship. *See* Home-school-
      community relationships
Family Science, 303
Family service centers (FSCs), 162
  Head Start FSCs, 296
Family support programs, 83, 123
Family systems, 7–8
Fandal, A. W., 356, 358
Farber, A., 485
Fathering Indicator Framework, 109
Father involvement
  1960s views, 75
  child care, 107–110
  helpful insights about, 111
  in schools and centers, 110–111
Fathers, resources, 504–505

Fehrmann, P. G., 150
Female householders, 95, 96
Fenichel, E., 300, 446–447
Ferdinand II, 54
Feudal society, 38
Field Theory, 286, 289
Field trips, 172–173, 181
Fierman, A. H., 126
Financial capital, 4
Finkelhor, D., 425, 431–432
Finlay, B. D., 124
Fischer, L., 463, 468, 469–471
Fisher, M., 59, 68, 420
Flag salute, 470
Flekkoy, M. G., 489
Fontana, V. J., 420, 421, 424, 438
Fraleigh, M., 285
Frank, L. R., 71, 148
Frankenburg, W. K., 358
Franklin, Benjamin, 132
Franklin, C. J., 232
Frede, E. C., 281, 484
Freedman, D., 115
Free press, 469
Free speech and expression, 467–468
Frelinghuysen, P. H., 34
French Revolution, 45
Freud, 58, 68
Froebel, Friedrich Wilhelm, 33, 41, 44, 46, 51,
   55–56, 57, 59, 87, 477
Frohman, A., 340
Froschi, M., 434
Frost, S. E., Jr., 37–38
Frye, K. F., 14
Fryer, G. E., Jr., 454
Furstenberg, F. F., Jr., 115

Gabbard, H. F., 69, 71
Galinsky, E., 5, 101, 107, 111, 434, 485, 487
Gallaudet, Thomas Hopkins, 371
Gallup, A. M., 152, 153, 155, 239, 285, 364
Gamble, M., 193
Gamble, T. K., 193
Gandini, L., 293
Garbarino, James, 434, 447
Gardner, H., 281
Gardner, N. D., 244
Garrity, C., 433
Gart, J., 79
Gartner, A., 23

Gay, E. C., 358
Gay households, 96, 101
Gelles, R. J., 419, 424
Gender discrimination, 472–473
Gesell, Arnold, 10, 66, 72
Ghirlandaio, Domenic (Domenico di Tommaso
   Curradi di Doffo Bigordi), 37
Gifted and talented children,
   385, 388
Giles-Sim, J., 119
Gilliland, H., 131, 133
Ginott, H. G., 76
Ginsberg, E., 76
Ginsburg, G., 482
Glick, P. C., 115
Goals 2000: Educate America, 83, 483–484
Goddard, 371
Goffin, S. G., 479
Goldenberg, D., 395
Goldman-Rakic, P., 16
Goncalvez, Antam, 54
Goodson, B. D., 79, 300
Goodykoontz, B., 69, 71
Gordon, I. J., 348–349
Gordon, T., 211–214, 213, 214, 220
Gotts, E. E., 23, 239, 274
Goya y Lucients, 40
Grady, K., 238
Grandparent maintenance families, 118–119
Gray, S. W., 77, 79
Graziano, A. M., 238
Great Depression, 68, 71
Great Society of the 1960s, 76, 78
Greece, ancient, 36–37
Green, F., 424, 435
Greenberg, P., 311
Greenberger, R. S., 469
Greene, B., 410
Greenleaf, B., 370
Greenspan, S. I., 15,
   18–19, 21, 27
Greenstein, R., 122
Grimes, Ann, 307, 310
Grissom, C. E., 227
Groups. *See* Parent education groups
Grow, C. R., 238
Gruenberg, B. C., 67
Gruenberg, S., 68, 72
Guillemeau, 45
Gun violence, 446–447

Gutek, G. L., 44
Gutenberg, Johannes, 41
Guterson, D., 359
Guthrie, 110
Guzick, 469
Guzzo, R., 126

Hagans, K. B., 430
Hagin, R. A., 392
Hale, J. E., 139–140
Hale-Benson, J. E., 138–139
Hall, G. Stanley, 58, 60, 63, 66, 88, 478
Hallahan, D. P., 369–371
Hallam, R. A., 300
Hall's child study movement, 60
Halmhuber, N., 405
Halperin, M., 442
Hamilton, L. R., 448–449, 453–454
Hammond, M., 238
Handbooks, 200–201
Handel, G., 38
Handicapped children. *See* Disabled children
Hanson, R. A., 79
Happoner, John, 46
"Happy grams," 197, 198
Harding, G., 180
Harkness, Edward S., 36
Harkness, Mary Stillman, 45
Harper, L. V., 35–38, 41
Harris, Dr. William, 57
Harris, L., 153
Hartman, 290
Hatch, Frederick H., 58
Hauge, E., 489
Hausner, L., 362, 367
Hawes, J. M., 462, 477
Haynes, N. M., 23, 26, 287–288, 289, 290
Head Start, 77, 296–299
    in the 1980s, 81
    disabled children in, 398–399
    Early Head Start, 85, 299
    Home Start, 79, 329, 352
Health care, 29
    resources, 507
Healthy Start program (Hawaii), 332, 334
Hedrich, V., 344
Helfer, R. E., 419, 426, 438
Helm, V. A., 125
Henderson, A. T., 23
Henry the Navigator, Prince, 54

Heredity, and brain development, 18
Hess, R. D., 23, 79, 174
Heurer, 359
Heward, W. L., 386
Hewett, V. M., 293
Hiebert, E. H., 23
High school dropouts, 105
Hildago, N., 25
Hill, Patty Smith, 60, 63
Hill, R. B., 74, 138
Hilliard, J., 340
Hippocrates, 370
Hispanics or Latinos
    1930s, substandard treatment, 69
    census 2000, 94
    child count, 104, 106
    college graduates, 104
    defined, 93
    diversity among, 134–135
    early Spanish explorers/settlers, 133–134
    helpful insights about, 135–136
    high school graduates, 103
    population count, 93, 94
    poverty rates, 120, 121, 122
History, 34, 40
    6000 B.C.–A.D. 1800, 57
    Africa, 40
    ancient societies. *See* Ancient societies
    Asia, 40
    family concept, development of, 48–49
    maltreatment of children, 418–419
    Middle Ages, 38–39
    Native Americans, in the 1700s and 1800s, 49–50
    North America, 40–41
    primitive societies, 35
    printing press, invention of, 41
    the Reformation, 41
    17th/18th century Europe, 44–47
    18th–20th century Europe, 49
    South America, 40–41
    Spanish Southwest, 48, 49
    special education, 368–372
    United States. *See* U.S. history
Hoare, Louise, 50
Hobson, C. J., 76
Hodapp, A. F., 362, 367
Hodapp, J. B., 362, 367
Hodges, J., 13, 14
Hoffman, S., 345
Holden, R., 126, 179

Holland, G., 469

Holloway, S. D., 23, 174

Holmes, S., 453

Holt, 65

Holzberg, R., 405

Home-based education, 327, 328–329. *See also* Home-learning activities

child's developmental progress, screening of, 355–357

choosing a program, 349–351

community resources, 354

a day in the life of one program, 341–344

evaluation of program, 354–355

Healthy Start program (Hawaii), 332, 334

Homebuilders, 336–337

Home Instruction Program for Preschool Youngsters (HIPPY), 331–332, 333, 334

Home Start, 79, 329, 352

inservice training, after program has started, 353–354

Parent-Child Home Program (PCHP), 335–336

parent questionnaires, 355

Parents as Teachers (PAT) program, 329–331

Portage Project, 337–341

recruitment of families, 352

visiting homes. *See* Home visiting/visitors

Homebuilders, 336–337

Home Instruction Program for Preschool Youngsters (HIPPY), 331–332

sample educational materials, 333, 334

Home-learning activities, 346–349

away-from-home activities, 348–349

file development, 346

five-step guide, 344

school workshops to introduce, 306–310, 311–312

Homelessness, 123–124, 486–487

in the 1980s, 81, 82

children's feelings, 125, 126

child welfare concerns, 125

educational support, for parents, 177–178

emotional support, for parents, 177–178

helpful insights about, 126–127

McKinney-Vento plan, 124–125

parents' desires, 125

student rights, 124–125

two-parent homeless family, 102, 124

Home Observation for Measurement of the Environment (HOME), 355–357

Home-Oriented Preschool Education (HOPE) programs, 26

Homer, Winslow, 56, 62

Home-school-community relationships

administrator's role, 160

after-school programs, 7, 107, 154, 156, 157, 177

before-school programs, 7, 107, 154, 156

book publishing, 169–170

building family strengths, 178–179

bus trips, 172

career day, 170

child care. *See* Child care

coffees, 172

crisis nursery, 176

extended school services. *See* Extended school services

family centers, 162

family literacy programs, 83, 123, 177

field trips, 172–173

improving, 151–156, 160–161

letters in August, 170–171

neighborhood visits, 172

open-door policy, 161–162

parent advisory councils, 162

parental attitudes, 150, 151

parent involvement. *See* Parent involvement

parent roles, 156–157

parents as partners, 170

parents as resources, 170

parent-school collaboration, 156, 157

parent-school cooperation, 149

parents-teachers-community collaboration, 7

parent-to-parent support, 176

picnics, 172–173

resources, 499–501

school activities and resources, 163–173

school climate and, 149–150, 161

open-door policy, 161–162

school-home support, 175

site-based management, 157, 162

collaborative decision making in, 235

skill training, 177

talent sharing, 170

teacher's role, 157–159

telephone trees, 176

transportation, 176

volunteers. *See* Volunteers
what works, 173–175
work-site seminars, 176
Home-school continuity, 154, 156
Homeschooling, 83, 357, 465. *See also* Home-based
    education
    characteristics of, 358
    children's characteristics, 358
    reasons for, 358, 359
    school-parent cooperation, 358–360
Home Screening Questionnaire (HSQ), 357
Home Start programs, 80, 329
    components of, 352
Home visiting/visitors, 327–328
    choosing visitors, 352–353
    evaluation of programs, 354
    guidelines for success, 353
    home-learning formulas, 348–349
    inservice training, 353–354
    Utah Home Visitor Guide, 345
Home visits, by teachers, 202
Homework, 360
    categories of, 362–363
    elementary schools, 362
    extension, 363
    hot lines, 201–202
        Parents in Touch (Indianapolis), 302
    how parents can help, 363–366
    practice, 362–363
    preparation, 363
    preschool and kindergarten, 361–362
    school-home collaboration, 360–361
    time spent on, 363
Homosexual households, 96, 101
Hong, E., 363–364, 367
Honig, A. S., 315–316
Horn, W. F., 109–111
Horton, C. B., 417, 419, 426–427
Hospitalized children, 15
Households, 95–96, 97, 98
Howell, Samuel G., 371
Howley, J. P., 288
Hughes, K. N., 23
Human attachment, 9–10
    Bowlby study, 12–13
    early deprivation, reversibility of, 13–14
    hospitalized children, 15
    maltreated children, 15
    parents posing concerns, 14–15
    Romanian orphanages, 13

Skeels study, 10–11
Spitz study, 11–12
Human capital, 4
Human Ecological Systems Theory, 286, 289
Hunt, D., 45
Hunt, J. M., 1, 18–21, 20, 32, 75–76
Huntington, Collis P., 51
Hurd, T. L., 301
Hyde, D., 26, 314
Hymes, J. L., Jr., 72, 81, 151, 220

Imber, M., 462–463
Immigrant families, 7
Immigration, 52, 144
    pre-1880, 52–53
    1880-1890, 59, 60
    1890-1914, 61–62, 63
    1990s to 2001, 87, 95
    Chinese Exclusion Act (1890), 52, 67
    German immigrants, 52–53
    Irish immigrants, 52, 53
    Italian immigrants, 52
    Johnson Reed Act (1924), 67
    Mexicans, 135
    settlement houses, 59
Individualism, overblown, 4
Individualized Education Plans (IEPs), 376
    cover, 386
    development of, 378–383
    disability determination, 380
    eligibility determination, 379
    goals and objectives, 387
    outline for review meeting, 377–378
    recommended placement, 381
Individuals with Disabilities Education Act (IDEA 97),
        84, 376, 378
    IEPs. *See* Individualized Education Plans (IEPs)
    infants and toddlers (Part C of IDEA 97), 395–397
    parents' rights and responsibilities, 382–385
    placement of child, 381, 385
Individuals with Disabilities Education Act (IDEA: P.L.
        101-476), 375, 473
    1997 amendments. *See* Individuals with
        Disabilities Education Act (IDEA 97)
Industrial Revolution, 45
Infanticide, 37–38
Infants and toddlers
    abuse, exposure to, 446. *See also*
        Abused/neglected children
    attachment. *See* Human attachment

Infants and toddlers, *continued*
  brain development. *See* Brain development
  child care. *See* Child care
  with disabilities
    Child Find Project, 395
    IDEA 97, Part C, 395–397
    parent-school partnerships, 399–401
    procedural rights, 397–398
    reaching out programs, 405–406
  mortality rates, 105
  nurturing, 8–9, 99
  shaken baby syndrome, 423
  swaddling of infants, 44–45
  thumb sucking, 65, 68
  "tight scheduling," of activities, 66
Intellectual development
  appropriate practices for, 21–22
  concrete stage, 20–21
  emotion and, 18–19
  formal stage, 21
  and general knowledge, 30
  Hunt on, 20
  Piaget on, 19–21
  sensorimotor stage, 20
  Vygotsky on, 19
Internet communications, 246
Internet connections, 515
Ireland, W. M., 50
Isaac, 47
Itard, Jean Marc Gaspard, 370
Iverson, T. J., 445, 448
I-you-we messages, 210–211

Jablow, M. M., 405
Jackson, B. L., 26, 314
Jackson, Carol, 344
Jackson, Jesse, 138
Jacobson, S. W., 14
Jenny, C., 427
Jesuit Order, 41, 48
Jesus, 41
John, R., 132
Johnson, Eastman, 58
Johnson, F., 340
Johnson, S. R., 432
Johnston, J. H., 102
Jones, L., 432
Journals and magazines, 515–517
Joyner, E. T., 26, 287–288, 289, 290
Just, Dr. Ernest, E., 138

Justice, B., 452
Justice, R., 452

Kaban, B. T., 79
Kagan, S. L., 6, 19, 23, 26, 29
Kaleidoscope, 128
Kamii, C., 348
Kaplan, G. P., 104
Karnes, F. A., 389
Karnes, Merle, 403
Karr-Morse, 446
Kauffman, J. M., 369–371
Kaufman, H. O., 154
Kawin, E., 257
Keith, T. Z., 150
Kellaghan, T., 24
Keller, Arthur H., 371
Keller, H., 368, 371
Kelley, M. L., 231
Kelly, 290
Kelly, C., 469–471
Kelly, P., 119
Kempe, C. H., 420, 431, 458
Kempe, R. S., 419, 426, 431, 438
Kennedy, John F., 53
Kennedys, 372
Kennell, J. S., 80
Kenoyer, C. E., 274
Kent, M. M., 486
Ker, C., 358
Kerber, K., 180
Kierstead, F. D., 469
Kilpatrick, William, 63
Kindergarten movement, 55, 58, 59
King, C. E., 252
King, Martin Luther, Jr., 138
Kirk, S. A., 371
Klass, C., 353
Klaus, M. H., 80
Klaus, R. A., 77
Klein, T., 126, 179
Knapp, P. A., 238
Knowledge, 30
Knowles, J. G., 359–360
Koch, P. K., 216
Kontos, S., 25
Kovach, B. A., 175, 179
Kozol, J., 92

Kraizer, S., 454
Kristensen, N., 300
Krugman, M. K., 436
Krugman, R. D., 431–432, 436
Kuhl, P. K., 17
Kullen, A. S., 40–41, 54, 61, 132, 144

LaConte, R. T., 362–364
Laissez-faire parents, 100, 101
La Leche League, 81
Lamaze classes, 81
Lamb, M. E., 109–111, 113
Lambie, D. A., 77
Lamison-White, L., 121
Lamont, Thomas W., 45
LaMorte, M. W., 463
Lamson, P. A., 360
Lancaster, J. B., 419, 424
Landers, A., 412
Langston, John Mercer, 138
Language development, 17–18, 30
Lao-tze, 234
Larner, M., 6
La Salle, 144
Latchkey children, 107
Latinos. See Hispanics or Latinos
Lawrence, Sir Thomas, 51
Layzer, J. I., 297–298
Lazar, I., 77, 79
Lazoritz, S., 420
Leadership. See Collaborative leadership
Learning, 16
    readiness, 27–28
    styles, 30
Learning centers, 167
Learning compacts, 305–306
Learning disabilities, 389, 390–392. See also Disabled
    children
LeDoux, J., 16
Lee, S. M., 140
Lehtinen, Laura, 371
Leiderman, P. H., 285
Leipzig, J., 314
Lenhoff, D. R., 86
Leong, D. J., 19
Lerner, J., 395
Lerner, R. M., 301
Letters to parents, 197, 199
    in August, 170–171
    disabled children's parents, 405

Levenstein, P., 23, 79, 337
Levine, A., 479
Levine, J. A., 111
Levine, M., 479
Levit, E. M., 486
Lewin, 290
Lewis, J. K., 115
Libraries, 168
Lines, P. M., 358–359, 463
Liontos, L. B., 174
Lipka, R., 281
Lipsky, D. K., 23
Listening, 209
    reflective, 210
Little Soldier, L., 131, 133
Local Education Agencies (LEAs), 124, 398
Locke, J., 33, 42–43, 46, 51, 57, 370, 477
Lombardi, J., 24–25, 479
Long, Jefferson, 138
Looking-Glass-Self, 207–209
Lopez, Dwight, 470
Lorence, B. W., 45
Loucks, H., 150, 153
Louis XIII, 45
Louis XV, 39
Love, J. M., 484
Lowenthal, B., 417
Lucus, R. D., 188
Luther, Martin, 41, 57
Lynch, John R., 138
Lyons, P., 175

Macchiarola, F. J., 23
MacDicken, R. A., 439
Magazines and journals, 515–517
Magnet schools, 22
Malaguzzi, L., 293
Male householders, 95, 96
Maltreatment of children. See Abused/
    neglected children
Mann, Horace, 55
Mann, T. L., 300
Manning, B. H., 216, 227
Manning, D. T., 117, 119
Manning, M. L., 111, 164
Mardell-Czudnowski, C., 395
Margolis, H., 229
Marquardt, R., 389
Married couples, 95
Marsh, D., 236

Marshall, 22
Marston, Stephanie, 281
Martin, 87
Martin Luther, 41, 57t
Mary, 41
Maslach, C., 412
Maslow, A. H., 151, 413–415
Maslow's hierarchy of needs, 412–413
Maternal deprivation, 12, 13. *See also*
    Human attachment
Mather, Cotton, 48
Mather, M., 486
Mattox, B., 173
Mauldin, T. A., 113
Mayberry, M., 359
Maynard, R. A., 317
McClave, Debra, 309
McClellan, S., 238
McCormick, L., 126, 179
McCourt, 290
McCoy, Elijah, 138
McDonald, 331
McDonough, M., 216
McKay, G. D., 211–212, 215, 220
McKinney-Vento plan, 124–125
McLearn, K. T., 29
McMillan, Margaret, 64
McNiel, D. E., 454
McPartland, J., 76
Mead, M., 70
Meadows, B. J., 161
Meckstrom, A., 484
Media communications, 200
Melaville, A. I., 319
Melcher, S. G., 485
MELD Young Moms (MYM), 317–318
Memory, 16
Mendes, Catulle, 52
Mendes, Claudine, 52
Mendes, Helyonne, 52
Mendes, Huguette, 52
Mental health
    1900-1910, 62
    1950s views, 72
    disabilities. *See* Disabled children
Mental retardation, 388, 392–393. *See also* Disabled
    children
    1920s concerns, 67
    1970s advocacy groups, 78–79

and homelessness, 124
    White House Conference Mental retardation
        (1963), 76
Mesosystem, 8
Messages, 192–193
    I-you-we, 210–211
    positive, 209
Mexican Americans, 135. *See also* Hispanics or
        Latinos
Mexican-American War, 53, 135
Mexican Revolution, 135
Meyer, D. J., 406
Meyerhoff, M. K., 150
Meyers, K., 227
Michel, G. J., 23
Microsystem, 8
Middle Ages, 38–39
Middlekauff, R., 48
Middle schools. *See* Secondary schools
Midgley, 87
Mikovsky, M., 79
Miller, 463
Miller, P., 194
Miller, S., 194
Millsap, M. A., 300
Minnesota Early Childhood
        Family Education
        Program, 299
Minnesota Early Learning Design (MELD), 317
Minnesota Mother-Child Project, 429
Minority students. *See also specific ethnic
        or racial group*
    1930-1954, substandard treatment, 69–70
    1980s, 81
    charter schools, 86
    equal educational opportunity, 76
Mischley, L., 238
Mischley, M., 238
Miscommunication, 193
Moles, O. C., 23, 116, 150, 201, 216, 238, 304, 311
Molnar, J., 126, 179
Montessori, Maria, 59, 63
Mood, A. M., 76
Moody, E., 47–48
Moore, E., 19, 26, 29
Moore, R. L., 46
Mork, O., 489–490
Morrison, G. S., 42
Motor development, 20, 29

Mullin-Rindler, N., 434
Mullins, J. B., 405–406
Murphy, D. T., 111
Murray, H., 77, 79

Nagi, S. Z., 419–420
Nain, Louis, 42
Natale, J. A., 359
National Association for the Education of Young
    Children (NAEYC), 82
National Association of Colored Women, 59
National Center on Child Abuse and Neglect
    (NCCAN), 420–421
National Congress of Mothers, 59
National Congress of Parents and Teachers (PTA), 59
    1920-1930, 66–67
    1950-1960, 71
National Education Goals Panel, 85–86
National Law Center on Homelessness and Poverty,
    124, 125
Native Americans
    Alaska Natives. See Alaska Natives
    American Indians. See American Indians
Neglected children. See Abused/neglected children
Negron, E. N., 288
Neighborhood visits, 172
New England schools (colonial times), 47
Newman, F., 15, 21
Newman, L., 18
Newsletters
    to disabled children's parents, 405
    district, 199
    elementary school, 197
    middle school, 197
    preschool, 194, 196–197
    sample layouts, 195, 196
    secondary school, 197
    simple, 194–197
Newspapers, 197–199
Nightingale, Forence, 328
Nimnicht, G. P., 169
Noble children, 38–39
No Child Left Behind Act of 2001, 85–86
Noller, P., 238
Nonfamily householders, 95
Nonfamily households, 95, 97, 98
North American history, 40–41
    United States. See U.S. history
Norton, A. J., 115

Notes to parents, 197, 198
Nunez, R. da Costa, 125, 127, 179
Nunnally, E., 194
Nuolet, Jean, 144
Nursery schools. See Preschools
Nurturing infants, 8–9
    attachment. See Human attachment
    familial role, 99
Nutrition resources, 507

O'Callaghan, J. B., 8, 23
O'Connell, M., 81
O'Donnell, N. S., 485
Ombudsmanship, 491
Open-door policies, 161–162
Open record policy, 465–467
Orlansky, M. D., 386
Osborn, A. F., 262
Osborn, D. K., 35, 37–38, 67
Osofsky, J. D., 446–447
Out-of-wedlock births, 101, 102, 105, 114

Pacific Islanders. See Asians/Pacific Islanders
Packer, A., 345
Papernow, P. L., 117–118
Pardeck, J. T., 453
Parent advisory councils, 162
Parental attitudes, 150, 151
Parent-Child Home Program (PCHP), 335–336
Parent cooperative movement, 67
Parent cooperatives
    first cooperative, 63, 64
    in the 1920s, 66
Parent education
    1920–1930, 67–68
    1930–1940, 68–70
    1950–1960, 71–73
    1970–1980, 79
    1980–1990, 81, 82
    Active Parenting program, 214–215
    child abuse and neglect, 451
    collaborative leadership. See Collaborative
        leadership
    college, 103–104
    groups. See Parent education groups
    high school, 103
    how parents learn best, 242
    needs assessment, 237–242
        sample, 274–278

Parent education, *continued*
  Parent Effectiveness Training (P.E.T.), 212–214
  parenting skills, 316–318
  programs, 212–215
    needs assessment, 237–242, 274–278
  resources, 511–514
  school-based programs. *See* School-based
    programs
  Systematic Training for Effective Parenting
    (STEP), 214
  for teenagers, 316–318
Parent education groups, 164–165. *See also*
    Collaborative leadership
  1940-1950, 70–71
  audiovisual presentations, 268–269
  book review discussions, 268
  brainstorming sessions, 261
  buzz sessions, 260
  centers, 261–263
  colloquies, 267
  concentric circles, 258–260
  debates, 267–268
  development of, 236
  dramatizations, 265–266
  dyad interaction and
    feedback, 264
  dyad introductions, 248–249
  end-of-meeting evaluations, 254, 255
  field trips, 263–264
  icebreakers, 246
  interest finders, 238–239
  lectures, 270–271
  meetings, 242–243
    arrangements for, 255–256
    bingo cards, 246, 248
    communication criteria, 243, 244
    dyad introductions, 248–249
    end-of-meeting evaluations, 254, 255
    icebreakers, 246
    informal discussion plan, 242–243
    "I've got a secret," 249
    problem-solving format, 243
    scrambled name tags, 248
    signature sheets, 246, 247
    types of, 255, 256–271
    "Who am I?", 248
  needs assessment, 237–242
    sample, 274–278
  objectives, development of, 239–242

    observations, 263–264
    panel presentations, 266–267
    productive/non-productive groups, 252
    roles of members, 249–250
      dynamics of, 250–255
      dysfunctional roles, 250–251, 252
      group-building roles, 250, 251–252
      individual roles, 250–251, 252
      maintenance roles, 250, 251–252
      playing roles, 253–255, 264–265
      task roles, 250, 251
    roundtable discussions, 256–258
    symposiums, 269–270
    triad interaction and feedback, 264
    workshops, 261–263
Parent Effectiveness Training (P.E.T.), 212–214
Parenting skills
  education, 316–318
  programs helpful in developing, 498–499
Parenting styles, 100–101
Parent involvement, 152
  administrator's role in, 160
  associations concerned with, 493–496
  book publishing, 169–170
  career day, 170
  collaborative leadership, 234, 237
  contacting parents, early in the school year,
    170–173
  disabled children, 401–402
  fathers. *See* Father involvement
  Head Start, 297–299
  parent questionnaire, 155
  Parents in Touch program (Indianapolis), 302–303
  in reading, support for, 515
  roles for, 156–157
  school-based programs, 282–286
  strategies for, 153
  talent sharing, 170
  teacher's role in, 157–159
  types of, 152–153
  what works, 173–175
Parent networks, 165
Parent questionnaires
  home-based education, 355
  home-school-community relationships, 155
Parent roles
  in the family, 99–100
  at school, 156–157
Parents Anonymous (1985), 452

Parents as partners, 170
Parents as resources, 170
Parents as Teachers (PAT) program, 329–331
Parent-school collaboration, 156, 157
Parent-school cooperation, 149
Parent-school relationship. *See* Home-school-
     community relationships
Parents' rights
     origin of, 460–461
     selection of child's education, 460–461
Parent-teacher associations (PTAs), 166
Parent-teacher conferences, 215
     angry parents, dealing with, 228, 230
     checklist, 229
     collaborative conversations, 215–216
     concrete examples, of child's work and behavior,
          227–228
     congruent beliefs about child, 221
     congruent conferences, 222–225
     contract arrangements, 230–231
     day of conference, 225–226
     invitation to attend, 216, 217
     language to use in, 219
     meeting place, 218
     objectives of, statement of, 225–226
     parent as part of team, recognition of, 226
     postconference plans, 228, 229
     practicing for, 219
     preconference workshops and guides, 220
     preparation for, 219, 225
     sandwich approach, 226
     schedules, 216, 217
     with student, 221, 222
     teacher preparation, 220–221
     team membership, 221–222, 226–227
     two-way communication in, 218–219
Parent-teacher organizations (PTOs), 166
Parent Team (PT), 287, 288
Parent-to-parent support, 176
Parker, Francis, 63
Parker, S., 29
Parks, C. C., 405
Partnerships for Family Involvement in
     Education, 85
Paulu, N., 362, 366, 367
Pawlas, G., 227
Peabody, Elizabeth, 33, 55–56, 57, 478
Pearl, P., 454
Penn, William, 144

Performances, 181
Perry Preschool Program, 79
Pestalozzi, Andrew, 43
Pestalozzi, Johann Heinrick, 33–34, 41, 43–44,
     46–51, 56, 57, 87, 477
Pettinelli, D., 353
Philippines, 62
Physical abuse. *See* Abused/neglected children
Physical development, 29
Piaget, J., 1, 18–21, 32, 59, 76, 347
Picnics, with parents, 172–173
Pierson, D. E., 301
Pittinsky, T. L., 111
Plato, 33, 36–37, 57, 370
Pledge of Allegiance, 470
Pocahontas, 144
Polybius, 37, 57
Ponce de Leon, 134
Popkin, M. H., 211–212
Popp, Judy, 344
Population
     census 2000, 93, 94, 96
     child count, 104, 106
     facts, 485
     growth from 1790, 103, 104
Population Adjustment Model, 286, 289
Portage Project, 337–341
Porter, W., 433
Positive speaking, 209
Post-Kammer, P., 453
Potts, M., 323
Poverty, 119–122, 485–486
     in the 1980s, 81
     counteracting, 123
     defined, 120
     destructive nature of, 120
     the Great Depression, 68, 71
     helpful insights about, 122–123
     homelessness. *See* Homelessness
     length of time in, 120
     statistics, 104–105, 119–122
     War on Poverty, 76–77, 121
Powell, D. R., 238
Powhatan, 144
Prehistoric societies, 35
Preschools
     abused/neglected children, 437, 453
     child care, 106–107
     first nursery school, 64

Preschools, *continued*
    homework, 361–362
    newsletters, 194, 196–197
Primitive societies, 35
Printing press, invention of, 41
Privacy
    Family Educational Rights and Privacy Act (FERPA),
        412, 465
    student records, 466
Private schools, public money for, 463–464
Pro-choice advocates, 82, 84
Pro-life advocates, 82, 84
Promising Practices Policies, 85
Protestant Reformation, 41
Pruett, K. D., 110
Puckett, 22
Puerto Rico, 61
Puritans, 47

Quinn, L. S., 115, 126

Race. *See also specific racial group*
    child count by, 106
    definitions of, 93
Racial discrimination, 470–472
Radencich, M. C., 362, 367
Raeburn, Sir Henry, 45
Raleigh, Sir Walter, 144
Rapier, James P., 138
Rauche-Elnekave, H., 489–490
Raudabaugh, J. N., 250, 252, 254
Ray, B. D., 359
Readiness to learn, 27–28
Reading First program, 305
Reed, J., 26, 314
Reflective listening, 210
The Reformation, 41
Reframing communications, 211
Reggio Emilia, 292
Rehnquist, Chief Justice, 465
Reich, K., 448
Reid, T., 427
Reiff, 290
Reimers, T. M., 150
Reinert, H. R., 370
"Related subfamilies," 114
Religious schools, public money for, 464
Renoir, Pierre-Auguste, 52
Rephrasing communications, 211
Reppucci, N. D., 453

Resource rooms, 167–168
Responsive school
    environment, 24
Revels, Hiram, 138
Reynolds, M. C., 23
Rich, D., 173, 174, 281
Richards, George N., 64
Richards, Helen M., 64
Rigaud, Hyacinthe, 39
Riggs, R. C., 431
Rights of children. *See* Children's/students' rights
Rights of parents. *See* Parents' rights
Rigsby, L. C., 23
Rioux, J. W., 23
Ritter, P., 285
Robbins, A., 175
Roberts, D. F., 285
Robinson, E. H., 219
Rochas, Benjie, 343–344
Rochas, Margaretta, 343–344
Rogers, C., 220
Rolfe, James, 144
Romanian orphanages, 13
Rome, ancient, 37–38
Ronstrom, A., 490
Room-parents, 156
Rose, L. C., 152, 153, 155, 239, 285, 364
Rosegrant, T., 25
Rosenblatt, P. C., 7
Rotter, J. C., 219
Rousseau, J. J., 33, 41, 43–44, 46, 51, 57, 59, 87,
    370, 477
Royce, J., 77, 79
Rubin, L., 126
Ruma, P. R., 238
Rural families, 7, 62
Rutter, M., 13–14, 174
Ryan, G., 432, 455

Sackville, 45
Salmond, K., 5, 434
Sanai Hospital, 300–301
Sandberg, D. N., 441
Sassetti, Francesco, 37
Sassetti, Teodoro, 37
Saturday School and Parents as Teachers (PAT)
    programs, 26
Saturday Schools, 294–296
"Scaffolding," 19
Scheeringa, M., 447

Schewinhart, L. J., 23
Schimmel, D., 463, 468, 469–471
Schlossman, S. L., 59–60, 66
Schmitt, Barton D., 417, 421, 428, 440
Schneider, B., 23
Schochet, P. Z., 484
Schoen, C., 29
School activities and resources, 163–173
School-based programs, 282
    Brookline Early Education Project, 300
    collaboration
        effective collaboration, characteristics of, 293
        middle and secondary schools, 292–293
    Comer's Program, 26–27, 286–289
    community resources, 323–325
    Early Childhood Longitudinal Study, 290–292
    elementary school, a walk through, 293–294
    Families and Schools Together (FAST), 320
    Family and Child Education (FACE), 320–321
    family literacy programs, 83, 123, 177, 322–323
    family resource centers, 83, 123, 318–323
    Family School Partnership, 304
    funding, 323
    Head Start. See Head Start
    helping parents work with children, 305–306
    home-learning activities, workshops to introduce, 306–310, 311–312
    League of Schools Reaching Out, 301–302
    learning compacts, 305–306
    math and science, 303
    middle and secondary schools, 292–293
    Minnesota Early Childhood Family Education Program, 299
    parenting skills, 316–318
    parent involvement, 282–286
    Parents in Touch (Indianapolis), 302–303
    reaching all families, 303–304
        reticent parents, 310, 313–315
    Reading First, 305
    Sanai Hospital, 300–301
    Saturday Schools, 294–296
    Teachers Involve Parents in Schoolwork (TIPS), 302–303
    teenagers, parent education for, 316–318
    Title programs. See Title programs
School climate, 149–150, 161
    open-door policy, 161–162
School conferences, 166
School-home activity packets, 165–166
School-home support, 175

School Planning and Management Team (SPMT), 287, 288
School programs, 166
School projects, 166
School vouchers, 464–465
School workshops, 166
Schorr, D., 81, 301, 338
Schorr, L. B., 81, 301, 338
Schumm, J. S., 362, 367
Schurz, Margaretha, 51, 53, 57
Schwab, L. O., 180
Scott, J. A., 23
Scott, S., 180
Search and seizure, 468–469
Secondary schools
    abused/neglected children indicators, 439
    newsletters, 197
Seefeldt, C., 24–26, 153
Seeley, D. S., 237
Segal, M., 445, 448
Self-esteem of child
    disabled children, 413
    promotion of, 279–280
Seligman, M., 404
September 11, 2001, 84–85
Sequin, Edouard, 370
Sereno, K. K., 250, 257
Sewell, P. M., 426
Sex discrimination, 472–473
Sexist textual references, 80
Sexual abuse of children, 429–432
    intervention in, 453–454
    prevention tips, 455–456
    resources, 508
Shaken baby syndrome, 423
Shapiro, B. B., 79
Shapiro, I., 122
Sharing reading, 164
Shaw, D. S., 112–113
Shearer, D., 340
Shearer, M., 340
Sheets, P., 252
Shields, M. K., 87
Shiono, P. H., 115
Shipman, V. C., 79
Shively, Henry L., M.D., 39
Shively, Mary Wetmore, 39
Shore, R., 14–18, 21–22
Shulman, S., 126

Sigel, I. E., 336
Silver, A. A., 392
Silver, H. K., 420
Silverman, F. N., 420
Silvern, S. B., 23, 25
Single-parent families, 102, 105, 113–114, 486
    father run, 109
    helpful insights about,
        114–116
    out-of-wedlock births,
        102, 114
    resources, 505–506
Site-based management,
        157, 162
    collaborative decision making in, 235
Sjostrom, L., 435
Skeels, H. M., 10, 13, 32,
        77, 454
Skeels study, 10–11
Skill training, for parents, 177
Skinner, B. F., 58, 72
"Skip-generation parenting," 101
Skyles, A., 118–119
Slavery, and the Civil War, 49, 53, 54
Sloane, K., 24
Smalls, Robert, 138
Smith, A., 175
Smith, V., 210
Smoking, 18, 22
Snipper, A., 77
Snow, D. L., 238
Social Action Model, 286, 289
Social capital, 4
Social development, 29
    Erikson's theory, 73
Societal challenges, 3
South American history, 40–41
Spain, D., 108, 487
Spanish-American War, 61
Spanish Southwest, 48
    families in, 49
Spanking, 73
Special education
    disabled children
        generally. See Disabled children
        Individualized Education Plans (IEPs). See
            Individualized Education Plans (IEPs)
        Individualized Family Service Plans (IFSPs),
            376, 397

Individuals with Disabilities Education Act
        (IDEA: P.L. 101-476), 375. See also
        Individuals with Disabilities Education
        Act (IDEA 97)
    gifted and talented children, 385, 388
    history of, 368–372
Special education, development of, 368–372
Specialized handbooks, 201
Spencer, 59
Spidel, J., 31, 368
Spitz, R. A., 10–11, 13, 32, 77, 80, 454
Spitz study, 11–12
Spock, B., 59, 70–71, 75
Spodek, B., 79
Sprung, B., 434
Squires, D. A., 288
St. Pierre, R. G., 297–298
Stacy, E. W., 238
Stahlman, B. R., 409, 411
Stahlman, Eric, 410–412
Stahlman, Jay, 410–411
Stahlman, K., 409, 411
Stahlman, Mark, 410–412
Statutory law, 461. See also specific name of act
        or statute
Steele, B. F., 418, 420, 448–449, 453–454
Stein, N., 435
Stendler, C. B., 61, 65, 68, 70
Stepparents
    blended families. See Blended families
    resources, 505
Stewart B. McKinney Homeless Assistance Act of
        1987, 124
Stinnett, N., 179
Stouffer, B., 294
Strauss, Alfred A., 371
Stronge, J. H., 125, 179
Student and Staff Support Team (SSST), 287, 288
Student-parent exchange day, 204
Student-parent-school exchange, 204
Student-parent-teacher conferences, 221, 222
Student records, 465–467
Student rights. See Children's/students' rights
Suess, Dr., 281
Suggestion boxes, 200
Sui, S., 25
Sullivan, Anne Mansfield, 371
Summer vacation activities, 168–169
Summit, R. C., 432

Sunley, R., 50–51
Suppers, 166
Suspension from school, 469–470
Swaddling of infants, 44–45
Swanberg, J. E., 107, 111, 487
Swap, S. M., 25
Swartz, J. P., 300, 301
Swick, K. J., 4, 5, 23, 100, 111, 126, 174–175, 179, 237–238, 238
Systematic Training for Effective Parenting (STEP), 214

Talented children, 385, 388
Talent sharing, 170
Taylor, K. W., 64, 67
Taylor, R., 238
Teachers Involve Parents in Schoolwork (TIPS) program, 302–303
Tebes, J. K., 238
Teenage Pregnancy and Parenting (TAPP) programs, 317
Teenagers
    parent education for, 316–318
    pregancy, 81
        unwed, single-teenage-mother family, 101, 102, 105, 114
    pregnancy, 315–316
Teen deaths, 105
Teen Outreach Program (TOP), 317
Telephone calls, to parents, 202, 203
Telephone trees, 176
Telephone tutor, 167
    Dial-a-Teacher (Indianapolis), 302
Temporary Assistance for Needy Families (TANF), 83–84
Terman, D. L., 486
Tessier, A., 370
Texts, selection of, 474–475
Thomas, E. J., 250
Thomas, Justice Clarence, 469
Thompson, F., 148
Thompson, R. W., 238
Thorndike, 60
Thornton, A., 115
Thumb sucking, 65, 68
Tinker, John F., 468
Tinker, Mary Beth, 468
Title IX, 472

Title programs
    Title I, 77, 83, 304–305
    Title IV, 77, 305
    Reading First, 305
Title VII, 470–471
Tivnan, T., 301
Tizard, J., 13, 32
Tobacco, 18, 22
Toddlers. *See* Infants and toddlers
Toth, S. L., 419, 449, 453
Touchpoints, 27
Tout, T., 107
Tower, C. C., 430, 435, 451, 453
Toy lending library, 168
Transportation, 176
Tubman, Harriet, 138
Turbiville, 110
Turnbull, A. P., 377, 386, 395, 405
Turnbull, H. R., 395
Turnbull, H. R., III, 377, 386, 405
Tutoring
    disabled children, parents of, 402–403
    telephone tutor, 167
        Dial-a-Teacher (Indianapolis), 302
Two-income family, 102–103
    father involvement, 109
    working mothers, 107
Two-parent families, 101
    homeless families, 102, 124

Umansky, W., 23
Umbarger III, 110
"Unrelated subfamilies," 114
Unwed, single-teenage-mother family, 101, 102, 105, 114
"Upslips," 197, 198
U.S. history
    pre-1880
        the Civil War, 53–55
        Colonial America, 47–48, 49
        the 1800s, 50–52
        immigration, 52–53
        Mexican-American War, 53
        Native Americans, in the 1700s and 1800s, 49–50
        Spanish Southwest, 48, 49
        Texas, annexation of, 53
    1880–1890, 59–61

U.S. history, *continued*
1890–1900, 61–62
1900–1910, 62–63
1910–1920, 63–66
1920–1930, 66–68
1930–1940, 68–70
1940–1950, 70–71
1950–1960, 71–74
1960–1970, 74–78
1970–1980, 78–80
1980–1990, 80–82
1990–2000, 82–84
2000—, 84–87
British explorations, 143
French explorations, 143
immigration. *See* Immigration
Native Americans
Alaska Natives. *See* Alaska Natives
American Indians. *See* American Indians
Pennsylvania, 143
Santa Fe, 143
Utriainen, S., 490

Valente, W. D., 462, 468, 471
Vandewalker, N. C., 56
Van Gogh, Vincent, 64
Van Valey, L., 104
Varner, J., 238
Vespucci, Amerigo, 134
Video lending library, 168
Vietnam War, 78
Vincent, C. E., 66, 70
Violence, 487
resources, 509–510
roots of, 445–447
in schools, 5, 432–434
Visher, E. B., 119
Visher, J. S., 119
Visual messages, 193
Vocational Rehabilitation Act of 1973 (Section 504),
372–373
Volk, D., 129
Volunteers, 179
action sheets, 185, 186
child performances, 181
field trips, 181
increasing usage of, 185
invitations that work, 181
invitations to share, 182, 184, 185
management techniques, 185

recruitment, by individual teachers, 180–181
recruitment, by schools and school systems,
188–189
responsibilities to teacher, 187–188
teacher's responsibilities to, 187–188
time schedules, 185
training of, 185, 187
used or users, 179
want ads, 181–182, 183
who should ask for, 179
Volunteer sheets, 185, 186
Vondra, J. I., 419, 449, 453
Vorrasi, J. A., 447
Vouchers, 464
Vygotsky, L. S., 1, 18–19,
32, 336

Wackman, S., 194
Wadsworth, B., 47–48
Wagner, P. A., 469
Walberg, H. F., 23
Waldessmuller, Martin, 134
Walker, D. K., 301
Wallerstein, J., 112
Walsh, M. E., 127
Walsh-Burton, S., 405
Walters, R. H., 220, 404–405, 407–408
Wanat, C. L., 117
Wang, M. C., 23
Ward, M. J., 406
Warner, I., 303
War on Poverty, 76–77, 121
Warren, V. B., 306
Wartes, J., 359
Wasik, B. J., 23, 329, 353
Watson, T., 10, 23, 58, 60, 66, 174–175
Weatherford, J., 132
Weber, E., 51, 59
Web sites, 246, 515
Webster-Stratton, C., 238
Weikart, D. R., 23, 77, 79–80
Weikart's Perry Preschool Program, 79
Weinfeld, F. D., 76
Wells, H. C., 281
Werber, B. Z., 23
Wesley, John, 46, 57
Wesley, Susanna, 46
Wet nurses, 45
Wheeler, P., 294
White, B. L., 79, 150, 332

White, Justice Byron R., 470
Whitebrook, M., 482
White House Conference(s)
    on Care of Dependent Children (1909), 63
    on Child Health and Protection (1930), 68
    on Children and Youth (1959), 63
    on Early Childhood Development and Learning
        (1997), 85
    on Families (1980), 80–81
    on Mental retardation (1963), 76
White House Summit on Early Childhood (2001), 85
Widgren, 87
Wiehe, V. R., 445
Wiley, M. S., 446
Wilkinson, I. A. G., 23
Williams, D. L., Jr., 153
Williams, Dr. Daniel Hale, 138
Williams, L. R., 129
Wilson, M., 23, 353
Wilson, S., 111
Winerip, M., 361
Winn, J., 220, 404–405, 407–408
Winter, M., 331, 332
Winters, D. G., 328
Witmer, Lightner, 478
Witte, S. S., 454
Wodarski, J. S., 432
Wolfenstein, M., 65–66, 68, 70
Women
    discrimination against, 472–473
    pre- and post-Civil War, 54–55

single-parent families. *See* Single-parent families
    working mothers. *See* Working mothers
Women's associations, 59
Women's Christian Temperance Union (WCTU), 59
Woolard, J. L., 453
Woolley, P. V., Jr., 420
Wootten, M. D., 117, 119
Working mothers, 107, 110
    father involvement, 109
    helpful insights about, 107
Working parents, 486
Workshops
    home-learning activities, 306–310, 311–312
    parent education groups, 261–263
    school, 166
    skill training, for parents, 177
Work-site seminars, 176
Wylan, 290f

Yoder, 462–463
Yogman, M. W., 14
Youngblade, L. M., 15
Young parents, 486
    unwed, single-teenage-mother family, 101, 102,
        105, 114
Yutzy, 463

Zabriskie, Christian A., 62
Zeanah, C. H., 447
Zigler, E. F., 23
Zill, N., 5